Applied Behavior Science in Organizations

Applied Behavior Science in Organizations provides a compelling overview of the history of Organizational Behavior Management (OBM) and the opportunity it presents for designing and managing positive work environments that can in turn have a positive impact on society.

The book brings together leading experts from industry and research settings to provide an overview of the historical approaches in Organizational Behavior Management. It begins with an introduction to recognized practices in OBM and the applications of fundamental principles of behavior analysis to a variety of performance problems in organizational settings. The book then highlights how organizational practices and consumers' behavior combine in a complex confluence to meet an organization's goals and satisfy consumer appetites, whilst often unintentionally affecting the wellbeing of organizational members. It argues that the science of behavior has a responsibility to contribute to the safety, health and wellbeing of organizational members, consumers of organizational products, and beyond. Finally, the book recognizes the essential role of organizations in initiating, shaping, and sustaining the development of more nurturing and reinforcing work environments, through discussion of the need for innovation while adapting and responding to growing social upheaval, technological advances, and environmental concerns, alongside crises in the global economy, health, education, and environment.

Showcasing emerging work by internationally recognized scholars on the application of behavior science in organizations, the book will be an essential read for all students and professionals of Organizational Behavior Management, as well as those interested in using organizational applications to create new models of management.

Ramona A. Houmanfar is Professor of Psychology and Director of the Behavior Analysis Program at the University of Nevada, Reno, USA.

Mitch Fryling is Interim Associate Dean in the Charter College of Education at California State University, Los Angeles, USA.

Mark P. Alavosius is President of Praxis^2 LLC and Graduate Faculty of Psychology in the Behavior Analysis Program at the University of Nevada, Reno, USA.

Behavior Science
Series Editor: The Association for Behavior Analysis International

Applied Behavior Science in Organizations: Consilience of Historical and Emerging Trends in Organizational Behavior Management
Edited by Ramona A. Houmanfar, Mitch Fryling & Mark P. Alavosius

Applied Behavior Science in Organizations

Consilience of Historical and Emerging Trends in Organizational Behavior Management

Edited by Ramona A. Houmanfar, Mitch Fryling, and Mark P. Alavosius

NEW YORK AND LONDON

First published 2022
by Routledge
605 Third Avenue, New York, NY 10158

and by Routledge
2 Park Square, Milton Park, Abingdon, Oxon, OX14 4RN

Routledge is an imprint of the Taylor & Francis Group, an informa business

Library of Congress Cataloging-in-Publication Data
A catalog record for this book has been requested

ISBN: 978-1-032-05735-4 (hbk)
ISBN: 978-1-032-05734-7 (pbk)
ISBN: 978-1-003-19894-9 (ebk)

DOI: 10.4324/9781003198949

Typeset in Minion
by Apex CoVantage, LLC

Contents

Introduction

Ramona A. Houmanfar, Mitch Fryling, and Mark P. Alavosius

Behavior analysts have been interested in improving behavior within organizational settings for many years (e.g., Dickinson, 2001; Gravina et al., 2018). This specific area of application within behavior analysis has come to be known as Organizational Behavior Management (OBM), and the *Journal of Organizational Behavior Management*, which focuses on behavior analysis in organizational settings, has been in existence since 1977. For behavior analysts interested in other areas, for example, clinical applications, the experimental analysis of behavior, or philosophical and conceptual issues, the importance of OBM may not be immediately apparent. However, it goes without saying that a substantial amount of human behavior occurs within an organizational context – most behavior analysts will work and participate in organizations throughout their careers, even if OBM is not their specific area of expertise. Given all that behavior analysis has to offer this area of application, in combination with the fact that organizations are ever-present in the day-to-day lives of humans, there is an increased call for training in the area of OBM in graduate training programs.

Indeed, content related to OBM is also present on the Behavior Analyst Certification Board's coursework requirements and exam task lists as well as the newly developed Culturo-Behavior Science verified course sequence from the Association for Behavior Analysis International. At the socio-cultural level, networks of interlocking behavioral contingencies (IBCs) shaping and sustaining the organizational actions, including leadership decision making (whether in the for-profit or other sectors) affect systemic arrangements, and influence practices of consumers within the associated communities (Houmanfar & Mattaini, 2016; Houmanfar & Mattaini, 2018).

Organizations are complicated, and OBM isn't simply an extension of what we already know about behavior to the area of organizations; OBM is a complex and dynamic area of study rich with opportunities for discovery. Consider the variety of organizations in which you may be a member – you buy goods and services from for-profit organizations, you receive education from public or private schools, you probably also buy from cooperatives (e.g., group purchase of health insurance, sporting goods from REI, etc.), and you may also participate in organizations related to your wellbeing and quality of life (e.g., an organization for a hobby or sport, meditation center, religious organization, etc.). You might promote social policies via advocacy associations; you belong to scientific/professional groups like Association for Behavior Analysis International (ABAI) and Association for Contextual Behavior Science (ACBS). You post what you ate for lunch on Facebook and count the number of views. You may vote in elections for government leaders (e.g., local, state, regional, national) or run for office yourself. You may play on sports teams or coach them, sing in a choir, read and discuss articles in a book club. Some of us protest on the steps of the oppressor. It is hard to imagine what we do that is not within the structure of some organization that supports our behavior. We socialize, consume, lead, follow, and lurk inside the boundaries of some organized activity most of the time. Indeed, organizational practices and consumers' behavior combine in a complex confluence to meet an organization's goals, satisfy consumer appetites, sustain established communities, and meet many human needs. These membership behaviors can often unintentionally affect the wellbeing of other organizational members (e.g., their safety, health, financial security, etc.), but our detection and comprehension of that is often incomplete or faulty (Houmanfar & Mattaini, 2018). The convergence of products and services to meet market demand may entail positive impacts on consumer wellbeing via their consumptive practices (e.g., adoption of new goods and services like healthier food, fuel-efficient transportation, renewable energy, less sedentary leisure choices, enriched social networks, etc.) but a negative impact on the collective community wellbeing is also possible (e.g., mis-education, obesity, cancer, unsafe, distracted or inefficient driving, poor energy conservation, faulty health care, invasion of privacy, etc.). In other words, organizational practices influence their members, employees and consumers in various ways, some of which are not easily anticipated or considered very thoroughly ahead of time. Organizations are not islands; rather, they interact with other organizations is a vast network of relations.

In 2020 it is widely accepted that how humans organize their communities, lifestyles, and activities is unsustainable in the face of dwindling resources. The global population is growing and much sustenance is currently dependent on organizations fueled by fossil fuels. Heavy consumption of resource-dependent goods and services requires mass production. This is organized in a just-in-time economy that relies on fragile supply chains. Witness the difficulty in 2020 in providing needed PPE (personal protective equipment) to citizens in the United States as virtually all PPE we purchase is manufactured in Asia. COVID-19 greatly disrupted supply chains in the Spring of 2020; health care workers in the US resorted to making their own masks, gowns, and face shields. Rates of COVID-19 in November 2020, as we write this Introduction, are at unprecedented levels despite lessons learned during the emergence and spread of the pandemic. Organized public health efforts are undermined by organized misinformation campaigns disseminated through communication networks. The developed countries are organized such that wealth inequality is increasing, not decreasing, as consumption spurs economic productivity. This spurs social unrest. Despite wealth, organizations providing education and public health, for examples of two crucial services, are underfunded. In the US, health care systems are organized to yoke medical care to employment. As the pandemic led to massive unemployment, millions lost needed health care. Automation is increasing and job losses will have the same effect unless we organize alternatives. Manufacturers replace workers with robots, universities release faculty and staff and develop online, digital education. Worldwide, there is a breakdown of weak nation-states (e.g., Syria, Lebanon, Venezuela, etc.) which leads to massive migration of populations to better-organized locations. In the US and elsewhere, sea-level rise, floods, and wildfires disrupt organized life. Insurance carriers shift liability to businesses and homeowners with underwriting policies that shield the insurer from losses. Businesses and citizens migrate to safer and more affordable locations. This complex organization of human life, and other stressors, multiplies conflicts. Governments invest in militaries rather than human welfare. Police arm themselves with military-grade weaponry. Citizens join militias, storm government offices, and defend against real and perceived infringements. All this is complicated to understand as social networks use media to spread and amplify misinformation to users. In recent years, institutional leaders charged with protecting the common good devalue expertise. Witness the undermining of climate science, public health, and behavioral sciences by some government leaders. Institutions like justice systems, education, finance, and healthcare exhibit structural biases that impoverish minorities and indigenous groups. The growing populations' consumption drives relentless expansion into wild spaces and the destruction of essential habitats. The way humans organize themselves in a race to resource depletion will lead to soaring greenhouse gas emissions, accelerated warming of the planet, and perhaps, innovation of alternative ways of living. OBM provides a behavior analytic perspective on much more than work behaviors in service to corporations. OBM contributes to understanding this trajectory of organized human behavior and offers an understanding of how selection processes might be managed (e.g., control and counter control) to avert much human suffering.

This text aims to provide an overview of behavior scientific contributions to the area of OBM. Some of these contributions have been studied and elaborated upon for many years and are already demonstrated to be associated with meaningful behavior change both in research and practice. These areas include the use of performance feedback, behavioral training methods, behavior-based safety, instructional design, behavioral systems analysis, and more. These areas of research and practice continue to evolve and develop and are the focus of the first half of the text. This first section of the text has the dual aim of providing an overview of the history of OBM in these areas of practice so that readers develop an appreciation of this context as well as to identify opportunities for continued research and practice.

The second half of the text focuses on emerging areas of research and practice within OBM. This includes areas where there has been some research and conceptual development and where there are many opportunities for research and application. Readers will also notice in this second half of the text a shift to areas that are perhaps less commonly included in behavioral work in organizations, though critically important to understanding the context in which organizational work occurs. These areas include consumer behavior, Acceptance and Commitment Training, cooperation, role of organizations in cultural change, values in organizations, and more. In our view this second part of the text represents what may be considered a next phase of research and development as OBM expands in crucial areas. This work is presented not as a replacement or as a "moving on" from what has been done so far, but rather as an additional layer to be added to our firm foundation, with specific attention to the expansion of the scope of the field of OBM. The complexity of organizational behavior requires us to continue to evolve – to develop a more and more comprehensive understanding of how to improve behavior in organizations and to influence society in meaningful ways.

Looking ahead from 2020, our behaviors within the organizations in which we work, play, consume, advocate, protest and do many of the things we value will transform in novel and complicated ways. For example, work will be increasingly automated displacing many workers, AI systems will function as partners in teamwork, entrants to organizations will be more diverse with expectations for tolerance and respect for variation, globalization of work will continue with supply chains expanding, home and work settings will blur as workers no longer are needed to labor in set locations, climate change will drive revolutions in how we feed, house, fuel, and sustain our communities. The future challenges are mounting, accelerating and likely to transform how humans organize themselves in ways many will experience as unsettling or worse. The importance of learning, flexibility and cooperation is evident now and this text offers a provocative view of how behavior science contributes to organizing our future.

REFERENCES

Dickinson, A.M. (2001). The historical roots of organizational behavior management in the private sector: The 1950s–1980s. *Journal of Organizational Behavior Management, 3–4*, 9–58. doi: 10.1300/J075v20n03_02

Gravina, N., Villacorta, J., Albert, K., Clark, R., Curry, S., & Wilder, D. (2018). A literature review of organizational behavior management interventions in human service settings from 1990–2016. *Journal of Organizational Behavior Management, 2–3*, 191–224. doi: 10.1080/01608061.2018.1454872

Houmanfar, R.A. & Mattaini, M.A. (2016). Leadership and cultural change: Implications for Behavior Analysis. *The Behavior Analyst, 39*(1), 41–46.

Houmanfar, R.A. & Mattaini, M. (Eds.) (2018). *Leadership & cultural change: Managing future wellbeing.* Taylor & Francis Group.

1

Performance Management in Organizations

David A. Wilder, Daniel Cymbal, and Nicole Gravina

Organizational Behavior Management (OBM) is a sub-discipline of applied behavior analysis (ABA) that focuses on the application of behavior analytic principles and procedures to improve performance in business, industry, government, and human service settings. This chapter describes the relationship between performance management (PM), a sub-discipline of OBM, and related disciplines and provides a brief history of PM (and OBM more generally). We then review performance analysis, the assessment component of PM, and describe various PM interventions. Finally, we conclude by noting the strengths and limitations of the field and by recommending future directions for PM research and practice.

PM IN CONTEXT

Although much behavior analytic work focuses on teaching skills to children or decreasing problem behavior exhibited by individuals with disabilities, behavior analytic principles have been applied to a variety of populations and settings. When these principles are studied and applied to organizations, the resulting discipline is called OBM (Wilder et al., 2009). PM is a replicable technology applied at the individual level in an organization; its focus is on all aspects of individual behavior in organizations. Performance is a function of an interaction between a person's behavior and her environment (Gilbert, 1978). Although PM is sometimes used as a synonym for OBM, it is better thought of as a sub-discipline of OBM; other OBM sub-disciplines include behavioral systems analysis (BSA) and behavioral safety. BSA focuses on processes and systems within an organization (e.g., Chapter 5), and behavioral safety focuses on assessing risk and increasing safe behavior, often at the individual level (e.g., Chapter 2). Table 1.1 provides a diagrammatic overview of the relationship between behavior analysis, ABA, OBM, and PM. A fourth area of behavior analysis, *behavior analytic practice*, is sometimes included in descriptions of the discipline, but has been excluded in Table 1.1 for efficiency.

OBM and PM are also related to Industrial-Organizational (I-O) Psychology (Bucklin et al., 2000). OBM and I-O Psychology both focus on the application of psychological (behavioral) knowledge to work settings. These disciplines also share a common history in that they were both influenced by the Hawthorne experiment, which is a series of studies conducted in the 1920s at an electric power plant outside of Chicago. One of the most important findings of the Hawthorne studies was that a variety of environmental changes in work settings, including simply observing employees, can affect worker performance and productivity.

DOI: 10.4324/9781003198949-1

TABLE 1.1

Relationship between Behavior Analysis, OBM, and OBM sub-disciplines

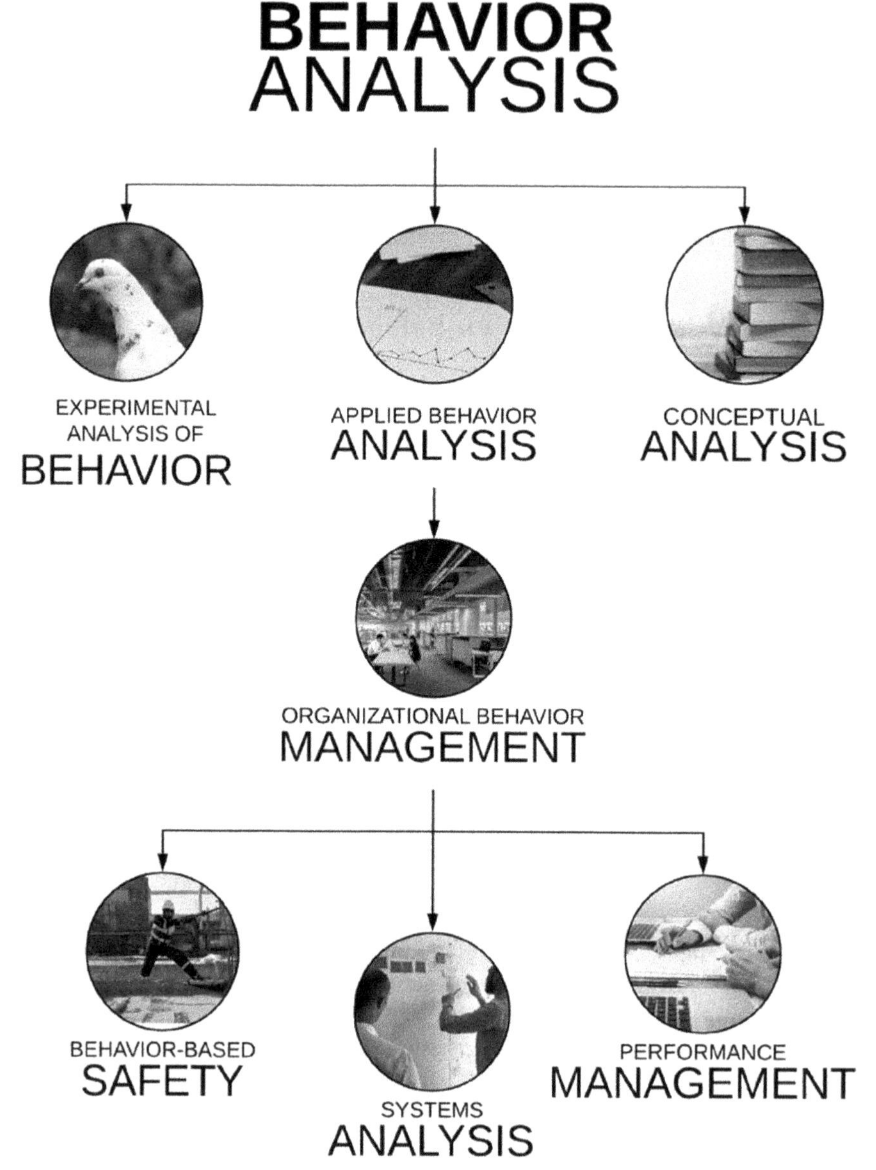

OBM and I-O Psychology differ in that I-O Psychology uses a more traditional, hypothetical deductive model of inquiry, in which a formal hypothesis is tested. OBM, in contrast, uses an inductive model of inquiry in which researchers study topics of interest as they arise. Formal hypothesis testing is generally not used. The use of the inductive approach is partially a result of one of the tenets of behaviorism (the philosophy of the science of behavior). That tenant says that the behavior of individual organisms is of primary interest. One of the benefits of the inductive approach is that it encourages studying topics of immediate interest, even if the findings upon which a study is based are accidental.

The two disciplines also differ in that, unlike I-O Psychology, OBM has a unified theoretical foundation (behaviorism). I-O Psychology has a more eclectic theoretical foundation, and draws mainly from cognitive and social psychology. Also, practitioners of I-O Psychology spend much of their professional time on selection and placement, whereas OBM practitioners focus on analyzing the variables that contribute to performance deficits and then implementing performance improvement programs with employees (Bucklin et al., 2000). Finally, I-O Psychology, which is represented by the Society for Industrial Organizational Psychology (SIOP), is quite large. It includes more than 8,000 members (http://www.siop.org/benefits/). In contrast, the OBM Network (OBMN), a special interest group of the Association for Behavior Analysis, International, includes just over 300 members.

BRIEF HISTORY OF OBM/PM

The history of PM largely mirrors the history of OBM. Although applications of behavior analysis to business and industry began to appear as early as the late 1960s, the precursors to the discipline of OBM date back even further (see Dickinson, 2001, for a detailed history of OBM). In the middle of the century, B.F. Skinner (1953) wrote about wage schedules and reinforcing high-quality work performance. Later, the first organization devoted to performance improvement, the International Society for Performance Improvement (ISPI), was established in 1962. Although not entirely behavior analytic in its approach, ISPI claimed many behavior analysts among its founding members (Dickinson, 2001). Edward Feeney started the first behavior analytic consulting firm in the mid-1960s; his success was even highlighted in the popular press, including the *Harvard Business Review and Fortune* magazines.

In the 1970s, the discipline expanded rapidly, with the founding and expansion of consulting firms. The flagship journal in the field, the *Journal of Organizational Behavior Management* (*JOBM*) was founded in 1977. Aubrey Daniels served as *JOBM*'s first editor; he was also the founder of one of the first OBM consulting firms (Behavioral Systems, Inc.). (Dickinson, 2001). In the years since, there have been many firms specializing in OBM and the practice is now also provided by some insurance companies.

JOBM's mission is to publish articles on "scientific principles to improve organizational performance through behavior change." Conceptual, experimental, and applied articles are published, and both academics and practitioners contribute to the journal. *JOBM* is the official journal of the OBMN, and many OBMN members meet bi-annually at an OBMN-specific conference.

Today, by many measures, OBM is doing quite well. The number of *JOBM* submissions has steadily increased, and the journal's impact factor has followed suit (R. Houmanfar, personal communication, June 20, 2019). OBM consulting firms, many of which focus on performance management, provide services to fortune 500 clients around the globe. The number of academic training programs in OBM has increased, and additional programs are planned.

PRINCIPLES UNDERLYING PM

PM is based upon the science of behavior, or behavior analysis. A number of basic principles constitute this science. A very basic description of these principles follows and will help to illustrate the importance of the scientific foundation of PM. Reinforcement is an increase in the future frequency of a behavior as a result of the addition of a stimulus (positive reinforcement) or the removal of a stimulus (negative reinforcement). As an example, a praise statement by a manager may function as positive reinforcement for an employee's performance. Removal of protective equipment, when it enables easier movement, may function as negative reinforcement for an employee's performance.

Punishment is a decrease in the future frequency of behavior as a result of the addition of a stimulus (positive punishment) or the removal of a stimulus (negative punishment). As an example, a reprimand from a manager may function as positive punishment for an employee's performance. Decreasing the amount of bonus money available may function as negative punishment for an employee's performance.

Stimulus control involves the control of behavior by environmental stimuli. These stimuli acquire control over behavior because they have been correlated with reinforcement or punishment in the past. For example, the presence of a manager may come to control employee performance because the manager himself has been correlated with punishment in the past. These principles, and others, guide decision making in PM.

GENERAL STEPS IN THE PM PROCESS

PM applications involve multiple formal steps. First, the performance of interest is pinpointed, or operationally defined. This is an important first step, as a poorly defined pinpoint may derail assessment and intervention. In some cases, pinpoints are precise descriptions of a behavior. These topographical pinpoints, or descriptions of what behavior looks like, enable PM practitioners to clearly identify the occurrence of behavior. However, the outcome of behavior, or an accomplishment, is often more important, so pinpoints describing results or accomplishments are more often used (Gilbert, 1978).

Next, the pinpoint(s) are measured repeatedly. Then, a performance analysis is conducted. Based on the results of the performance analysis, a PM intervention or performance improvement plan is devised and implemented. Measurement of the pinpoint continues during this phase. If the plan is effective, management is trained to implement it. Finally, the cost–benefit ratio and the social validity of the plan are assessed. Although each step is important, much of PM centers around two major phases: conducting a performance analysis and implementing a PM intervention. These phases are crucial; poor execution of either may lead to a suboptimal outcome.

PERFORMANCE ANALYSIS

Performance analysis (PA) focuses on the assessment of contingencies affecting individual performance in organizations. Although there are some differences, PA is akin to functional assessments in clinical applications of behavior analysis. Clinical applications of behavior analysis focus on behavioral excesses or problematic behavior, such as aggression or property destruction that occurs too often. In PA, the focus of assessment is typically an employee performance problem, such as inadequate job completion, tardiness, or unsafe performance. PA is typically conducted before a performance management intervention or performance improvement plan is implemented; PA results are used to inform the performance improvement plan. Although focusing on the organization as a system is preferable to focusing only on a specific performance deficit exhibited by an employee (Abernathy, 2010), it is nevertheless important to describe PA and PM as part of an overall systems approach.

Three methods of PA exist: indirect, descriptive, and experimental. Indirect methods include interviews, checklists, and questionnaires completed by a supervisor or manager. Largely due to their efficiency, indirect methods have become the most popular method of PA (conducted in about 14% of studies describing an intervention in *JOBM*; Wilder et al., 2018). Austin (2000) describes a number of indirect tools that have been developed. For example, Mager and Pipe (1970) utilized a flowchart consisting of questions designed to determine whether a performance problem was due to a skill deficit or a problem with motivation. Based on the results, the consultant is instructed to design an intervention to address one or both of these issues. Gilbert (1978) provided another informant-based troubleshooting method to be used when consultants initially assess performance. This method includes questions in six areas, including information, equipment, incentives, motivation, knowledge, and the capacity of the performer. Finally, Kent (1986) provides a "problem diagnosis algorithm" that includes 25 questions designed to identify some of the reasons for poor performance. Questions about priorities, distractions, and motivation are included. Marilyn Gilbert (2019) cautions against the sole use of verbal report to assess performance and suggests direct observation should also be used; some recent informant methods have incorporated this.

Perhaps the most common, empirically-supported indirect method of PA is the Performance Diagnostic Checklist (PDC; Austin, 2000). The PDC is an informant-based tool designed to identify the variables contributing to poor employee performance. The PDC was developed based on research examining the ways in which experts solve performance problems. The tool includes four domains, each with five questions. The domains are *Antecedents and Information, Equipment and Processes, Knowledge and Skills*, and *Consequences*. The PDC was designed to be conducted during an interview. That is, the consultant or behavior analyst interviews a supervisor or manager about an employee performance problem. The original PDC includes no formal scoring mechanism, but consultants are instructed to count the number of questions indicating a problem in each domain. Based on PDC results, consultants then design an intervention that addresses the domains that are problematic. The PDC has been used in health care, restaurant, and retail settings.

Shier et al. (2003), in the first empirical evaluation of the PDC, used a package intervention to increase compliance with cleaning tasks at a grocery store. The PDC was used to assess and determine intervention components, and indicated problems related to *Antecedents and Information* as well as *Consequences*. Two intervention components, task clarification and feedback, were implemented, resulting in performance increases in all departments.

Doll et al. (2007) evaluated the PDC at a ski shop. The PDC was one of two performance analyses conducted. Though researchers did not identify the deficient domains indicated by the PDC, they concluded that both antecedents and consequences were needed to occasion and maintain the desired performance. The researchers implemented a package intervention consisting of task clarification, graphed and task-specific feedback; cleaning behaviors improved.

Gravina et al. (2008) used the PDC to inform an intervention to increase task performance at a physical therapy clinic. A package intervention was implemented based on PDC results, with a component from three indicated domains: task clarification, equipment manipulations, and feedback, which corresponded to *Antecedents and Information, Equipment and Processes*, and *Consequences*, respectively. The percentage of completed tasks increased and was maintained following intervention.

The success of the PDC has spawned some variations of the tool. The first variation of the PDC, which was developed to assess employee performance problems specifically occurring in human service settings such as schools, group homes, and clinics, is the Performance Diagnostic Checklist-Human Services (PDC-HS; Carr et al., 2013). The authors noted that human service settings are sufficiently different to warrant a specialized version of the PDC. The PDC-HS is similar to the original tool in that it has the same purpose and includes the same domains. However, it differs in that it also includes some direct observation requirements. Unlike the PDC, the PDC-HS includes a scoring page and suggested intervention page.

The first evaluation of the PDC-HS was conducted by Carr and colleagues (2013) to address staff members' inadequate cleaning of treatment rooms in a center-based autism program. In this study, an intervention was developed based on PDC-HS results. The intervention, which consisted of training and graphed feedback, was compared to a non-indicated intervention (increased availability of cleaning materials). The results of the study showed that completion of the cleaning checklist improved only when the PDC-HS indicated intervention was implemented.

More recently, Bowe and Sellers (2018) used the PDC-HS to identify and address the factors contributing to four paraprofessionals' inaccurate implementation of error correction procedures during discrete trial teaching sessions with young children. The researchers implemented a PDC-HS non-indicated intervention (task clarification and a vocal prompt) first, followed by a PDC-HS indicated intervention (training). All four paraprofessionals met the mastery criteria immediately following the implementation of the training. However, they did not meet the mastery criterion when the non-indicated intervention was implemented.

Smith and Wilder (2018) trained individuals with intellectual disabilities to use the PDC-HS to increase accurate pricing in a community thrift and retail store. This study was unique; the managers who completed the PDC-HS and implemented the intervention had intellectual disabilities. In addition, their job involved supervision of other employees with disabilities. The results showed that training and consultation on the PDC-HS enabled participants to suggest an effective intervention to increase supervisee performance. Thus, these results imply that the PDC-HS may even be useful for supervisors or managers who have a disability themselves.

More recently, Wilder et al. (2019) assessed the reliability and validity of the PDC-HS. These researchers had participants use the tool to score brief videos simulating a performance problem. Each of the three videos indicated a different problematic domain, and some videos depicted problems that were due to more than one domain. Participants generally scored the videos accurately. They were also able to duplicate this performance two to four weeks later, suggesting that the PDC-HS may be a valid and reliable tool. Interestingly, the authors also examined accuracy across three training levels in ABA (high school diploma, bachelor's degree, and master's degree); results suggested that even those with very little training in ABA accurately identified an appropriate intervention. Although these results are encouraging, assessing validity via videos is not ideal. Research on the validity of the tool in the context of actual consults is needed.

Another variation of the PDC was recently developed. The Performance Diagnostic Checklist-Safety (PDC-Safety) is designed to assess the variables which contribute to dangerous behaviors. Martinez-Onstott et al. (2016) noted that safe behavior at work is distinct from other types of performance, and is overseen by the federal government through the Occupational Safety and Health Administration (OSHA), which justifies a separate tool. To create the tool, the authors asked experts in behavioral safety to describe how they assess both safe and dangerous behavior. The authors retained the same domains but, with expert help, designed specific questions for consultants and managers responsible for employee safety. The authors then evaluated the tool with three employees who rarely used personal protective equipment (PPE) in a Grounds Maintenance Department at a University. The PDC-Safety suggested that the relevant consequences were insufficient to maintain safe performance; the authors then devised a feedback intervention to remediate the deficit. PPE usage increased for all three participants. One limitation of this tool is the extent to which it relates to OSHA standards and recommendations; future iterations of the PDC-Safety should address this.

Finally, Cruz et al. (2019) extended the original PDC-Safety study by comparing a non-indicated intervention to an indicated intervention to increase safe hygiene among employees. In this study, the *Antecedents and Information* domain was noted as most problematic for impeding safe performance. The researchers implemented a non-indicated intervention, increased access to resources, but it failed to improve performance. However, when the researchers added an indicated intervention, task clarification and prompting, performance increased for two of three participants.

Descriptive methods of PA involve directly observing performance to examine correlations between relevant variables and performance. Although not as common as informant methods of PA, descriptive methods have been used to identify the variables that contribute to performance problems. For example, Gilbert (1978) described directly observing performance, in addition to using informant methods, to compare exemplary performance with average performance. Pampino et al. (2005) utilized a descriptive assessment to identify the specific skill deficits responsible for poor billing performance among four foremen working at a construction site. The researchers first developed three hypotheses regarding the reasons for poor performance. They then tested each of these hypotheses directly by observing the foremen perform the task and noting the points at which problematic performance occurred. Based on assessment results, the authors concluded that the foremen were deficient in product knowledge and data entry, and that these were responsible for poor billing. An intervention designed to teach each foreman both skills was then implemented and evaluated using a multiple baseline design. The results showed that foremen were deficient in two of the three skills evaluated. A multi-component intervention, targeting both skills, was effective to increase performance for all four foremen.

Fienup et al. (2013) conducted a descriptive assessment as part of a broader performance analysis to identify the variables responsible for late meeting attendance by employees in a human service organization. The authors observed pre-meeting and meeting behavior among employees and found that meeting organization and duration appeared to be related to attendance. Their intervention consisted of additional meeting organization and strict meeting duration criteria. The results suggested that these were effective to improve meeting attendance.

Descriptive methods of PA are utilized less often because directly observing a performance problem and its antecedent and consequent events is sometimes difficult, or even impossible. Performance problems may only occur when specific tasks are performed, and these tasks may be done infrequently and irregularly. In addition, some employee performance problems are created by faulty rules, which may not be documented. However, if descriptive methods are feasible, they should be conducted, as they provide a more valid way of identifying the variables contributing to performance problems. Recent technological developments such as high definition cameras, motion detectors, and sensors have made it easier to observe performance, however. Alavosius et al. (2017) describe the use of these technologies in high-reliability organizations. Future research on descriptive methods of PA should take advantage of these technological advances.

Experimental methods of PA involve manipulating variables to identify those that affect performance. Due to the difficulty involved in manipulating specific variables in organizations, experimental methods of PA are not often conducted. Nevertheless, examples of experimental methods do exist. Therrien et al. (2005) conducted an experimental analysis of some of the variables which contributed to poor customer greeting by employees at a sandwich restaurant chain. The researchers first pinpointed greeting as saying something to customers within 3 seconds of their entry into the store. They then manipulated the presence of a manager, the use of a door chime, and the volume of a radio to determine the extent to which each of these stimuli affected customer greeting by employees. The results showed that greeting occurred more often in the presence of a manager and when a door chime was used. A subsequent intervention, consisting of the presence of a manager combined with the use of a door chime, increased greeting to moderate levels. The researchers then added feedback, which increased greeting even further. These data suggest that although experimental methods may be difficult to implement, they can be particularly useful to identify the variables which affect performance. Future research on experimental methods should take advantage of computer simulations to study behavior in controlled environments and test generalization to work sites.

Given the utility of PA, it is somewhat surprising that it is not used more often as a first step in PM. Only in the last 15 years or so has PA appeared in the PM literature. Austin et al.

(1999) provide three reasons for the lack of PA in PM. The first reason is that OBM/PM has been successful without PA. The second reason is that much of organizational behavior is rule-governed and assessing the impact of rules is difficult. The third reason is that PM practitioners are generally interested in increasing, rather than decreasing, performance. Performance to be increased often does not occur or occurs only infrequently, which makes it difficult to observe or manipulate. It is also possible that PA is used by PM practitioners, but underreported. Many consultants may informally assess performance before implementing an intervention.

Although these reasons may be somewhat valid, they don't mean that PA is without merit. First, PM may be even more effective than it already is with additional PA. Also, rules are not immeasurable, can be manipulated, and adherence precisely measured. Finally, environmental stimuli and events affect skill deficits just as they do performance that occurs too much. Many performance problems can be assessed, despite the difficulty involved in doing so.

The alternative to PA is the use of arbitrarily selected interventions, or interventions consisting of antecedent versus consequence components. Although some in the field of PM utilized this approach for decades, further advances may be possible with the use of PA. Clinical applications of behavior analysis have been revolutionized using pre-intervention assessment procedures; PM may be as well.

PERFORMANCE MANAGEMENT INTERVENTIONS

PM interventions have historically been categorized into antecedent-based procedures and consequence-based procedures. Although this distinction may be valuable when describing what a supervisor or manager should do to address a performance problem, it may also be problematic because antecedent interventions are often linked to consequences. For example, a goal provided by a supervisor is an antecedent to the performance, but goals often specify an outcome for meeting the goal. Thus, a consequence is inherently linked to the goal. Growth in PA has prompted an alternative approach to intervention categorization. PM interventions may now be best organized according to the stimuli and events responsible for problematic or deficient performance. In general, problematic performance is a result of insufficient training, prompts that are either absent or too weak to evoke proper performance, problems with the equipment necessary to perform the job, or deficient contingencies to support appropriate performance.

TRAINING

Training is a common PM intervention that involves teaching employees how to properly perform the task. When done effectively, training provides staff members with the knowledge and skills to perform their jobs appropriately (Reid et al., 2012). Interestingly, Mager and Pipe (2004) caution against using training as a catchall to remediate all skill deficits. For instance, if an organization misaligns contingencies or fails to provide adequate equipment, training will likely fail. Of course, there are many instances in which training may be the prescribed remedy or, in the case of novice performers, necessary to produce adequate job performance.

One of the most commonly used and evaluated behavior analytic methods of training is Behavioral Skills Training (BST). The four key components of BST are instructions, modeling, rehearsal, and feedback (Miltenberger, 2018). Several studies have verified the effectiveness of BST in a variety of different organizations. BST has been used to train staff to complete myriad tasks, ranging from basic job duties like data collection (Hine, 2014) to complex skills such as conducting a clinical assessment (Jenkins & DiGennaro Reed, 2016). Although some supervisors report using only some BST components, it may be critical to include all components of

BST; Jenkins and DiGennaro Reed (2017) found that instructions alone were insufficient to train skills. Moreover, they found that rehearsal need not be repeated excessively so long as performance evaluation includes a mastery criterion and feedback.

Given the high costs associated with training staff, maintaining the changes and skills produced by training may not always be financially feasible. Even when using a potentially costly expert trainer, training that lacks ongoing feedback may fare poorly. Pyramidal training, which includes a train-the-trainer model, may partially circumvent training expenses and promote skill maintenance among trainees. Haberlin et al. (2012) found that pyramidal training produced greater skill gains and more durable skills after a three-month follow-up. Some solutions omit the presence of an expert entirely; other training modalities incorporate self-guided instruction as well as computer-based instruction (Shapiro & Kazemi, 2017).

TASK CLARIFICATION

Task clarification generally refers to some antecedent stimulus (verbal, written, or visual) that defines or describes the performance required of the employee (Anderson et al., 1988). In other words, task clarification helps operationally define performer behaviors to better occasion competent job performance. Often, task clarification is used interchangeably with job aids. Task clarification interventions comprise a range of different mediums to specify performance, including checklists, flowcharts and signs (Parnell et al., 2017).

Task clarification is a relatively simple intervention and has been utilized in a variety of settings and situations. For example, it has been used to increase police courtesy (Wilson et al., 1997), improve wait staff performance in restaurants (Amigo et al., 2008; Austin et al., 2005; Reetz et al., 2016; Rodriguez et al., 2005; Squires et al., 2007), and improve customer service in medical settings (Cunningham & Austin, 2007; Gravina et al., 2008; Slowiak et al., 2005). In most research, task clarification is implemented as part of a treatment package. Components commonly used with task clarification include feedback (Durgin et al., 2014; Gravina et al., 2008; Palmer & Johnson, 2013; Reetz et al., 2016) and goal setting (Amigo et al., 2008; Cunningham & Austin, 2007).

Anderson et al. (1988) conducted a study to increase cleaning at a student-run bar where task clarification was implemented apart from other interventions. The authors noted that performance increased 13% over the baseline. Performance increases were even greater when consequences were implemented in subsequent phases. Parnell et al. (2017) found similar results when introducing varying levels of job aids to increase staff implementation of discrete trial instruction in a human service agency. That is, the job aids were somewhat effective, but the authors found that performance feedback was necessary to maintain adequate levels of performance. Unfortunately, there is limited research examining task clarification independent of other interventions.

PROMPTING

At a glance, prompting and task clarification may appear identical; both are antecedent procedures intended to occasion accurate performance. Like task clarification, prompts are often visual, verbal, or written. However, it is worth noting that the primary intent of task clarification is to address knowledge deficits impeding performance (e.g., task clarification often consists of a checklist specifying job duties), whereas prompts are antecedent stimuli that have already acquired some control over the response. The goal of prompting is to evoke responding in the presence of a neutral stimulus that will, in time, evoke the desired behavior (Karlsson & Chase, 1996). That is, the prompt should facilitate the transfer of control from one antecedent stimulus (i.e., the prompt) to another (the neutral stimulus). As an example, a manager may initially need to be prompted to comment on outstanding performance by an employee. Over time, however, the employee's performance itself should evoke the manager's praise.

Prompting has been used as a strategy in multiple organizational contexts, including restaurants (Ralis & O'Brien, 1986; Squires et al., 2007), retail (Clayton et al., 2014; Rafacz et al., 2011), and within universities (Clayton & Blaskewicz, 2012; Reetz et al., 2014). Research has provided some insight on the most effective use of prompting. Modality may not matter; research has demonstrated effective use of prompting in multiple modalities (e.g., verbal, written, visual). Moreover, Reetz et al. (2014) found that passive prompts (i.e., signs) and mediated prompts (i.e., people providing verbal prompts) both provided a significant increase above no prompts when monitoring pedestrian and bike traffic on a college campus. Conversely, the placement of the prompt may be a critical feature. Austin et al. (1993) found that prompts to recycle paper tended to produce more substantial effects when placed in proximity to the area where the target response occurs (i.e., within close distance to the recycling bins).

Even with significant behavioral gains, prompts are not intended to support performance in the long run. They may eventually produce responses that lead to reinforcement opportunities, and it is prudent to fade prompts once the naturally occurring event that should evoke performance has acquired control over the response. In the studies described above, no formal evaluation of the maintenance of intervention effects was conducted; future research should evaluate how long the effects of prompts are likely to maintain.

RESPONSE EFFORT MANIPULATIONS

Manipulating the effort involved in a task refers to making the task easier or more difficult to perform. When effort is manipulated in basic behavior analytic research, typically the force required to engage in a response (e.g., a lever press) is changed. In PM, both force (Casella et al., 2010; Van Houten et al., 2011) and distance (Abellon & Wilder, 2014; Casella et al., 2010; Fritz et al., 2017; Ludwig et al., 1998; Miller et al., 2016; O'Connor et al., 2010) have been manipulated. Friman and Poling (1995) noted that manipulating response effort as an independent variable is a generally untapped intervention in ABA; this remains generally true in PM to date.

Casella et al. (2010) evaluated response effort as an independent variable across three different staff behaviors in an autism treatment clinic. Behaviors targeted included glove-wearing, replacement of electrical outlet covers, and hand sanitizer usage. Distance to available gloves and the effort required to use outlet covers and sanitizer pumps were manipulated at two levels, with higher response effort resulting in a lower occurrence of safe performance.

In another evaluation, Van Houten et al. (2011) manipulated accelerator pedal force when seatbelt usage was not occurring. When drivers failed to buckle up, additional force was required to depress the accelerator, resulting in increased seatbelt usage. In another study, Abellon and Wilder (2014) examined the use of personal protective equipment (PPE) when the distance to access equipment was manipulated. Employee performance increased when physical proximity was reduced. Finally, multiple studies have examined the impact of reducing the response requirement to emit recycling behaviors (Ludwig et al., 1998; Miller et al., 2016; O'Connor et al., 2010) as well as increasing the effort to emit incorrect waste disposal (Fritz et al., 2017). In general, by adding receptacles for recycling and removing receptacles for trash, thereby reducing the effort, correct recycling increased.

GOAL SETTING/RULES

A goal provides a defined level of desired performance, often within a time criterion (Latham & Locke, 2006). Goal setting is a common intervention within and outside of PM; estimates suggest well over 1,000 studies dedicated to the analysis of goals' effect on human performance. While most psychological explanations of goals rely on cognition, behavior analytic conceptualizations have posited goals as discriminative stimuli (Fellner & Sulzer-Azaroff, 1984) and establishing operations (Malott, 1992). Goals can also be described as rules, which establish relations between goal statements and current performance; performers act to reduce "less than" relations with the goal statement and derive reinforcement from goal attainment (O'Hora & Maglieri, 2006).

In PM literature, goal setting has been used to solve a variety of performance problems, including customer service (Loewy & Bailey, 2007; Slowiak et al., 2005), energy conservation (Clayton & Nesnidol, 2017), preventing fraud (Downing et al., 2018), and manufacturing (Jessup & Stahelski, 1999). Best practices when setting performance goals is often the subject of research and, in general, goals may be best achieved when they are specific, tied to reinforcement, and relatively difficult. Goals are antecedents and, provided alone, may not be sufficient to maintain performance (Fellner & Sulzer-Azaroff, 1984; Fellner & Sulzer-Azaroff, 1985).

Introducing difficult goals (sometimes called "stretch goals") is often common practice both to produce higher levels of performance and avoid performance ceilings (Latham & Locke, 2006). PM literature is consistent with caveats: high goals tend to produce higher performance (Tammemagi et al., 2013) though extremely difficult goals eventually result in stalled or declining performance (Roose & Williams, 2018). Moreover, setting goals according to performer ability may produce a greater effect than merely assigning one goal for all individuals (Jeffrey et al., 2012).

MONETARY INCENTIVES

Conventional pay schemes compensate employees for their time, rather than output. However, many companies provide some form of monetary bonus, including distributing a percentage of organizational profits (profit-sharing) or distributing money based on a department's economic or functional health (gain-sharing). Performance-based pay ties some portion of the performer's wage or salary directly to their work output. In contrast to hourly wages, performance pay systems provide compensation for specific output and pay out with frequency and certainty (Bucklin & Dickinson, 2001).

Empirical validation of performance-based pay systems is relatively sparse, and establishing best practices is largely built on a few studies and anecdotal information. Moreover, conceptualizing the work environment in terms of basic reinforcement schedules is difficult due to the significant number of schedules to which performers respond (Bucklin & Dickinson, 2001). Studies have generally indicated that any percentage of performance-based pay produces performance over and above fixed wages. Moreover, Frisch and Dickinson (1990) found that adjustments to the incentive to base pay ratio did not significantly impact performance, suggesting that the link between performance and pay is adequate, and that incentives beyond this may be unnecessary. This was borne out in further studies, when 100% pay was contrasted with a mixture of base pay and incentive pay, suggesting that performance pay schematics simply increase the frequency with which performers engage in the desired behavior (Dickinson & Gillette, 1993; Matthews & Dickinson, 2000). However, more research is required as most studies have used small incentive percentages, feature other intervention components (i.e., feedback), and have occurred in analog settings (Bucklin & Dickinson, 2001).

LOTTERIES

One of the main difficulties when establishing performance-based pay is limited resources. Lotteries or raffles are "probabilistic performance contingencies," providing performers chances to win monetary or tangible bonuses contingent on pinpointed behaviors. Lotteries can be used to increase the overall frequency of performance rewards within an organization while decreasing the frequency of payouts. In clinical settings, revenue is tied to funding streams and provides a fertile setting to implement lotteries, evidenced by the frequency of lottery/raffle intervention (Cook & Dixon, 2005; Griffin et al., 2019; Miller et al., 2014). Multiple studies have found that odds of winning had no significant impact on performance (Cook & Dixon, 2005; Gravina et al., 2005). Overall, odds as low as 6% have been found to produce steady responding, suggesting that lotteries may potentially provide a significant cost savings to organizations (Wine et al., 2017).

PERFORMANCE FEEDBACK

Feedback is the most common PM intervention, accounting for a large portion of studies published in the *JOBM*. Feedback can be defined as information describing a performance (Alvero et al., 2001). While this rather broad definition works well when classifying interventions, much debate on the behavioral function of performance feedback exists.

Behavioral Function of Feedback

Performance feedback has been described as a prompt to evoke future performance, as a reinforcer to increase desired performance or as both (Alvero et al., 2001). Researchers have attempted to identify the function of feedback, however results have been inconsistent. Anderson et al. (1988) appeared to produce expected patterns of reinforcement in bank tellers' behavior, though the authors conceded that the feedback may serve multiple stimulus functions. More recently, Aljadeff-Abergel et al. (2017) assessed the delivery of feedback pre- and post-session. The authors found that feedback provided as an antecedent was more effective at increasing behavior than feedback delivered directly following a session. Moreover, participants reported that pre-session feedback was more useful. While the debate over function will likely continue, some other aspects of performance feedback are more firmly established.

Feedback may be delivered in multiple formats, be it written, verbal, or graphed. It can also be delivered privately, via electronic correspondence or even publicly posted. Alvero et al. (2001) found that a combination of modalities (i.e., graphed, written and verbal) had the largest impact on performance, but that the most frequent delivery medium was feedback alone with no clear difference in effectiveness regarding modality.

Feedback shows the most consistent effects when it is delivered daily or in tandem with other delivery schedules (e.g., daily and monthly, daily and weekly). Pampino et al. (2003) directly compared weekly feedback against daily feedback and found similar results: daily feedback was more effective, but weekly feedback was more efficient. However, it should be noted that previous investigations of staff preference in feedback notes an overwhelming choice for daily feedback (Reid & Parsons, 1996).

Content and Source of Feedback

In terms of content, feedback in research is most commonly delivered as a comparison between the performer's current and past performance or as a measure against a performance standard, with performance impacts remaining relatively similar (Alvero et al., 2001). In general, for maximal effects, feedback should comprise evaluative (i.e., qualitatively rating performance) and objective (i.e., placing performance relative to goals/contingencies) statements relative to the performance (Johnson, 2013; Johnson et al., 2015). Feedback in research is most often delivered via a supervisor, which has been shown to be effective to improve performance; this may be due to supervisors having some measure of control over contingencies. However, the strongest effects were observed when a supervisor or researcher delivered feedback, suggesting that perhaps procedural fidelity wanes in their absence (Alvero et al., 2001).

CONCLUSIONS

PM offers several strengths compared to other approaches for understanding and improving organizational performance. For example, compared to I-O Psychology, PM retains high practical significance, demonstrated by the large proportion of PM research studies conducted in applied settings that produce meaningful changes (Bucklin et al., 2000). Furthermore, most of the interventions used in PM are viewed favorably by employees and supervisors (Hantula, 2015). As Crowell (2004) points out, PM interventions allow for individual differences while also creating accountability. Further, they increase the clarity of expectations and encourage management through appreciation rather than by exception. Using PM, organizations can better achieve their desired results while also improving employee satisfaction and work relationships.

Despite PM's practical utility, there are still opportunities for growth in the field. For example, a large portion of PM research is conducted with front-line employees rather than managers and supervisors (Gravina et al., 2018; VanStelle et al., 2012). Relatedly, although PM practitioners often seek to make large scale improvements in organizations, much of the research is still conducted at the performer level (Hyten, 2009; Vanstelle et al., 2012). Thus, PM research may not inform practice as well as it could. PM is also not currently well-recognized in business, which can present challenges for marketing services and obtaining employment. Individuals trained in PM must learn to describe their skills using more well-recognized business terms (Brown, 2001). Finally, unlike similar fields, there is no certification specific to OBM/PM training. Thus, it can be difficult to distinguish which practitioners have adequate OBM/PM training to practice and train others. The absence of an OBM/PM-specific certification may contribute to the lack of recognition for the field and the need to translate the OBM/PM skillset into business language to fit employment opportunities.

Practice Issues

One way to get behavior science more involved in organizations is to hire experienced managers and teach them about PM. Another approach is to train college students preparing for business and managerial careers in PM. Although there are relatively few employment opportunities with OBM in the title, PM training lends itself to several career paths. Training in PM provides a distinct advantage for working in a variety of industries and jobs because most jobs, to some extent, require employees to supervise or influence others. Further, being more effective at influencing others can increase an employee's overall effectiveness. Moreover, PM teaches a systems approach and understanding the greater system can lead to improved processes and innovation. PM techniques can be applied to any industry, and allow individuals to specialize in a variety of careers.

For instance, individuals with PM training could work in human resources, training and instructional design, organizational development, operations, safety, healthcare, user experience and design, management, and other careers. However, those with PM training may need to seek additional training or certifications to obtain some of these positions. For example, acquiring training and certification in Lean Healthcare may benefit individuals seeking performance improvement positions in healthcare. This certification is commonly listed in job advertisements for continuous improvement and organizational development positions in healthcare settings. Individuals hoping to work in operations or management may need to obtain additional training on the specific industry of interest. They might also find that certification in project management increases their marketability. Individuals interested in user experience and design jobs could be more marketable with training in block coding, web design, or graphic design. The appropriate training and certifications can be identified by examining a number of job advertisements for the candidate's desired position. Commonly required or desired qualifications are good indicators of additional training and certifications that can help with obtaining positions in these areas. The addition of PM training can prepare employees to take leadership positions upon entry or soon after entering the career area.

There are several organizations that represent fields closely related to PM, and many offer job boards online and recruitment sessions at their conferences. For example, as described above, ISPI was founded by individuals with training in behavior analysis and most of their members work in training, instructional design, and process improvement (Dickinson, 2001). They list job postings, offer training and coaching for job seekers, and allow applicants to list post their resume online. ISPI also offers a certification called Human Performance Technologist (HPT) that could be useful for individuals interested in training and instructional design. The Association for Training and Development (ASTD) also supports practitioners who work in training and instructional design and provides a certification option. Professional associations exist for every industry and general job function. Job seekers will benefit from connecting to the professional organizations within their career path. In addition, continuing to network within these associations can increase opportunities for learning and career growth.

PM practitioners may also wish to become Board Certified Behavior Analysts (BCBA®s) for a number of reasons (Luke et al., 2018). Some clinical behavior analysis organizations seek PM professionals to manage employee performance and they may prefer individuals who are board certified. Also, some states have licensure laws that may include PM practitioners; this could make practicing PM without certification in those states tenuous, although this has been debated. Further, many faculty positions in behavior analysis programs require or strongly desire job candidates to be board certified. In some cases, obtaining a BCBA® could be an important differentiator, but it is not always necessary. Currently, the BCBA® designation is not a widely recognized certification in business and thus, it will not increase the chances of obtaining employment in most industries. However, this may change as the field of behavior analysis grows, and certification may prove useful for PM practitioners in the future.

Of course, certification may also have some drawbacks. For example, because certification has historically focused on human service practitioners, certificants may be more likely to seek and obtain jobs in human service settings, which may limit the number of certificants who might seek employment in business and industry. Also, certification exams without specialized PM questions may not ensure well-trained PM consultants; perhaps future iterations of certification exams should include PM-specific content.

Future Research Needs

Although the body of research in PM is consistently growing, there are a number of research topics that require further investigation. For example, as described above, while assessment is ubiquitous in clinical behavior analysis, PM researchers and practitioners have just begun to develop and incorporate assessment tools into their practice (Wilder et al., 2018). Although a few assessment tools exist for identifying appropriate performance improvement interventions (e.g., the PDC and PDC-HS), these tools need further refining to identify the best strategies for conducting the assessment interview and selecting interventions. Further, PM practitioners could benefit from tools that target specific performances or processes to improve (e.g., meetings, time management) and from tools that help identify appropriate performance targets (Cunningham & Geller, 2012).

Another opportunity for PM research lies in leadership development and large scale change. Many of the current PM interventions found in research target front-line staff. It is difficult for those interventions to maintain after the research or consulting engagement is complete, without supervisors engaging in a new set of behaviors to support the intervention. It can be difficult to identify the most appropriate leader behaviors to target targets and even more challenging to measure them. Still, including leaders in PM research will promote larger-scale change and intervention maintenance. Also, designing precise and insightful measurement and intervention tools for leaders could advance the field.

There is also increasing recognition in PM for the role of technology in implementing and maintaining interventions. In-person, lecture-based training may be inefficient and ineffective, especially for large organizations with employees spread across multiple locations. Instead, computer-based instruction (Johnson & Rubin, 2011), video-modeling (Loughrey et al., 2013), and virtual environment training (Arnold & VanHouten, 2011) may be more cost-effective, consistent, and time-efficient alternatives for training employees. Videoconferencing could result in more cost-effective training and coaching from expert PM consultants, as well. Finally, technology can automate data collection as well as intervention delivery. For example, prompts and feedback can be delivered through technology (Berger & Ludwig, 2007).

Lastly, there are many opportunities for PM researchers and practitioners to address problems plaguing society with roots in organizational systems. For example, PM can offer solutions for high need industries such as healthcare (Cunningham & Geller, 2012; Kelley & Gravina, 2018) and education (Witt et al., 1997). PM researchers and practitioners can also contribute solutions for difficult problems that span across many industries, such as reducing catastrophic safety events (Bogard et al., 2015) and improving employee health and wellbeing (Olson et al., 2015). Addressing these and other high impact issues will strengthen PM's reputation and increase recognition for the field, and will also go a long way toward solving these socially important behavioral issues

PM practitioners and researchers should not lose sight of the larger organizational problems when conducting PM. A broad approach, wherein individual-level performance is addressed in the context of a systemic organizational analysis, will move all of OBM forward. Relatedly, although research on specific interventions (e.g., feedback) is important, PM researchers should address a wider variety of performance issues in organizations. Recent work on topics such as rumor and gossip (Houmanfar & Johnson, 2004) illustrate this.

PM offers organizations and employees myriad tools and technologies for achieving desired business outcomes, which benefits both the organization and the employee. Yet, many opportunities still exist for creating new tools and techniques and disseminating that work in a digestible way to the business community. As interest in and recognition for PM grows, so will its impact.

STUDY QUESTIONS

1. Comment on the difference between Organizational Behavior Management, Performance Management, and Behavior Systems Analysis.
2. What are some differences between OBM and Industrial Organizational Psychology?
3. What steps are involved in the performance management process?
4. Describe the four domains assessed with the Performance Diagnostic Checklist.
5. Explain how two of the performance management interventions reviewed in the chapter are linked to domains of the Performance Diagnostic Checklist.

REFERENCES

Abellon, O.E. & Wilder, D.A. (2014). The effect of equipment proximity on safe performance in a manufacturing setting. *Journal of Applied Behavior Analysis, 47*(3), 628–632. doi: 10.1002/jaba.137

Abernathy, W. (2010). A comprehensive performance analysis and improvement method. *Performance Improvement, 49*(5), 5–17.

Alavosius, M.P., Houmanfar, R.A., Anbro, S.J., Burleigh, K., & Hebein, C. (2017). Leadership and crew resource management in high-reliability organizations: A competency framework for measuring behaviors. *Journal of Organizational Behavior Management, 37*(2), 142–170. doi: 10.1080/01608061.2017.1325825

Aljadeff-Abergel, E., Peterson, S.M., Wiskirchen, R.R., Hagen, K.K., & Cole, M.L. (2017). Evaluating the temporal location of feedback: Providing feedback following performance vs. prior to performance. *Journal of Organizational Behavior Management, 37*(2), 171–195. doi:10.1080/01608061.2017.1309332

Alvero, A.M., Bucklin, B.R., & Austin, J. (2001). An objective review of the effectiveness and essential characteristics of performance feedback in organizational settings. *Journal of Organizational Behavior Management, 21*(1), 3–29. doi:10.1300/J075v21n01_02

Amigo, S., Smith, A., & Ludwig, T. (2008). Using task clarification, goal setting, and feedback to decrease table busing times in a franchise pizza restaurant. *Journal of Organizational Behavior Management, 28*(3), 176–187. doi: 10.1080/01608060802251106

Anderson, D.C., Crowell, C.R., Hantula, D.A., & Siroky, L.M. (1988). Task clarification and individual performance posting for improving cleaning in a student-managed university bar. *Journal of Organizational Behavior Management, 9*(2), 73–90. doi: 10.1300/J075v09n02_06

Arnold, M.L. & VanHouten, R. (2011). Increasing following headway with prompts, goal setting, and feedback in a driving simulator. *Journal of Applied Behavior Analysis, 44*(2), 245–254. doi: 10.1901/jaba.2011.44-245

Austin, J. (2000). Performance analysis and performance diagnostics. In J. Austin, & J. E. Carr (Eds.), *Handbook of Applied Behavior Analysis* (pp. 321–350). Context Press.

Austin, J., Carr, J.E., & Agnew, J.L. (1999). The need for assessment of maintaining variables in OBM. *Journal of Organizational Behavior Management, 19*(2), 59–87. doi: 10.1300/J075v19n02_05

Austin, J., Hatfield, D.B., Grindle, A.C., & Bailey, J.S. (1993). Increasing recycling in office environments: The effects of specific, informative cues. *Journal of Applied Behavior Analysis, 26*(2), 247–253. doi: 10.1901/jaba.1993.26-247

Austin, J., Weatherly, N.L., & Gravina, N. E. (2005). Using task clarification, graphic feedback, and verbal feedback to increases closing-task completion in a privately owned restaurant. *Journal of Applied Behavior Analysis, 38*(1), 117–120. doi: 10.1901/jaba.2005.159-03

Berger, S.M. & Ludwig, T.D. (2007). Reducing warehouse employee errors using voice-assisted technology that provided immediate feedback. *Journal of Organizational Behavior Management, 27*(1), 1–31. doi: 10.1300/J075v27n01_01

Bogard, K., Ludwig, T.D., Staats, C., & Kretschmer, D. (2015). An industry's call to understand the contingencies involved in process safety: Normalization of deviance. *Journal of Organizational Behavior Management, 35*(1–2), 70–80. doi: 10.1080/01608061.2015.1031429

Bowe, M. & Sellers, T.P. (2018). Evaluating the Performance Diagnostic Checklist-Human Services to assess incorrect error-correction procedures by preschool paraprofessionals. *Journal of Applied Behavior Analysis, 51*(1), 166–176. doi:10.1002/jaba.428

Brown, P.L. (2001). Communicating the benefits of the behavioral approach to the business community. *Journal of Organizational Behavior Management, 20*, 59–72. doi: 10.1300/J075v20n03_03

Bucklin, B.R. & Dickinson, A.M. (2001). Individual monetary incentives: A review of different types of arrangements between performance and pay. *Journal of Organizational Behavior Management, 21*(3), 45–137. doi: 10.1300/J075v21n03_03

Bucklin, B.R., Alvero, A.M., Dickinson, A.M., Austin, J., & Jackson, A.K. (2000). Industrial-Organizational Psychology and Organizational Behavior Management: An objective comparison. *Journal of Organizational Behavior Management, 20*(2), 27–75. doi: 10.1300/J075v20n02_03

Casella, S.E., Wilder, D.A., Neidert, P., Rey, C., Compton, M., & Chong, I. (2010). The effects of response effort on safe performance by therapists at an autism treatment facility. *Journal of Applied Behavior Analysis, 43*(4), 729–734. doi: 10.1901/jaba.2010.43-729

Carr, J.E., Wilder, D.A., Majdalany, L., Mathisen, D., & Strain, L.A. (2013). An assessment-based solution to a human-service employee performance problem. *Behavior Analysis in Practice, 6*(1), 16–32. doi:10.1007/bf03391789

Clayton, M.C. & Blaskewicz, J. (2012). The use of visual prompts to increase the cleanliness of restrooms on a college campus. *Journal of Organizational Behavior Management, 32*(4), 329–337. doi: 10.1080/01608061.2012.729393

Clayton, M.C., Boron, J.B., & Mattila, L. (2014). Child safety in grocery stores: The impact of verbal prompts and reinforcement on safety strap use in shopping carts. *Journal of Organizational Behavior Management, 34*(1), 52–58. doi:10.1080/01608061.2013.873380

Clayton, M. & Nesnidol, S. (2017). Reducing electricity use on campus: The use of prompts, feedback, and goal setting to decrease excessive classroom lighting. *Journal of Organizational Behavior Management, 37*(2), 196–206. doi: 10.1080/01608061.2017.1325823

Cook, T. & Dixon, M.R. (2005). Performance feedback and probabilistic bonus contingencies among employees in a human service organization. *Journal of Organizational Behavior Management, 25*(3), 45–63. doi: 10.1300/J075v25n03_04

Crowell, C.R. (2004). Beyond positive reinforcement: OBM as a humanizing approach to management practices. *Journal of Organizational Behavior Management, 24*(1–2), 195–202. doi: 10.1300/J075v24n01_13

Cruz, N.J., Wilder, D.A., Phillabaum, C., Thomas, R., Cusick, M., & Gravina, N. (2019). Further evaluation of the Performance Diagnostic Checklist-Safety (PDC-Safety). *Journal of Organizational Behavior Management,* 39(3–4), 266–279. doi: 10.1080/01608061.2019.1666777

Cunningham, T.R. & Austin, J. (2007). Using goal setting, task clarification, and feedback to increase the use of the hands-free technique by hospital operating room staff. *Journal of Applied Behavior Analysis, 40*(4), 673–677. doi: 10.1901/jaba.2007.673-677

Cunningham, T.R. & Geller, E.S. (2012). A comprehensive approach to identifying intervention targets for patient-safety improvement in a hospital setting. *Journal of Organizational Behavior Management, 32*(3), 194–220. doi: 10.1080/01608061.2012.698114

Dickinson, A.M. (2001). The historical roots of Organizational Behavior Management in the private sector. *Journal of Organizational Behavior Management, 20*(3–4), 9–58. doi: 10.1300/J075v20n03_02

Dickinson, A.M. & Gillette, K.L. (1993). A comparison of the effects of two individual monetary incentive systems on productivity: Piece rate pay versus base pay plus incentives. *Journal of Organizational Behavior Management, 14*(1), 3–82. doi: 10.1300/J075v14n01_02

Doll, J., Livesey, J., McHaffie, E., & Ludwig, T.D. (2007). Keeping an uphill edge: Managing cleaning behaviors at a ski shop. *Journal of Organizational Behavior Management, 27*(3), 41–60. doi:10.1300/j075v27n03_04

Downing, C.O., Jr., Capriola, N., & Geller, E.S. (2018). Preventing credit-card fraud: A goal-setting and prompting intervention to increase cashiers' ID-checking behavior. *Journal of Organizational Behavior Management, 38*(4), 335–344. doi: 10.1080/01608061.2018.1514349

Durgin, A., Mahoney, A., Cox, C., Weetjens, B.J., & Poling, A. (2014). Using task clarification and feedback training to improve staff performance in an east African nongovernmental organization. *Journal of Organizational Behavior Management, 34*(2), 122–143. doi: 10.1080/01608061.2014.914007

Fellner, D.J. & Sulzer-Azaroff, B. (1984). A behavioral analysis of goal setting. *Journal of Organizational Behavior Management, 6*(1), 33–51. doi: 10.1300/J075v06n01_03

Fellner, D.J. & Sulzer-Azaroff, B. (1985). Occupational safety: Assessing the impact of adding assigned or participative goal-setting. *Journal of Organizational Behavior Management, 7*(1–2), 3–24. doi: 10.1300/J075v07n01_02

Fienup, D., Luiselli, J., Joy, M., Smyth, D., & Stein, R. (2013). Functional assessment and intervention for organizational behavior change: Improving the timeliness of staff meetings at a human services organization. *Journal of Organizational Behavior Management, 33*(4), 252–264. doi: 10.1080/01608061.2013.843435

Friman, P.C. & Poling, A. (1995). Making life easier with effort: Basic findings and applied research on response effort. *Journal of Applied Behavior Analysis, 28*(4), 583–590. doi: 10.1901/jaba.1995.28-583

Frisch, C.J. & Dickinson, A.M. (1990). Work productivity as a function of the percentage of monetary incentives to base pay. *Journal of Organizational Behavior Management, 11*(1), 13–33. doi:10.1300/J075v11n01_03

Fritz, J.N., Dupuis, D.L., Wu, W., Neal, A.E., Rettig, L.A., & Lastrapes, R.E. (2017). Evaluating increased effort for item disposal to improve recycling at a university. *Journal of Applied Behavior Analysis, 50*(4), 825–829. doi: 10.1002/jaba.405

Gilbert, M.B. (2019) Human Performance Technology: Further Reflections on Human Competence. *Journal of Organizational Behavior Management, 39*(1–2), 7–112, doi: 10.1080/01608061.2019.1596864

Gilbert, T.F. (1978). *Human competence.* McGraw-Hill.

Gravina, N., VanWagner, M., & Austin, J. (2008). Increasing physical therapy equipment preparation using task clarification, feedback and environmental manipulations. *Journal of Organizational Behavior Management, 28*(2), 110–122. doi:10.1080/01608060802100931

Gravina, N., Villacorta, J., Albert, K., Clark, R., Curry, S., & Wilder, D. (2018). A literature review of organizational behavior management interventions in human service settings from 1990 to 2016. *Journal of Organizational Behavior Management, 38*(2–3), 191–224. doi: 10.1080/01608061.2018.1454872

Gravina, N., Wilder, D.A., White, H., & Fabian, T. (2005). The effect of raffle odds on signing in at a treatment center for adults with mental illness. *Journal of Organizational Behavior Management, 24*(4), 31–42. doi: 10.1300/J075v24n04_02

Griffin, M., Gravina, N.E., Matey, N., Pritchard, J., & Wine, B. (2019). Using scorecards and a lottery to improve the performance of behavior technicians in two autism treatment clinics. *Journal of Organizational Behavior Management, 39,* 45–57. doi: 10.1080/01608061.2019.1632241

Haberlin, A.T., Beauchamp, K., Agnew, J., & 'O'Brien, F. (2012). A comparison of pyramidal staff training and direct staff training in community-based day programs. *Journal of Organizational Behavior Management, 32*(1), 65–74. doi: 10.1080/01608061.2012.646848

Hantula, D.A. (2015). Job satisfaction: The management tool and leadership responsibility. *Journal of Organizational Behavior Management, 35*(1–2), 81–94. doi: 10.1080/01608061.2015.1031430

Hine, K.M. (2014). Effects of behavioral skills training with directed data collection on the acquisition of behavioral practices by workers in a private, not-for-profit child care center. *Journal of Organizational Behavior Management, 34*(3), 223–232. doi: 10.1080/01608061.2014.944744

Houmanfar, R. & Johnson, R. (2004). Organizational implications of gossip and rumor. *Journal of Organizational Behavior Management, 23*(2–3), 117–138, doi: 10.1300/J075v23n02_07

Hyten, C. (2009). Strengthening the focus on business results: The need for systems approaches in organizational behavior management. *Journal of Organizational Behavior Management, 29*(2), 87–107. doi: 10.1080/01608060902874526

Jeffrey, S.A., Schulz, A., & Webb, A. (2012). The performance effects of an ability-based approach to goal assignment. *Journal of Organizational Behavior Management, 32*(3), 221–241. doi: 10.1080/01608061.2012.698116

Jenkins, S.R. & DiGennaro Reed, F.D. (2016). A parametric analysis of rehearsal opportunities on procedural integrity. *Journal of Organizational Behavior Management, 36*(4), 255–281, doi: 10.1080/01608061.2016.1236057

Jessup, P.A. & Stahelski, A.J. (1999). The effects of a combined goal setting, feedback and incentive intervention on job performance in a manufacturing environment. *Journal of Organizational Behavior Management, 19*(3), 5–26. doi:10.1300/J075v19n03_02

Johnson, D.A. (2013). A component analysis of the impact of evaluative and objective feedback on performance. *Journal of Organizational Behavior Management, 33*(2), 89–103. doi: 10.1080/01608061.2013.785879

Johnson, D.A., Rocheleau, J.M., & Tilka, R.E. (2015). Considerations in feedback delivery: The role of accuracy and type of evaluation. *Journal of Organizational Behavior Management, 35*(3–4), 240–258. doi: 10.1080/01608061.2015.1093055

Johnson, D.A. & Rubin, S. (2011). Effectiveness of interactive computer-based instruction: A review of studies published between 1995 and 2007. *Journal of Organizational Behavior Management, 31*(1), 55–94. doi: 10.1080/01608061.2010.541821

Karlsson, T. & Chase, P.N. (1996). A comparison of three prompting methods for training software use. *Journal of Organizational Behavior Management, 16*(1), 27–44. doi: 10.1300/J075v16n01_03

Kelley, D.P. & Gravina, N. (2018). A paradigm shift in healthcare: An open door for organizational behavior management. *Journal of Organizational Behavior Management, 38*(1), 73–89. doi: 10.1080/01608061.2017.1325824

Kent, R.S. (1986). *25 steps to getting performance problems off of your desk ... and out of your life!* Dodd, Mead, and Company Latham, G.P. & Locke, E.A. (2006). Enhancing the benefits and overcoming the pitfalls of goal setting. *Organizational Dynamics, 35*(4), 332–340. doi: 10.1016/j.orgdyn.2006.08.008

Loewy, S. & Bailey, J. (2007). The effects of graphic feedback, goal-setting, and manager praise on customer service behaviors. *Journal of Organizational Behavior Management, 27*(3), 15–26. doi: 10.1300/J075v27n03_02

Loughrey, T.O., Marshall, G.K., Bellizzi, A., & Wilder, D.A. (2013). The use of video modeling, prompting, and feedback to increase credit card promotion in a retail setting. *Journal of Organizational Behavior Management, 33*(3), 200–208. doi:10.1080/01608061.2013.815097

Ludwig, T.D., Gray, T.W., & Rowell, A. (1998). Increasing recycling in academic buildings: A systematic replication. *Journal of Applied Behavior Analysis, 31*(4), 683–686. doi: 10.1901/jaba.1998.31-683

Luke, M.M., Carr, J.E., & Wilder, D.A. (2018). On the compatibility of organizational behavior management and BACB certification. *Journal of Organizational Behavior Management, 38*(4), 288–305. doi: 10.1080/01608061.2018.1514347

Mager, R.F. & Pipe, P. (2004). *Analyzing performance problems: Or, You Really Oughta Wanna.* The Center for Effective Performance.

Mager, R.F. & Pipe, P. (1970). *Analyzing performance problems.* Fearon Publishers.

Malott, R.W. (1992). A theory of rule-governed behavior and organizational management. *Journal of Organizational Behavior Management, 12*(2), 45–65. doi: 10.1300/J075v12n02_03

Martinez-Onstott, B., Wilder, D., & Sigurdsson, S. (2016). Identifying the variables contributing to at-risk performance: Initial evaluation of the Performance Diagnostic Checklist–Safety (PDC-Safety). *Journal of Organizational Behavior Management, 36*(1), 80–93. doi:10.1080/01608061.2016.1152209

Matthews, G.A. & Dickinson, A.M. (2000). Effects of alternative activities on time allocated to task performance under different percentages of incentive pay. *Journal of Organizational Behavior Management, 20*(1), 3–27. doi: 10.1300/J075v20n01_02

Miller, M.V., Carlson, J., & Sigurdsson, S. O. (2014). Improving treatment integrity in a human service setting using lottery-based incentives. *Journal of Organizational Behavior Management, 34*(1), 29–38. doi: 10.1080/01608061.2013.873381

Miller, N.D., Meindl, J.N., & Caradine, M. (2016). The effects of bin proximity and visual prompts on recycling in a university building. *Behavior and Social Issues, 25*, 4–10. doi: 10.5210/bsi.v25i0.6141

Miltenberger, R.G. (2018). *Behavior modification: Principles and procedures.* Cengage Learning.

O'Connor, R.T., Lerman, D.C., Fritz, J.N., & Hodde, H.B. (2010). Effects of number and location of bins on plastic recycling at a university. *Journal of Applied Behavior Analysis, 43*(4), 711–715. doi: 10.1901/jaba.2010.43-711

O'Hora, D. & Maglieri, K.A. (2006). Goal statements and goal-directed behavior: A relational frame account of goal setting in organizations. *Journal of Organizational Behavior Management, 26*(1–2), 131–170. doi: 10.1300/J075v26n01_06

Olson, R., Wright, R.R., Elliot, D., Hess, J., Thompson, S., Buckmaster, A., Luther, K., & Wipfli, B. (2015). The COMPASS Pilot Study: A Total Worker Health™ Intervention for Home Care Workers. *Journal of Occupational and Environmental Medicine, 57* (4), 406–416. doi: 10.1097/JOM.0000000000000374

Palmer, M.G. & Johnson, C.M. (2013). The effects of task clarification and group graphic feedback on early punch-in times. *Journal of Organizational Behavior Management, 33*(4), 265–275. doi: 10.1080/01608061.2013.843492

Pampino, R.N., Jr., MacDonald, J.E., Mullin, J.E., & Wilder, D.A. (2003). Weekly feedback vs. daily feedback: An application in retail. *Journal of Organizational Behavior Management, 23*(2–3), 21–43. doi: 10.1300/J075v23n02_03

Pampino, R.N., Wilder, D.A., & Binder, C. (2005). The use of functional assessment and frequency building procedures to increase product knowledge and data entry skills among foremen in a construction organization. *Journal of Organizational Behavior Management, 25*(2), 1–36. doi: 10.1300/J075v25n02_01

Parnell, A.M., Lorah, E.R., Karnes, A., & Schaefer-Whitby, P. (2017). Effectiveness of job aids and post performance review on staff implementation of discrete trial instruction. *Journal of Organizational Behavior Management, 37*(2), 207–220. doi: 10.1080/01608061.2017.1309333

Rafacz, S.D., Boyce, T.E., & Williams, W.L. (2011). Examining the effects of a low-cost prompt to reduce retail theft. *Journal of Organizational Behavior Management, 31*(2), 150–160. doi: 10.1080/01608061.2011.570087

Ralis, M.T. & O'Brien, R.M. (1986). Prompts, goal setting and feedback to increase suggestive selling. *Journal of Organizational Behavior Management, 8*(1), 5–18. doi: 10.1300/J075v08n01_02

Reetz, N.K., Loukus, A.K., Taylor, K.M., & Dixon, M.R. (2014). Investigating the effects of mediated and passive prompts on pedestrian and bicycle lane adherence on a college campus footbridge. *Journal of Organizational Behavior Management, 34*(2), 144–155. doi: 10.1080/01608061.2014.914008

Reetz, N.K., Whiting, S.W., & Dixon, M.R. (2016). The impact of a task clarification and feedback intervention on restaurant service quality. *Journal of Organizational Behavior Management, 36*(4), 322–331. doi: 10.1080/01608061.2016.1201035

Reid, D.H. & Parsons, M.B. (1996). A comparison of staff acceptability of immediate versus delayed verbal feedback in staff training. *Journal of Organizational Behavior Management, 16*(2), 35–47. doi: 10.1300/J075v16n02_03

Reid, D.H., Parsons, M.B., & Green, C.W. (2012). *The supervisor's guidebook: Evidence-based strategies for promoting work quality and enjoyment among human service staff.* Habilitative Management Consultants.

Rodriguez, M., Wilder, D.A., Therrien, K., Wine, B., Miranti, R., Daratany, K., ... Rodriguez, M. (2005). Use of the performance diagnostic checklist to select an intervention designed to increase the offering of promotional stamps at two sites of a restaurant franchise. *Journal of Organizational Behavior Management, 25*(3), 17–35. doi: 10.1300/J075v25n03_02

Roose, K.M. & Williams, W.L. (2018). An evaluation of the effects of very difficult goals. *Journal of Organizational Behavior Management, 38*(1), 18–48. doi: 10.1080/01608061.2017.1325820

Shapiro, M. & Kazemi, E. (2017). A review of training strategies to teach individuals implementation of behavioral interventions. *Journal of Organizational Behavior Management, 37*(1), 32–62. doi: 10.1080/01608061.2016.1267066

Shier, L., Rae, C., & Austin, J. (2003). Using task clarification, checklists and performance feedback to improve the appearance of a grocery store. *Performance Improvement Quarterly, 16*(2), 26–40. doi:10.1111/j.1937-8327.2003.tb00277.x

Skinner, B.F. (1953). *Science and human behavior.* Macmillan.

Slowiak, J.M., Madden, G.J., & Mathews, R. (2005). The effects of a combined task clarification, goal setting, feedback, and performance contingent consequence intervention package on telephone customer service in a medical clinic environment. *Journal of Organizational Behavior Management, 25*(4), 15–35. doi: 10.1300/J075v25n04_02

Smith, M. & Wilder, D.A. (2018). The use of the Performance Diagnostic Checklist-Human Services to assess and improve the job performance of individuals with intellectual disabilities. *Behavior Analysis in Practice, 11*(2), 148–153. doi:10.1007/s40617-018-0213-4

Squires, J., Wilder, D.A., Fixsen, A., Hess, E., Rost, K., Curran, R., & Zonneveld, K. (2007). The effects of task clarification, visual prompts, and graphic feedback on customer greeting and up-selling in a restaurant. *Journal of Organizational Behavior Management, 27*(3), 1–13. doi: 10.1300/J075v27n03_01

Tammemagi, T., O'Hora, D., & Maglieri, K. A. (2013). The effects of a goal setting intervention on productivity and persistence in an analogue work task. *Journal of Organizational Behavior Management, 33*(1), 31–54. doi: 10.1080/01608061.2013.758001

Therrien, K., Wilder, D A., Rodriguez, M., & Wine, B. (2005). Preintervention analysis and improvement of customer greeting in a restaurant. *Journal of Applied Behavior Analysis, 38*, 411–415. doi:10.1901/jaba.2005.89-04

Van Houten, R., Hilton, B., Schulman, R., & Reagan, I. (2011). Using accelerator pedal force to increase seat belt use of service vehicle drivers. *Journal of Applied Behavior Analysis, 44*(1), 41–49. doi: 10.1901/jaba.2011.44-41

VanStelle, S.E., Vicars, S.M., Harr, V., Miguel, C.F., Koerber, J.L., Kazbour, R., & Austin, J. (2012). The publication history of the Journal of Organizational Behavior Management: An objective review and analysis: 1998–2009. *Journal of Organizational Behavior Management, 32*, 93–123. doi: 10.1080/01608061.2012.675864

Wilder, D.A., Austin, J., & Casella, S. (2009). Applying behavior analysis in organizations: Organizational behavior management. *Psychological Services, 6*(3), 202–211. doi: 10.1037/a0015393

Wilder, D., Lipschultz, J., Gehrman, C., Ertel, H., & Hodges, A. (2019). A preliminary assessment of the reliability and validity of the Performance Diagnostic Checklist-Human Service. *Journal of Organizational Behavior Management, 39*(3–4), 194–212. doi: 10.1080/01608061.2019.1666772

Wilder, D., A., Lipschultz, J., King, A., Driscoll, S., & Sigurdsson, S. (2018) An analysis of the commonality and type of preintervention assessment procedures in the Journal of Organizational Behavior Management (2000–2015). *Journal of Organizational Behavior Management, 38*(1), 5–17. doi: 10.1080/01608061.2017.1325822

Wilson, C., Boni, N., & Hogg, A. (1997). The effectiveness of task clarification, positive reinforcement and corrective feedback in changing courtesy among police staff. *Journal of Organizational Behavior Management*, *17*(1), 65–99. doi: 10.1300/J075v17n01_04

Wine, B., Edgerton, L., Inzana, E., & Newcomb, E.T. (2017). Further effects of lottery odds on responding. *Journal of Organizational Behavior Management*, *37*(1), 75–82. doi: 10.1080/01608061.2016.1267064

Witt, J.C., Noell, G.H., LaFleur, L.H., & Mortenson, B.P. (1997). Teacher use of interventions in general education settings: Measurement and analysis of the independent variable. *Journal of Applied Behavior Analysis*, *30*(4), 693–696. doi: 10.1901/jaba.1997.30-693

2

Behavior-Based Safety as a Replicable Technology

Mark P. Alavosius and Ken Burleigh

BEHAVIOR-BASED SAFETY

a) Origin

Behavior analysts initiated efforts in the 1970s by applying the concepts, procedures, and analyses of applied behavior analysis toward understanding and managing behaviors involved in occupational injuries and illness. This decade was notable for behavior analysis as many applications of behavior analysis were emerging, in line with the dimensions of applied behavior analysis described by Baer et al. (1968), to address a wide range of social problems. Besides the expansion of effort to treat and educate dependent populations, applications emerged and/or expanded in community psychology, public health, behavioral medicine, industrial/organizational psychology, environmental protection, education, and other socially significant areas.

Journals such as the *Journal of Applied Behavior Analysis* (*JABA*), *Behavior Modification, Education and Treatment of Children*, the *Journal of Organizational Behavior Management* (*JOBM*), and others provided peer-reviewed outlets for reports of applied research, demonstration projects, conceptual analyses, and calls for more research, training, and dissemination. The Association for Behavior Analysis (not yet international) provided a venue for the relatively small membership to gather and share efforts across many fronts. Integration of subfields within behavior analysis was evident in the transfer and sharing of findings across applications. The ABA presidential addresses of Jack Michael (Michael, 1980) and Don Baer (Baer, 1981) revealed tensions between basic laboratory researchers seeking to discover and articulate principles of behavior and applied practitioners seeking practical solutions to socially valid problems. Concern was over drift away from scientific foundations by those focusing on technology development and how this affected prospects for future directions in the field. Drift toward technology was a topic of debate as some worried that applications rushed ahead of scientific discovery.

The first author of this chapter entered graduate school in 1983 (University of Massachusetts, Amherst – UMASS) and joined Beth Sulzer-Azaroff's research group. This was an opportune time and setting as Beth was President of the ABA in 1982 (the first woman to hold that office). Her presidential address to the ABA celebrated leaders in behavior analysis (her heroes in both basic and applied areas) and sought to calm the emerging rift splitting basic and applied researchers. Beth led a grant-funded doctoral training program to generate leaders in behavior analysis at this time. Her students were federally funded throughout their doctoral

DOI: 10.4324/9781003198949-2

training to complete their studies, conduct research, and disseminate results. Beth's training approach was highly influenced by Fred Keller's Personalized System of Instruction (PSI) model (Keller, 1968) and structured as a competency-based curriculum that guided students to demonstrate mastery on core competencies in behavior analysis. The learning curve was steep and the pace was brisk. A number of leaders in behavior analysis at the time (e.g., Skinner, Sidman, Baer, Hopkins, Wolf, Risley, Bijou, and others) visited Beth's program, reviewed the competency framework, and advised on refinements. These were exciting times to be a doctoral student in behavior analysis, and Beth took effort to bridge the diverse interests in behavior analysis. Her teaching methods immersed her students in behavior management as Beth applied what she professed.

Behavior-based safety in 1983 was in its infancy. Three people stand out as the pioneers of this field – Judy Komaki, Bill Hopkins, and Beth Sulzer-Azaroff. Judy had published in 1978 on behavior analysis applied to safety in a meatpacking plant in the Midwest (Komaki et al., 1978). Workers were exposed to various risks (e.g., lacerations, contaminates, slips and falls, etc.) as they eviscerated, processed and packed poultry. In 1978 Bill began an analysis of incentives applied to safety behaviors in open-pit coal mining in the southwest where risks involved vehicle operations, exposure to dust, and material handling hazards (Fox et al., 1987). In 1978 Beth published (Sulzer-Azaroff, 1978) on safety behaviors in a materials science laboratory in a university in New England. Personnel in this lab handled a variety of hazardous materials, wore personal protective equipment (PPE), and needed to adhere to chemical safety protocols. These fledgling efforts, across quite different work environments, demonstrated the utility of applying behavior analysis to assess and manage variations in work safety behaviors. Much was yet to be learned, but these early projects showed the promise of improving workplace safety by behavior assessment, contingency management, controlled program evaluation, and organized behavior management aligned with safety engineering.

Graduate students in behavior analysis in 1983 had a few published examples of the emerging behavior-based safety approach and many examples of the forward march of applied behavior analysis in other settings and with other populations. As a student working with Beth, the experience might be described as "learning to fly with Orville." Looking back, behavioral safety was taking flight and opportunities were everywhere. Under her tutelage, the emphasis was to embrace the contributions of basic and applied research and find opportunities possible within the community to transfer behavior science toward socially important applications. This outreach was conducted as applied research with rigorous evaluation using experimental designs for field settings (Cook & Campbell, 1979).

Beth articulated her thoughts of the scope of behavioral safety in several papers and chapters and looked to see advances in research, understanding of the context for safety, and development of a replicable technology. This required competencies to integrate real-world applications with scientific foundations and use rigorous methodologies for testing implementations. Training at UMASS under her mentorship entailed a breadth of experiences arranged toward that end guided by the available scholarly publications. Bill Hopkins commented that Beth, more than anyone, promoted coherent scientific development for behavioral safety as opposed to some that focused almost exclusively on technological features. He reported that Beth was persuasive with safety professionals who might favor development of treatment packages over scientific understanding of risky work behaviors and analysis of the sources of variation that produced them. A concern among behavior analysts working in safety in the early 1980s was that behavior-based safety might become a cookbook, rote approach to safety and rise and fade as many management fads do. This drift was a central concern expressed by Michael (1980) in regards to all applications of behavior analysis. Baer (1981) observed that "the cat was out of the bag" and a grand experiment was underway as applications could not be stopped and lessons were learned via applying science. Thus, the development of behavior-based safety (BBS) over more than 40 years reveals if those concerns were warranted.

The first author of this chapter worked in developmental disability treatment centers for a number of years before entering graduate school and witnessed, firsthand, the occupational injuries incurred by caregivers and clients in part due to behavioral variation in work practices. Particularly serious were the injuries incurred in nursing and healthcare services provided to medically frail individuals. Caregivers suffered sprains and strains from the biomechanical pressures of lifting patients. Patients were injured in slips and falls and from sedentary positioning leading to skin breakdowns and difficulty breathing. Settings near campus provided the resources, interests, and opportunity to extend behavior analysis to the prevention of injury incurred during health routines provided to dependent populations. His thesis and doctoral research examined BBS applied to behavioral assessments and interventions to improve patient handling behaviors and reduce injuries to caregivers and patients. The durability of behavior change achieved with BBS contingency management was relatively untested at that time. The opportunity to examine schedules or density of feedback in the context of shaping caregivers' safety behaviors allowed examination of variations in implementation regimens in light of research into humans' response under schedules of reinforcement (Weiner, 1983) and the early studies of behavioral momentum (Nevin, 1988). A field study of BBS enabled us to assess the durability of behavior change achieved with practical BBS interventions (Alavosius & Sulzer-Azaroff, 1990) and perhaps reveals something about the partial reinforcement extinction effect.

Much research and application of BBS has been completed in the 40 years since the founding work in the late 1970s. This chapter highlights the growth in interest in BBS and the accumulation of knowledge amassed in over 300 publications addressing BBS. Our plan is to provide readers with an account of BBS, an extensive reading list to explore, and a discussion of the status of BBS in 2020. We seek to suggest what is ahead for graduate students and young researchers interested in creating further advances.

b) Basic BBS conceptual framework

Sulzer-Azaroff (1978, 1982) described behavioral safety as the prevention of occupational accidents in part resulting from the interaction of work behavior and the physical environment. She labeled this an "ecological" perspective as the frame of analysis. This conceptualization leads to analysis of work environments and the behaviors of workers as they perform tasks within a job to identify sources of variation that contribute to injury and illness. From this view, unsafe work behaviors may be seen as deviations from safe behaviors at granular levels of quite molecular behaviors to larger composite units such as acts, practices, and techniques needed to complete a job. Variations may result from faulty or incomplete learning, distraction, fatigue, improper or misaligned reinforcement, and a host of other sources of variability. Some of these reside in the environment; some are in the repertoire of the performer. Gilbert (1978, 2007) succinctly articulated this distinction in his behavioral engineering matrix. Analyses may reveal that people engage in unsafe conduct because they have not acquired the requisite competencies to act safely, and in other cases people may have acquired the competencies, but the work environment differs from the learning setting and fails to select and maintain the needed safety performance.

Safety performance management is a replicable technology based on experimentally derived principles of behavior. The antecedents and consequences of behavior influence behavior, and these conditions can be identified and managed to influence performance (Skinner, 1953). Considerable research (see the reading list of 300 papers) shows that safety and health performance management can be accomplished in a variety of work settings such that it is hard to imagine an industry in which it has not been applied effectively. A number of texts are available describing behavioral procedures for improving safety performance. Various user conferences showcase applications and a number of consultant companies commercialize BBS services and technologies. A variety of behavior change procedures incorporating reinforcement, punishment, and stimulus control are demonstrated to be effective in improving work safety. An impressive research base and series of project reports, spanning over 40 years, supports the merit of applying behavior analysis to improve work safety.

c) Basic BBS procedures

Practicing safety performance management effectively requires skill in analyzing and managing the complex contingencies operative in work environments. Successful application is accomplished by organizing work contingencies (the relationships among antecedents, behaviors, consequences) to primarily strengthen safe behaviors and secondarily discourage at-risk ones. Practically, this entails identifying sources of variation in work tasks and processes and the organization of a work environment that supports safety. Typically, the development of a BBS process begins with data analyses guiding the identification of losses (trends in health, safety, environmental events) and the risk exposures that organizational members confront (Sulzer-Azaroff & Fellner, 1984). Workers compensation risk managers, via analysis of insurance claims, typically conduct analyses of loss history and provide data on injury/illness frequencies, characteristics, and costs. These data are, in part, measures of the human and organizational impact of unsafe work conditions and practices. Additional data may be available from incident investigations that examine the chain of events leading to serious industrial accidents. In the United States, the federal government requires employers to record and post annual reports of recordable injuries (Occupational Safety and Health Administration (OSHA) logs). These records of loss events provide a starting place to identify at-risk behaviors and desired safety practices. Reviewing an organization's accident log and other records is often a starting point in the search for behavioral safety targets. Incident reports describing both work injuries, illnesses, and "near-misses" can reveal characteristics of risky work behaviors and their context. These reports, often available from the insurance company's claims and underwriting databases, profile the experience of an organization in many useful ways. These show the general features of the company (size, payroll, insurance premiums, and claims' cost as a percentage of premium, etc.), its detailed history of losses, configuration of management and the workforce, and other important measures of organizational context related to health and safety. The insurance carrier benchmarks the company against its industry and sets the premium based on the comparisons. Analyses of these metrics suggest behaviors that expose workers to the greatest risk for injury and help specify safety practices that should replace risky alternatives.

d) Behaviors relevant to safety and health

Specifying optimally safe behavior is usually the most challenging activity for developing a behavioral safety program, as in many cases the safest way to perform a job is not easily determined, as many actions combine in a chain of activities to complete a task. This is further complicated as tasks combine in a sequence of steps to complete a process. Where to focus examination is often a matter of opinion as to the level of granularity most useful to detecting meaningful variation. Subject matter experts (e.g., those who design the tasks and processes, write instructions and standard operating procedures, and create measures of output, etc.) are helpful in ascertaining the deviations in behaviors that are associated with losses and what dimensions of responding are related to risk. Consider repetitive motion tasks such as packing products for shipment after their assembly. The movements of a packer that exposes her to cumulative trauma include repetitive reaching, grasping, twisting, and other manipulations of materials. The rotation of the fingers, wrist, arms, and shoulders, the force of the pinch grip to grasp products, the length of the reach, and the dynamics of the motions are topographical differences. All might play a part in cumulative trauma. Specifying the safest topography and rate of these movements is a challenging assignment that probably exceeds the expertise of most safety and production managers. Those with training in ergonomics, biomechanics, and physiology can define the stressors to which workers are exposed and define the optimal technique for completing the task and avoiding trauma. Note in this example that our lens is set on the dimensions of behaviors of the packer. Other workers behaviors are impactful as well. Scheduling workers to jobs, setting their break schedule, arranging job rotation, and other manipulations of temporal factors are behaviors of supervisors and managers that affect risk for injury. The designs of the physical work environment (e.g., height of workstation, lighting, temperature, size of packaging, distance carried, pace of production, etc.) are the result of behaviors by industrial planners. The instructions, feedback, and incentives (if any) provided to the packers from peers, supervisors, and managers affects the pace of their work. The risk of cumulative trauma in this example is affected by the interlocked measurable behaviors of many organizational members that influence risk exposure with the rate of packing behaviors and their biomechanical stressors being most relevant to cumulative trauma injuries.

e) BBS observation systems

Given the specification of work behaviors related to injuries and illnesses, the typical BBS development process moves to designing an observation system to measure variation, over time, of the designated behaviors. Often times, trained human observers score the behaviors they observe along dimensions of safety. These scores are plotted as time-series data. This can be a simple rating of observed behavior as being "safe" or "at-risk." Observers might directly observe workers as they conduct the task or score video-taped samples of their work. Plotting these data provide for visual analysis of the level, trend, and variation of samples. Note that this method entails judgment by the observers as to the safety of observed conduct. This appears to be the most common configuration of BBS observation systems – trained observers use a checklist to score samples of actual work behavior and these data are plotted along a timeline. Other observation systems such as sensors, monitors, mechanical logs, and self-observation are possible and might replace or supplement direct observation by BBS observers. In some cases, the results of behaviors might be measured (e.g., spills, blocked fire escape routes, disconnected safety alarms, etc.) as indirect evidence of the behavior that created the hazard. These hazards are observed in safety audits of work settings and provide an indication of at-risk behaviors. Who actually completed the behavior to yield the result may be difficult to determine, but such evidence does contribute to safety behavior assessment in context.

BBS observations are generally announced to those observed and workers are given the opportunity to decline observation. Many systems include gathering workers' input and commentary on the observation as part of data collection. Comments from workers might include reasons for the "at-risk" conduct, recommendations for safety improvements, and other suggestions. While surveillance systems might operate without workers' awareness of them, most BBS observation systems aspire to full disclosure of data collection with an emphasis on promoting safety over punishing misconduct. Many mechanical observation systems, such as instrumentation on vehicles, sensors on oil rigs, monitors on warehouse workers, and many others gather much data on workers' behaviors such as their movements, location, pace, reaction times to signals, physiological state, and so on. These data provide a wealth of objective information on adherence to safety protocols and do not require human observers to rate risk. Incorporation of these measures in BBS protocols is emerging in organizations that can afford the required technology. Aerospace, nuclear power, transportation systems, oil and gas exploration, and medicine are examples where such observations are used to measure workers' adherence to safety standards in both simulated and actual work environments. These instruments gather and stream data to analytic systems that visualize the data, often in complex arrays, and save records for post hoc analyses (e.g., incident investigations of catastrophic events).

Many design considerations in behavioral observation are important to capture or realize the behavioral variation in work sites. The level of granularity required is determined by the risk profile of the work, range of behavioral variation likely to occur, and risk tolerance of the organization. High reliability organizations (HROs) aspire to high levels of precision in repeated operations that entail considerable risk if systems fail (e.g., commercial aviation). HROs engineer control systems, including behavior management, to permit rapid detection and correction of behavioral variation that undermines operational integrity. These organizations offer venues to study refinements in BBS and perhaps discover more about interlocking behavioral contingencies acting on complex work behaviors by individuals and teams.

f) Sources of behavioral variation

One objective of the task specification process is to identify the task/process components in sufficient detail to permit development of an observational system that detects meaningful variation in how workers actually perform the work. This enables for the establishment of a baseline that could be said to "realize" the trend and patterns in behavior over time, across settings, and in relation to other contextual variables. To be maximally useful, the observation system collects sufficient data to reveal practically important variation in behaviors in relation to sources of that variation. Note that this requires measuring behavior (e.g., use of PPE) and measuring context (e.g., social situations where there is potential to contact COVID-19 from surfaces, other people, etc.) and examining covariation. Some sources of behavioral variation might be time dependent, so a schedule of observations that samples at identified time points permits detection of cycles, periods, and seasonal variation in behavior. For example, safety behavior deteriorating due to fatigue would be more evident later in a shift than earlier. This might be detected during the workday, work week, or job rotation. A physician might be more likely to commit a medical error at the end of her 12-hour shift than during the middle of the shift. An oil field worker may make faulty decisions on day 20 of a three-week stay on a rig than upon arrival. Other sources of variation may be in the immediate environment (e.g., distractors) that occasion at-risk behaviors. The contextual factors that stimulate or occasion at-risk behavior and safe alternatives are ideally identified during baseline observations, and these factors are considered in the design of interventions.

Interviewing workers and supervisors about their observations of others' work behavior and seeking recommendations regarding safe performance can obtain additional information. Subject matter experts provide guidelines to inform decisions as to how to best conduct these tasks, but this information may not be written as behavioral definitions. Often, consultation with content-area experts (e.g., ergonomists, industrial hygienists, industrial engineers, etc.) is needed to articulate optimal work practices as response classes and the context in which variation is observed.

Within BBS initiatives, workers' own behaviors (i.e., those behaviors proximate to the injury) are most frequently identified as the primary contributor to work accidents. Less frequently identified are the behaviors of supervisors, managers, and executives as contributing to work-related injuries. As one examines the proximate behaviors leading to injuries and illnesses, more distal behaviors are found that set the stage for their occurrence. A comprehensive assessment of an organization's safety program will typically reveal a lattice-work of behaviors from those of the top executives through management levels to front-line workers that operate to assess and control risks for work accidents. An even broader assessment would consider the culture of work and explore how marketplace contingencies, industry traditions, and cultural practices influence self-protective behaviors and safety practices. Much research in behavioral safety has tended to focus on the behaviors of workers that are proximate to injury or illness (e.g., examine lifting technique in efforts to prevent back injuries) and have not examined the complexity of organizational behaviors (e.g., setting work schedules, production goals, staffing patterns, etc.) and cultural practices (e.g., risk-taking) that are the context for work-related injury.

These classes of behavior influence safety often in unplanned ways. For example, consider a nurse aide's caring for non-ambulatory patients in a residential care facility. (Note: A job leading to high rates of back injuries and often targeted for safety interventions.) The technique this person uses to lift, carry, and transfer patients is crucial to the success and safety of the patient handling assignments within the context of nursing care. Using variable, uncoordinated, or otherwise faulty lifting technique can lead to injury to both the caregiver and the patient. The observation system detects variation in the topography of behaviors (in this case, the movements of the caregiver and patient through the sequence of transfer), their function (relocation from one surface to another without harm), and features of the context (e.g., time of day, location, obstacles such as IV's (intravenous catheters), confined space, work schedule demands, etc.). An added complexity is the importance of infection control during patient contact. The spread of infection is a risk factor that must also be addressed by improving adherence to hygiene guidelines. Collection of many observations reveal variations in behavior correlated with environmental variables so that potential sources of variation can be identified.

One approach to improve the safety of patient handling is to shape caregivers' transfer technique to reduce biomechanical stressors, standardize practices, and promote cooperation by the patient. The patient transfer entails communication between the caregiver and patient to coordinate steps. Often, but not always, the patient bears some weight by standing and pivoting during the move from one surface to another. Clear communication and coordinated, interlocked behavior reduce the probability of slips, falls, and awkward movements that contribute to sprains and strains. This can be accomplished by task analyzing transfer procedures, arranging for on-the-job observation of work practices, and providing performance feedback to caregivers on the safety of their work (Alavosius & Sulzer-Azaroff, 1985, 1986, 1990; Luke & Alavosius, 2011). Whereas this has proven to be an effective method to establish work safety practices, it is an approach that requires acceptance of observation and intervention by workers, commitment from management and allocation of supervisory time to sustain its operation. Lacking these support systems, feedback systems tend to falter and behavior may revert to baseline levels if the intervention does not establish fluency.

g) BBS interventions

A useful baseline coupled with input from people conducting the task and experts in the process leads to the formulation of an intervention when behavioral variability is unacceptable and deemed under the control of performers. Gilbert's (1978) behavioral engineering matrix offers a logic map to organize interventions from relatively low-cost, easy adjustments to the work environment such as improving tools, equipment, instructions, feedback, and incentives to guide safer behavior within context. More costly and effortful interventions like training competencies, selecting workers whose values align with the work, and motivational campaigns are considered if simple environmental changes are inadequate. BBS interventions are generally organized with the buy-in and commitment of key organizational members (e.g., workers, supervisors, labor leaders, managers, and executives) and operate as an open system. That is, everyone is informed of the purpose, goals, objectives, procedures, and measures. Other diagnostic assessments (e.g., the Performance Diagnostic Checklist; Chapter 1 of this text) provide similar methods to develop interventions from surveys of potential sources of behavioral variability.

The test of an intervention is observation that behavior changes, when and only when, the intervention is applied. Various evaluation designs for field settings (e.g., multiple baselines, changing criterion, withdrawals, and group comparisons) are suitable to evaluate BBS interventions. These coupled with social validity assessments determine if the BBS is effective in changing behavior and acceptable to the participants. The ultimate test is demonstration that the behavior change leads to a reduction in reported loss events. Tracking near-hits, first aid cases, and serious and catastrophic events reveals if the behaviors selected for change are in fact related to loss prevention. OSHA logs, insurance loss runs, accident investigation reports, incident reports, and other data sources within organizations are correlated with the behavioral time-series data to assess impact. There is no question that across the decades, various BBS interventions, used in a wide range of industries and settings, have prevented countless injuries, illnesses, fatalities, and much human suffering.

Institutionalizing proven effective BBS interventions within the communication, supervisory, and incentive systems of the organization is a preferred strategy as this likely sustains the managed contingencies and reduces the disruption caused when key personnel depart, and new hires enter the organization. Codified BBS interventions (e.g., descriptions of the instructions, signaling, coaching, feedback, incentives, etc.) and supports (e.g., data displays, briefings, reports, etc.) enable replication across behaviors, personnel, locations, and organizations. A search of the reading list in this chapter reveals many examples of BBS applied, extended, and sustained in a wide range of organizations and industries.

REVIEW OF THE BBS LITERATURE (1954 TO PRESENT)

The literature search for this chapter began with a reference list from the Cambridge Center for Behavioral Studies (CCBS; www.behavior.org) website of approximately 200 articles from 1954–2008. We supplemented the CCBS list with web searches using the University of Nevada, Reno's One Search function of the online library system that pulled from PsychINFO and PsychARTICLES, among many other databases. The keywords: behavior-based safety, BBS, behavior safety, safety, EHS (Environment, Health, Safety), and safety programs were used to locate articles. The search included the years 1950–2020. This was supplemented with a follow-up search on Google Scholar using the same key words and date restrictions. This also listed the number of times the publication was cited. The results were reviewed for their relevance to BBS using an ad hoc review of the titles and abstracts to determine inclusion in the reading list. A good starting point for BBS publications is Heinrich's (1954) text *Industrial accident prevention: A scientific approach*, 4th Edition, that is seen by many as the first articulation of the importance of human behavior in industrial accidents. Heinrich reviewed many incident reports and observed that human error contributed to upwards of 90% of accidents. His approach to prevention included the design of safer work environments and management of human behavior. By the late 1970s, BBS publications began to show up with regularity and reached their current rate after 1980 and have been relatively consistent through 2020 (approximately 35 publications per year).

Readers are encouraged to review this list of articles ($n = 317$), presented in chronological order, and observe the expansion of topics, journals serving as outlets, number of times each

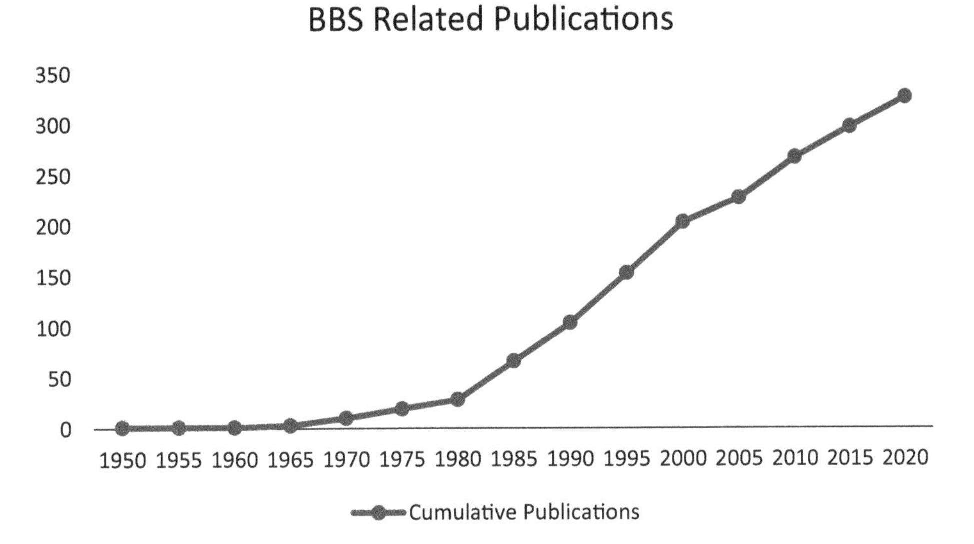

FIGURE 2.1 Cumulative count of BBS publications.

TABLE 2.1
Top five journals publishing BBS papers

Journal	*Publications*	*Impact Factor*
Journal of Organizational Behavior Management	42	1.09
Journal of Applied Behavior Analysis	33	1.53
Journal of Safety Research	28	2.4
Professional Safety	18	N/A
Journal of Applied Psychology	12	5.07

publication has been cited, and proliferation of researchers and practitioners developing BBS. This list conveys the wide application of BBS in the industrial, healthcare, transportation, service, construction, and energy sectors of the economy and in community settings. The implementations across organizations, settings and decades make a compelling case that BBS is a socially valid, widely adopted method to improve safety.

The top five outlets for BBS publications are noted with their current (October, 2020) impact factor. Readers are encouraged to explore the list for examples relevant to projects they conduct. The search will yield nuances in how principles of behavior are applied creatively in a vast number of replications.

BBS TECHNOLOGY

The dissemination of BBS depicted in the published literature reveals that BBS technology is massively deployed worldwide. This speaks clearly to its demonstrated utility, cost-effectiveness, and user satisfaction. Within the area of OBM, BBS stands out as an example of a replicable technology for behavior change that enjoys widespread and lasting support. Numerous consulting firms and management services offer some version of BBS and have developed significant markets for the technology.

a) Direct and indirect contingency management

BBS interventions predominantly entail management of direct and indirect contingencies within the boundaries of an organizational setting. Antecedent manipulations like instructions, signals, prompts, alerts, training, and values alignment are common elements of interventions. Consequences like feedback on performance, praise, correction, and incentives are ubiquitous. Contingency management includes interlocking elements in teamwork where the behavior of one person is antecedent to the behavior of another and team members' combined behaviors are coordinated by the environmental variables managed in the intervention. Some of the intervention components are present in the work environment and are immediately and directly influential on workers' behavior. For example, standard work instructions viewed during the completion of a task are directly acting to guide behavior. Other components are delayed and follow behavior, sometimes at much later times. Thus, these are indirect acting. For example, a monthly posting of charts depicting behavioral variation observed by a group of workers over time is an indirect influence on future behavior. The mechanism of action for both direct- and indirect-acting contingencies is explained by appeal to principles of behavior such as reinforcement, punishment, stimulus control, rule governance, and selection processes of interlocking behavioral contingencies.

While a few basic principles of behavior underlie all effective BBS interventions, variations in intervention development and implementation abound. The papers and reports in the reading list convey the diversity of approaches and customization that is prevalent in applications. Skillful coordination by managers of treatment components (e.g., training, instructions, coaching, feedback, and reinforcement) differentiates BBS interventions that have a weak and short-lived impact from those that have large, sustained effects.

b) Controversies and misperceptions

As practitioners deployed BBS during the early decades (the 1980s and 1990s), criticisms were advanced by some labor organizations that BBS was an instrument used by management to assign blame to the workers for their injuries creating resistance to BBS within some industries. Resisting transference of effective behavior science solutions to settings that would benefit from reducing variation in safety behaviors remains an issue, although the prevalence is limited. The controversy was a misperception of behavioral principles that describe behavioral variation as a function of the environmental variables. Some critics viewed at-risk behavior as a choice made by workers and therefore any injury was due to human error (i.e., a stance that blames the worker for their behavior). The stance completely failed to see behavior as under the influence of context and that is under the organization's manager's control. A common method to alleviate this resistance is to have BBS design and management teams comprised of representatives of levels of the organization so that workers participate in the design, implementation, evaluation and refinement of BBS processes.

Another related resistance to BBS is fear that observations of at-risk behaviors may occasion disciplinary action from management. Often, the identities of those observed are not recorded and therefore not entered into organizational safety records. Maintaining the anonymity of those observed ensures that the BBS process is instructive and not disciplinary in operation. This protection is challenged by the increasing use of automated surveillance systems such as vehicle black boxes, video cameras, voice recorders, motion detectors, proximity detectors, and other sensors that record behavioral observations and stream data to analytic systems. These data records may contain fields that identify those observed and permit tagging data to personal identity. This is an area for further examination as anonymous behavioral data are often featured as a way to insulate workers from blame for their own at-risk actions.

c) Competencies needed for implementation

The brief discussion above illuminates the core knowledge of behavioral principles and technologies at the foundation of BBS systems. Review of the many reports of effective implementation suggests that a rudimentary understanding of behavioral principles coupled with practical expertise in managing work tasks and processes is adequate. Few of the effective, sustained BBS programs deployed worldwide in a multitude of industries are managed by personnel with advanced training in behavior analysis. This is remarkable. A relatively small cadre of BBS consultants, some of whom have little schooling in behavior science, have acquired the necessary competencies to transfer BBS solutions to end-users. This suggests that the competencies needed for implementation in work organizations are those acquired in the successful management of work processes. The complexities of BBS solutions are readily learned by those with a learning history in which they acquire skills in arranging work environments, detecting the impact of adjustments, and industrializing solutions. The availability of many reports of successful implementations, published guidelines for contingency management, popular books, data tracking software (or easily crafted behavioral measures added to internal data systems) and user conferences where BBS managers share their approaches provide sufficient support to those implementing BBS solutions. This is an interesting observation of the maturity of BBS as a technology and worthy of more consideration as it may inform the development process possible with other OBM focus areas.

d) Features of market-driven development

The origins of BBS were within academic programs by Ph.D. level faculty aspiring to extend behavior analysis to socially important problems, namely occupational injury and illness. Sulzer-Azaroff, Komaki, and Hopkins in their pioneering initiatives used experimental designs for field settings to enable rigorous evaluation of behavior change as a function of manipulated variables. This methodological rigor enabled peer review and publication in scientific journals. The early work developing BBS proceeded in similar fashion. The initial projects demonstrated behavior change with socially valuable impact. The risk for injury and illness was reduced when behavioral variability in safety practices was effectively managed. The human suffering and financial cost of occupational injury/illness could be lowered by BBS and market forces selected practical solutions. BBS providers emerged to respond to the demand.

e) Social validity

Wolf (1978), Hawkins (1991), and Houmanfar et al. (2015) among others discuss social validity as a distinguishing feature of behavioral technologies. Examination of BBS replicating in numerous industries over the decades reveals that it is an effective, user-friendly, affordable, practical solution that reliably reduces costly losses across many populations and settings. BBS procedures address important organizational goals to maintain safety, improve wellbeing at work, and generally align with existing organizational functions like human resources, safety, production, and professional development. Thus, the goals and procedures are acceptable to audiences. Safety professionals employ three basic directions to improve workplace safety. First, they engineer environments to reduce hazards by designing equipment and processes, eliminating hazardous materials and exposures, installing guards to isolate dangers, and so on. Second, they employ administrative controls like selecting workers for tasks, training workers in safety standards, scheduling work with consideration of human abilities, and other management initiatives to administer work. When these two are not fully effective, they provide PPE that essentially is armor worn by workers as a last line of defense against injury. Behavior-based safety blends with safety engineering as it provides a practical method to measure variation in important safety behaviors, identify sources of that variation that might be managed, and interventions that embed within management practices.

f) BBS as a service commodity

1) Definition of commodity

A commodity is a commercial good that is interchangeable with other goods of the same type. There is little differentiation between a commodity coming from one producer and the same commodity from another producer. A bushel of wheat is basically the same product, regardless of the producer. One generally thinks of commodities as products (e.g., things) that tend to be sold at a relatively consistent price. Barrels of oil, regardless of producer, are traded at an established price. That price may vary over time, depending on supply and demand, but at any one time, buyers generally see little variation in cost. Services are different in that a given service (e.g., landscape maintenance, plumbing, college instruction) varies in duration and quality. Customers may encounter quite a range in quality and cost. But some services become standardized and replicable to the point they approach commodity level placement in a market. Fee schedules, for example, may set the standards and cost of a service (e.g., a dental procedure) so that the customers encounter little variation in these features and may choose a dentist based on qualitative factors. The end customer experience affects the way the good or service is sold.

2) Receiving system: organizational context

BBS is typically purchased by agents within organizations in search of programs reducing injury and illness attributed to human factors and variation in safety behaviors. The agent may be an owner, executive, production manager, or HSE manager. Large companies with developed and structured management systems likely have an HSE or HSSE department (health, safety environment or health, safety, security, environment) with authorization to purchase support to their internal capability. Smaller companies may not have such departmentalization and owners/leaders may make the purchasing decision. The value BBS brings to the organization is probably viewed along several avenues. One frame is the values of the organization's leaders in terms of understanding that human behavior within the organization contributes to losses like injuries and illnesses to workers. The organization's leaders understand that behaviors can be changed to prevent future occurrences. The organizational leaders see value in preventing human suffering. A related frame is the financial cost of occupational injury and illness. This is a known cost in organizations. Workers compensation insurance manages the expense (e.g., medical costs, wage replacement, disability, etc.) of work-related injury/illness and charges the company an annual premium to cover those estimated costs. Underwriters, who consult actuarial data on the industry in general and a company in particular, set a fee likely to cover expected losses. The insurance companies insure multiple organizations and essentially play the odds that their estimates of loss and premiums charged are calculated so that premiums cover all losses and transaction expense. Insurance companies profit in several ways. They invest the collected premiums in interest-earning investments and accumulate wealth. They pay for claims' incurred losses from the insured's premium. Often losses are less than expected and the residual is profit to the insurer.

Deeper discussion of this is beyond the scope of this chapter on BBS. It is relevant as the insurance industry is a key factor in measuring losses, calculating financial costs, and selecting organizational models that effectively limit losses. In many industries, safety engineering has advanced steadily to control many known hazards and incidence rates have plateaued. Variation in human behavior is one of the last challenges to a step change in safety performance. Thus, BBS finds purchase within the organizational marketplace for management improvements. The purchaser faces two basic choices. The organization can engage external resources, as hired hands, to enter, develop, and implement behavioral controls; or the organization can acquire the needed expertise or train internal personnel in the needed competencies and embed the solution within established functions.

3) Consultant model

BBS consultants entered the marketplace in the 1980s and soon proliferated so that a small number of providers competed in the safety marketplace. The operating model most selected by purchasers was for a trained BBS specialist to consult with safety personnel and managers within the host company to assess behavioral safety needs, develop an intervention typically involved behavioral observation and feedback, and guide the establishment of a working system. The consultation process entailed advising a design team of internal personnel representing key functions within the organization to evaluate safety data (e.g., incident reports, audit reports, investigation reports, etc.) and select critical behaviors likely important to reduce losses. For example, workers' use of PPE, proper body mechanics during material handling, and staying out of the line of fire were behaviors commonly seen as involving risk of injury. The design team proceeded to develop an observation system involving human observers using checklists to score actual behavior at work, and these data were fed back to observed personnel. Sometimes feedback was immediate, personal, and on the job. Other procedures used delayed feedback like posting summaries of observations in break rooms and on bulletin boards. The consultant often followed a planned series of workshops, with workbooks to guide assignments, to support the design team.

Some consultants developed tracking software to tabulate scores and generate graphic depictions of observation trends. The ongoing BBS operations were then managed by an internal BBS team, perhaps part of a larger safety committee, who tended to the behavioral data, planned refinements, and communicated results within the organization. The BBS systems are elegant, replicable procedures to observe behavior in context, manage antecedents like training and coaching to instruct safe work practices, and consequences like praise, acknowledgment, and incentives to celebrate improvements. The consultant groups were often led by practitioners with advanced degrees in behavior analysis or psychology and complemented by seasoned managers, perhaps lacking training in behavior science, who were adept at management and consultation. Once BBS procedures became routine in the organization, the consultant dialed back engagement to advise on refinements. Implementations were often to selected areas within an organization (e.g., a unit or department experiencing losses and willing to attempt behavior management as a remedy) and these served as pilot tests proving the concept. Successful rollout to other areas may have been aided by contracting for additional consultation, but the replicability of procedures permitted this to be done with internal resources. Often the external consultant relationship reduced to periodic contact or terminated altogether.

4) Safety professional as internal consultant

As BBS diffused within an industry (e.g., petro-chemical refiners were early adopters) and reports within trade journals described the benefits of the procedures, some organizations elected to develop their internal competencies in BBS. Some of the BBS consultants published textbooks, manuals, worksheets, and videos to enable this. In the 1990s, one consultant's videos and materials were marketed by a provider of safety equipment and training supplies with the promise that managers "no longer needed a team of BBS consultants. Our safety videos are all you need." While this advertisement may not have been substantiated by clinical trials, it did reflect the growing interest in the safety profession to acquire low-cost, easily acquired competencies. The extent to which safety professional acquired BBS competencies via self-study is indicated by the success of the CCBS (see www.behavior.org) behavioral safety accreditation that provides an external review of organizations BBS processes. As of this writing, nearly 50 site assessments are posted on the CCBS website describing the effectiveness of BBS processes. Most of these accredited BBS implementations are done with internal managers with little or no formal ongoing support from BBS consultants. Some were initiated with help by external BBS consultants, but continuation was executed with internal resources; some were entirely developed and implemented with internal resources.

It is unknown by the authors as to how many BBS processes were developed by internal consultants who followed published reports and manuals. There is no OSHA standard or requirement to incorporate BBS in safety programs and no registry of providers to quality assure provision. Sales of safety and BBS materials are sizable and diffusion of BBS via this method is likely significant.

5) BBS as replicable service and product

The proliferation of BBS globally is a testament to the maturity of BBS as a replicable service supported by-products such as manuals, checklists, scorecards, observation protocols, video examples, online training, and data analysis/reporting applications such that purchasers are afforded a variety of ways to access the technology. The principles of behavior underlying BBS applications are well understood and generally uniform across implementations. Variation in how the principles are organized and packaged for use is a function of the skill and ingenuity of consultants and managers who install and tend the BBS processes. The principles of behavior are products of scientific enterprise and in the public domain. The packaging, branding, and tools of BBS technologies are the intellectual property of developers and protected by trademark and copyright. As expertise with implementation is acquired via experience, it is relatively easy for end-users to customize elements to fit their needs, and much innovation occurs in the field. Savvy consultants detect these variations and incorporate them in their latest versions.

6) Contract, fee structures and branding

End-users purchasing BBS services and products encounter a range of options from the self-study of published materials to guide "homegrown" BBS processes through hiring external experts to develop and install working systems. The purchasers of BBS via consultants likely entertain a selection of proposals from providers and choose one best fitting the organization's needs and budget. Vetting a provider by examining references, reviewing proposals, and comparison-shopping has shaped BBS providers to brand their deliverables to distinguish themselves from their competitors. Branding BBS processes, which all rely on a relatively small set of principles of behavior, has emphasized topographical features as critical to effectiveness. The purchasers must weigh the evidence of effectiveness (e.g., likely effects size, speed, durability of behavior change, and concomitant reduction in losses) with qualitative features such as reputation of the provider, the appearance of service marketing materials, and other difficult to objectively judge dimensions. The branding exaggerates differences in BBS processes and highlights form over function. Coherently applied behavior analysis of safety behavior employs evaluation methods to refine procedures toward increasing effectiveness. Field evaluation of behavior analysis is a hallmark of applied behavior analysis. This drives refinement to converge toward functional elements and the value of cosmetic variations likely diminishes over time.

A BBS contract defines the consulting relation into a series of steps from initial entry, assessment of need, development of a process, installation, and evaluation leading to refinements. The phases of this may vary somewhat across providers, but this scheme is likely typical. The purchaser seeks a cost estimate, timeline, and determines how to budget for services. As BBS has matured, the contracting process tends to fix the price within a certain range. The market has commodified BBS as a relatively defined product (application of behavioral principles) embedded within organizational operations (e.g., manufacturing, transportation, refining, etc.) so that those operations are improved. One might see this as similar to how a product (e.g., wheat or oil) is traded at an established price, used in making some other product (e.g., wheat is made into bread, oil is made into jet fuel), and market forces stabilize the trade. Often, price is a deciding factor influencing the purchase of BBS.

7) Gains and losses when behavior technology achieves the status of a commodity

If BBS has reached the status of a commodity within a market, this has implications for future directions. The receiving system (host organizations buying BBS) will select for the lowest cost-effective service. The BBS consultant is retained for a limited time as the organization's internal capabilities grow, and hired help is no longer needed. BBS providers will invest in streamlining and standardizing services (e.g., into a set series of workshops and supplemental products) that are reliably and efficiently installed. They engage in much effort to find new business or expand product lines to go beyond safety/health behaviors and address other critical activities. BBS user conferences show both directions are prevalent, although generalization of BBS toward critical non-safety behaviors is hampered when BBS is compartmentalized as an EHS function. The trajectory appears to be characterized by the widespread adoption of BBS across many industries, with evidence of market saturation in wealthy top tier organizations able to afford niche, specialized consultants. Some insurance companies incorporate BBS into their loss control and safety services, so companies have access to the service via insurance product lines. Smaller companies, with less sophisticated and advanced safety departments, are markets for BBS if the price is affordable. This selects for development of low-cost, self-installed variations that streamline installation by internal resources. Service companies providing management supports (e.g., financial services, accounting, safety, environmental consultation) might bundle BBS with other product lines to differentiate themselves from competitors. The selection process promotes variation in the delivery of codified interventions resting on tested principles of behavior. This alters the business model for BBS specialists and opens the market to the more massive transference of behavior science to end-users.

FUTURE TRENDS

Behavior-based safety is a replicable and effective method to improve workplace health and safety. Over 40 years of research, development, and dissemination provide indisputable evidence of social benefit. BBS has reached a level of maturity, perhaps unmatched in behavior analysis except for services to individuals with autism spectrum disorder, and stands as an example of the birth, development, and maturity of behavioral technologies. A recent analysis of future trends in occupational safety and health published in June, 2020 in *Occupational Safety and Health* (Columbia Southern University, 2020) projected the following:

1. High-tech workplace safety programs

Online technologies, tools and methods of training and leadership will increasingly be used to introduce workers to work safety. In behavioral analysis, personalized systems of instruction, fluency training assessments, self-paced modules, and applications to track learning and behavior will provide learners with more autonomy over their own health and safety. Young people entering the workplace seek personalized experiences and applications that stream customized content. In 2020 and beyond, expect to see more safety programs offering individualized coaching and feedback during real-life learning situations.

2. Safety professionals become generalists

In the US, there are approximately 49,600 Certified Safety Professionals (CSP) according to the Board of Certified Safety Professionals' (BCSP) 2018 annual report (see https://www.bcsp.org). CSP are experts in industrial hygiene, safety engineering, contractor safety, and other professional fields such as fire prevention and ergonomics. Inclusion of knowledge of behavioral principles and BBS has been identified for years as an important addition to their training (e.g., Lischeid et al., 1997). As companies look to streamline their teams and improve efficiencies, we might expect safety professional to see value in BBS in particular and behavior science in general and seek training and certification to better approach their work from multiple perspectives.

3. Focus on total health

Occupational safety and health focuses on keeping workers safe at work and reducing the risks of their job. In other words, like BBS, the health and safety field has focused on preventing injuries and illness on the job, and less so in other contexts. The National Institute for Occupational Safety and Health launched an initiative in 2011 to support the overall health and wellbeing of workers. It is consistent with our understanding of how behavioral change demonstrated in one setting may be generalized to other settings by managing contingencies that bridge similar but separate environments. As we move past 2020, expect to see this emphasis supporting all aspects of employee wellbeing – including physical, mental, social, and financial health – rising in occupational safety programs within leading workplaces. Workers will expect their employers to better care for their wellbeing and employers seeking to retain top talent will organize systems to that end.

4. Changing workplace environments

The workplace of 2020 looks little like the workplace of 40 years ago when BBS began. Now there is telecommuting, flexible scheduling, the gig economy, and many more automated work processes. These advancements created new safety concerns and potential liabilities for companies, challenging how workers are selected, trained, and advanced in their jobs. Temporary, short-term, or independent contractors are common in companies and may not mesh with safety protocols designed for in house personnel. Automation and AI systems in HROs like nuclear power, transportation systems, advanced medicine, warehousing, and distribution and others require workers to interact with learning systems that provide them with instructions and feedback. The workers' behaviors are shifting from the completion of repetitious behaviors now done robotically to oversight and review functions of complex systems. This shift entails new risks and exposures at the boundaries of the human–machine interaction. Process safety (Hyten & Ludwig, 2017; Ludwig, 2017) is relatively unexplored by behavior analysis. This refers to safety within complex, dynamic processes, like chemical refining, where catastrophic events can result when engineered systems fail to control deviation from needed procedures.

5. Changing demographics of the workforce

Younger people are entering the workforce with different learning experiences than the seasoned workers they replace. Safety systems and protocols developed for workers now reaching retirement age require adjustment to optimize learning by individuals at ease with digital communications but perhaps not trained in the subtle nuances of work processes. Some industries face a changing of the guard characterized by a jump over generations. Oil and gas exploration, for example, saw a long period of relatively small growth in their workforce as seasoned workers remained on the job and hiring was slow during a turn down in the business. Once the current downturn is over, expect to see an influx of new, young workers to replace the many senior people now exiting the industry during COVID-19. This is true in the safety profession as well, and a younger generation will replace the senior leaders entering retirement. The new workforce is likely to be more diverse and expect an experience different from that of the older workers. BBS may play a part in integrating these workers to work via behavioral technologies that promote effective, safe, and healthy work practices.

SUMMARY AND CONCLUSIONS

BBS has matured over a period of 40 years and can be viewed as an established, replicable technology that is adopted globally. Future development is likely to see BBS expanding in scope and depth as behavioral targets grow from the relatively focused look at workers' behaviors (e.g., PPE use, avoid line of fire, use sound lifting techniques, etc.) examined in the early decades to analysis of complex, interlocked behaviors required for health and safety in contemporary organizations. Managing human behavioral variation will increasingly be part of process safety that seeks to maintain the integrity of hazardous operations. Work environments are evolving with more automation and massive data collection and analysis capabilities. Workers entering these environments are products of learning histories that developed their competencies in rapid communications via social media, and problem-solving learned in engagement with gamified environments. These new entrants to work perhaps acquired different expectations of employers than their predecessors. The published literature base on BBS offers a wealth of accumulated knowledge to guide those entering the field of behavioral safety to build upon success, introduce new findings, and grow the enterprise. The term "BBS" is no longer descriptive of the range of applications of behavior science to occupational health and safety. Better descriptors are possible to capture the richness of the contributions. The commercialization of BBS has led to wide-scale adoption, but the business model developed by consultants to serve end-users may be limiting expansion. The challenges ahead create opportunities to conduct research in both field settings and simulations to not only advance technical applications but also understand complex contingency networks that select socially important behavior beyond those relevant to health and safety. The analysis of safety and health behaviors will expand to embrace the economic shifts underway by extending to other response classes (e.g., those related to sustainability of organizations and communities). The mechanisms for measuring behavior will take advantage of surveillance systems collecting and streaming real-time data to powerful analytic software. Variations in behaviors as a function of multiple sources of variance will be visualized in a variety of graphic data displays and animations that reveal dynamic patterns. Interventions will entail increasingly complex interlocked variables, some of which will be automated. The preferred methodologies transferring behavior science to end-users, popularized by BBS consultants, will expand to make full use of emerging technologies. Travel bans implemented under COVID-19 are forcing companies to accelerate management via remote contacts. This will maintain where organizational leaders see that work productivity and efficiency is achieved with these systems. Young people entering behavior analysis with an interest in promoting health and safety inherit a legacy of sound behavior science, a worldwide marketplace, and many opportunities to innovate.

STUDY QUESTIONS

1) Briefly summarize basic principles of behavior that underlie BBS interventions and give an example of each.
2) Summarize Beth Sulzer-Azaroff's approach to training graduate students. How do you evaluate her teaching model?
3) BBS is a widely used replicable service/product. BBS might be viewed as maturing to the status of a commodity. Evaluate this assessment. If BBS is a commodity, what are the implications for purchasers? For providers? For researchers?
4) Speculate how you might automate management of interlocking behavioral contingencies relevant to some class of occupational safety behaviors. Give an example. What research questions interest you when considering automating BBS within the context of work?
5) Behaviors to contain COVID-19 occur across settings (home, community, school, work, etc.). Why might people not engage in COVID-19 safety behaviors? What behavioral assessments are useful? How might BBS be expanded to address the pandemic?

REFERENCES

Alavosius, M.P. & Sulzer-Azaroff, B. (1985). An on-the-job method to evaluate patient lifting techniques. *Applied Ergonomics, 16*(4), 307–311.

Alavosius, M.P. & Sulzer-Azaroff, B. (1986). The effects of performance feedback on the safety of client lifting and transfer. *Journal of Applied Behavior Analysis, 19*, 261–267.

Alavosius, M.P. & Sulzer-Azaroff, B. (1990). Acquisition and maintenance of health-care routines as a function of feedback density. *Journal of Applied Behavior Analysis, 23*, 151–162.

Baer D. M. (1981). A flight of behavior analysis. *The Behavior Analyst, 4*(2), 85–91. https://doi.org/10.1007/BF03391857

Baer, D.M., Wolf, M.M., & Risley, T.R. (1968). Some current dimensions of applied behavior analysis. *Journal of Applied Behavior Analysis, 1*, 91–97.

Columbia Southern University. (2020). 5 Occupational safety and health trends to watch in 2020. *Occupational Health and Safety. June, 2020.* Retrieved October 20, 2020, **https://ohsonline.com/articles/2020/06/15/5-occupational-safety-and-health-trends-to-watch-in-2020.aspx**

Cook, T.D. & Campbell, D.T. (1979). *Quasi-Experimentation: Design and Analysis Issues for Field Settings.* Houghton Mifflin.

Fox, D.K., Hopkins, B.L., & Anger, W.K. (1987). The long-term effects of a token economy on safety performance in open-pit mining. *Journal of Applied Behavior Analysis, 20*(3), 215–224. https://doi.org/10.1901/jaba.1987.20-215

Gilbert, T.F. (1978, 2007). *Human competence: Engineering worthy performance.* Publication of the International Society for Performance Improvement. Pfeiffer.

Hawkins R.P. (1991). Is social validity what we are interested in? Argument for a functional approach. *Journal of Applied Behavior Analysis, 24*(2), 205–213. https://doi.org/10.1901/jaba.1991.24-205

Heinrich, H.W. (1954). *Industrial Accident Prevention: A scientific approach* (4th ed). McGraw-Hill.
Houmanfar, R., Alavosius, M.P., Morford, Z.H., Reimer, D., Herbst, S.A. (2015). Functions of organizational leaders in cultural change: Financial and social well-being. *Journal of Organizational Behavior Management, 35*, 4–27.
Hyten, C. & Ludwig. T. (2017). Complacency in Process Safety: A behavior analysis toward prevention strategies. *Journal of Organizational Behavior Management, 37*(3–4), 240–260. doi: 10.1080/01608061.2017.1341860
Keller, F.S. (1968). "Good-bye, teacher..." *Journal of applied behavior analysis, 1*(1), 79–89. https://doi.org/10.1901/jaba.1968.1-79
Komaki, J., Barwick, K.D., & Scott, L.R. (1978). A behavioral approach to occupational safety: Pinpointing and reinforcing safe performance in a food manufacturing plant. *Journal of Applied Psychology, 63*(4), 434–445. https://doi.org/10.1037/0021-9010.63.4.434
Lischeid, W., Sulzer-Azaroff, B., & Alavosius, M. (1997). Behavior-based safety: Who will train the safety profession? *Professional Safety. October*, 32–36.
Ludwig, T. (2017). Process safety: Another opportunity to translate behavior analysis into evidence-based practices of grave societal value. *Journal of Organizational Behavior Management, 37*(3–4), 221–223. doi: 10.1080/01608061.2017.1343702
Luke, M. & Alavosius, M.P. (2011). Adherence with Universal Precautions after immediate, personalized performance feedback. *Journal of Applied Behavior Analysis, 44*, 967–971.
Michael J. (1980). Flight from behavior analysis. *The Behavior Analyst, 3*(2), 1–21. https://doi.org/10.1007/BF03391838
Nevin, J. A. (1988). Behavioral momentum and the partial reinforcement extinction effect. *Psychological Bulletin, 103*, 44–56.
Skinner, B.F. (1953). *Science and human behavior*. Macmillan.
Sulzer-Azaroff, B. (1978). Behavioral ecology and accident prevention. *Journal of Organizational Behavior Management, 2*, 11–44.
Sulzer-Azaroff, B. (1982). Behavioral approaches to occupational health and safety. In Lee Fredricksen (Ed.), *Handbook of organizational behavior management* (pp. 505–538). Wiley.
Sulzer-Azaroff, B. & Fellner, D. (1984). Searching for performance targets in the behavioral analysis of occupational health and safety: An assessment strategy. *Journal of Organizational Behavior Management, 6*, 53–65.
Weiner, H. (1983). Some thoughts on discrepant human-animal performances under schedules of reinforcement. *The Psychological Record, 33*, 521–532.
Wolf, M.M. (1978). Social validity: The case for subjective measurement or how applied behavior analysis is finding its heart. *Journal of Applied Behavior Analysis, 1*, 203–214.

TABLE 2.2
BBS reading list in chronological order (n = 317)

Date	*Reference*	*Cited*	*Text, Journal, Talk*
1954	Heinrich, H. W. (1954). Industrial Accident Prevention: A scientific approach (4th ed). New York: McGraw-Hill.	4030	Text
1969	Haskins, J. B. (1969). Effects of safety information campaigns: A review of the research evidence. Journal of Safety Research, 1, 58–66.	31	Journal of Safety Research
1970	Altman, J.W. (1970). Behavior and accidents. Journal of Safety Research, 2, 109–122.	23	Journal of Safety Research
1970	Bird, F. E., Jr., & Schlesinger, L. E. (1970, June). Safe behavior reinforcement. American Society of Safety Engineers Journal, 16–24.	27	American Society of Safety Engineers Journal
1970	Grimaldi, J. V. (1970). The measurement of safety performance. Journal of Safety Research, 2, 137–159.	29	Journal of Safety Research
1970	Haskins, J. B. (1970). Evaluative research on the effects of mass communication safety campaigns: A methodological critique. Journal of Safety Research, 2, 86–96.	31	Journal of Safety Research
1970	Jacobs, H. H. (1970). Towards more effective safety measurement systems. Journal of Safety Research, 2, 160–175.	0	Journal of Safety Research

(*Continued*)

TABLE 2.2
(Continued)

Date	*Reference*	*Cited*	*Text, Journal, Talk*
1973	McKelvey, R. K., Engen, T., & Peck, M. B. (1973). Performance efficiency and injury avoidance as a function of positive and negative incentives. Journal of Safety Research, 5, 90–96.	26	Journal of Safety Research
1974	Chelius, J. R. (1974). The control of industrial accidents: Economic theory and empirical evidence. Law and Contemporary Problems, 80, 700–729.	113	Law and Contemporary Problems
1975	Ellis, L. (1975). A review of research efforts to promote occupational safety. Journal of Safety Research, 7, 180–189.	31	Journal of Safety Research
1975	Goldstein, I. L. (1975). Training. In B. L. Margolis & W. H. Kroes (Eds.) The Human Side of Accident Prevention (pp. 92–113). Springfield, IL: Charles C. Thomas.	0	Text
1975	Grimaldi, J. V., & Simonds, R. H. (1975). Safety management (3rd. edition). Homewood, IL: Irwin.	237	Text
1976	Fitch, H. G., Herman, J., & Hopkins, B. L. (1976). Safe and unsafe behavior and its modification. Journal of Occupational Medicine, 18, 618–622.	35	Journal of Occupational Medicine
1976	Fox, D. K. (1976). Effects of an incentive program on safety performance in open-pit mining at Utah's Shirley Basin Mine Wyoming. Paper presented at the annual meeting of the Midwestern Association of Behavior Analysis, Chicago.	4	Conference Talk
1978	Komaki J., Barwick, K., & Scott, L. (1978). A behavioral approach to occupational safety: Pinpointing and reinforcing safety performance in a food manufacturing plant. Journal of Applied Psychology, 63, 434–445.	616	Journal of Applied Psychology
1978	Smith, M. J., Anger, W. K., & Uslan, S. S. (1978). Behavioral modification applied to occupational safety. Journal of Safety Research, 10, 87–88.	79	Journal of Safety Research
1978	Sulzer-Azaroff, B. (1978). Behavioral ecology and accident prevention. Journal of Organizational Behavior Management, 2, 11–44.	113	Journal of Organizational Behavior Management
1979	Ilgen D. R., Fisher, C. D., & Taylor, M. S. (1979). Consequences of individual feedback on behavior in organizations. Journal of Applied Psychology, 64 (4), 349–371.	2337	Journal of Applied Psychology
1980	Houten, R. V., Nau, P., & Marini, Z. (1980). An analysis of public posting in reducing speeding behavior on an urban highway. Journal of Applied Behavior Analysis, 13(3), 383–395.	147	Journal of Applied Behavior Analysis
1980	Heinrich, H. W., Peterson, D., & Roos, R. (1980). Industrial accident prevention. New York: McGraw-Hill.	16	Text
1980	Komaki, J. L., Heinzmann, A. T., & Lawson, L. (1980). Effect of training and feedback: Component analysis of a behavioral safety program. Journal of Applied Psychology, 65, 261–270.	379	Journal of Applied Psychology

Date	*Reference*	*Cited*	*Text, Journal, Talk*
1980	Larson, L. D., Schnelle, J. F., Kirchner, Jr., R., Carr, A., Domash, M., & Risley, T. R. (1980). Reduction of police vehicle accidents through mechanically aided supervision. Journal of Applied Behavior Analysis, 13, 571–581.	57	Journal of Applied Behavior Analysis
1980	Rhoton, W. W. (1980). A Procedure to improve compliance with coal mine safety regulations. Journal of Organizational Behavior Management, 4 (4), 243–249.	51	Journal of Organizational Behavior Management
1980	Sulzer-Azaroff, B., & de Santamaria, M. C. (1980). Industrial safety hazard reduction through performance feedback. Journal of Applied Behavior Analysis, 3, 287–295.	175	Journal of Applied Behavior Analysis
1980	Zohar, D. (1980). Safety climate in industrial organizations: Theoretical and applied implications. Journal of Applied Psychology, 65, 96–101.	3108	Journal of Applied Psychology
1980	Zohar, D. (1980). Promoting use of personal protective equipment by behavior modification techniques. Journal of Safety Research, 12, 78–85.	68	Journal of Safety Research
1980	Zohar, D., Cohen, A., & Azar, N. (1980). Promoting increased use of ear protection in noise through information feedback. Human Factors, 22, 69–79.	171	Human Factors
1981	Zohar, D., & Fussfield, H. (1981). Modifying earplug wearing behavior by behavior modification techniques: An empirical evaluation. Journal of Safety Research, 3, 41–52.	32	Journal of Safety Research
1982	Haynes, R., Pine, R. C., & Fitch, H. G. (1982). Reducing accident rates with organizational behavior modification. Academy of Management Journal, 25, 407–416.	92	Academy of Management Journal
1982	Komaki, J. L., Collins, R. L., & Penn, P. (1982). The role of performance antecedents and consequences in work motivation. Journal of Applied Psychology, 67, 334–340.	163	Journal of Applied Psychology
1982	Peterson, D. (1982). Human error reduction and safety management. New York: Garland STPM Press.	0	Text
1982	Sulzer-Azaroff, B. (1982). Behavioral approaches to occupational health and safety. In L., Fredericksen (Ed.), Handbook of Organizational Behavior Management (pp. 505–538). New York: John Wiley & Sons.	64	Text
1983	Kjellen, U., & Baneryd, K. (1983). Changing local health and safety practices at work within the explosives industry. Ergonomics, 26, 863–877.	15	Ergonomics
1984	Chhokar, J. S., & Wallin, J. A. (1984). A field study of the effect of feedback frequency on performance. Journal of Applied Psychology, 69, 524–530.	170	Journal of Applied Psychology
1984	Chhokar, J. S., & Wallin, J. A. (1984). Improving safety through applied behavior analysis. Journal of Safety Research, 15, 141–151.	98	Journal of Safety Research
1984	Cohen, H. H. & Jensen, R. C. (1984). Measuring the effectiveness of an industrial lift truck safety training program. Journal of Safety Research, 15 (3), 125–135.	87	Journal of Safety Research

(Continued)

TABLE 2.2
(Continued)

Date	*Reference*	*Cited*	*Text, Journal, Talk*
1984	Fellner, D. J., & Sulzer-Azaroff, B. (1984). A behavioral analysis of goal setting. Journal of Organizational Behavior Management, 6, 33–51.	108	Journal of Organizational Behavior Management
1984	Fellner, D. J., & Sulzer-Azaroff, B. (1984). Increasing industrial safety practices and conditions through posted feedback. Journal of Safety Research, 15, 17–21.	137	Journal of Safety Research
1984	Geller, E. S. (1984). A delayed reward strategy for large-scale motivation of safety belt use: A test of long-term impact. Accident Analysis and Prevention, 16 (5/6), 457–463.	43	Accident Analysis and Prevention
1984	Geller, E. S., & Hahn, H. A. (1984). Promoting safety belt use at industrial sites: An effective program for blue-collar employees. Professional Psychology: Research & Practice, 15, 553–564.	62	Professional Psychology: Research & Practice
1984	Krause, T. R. (1984). Behavioral science applied to accident prevention. Professional Safety Journal, 229, 21–27.	44	Professional Safety Journal
1984	Krause, T.R., Hidley, J. H., & Lareau, W. (1984). Behavioral science applied to industrial accident prevention. Professional Safety, 29 (7).	44	Professional Safety
1984	Peterson, D. (1984). An experiment in positive reinforcement. Professional Safety, 29 (5), 30–35.	14	Professional Safety
1984	Reber, R. A., & Wallin, J. A. (1984). Validation of Behavioral Measures of Occupational Safety. Journal of Organizational Behavior Management, 7, 69–77.	47	Journal of Organizational Behavior Management
1984	Reber, R. A., & Wallin, J. A. (1984). The effects of training, goal setting, and knowledge of results on safe behavior: A component analysis. Academy of Management Journal, 27, 544–560.	184	Academy of Management Journal
1984	Reber, R. A., Wallin, J. A., & Chhokar, J. (1984). Reducing industrial accidents: A behavioral experiment. Employee Relations, 23, 119–124.	59	Employee Relations
1984	Sulzer-Azaroff, B., & Fellner, D. (1984). Searching for performance targets in the behavior analysis of occupational safety: An assessment strategy. Journal of Organizational Behavior Management, 6, 53–65.	54	Journal of Organizational Behavior Management
1985	Jonah, B. A., & Grant, B. A. (1985). Long-term effectiveness of selective traffic enforcement programs for increasing seat belt use. Journal of Applied Psychology, 70(2), 257.	92	Journal of Applied Psychology
1985	Alavosius, M.P., & Sulzer-Azaroff, B. (1985). An on-the-job method to evaluate patient lifting technique. Applied Ergonomics, 16 (4), 307–311.	32	Applied Ergonomics
1985	Carter, N., & Menckel, E. (1985). Near accident reporting: A review of Swedish research. Journal of Occupational Accidents, 7, 41–64.	34	Journal of Occupational Accidents
1985	Fellner, D. J., & Sulzer-Azaroff, B. (1985). Occupational safety: Assessing the impact of adding assigned or participative goal setting. Journal of Organizational Behavior Management, 7, 3–24.	56	Journal of Organizational Behavior Management

Date	Reference	Cited	Text, Journal, Talk
1985	Van Houten, R., Malenfant, L., & Rolider, A. (1985). Increasing driver yielding and pedestrian signaling with prompting, feedback, and enforcement. Journal of Applied Behavior Analysis, 18, 103–110.	46	Journal of Applied Behavior Analysis
1986	Alavosius M.P., & Sulzer-Azaroff, B. (1986). The effects of performance feedback on the safety of client lifting and transfer. Journal of Applied Behavior Analysis, 19, 261–267.	134	Journal of Applied Behavior Analysis
1986	Balcazar F., Hopkins, B. L., & Suarez, Y. (1986). A critical objective review of performance feedback. Journal of Organizational Behavior Management, 7, 65–89.	523	Journal of Organizational Behavior Management
1986	Hopkins, B. L., Conard, R. J., Dangel, R. G., Fitch, H. G., Smith, M. J., & Anger, W. K. (1986). Behavioral technology for reducing occupational exposures to styrene. Journal of Applied Behavior Analysis, 19, 3–11.	63	Journal of Applied Behavior Analysis
1986	Hopkins, B. L., Conard, R. J., & Smith, M. J. (1986). Effective and reliable behavioral control technology. American Industrial Hygiene Association Journal, 47 (12), 775–781.	27	American Industrial Hygiene Association Journal
1986	Komaki, J. L. (1986). Toward effective supervision: An operant analysis and comparison of managers at work. Journal of Applied Psychology, 71, 270–279.	314	Journal of Applied Psychology
1986	Komaki, J. L., Zlotnick, S., & Jensen, M. (1986). Development of an operant-based taxonomy and observational index of supervisory behavior. Journal of Applied Psychology, 71 (2), 260–269.	152	Journal of Applied Psychology
1986	Sulzer-Azaroff, B., & Mayer, G. R. (1986). Achieving educational excellence using behavioral strategies. Chicago: Holt Rinehart & Winston.	211	Text
1987	Baer, D. M., Wolf, M. M., & Risley, T. R. (1987). Some still-current dimensions of applied behavior analysis. Journal of Applied Behavior Analysis, 20, 313–327.	787	Journal of Applied Behavior Analysis
1987	Chhokar, J. S. (1987, Mar-Apr). Safety at the workplace: A behavioral approach. International Labour Review, 169–178.	19	International Labour Review
1987	Fox, C. J., & Sulzer-Azaroff, B. (1987). Increasing the completion of accident reports. Journal of Safety Research, 18, 65–71.	21	Journal of Safety Research
1987	Fox, D. K., Hopkins. B. L., & Anger, W. K. (1987). The long-term effects of a token economy on safety performance in open-pit mining. Journal of Applied Behavior Analysis, 20, 215–224.	217	Journal of Applied Behavior Analysis
1987	Karan, B. S., & Kopelman, R. E. (1987). The effects of objective feedback on vehicular and industrial accidents: A field experiment using outcome feedback. Journal of Organizational Behavior Management, 8, 45–56.	26	Journal of Organizational Behavior Management
1987	Naesaenan, M., & Saari, J. (1987). Effects of positive feedback on housekeeping and accidents at a shipyard. Journal of Occupational Accidents, 8, 237–250.	56	Journal of Occupational Accidents

(Continued)

TABLE 2.2
(Continued)

Date	*Reference*	*Cited*	*Text, Journal, Talk*
1987	Roberts, M. C., Fanurik, D., & Layfield, D. A. (1987). Behavioral approaches to prevention of childhood injuries. Journal of Social Issues, 23, 105–118.	72	Journal of Social Issues
1987	Sulzer-Azaroff, B. (1987). The modification of occupational safety behavior. Journal of Occupational Accidents, 9, 177–197.	71	Journal of Occupational Accidents
1987	Sulzer-Azaroff, B., Fox, C., Moss, S. M., & Davis, J. M. (1987). Feedback and safety: Involving workers. Unpublished paper.	10	Paper
1987	Tolsma, D. D. (1987, November–December). Behavioral aspects of injury. Proceedings of the 1987 Conference on Injury in America, U.S. Department of Health and Human Services, Public Health Service, 102, 605–606.	49	Paper
1988	Van Houten, R. (1988). The effects of advance stop lines and sign prompts on pedestrian safety in a crosswalk on a multilane highway. Journal of Applied Behavior Analysis, 21(3), 245–251.	63	Journal of Applied Behavior Analysis
1988	Geller, E. S. (1988). Managing occupational safety. Blacksburg, VA: Make-A-Difference, Inc.	3	Text
1988	Lopez-Mena, L., Rodriguez-Moya, C., Soto-Elgueta, J., & Soto-Leconte, H. (1988). Beneficios economicos obtenidos con una programa conductual en seguridad del trabajo. (Economic benefits obtained with a behavioral program in job safety.) Psicologia del Trabajo y de las Organizaciones, 4, 74–86.	8	Psicologia del Trabajo y de las Organizaciones,
1988	Mattila, M. & Hyödynmaa, M. (1988). Promoting job safety in building: An experiment on the behavior analysis approach. Journal of Occupational Accidents, 9, 255–267.	85	Journal of Occupational Accidents
1988	Saari, J. (1988). Successful accident prevention: An intervention study in the Nordic countries. Scandinavian Journal of Work and Environmental Health, 14, 121–123.	16	Scandinavian Journal of Work and Environmental Health
1988	Sulzer-Azaroff, B., & Alavosius, M. C. (1988). Preventing back injuries at an institutional infirmary. Performance Management Magazine, 6 (4), 14–16.	2	Performance Management Magazine
1988	Vilardo, F. J. (1988). The role of the epidemiological model in injury control. Journal of Safety Research, 19, 1–4.	9	Journal of Safety Research
1989	McAfee, R. B., & Winn, A. R. (1989). The use of incentives/feedback to enhance workplace safety: A critique of the literature. Journal of Safety Research, 20(1), 7–19.	292	Journal of Safety Research
1989	Fox, C. J., & Sulzer-Azaroff, B. (1989). The effectiveness of two different sources of feedback on staff teaching of fire evacuation skills. Journal of Organizational Behavior Management, 10, 19–35.	37	Journal of Organizational Behavior Management
1989	Geller, E. S. (1989). Managing Occupational Safety Marketing and the Human Element. Paper presented at the Fifteenth Annual Convention of the Association for Behavior Analysis, Milwaukee, WI.	0	Paper

Date	*Reference*	*Cited*	*Text, Journal, Talk*
1989	Kalsher M. J., Geller, E. S., Clarke, S. W., & Lehman, G. R. (1989). Safety belt promotion on a naval base: A comparison of incentives vs. disincentives. Journal of Safety Research, 20, 103–113.	38	Journal of Safety Research
1989	Komaki, J. L., Desselles, M. L., & Bowman, E. D. (1989). Definitely not a breeze: Extending an operant model of effective supervision to teams. Journal of Applied Psychology, 74 (3), 522–529.	193	Journal of Applied Psychology
1989	McAfee, R. B., & Winn, A. R. (1989). The use of incentives/feedback to enhance workplace safety. Journal of Safety Research, 20, 7–19.	292	Journal of Safety Research
1989	Petersen, D. (1989). Safe behavior reinforcement. Goshen. NY: Aloray, Inc.	52	Text
1989	Ray, P. S., Purswell, J. L., & Schlegel, R. E. (1989). Evaluating and improving safety behavior at the workplace. Advances in Industrial Ergonomics and Safety I. In Proceedings of the International Foundation for Industrial Ergonomics and Safety Research Conference, 375–381.	0	Paper
1989	Saari, J., & Naesaenan, M. (1989). The effect of positive feedback on industrial housekeeping and accidents: A long term study at a shipyard. International Journal of Industrial Ergonomics, 4, 201–211.	102	International Journal of Industrial Ergonomics
1990	Krause, T. R., Seymour, K. J., & Sloat, K. C. M. (1999). Long-term evaluation of a behavior-based method for improving safety performance: a meta-analysis of 73 interrupted time-series replications. Safety Science, 32(1), 1–18.	251	Safety Science
1990	Krause, T., & Hidley, J. H. (1990). The behavior-based safety process. J.Wiley	426	Text
1990	Alavosius, M.P., & Sulzer-Azaroff, B. (1990). Acquisition and maintenance of health-care routines as a function of feedback density. Journal of Applied Behavior Analysis, 23, 151–162.	144	Journal of Applied Behavior Analysis
1990	Chhokar, J. S. (1990). Behavioral safety management, Vikalpa, 15, 15–22.	18	Vikalpa
1990	Mattila, M. (1990). Improving working practices and workplace safety through behavior analysis in the veneer industry. In B. Das (Ed.) Advances in Industrial Ergonomics and Safety, 11, 957–961.	16	Advances in Industrial Ergonomics and Safety
1990	Mortimer, R. G., Goldstein, K., Armstrong, R. W., & Macrina, D. (1990). Effects of incentive and enforcement on the use of seat belts by drivers. Journal of Safety Research, 21, 25–37.	36	Journal of Safety Research
1990	Ray, P. S., Purswell, J. L., & Schlegel, R. E. (1990). A behavioral approach to improve safety at the workplace. Advances in Industrial Ergonomics and Safety I. In Proceedings of the International Foundation for Industrial Ergonomics and Safety Research Conference, 983–988.	11	Paper
1990	Reber, R. A., Wallin, J. A., & Chhokar, J. (1990). Improving safety performance with goal setting and feedback. Human Performance, 3, 51–61.	53	Human Performance

(*Continued*)

TABLE 2.2
(Continued)

Date	*Reference*	*Cited*	*Text, Journal, Talk*
1990	Saarela, K. L. (1990). An intervention program utilizing small groups: A comparative study. Journal of Safety Research, 21, 149–156.	40	Journal of Safety Research
1990	Sulzer-Azaroff, B., Loafman, B., Merante, R. J., & Hlavacek, A. C. (1990). Improving occupational safety in a large industrial plant: A systematic replication. Journal of Organizational Behavior Management, 11, 99–120.	100	Journal of Organizational Behavior Management
1990	Veltri, A. (1990). Accident cost impact model: The direct cost component. Journal of Safety Research, 21, 67–73.	19	Journal of Safety Research
1991	Blake, K. E. (1991). Toward the reduction of risk of carpal tunnel syndrome in video display terminal users through feedback. Unpublished master's thesis, University of Massachusetts, Amherst.	1	Paper
1991	Chilton, D. A., Lombardo, G. J., & Pater, R. F. (1991). Effective safety program design. Proceedings of the First International Conference on Health, Safety and Environment in Oil and Gas Exploration and Production, 1, 397–405.	0	Paper
1991	DeVries J. E., Burnette M. M., & Redirion, W. K. (1991). AIDS: Improving nurses' compliance with glove wearing through performance feedback. Journal of Applied Behavior Analysis, 24, 705–711.	82	Journal of Applied Behavior Analysis
1991	Geller, E. S., & Lehman, G. R. (1991). The buckle-up card: A versatile intervention for large-scale behavior change. Journal of Applied Behavior Analysis, 24, 91–94.	59	Journal of Applied Behavior Analysis
1991	Hale, A. R., Oortman-Gerlings, P., Swuste, P., & Heimplaetzer, P. (1991). Assessing and improving safety management systems. Proceedings of the First International Conference on Health, Safety and Environment in Oil and Gas Exploration and Production, 1, 381–388.	7	Paper
1991	Harshbarger, D., & Rose, T. (1991). New possibilities in safety performance and the control of worker's compensation costs. Journal of Occupational Rehabilitation, 1, 133–143.	23	Journal of Occupational Rehabilitation
1991	Ludwig, T. D., & Geller, E. S. (1991). Improving the driving practices of Pizza deliverers: Response generalization and moderating effects of driving history. Journal of Applied Behavior Analysis, 24, 31–44.	102	Journal of Applied Behavior Analysis
1991	National Safety Council. (1991). Accident Facts. Chicago.	8	
1991	Peters, R. H. (1991). Strategies for encouraging self-protective employee behavior. Journal of Safety Research, 22, 53–70.	68	Journal of Safety Research
1991	Pidgeon (1991). Safety culture and risk management in organizations. Special Issue: Risk and culture., 22 (1), 129–140.	638	Risk and culture

Date	*Reference*	*Cited*	*Text, Journal, Talk*
1991	Ray, P. S., Purswell, J. L., & Bowen, D. J. (1991). Long-term effect of a behavioral safety program. In W. Karwowski & J. W. Yates (Eds.) Advances in Industrial Ergonomics and Safety, pp. 725–730. Taylor & Francis.	7	Advances in Industrial Ergonomics and Safety
1991	Sulzer-Azaroff, B., & Mayer, G. R. (1991). Behavior analysis for lasting change. Fort Worth, TX: Harcourt Brace.	772	Text
1991	Turner, B. A. (1991). The development of a safety culture. Chemistry and Industry, 7, 241–243.	0	Chemistry and Industry
1992	Babcock, R., Sulzer-Azaroff, B., Sanderson, M., & Scibek, J. (1992). Increasing nurses' use of feedback to promote infection control practices in a head injury treatment center. Journal of Applied Behavior Analysis, 25, 621–627.	68	Journal of Applied Behavior Analysis
1992	Baker, S. P., Conroy, C., & Johnston, J. J. (1992, Summer). Occupational injury prevention. Journal of Safety Research, 23 (2), 129–133.	0	Journal of Safety Research
1992	Feuerstein, P. (1992, January). Incentives inspire safe behavior. Safety and Health, 42–45.	0	Safety and Health
1992	Fleming, R., & Sulzer-Azaroff, B. (1992). Reciprocal peer management: Increasing and maintaining beneficial staff-client interactions. Journal of Applied Behavior Analysis, 25, 611–620.	36	Journal of Applied Behavior Analysis
1992	Saari, J. (1992). Scientific housekeeping studies. In Bird, Jr., F.E. (Ed.) Profits are in Order. International Loss Control Institute, Atlanta, 27–42.	8	Text
1992	Sulzer-Azaroff, B. (1992). Making a difference in occupational safety with behavior management. Journal of Applied Behavior Analysis, 25, 653–654.	4	Journal of Applied Behavior Analysis
1993	Bailey, C. (1993, October). Improve safety program effectiveness with perception surveys. Professional Safety, 28–32.	25	Professional Safety
1993	Krause, T. R., Hidley, J. H., & Lareau, W. (1993). Implementing the behavior-based safety process in a union environment: A natural fit. Professional Safety, 38 (6), 26–31.	7	Professional Safety
1993	McSween, T. E. (1993). Improve your safety program with a behavioral approach. Hydrocarbon Processing, 72 (8), 119–128.	5	Hydrocarbon Processing
1993	McSween, T. E. (1993). Behavior and safety – The critical link. Performance technology – 1993. Selected Proceedings of the 31st NSPI Conference. National Society for Performance and Instruction, Washington, DC, 191–205.	3	Paper
1993	Menkel, E., Carter, N., & Hellbom, M. (1993). The long-term effects of two group routines on accident prevention activities and accident statistics. International Journal of Industrial Ergonomics, 12, 301–309.	6	International Journal of Industrial Ergonomics
1993	Montero, R. (1993). Reducción de accidentes de trabajo mediante el cambio de conducta hacia la seguridad. (Reduction of work accidents mediated by safety behavior change.) Mafre Seguridad, 52 (4), 31–37.	33	Mafre Seguridad

(*Continued*)

TABLE 2.2
(Continued)

Date	*Reference*	*Cited*	*Text, Journal, Talk*
1993	Montero, R. (1993). Un procedimiento para el perfeccionanidento de la seguridad del trabajo. (A procedure leading toward the perfection of job safety.) Revista Brasileira de Sdude Ocupacional, 21 (78), 51–56.	0	Revista Brasileira de Sdude Ocupacional
1993	Montero, R., & Molina, A. (1993). Resultados de la aplicación de una campaña informativa Sobre la seguridad. (Results of the application of an informational campaign on safety.) Salud y Trabajo, 97 (3), 30–32.	4	Salud y Trabajo
1993	Ray, P. S., Purswell, J. L., & Bowen, D. J. (1993). Behavioral safety program – Creating a new corporate culture. International Journal of Industrial Ergonomics, 12, 193–198.	38	International Journal of Industrial Ergonomics
1993	Reber, R.A., Wallin, J.A., & Duhon, D.L. (1993). Preventing occupational injuries through performance management. Public Personnel Management, 22 (2), 301–311.	24	Public Personnel Management
1993	Streff, F. M., Kalsher, M. J., & Geller, E. S. (1993). Developing efficient workplace safety programs: Observations of response covariation. Journal of Organizational Behavior Management, 13, 3–15.	63	Journal of Organizational Behavior Management
1994	Brown, C. S., & Sulzer-Azaroff, B. (1994). An assessment of the relationship between customer satisfaction and service friendliness. Journal of Organizational Behavior Management, 14, 55–75.	144	Journal of Organizational Behavior Management
1994	Cooper, S. E., & Newbold, R. C. (1994). Combining external and internal behavioral system consultation to enhance plant safety. Consulting Psychology Journal, 32–41.	11	Consulting Psychology Journal
1994	Cooper, M. D., Phillips, R. A, Sutherland, V. J., & Maldn, P. J. (1994). Reducing accidents using goal setting and feedback: A field study. Journal of Occupational Psychology, 67, 219–240.	247	Journal of Occupational Psychology
1994	Johnston, J. J., Cattledge, G.G.H., & Collins, J.W. (1994). The efficacy of training for occupational injury control. Occupational Medicine, 9, 147–158.	64	Occupational Medicine
1994	Killimet P. T., & Hidley, J. H. (1994, April). Strategy versus tactics in safety performance improvement. Occupational Hazards, 43–47.	0	Occupational Hazards
1994	Mattilla, M., Rantanen, E., & Hyttinen, M. (1994). The quality of supervision and safety work environment in building construction. Safety Science, 17, 257–268.	59	Safety Science
1994	Saari, J. (1994). When does behavior modification prevent accidents? Leadership and Organizational Development Journal, 15, 11–15.	32	Leadership and Organizational Development Journal
1994	Sulzer-Azaroff, B., Harris, T. C., & McCann, K. (1994). Beyond training: Organizational performance management techniques. Occupational Medicine: State of the Art Reviews, 9, 321–339.	67	Occupational Medicine: State of the Art Reviews
1995	Brigham, T. A., Meier, S. M., & Goodner, V. (1995). increasing designated driving with a program of prompts and incentives. Journal of Applied Behavior Analysis, 28(1), 83–84. doi:10.1901/jaba.1995.28-83	27	Journal of Applied Behavior Analysis

Date	*Reference*	*Cited*	*Text, Journal, Talk*
1995	Laitinen, H., & Järvinen T. (1995). Accident risks and the effect of performance feedback with industrial CO_2 lasers. Optics Laser Technology, 27 (1), 25–30.	2	Optics Laser Technology
1995	McSween, T. E. (1995). The values-based safety process. Improving your safety culture with a behavioral approach. New York: Van Nostrand Reinhold.	373	Text
1995	McSween, T. E. (1995, October). Making Sense of Different Safety Approaches. Industrial Safety and Hygiene News, 44.	0	Industrial Safety and Hygiene News
1995	Montero, R. (1995). Reducción de los accidentes de trabajo utilizando ana estrategia de gestion participativa en la seguridad industrial. (Reduction of job accidents utilizing a participative strategy in industrial safety.) Doctoral Dissertation, 96 pp + xxv pp ed. ISPJAE La Habana.	7	Paper
1995	Montero, R. (1995). Psicosociología preventiva aplicada a la accidentabilidad laboral. (Psychosocial prevention applied to work accidents.) Estudios Empresariales, 88 (2), 64–68.	24	Estudios Empresariales
1995	Ray, P. S. & Bishop, P. A. (1995). Why safety in the workplace is still an illusion? In proceedings of the International Industrial Engineering 46th Annual Conference, Norcross, GA.	0	Paper
1995	Ray, P. S., & Bishop, P. A. (1995, April). Can training alone ensure a safe workplace? Professional Safety, 56–59.	28	Professional Safety
1995	Sulzer-Azaroff, B. (1995). Lessons learned in enhancing safety performance in a paper mill. In T. E. McSween, The values based safety process: Improving your safety culture with a behavioral approach. New York: Van Nostrand Reinhold.	0	Text
1996	Austin, J., Kessler, M.L., Riccobono, J. E., & Bailey, J. S. (1996). Using feedback and reinforcement to improve the performance and safety of a roofing crew. Journal of Organizational Behavior Management, 16 (2), 49–75.	167	Journal of Organizational Behavior Management
1996	Geller, E. S. (1996). The psychology of safety. Radnor, PA: The Chilton Book Company.	338	Text
1996	Geller, E. S. (1996). Working safe: How to help people actively care for health and safety. Boca Raton: CRC Press.	211	Text
1996	Krause, T. R., Hidley, J. H., & Hodson, S. J. (1996). The behavior-based safety process: Managing involvement for an injury free culture (Second Edition). New York: Van Nostrand Reinhold.	0	Text
1996	Krause, T. R., & McCorquodale, R. J. (1996). Transitioning away from safety incentive programs. Professional Safety, 41 (3), 32–36.	11	Professional Safety
1996	Laitinen, H., & Ruohomaki, I. (1996). The effects of feedback and goal setting on safety performance at two construction sites. Safety Science, 24, 61–73.	111	Safety Science
1996	McCann, K. B., & Sulzer-Azaroff, B. (1996). Cumulative trauma disorders: Behavioral injury prevention at work. Journal of Applied Behavioral Science, 32 (3), 277–291.	75	Journal of Applied Behavioral Science

(Continued)

TABLE 2.2
(Continued)

Date	*Reference*	*Cited*	*Text, Journal, Talk*
1996	McSween, T. E., & Mathis, T. L. (1996, February). The infamous quick fix. Industrial Safety and Hygiene News, 26–27.	0	Industrial Safety and Hygiene News
1996	Montero, R. (1996). La investigación de acción participativa una estrategia de intervención organizacional. (The investigation of a participative action: An organizational intervention strategy). Estudios Finpresariales, 91 (2), 45–52.	0	Estudios Finpresariales
1996	Montero, R. (1996). How much "participation" does a behavior modification program need for improving safety? International Conference on Occupational Health, Septiembre Estocolmo Suecia.	2	Paper
1996	National Safety Council. (1996). Accident Facts. Chicago.	258	Text
1996	Ray, P. S., & Bishop, P. A. (1996). How to ensure a safe workplace? In Proceedings of the Third International Conference on Injury Prevention and Control, Melbourne, Australia, 184.	0	Paper
1996	Ray, P. S., & Frey, A. (1996, September). Measurement of safety level in an industrial set-up. Presented at the International NIET96 Conference, Pittsburgh.	0	Paper
1997	Krause, T. R. (1997). The Behavior-Based Safety Process: Managing Involvement (Industrial Health and Safety).	1	Industrial Health and Safety
1997	Lingard, H., & Rowlinson, S. (1997). Behavior-based safety management in hong kong's construction industry. Journal of Safety Research, 28(4), 243–256. doi:10.1016/S0022-4375(97)00010-8	225	Journal of Safety Research
1997	Bailey, C. (1997, August). Managerial factors related to safety program effectiveness: An update on the Minnesota Perception Survey. Professional Safety, 33–35.	71	Professional Safety
1997	Bird, F. E., Jr., & Germain, G. L. (1997). The property damage accident: The neglected part of safety. Loganville, GA: Institute Publishing Inc.	13	Text
1997	Geller, E. S. (1997). Understanding behavior-based safety: Step-by-step methods to improve your workplace. Neenah, WI: J. J. Keller & Associates Inc.	0	Text
1997	Harris, T. C. (1997). Predicting workplace safety outcomes through subordinate and supervisor involvement in safety issues. Unpublished doctoral dissertation, University of Connecticut, Storrs.	7	Paper
1997	Laitinen, H., Saari, J., & Kuusela, J. (1997). Initiating an innovative change process for improved working conditions and ergonomics with participation and performance feedback: A case study in an engineering workshop. International Journal of Industrial Ergonomics, 19, 299–305.	54	International Journal of Industrial Ergonomics
1997	Lischeid, W. E., Sulzer-Azaroff, B., & Alavosius, M. (1997, October). Behavioral safety: Who will train the safety profession? Professional Safety, 32–36.	7	Professional Safety

Date	Reference	Cited	Text, Journal, Talk
1997	Ludwig, T. D., & Geller, E. S. (1997). Assigned versus participative goal setting and response generalization: Managing injury control among professional pizza deliverers. Journal of Applied Psychology, 82 (2), 253–261.	161	Journal of Applied Psychology
1997	Montero, R. (1997). Caso Practico reforzar las conductas para mejorar la calidad. (Practical example: Reinforcing behavior to improve quality). Estudios Empresariales, 94 (2), 52–60.	4	Estudios Empresariales
1997	Montero, R. (1997). Por que la gestion de la seguridad se basa hoy en dia en la conducta hacia el riesgo? (Why is the safety question based today on risk behavior?) Simposio Internacional Salud y Trabajo. Cuba '97 Diciembre, C. Habana.	0	Paper
1997	Ray, P. S., & Bishop, P. A. (1997). Efficacy of the components of a behavioral safety program. International Journal of Industrial Ergonomics, 19, 19–29.	62	International Journal of Industrial Ergonomics
1997	Ray, P. S., & Frey, A. (1997). Validation of the behavioral safety index. Submitted for publication to the International Journal of Industrial Ergonomics.	14	Professional Safety
1997	Saari, J. (1997). Participatory workplace improvement process. In: Stellman, J. M. (Ed.) Encyclopedia of Occupational Health and Safety 4th edition International Labour Office, Geneva 59. 11–59. 15.	8	Text
1997	Salminen, J., & Saari, J. (1997). Improving working conditions and work performance in temporary work sites. In: Das, B. & Karwoski, W. (Eds.): Advances in occupational ergonomics and safety 1997. IOS Press Amsterdam, 459–462.	2	Text
1997	Sulzer-Azaroff, B. (1997). Ten ways to heighten the safety culture of your organization. The Safety & Health Practitioner, 15 (7), 18–20.	3	The Safety & Health Practitioner
1998	Austin JAustin, J., Alvero, A. M., & Olson, R. (1998). prompting patron safety belt use at a restaurant. Journal of Applied Behavior Analysis, 31(4), 655–657. doi:10.1901/jaba.1998.31-655, Alvero A.M, Olson R. Prompting patron safety belt use at a restaurant. (n.d.).	39	Journal of Applied Behavior Analysis
1998	Blair, E. H. (1998). Practical Behavior-Based Safety: Step-By-Step Methods to Improve Your Workplace. Professional Safety, 43(5), 20.	0	Professional Safety
1998	Geller, E. S., Boyce, T., DePasquale, J., Pettinger, C., & Williams, J. (1998). Critical success factors for behavior-based safety. In Proceedings of Light Up Safety in the New Millennium: A Behavioral Safety Symposium (pp. 83–111).	1	Paper
1998	Boyce, T. E., & Geller, E. S. (1998). Applied behavior analysis and occupational safety: The challenge of response maintenance (under review).	78	Under review
1998	Laitinen, H., Saari, J., Kivistd, M., & Rasa, P. L. (1998). Improving physical and psychosocial working conditions through a participatory ergonomic process: A before-after study at an engineering workshop. International Journal of Industrial Ergonomics, 21, 35–45.	72	International Journal of Industrial Ergonomics

(*Continued*)

TABLE 2.2
(Continued)

Date	*Reference*	*Cited*	*Text, Journal, Talk*
1998	Ray, P. S. (1998, May). Integrated approach to hazard analysis. IERC 7 Conference.	0	Paper
1998	Sulzer-Azaroff, B. (1998). Who killed my daddy? A behavioral safety fable. Cambridge, MA: Cambridge Center for Behavioral Studies.	27	Text
1998	Sulzer-Azaroff, B. (1998). Center works toward making the world a safer place. The Cambridge Center for Behavioral Studies, Current Repertoire, 14, 4.	0	Article
1999	Krause, T. R., Seymour, K. J., & Sloat, K. C. M. (1999). Long-term evaluation of a behavior-based method for improving safety performance: A meta-analysis of 73 interrupted time-series replications. Safety Science, 32, 1–18.	251	Safety Science
1999	Ludwig, T. D., & Geller, E. S. (1999). Behavioral impact of a corporate driving policy: Undesirable side-effects reflect countercontrol. Journal of Organizational Behavior Management, 19, 3–24.	23	Journal of Organizational Behavior Management
1999	Ludwig, T. D., & Geller, E. S. (1999). Behavior change among agents of a community safety program: Pizza deliverers advocate community safety belt use. Journal of Organizational Behavior Management, 19, 3–24.	43	Journal of Organizational Behavior Management
1999	Sulzer-Azaroff, B. (1999). Activities manual for who killed my daddy? A behavioral safety fable. Cambridge, MA: Cambridge Center for Behavioral Studies.	2	Text
2000	Alavosius, M. P., Adams, A.E., Ahern, D.K., & Follick, M.J. (2000). Chapter 15: Behavioral approaches to organizational safety. In Austin, J. & Carr, J. (Eds.), *Handbook of Applied Behavior Analysis,* Context Press, Reno, NV.	16	Text
2000	Frederick, James, and Nancy Lessin. "Blame the Worker: The Rise of Behavioral-Based Safety Programs." Multinational Monitor, vol. 21, no. 11, 2000, p. 10. Gale Academic Onefile, Accessed 17 Dec. 2019.	45	Text
2000	Grant, J. G. (2000). Involving the total organization. Occupational health & safety (Waco, Tex.), 69(9), 64–65.	3	Occupational health & safety
2000	Grindle, A. C., Dickinson, A. M., & Boettcher, W. (2000). Behavioral safety research in manufacturing settings: A review of the literature. Journal of Organizational Behavior Management, 20(1), 29–68.	109	Journal of Organizational Behavior Management
2000	Manuele, F. A. (2000). Behavioral safety: looking beyond the worker. Occupational Hazards, 62(10), 86–91.	12	Occupational Hazards
2000	Williams, J. H., & Geller, E. S. (2000). Behavior-based intervention for occupational safety: Critical impact of social comparison feedback. Journal of Safety Research, 31(3), 135–142.	138	Journal of Safety Research
2000	Ludwig, T. D., & Geller, E. S. (2000). Intervening to improve the safety of delivery drivers: A systematic behavioral approach [Monograph]. Journal of Organizational Behavior Management, 19, 1–124.	65	Journal of Organizational Behavior Management
2000	Sulzer-Azaroff, B., & Austin, J. (2000). Does BBS work? Behavior-based safety and injury reduction: A survey of the evidence. Professional Safety, 19–24.	213	Professional Safety

Date	*Reference*	*Cited*	*Text, Journal, Talk*
2001	Baer, D. M. (2001). Since safety maintains our lives, we need to maintain maintaining. Journal of Organizational Behavior Management, 21(1), 61–64. doi:10.1300/J075v21n01_04	7	Journal of Organizational Behavior Management
2001	Boyce, T. E., & Geller, E. S. (2001). Applied behavior analysis and occupational safety: The challenge of response maintenance. Journal of Organizational Behavior Management, 21(1), 31–60. doi:10.1300/J075v21n01_03	78	Journal of Organizational Behavior Management
2001	Geller, E. S. (2001). A total safety culture: From a corporate achievement to a global vision. Behavior and Social Issues, 11(1), 18.	10	Behavior and Social Issues
2001	Geller, E. S. (2001). Behavioral safety: Meeting the challenge of making a large-scale difference. The Behavior Analyst Today, 2(2), 64.	7	The Behavior Analyst Today
2001	Geller, E. S. (2001). Behavior-based safety in industry: Realizing the large-scale potential of psychology to promote human welfare. Applied and Preventive Psychology, 10(2), 87–105.	102	The Behavior Analyst Today
2001	Malott, R. W. (2001). Occupational safety and response maintenance: An alternate view. Journal of Organizational Behavior Management, 21(1), 85–102.	24	Journal of Organizational Behavior Management
2001	McSween, T., & Matthews, G. A. (2001). Maintenance in behavior safety management. Journal of Organizational Behavior Management, 21(1), 75–83.	23	Journal of Organizational Behavior Management
2001	Alvero, A. M., Bucklin, B. R., & Austin, J. (2001). An objective review of the effectiveness and essential characteristics of performance feedback in organizational settings. Journal of Organizational Behavior Management, 21(1), 3–29.	534	Journal of Organizational Behavior Management
2001	Ludwig, T. D., Biggs, J., Wagner, S., & Geller, E. S. (2001). Using public feedback and competitive rewards to increase the safe driving behaviors of pizza deliverers. Journal of Organizational Behavior Management, 21, 75–104.	56	Journal of Organizational Behavior Management
2001	Olson, R. & Austin, J. (2001). Behavior-based safety and working alone: The effects of a self-monitoring package on the safe performance of bus operators. Journal of Organizational Behavior Management, 21 (3), 5–43.	101	Journal of Organizational Behavior Management
2002	Zohar, D. (2002). Modifying supervisory practices to improve subunit safety: a leadership-based intervention model. Journal of Applied psychology, 87(1), 156.	637	Journal of Applied psychology
2003	Gras, M. E., Cunill, M., Planes, M., Sullman, M. J., & Oliveras, C. (2003). Increasing safety-belt use in Spanish drivers: A field test of personal prompts. Journal of Applied Behavior Analysis, 36(2), 249–251.	24	Journal of Applied Behavior Analysis
2004	Van Houten, R., & Malenfant, J. L. (2004). Effects of a driver enforcement program on yielding to pedestrians. Journal of Applied Behavior Analysis, 37(3), 351–363.	44	Journal of Applied Behavior Analysis
2004	Alvero, A. M., & Austin, J. (2004). The effects of observing on the behavior of the observer. Journal of Applied Behavior Analysis, 37, 457–468.	98	Journal of Applied Behavior Analysis

(*Continued*)

TABLE 2.2
(Continued)

Date	*Reference*	*Cited*	*Text, Journal, Talk*
2004	McSween, T. (2004). The value-based safety process: Improving your safety culture with a behavioral approach. (2nd ed.) New York, NY: John Wiley & Sons, Inc.	374	Text
2004	Sasson, J. R., & Austin, J. (2004). The effects of training, feedback, and participant involvement in behavioral safety. Journal of Organizational Behavior Management, 24(4), 1–30.	54	Journal of Organizational Behavior Management
2005	Bumstead, A., & Boyce, T. E. (2005). Exploring the effects of cultural variables in the implementation of behavior-based safety in two organizations. Journal of Organizational Behavior Management, 24(4), 43–63.	17	Journal of Organizational Behavior Management
2005	DeJoy, D. M. (2005). Behavior change versus culture change: Divergent approaches to managing workplace safety. Safety Science, 43(2), 105–129.	357	Safety Science
2005	Geller, E. S. (2005). Behavior-based safety and occupational risk management. Behavior modification, 29(3), 539–561.	181	Behavior Modification
2005	Geller, E. S. (2005). People-based safety: The source. Coastal Training Technologies.	85	Text
2005	Houten, R. V., Malenfant, J. L., Austin, J., & Lebbon, A. (2005). The effects of a seatbelt-gearshift delay prompt on the seatbelt use of motorists who do not regularly wear seatbelts. Journal of Applied Behavior Analysis, 38(2), 195–203.	32	Journal of Applied Behavior Analysis
2005	Johnson, B. M., Miltenberger, R. G., Egemo-Helm, K., Jostad, C. M., Flessner, C., & Gatheridge, B. (2005). Evaluation of behavioral skills training for teaching abduction-prevention skills to young children. Journal of Applied Behavior Analysis, 38(1), 67–78.	134	Journal of Applied Behavior Analysis
2005	Johnston, M. R., & Hayes, L. J. (2005). Use of a simulated work setting to study behavior-based safety. Journal of Organizational Behavior Management, 25(1), 1–34.	15	Journal of Organizational Behavior Management
2005	Sasson, J. R., & Austin, J. (2005). The effects of training, feedback, and participant involvement in behavioral safety observations on office ergonomic behavior. Journal of Organizational Behavior Management, 24(4), 1–30.	54	Journal of Organizational Behavior Management
2005	Bumstead, A., & Boyce, T. E. (2005;2004;). Exploring the effects of cultural variables in the implementation of behavior-based safety in two organizations. Journal of Organizational Behavior Management, 24(4), 43–63. doi:10.1300/J075v24n04_03	17	Journal of Organizational Behavior Management
2005	Austin, J., Sigurdsson, S., & Schpak, Y. (2005). An examination of the effects of delayed versus immediate prompts on seat belt use. Environment and Behavior.	17	Environment and Behavior
2005	Culig, K., Dickinson, A. M., McGee, H., & Austin, J. (2005). An objective comparison of applied behavior analysis and organizational behavior management research. Journal of Organizational Behavior Management, 25(1).	14	Journal of Organizational Behavior Management

Date	*Reference*	*Cited*	*Text, Journal, Talk*
2005	Ludwig, T. D., Buchholz, C., & Clarke, S. W. (2005). Using social marketing to increase the use of helmets among bicyclists. Journal of American College Health, 54(1), 51–58.	52	Journal of American College Health
2005	Nielsen, D., & Austin, J. (2005). Improvement opportunities in hospital safety. Professional Safety, 50(2).	3	Professional Safety
2005	Olson, R., & Austin, J. (2005). A step toward early PC-based training that reduces risk: The effects of practicing an "instrument referenced" skill pattern on "visually referenced" performance of beginning flight students. Journal of Aviation/Aerospace Education and Research, 14(2), 47–61.	4	Journal of Aviation/Aerospace Education and Research
2005	Stephens, S.D., & Ludwig, T.D. (2005). Improving anesthesia nurse compliance with Universal Precautions using group goals and public feedback. Journal of Organizational Behavior Management, 25 (2), 37–71.	41	Journal of Organizational Behavior Management
2005	Van Houten, R., Malenfant, J.E.L., Austin, J., & Lebbon, A. (2005). The effects of a seatbelt-gearshift delay prompt on the seatbelt use of motorists who do not regularly wear their seatbelt. Journal of Applied Behavior Analysis, 38, 198–203.	32	Journal of Applied Behavior Analysis
2006	Cooper, M. D. (2006). Exploratory analyses of the effects of managerial support and feedback consequences on behavioral safety maintenance. Journal of Organizational Behavior Management, 26(3), 1–41. doi:10.1300/J075v26n03_01	91	Journal of Organizational Behavior Management
2006	Al-Hemoud A.M. and Al-Asfoor M.M. 2006 A behaviour-based safety approach at a Kuwait research institution Journal of Safety Research 37 201-206	78	Journal of Safety Research
2006	Al-Hemoud, A. M., & Al-Asfoor, M. M. (2006). A behavior-based safety approach at a Kuwait research institution. Journal of Safety Research, 37(2), 201–206. doi:10.1016/j.jsr.2005.11.006	78	Journal of Safety Research
2006	Alvero, A.M., & Austin, J. (2006). An implementation of protocol analysis and the silent dog method in the area of behavioral safety. Analysis of Verbal Behavior, 22, 61–79.	23	Analysis of Verbal Behavior
2006	Austin, J., Hackett, S., Gravina, N., & Lebbon, A. (2006). The effects of prompting and feedback on drivers' stopping at stop signs. Journal of Applied Behavior Analysis, 39, 117–121.	24	Journal of Applied Behavior Analysis
2007	Geller, E. S. (2007, January). People-Based Leadership: Gaining and Sustaining Engagement in Occupational Safety. In ASSE Professional Development Conference. American Society of Safety Engineers.	0	American Society of Safety Engineers
2007	Geller, E. S., & Johnson, D. (2007). The anatomy of medical error: Preventing harm with people-based patient safety. Coastal.	4	Coastal
2007	Sasson, J. R., Austin, J., & Alvero, A. M. (2007). Behavioral observations effects on safe performance. Professional Safety, 52(04).	11	Professional Safety

(*Continued*)

TABLE 2.2
(Continued)

Date	*Reference*	*Cited*	*Text, Journal, Talk*
2007	Van Houten, R., Van Houten, J., & Louis Malenfant, J.. (2007). Impact of a Comprehensive Safety Program on Bicycle Helmet Use Among Middle-school Children. Journal of Applied Behavior Analysis, 40(2), 239–247. https://doi.org/10.1901/jaba.2007.62-06	26	Journal of Applied Behavior Analysis
2007	HL, K. (2007). Behaviour-based safety in organizations. Indian Journal of Occupational and Environmental Medicine, 10(3)	16	Indian Journal of Occupational and Environmental Medicine
2007	Brown, G. D., & Barab, J. (2008;2007;). "Cooking the Books" – Behavior-based safety at the San Francisco bay bridge. NEW SOLUTIONS: A Journal of Environmental and Occupational Health Policy, 17(4), 311–324. doi:10.2190/NS.17.4.g	18	A Journal of Environmental and Occupational Health Policy
2007	Gravina, N., Hazel, D., & Austin, J. (2007). Evaluating the effects of workstation changes, the Rollermouse keyboard and behavioral safety on performance in an office setting. Work: A Journal of Prevention, Assessment, & Rehabilitation, 29, 245–253.	27	A Journal of Prevention, Assessment, & Rehabilitation
2007	Sasson, J. R., Austin, J., & Alvero, A. M. (2007). Behavioral observations: Effects on safe performance. Professional Safety, 52, 26–32.	11	Professional Safety
2008	Alvero, A. M., Rost, K., & Austin, J. (2008). The safety observer effect: The effects of conducting safety observations. Journal of Safety Research, 39(4), 365–373.	59	Journal of Safety Research
2008	Dagen, J. C., & Alavosius, M. P. (2008a). Bicyclist and Motorist Environments: Exploring Interlocking Behavioral Contingencies. Behavior and Social Issues; New York, 17(2), 139–160. Retrieved from https://search.proquest.com/docview/229300236/abstract/F4B1778A3C974F10PQ/1	10	Behavior and Social Issues
2008	Geller, E. S. (2008). People-Based Leadership Enriching a Work Culture For World-class Safety. Professional Safety, 53(03).	22	Professional Safety
2008	Geller, E. S., & Johnson, D. (2008). People-based patient safety: Enriching your culture to prevent medical error. Coastal Training Technologies.	10	Coastal Training Technologies
2008	Dağdeviren, M., & Yüksel, İ. (2008). Developing a fuzzy analytic hierarchy process (AHP) model for behavior-based safety management. Information Sciences, 178(6), 1717–1733. doi:10.1016/j.ins.2007.10.016	430	Information Sciences
2008	Gravina, N., Yueng-hsiang, H., Robertson, M., Blair, M., & Austin, J. (2008, November). Using self-monitoring to promote behavior change of computer users. Professional Safety.	0	Professional Safety
2009	Christian, M. S., Bradley, J. C., Wallace, J. C., & Burke, M. J. (2009). Workplace safety: A meta-analysis of the roles of person and situation factors. Journal of Applied Psychology, 94(5), 1103–1127. https://doi.org/10.1037/a0016172	1191	Journal of Applied Psychology
2009	Geller, E. S., & Veazie, B. (2009). The courage factor: Leading people-based culture change. Coastal Training Technologies Corporation.	15	Coastal Training Technologies

Date	*Reference*	*Cited*	*Text, Journal, Talk*
2009	Yiannas, F. (2009). Food safety culture: Creating a behavior-based food safety management system. New York: Springer.	173	Text
2009	Alavosius, M. P., Getting, J., Dagen, J., Newsome, W. D., Hopkins, B. (2009). Use of a cooperative to interlock contingencies and balance the commonwealth. *Journal of Organizational Behavior Management*, *29*, 193–211.	23	Journal of Organizational Behavior Management
2009	Kaila, H. L. (2009). Behaviour-based safety in Indian organisations. Journal of Health Management, 11(3), 489–500. doi:10.1177/097206340901100303	6	Journal of Health Management
2009	Kaila, H. L. (2009). Behaviour-based safety management: Case studies across industries in India. The Indian Journal of Social Work, 70(3), 499–511.	1	The Indian Journal of Social Work
2010	Cornwell-Smith, N. (2010). Behavioral safety--A framework for success. Borehamwood: UBM Information Ltd.	0	Text
2010	Cox, M. G., & Geller, E. S. (2010). prompting safety belt use: Comparative impact on the target behavior and relevant body language. Journal of Applied Behavior Analysis, 43(2), 321–325. doi:10.1901/jaba.2010.43-321	11	Journal of Applied Behavior Analysis
2010	Hermann, J. A., Ibarra, G. V., & Hopkins, B. L. (2010). A safety program that integrated behavior-based safety and traditional safety methods and its effects on injury rates of manufacturing workers. Journal of organizational behavior management, 30(1), 6–25.	39	Journal of Organizational Behavior Management
2010	Kazbour, R. R., & Bailey, J. S. (2010a). An analysis of a contingency program on designated drivers at a college bar. Journal of Applied Behavior Analysis, 43(2), 273–277. https://doi.org/10.1901/jaba.2010.43-273	7	Journal of Applied Behavior Analysis
2010	Myers †, W. V., McSween, T. E., Medina, R. E., Rost, K., & Alvero, A. M. (2010). The Implementation and Maintenance of a Behavioral Safety Process in a Petroleum Refinery. Journal of Organizational Behavior Management, 30(4), 285–307. https://doi.org/10.1080/01608061.2010.499027	31	Journal of Organizational Behavior Management
2010	The Additive Impact of Group and Individual Publicly Displayed Feedback: Examining Individual Response Patterns and Response Generalization in a Safe-Driving Occupational Intervention - Timothy D. Ludwig, E. Scott Geller, Steven W. Clarke, 2010. (n.d.). Retrieved December 17, 2019, from https://journals.sagepub.com/doi/abs/10.1177/0145445510383523	9	Text
2010	Van Houten, R., Malenfant, J. E. L., Reagan, I., Sifrit, K., Compton, R., & Tenenbaum, J. (2010a). Increasing seatbelt use in service vehicle drivers with gearshift delay. Journal of Applied Behavior Analysis, 43(3), 369–380. https://doi.org/10.1901/jaba.2010.43-369	14	Journal of Applied Behavior Analysis
2010	Dagen, J. C. (2010). The effects of feedback on safety observations and related behaviors. Unpublished dissertation	0	Paper
2010	Nielsen, D. (2010). Behavior-based safety in health care environments. Giornale Italiano Di Medicina Del Lavoro Ed Ergonomia, 32(1 Suppl A), A33.	1	Paper

(*Continued*)

TABLE 2.2
(Continued)

Date	*Reference*	*Cited*	*Text, Journal, Talk*
2010	Vaughen, B. K., Lock, K. J., & Floyd, T. K. (2010). Improving operating discipline through the successful implementation of a mandated behavior-based safety program. Process Safety Progress, 29(3), 192–200. doi:10.1002/prs.10376	14	Process Safety Progress
2010	Kaila, H. L. (2010). Behavior-based safety programs improve worker safety in India. Ergonomics in Design: The Quarterly of Human Factors Applications, 18(4), 17–22. doi:10.1518/106480410X12887326203031	15	Quarterly of Human Factors Applications
2010	Hermann, J. A., Ibarra, G. V., & Hopkins, B. L. (2010). A safety program that integrated behavior-based safety and traditional safety methods and its effects on injury rates of manufacturing workers. Journal of Organizational Behavior Management, 30(1), 6–25. doi:10.1080/01608060903472445	39	Journal of Organizational Behavior Management
2010	Turnbeaugh, T. M. (2010). Improving business outcomes: Behavior-based safety techniques can influence organizational performance. Professional Safety, 55(3), 41–49.	22	Professional Safety
2011	Okinaka, T., & Shimazaki, T. (2011a). The effects of prompting and reinforcement on safe behavior of bicycle and motorcycle riders. Journal of Applied Behavior Analysis, 44(3), 671–674. https://doi.org/10.1901/jaba.2011.44-671	5	Journal of Applied Behavior Analysis
2011	Scott Geller, E. (2011a). Psychological Science and Safety: Large-Scale Success at Preventing Occupational Injuries and Fatalities. Current Directions in Psychological Science, 20(2), 109–114. https://doi.org/10.1177/0963721411402667	30	Current Directions in Psychological Science
2011	Luke, M. & Alavosius, M.P. (2011). Adherence with Universal Precautions after immediate, personalized performance feedback: An experimental analysis. *Journal of Applied Behavior Analysis*. 44, 967–971.	26	Journal of Applied Behavior Analysis
2011	Kaila, H. L. (2011). Organizational cases on behaviour-based safety (BBS) in India. The International Journal of Human Resource Management, 22(10), 2135–2146. doi: 10.1080/09585192.2011.580180	3	The International Journal of Human Resource Management,
2012	Alavosius, M.P. (2012). Best-practice in behavior-based safety applications in hospital settings. Proceedings of the 8th International Conference published in *Journal of Applied Radical Behavior Analysis*. 27–32.	0	Journal of Applied Radical Behavior Analysis.
2012	Tauseef, A., Villegas Bello, M., Bordage, P., & Turner, L. A. (2012, January). Behavior Management: A Successful Approach. In International Conference on Health, Safety and Environment in Oil and Gas Exploration and Production. Society of Petroleum Engineers.	0	Society of Petroleum Engineers
2012	Chen, D., & Tian, H. (2012). Behaviour-based safety for accidents prevention and positive study in China construction project. Procedia Engineering, 43, 528–534. doi:10.1016/j.proeng.2012.08.092	41	Procedia Engineering
2013	Han, S., & Lee, S. (2013). A vision-based motion capture and recognition framework for behavior-based safety management. Automation in Construction, 35, 131–141. doi:10.1016/j.autcon.2013.05.001	185	Automation in Construction

Date	Reference	Cited	Text, Journal, Talk
2013	Zhang, M., & Fang, D. (2013). A continuous behavior-based safety strategy for persistent safety improvement in construction industry. Automation in Construction, 34, 101–107. doi:10.1016/j.autcon.2012.10.019	85	Automation in Construction
2014	Abellon, O. E., & Wilder, D. A. (2014). The effect of equipment proximity on safe performance in a manufacturing setting. Journal of Applied Behavior Analysis, 47(3), 628–632. https://doi.org/10.1002/jaba.137	4	Journal of Applied Behavior Analysis
2014	Dean, J. (2014). Personal Protective Equipment: An antecedent to Safe behavior? Professional Safety, 59(02), 41–46. Retrieved from https://www.onepetro.org/journal-paper/ASSE-14-02-41	24	Professional Safety
2014	Himle, M. B., & Wright, K. A. (2014). Behavioral skills training to improve installation and use of child passenger safety restraints. Journal of Applied Behavior Analysis, 47(3), 549–559. https://doi.org/10.1002/jaba.143	22	Journal of Applied Behavior Analysis
2014	Hystad, S. W., Bartone, P. T., & Eid, J. (2014). Positive organizational behavior and safety in the offshore oil industry: Exploring the determinants of positive safety climate. The Journal of Positive Psychology, 9(1), 42–53. https://doi.org/10.1080/17439760.2013.831467	55	The Journal of Positive Psychology
2014	Vanselow, N. R., & Hanley, G. P. (2014a). An Evaluation of Computerized Behavioral Skills Training to Teach Safety Skills to Young Children. Journal of Applied Behavior Analysis; Malden, 47(1), 51–69. Retrieved from https://search.proquest.com/docview/1517530267/abstract/BB52BC187A994581PQ/1	29	Journal of Applied Behavior Analysis
2014	Choudhry, R. M. (2014). Behavior-based safety on construction sites: A case study. Accident Analysis and Prevention, 70, 14–23. doi:10.1016/j.aap.2014.03.007	147	Accident Analysis and Prevention
2014	Yeow, P. H. P., & Goomas, D. T. (2014). Outcome-and-behavior-based safety incentive program to reduce accidents: A case study of a fluid manufacturing plant. Safety Science, 70, 429–437. doi:10.1016/j.ssci.2014.07.016	17	Safety Science
2014	Kaila, H. L. (2014). Outcomes of behaviour-based safety (BBS) implementation. The Indian Journal of Social Work, 75(4), 595–602.	0	The Indian Journal of Social Work
2014	Möller, G., & Rothmann, S. (2014). The implementation and evaluation of a behaviour-based safety intervention at an iron ore mine. South African Journal of Economic and Management Sciences, 9(3), 299–314. doi:10.4102/sajems.v9i3.1089	4	South African Journal of Economic and Management Sciences
2014	Kaila, H. L. (2014). A case of behaviour-based safety (BBS) implementation at a multinational organization. Journal of Psychosocial Research, 9(2), 337.	3	Journal of Psychosocial Research
2015	Shin, D.-P., Gwak, H.-S., & Lee, D.-E. (2015). Modeling the predictors of safety behavior in construction workers. International Journal of Occupational Safety and Ergonomics, 21(3), 298–311. https://doi.org/10.1080/10803548.2015.1085164	28	International Journal of Occupational Safety and Ergonomics

(Continued)

TABLE 2.2
(Continued)

Date	*Reference*	*Cited*	*Text, Journal, Talk*
2015	Li H., Lu M., Hsu S.C., Gray M. and Huang T. 2015 Proactive behavior-based safety management for construction safety improvement. Safety Science, 75, 107–117	147	Safety Science
2015	Grzybowski, E. P., Jr. (2015). Behavior-based safety and the multi-generational workforce. Unpublished thesis	0	Paper
2016	Guo, S. Y., Ding, L. Y., Luo, H. B., & Jiang, X. Y. (2016). A big-data-based platform of workers' behavior: Observations from the field. Accident Analysis and Prevention, 93, 299–309. doi:10.1016/j.aap.2015.09.024	52	Accident Analysis and Prevention
2016	Killingsworth, K., Miller, S. & Alavosius, M. P. (2016) A behavioral interpretation of Situational Awareness and prospects for OBM. *Journal of Organizational Behavior Management*, 36(4), 301–321	15	Journal of Organizational Behavior Management
2016	Lopez, J.C., Barragan, M., Jeffries, J., Capote, W., Bordage, P., Martinez, L., Boz, A., Gonzalez, J. Alavosius, M. & Houmanfar, R. (2016) Applying behavior engineering to procedural adherence. *Proceedings of 2018 SPE Conference on Health, Safety, Security, Environment and Social Responsibility.* Stavanger, Norway.	0	Proceedings of 2018 SPE Conference on Health, Safety, Security, Environment & Social Responsibility
2017	Wang B., Wu C., Shi B. and Huang L. 2017 Evidence-based safety (EBS) management: A new approach to teaching the practice of safety management (SM) Journal of Safety Research, 63, 21–28.	24	Journal of Safety Research
2017	Zhang P., Li N., Fang D. and Wu H. 2017 Supervisor-Focused Behavior-Based Safety Method for the Construction Industry: Case Study in Hong Kong Journal of Construction Engineering and Management, 143.	24	Hong Kong Journal of Construction Engineering and Management
2017	Hagge, M., McGee, H., Matthews, G., & Aberle, S. (2017). Behavior-based safety in a coal mine: The relationship between observations, participation, and injuries over a 14-year period. Journal of Organizational Behavior Management, 37(1), 107–118. doi:10.1080/01608061.2016.1236058.	14	Journal of Organizational Behavior Management
2017	Alavosius, M.P., Houmanfar, R., Anbro, S. Burleigh, K, & Hebein, C. (2017). Leadership and crew resource management in high reliability organizations: A competency framework for measuring behaviors. *Journal of Organizational Behavior Management*, 37(2) 142–170.	14	Journal of Organizational Behavior Management
2017	Sussman, A. (2017). Buying into behavior-based safety. Ishn, 51(8), 16.	0	Ishn
2017	Hyten, C. & Ludwig. T., (2017) Complacency in Process Safety: A behavior analysis toward prevention strategies. Journal of Organizational Behavior Management, 37:3–4, 240–260, doi: 10.1080/01608061.2017.1341860	12	Journal of Organizational Behavior Management
2017	Ludwig, T., (2017) Process Safety: Another opportunity to translate behavior analysis into evidence-based practices of grave societal value. Journal of Organizational Behavior Management, 37:3–4, 221–223, doi: 10.1080/01608061.2017.1343702	6	Journal of Organizational Behavior Management

Date	*Reference*	*Cited*	*Text, Journal, Talk*
2017	McSween, T., & Moran, D. J. (2017). Assessing and preventing serious incidents with behavioral science: Enhancing Heinrich's triangle for the 21st century. Journal of Organizational Behavior Management, 37(3–4), 283–300. doi:10.1080/01608061.2017.1340923	11	Journal of Organizational Behavior Management
2018	Wu, C., & Wang, B. (2018). Research on meta-model of behavior-based safety management. Zhongguo Anquan Shengchan Kexue Jishu = Journal of Safety Science and Technology; Beijing, (2), 5. Retrieved from https://search.proquest.com/docview/2044638345?pq-origsite=summon	0	Journal of Safety Science and Technology
2018	YU, Y., & Yanyan, L. V. (2018). Application Study of BBS on Unsafe Behavior and Psychology of Coal Miners. NeuroQuantology; Bornova Izmir, 16(4). http://dx.doi.org/10.14704/nq.2018.16.4.1188	1	NeuroQuantology
2018	Wang, X., Xing, Y., Luo, L., & Yu, R. (2018). Evaluating the effectiveness of behavior-based safety education methods for commercial vehicle drivers. Accident Analysis and Prevention, 117, 114–120. doi:10.1016/j.aap.2018.04.008	8	Accident Analysis and Prevention
2018	Guo, B. H. W., Goh, Y. M., & Le Xin Wong, K. (2018). A system dynamics view of a behavior-based safety program in the construction industry. Safety Science, 104, 202–215. doi:10.1016/j.ssci.2018.01.014	16	Safety Science
2018	Nunu, W. N., Kativhu, T., & Moyo, P. (2018). An evaluation of the effectiveness of the behaviour-based safety initiative card system at a cement manufacturing company in zimbabwe. Safety and Health at Work, 9(3), 308–313. doi:10.1016/j.shaw.2017.09.002	6	Safety and Health at Work
2018	Da Silva, J. P. (2018). Combining safety climate and behavior-based safety to achieve compliance: A sociotechnical systems model. Proceedings of the Human Factors and Ergonomics Society Annual Meeting, 62(1), 1619–1623. doi:10.1177/1541931218621366	0	Paper
2018	McKenzie, L. B., Roberts, K. J., Clark, R., McAdams, R., Abdel-Rasoul, M., Klein, E. G.,... Shields, W. C. (2018). A randomized controlled trial to evaluate the make safe happen® app – a mobile technology-based safety behavior change intervention for increasing parents' safety knowledge and actions. Injury Epidemiology, 5(1), 1–9. doi:10.1186/s40621-018-0133-3	4	Injury Epidemiology
2018	Li, H., Li, Y., Hu, Y., Xia, B., & Skitmore, M. (2018). Proactive behavior-based system for controlling safety risks in urban highway construction megaprojects. Automation in Construction, 95, 118–128. doi:10.1016/j.autcon.2018.07.021	4	Automation in Construction
2018	Nunu, W. N., Kativhu, T., & Moyo, P. (2018). An evaluation of the effectiveness of the behaviour-based safety initiative card system at a cement manufacturing company in zimbabwe. Safety and Health at Work: SH@W, 9(3), 308–313.	6	Safety and Health at Work

(*Continued*)

TABLE 2.2
(Continued)

Date	*Reference*	*Cited*	*Text, Journal, Talk*
2018	Capote, W., Boz, A., Lopez, J.C., Noya, V., Bordage, P., Febles, N., Hebein, C., Houmanfar, R., Alavosius, M., (2018). An applied behavior science project; Rig floor safety. In: *Proceedings of 2018 SPE Conference on Health, Safety, Security, Environment, and Social Responsibility*. Abu Dhabi, UAE. https://doi.org/10.2118/190610-MS	0	Proceedings of 2018 SPE Conference on Health, Safety, Security, Environment, and Social Responsibility
2018	Yue, Y., & Yanyan, L. (2018). Application study of BBS on unsafe behavior and psychology of coal miners. Neuroquantology, 16(4) doi:10.14704/nq.2018.16.4.1188	1	Neuroquantology
2019	Kaila, H. L., & Founder Director – Forum of Behavioural Safety, Mumbai, Professor of Psychology (retd.) SNDT Women's University, Mumbai & Advisor & Professor Emenities, Shri JJT University, Rajasthan. (2019). Journey of behaviour-based safety in India: An overview. Journal of Psychosocial Research, 14(1), 81–94. doi:10.32381/JPR.2019.14.01.9	0	Journey of behaviour-based safety in India
2019	Roberts, K. J., McAdams, R. J., Kristel, O. V., Szymanski, A. M., & McKenzie, L. B. (2019). Qualitative and quantitative evaluation of the make safe happen app: Mobile technology-based safety behavior change intervention for parents. JMIR Pediatrics and Parenting, 2(1), e12022. doi:10.2196/12022	0	JMIR Pediatrics and Parenting
2019	Lee, P., Wei, J., Ting, H., Lo, T., Long, D., & Chang, L. (2019). Dynamic analysis of construction safety risk and visual tracking of key factors based on behavior-based safety and building information modeling. KSCE Journal of Civil Engineering, 23(10), 4155–4167. doi:10.1007/s12205-019-0283-z	0	KSCE Journal of Civil Engineering
2019	Li, X., & Long, H. (2019). A review of worker behavior-based safety research: Current trends and future prospects. IOP Conference Series: Earth and Environmental Science, 371, 32047. doi:10.1088/1755-1315/371/3/032047	0	Paper
2019	Gravina N.E., King A. and Austin J. 2019 Training leaders to apply behavioral concepts to improve safety. Safety Science 112 66–70	7	Safety Science
2019	Guo, S., Ding, L., Zhang, Y., Skibniewski, M. J., & Liang, K. (2019). Hybrid recommendation approach for behavior modification in the Chinese construction industry. Journal of Construction Engineering and Management, 145(6), 4019035. doi:10.1061/(ASCE)CO.1943-7862.0001665	0	Journal of Construction Engineering and Management
2019	Hussain, U., Shoukat, M. H., & Shamail Haider, M. (2019). Analysis of safety awareness, accident prevention and implementation of behavior-based safety program in energy utility. Paper presented at the, 84–88. doi:10.1109/ICFIE.2019.8907683	0	Paper
2020	Fang, W., Love, P. E. D., Luo, H., & Ding, L. (2020). Computer vision for behaviour-based safety in construction: A review and future directions. Advanced Engineering Informatics, 43, 100980. doi:10.1016/j.aei.2019.100980	3	Advanced Engineering Informatics

Date	*Reference*	*Cited*	*Text, Journal, Talk*
2020	Ting, H., Lee, P., Chen, P., & Chang, L. (2020). An adjusted behavior-based safety program with the observation by front-line workers for mitigating construction accident rate. Journal of the Chinese Institute of Engineers, 43(1), 37–46. doi:10.1080/02533839.2019.1676654	0	Journal of the Chinese Institute of Engineers
2020	Tripathy, D. P. (2020). Behavior-based safety. (1st ed., pp. 45–55) CRC Press. doi:10.1201/9781315162294-3	0	Text
2020	Lopez, J.C., Gonzalez, J., Capote, W., Jeffries, J., Martinez Sistiva, L.M., Sanabria Morales,J.S., Del Socorro Claros Rojas, L., Pazmino Aldaz, K., Miranda, G., Alavosius, M., Houmanfar, R. (2020). Behavior engineering applied to procedural adherence in global operations. In: *SPE proceedings of 2020 SPE Conference on Health, Safety, Environment, and Sustainability.* Bogota, Colombia. Publisher: Society for Petroleum Engineers. doi: March 2020 publication	0	SPE proceedings of 2020 SPE Conference on Health, Safety, Environment, and Sustainability

3

The Foundations of Behavior-Based Instructional Design Within Business

Douglas A. Johnson

> But how could a teacher reinforce the behavior of each of twenty or thirty students at the right time and on the material for which he or she was just ready? I had solved a similar problem in the laboratory. When I was a graduate student, almost all animal psychologists watched their animals and recorded their behavior by hand. They could make only a few observations, many of them not too reliable. Mechanization had made a great difference.
>
> (Skinner, 1983, pp. 64–65)

If one were interested in fully understanding the behavior analytic approach for creating instructional design in business and industry, it would be informative to understand the history that shaped and evolved the perspectives and practices of the field. Such a history would first involve early efforts to revolutionize education before transitioning to workplace concerns. Like many developments in behavior analysis, much of the origin behind behavior-based instructional design can be traced back to the efforts of B.F. Skinner.

AN IMPETUS TO EXTEND LABORATORY FINDINGS

Although Skinner had long shown an interest in speculating about the possible role of using behavioral science to shape social concerns (Skinner, 1948), it is probably fair to say that during the early stages of his career he was largely content to investigate basic phenomenon under controlled laboratory conditions. When discussing real-world applications during a lecture in 1951, Skinner spoke of the importance of isolating the component variables of complex behavior as part of basic research, with the notion that behavioral science would eventually find some practical applications at a later date, just as other sciences had done (Skinner, 1953). While speculative extrapolation was worthwhile and encouraged, actual extensions needed to wait until we had a stronger empirical foundation.

An important change in priorities occurred in late 1953 for Skinner. As part of a Father's Day event at his daughter's elementary school, Skinner found himself observing the math lesson of a fourth-grade class (Skinner, 1983). Students worked at various levels of readiness and engagement, with some students appearing to be adrift in confusion and others being artificially held back. The pace of lessons had to be shackled to the needs of an ideal average student, ensuring that the actual student was always at the mercy of instruction that was likely either too fast or too slow for them as an individual. Errors in comprehension were allowed to persist and strengthen during the time period before the correction was provided (after

DOI: 10.4324/9781003198949-3

which a certain amount of unlearning must take place). Instances of reinforcement in the classroom appeared to be few and far between. Skinner's observation of reinforcement rates was confirmed by later researchers, who noted across observational studies that teachers use infrequent rates of approval and that these rates tend to decline as children progress in school (Merrett & Wheldall, 1987; White, 1975).

It was likely a disturbing sight for a scientist such as Skinner, watching young pupils like his daughter being educated less efficiently than the rats and pigeons he was accustomed to working with. Just as a rat should not be blamed for the conditions that the experimenter has arranged, the students could not be held responsible for the conditions of the classroom they found themselves in. Although he saw obvious shortcomings in how his daughter was being taught, his solution was not to blame the classroom's teacher. Instead, he noted that the teacher's classroom practices were a product of her learning history and the current available resources, just as the behaviors of the students were a product of their learning history and current available resources. Ultimately, the educational system had produced circumstances in which the neglect of many students was all but guaranteed regardless of the intentions or aspirations of the teacher. At the heart of the problem was the fact that there were too many students for each individual teacher (Skinner, 1961). If a laboratory researcher was forced to shape the behavior of several rats and pigeons simultaneously, the process would be guaranteed to be inefficient in comparison to the one-on-one experimentation often being done. Even with something as simple as shaping a lever press response with rats, group management would be disastrously cumbersome if the reinforcers were delivered simultaneously to all rats regardless of their individual progress with the lever or if the experimenter skillfully shaped up one rat's responding while the behavior of the other rats inadvertently underwent extinction. If there was a limited time frame to complete this shaping process, an experimenter might be lucky if a select few of the rats mastered the desired response. The educational system routinely put teachers in this unfortunate position of simultaneously shaping the educational repertoires of several learners with limited time and resources. In other words, it was a problem of mass production.

COMBINING BEHAVIORAL THEORY AND MECHANICAL TECHNOLOGY TO ADVANCE EDUCATION

Skinner had observed that in other industries, the most effective way to solve a production problem would be to automate parts of the production process (Skinner, 1954). For example, the automobile industry could never meet the demands of customers if several cars had to be assembled by a single person without the aid of automation. Instead, production lines were created in which machines helped cut, mold, assemble, weld, and move vehicles through various stages of production. From this perspective, education could be viewed as an enterprise aimed at producing large quantities of well-educated citizens. Of course, developing the skills of students is a much more complex, multi-faceted, and sensitive endeavor than the assembly of a vehicle, but the quantitative similarities are relevant. If more educated youth were needed, then perhaps teaching machines could be enlisted to increase the output of well-educated people. Although other educational reformers had already developed machines that could test students on what they already knew (Pressey, 1926, 1927, 1932), Skinner was likely the first to take comprehensive steps to create machines that would teach students new behavior.

He also thought mechanization could solve several of the problems inherent in typical educational methods (Skinner, 1958, 1961). Skinner noted that most of the contingencies employed throughout the history of education were primarily aversive in nature. Although he did not completely rule out the use of aversive stimulation to develop academic repertoires, he felt that it was critical to capitalize on more positive methods of refining performance (Skinner, 1954). Positive affirmations for correct responding and gentle corrections for errors could be designed in advance when using an automated sequence. Such feedback could be delivered immediately after each students' response, unlike traditional education, in which students' work on homework, worksheets, quizzes, and exams would not receive feedback until minutes, hours, days, and perhaps weeks later. In his laboratory work Skinner had noted the detrimental effects of reinforcement being delayed by even a few seconds.

Of course, verbally sophisticated organisms may be better prepared to suffer delays in consequences, thanks in part to rule-governed behavior producing stimuli to mediate the gap between performance and outcome (Blakely & Schlinger, 1987; Malott, 1992). That is, a person may generate a verbal description of the relationship between their behavior and the consequences for that behavior. That verbal description begins to directly exert functional control over behavior related to delayed outcomes. The individual may follow a rule and immediately provide direct reinforcement to themselves in the form of self-statements. For example, they may say, "Now that I've done a good job on that report, I'll probably get a good grade in the class." Although the good grade is delayed, the verbal stimuli arising from their own verbal descriptions may have direct reinforcing properties for the academic behavior. Furthermore, others in their verbal community may provide direct reinforcement when they observe that an individual's behavior is in compliance with the rule (or direct punishment when they observe behavior that is out of compliance with the rule).

However, rule governance may not help when the organism is uncertain of the accuracy of their performance (i.e., they cannot talk to themselves about the eventual consequence due to their uncertainty regarding the outcome of evaluation). That is, events in the environment generate descriptive verbal behavior on the part of the individual and the response products arising from such descriptions serve as verbal stimuli that may exert a strengthening or weakening effect on prior responding. In addition, these verbal stimuli describing the relations among events can also evoke or abate subsequent behavior, as well as alter the function of other stimuli. For example, when completing a homework assignment that the individual lacks expertise in, the generated rules are more likely to be vague and less likely to result in verbal stimuli with reinforcing properties (e.g., "I've finally finished that report – who knows what grade I'll get"). As such, prior behavior is less likely to be strengthened, and any potential evocative properties will be weaker. When it comes to acquisition of new skills, immediacy may be equally critical for both verbal and non-verbal organisms. In fact, a lack of immediacy could potentially be more challenging for verbal organisms, who may make erroneous inferences that in turn strengthen problematic rules during the delay until disconfirmation (e.g., a student who rehearses an inaccurate flashcard and tells themselves that they will get a good grade for practicing their material, when in fact the subsequent examination will result in poor marks). Such mislearning may then need to be undone before the next lesson can be effective. The typical educator is faced with far too many students to allow them to supply accurate and individualized feedback during the critical time when response relations are initially being developed.

Not only could teaching machines potentially fix the issues related to the timing and nature of consequences, but they could also require meaningful responding and improve the provision of antecedents (D.A. Johnson & Rubin, 2011). Too often education is a passive affair, with students listening, watching, or reading (assuming they are even orienting to the relevant material during instruction) but not frequently demonstrating their comprehension of the material they are being exposed to (i.e., overtly responding in a differential manner to various instructional stimuli). A teaching machine could include a response requirement that would require a student to master basic material before being allowed to progress to more complex material. It has often been shown that the probability of success on advanced material can be greatly increased by ensuring fluent mastery of foundational material (Binder, 1996; K.R. Johnson & Layng, 1992). When accurate responding is occurring at a high rate, it better prepares individuals to function in natural environments and facilitates components of performance combining into more complex forms (K.R. Johnson & Street, 2012; Twarek et al., 2010). The increased rate in responding also provides an opportunity for an increased frequency of reinforcer delivery (after all, contingent reinforcement can only be delivered if the organism is active).

Regarding antecedents, the fact that the material was programmed in advance allowed for the development of a careful sequence of skillful progression, a feature lacking in most textbooks and classrooms. Material could prompt students in a manner that all but guaranteed correct responding, thus reducing the embarrassment and frustration from incorrect answers (Terrace, 1963). Such errorless learning may not always be ideal, as it might inhibit the transfer of training or lead to an excessive dependence on prompts (Jones & Eayrs, 2010), but such considerations could be factored into the types of response opportunities built into the program. Response requirements could be provided much more frequently than any classroom instructor could reasonably manage, thus breaking the instructional process into a series of small steps. In other words, the effective contingencies often seen with one-to-one tutoring sessions could be replicated on a larger scale (Markle, 1964; Skinner, 1958). Effective tutors constantly check on the progress of their pupils, break information into manageable amounts, provide hints as needed, challenge and test comprehension, and adjust the speed of instruction to the readiness of the individual. Any human teaching a group of students could never customize their instruction to such an individualized degree, but machines have the potential to do so.

The machines Skinner invented were often simple in design, but still possessed the basic elements of presenting an instructional antecedent, requiring a behavior from the student, and providing consequent feedback (Skinner, 1954, 1958). Students rotated knobs and pulled levers to see a small unit of instruction with a response request. Students would then write or select their answers, operate the machine, and immediately receive feedback regarding their understanding. Students could move as fast or as slow as they needed to progress through material, a feature absent in typical group instruction. Pilot tests with the machines were encouraging, with prototypes showing students giving positive evaluations and acquiring knowledge faster than standard classroom instruction permitted (Skinner, 1963, 1983). The science of behavior seemed poised to revolutionize the world of education and to bring an empirical approach to teaching and training. Yet this revolution would fail during Skinner's time.

DEVELOPING A PROGRAM OF INSTRUCTION WITHOUT MACHINERY

If one was feeling charitable, Skinner's attempt to transform instructional practices could be viewed as simply ahead of its time rather than as a complete failure. The reasons that teaching machines failed are varied. Production issues plagued Skinner's attempts to mass produce reliable machines of sound quality (Skinner, 1963, 1983). Skinner's vision for education ran counter to long-held and deeply entrenched educational philosophies. Some of these viewpoints proposed that change must ultimately come from inside the student and that to intentionally and extensively modify the environment is to deny essential freedoms. Some perspectives saw the use of technology in the educational process as inherently dehumanizing. In the final summary, his vision for education may have been too much of a radical departure to be embraced by society in general. Of course, what was a radical departure during the 1950s and 1960s may be less of a departure from the norms today. The notion of integrating technology into classes has become progressively less controversial over the subsequent decades. Although Skinner's dream of automated education was never realized during his life, it was not without impact – both immediate and long-term.

An attempt to attain the outcomes of teaching machines with a smaller deviation from typical educational practices was seen with the Programmed Instruction movement. This movement involved the development of textbooks that broke instructional material into smaller units than typical textbook chapters, often just a few sentences, before a request for a student response was presented. As such, these textbooks immediately looked quite different, with material in little chunks that included space for student answers on every page of the text (in contrast to textbooks that typically have no student response requests or save potential interactions for the occasional note in the margin or discussion questions at the end of a chapter). Essentially, Programmed Instruction textbooks allowed designers to replicate many of the conditions of teaching machines without relying on manufacturers who had proven unreliable at making quality machines (D.A. Johnson, 2014; Vargas, 2014). Unlike teaching machines, the Programmed Instruction movement exploded and became popular enough that professional organizations such as the National Society for Programmed Instruction were formed during the early 1960s. The format of Programmed Instruction textbooks will be illustrated by briefly switching the format of this chapter below (please cover the right side of the following table with a piece of paper, moving the paper downward only after answering in the blank or on a separate paper):

TABLE 3.1
Sample of programmed instruction

Unlike the passive exposure seen in traditional education (both written and spoken), one of the tenets of Programmed Instruction was the importance of _____ responding on the part of the learner. It was also critical that a consequence was provided for each response made by the learner.	active
Following a learner response, a consequence was immediately provided. That is, the student would receive _____ for their response by reading the correct answer and comparing it with what they had written.	feedback (acceptable: confirmation)
Also critical was the idea of _____-pacing, which allowed fast learners to advance rapidly and slow learner to take their time.	self
Although the pace was student determined, the sequencing often was not. As such, students often had to show _____ of basic concepts before attempting more complex concepts.	mastery
By ensuring that students _____ concepts across a variety of examples and different sentence structures before progressing and allowing them to _____ at their own speed, it was more likely that students would generalize the concept to other situations.	(1) mastered (2) self-pace
Books were designed so that the learner would always be right, so the previously mentioned features of _____, _____, _____, and _____ were necessary to guarantee learner success.	(1) active responding (2) feedback (3) self-pacing (4) mastery (ANY ORDER)
_____ responding also had another benefit for instruction. It could produce a record of responding that a programmer could use to revise the material.	Active
Only through continual _____ and refinement based on past student responses through testing could the published textbook sequences be guaranteed to be effective with future students.	revision

Like teaching machines, Programmed Instruction textbooks were meant to replicate the conditions of a competent one-on-one tutor (Holland & Skinner, 1961). Unlike teaching machines, Programmed Instruction textbooks could not require the response to be made before allowing students to look at the answer and continue onward (as some current readers might admit to doing just a few moments ago), but designers still attempted to induce continual interactions. Students were frequently reminded to respond to the material; answers were placed in margins with instructions to keep the margin covered until after a response or placed on different pages to be read later (Hetzel & Hetzel, 1969; Holland & Skinner, 1961). Another difference from teaching machines was that Programmed Instruction textbooks were easier to produce. Unfortunately, this may have also been a drawback, in that even people with little expertise in instructional design or behavioral theory could rush poorly designed books to market (Vargas, 2014). Some people less versed in analysis and empirical revisions simply assumed that any book with many response requests would be effective (Markle, 1965). Unfortunately, this often led to busy work on the part of the pupil, in which the learner was actively responding but not in any meaningful manner (Markle, 1990). The form of Programmed Instruction was being replicated, but not the underlying theoretical framework that had initially made such material effective. The process by which students came to acquire new skills was understood in only a superficial manner, as seen by the following lesson:

TABLE 3.2
Superficial program instruction

Correct responses were often seen as essential to the acquisition process. As such, material progressed slowly and in tiny chunks, so that student responses would be ______.	correct
Frequent correct answers were intended to provide a steady supply of reinforcement, but this meant that student progress was often ______. Often a frustrating degree of redundancy were built into the books.	slow
The redundancy and small incremental progress were probably quite ______ for an adept student who was ready for more ambitious response requests.	frustrating
Despite being frustrated and ready to move on, the design of the material still forced the student into ______ steps. Confirmation of correct answers may have had little reinforcing value under such conditions.	small
To increase the probability of a correct r______nse, sometimes additional prompts would be supplied to the response requests.	response
In a rush to capitalize on the new Programmed Instruction format, untrained designers often would randomly drop words from ______ blocks of instruction.	typical
The dropped words may have done little to establish a useful repertoire in the student, but they were ______ for designers to implement.	easy
Easy implementation meant many textbooks were produced that had questionable value for the ______.	student
Of course, extensive testing could have fixed some of the problematic features of these textbooks, but testing requires ______ and therefore was often ______ from the development of the material.	(1) time (acceptable: effort) (2) omitted (acceptable: absent)
Since the material had frequent response requests, it certainly had the appearance of a Pr______ Instruction textbook.	Programmed
The frequent holes in sentences gave publishers books that had the ______ cheese appearance resulting from Programmed Instruction recommendations, but the functional value behind such recommendations was absent.	Swiss
Perhaps unsurprisingly, the Swiss cheese approach to textbook design led to a general dissatisfaction with Programmed ______.	Instruction

RETURNING TO MACHINERY THROUGH COMPUTER-BASED INSTRUCTION

Another way in which Skinner's teaching machines were impactful – although this impact would be more delayed – was through computer-based instruction. Unlike the teaching machines of the 1950s, the computers of today are quite commonplace and easier to develop programs for without the intervention of manufacturers. Furthermore, all the guidelines that Skinner recommended for teaching machines and Programmed Instruction apply to computer-based instruction (D.A. Johnson & Rubin, 2011). In fact, computer-based instruction may be better positioned than teaching machines or Programmed Instruction to replicate the interactions of a good tutor. This is because computer-based instruction can more easily adjust the presented material based on learner responses than the scripted programs employed with older machines and programs. Business and industry have increasingly embraced computer-based instruction to meet the needs of employee training (Marroletti & Johnson, 2014; McCalpin et al., 2018). Like teaching machines, computer-based instruction opens the possibility of active learning that is self-paced, mastery-enforced, and feedback-rich. Many of the individuals who saw the entrenchment of traditional philosophies within education thought that the workplace might prove more receptive to the behavioral innovations in instruction (Lindsley, 1992). Skinner himself saw business and industry as one of the areas ripe for the application of automated instruction (Skinner, 1958). Computer-based instruction also allows for easier training of remote employees and consistency of standards in comparison to typical training standards. Unfortunately, computer-based training, much like the Programmed Instruction movement before it, can be subject to superficial considerations of design as programmers and managers become preoccupied with flashy bells and whistles and lose sight of the behavioral underpinnings relevant to changing employee repertoires (D.A. Johnson & Rubin, 2011; Zemke & Armstrong, 1997). As such, it became critical for researchers and practitioners to familiarize themselves with best practices for designing instruction, regardless of the medium employed. Even when designers adhered to the aforementioned guidelines, this did not guarantee successful outcomes for all types of learning that were of interest. This further highlights the need for behavioral researchers to study instructional design independent of the particular medium, later termed behavior-based instructional design (D.A. Johnson, 2014).

DESIGNING TRAINING TO ESTABLISH APPROPRIATE STIMULUS CONTROL

Much of early behavior-based instructional design originated from Skinner's work on teaching machines and verbal behavior. An early noteworthy contributor to this approach was Susan Markle. Markle had been one of the people in charge of pilot testing Skinner's teaching machines with children and had helped edit his book on the topic of verbal behavior (Skinner, 1957, 1983). One important concept within Skinner's approach to verbal behavior was the idea of behavioral semantics, which entailed conceptualizing the meaning of words by analyzing the conditions under which verbal responses are emitted (Skinner, 1945). For example, if one wanted to understand what words such as "love" or "creativity" meant, then one only needs to identify the circumstances that typically cause people to say such words. Once you have identified the relevant discriminative stimuli, then the meaning of words and concepts can be understood (Keller & Schoenfeld, 1950). Since conceptual understanding is established via stimulus control using classes of stimuli (as opposed to a single stimulus), this meant that designing instruction to teach a concept would require multiple examples (to promote generalization within the relevant stimulus class) *and* multiple non-examples (to promote discrimination between stimulus classes). This also suggests that teaching someone to recite a definition in the presence of a prompt may not be enough to conclude that a concept is understood (Markle, 1975; Markle & Tiemann, 1970). One of the primary lessons is that different learning outcomes may necessitate different teaching and assessment strategies.

Markle wrote extensively about the process of using instructional design to develop distinct learning outcomes. Unlike many traditional and cognitive approaches to instructional design, Markle's approach was predicated on the idea that effective designs involve the development of stimuli that will reliably evoke desirable responses from the target population, rather than inferences about perceptions, schemas, processing systems, and other constructs that mediate the internal mind. Effective instruction should be under the control of the designer, rather than deciding that the trainee's shortcomings should be faulted. Ultimately, it is up to the designer to engineer learning conditions so that trainees are eventually able to perform in the same manner as experts while under the same conditions that the experts encounter (Markle & Tiemann, 1970). Along with her husband, Philip Tiemann, Markle outlined four general categories of learning relationships. The names of the categories and sub-categories are slightly modified for this chapter to incorporate features of both the original conceptualizations (Tiemann & Markle, 1990) and later adaptations (Sota et al., 2011). The basic categories are psychomotor responses, simple discriminative relations, complex extended relations, and emotional relations. Each of these basic categories would necessitate distinct training and assessment strategies.

PSYCHOMOTOR RESPONSES: GETTING THE PROPER RESPONSE

For the category of psychomotor responses, the objective is to differentiate responding into more precise or different forms. Behaviors within this category have no particular relation to external stimuli; rather, the emphasis is on developing specific response topographies. Responding is developed until it becomes fluent (i.e., both accurate and fast), and the trainee can differentiate between accurate and inaccurate response forms. Psychomotor responses can be broken down into sub-categories of basic units (responses), linked units (chained responses), or a combination of units (kinesthetic repertoires). Examples of responses would include learning the correct pronunciation of a client's name or learning to twist one's wrist to curve a bowling ball. To a novice trainee, it may be difficult to notice the differences in the production of various sounds or various ball throws. Several distinct variations in performance all look, sound, and feel the same to the neophyte. However, as expertise develops, correct pronunciations and correct throws begin to feel distinct from incorrect variants. Furthermore, it becomes easier to reliably produce the correct variations (Tiemann & Markle, 1990).

Chained responses are similar to responses, except that several distinct units of behavior are linked together. Examples would include the steps in maintaining a piece of equipment or preparing a chocolate souffle. Kinesthetic repertoires involve the most elaborate psychomotor responses, in which several combinations of basic and/or linked units are drawn upon during successful performance. For example, the movement of a forklift driver operating a vehicle to move several pieces of cargo across a warehouse or a painter prepping and painting the interior walls of a house. Despite the increasing complexity, the criterion remains the same: to produce the correct forms of behavior without hesitation. When this criterion is met, the performer should be able to consistently describe when there is a qualitative difference between their correct and incorrect performances, and these self-appraisals should match the evaluations of a competent observer. Obviously, it is rarely the case that it is satisfactory to only have trainees know how to perform accurately if they don't also know when to perform accurately. Proper stimulus control is essential in the real world, but it is easier to establish stimulus control if behavior is already occurring with an appropriate topography. In other words, mastery of psychomotor responses aids in the later mastery of different types of discriminative relations.

DISCRIMINATIVE RELATIONS: GETTING THE PROPER RESPONSE AT THE PROPER TIME

For the category of simple discriminative relations, it becomes critical that responding is under the control of appropriate external stimuli. Learners are not simply learning *how* to make an appropriate response, but they are also learning *when* to make an appropriate response. Simple discriminative relations can also be broken down into sub-categories of basic units (associations), linked units (discriminative sequences), and a combinations of units (verbal repertoires). Examples of associations would include writing the correct English translation when seeing a Chinese word (writing "hello" in the presence of the discriminative stimulus of "你好") or saying a client's name when seeing a client's face (as opposed to someone else's name or no name). An important part of the process is discrimination training that firmly establishes stimulus control, so that a familiar stimulus reliably evokes that desired response. This can be conducted using flashcards, examinations, one-on-one trainer drills, and other options that involve presenting the test item, having the trainee respond, and then providing feedback on the accuracy of their response.

Much like chained responses from the psychomotor category, discriminative sequences involve the linking together of several distinct units of behavior, except this time responding is under the control of a particular stimulus. For example, having a taste of wine (as a discriminative stimulus) evokes a well-practiced series of colorful adjectives and historical accounts of grapes, whereas the sight of an algebra problem (as a discriminative stimulus) evokes solving the equation through a familiar set of steps. Verbal repertoires are the most developed of the simple discriminative relations, combining basic units and linked units into an elaborate verbal pattern. Examples would include an expert witness at trial who explains the details of forensic evidence upon being asked a question or a professor who relays the historical background related to a topic upon seeing a presentation slide. As mentioned earlier, simply being able to recite the appropriate information on command is not the same as understanding a concept. Someone could memorize a definition or an entire speech without comprehending the words they are using. However, this does not mean there is no utility to such skills. For example, stating a definition in the presence of a technical term is a common assessment procedure in higher education. Once established, knowledge of a good definition can aid in the inspection and classification of novel instances (Markle & Tiemann, 1970). As such, mastery of simple discriminative relations can foster mastery of more complex relations, such as complex extended relations.

EXTENDED RELATIONS: GETTING THE PROPER RESPONSE UNDER NOVEL CIRCUMSTANCES

For the category of complex extended relations, responding is no longer rote in nature and can be abstracted into more diverse forms of discriminative control. Learners are no longer simply making correct responses to familiar stimuli from training. Instead, test situations involve novel stimuli and situations that require the learner to respond appropriately. Complex extended relations can also be broken down into the sub-categories of basic units (conceptual relations), linked units (principles), and combinations of units (generative repertoires). Examples of conceptual relations would include a welder inspecting new welds and classifying them as "good" or "bad." Another example would include an art critic deciding which genre a new painting belongs to. Since the controlling variables of interest are unique stimulus conditions not previously encountered, it would not be appropriate to train this category using the same items for both training and testing, and it would also be inappropriate to have a narrow range of training items. Necessarily, the controlling variables involve stimulus classes rather than specific stimuli, so a wide range of examples are needed to promote generalization to new members within the class. Furthermore, a wide range of non-examples will be needed to prevent overgeneralization of the concept.

Much like discriminative sequences, principles involve the linking together of several distinct units of behavior (i.e., the relations between different concepts). The established relations can take a wide variety of forms. For example, a hierarchical relation could be established in which the learner is taught that one concept is subordinate to another concept. A conditional or causality relation could be established in which one concept is necessary for the occurrence of another concept. With sufficient training, abstract control can develop (such as "if ___, then ____," "____ is the opposite of ____," etc.) such that the verbal patterns can become generalized operant "frames" that get used in multiple contexts (Alessi, 1987; Hayes et al., 2001; Skinner, 1957). Such abstracted control helps to pattern additional forms of verbal responding even in the absence of direct teaching. Examples of principles being applied would be someone making predictions after hearing stock market news or an engineer deciding on how to implement supports for a vertical dwelling in a unique environment. Generative repertoires are the most complex of all the learning relations, in that learner performance involves combinations of basic and linked units that allow for appropriate actions under novel circumstances. For example, needing to invent a new type of programming language to solve problems generated by advancing technology or conducting research to investigate the etiology of psychological phenomenon. Whether one should train performance to mastery under psychomotor, simple discriminative relations, or complex extended relations depends upon how established experts perform under representative conditions (M.B. Gilbert, 2019). If an expert rehearses the same speech every time upon hearing the anticipated cue, then training mastery of simple discriminative relations will suffice. If an expert must think on their feet in new situations, sorting new encounters into the appropriate labels, or problem-solve unique challenges, then mastery of complex extended relations will be necessary.

EMOTIONAL RELATIONS: CONSIDERATION OF FEELINGS DURING TRAINING

The last category may be simpler in comparison to the preceding categories, but it may have the greatest reach. That category is emotional relations, which are present during other types of learning. Since emotional learning can happen simultaneously with other types of learning, it may be worthwhile to take this into consideration while establishing other learning outcomes. If instructional designers make reinforcement too infrequent or provide too many aversive stimuli during the learning process, it is likely that trainees will feel a negative emotional reaction to the training tasks and instructional environment in general. Such negative emotions may interfere with the acquisition of knowledge and generate escape and avoidance behaviors. Trainees may become inattentive, convince decision-makers to abandon instructional solutions, or even aggress in order to terminate the learning situation. Alternatively, a well-designed instructional plan that integrates an appropriate amount of reinforcement may result in positive word of mouth, approach behaviors, and a general positive reaction to further trainings. Of course, excessive reinforcement may be problematic as well in that it may be disruptive (e.g., near-constant praise means less time for the presentation of instructional material) or create a density of reinforcement unrepresentative of the actual work environment (and therefore the new work behavior may quickly extinguish outside of the

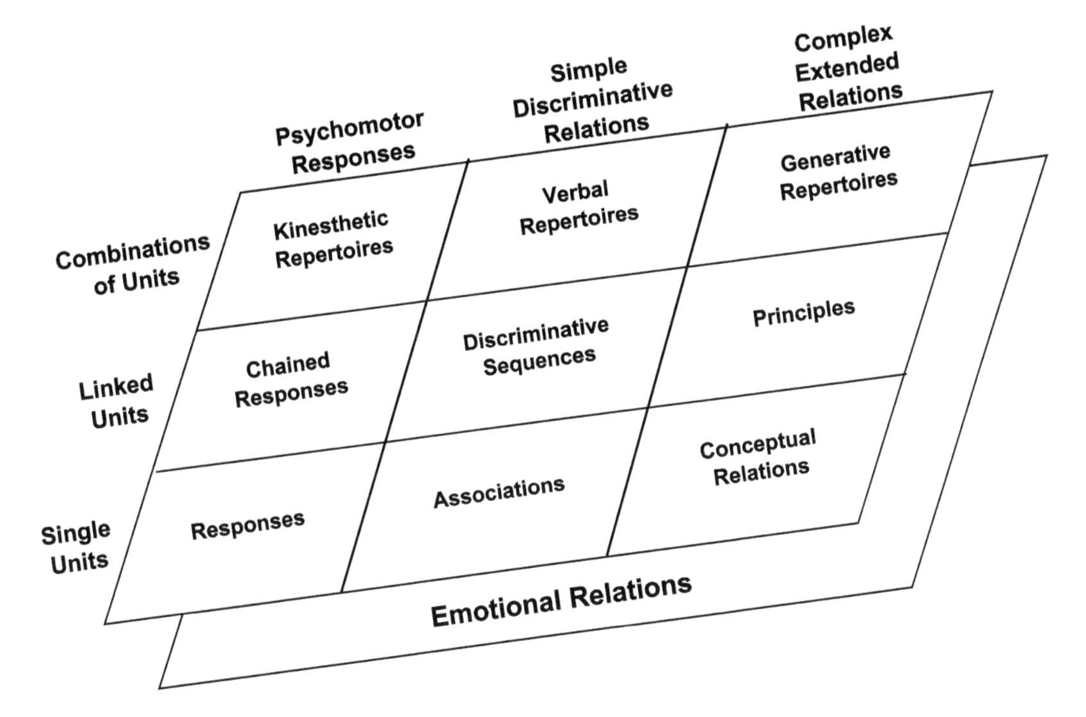

FIGURE 3.1 Types of Learning Diagram—based on Tiemann and Markle (1990) and revisions by Sota, Leon, and Layng (2011)

instructional context). These learning outcomes are summarized in Figure 3.1, which arranges the categories based upon how the learning types build upon one another.

EMPIRICAL TESTING OF INSTRUCTIONAL LESSONS

The only way to ensure that training has a proper amount of reinforcement built in, that examples and non-examples are well selected, or that the rates of performance are sufficient enough to achieve fluency is through the empirical testing of programs. The basic process of development, validation, and field testing has been outlined by several other authors (Markle, 1967, 1990; Twyman et al., 2004). One of the first important steps during development is to decide if training is even worth doing. Decision-makers first need to decide if the cost of untrained employees outweighs the cost of developing a training program. If the problem is a minor one with little impact, it may be in the best interest of the organization to allow the problem to persist. If the problem is worthy of being tackled, it must also be determined whether training can solve it or whether motivational strategies may be more appropriate. If the employee can perform correctly given that motivation was high enough (such as if their life depended on it), then training will not solve the organizational problem (Mager & Pipe, 1970). If a lack of knowledge is the primary problem, then the training development process should continue. There are a multitude of tools that have been developed to identify the nature of the performance concern (Austin, 2000; Diener et al., 2009; T.F. Gilbert, 1978; D.A. Johnson et al., 2014; Rummler & Brache, 2013) that range from simple assessments at the individual level of performance to a multi-level analysis of the entire organizational system (more on this in Chapter 5 of this text). If a lack of knowledge is the primary concern, training objectives need to be developed that take into consideration the type of learning outcome that is necessary (see Figure 3.1). Subject matter experts should be recruited to help develop such objectives, since they best understand the behaviors necessary for expertise and the conditions under which experts will need to perform. Next, a sequence of instruction should be laid out in a logical fashion that will achieve the objectives and is necessary to support excellent on-the-job performance. Trivial information, information not typically possessed by experts, and prerequisite knowledge that novice trainees already possess should be eliminated.

Probably the most critical aspect of the validation process is the collection of performance data using representative untrained learners and continually revising the program based upon this data until the training outcomes can be reliably met by any trainee with the minimal prerequisite skills. This step of continual revision is also typically neglected in practice. Instead, training often involves a very linear approach of an instructional designer developing a sequence of instruction that makes sense from their perspective and then implementing that instruction serving as both the first and final drafts (Dutch, 2005; Engelmann, 1992). Designers such as Markle frequently cautioned against such an approach, stating that one cannot tell if training will work simply by looking at it (Markle, 1990). All designer assumptions must be challenged by actual trainees working with the instructional material. A nonlinear approach emphasizes continually repeating steps of the process (i.e., test and revise) until mastery can be achieved. How many iterations it will take until the program is complete cannot be determined in advance using a nonlinear approach, although even a few iterations of testing and revising can greatly improve a program if practical concerns prevent ideal development. The process of testing should be conducted under a variety of conditions to ensure generalization across settings and individuals.

CONNECTING INSTRUCTIONAL DESIGN TO THE BROADER ORGANIZATIONAL CONTEXT

Even if one follows a careful testing and development sequence, it does not guarantee that such a process will result in value for the organization unless the design is well connected to other organizational considerations. For example, if new employees master the aims of the training process, but their newfound repertoire is not actually utilized in the actual performance of the job, then the entire training process was ultimately worthless (at least from the perspective of relevant performance improvement). Deciding what outcomes represent the appropriate knowledge, skills, and abilities cannot be decided in a vacuum. Instead, instructional designers need to collaborate with other invested parties within an organization. This involves talking to managers and supervisors, subject matter experts, employees, trainees, and possibly customers themselves. Once these external sources of feedback are added to the design process, training goals can be adjusted to be appropriate to the actual demands and needs of the organization (Goldstein & Ford, 2002).

It was this realization that instructional designers cannot be successful without a sufficient degree of collaboration and outreach that lead organizations such as the National Society for Programmed Instruction to broaden their scope beyond just Programmed Instruction (the National Society for Programmed Instruction eventually renamed itself as the International Society for Performance Improvement to better capture the expansion in scope). Even if the training process became perfect, it would still be insufficient if the training outcomes are not maintained through the daily consequences of the on-the-job environment. This has been frequently demonstrated with the failure to enact lasting change as seen by businesses that bring in seemingly endless workshops, with trainers teaching employees new practices, but ultimately the organization does not change its daily functioning.

Ideally, training will be designed to promote generalization by ensuring the training environment is either similar to the on-the-job environment or slowly fading the controlling variables to the natural contingencies (Brethower & Smalley, 1998; Stokes & Baer, 1977).

This strategy can only work if there are reinforcers already built into the preexisting natural contingencies. If such reinforcement is absent, then training innovations are doomed to fail. Under these circumstances it becomes critical to change others in the environment and train them to support desirable performance change. Managers and supervisors need to provide coaching and feedback on a regular basis, not only when employees are learning new skills (D.A. Johnson, 2013; Tilka & Johnson, 2018). As such, successful instructional design is integrally tied to successful performance management.

Ensuring that appropriate consequences are provided often entails changing how managers monitor and interact with subordinates. Of course, changes in managerial practices also need to be sustained through consequences for the managers themselves, which entails changing how upper administration interacts with lower administration. If a good instructional designer is pitted against a bad management system, then training innovations will end up being undercut and eventually fail to result in long-term change (Rummler & Brache, 2013). It does not take long before a behavior analyst working with an organization realizes that systemic reform may be necessary to sustain lasting change. Therefore, successful instructional design is also integrally tied to successful systems assessment and changes.

CONCLUSION

This foundation for instructional design informs the practices of behavior-based instructional designers and have produced many successful applications (K.R. Johnson & Street, 2012; Layng et al., 2004; Twyman et al., 2004). Unfortunately, much of the exemplary work done in corporate environments has had an invisible impact due to concerns related to internal politics (e.g., such as when baseline and control measures make some aspect of an organization look substandard) or proprietary interests (e.g., when an innovative training process is seen as a competitive edge that must be kept confidential) that prevent the public dissemination of the accomplishments. Despite such confines, many best practices are known for behavior-based instructional designers working within business and industry. Successful designers use carefully designed antecedents that establish organizationally relevant repertoires and help ensure that these outcomes are maintained through consequences built into the organizational policies and practices. Instruction needs to be designed to induce frequent learner activity, minimize errors, and provide feedback (Markle, 1990). A successful behavior-based instructional designer needs to either be sophisticated in the subject matter themselves or be able to collaborate with subject matter experts. This entails an investigation of the conditions under which experts eventually perform, precisely defining the needed performance, and establishing the appropriate type of responding and stimulus control during instruction. Given the degree to which training intersects with other job functions, good communication and persuasion skills are necessary for an instructional designer (and consultants in general). A behavior-based instructional designer needs extensive training in behavior analysis, instructional design, technology, and experimental design and testing. Most importantly, a behavior-based instructional designer needs to remember that the learner is always right (Keller, 1968; Skinner, 1948). The learner behaves in lawful ways given their past learning history and the current environmental stimuli. Although the instructional designer does not control the learning history of the people they work with, they have a significant impact on the current instructional contingencies. Instruction and training can be better than what is typically seen and behavior analysts have the techniques to do something about it. Many recent popular trends in instruction have shown evidence of behavioral guidelines in action (K.R. Johnson, 2015), such as greater emphases on mastery of skills, self-pacing, and corrective feedback. Even among the successful approaches, there is still evidence that behavior analysis could contribute to a refinement of the instructional lessons (Vargas, 2014). Enacting such changes will likely be difficult, time-consuming, and involve a push against the status quo. This ongoing struggle began in a small classroom back in 1953 and has continued every day ever since. Such struggles will likely continue onward into the future but will ultimately be worth it if they lead to better education and training for both business and beyond.

STUDY QUESTIONS

1. In what way is the number of students being taught by one teacher the "heart of the problem" as described by the author?
2. From the perspective of behavioral semantics, how does one decide the meaning of words? Provide an example of a vague term and how it might be defined more precisely.
3. Why is it important to include both examples and non-examples when designing instruction? Explain in behavior analytic terms.
4. How do psychomotor responses, discriminative relations, and extended relations contrast with one another? Give examples in each category.
5. Explain the importance of empirical testing of instructional lessons. What are the reasons why following a behavior-based instructional design approach could still produce outcomes that are not valuable to the organization?

REFERENCES

Alessi, G. (1987). Generative strategies and teaching for generalization. *The Analysis of Verbal Behavior, 5*, 15–27. https://doi.org/10.1007/bf03392816

Austin, J. (2000). Performance analysis and performance diagnostics. In J. Austin & J. E. Carr (Eds.), *Handbook of applied behavior analysis* (pp. 321–349). Context Press.

Binder, C. (1996). Behavioral fluency: Evolution of a new paradigm. *The Behavior Analyst, 19*, 163–197. https://doi.org/10.1007/bf03393163

Blakely, E. & Schlinger, H. (1987). Rules: Function-altering contingency-specifying stimuli. *The Behavior Analyst, 10*, 183–187. https://doi.org/10.1007/bf03392428

Brethower, D.M. & Smalley, K.A. (1998). *Performance-based instruction: Linking training to business results*. Jossey-Bass.

Diener, L.H., McGee, H.M., & Miguel, C.F. (2009). An integrated approach for conducting a behavioral systems analysis. *Journal of Organizational Behavior Management, 29*, 108–135. https://doi.org/10.1080/01608060902874534

Dutch, S.I. (2005). Why textbooks are the way they are. *Academic Questions, 18*, 34–38.

Engelmann, S. (1992). *War against the schools' academic child abuse*. Halcyon House.

Gilbert, M.B. (2019). Human performance technology: Further reflections on Human Competence. *Journal of Organizational Behavior Management, 39*, 7–112. https://doi.org/10.1080/01608061.2019.1596864

Gilbert, T.F. (1978). *Human competence: Engineering worthy performance*. McGraw-Hill.

Goldstein, I.L. & Ford, J.K. (2002). *Training in organizations: Needs assessment, development, and evaluation*. Wadsworth.

Hayes, S.C., Barnes-Holmes, D., & Roche, B. (2001). *Relational frame theory: A post-Skinnerian account of human language and cognition*. Kluwer Academic/Plenum Publishers.

Hetzel, M.L. & Hetzel, C.W. (1969). *Relay circuits for psychology*. Appleton-Century Crofts

Holland, J.G. & Skinner, B.F. (1961). *The analysis of behavior*. McGraw-Hill.

Johnson, D.A. (2013). A component analysis of the impact of evaluative and objective feedback on performance. *Journal of Organizational Behavior Management, 33*, 89–103. https://doi.org/10.1080/01608061.2013.785879

Johnson, D.A. (2014). The need for an integration of technology, behavior-based instructional design, and contingency management: An opportunity for behavior analysis. *Revista Mexicana de Análisis de la Conducta* [*Mexican Journal of Behavior Analysis*], *40*, 58–72.

Johnson, D.A., Casella, S.E., McGee, H., & Lee, S.C. (2014). The use and validation of preintervention diagnostic tools in organizational behavior management. *Journal of Organizational Behavior Management, 34*(2), 104–121. https://doi.org/10.1080/01608061.2014.914009

Johnson, D.A. & Rubin, S. (2011). Effectiveness of interactive computer-based instruction: A review of studies published between 1995 and 2007. *Journal of Organizational Behavior Management, 31*, 55–94. https://doi.org/10.1080/01608061.2010.541821

Johnson, K. (2015). Behavioral education in the 21st century. *Journal of Organizational Behavior Management, 35*, 135–150. https://doi.org/10.1080/01608061.2015.1036152

Johnson, K. & Street, E.M. (2012). From the laboratory to the field and back again: Morningside Academy's 32 years of improving students' academic performance. *The Behavior Analyst Today, 13*, 20–40. https://doi.org/10.1037/h0100715

Johnson, K.R. & Layng, T.V.J. (1992). Breaking the structuralist barrier: Literacy and numeracy with fluency. *American Psychologist, 47*, 1475–1490. https://doi.org/10.1037//0003-066x.47.11.1475

Jones, R.S.P. & Eayrs, C.B. (2010). The use of errorless learning procedures in teaching people with a learning disability: A critical review. *Mental Handicap Research, 5*, 204–212. https://doi.org/10.1111/j.1468-3148.1992.tb00045.x

Keller, F.S. & Schoenfeld, W.N. (1950). *Principles of psychology: A systematic text in the science of behavior.* Appleton-Century-Crofts.

Keller, F.S. (1968). "Good-bye, teacher ..." *Journal of Applied Behavior Analysis, 1*, 79–89. https://doi.org/10.1901/jaba.1968.1-79

Layng, T.V.J., Twyman, J.S., & Stikeleather, G. (2004). Selected for success: How Headsprout Reading Basics teaches children to read. In D.J. Moran & R.W. Malott (Eds.), *Evidence-based educational methods* (pp. 171–197). Elsevier/Academic Press.

Lindsley, O.R. (1992). Why aren't effective teaching tools widely adopted? *Journal of Applied Behavior Analysis, 25*, 21–26. https://doi.org/10.1901/jaba.1992.25-21

Mager, R.F. & Pipe, P. (1970). *Analyzing performance problems, or, "you really oughta wanna."* Fearon Publishers.

Malott, R.W. (1992). A theory of rule-governed behavior and organizational behavior management. *Journal of Organizational Behavior Management, 12*(2), 45–65. https://doi.org/10.1300/J075v12n02_03

Markle, S.M. (1964). Individualizing programed instruction: The programmer. *Teachers College Record, 66*, 219–228.

Markle, S.M. (1965). The wastebasket reflex: A response to some exemplars of the art. *NSPI Journal, 4*, 8–11. https://doi.org/10.1002/pfi.4180040507

Markle, S.M. (1967). Empirical testing of programs. In P. C. Lange (Ed.), *Programmed instruction: Sixty-sixth yearbook of the National Society for the Study of Education* (pp. 104–138). University of Chicago Press.

Markle, S.M. (1975). They teach concepts, don't they? *Educational Researcher, 4*, 3–9.

Markle, S.M. (1990). *Designs for instructional designers.* Stipes Publishing Company.

Markle, S.M., & Tiemann, P.W. (1970). "Behavioral" analysis of "cognitive" content. *Educational Technology, 10*, 41–45.

Marroletti, K. & Johnson, D.A. (2014). Current best practices for creating effective and palatable eLearning. *Revista Mexicana de Análisis de la Conducta* [*Mexican Journal of Behavior Analysis*], *40*, 73–84.

McCalpin, A.L., Johnson, D.A., & Ferragut, T.N. (2018). Using feedback and postfeedback delays to improve performance with online lessons. *The Psychological Record, 68*, 489–499. https://doi.org/10.1007/s40732-018-0295-y

Merrett, F. & Wheldall, K. (1987). Natural rates of teacher approval and disapproval in British primary and middle school classrooms. *British Journal of Educational Psychology, 57*, 95–103. https://doi.org/10.1111/j.2044-8279.1987.tb03064.x

Pressey, S.L. (1926). A simple apparatus which gives tests and scores – and teaches. *School and Society, 23*, 373–376.

Pressey, S.L. (1927). A machine for automatic teaching of drill material. *School and Society, 25*, 549–552.

Pressey, S.L. (1932). A third and fourth contribution toward the coming "industrial revolution" in education. *School and Society, 36*, 668–672.

Rummler, G.A. & Brache, A.P. (2013). *Improving performance: How to manage the white space on the organizational chart* (3rd ed.). Jossey-Bass.

Skinner, B.F. (1945). The operational analysis of psychological terms. *Psychological Review, 52*, 270–277. https://doi.org/10.1037/h0062535

Skinner, B.F. (1948). *Walden two.* Prentice-Hall, Inc.

Skinner, B.F. (1953). Some contributions of an experimental analysis of behavior to psychology as a whole. *American Psychologist, 8*, 69–78. https://doi.org/10.1037/h0054118

Skinner, B.F. (1954). The science of learning and the art of teaching. *Harvard Educational Review, 24*, 86–97.

Skinner, B.F. (1957). *Verbal behavior.* Appleton-Century-Crofts.

Skinner, B.F. (1958). Teaching machines. *Science, 128*, 969–977. https://doi.org/10.1126/science.128.3330.969

Skinner, B.F. (1961). Why we need teaching machines. *Harvard Educational Review, 31*, 377–398.

Skinner, B.F. (1963). Reflections on a decade of teaching machines. *Teachers College Record, 65*, 168–177.

Skinner, B.F. (1983). *A matter of consequences.* New York University Press.

Sota, M., Leon, M., & Layng, T.V.J. (2011). Thinking through text comprehension II: Analysis of verbal and investigative repertoires. *The Behavior Analyst Today, 12*, 12–20. https://doi.org/10.1037/h0100707

Stokes, T.F. & Baer, D.M. (1977). An implicit technology of generalization. *Journal of Applied Behavior Analysis, 10*, 349–367. https://doi.org/10.1901/jaba.1977.10-349

Terrace, H.S. (1963). Discrimination learning with and without "errors." *Journal of the Experimental Analysis of Behavior, 6*, 1–27. https://doi.org/10.1901/jeab.1963.6-1

Tiemann, P.W. & Markle, S.M. (1990). *Analyzing instructional content: A guide to instruction and evaluation.* Stipes Publishing Company.

Tilka, R. & Johnson, D.A. (2018). Coaching as a packaged intervention for telemarketing personnel. *Journal of Organizational Behavior Management, 38*, 49–72. https://doi.org/10.1080/01608061.2017.1325821

Twarek, M., Cihon, T., & Eshleman, J. (2010). The effects of fluent levels of big 6 + 6 skill elements on functional motor skills with children with autism. *Behavioral Interventions, 25*, 275–293. https://doi.org/10.1002/bin.317

Twyman, J.S., Layng, T.V.J., Stikeleather, G., & Hobbins, K. (2004). A non-linear approach to curriculum design: The role of behavior analysis in building an effective reading program. In: W.L. Heward et al. (Eds.), *Focus on behavior analysis in education, Vol. 3*. Merrill/Prentice Hall.

Vargas, J.S. (2014). Programmed Instruction's lesson for xMOOC designers. *Revista Mexicana de Análisis de la Conducta [Mexican Journal of Behavior Analysis]*, *40*, 7–19.

White, M.A. (1975). Natural rates of teacher approval and disapproval in the classroom. *Journal of Applied Behavior Analysis*, *8*, 367–372. https://doi.org/10.1901/jaba.1975.8-367

Zemke, R. & Armstrong, J. (1997). Timeless rules for good instruction. *Training*, *34*, 55–60.

4

From Fluency-Based Instruction to Accomplishment-Based Performance Improvement[1]

Carl Binder

INTRODUCTION

This is an evolutionary history that recounts how the author began as a student with B.F. Skinner focused on accelerating behavior frequency (rate of response), and over more than four decades developed a user-friendly approach to performance improvement informed by the work of Thomas F. Gilbert (1978) and inspired in part by the operating philosophy of Steve Jobs. It reflects an evolution from basic science to performance engineering, from instruction to systemic performance improvement, and from academic vocabulary to user-tested plain English labels on simple visual models. The approach, rather than being an "open source" academic field of study, has emerged in the form of packaged programs of instruction, job aids, and coaching that can be introduced in any organization, with virtually any function or department, at any level – from front-line contributor to CEO.

This is also a story of contributions by a host of thought leaders and mentors, scientists and practitioners, consultants and methodologists to an evolutionary stream that has developed, and continues to develop, by means of the usual principles: *variation* and *selection*.

A PERSONAL HISTORY

The author began his career in behavior science, fortuitously and with a remarkable series of events, as one of B.F. Skinner's last graduate students in the Harvard Department of Experimental Psychology. For more details about this history, refer to Binder (2014) in a collection of professional biographies published by the Cambridge Center for Behavioral Studies.

After several semesters of independent study with Skinner, an introduction to Joseph R. Cautela, then a prominent figure in the field of Behavior Therapy, led to B.H. Barrett, whose pioneering laboratory and classroom for institutional residents with severe disabilities provided a perfect venue for basic research and application of Skinner's variable, rate of response, with humans. Barrett had completed postdoctoral training with Skinner and Ogden Lindsley in their lab at the Metropolitan State Hospital and Harvard Medical School, where she extended the methods of free operant conditioning in laboratory studies, and turned from the Skinner-Lindsley focus on adult psychotic and normal subjects to learners with severe disabilities, including children in and out of the institution (Barrett, 1977).

After I had conducted basic laboratory research with institutional residents for several years, Barrett asked me to transform her pioneering behavioral classroom for institutionalized

DOI: 10.4324/9781003198949-4

learners from a discrete trial programmed instruction methodology to one applying O.R. Lindley's new tool, then called the standard behavior chart (Pennypacker, Koenig, & Lindsley, 1972). The power of Skinner's variable – rate of response – combined with a standard visual display on Lindsley's chart enabled us to make discoveries that would have been impossible using percent correct measures and trials-based programmed instruction. We developed instructional strategies and created curriculum sequences that contributed to the early development of Precision Teaching. The work that began in Barrett's lab and continued beyond in teacher training, consulting, and evangelism, under the tutelage of Barrett, Lindsley, and Eric Haughton, has been documented in a widely read paper (Binder, 1996) on the evolution of what became known as *behavioral fluency* and the practice of fluency-based instruction.

By the late 1970s, those in the field of behavioral education, which included Precision Teaching as well as Siegfried Engelmann's Direct Instruction programs and methodology (Binder, 1988, 1990a, 1991; Binder & Watkins, 1989, 1990), were becoming frustrated with their inability to penetrate the educational establishment. Watkin's (1988, 1997) analysis of the contingencies that determine the adoption of educational materials and programs in regular education made clear that non-behavioral professors of education, who train teachers, write textbooks, develop or guide curriculum, and consult with schools had a lock on public education. This was perhaps a first inkling that we would need to take a more *systemic* approach to change management if we wanted our methods and discoveries to be adopted outside of a small sub-community of applied behavior scientists. Leaders in behavioral instruction, including Ogden Lindsley and Henry Pennypacker, who were ABA Presidents in successive years at that time, encouraged their proteges and members of the broader behavior science community to "go private" – to create commercial offerings from our applications, expose ourselves to selection based on the "contingencies of the marketplace," and thereby increase the likelihood that we would adapt to and thrive in the natural environment of a market economy (Pennypacker, 1986).

As an extension of this push into commercial applications, Lindsley strongly encouraged me to move from educational research and teacher training to find business applications of what we had learned from Precision Teaching and fluency-based instruction. After establishing my first consulting firm (Precision Teaching & Management Systems, Inc.), and subsequently learning about sales, marketing, business, and a host of factors in this new market for our work, while promoting the value of behavioral fluency in the business training market (Binder, 1990b, 1999, 2003), my colleagues and I developed and promoted fluency-based instruction and coaching programs for sales, customer service, and other working professionals (Binder, 1987; Binder & Bloom, 1989; Binder & Sweeney, 2002). The addition of a fluency-building (or rate-building) practice phase to conventional training dramatically accelerated results. Introduction of practice aimed at achieving behavioral fluency, plus a focus on core fundamentals rather than including nice-to-know, typically cut training time by a factor of 2 or 3 and achieved productivity levels on the job that were considerably higher than what was achieved with conventional training and coaching methods that rely on percent correct measurement without taking the time dimension (with rate of response) into account.

However, on-the-job results occurred *only* if learners actually *used* practice routines that involved self-management and self-measurement on the job; and *only* if other factors in the workplace prompted, provided tools, and delivered feedback and reinforcing consequences for using new methods, procedures, skills and knowledge. Arranging contingencies beyond conventional "spray and pray" training was not always easy in the face of business-as-usual for training departments. But optimizing impact required us as consultants to plan and work with clients to implement conditions that would support performance on the job, after training. This almost always involved ensuring that leaders, managers, and supporting departments

	S^D *Information*	*R* *Response*	S_r *Motivation*
E *Environmental support*	(Data) ①	(Instruments) ②	(Incentives) ③
P *Behavior repertory*	(Knowledge) ④	(Capacity) ⑤	(Motives) ⑥

FIGURE 4.1 The Behavior Engineering Model (from Gilbert, 1978).

would do their parts to encourage and support practice and desired application on the job. It was perhaps fortuitous that this work began in the field of sales performance, since sales leaders and managers tend to be more engaged with their people, and are more results-focused than in some other areas of corporate management, training, and development.

This is where we first used Gilbert's (1978) Behavior Engineering Model. Eric Haughton (1972), one of the pioneers and my personal mentor in the development of Precision Teaching methods and curriculum, had worked at Harvard's Office of Programmed Instruction when Skinner and his colleagues were first developing teaching machines and programs. He met Tom Gilbert while the latter was doing postdoctoral work with Skinner. When Gilbert's (1978) groundbreaking book, *Human Competence*, came out, Haughton had gifted me with a copy, but I had not paid close attention to it until the early 1980s when we were first introducing fluency-based instruction and coaching in banks and other organizations. At that point, Gilbert's Behavior Engineering Model provided a perfect framework for my consulting teams to use for planning with clients how to support self-managed practice and application of new skills and knowledge on the job.

Our work developing and implementing training programs fit the *Knowledge* cell of Gilbert's model. Our fluency-based practice procedures dramatically accelerated new learners toward true mastery. However, in the absence of variables identified in the top three cells of the Behavior Engineering (*Data*, *Instruments*, and *Incentives*) arranged in the work environment, we could not be sure that trainees would practice daily on their own, measure their own performance and work toward fluency goals. Moreover, once on the job, we could not ensure that, for example, newly trained salespeople would actively engage prospective customers in discussions about new products they had practiced to sell, but instead might revert to old habits in the work environment. The Behavior Engineering Model gave those in our consulting teams a tool for designing implementation plans that would optimize return on investment in fluency-based training and practice methods.

However, as we began to engage clients as partners in program roll-outs, we found that the language of Gilbert's model was often confusing, limiting, and likely to produce errors of application. *Data*, for example, could be understood in many ways, and often our clients would wonder aloud if we were speaking about databases or spreadsheets, charts or graphs. We would explain that sometimes quantitative data can be helpful in setting goals and providing feedback, but that the *Data* cell in Gilbert's model could extend far beyond its label in the conventional sense to include qualitative information to set expectations, corrective feedback, and other forms of information. Similarly, *Instruments* was confusing to people. They asked if it meant some kind of physical instrument, like an ohm meter, or perhaps a personality profiling tool. *Incentives* prompted people to ask about consequences of which people are

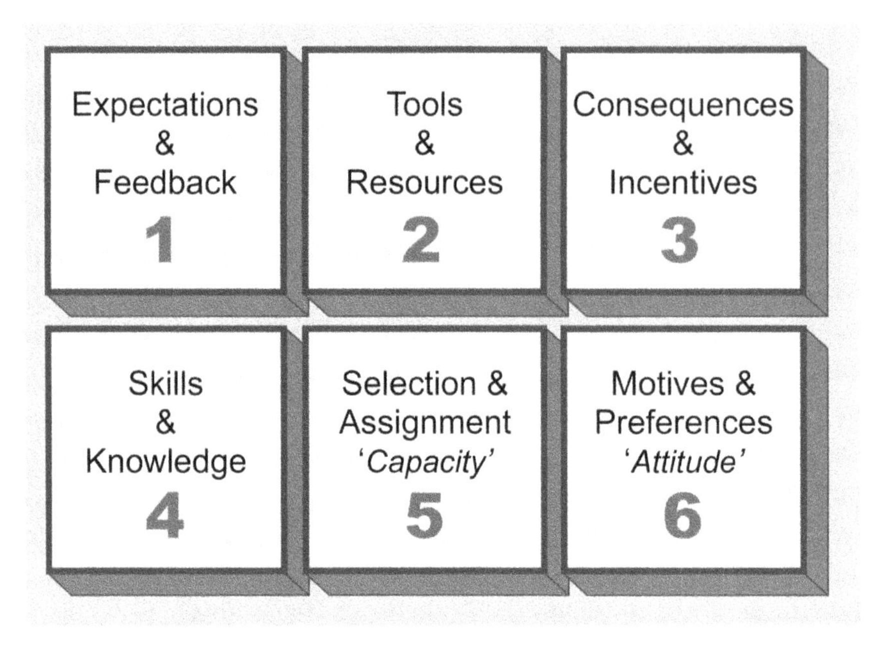

FIGURE 4.2 The Six Boxes® Model.

unaware before they occur, for example, unintended consequences. What about skills? Is that included in the *Knowledge* cell? And so forth.

I and my colleagues began in the mid-1980s to try different language with clients, and to test various words and phrases for labeling the cells of the model. This continued until I found a language that people could initially understand, apply the concepts as intended, and make fewer errors that we needed to correct. By the late 1980s, we had arrived at the labels we now use in our version of the model. We always referred to Gilbert (1978) when describing the origins of our model, but because the language had changed significantly we were not clear about what we should call it. Finally, a client named Tom Hogan, who was Vice President of Sales Training at Dun and Bradstreet, said, "You're always talking about those boxes. Why don't you just call it the Six Boxes Model?" We took his advice (Binder, 1998) and subsequently formally named our model the Six Boxes Model, eventually registering its name as a trademark.

For at least a decade, while working with sales, marketing, customer service, manufacturing, and other functions in organizations around the globe, we used the Six Boxes Model, taught it to our clients, and made many presentations that included the model at conferences and corporate meetings. The name of the model spread widely, and was even mistakenly used to refer to Gilbert's model and other variants or descendants of it (Binder, 2019). Using plain English was a communication strategy we had learned from Ogden Lindsley (1971), who developed plain English equivalents for terms from the experimental analysis of behavior when he first worked with special education teachers. User-testing was something we adopted by studying the early work of Steve Jobs, at Lindsley's suggestion in the late 1970s, because Jobs had focused on user experience and *simplicity* (Segall, 2013) in his creation of the Apple II computer. The Apple II was accessible for ordinary people rather than only for nerdy computer hobbyists, and represented an enormous shift from complicated configurations of technology to products that are easy to use for virtually anyone.

EVOLUTION OF PERFORMANCE THINKING® MODELS AND METHODS

As we continued to apply what we learned from Gilbert (1978) through his book and for several years in an informal mentoring relationship, we recognized that the most important aspect of his work was the insistence on a paradigm shift from a focus by leaders, managers, trainers, and performance professionals on *behavior* and behavioral objectives to focus on the valuable products of behavior, what Gilbert called *accomplishments*. Another important influence on our evolution toward an easy-to-use accomplishment-based approach was Joe Harless, a protégé and one-time business partner of Gilbert. Harless led a successful performance consulting and training company for decades, later deciding to focus on training instructional designers and performance consultants in methods that anchor performance analysis to accomplishments. Mentored by Harless (1975, 1987) and his packaged programs, we began to see the power of an accomplishment-based approach, and during the late 1990s we developed a simplified model called the *Performance Chain* to depict the elements of performance.

Following what we had learned about the usability of plain English terminology and testing it to minimize initial category errors, we changed the word *accomplishment* to *work output* for two reasons. First, most dictionary definitions of *accomplishment* refer to either behavior or ability, not to the products of behavior. Second, many of our colleagues in the fields of performance improvement and organizational behavior management, although claiming to follow Gilbert's lead by focusing on accomplishments, often used the terms *outcomes*, *results*, and *accomplishments* more or less interchangeably and with varying meanings. Sometimes they referred to organization-level results. Other times they referred to changes in behavior (often using passive voice nouns, as in "procedure completed"). And often they failed to name specific things, or nouns, that one might *produce* with behavior. We found that the phrase *work outputs* produced fewer initial errors in our training programs for performance consultants, and by carefully defining it in the beginning we were able to teach its use to avoid errors or lack of clarity about the valuable products of behavior.

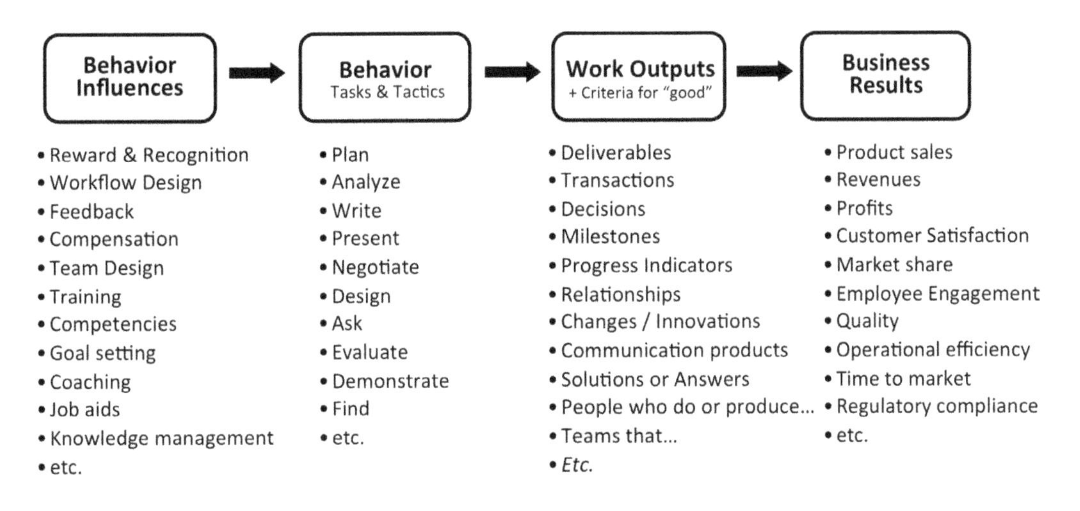

FIGURE 4.3 The Performance Chain.

After years of including these two models (the Six Boxes Model and the Performance Chain) in presentations at conferences and in work with clients, we realized that many of our clients and colleagues appreciated the simplicity and plain language of our models. We saw that the plain English language and simple visual models often spread "virally" across organizations, and that we could nurture that diffusion to expand verbal communities of use. We discovered, in short, that our models and language provided an effective communication framework, not merely a technical vocabulary.

In about 2005 we decided to create a series of programs to teach people how to use these models. We re-named our consulting firm, then called Binder Riha Associates, to be The Performance Thinking Network, because we saw that the easy communication fostered by our models and language provided a foundation for creating verbal communities, networks of users who could learn with and from one another using a shared language. Our clients told us that we not only gave them a set of models and tools for improving performance, but that we were teaching them "a new way of thinking" about performance. We shifted from referring to our methodology as the *Six Boxes® Approach* to using and trademarking the term *Performance Thinking®* to brand our methods, tools, programs (Binder, 2019), and our Company.

One of the more important developments in this work involved precise definitions of terms to optimize the flexibility of application while ensuring technical consistency. This statement may, at first, seem inherently contradictory since a focus on precision could conceivably limit application. On the contrary, once we had crystal clear language guidelines for "good" descriptions of business results, work outputs, criteria, behavior, and behavior influences, we found that we could apply these guidelines while maintaining precision across an enormous range of applications and users. Perhaps more importantly, insisting on precise descriptions of elements of performance defined by our two models (e.g., that descriptions of work outputs include countable nouns and no verbs, not even passive verbs) makes it more likely that individuals and teams from widely varying disciplines and functions will communicate with one another effectively. When executives, staff performance professionals, middle managers, and individual contributors all use labels and terminology in the ways that our guidelines specify, then communication and effective collaboration across the enterprise is more likely. We highlight this problem, and solution, with a metaphor from the Bible story about the Tower of Babel (Binder, 2009a). When language differs, communication and collaboration become difficult, if not impossible. With consistent language, people can work more effectively and efficiently across the usual silos and sub-groups.

THE LOGIC OF ACCOMPLISHMENT-BASED PERFORMANCE IMPROVEMENT

Teaching others to apply this approach, we defined what we call *performance improvement logic*. A flexible approach, there is nonetheless a sequential dependency in the steps that one takes to arrive at an intervention, plan, or performance design. One first uses the Performance Chain model to deconstruct performance, following a series of questions:

1. What is at stake for the organization? (business or organizational results)
2. What are the actual or desired accomplishments produced by performers as individuals, teams, or contributors in a process? (work outputs)
3. To what organizational or business results does each accomplishment contribute? (link from work outputs to business results)
4. What characteristics of each work output define a "good" instance of that work output? (criteria for a "good one")
5. What tasks and tactics are needed to produce desired work outputs at the highest level? (behavior)

Once having defined performance using the Performance Chain, we then turn to behavior influences, framed by the Six Boxes Model. We ask a series of questions about behavior influences affecting the behavior needed to produce each accomplishment:

1. What behavior influences in each cell of the Six Boxes Model currently enable and obstruct desired behavior needed to produce the work output? (Analyze)
2. What improvements might we make in behavior influences, based on what we learn from successful performers, from evidence-based practice, or from other sources? (Brainstorm)
3. What combination of behavior influences should we ultimately configure as our best guess at what will optimize desired behavior and work outputs? (Choose)

Once we choose behavior influences, we implement our plan, measure performance, and iterate until we achieve optimal results. The Performance Chain provides a guide for what we can measure: business results, work outputs, and/or behavior (Binder, 2009b).

This "logic" is straightforward and relatively easy to teach, although it is not always easy to apply, since performance in organizations can be complex, and conducting analyses of actual or desired performance may not be simple. Nonetheless, we have found very few individuals in any function or at any level of an organization unable to learn and apply this approach in at least a rudimentary way. Some organizations that have adopted this approach, such as one of the largest global biotechnology firms, support hundreds of performance consultants in facilities around the globe who apply this approach to huge, multi-year projects. Other organizations have trained hundreds of front-line managers who use this approach to coach and continuously develop the performance of their people.

THE POWER OF BEING ACCOMPLISHMENT-BASED

Most people, independent of their background, find it challenging to make the shift from a focus on behavior to a focus on accomplishments during analysis and description of performance. We once thought that this was because many of those with whom we work had backgrounds in training or, in some cases, in behavior science, and consequently were accustomed to focusing on behavior, creating behavioral objectives, and so on. We have concluded after several decades, however, that we humans are more accustomed to observing, discussing, and trying to influence our own behavior and that of others, while we are not so accustomed to identifying the valuable *products* of behavior, except in the most concrete examples. Accomplishments such as decisions, relationships, and recommendations, particularly if they are not concrete and visible, are often harder to recognize than more tangible accomplishments like documents or widgets. Thus, one of the biggest obstacles in the initial learning process is to eliminate verbs when describing accomplishments while focusing on what we call "countable nouns."

Once a focus on accomplishments becomes routine with users, the power of an accomplishment-based approach is obvious.

First, by focusing on the valuable products of behavior, and linking them to business results, we draw a "line of sight" from the behavior of people to results for the organization that they serve "through" their accomplishments. This is one reason we sometimes use the term *contributions* when referring to people's accomplishments. As Gilbert (1978) pointed out repeatedly, accomplishments are *valuable* while behavior is *costly*. An accomplishment-based approach focuses everyone on the value delivered.

Second, when we pinpoint valuable accomplishments, it is easier to identify the behavior needed to produce them. Particularly if we observe and interview exemplary performers – those who consistently deliver desired accomplishments at higher levels of productivity or quality than average – we can discover specific tasks and tactics that deliver accomplishments most efficiently. This is in contrast to competencies or other abstractions describing categories of behavior, which are not specific enough to pinpoint, measure, or manage if we choose to follow a natural science approach to measurement.

Finally, when we define job titles, processes, or team contributions by listing the accomplishments they produce, we can more precisely set expectations for what a particular job title contributes, measure performance more easily by counting work outputs that do and do not meet criteria, and provide feedback based on whether behavior produces desired accomplishments or not. Anchoring performance analysis in accomplishments rather than in behavior per se offers these advantages, and more.

USERS AND APPLICATIONS OF PERFORMANCE THINKING® MODELS AND METHODS

One of the benefits of using plain English and simple visual models is that it makes our methodology accessible for anyone who might have an interest in understanding or improving performance, no matter their education, their level in the organization, or their function. We have enabled high-school-educated employees working on production lines in small manufacturing organizations to help improve performance in the processes to which they contribute. We've enabled CEOs to better understand their own performance in the form of their major accomplishments, and that of their teams, to adjust priorities and to implement new strategies and tactics. The majority of users of this approach are either "performance professionals" in Training, Quality, Human Resources, Organizational Development, or other departments who seek to improve their impact on performance; or leaders and managers responsible for the performance of their direct reports, teams, departments, and business units. Early in the development of Performance Thinking programs, we created various matrices of Users x Applications to better understand and define the potential scope of application and to guide the development of programs and tools.

With ease of communication and instruction supported by simple visual models and plain English, we could vary the tools offered to different users for different programs, and create program modules to teach different users how to produce accomplishments of value to them (e.g., program design documents for performance consultants, agreed-upon-action steps for managers and their direct reports, strategy execution plans for senior leaders). This led to tools and guidelines for approaching five distinctly different types of performance opportunities, where specific applications might represent one of these types or a combination of them. The five types of performance opportunities are:

1. Defining and supporting the performance of an individual, role or team.
2. Defining and supporting performance in a process.
3. Ensuring that training is applied on the job and that performance sustains.
4. Implementing or managing change for a program, system, process, etc.
5. Defining and strengthening the practice of organizational values.

We use these categories, especially with performance consultants, to help them "frame" projects and know how and where to look for work outputs as they conduct performance analyses.

CLIENT EXAMPLES

While few of our clients will allow us to use their names or to share their data, the following examples are real client stories about the evolution and impact of Performance Thinking® programs and applications in different organizations.

Applications of the Performance Thinking® Methodology for Different Types of Users

Users / Applications	Executives & Leaders	Middle Managers	Front Line Managers Supervisors Team Leaders	Staff Professionals (Training, OD, HR, Process, etc.)	Individual Contributors
Organizational or Team Alignment	X	X	X	X	
Implementation Planning	X	X	X	X	
Strategy Execution	X	X			
Employee Engagement Planning	X	X	X	X	
Best Practices Documentation & Continuous Improvement	X	X		X	
Performance Needs/Opportunity Analysis	X	X		X	
Performance Design / Training Support		X	X	X	
Management or Supervisor Development	X	X		X	
Leadership Development	X	X	X		
Performance Consulting				X	
Performance Problem-Solving	X	X	X	X	X
Process & Quality Improvement/Management	X	X	X (Lean teams)	X	X
Career Self-Development	X	X	X	X	X
Specialized Applications	X	X	X	X	X
Performance Coaching	X	X	X	X	X
Executive Performance Coaching	X			X	
Agile Talent Development	X	X	X	X	X
Job Descriptions/Requirements & Hiring / Succession	X	X	X	X	X

FIGURE 4.4 A Users X Applications matrix for performance thinking applications.

From Training to Performance Consulting at a Biotechnology Firm

The organization with the longest continuous use of Performance Thinking programs is a major biotech firm with facilities around the globe. In 2009 we trained the first performance professionals from their Operations Learning and Performance group, an organization that delivers training and non-training performance interventions to factories worldwide. Starting with a small team of about a dozen learning and development professionals, the leader of that group began a multi-year effort to spread Performance Thinking models and language like a virus. After he became certified to teach the *Six Boxes® Practitioner Program* and to provide ongoing project coaching of performance consultants certified in that program, he and his colleagues worked to deliver valuable results to internal clients, one project at a time. They collected and communicated success stories from projects that they undertook, and slowly became a recognized resource within the organization for addressing performance improvement and implementation opportunities, not merely providing training. The leader continued to certify Six Boxes Practitioners, licensing our program for delivery to his company's employees, and built teams of performance consultants in facilities around the world. By the time he retired, he had sufficiently impressed senior executives with results of projects that some occasionally used the language of Performance Thinking, and Six Boxes Performance Thinking had become a *de facto* standard for performance improvement in the Company.

A seasoned member of the group succeeded the first leader, and was charged with expanding and strengthening the community of practice. She became certified to deliver the program, and to date coordinates and supports nearly 300 Six Boxes Practitioners, both within Learning and Performance and in other organizations, including Sales, and Research and Development. Each year she drives initiatives to strengthen the sharing of results and methods, working with clients to sustain and continuously improve impact over time, and building fluency in applying the models and methodology to allow scaling of applications from small "quick hits" to multi-year implementation and change management projects. Performance Thinking methods have come together with a specialized error reduction methodology used in factories to ensure quality. Currently, the position of this group is strong, illustrated by confident statements to stakeholders that "this just works," and the message that if stakeholders are unable or unwilling to engage fully in the process, the group has sufficient standing in the organization, and so much demand on their time, that they can occasionally refuse project requests when stakeholders are not ready to fully engage.

Performance Thinking for Organizational Development

Another organization, in the health insurance industry, with a strong organizational development orientation, approached us to develop a team of performance consultants. They viewed the models and language of Performance Thinking as vehicles for building a shared understanding of performance and a culture and vocabulary across the organization that could make continuous performance improvement more likely. After completing a program to certify a dozen Six Boxes Practitioners, they continued working with The Performance Thinking Network for a year, with ongoing support and coaching for high visibility and important projects, and with various interventions designed to bring stakeholders – the performance consultants' clients – into the shared perspective based on the models and language of Performance Thinking. They also conducted a series of projects designed to improve their own processes and performance in work with clients (Gilbert et al., 2014). By the time their Company was acquired by a larger organization, there was a seasoned team of performance consultants, many of whose internal clients had become partners in performance improvement with a shared vocabulary and understanding of performance that enabled them to work more closely together.

The Performance Thinking® Manager at an ABA Organization

A rapidly growing organization in the Applied Behavior Analysis/Autism field sought to develop their managers and leaders with a Performance Thinking approach. Certifying one staff member to facilitate a program for managers, and several internal program coaches to help managers apply what they learned after completing the program, the organization developed several 100 managers using our programs. The focus on accomplishments, or work outputs, underlying this program led to the organization's creating job descriptions built around major work outputs rather than competencies or more traditional descriptions of performance. They use these job descriptions to drive performance management and coaching.

After observing the impact of management and coaching based on work outputs, the CEO requested assistance from The Performance Thinking Network to develop a list of work outputs to support measurement by the Board of Directors of her performance. This was an early example in our work of defining the jobs of senior executives based on their work outputs. This led has led to our developing an entirely new approach to Executive Performance Coaching that helps senior leaders clarify their work outputs, some of which often do not make it onto the "radar screen" of executive evaluation or self-management, but which exert significant leverage on performance across the organization. Accomplishments such as key *relationships* that leaders establish and maintain, *decisions* or *approvals* of various kinds that are part of budgeting, hiring, and strategic planning processes, and *recommendations* or *directives* they pass on to their teams often fill much of senior leaders' time but can go almost unnoticed as they occur in the context of meetings and conversations. With all of the major work outputs of a leader on paper, the leaders themselves can better decide how to allocate their time, what work outputs they might be able to delegate to others, and how their contributions influence the performance of those who report to them, etc.

In many organizations that adopt our approach, we see discoveries and insights that would probably not have occurred without the language and models of Performance Thinking. In addition to the operational impact of better management and performance improvement, these insights can lead to new and innovative approaches to human resource management, leadership development, measurement, and implementation planning.

Building a Performance Coaching Culture

A Senior Vice President of Talent Management and Chief Culture Officer, who had introduced our Six Boxes Practitioner Program to build a team of performance consultants in another organization, decided to adopt *Six Boxes® Performance Coaching* at a software company in the medical field. After certifying training and development staff to deliver the program, plus a few program coaches to support application on the job by program participants, the organization has trained around 500 managers, with roughly 1500 more to come. While implementation across the organization has been inconsistent due to differing levels of support from business unit leaders and managers, in groups where all managers complete the program and a senior leader is supportive, Performance Thinking models and vocabulary have been seen as "changing the conversation" about performance and how to improve it. While the Company is still in a multi-year process of rolling out the program, the goal is to use it as a foundation for creating a management and leadership culture focused on accomplishments and on agreed-upon action steps between managers and their direct reports for continuous performance improvement and career development.

In an interview with the author, the SVP who introduced the program said how pleased she is to hear managers and their teams discussing performance with the shared language of Performance Thinking. She recounted how often she, as a senior leader, finds herself sketching and labeling the Performance Chain and Six Boxes models on whiteboards in meetings with individuals and groups to guide conversations about operational challenges and performance improvement opportunities. When asked what she would say about this approach to her C-level colleagues, she said, "If aligning your people with business results is an important goal of yours, then Performance Thinking is a strategic imperative."

These examples illustrate what can happen in organizations that adopt the 21 plain English words and two simple visual models as a framework for teaching leaders, managers, staff professionals, and individual contributors how to analyze performance and configure plans for improving it at the organizational or individual level. This work is still very much an experiment in progress. But to date, the impact is quite gratifying. It's important to note that in the corporate human resources and development arena, where many companies adopt new programs and approaches every few years, Performance Thinking has so far proven to be sustainable, with some organizations maintaining their commitment and continuing to develop their internal capabilities for 5–10 years. We also see individuals returning to The Performance Thinking Network's annual Summer Institute year after year, based on the impact this approach has had in their organizations and their own professional development.

ALIGNING WITH TRENDS AND ISSUES IS THE PERFORMANCE IMPROVEMENT MARKETPLACE

The evolution of Performance Thinking models and programs continues, and is now on the cusp of scaling to more companies around the world and to larger implementations. In the process, we are aligning with or "riding the tail" of several trends that have been visible in the human resource development and performance improvement markets in recent years.

Agile Talent Development

The term *agile* is being applied to many different types of activities and functions in organizations these days. Emerging from the software development field, where iterative development and building applications with smaller chunks has been shown to accelerate development and allow for more rapid adaptation to changing business needs, the term has recently been applied to human resources and talent development in organizations. A 2018 *Harvard Business Review* article (Cappelli & Tavis, 2018) summarized the trend toward agile talent development that is affecting how companies improve and expand the performance of their employees over time. The concept of *agile*, as it relates to training and development, highlights the fact that the pace of business has become too quick for traditional quarterly reviews and learning plans, pre-defined course sequences and learning management systems, and other slow, calendar-driven efforts to develop people. As the authors state, organizations most successful in adopting agile talent development have invested in coaching, collaboration between individuals and their managers to provide learning and development in response to individual and company needs, which might change monthly, or even weekly in some cases.

A challenge with most coaching models is that they are relatively non-directive (Binder, 2019), engaging those being coached in conversations designed to help the individual identify their own problems or issues and then arrive at their own solutions. While this form of coaching can be useful, it is seldom truly performance-focused. Coaching and development models that link to competency models are another option, but competencies are abstractions, referring to categories of behavior rather than to specific behavior (Teodorescu & Binder,

2004). Even behavior-based coaching may not focus on accomplishments, and consequently might or might not enable those being coached to improve their ability to produce valuable contributions (accomplishments or work outputs) for their organizations.

Our accomplishment-based coaching model (*Six Boxes® Performance Coaching*) offers a compelling alternative to more traditional coaching programs. We intend to ride this trend in the human resources field and demonstrate the power of an accomplishment-based approach for driving individual performance development in line with the immediate business, project, and career path needs of individuals.

Beyond Competency Modeling

Many large organizations long ago adopted competency models as frameworks for recruitment, performance evaluation, learning management, and career path design. They have spent millions of dollars formulating competency models and embedding them in their performance evaluation and management processes, their learning management systems, and in other human resources functions and systems. Thomas F. Gilbert (1978) and Marilyn Gilbert (2019) have used the term *competence* to describe behavior producing valuable accomplishments, or what we call *work outputs*. The value of the accomplishment is related to how it contributes to organizational or societal results. *Competency*, on the other hand, is a term used for several decades by Human Resources and Training professionals to label abstract categories of skills, knowledge, and personal attributes, often used in performance management and learning management systems instead of specific descriptions of performance. See Teodorescu and Binder (2004) for a more detailed discussion.

But let us be clear: Competency models are a disaster, and they are harmful to individuals and organizations (Binder, 2018). This is a controversial position to take in public because so many millions of dollars, careers, consulting firms, and off-the-shelf training providers have been devoted to competency modeling over the last several decades. However, so-called competencies are at best category names for large clusters of behavior, sorted into categories for convenience. When organizations add Likert rating scales to competencies, so that managers "rate" their employees on competencies such as *strategic thinking* or *customer focus* on 1-to-5 scales, the entire enterprise collapses in a heap of subjective judgment. While most HR organizations still seem to defend their use of competency modeling, many senior HR leaders will admit in private that competencies are not helpful. In the worst cases, they introduce a level of cynicism into performance evaluation rituals, where employees feel that the ratings they receive might be dependent on whether their bosses have had their cup of coffee or been in an argument with their spouse that morning. Rating people on abstractions that are, at best, conceptually related to some aspect of an employee's performance, does not meet any criterion that an applied behavior scientist, let alone a pragmatic leader, might apply. For years I have asked employees and senior executives what they really think of rating scales combined with competencies for determining promotions and pay raises. I generally get lots of eye-rolling in the audience. And these days the eye-rolling is more public.

But organizations do not know what else do to. Some HR professionals (Lambert, 2018) have suggested developing competency models based on *talents* described as recurring patterns of thought, feeling, and behavior. Lambert argues that with artificial intelligence it should be possible to refine definitions of talents across many individuals in ways that will be more useful than current competency models. I would argue that no amount of refinement will change the fact that a competency is an abstract concept based on a wide variety of examples, and therefore cannot by definition be precise enough to pinpoint in the performance of an individual. In our view, any effort to refine competency modeling will be inherently flawed

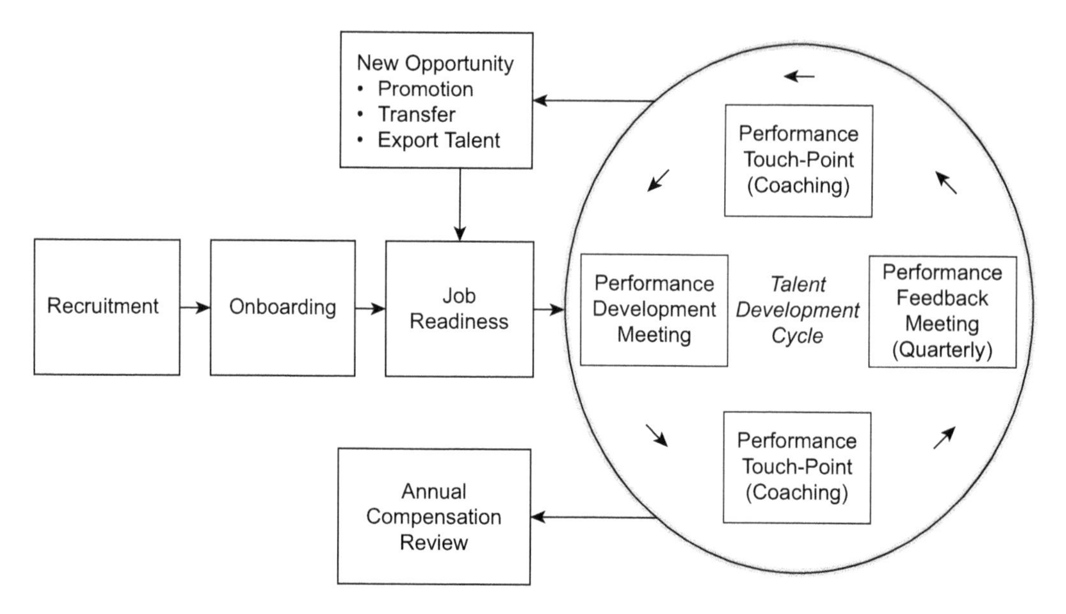

FIGURE 4.5 An accomplishment-based talent development process.

because competencies neither define behavior nor accomplishments with sufficient detail to be managed, developed, or measured, except with rating scales, which some have referred to as "refined opinion."

We believe that accomplishments provide an alternative to competencies for creating job descriptions, driving the development of individuals based on their own and their organizations' immediate and long-term needs, planning succession, and every other aspect of talent development.

In organizations as diverse as Easter Seals Bay Area, the Al Futtaim Group in Dubai, and Insperity, HR professionals have created job descriptions that list the major work outputs or accomplishments of jobs. In some organizations, coaches who use the Performance Thinking approach conduct their initial coaching sessions with individuals by creating with the employee a list of the major work outputs (or "contributions") that the employee produces as part of his or her job. Based on that list, coaches can collaborate with those whom they coach to target specific work outputs for improvement or development, identify additional work outputs that will be required for their next career level, or add and make plans to develop new work outputs based on the needs of the company or workgroup. We believe that focusing on accomplishments can help organizations move beyond competency modeling in a way that will be more performance-focused, and less open to subjective interpretation during the evaluation process.

COMMUNITIES OF PRACTICE

While the phrase "community of practice" is not new, it has taken on a more prominent role in many organizations over the last decade. In part due to software, such as Microsoft's SharePoint and many other platforms for collaboration, networking, and document sharing that have followed, organizations often designate communities of practice to accelerate collective learning and development across groups who share interests, areas of focus, disciplines, functional roles, and so on.

At companies that adopt Performance Thinking® programs and methods, the two simple pictures and 21 plain English words that comprise its models offer a shared vocabulary to support communities of practice. Organized brown bag lunches among managers who coach using our accomplishment-based approach, online web meetings, SharePoint applications, and concerted efforts from community of practice leaders to harvest what leaders, managers, and performance professionals learn with and from one another empower communities of practice. Focusing on accomplishments, and using a shared vocabulary for the elements of performance and behavior influences, facilitates communication across otherwise diverse groups and individuals.

At a global level, a community of practice is emerging among users of Performance Thinking[2] programs and models. The annual Six Boxes Summer Institute (www.SixBoxes.com), having completed its tenth year, brings together people from many different industries, geographies and roles. We have had participants in human services, professional athletic organizations, corporations across multiple industries, from North America, Europe, South Korea, Africa, and elsewhere. We've had training and development professionals, management consultants, safety and error reduction specialists, leaders, managers, and executives from many different organizations, all sharing insights and applications related to performance using the shared models and language of this approach. The potential for communities of practice that leverage plain English and simple models is significant, and offers a way to get beyond the common silos created by different vocabularies, areas of application, and professional specialties.

SUMMARY AND CONCLUSIONS

Approaching human performance with a focus on the valuable products of behavior, called accomplishments or work outputs, changes the conversation in organizations about how individuals, teams, and processes deliver value toward common business and societal goals. When we discipline ourselves to first identify the "countable nouns" representing value delivered, it becomes possible to agree on criteria for "good" instances of those accomplishments and to zero in on the behavior needed to produce the accomplishments with high degrees of quality and productivity. When we expand our framework of behavior influences from the three-term contingency to the categories originally identified by Gilbert (1978) in his Behavior Engineering Model, we facilitate discussion about variables that might otherwise not be considered, at both the organizational and individual level. And when we communicate about the elements of performance and behavior influences in plain English that everyone can quickly understand and adopt, we accelerate the pace at which individuals from many different levels and functions in an organization can collaborate to create solutions and drive continuous performance improvement. Those have been the lessons learned on the evolutionary path described in this article.

We might summarize what we have learned in several key points:

- Gilbert's insight that accomplishments are valuable while behavior is costly has the potential for transforming how we approach organizational performance.
- User-tested plain English terminology for technical concepts, first modeled by Lindsley when he took behavior science from the laboratory to special education classrooms, can broaden the application of behavior science to a wider audience of users.
- When we place behavior science in the hands of people at all levels and in all functions, with simple models and language and a focus on the valuable accomplishments that people contribute to organizations, we can accelerate continuous performance improvement and support agile talent development, more likely able to keep up with the rapid pace of change in today's business and work environments.

STUDY QUESTIONS

1. Describe the "paradigm shift" that Gilbert's work was associated with.
2. How did the use of precise definitions/specific language contribute to the author's work?
3. Why does the author believe people have a hard time shifting from a focus on behavior to a focus on accomplishments?
4. What is the author's main concern with competency-based models?
5. Summarize the three key points the author described at the end of the chapter.

NOTES

1. We have refrained from naming client organizations in this article because most of our clients specified in contracts and master service agreements that we cannot use their names in publications or marketing without specific permission, which can require lengthy legal reviews and documentation.
2. *Performance Thinking®* and *Six Boxes®* are registered trademarks of The Performance Thinking Network and should not be used to label products or services provided by other organizations or individuals. We request that those who cite these models or this approach acknowledge copyright and trademarks, as applicable, and refer to www.SixBoxes.com in their citation.

REFERENCES

Barrett, B.H. (1977). Behavior analysis. *Mental Retardation and Developmental Disabilities, 9*, 139–202.

Binder, C. (1987, September). Computing "fluency" and productivity. *Managing End User Computing*, 4–5.

Binder, C. (1988). Precision Teaching: Measuring and attaining exemplary academic achievement. *Youth Policy Journal, 10*(7), 12–15.

Binder, C. (1990a). Efforts to promote measurably superior instructional methods in schools. *Performance & Instruction, 29*(9), 32–34.

Binder, C. (1990b, September). Closing the confidence gap. *Training Magazine*, 49–56.

Binder, C. (1991). Marketing measurably effective instructional methods. *Journal of Behavioral Education, 1*(3), 317–328.

Binder. C. (1996). Behavioral fluency: evolution of a new paradigm. *The Behavior Analyst, 19*(2), 163–197.

Binder, C. (1998). The Six Boxes™: A descendent of Gilbert's Behavior Engineering Model. *Performance Improvement, 37*(6), 48–52.

Binder, C. (1999). Fluency development. In D.G. Langson, K.S. Whiteside, & M.M. McKenna (Eds.), *Intervention resource guide: 50 performance improvement tools* (pp. 176–183). Jossey-Bass/Pfeiffer.

Binder, C. (2003, March). Doesn't everybody need fluency? *Performance Improvement, 42*(3), 14–20.

Binder, C. (2009a). *A view from the top: human performance in organizations.* White paper published by The Performance Thinking Network, LLC, available in the online SixBoxes.com Resource Library at https://bit.ly/2Y59UY2.

Binder, C. (2009b). Measurement, evaluation, and research: Feedback for decision making. In J.L. Mosley & J.C. Dessinger (Eds.), *Handbook of improving performance in the workplace Volume 3: measurement and evaluation* (pp. 3–24). Pfeiffer and the International Society for Performance Improvement.

Binder, C. (2014). Teachers and students passing it on. In R.D. Holdsambeck and H.S. Pennypacker (Eds.), *Behavior science: Tales of inspiration, discovery, and service* (pp. 263–288). Cambridge Center for Behavioral Studies.

Binder, C. (2018). Why competency based HR systems are unfair and ineffective. Blog post in *Performance improvement from the inside out.* www.SixBoxes.com.

Binder, C. (2019, June). Why trademark a performance improvement methodology? ISPI. The International Society for Performance Improvement. https://bit.ly/2Z2McbN

Binder, C. & Bloom, C. (1989). Fluent product knowledge: application in the financial services industry. *Performance and Instruction, 28*(2), 17–21.

Binder, C. & Sweeney, L. (2002). Building fluent performance in a customer call center. *Performance Improvement, 41*(2), 29–37.

Binder, C. & Watkins, C.L. (1989, December). Promoting effective instructional methods: solutions to America's educational crisis. *Youth Policy, 1*(3), 33–39.

Binder, C. & Watkins, C.L. (1990). Precision teaching and direct instruction: Measurably superior instructional technology in schools. *Performance Improvement Quarterly, 3*(4), 74–96.

Cappelli, P. & Tavis, A. (2018, March–April). HR goes agile. *Harvard Business Review*, 3–8.

Gilbert, T. F. (1978). *Human competence: Engineering worthy performance.* McGraw-Hill Book Company.

Gilbert, M.B. (2019). Human performance technology: Further reflections on Human Competence. *Journal of Organizational Behavior Management, 39*(1), 7–112.

Gilbert, L.M., Weersing, S., Patterson, S., Fisher, L. R., & Binder, C. (2014). The cobblers' children: Improving performance improvement at Amerigroup. *Performance Improvement, 53*(2), 22–33.

Harless, J.H. (1975). *An ounce of analysis (is worth a pound of objectives): A Self-instructional lesson.* Harless Performance Guild.

Harless, J.H. (1987). *Front end analysis workshop materials.* Harless Performance Guild.

Haughton, E. (1972). Aims – growing and sharing. In J.B. Jordan & L.S. Robbins (Eds.), *Let's try doing something else kind of thing: behavioral principles and the exceptional child.* A report from the Invisible College Conference on Application of Behavioral Principles in Exceptional Child Education, March, 1971 (pp. 20–39). The Council for Exceptional Children.

Lambert, E. (2018). *A case for talent-based competency models (and how AI can help).* Talent Take Five, a blog from Plum, Inc. November 2, 2018. https://www.plum.io/blog/a-case-for-talent-based-competency-models

Lindsley, O.R. (1971). From Skinner to precision teaching: The child knows best. In J.B. Jordan & L.S. Robbins (Eds.), *Let's try doing something else kind of thing: Behavioral principles and the exceptional child.* The Council for Exceptional Children, 1-11.

Pennypacker, H.S., Koenig, C.H., & Lindsley, O.R. (1972). *Handbook of the standard behavior chart.* Precision Media.

Pennypacker. H.S. (1986). The challenge of technology transfer: Buying in without selling out. *The Behavior Analyst, 9*(2), 147–156.

Segall, K. (2013). *Insanely simple: The obsession that drives Apple's success.* Portfolio/Penguin.

Teodorescu, T.M. & Binder, C. (2004). Competence is what matters. *Performance Improvement, 43*(8), 8–12.

Watkins, C.L. (1988). Project Follow Through: A story of the identification and neglect of effective instruction. *Youth Policy, 10*(7), 7–11.

Watkins, C.L. (1997). *Project Follow Through: A case study of contingencies influencing instructional practices of the educational establishment.* The Cambridge Center for Behavioral Studies. Available at www.behavior.org.

5

Behavioral Systems Analysis in Organizations

Heather M. McGee and Brian J. Crowley-Koch

BEHAVIORAL SYSTEMS ANALYSIS IN ORGANIZATIONS

The field of behavior analysis exists within the larger field of psychology (APA Division 25) and is typically viewed as comprising two large subfields: the Experimental Analysis of Behavior (EAB; basic research and science) and Applied Behavior Analysis (applied research and science or practice). Poling et al. (2000) described EAB as providing "information about behavior and the variables that control it. A basic research study does not directly attempt to solve a problem, and need not benefit participants" (p. 297). Alternatively, Applied Behavior Analysis is concerned with the prediction and control of socially important behaviors and in addressing socially important problems through behavior change (Baer et al., 1968; Bailey & Burch, 2002).

Because Applied Behavior Analysis is concerned with socially important behaviors, scientists and practitioners working within the various areas of application (e.g., developmental disabilities, sports psychology, applied animal behavior, etc.) strive to improve socially important behaviors relevant to the population of interest in those particular areas. While each area is then unique in serving the needs of a specific population of interest, the science of behavior is consistent across all areas of application. When viewed this way, the various areas of Applied Behavior Analysis are more similar than dissimilar: they all attempt to change behavior by altering environmental variables that affect socially important behaviors.

One application area of Applied Behavior Analysis is Organizational Behavior Management (OBM). Within OBM, the behaviors and variables of interest occur within the context of the workplace. Said another way, OBM is the field of study concerned with the performance of people at work. Hall (1980), in an early editorial for the *Journal of Organizational Behavior Management (JOBM)*, offered the following goal for the field of OBM: "establish a technology of broad-scale performance improvement and organizational change so that employees will be more productive and happier, and so that our organizations and institutions will be more effective and efficient in achieving their goals" (p. 145).

The subfield of OBM generally comprises two main analysis/assessment and intervention frameworks based on scope: Performance Management and Behavioral Systems Analysis (Sigurdsson & McGee, 2015). Performance Management (PM) involves analyzing and improving the performance of individuals or groups within the organization. Behavioral Systems Analysis (BSA) involves analyzing and improving the performance of individuals or groups within the organization, as well as organizational factors across multiple individuals or groups. Because the scope of BSA includes analyzing and improving the performance of individuals

DOI: 10.4324/9781003198949-5

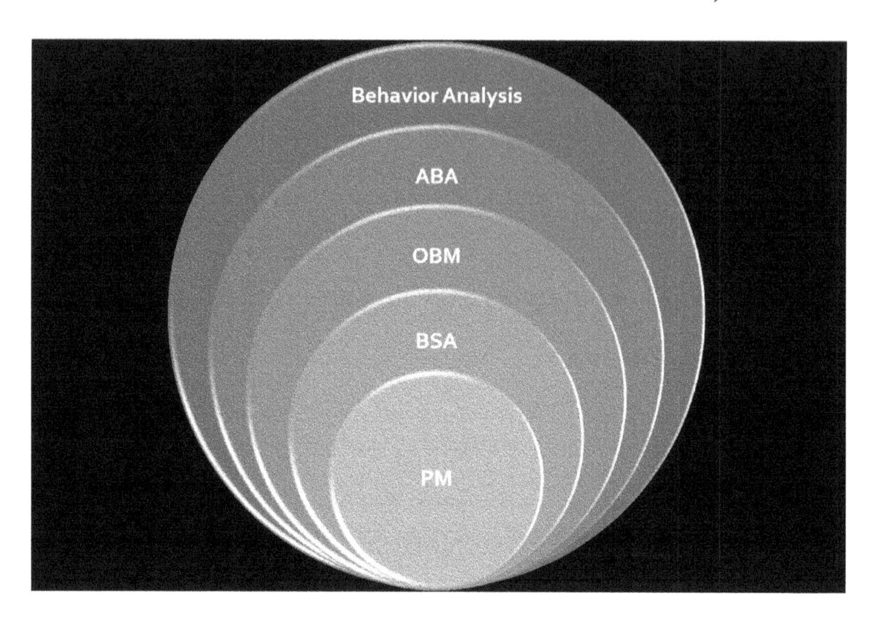

FIGURE 5.1 Behavior analysis drill down.

and groups within the organization (PM), we would consider PM to be part of BSA. In other words, BSA includes PM, but PM does not include BSA (see Figure 5.1).

While some have presented specific topics within OBM (e.g., behavior-based safety) as distinct areas of OBM (Wine & Pritchard, 2018), we would argue that these are better viewed as specific analyses/assessments and/or interventions/intervention targets that are implemented within one of the two OBM frameworks (PM or BSA). For example, behavior-based safety (see Chapter 2 of this text) is a collection of assessments and interventions (which would fall under PM or BSA, depending on scope) targeting safety-related behaviors and conditions. Instructional design (see Chapter 3 of this text) is the analysis of workplace performance (within OBM – instructional design also applies to the non-organization based education area) with the explicit goal of creating effective educating/training (intervention) for employees and employers. The focus of this chapter will be on the BSA framework of performance analysis and improvement (as opposed to the PM framework).

THE HISTORICAL ROOTS OF BEHAVIORAL SYSTEMS ANALYSIS

To understand the complex history of BSA, it is helpful first to understand the relationship between two fields of performance improvement: OBM and Human Performance Technology (HPT). We have already defined OBM as an application area of Applied Behavior Analysis dedicated to improving the performance of people at work. The professional network most associated with OBM is the OBM Network, which is a special interest group of the Association for Behavior Analysis International (ABAI). Pershing (2006) defined HPT as "the study and ethical practice of improving productivity in organizations by designing and developing effective interventions that are results-oriented, comprehensive, and systemic" (p. 6). The professional network most associated with HPT is the International Society of Performance Improvement (ISPI).

Colloquially speaking, we could consider the fields of OBM and HPT siblings in that they share a common "father." Both OBM and HPT claim roots in Skinner's analysis of behavior. Dickinson (2000) cited Skinner's (1953) analysis of work behavior and economics in *Science and human behavior*, as well as his Programmed Instruction (PI) articles (Skinner, 1954, 1958), as influences on OBM's development, while Tosti and Kaufman (2007) cite Skinner's (1954) *The science of learning and the art of teaching* as the precursor to HPT. In fact, the National Society of Programmed Instruction (NSPI), which would later become the National Society for Performance and Instruction and, eventually, the ISPI that we know today, was formed in January 1962 by a group of military, public school, and university professionals interested in Programmed Instruction. For context, the Midwest Association of Behavior Analysis (MABA), which would go on to become the Association for Behavior Analysis (ABA) and eventually ABAI, was not formed until 1974 (Dickinson, 2000). In April, 1962, NSPI held its first "Programmed Instruction Institute" in San Antonio, Texas, during which the NSPI president outlined "three nation-wide problems of modern education: high-school dropouts, industrial retraining, and teacher procurement" (Ofiesh & Meierhenry, 1964, p. v). In 1963, NSPI held its first annual conference with several notable speakers who would go on to be leaders within the OBM/HPT fields, including Thomas Gilbert, Robert Mager, Roger Kaufman, along with several other experts and leaders within PI and instructional systems design.

Ofiesh and Meierhenry (1964) published the papers presented at that first conference in a volume titled *Trends in Programmed Instruction*. They organized the papers into the following sections: (1) Introduction, (2) Education, (3) Development of Systems Applications, (4) The Teacher, (5) The Exceptional Student, (6) Industrial Applications, (7) Military and Government Applications, (8) The Health Sciences, (9) Instructional Programming, (10) Evaluations, (11) Future Trends, and (12) A Point of Transition. These sections are noteworthy in that they demonstrate that (a) PI was being applied in both educational and business settings, and (b) practitioners of PI were already using a systems approach (BSA, though the term would not appear until several years later) for performance analysis and improvement, though applied specifically within the context of PI. In the first paper of the systems section, Kaufman (1964) defined the systems approach as "the notion that anything we consider is a dynamic whole constituted of interacting factors or variables" (p. 33).

In the second systems section paper, Corrigan (1964) described the systems approach from the historical context of military application:

> The terms "system" and "systems approach," when originally conceived, related to applied methods for increasing the efficiency of overall planning, organization, and coordination in the development of our national weapon systems. The "systems approach" considers each of the many individuals and groups developing a particular weapon (like the Atlas missile) as individual components like cogs in a machine working together to achieve a common goal. This approach requires: (1) defining in advance the job of each person or "cog" in terms of his assigned responsibilities, (2) detailing the task, (3) specifying performance requirements, and (4) stating the necessary interactions and communications to be carried out between groups, each requirement tailored and defined to meet the preset system goal. (p. 36)

In the following paper, Smith (1964) described how the Human Resources Research Organization (HumRRO) used a systems approach to improve Army training procedures. He stated that HumRRO had successfully reduced training time while increasing proficiency through the development of a "Technology of Training" process.

> These steps are (1) Analysis of the operational system and the training system; (2) Analysis of the job; (3) Analysis of the Tasks to specify required knowledges and skills; (4) Determination of

> training objectives; (5) Construction of the training program; (6) Development of measures of proficiency; and (7) Evaluation of the training program. (p. 46)

The picture that emerged from these papers was that a systems approach could, and should, be used to design effective PI and workplace training. This picture was also emerging at the University of Michigan, with the Center for Programmed Learning for Business (CPLB), created by Geary Rummler and Dr. George Odiorne in 1962 within the university's Graduate School of Business (Dickinson, 2000; Rummler, 2007). They began running the monthly, weeklong "Performance Learning Workshop." That same year, Dale Brethower joined their faculty. Brethower had been at the University of Michigan since 1960 and had worked with Rummler over the previous year (1961) at the Institute for Behavioral Research and Programmed Instruction (that particular organization only operated for one year). Prior to coming to the University of Michigan, Brethower earned his M.A. with Dr. B.F. Skinner at Harvard, and his B.A. at the University of Kansas, where he was first introduced to behavior analysis by Dr. Jack Michael (Dickinson, 2000).

Over the next few years, the CPLB faculty would expand their workshop offerings, adding expert staff (e.g., Karen Brethower, David Markle) and guest speakers (e.g., Tom Gilbert, Joe Harless, Roger Kaufman). These experts, along with workshop graduates (e.g., Ed Feeney), would go on to disseminate the workshops at conferences and in books, journal articles, and other publication outlets, thereby broadening the reach and impact of BSA. Two of these workshops warrant particular attention: the "Applied Learning Theory" workshop (1963), and the "Training Systems Workshop" (1965).

The "Applied Learning Theory" workshop was a response to Rummler's and Brethower's growing concerns regarding why "learning did not always result in improved performance on the job" (Rummler, 2007, pp. 5–6). This workshop asserted that knowledge and skill-building are not the only factors relevant to successful job performance. Other factors, such as feedback, resources, and consequences, are also necessary. Brethower led the charge of adapting the workshop to become the "Management of Behavior Change Workshop." This appears to be one of, if not the first, applied examples of a behavior analytic/behavioral systems workshop targeting workplace performance change beyond improving and implementing instruction and training. As a reminder, this was the same year that the NSPI held its first programmed instruction conference, with a section on the "systems approach" (Ofiesh & Meierhenry, 1964). In other words, by 1963, a full 14 years before the first issue of *JOBM* would be published, learning and performance experts were using behavior analysis and systems analysis to analyze and improve workplace performance, both within and outside of training.

In 1965, Brethower and Rummler developed the "Training Systems Workshop" founded on the framework that would go on to define the BSA framework as we know it today: (a) Brethower's Total Performance System (TPS) and (b) Rummler's three levels of performance (organization, process, job/performer). The focus of the workshop was on results, and improving systems to achieve those results. It was in this workshop that Brethower and Rummler introduced the concept of "performance engineering" and organization mapping (Rummler, 2007). Additionally, they furthered the central theme of the "Management of Behavior Change Workshop" by advocating for performance departments, rather than training departments, within organizations. Also in 1965, CPLB presented for the first time at the third annual NSPI conference.

In 1967, CPLB won the NSPI award for Outstanding Public Organization and organized the first NSPI conference business and industry track. This track expanded the NSPI offerings and audience, which had been primarily academics, military, professionals in the medical and education fields, and consultants (Rummler, 2007), and represents a major shift toward what we now know as ISPI.

Over the next several years, Brethower and Rummler continued to collaborate with other systems thinkers to further apply and disseminate the systems approach. Brethower began collaborating with Richard "Dick" Malott of Western Michigan University (WMU) in the mid to late 1960s, while Rummler formed the consulting firm Praxis with Tom Gilbert in 1969. These collaborations resulted in more widespread education and adoption of systems concepts and principles. By 1969, Malott had begun incorporating OBM and BSA into the undergraduate and graduate curriculum at WMU (Dickinson, 2000; R.W. Malott, 2016). In 1970, Brethower completed his dissertation, "The classroom as a self-modifying system," which was the first published application of the Total Performance System.

Throughout the 1970s, several articles and books were written on BSA (Dickinson, 2000; Rummler, 2007). Two books are of particular note: Brethower's (1972) *Behavioral analysis in business and industry: A total performance system*, and Maley and Harshbarger's (1974) *Behavior analysis and systems analysis: An integrated approach to mental health*, both published by Malott's Behaviordelia, Inc. (Dickinson, 2000). These were the first books dedicated to a behavioral systems approach to performance analysis and improvement. In 1973, Dick Malott and Dwight Harshbarger first introduced the term "behavioral systems analysis" to describe the systems approach (Brethower, 2002). This was also the year that NSPI changed its name from the National Society for Programmed Instruction to the National Society for Performance and Instruction. Either 1974 (R.W. Malott, 2016) or 1975 (Dickinson, 2000) heralded the first MABA conference, which boasted three OBM/BSA talks. According to R.W. Malott (2016), Jerry Mertens had organized a small, behavior analytic conference the year before at the University of Chicago and it was at that unnamed conference that attendees came up with the MABA name and organization. The MABA organization was housed on WMU's campus, where it remained until 2002 (it is still located in the greater Kalamazoo area, just not on the WMU campus).

The late 1970s saw the birth of formal OBM graduate training. Up to this point, individual faculty had already been teaching OBM courses at several universities, but there were no cohesive OBM programs (Dickinson, 2000). Harshbarger was faculty at West Virginia University (WVU) and, around 1976, WVU started its Community/Systems graduate program (Hawkins et al., 1993). While BSA in business and industry was not the primary focus of the program – applications in mental health settings was – it was one area of application and, in fact, several of the faculty eventually left academia to do private consulting (Dickinson, 2000). The next year (1977) Phil Duncan joined the behavior analysis faculty at Drake University and established OBM coursework, practical, and the Behavioral Systems Administration program, which he also directed. In 1978, Dale Brethower joined the faculty at WMU "to behavioralize the already-existing master's program in industrial/organizational psychology and contribute to doctoral training in OBM" (Dickinson, 2000, p. 37).

By the end of the 1970s, the behavioral systems analysis approach to performance analysis and improvement could be found in books, articles, among the services provided by consulting firms, and in graduate coursework. In 1977, the first issue of *JOBM* was published, though the first BSA article would not appear until Krapfl's (1982) *Behavior management in state mental health systems* (Johnson et al., 2014). In 1978, Tom Gilbert published *Human competence*, which recently enjoyed its 40th anniversary and is currently in its third edition (Gilbert, 2007). Rummler and Gilbert sold Praxis and went their separate ways that year. In 1979, Duncan organized the first national OBM conference at Drake University. That same year, the MABA became the ABA (the "I" would not be added until 2008), and the annual conference included a special program track for OBM/BSA (Dickinson, 2000).

In 1982, the Organizational Behavior Network (now the OBM Network) became an official special interest group of the ABA, though it had been meeting annually, informally, since 1979 (Dickinson, 2000). Also that year, Rummler formed The Rummler Group, working with his son, Rick Rummler, and Carol Panza (Rummler, 2007). The Rummler Group operated between 1982–1986 and, during that time, Rummler worked with such companies as Motorola and GTE, teaching the three levels of performance view to executives of these organizations. Of particular importance is Rummler's work with Motorola.

Throughout 1984–1985, Rummler and Alan Ramias, a Motorola training manager and internal consultant for the Semiconductor Products business groups, did extensive process analysis and improvement work (Rummler et al., 2009). They were invited to present their work at the April 1985 NSPI conference, where they described their exciting new methodology, but did not yet have any results to demonstrate the true power of the methodology. That changed in June 1985: "It turned out that cycle time had been cut from fourteen weeks to seven weeks in nine months. The business – addressing a vital new segment for the sector – had turned completely around, and now the competition was chasing them" (Rummler et al., 2009, p. 7). Motorola eventually rolled out Rummler and Ramias' methodology to most major business units, eventually integrating it into their existing Total Quality Management (TQM) system and rolling it out in the late 1980s as Six Sigma.

Throughout the 1980s and 1990s, OBM and HPT would continue to develop, but as separate "sibling" fields of performance improvement. While they shared this history, OBM remained firmly rooted in behavior analysis, while HPT would expand its theoretical ties to become a more interdisciplinary approach to performance analysis and improvement. While both fields continue to practice BSA, NSPIs/ISPIs strong instructional design roots may be partially responsible for its expansion into non-behavioral approaches, especially as they relate to the training side of the field. Conversely, OBM's firm foundation in behavior analysis might explain why the PM framework is seemingly so much more popular than the BSA framework, even though the BSA framework was as integral to the development of the field as the PM framework.

This brief historical account is by no means all-encompassing of BSA, HPT, or OBM. The history is rich and complex, with branches coming in and out, perhaps running parallel for some time. In fact, BSA could be seen as a branching off from the application area of instructional design since its roots are in programmed instruction. Readers are encouraged to read Rummler's (2007) *The past is prologue: An eyewitness account of HPT*; Tosti and Kaufman's (2007) *Who is the "real" father of HPT?*; Dickinson's (2000) *The historical roots of Organizational Behavior Management in the private sector*; and R.W. Malott's (2016) *Why is Dick so weird?* for more detailed accounts, from varying perspectives. We have tried to compile these accounts as best we can, while at the same time reserving chapter space to cover BSA concepts, applications, research, and future directions.

BSA CONCEPTS AND PRINCIPLES

As previously stated, BSA involves analyzing and improving the performance of individuals or groups within the organization, as well as organizational factors across multiple individuals or groups. The BSA history provided in the previous section highlights the behavior analysis concepts inherent in the BSA approach. Therefore, at its core, many BSA concepts are simply behavior analysis concepts. In fact, any changes made to an organizational system will only be as successful as the behavior changes that support the system change. If you change an organizational process, you are changing the way work gets done. If you are changing the way work gets done, you are changing behavior. In order to change behavior, you must change antecedents and consequences.

While many BSA concepts are behavior analysis concepts and, therefore, are familiar to our readers, BSA is not merely behavior analysis in the workplace. You can change contingencies without changing larger system factors (e.g., processes). BSA is the combination of behavior analysis and general systems theory (GST, the systems piece of BSA). Therefore, the remainder of this section will focus on defining and describing key GST and BSA concepts and discussing how these concepts guide the practice of BSA.

SYSTEMS AND OPEN/ADAPTIVE VERSUS CLOSED SYSTEMS

The most basic systems concept is that of the system itself. Von Bertalanffy (1972) defined a system as "a set of elements standing in interrelation among themselves and with the environment" (p. 417). Inherent in this particular definition is the notion of the open or adaptive system. An open system is one that interacts with the external environment, while a closed system interacts only with other internal elements. Due to the fact that all organizations produce products and/or services to be received by outside customers or consumers, they must be viewed as open or adaptive systems, not closed systems. It should be noted, however, that just because an organizational system is an adaptive system does not meet that it operates effectively as an adaptive system. If all organizational systems were effective in being truly adaptive systems, there would be no need for OBM at all!

Given that organizational systems comprise elements that interact with each other and the external environment, a change in one part of the system has the potential to impact other parts of the system as well as the external environment. Additionally, changes in the external environment have the potential to impact the organization. Therefore, we can use a BSA approach to analyze how an organization change in one department or function (one system element) affects other departments or functions (other system elements) as well the external environment (customers and other external factors). For example, an organization – or more accurately, organizational leaders – might decide to change up its/their marketing strategy (as organizations often do). This system element change, which occurs in the marketing function of the organization, has the potential to impact the sales function (possible increase in the number of sales), the manufacturing function (possible increase in production requirements), the logistics function (possible increases in order fulfillment), etc. Additionally, the marketing strategy, if effective, has an impact on the behavior of the consumer, thereby changing the external environment. It could also impact other external elements, such as suppliers, who might need to produce more raw materials to meet demand increases, competition, which might need to change its own marketing strategy to remain competitive, etc.

FEEDBACK LOOPS

Within GST as well as BSA, feedback looks are considered requirements for maintaining the overall health and adaptiveness of the organization. Von Bertalanffy (1972) defined these feedback loops or "schemes" as follows: as follows:

> In a system responding to disturbance from outside, part of the output is monitored back to the input so as to control the system's function, either to maintain a desired state or to guide the system toward a goal. Both in technology and in living nature, feedback systems can be of any degree of complexity, but can always be analyzed into feedback loops according to the scheme. (pp. 132–133)

Brethower and Wittkopp (1988) further differentiated *external* feedback loops from *internal* feedback loops, and described the specific data gathered and analyzed through each loop:

> The external loop symbolizes the feedback the organization needs from the marketplace, broadly conceived: It symbolizes data on sales, on customer satisfaction, on market share, on social and

> economic trends, on technological developments, on any other variables the organization needs to be aware of to function well in the long run. The internal loop symbolizes the internal feedback the organization needs to function well in the short run. It symbolizes data on unit costs, on scrap rates, on absenteeism, on costs of labor and materials, on performance relevant to production or service standards, on all the variables the organization needs to monitor to function well. (p. 86)

Regardless of the definitions used, feedback is an important concept in both GST and BSA and represents how the system feeds information back into itself, to be used for the purpose of adaptation and, ultimately, survival.

AGGREGATE PRODUCTS, INTERLOCKING BEHAVIORAL CONTINGENCIES, AND METACONTINGENCIES

Some have argued that BSA should not be considered part of behavior analysis. Part of this argument seems to stem from the fact that BSA practitioners are often concerned with changing processes and organizational factors. However, these changes always require changes to behavioral contingencies (at least they do if they are to be successful in the long term). Additionally, some have argued that, because BSA practitioners are typically concerned with aggregate products rather than or in addition to specific behavioral outputs of the individual worker, BSA is not behavior analysis.

The aggregate products of organizations are those products (or services) received – or selected – by the organizations' customers. Aggregate products are not typically produced by a single individual or even a single job position (with multiple job holders) within the organization. Rather, they are produced through work done across job positions and individuals within the organization. There are contingencies operating on each individual's behavior, but it is the complex interconnectedness of those contingencies and the products of behavior supported by those contingencies that are responsible for the final (aggregate) product that is received by the customer. These interconnected contingences are referred to as interlocking behavioral contingencies (Glenn & Malott, 2004; M.E. Malott, 2016; Malott & Glenn, 2006).

Taken together, the interlocking behavioral contingencies, the aggregate products produced by those contingencies, and the customers (i.e., the receiving system or selecting environment) who select those products make up what Glenn and Malott (2004) referred to as the "metacontingency." Understanding and improving these metacontingencies is critical to organizational success and also allows for an approach to organizational improvement that is "analogous to operant reinforcement in individual behavior" (Glenn & Malott, 2004, p. 100). Metacontingencies can (and should) also be analyzed and understood in the context of organizational processes, which typically cut across organizational functions. In fact, Rummler and Brache (2013) defined a process as "a series of steps designed to produce a product or service" (p. 43). Therefore, a cross-functional organizational process can be defined as a series of steps, conducted by individuals across multiple functions, designed to produce a product or a service. This is very similar to the definition of a metacontingency (though the receiving system is not explicitly identified). In BSA, it is important to analyze and improve both the interlocking contingencies operating on the behavior of individuals throughout the process, but also the process itself. Of course, any changes made to the process itself would require changes in behavior and therefore changes to the interlocking behavioral contingencies.

BSA APPLICATION AND RESEARCH

While the previous discussion of concepts and principles illustrates how BSA fits into the larger field of behavior analysis, it is the application of BSA that demonstrates how it fits into

OBM specifically. This section will describe how BSA is performed across multiple levels of organizational performance. Additionally, we will describe the OBM research relevant to each level of performance.

The BSA Process

Central to any applied work in behavior analysis is a commitment to the *analysis*, and this is as true in BSA as any other application. In fact, analysis is the heart of BSA – it is called behavioral systems *analysis*, after all. In our experience, this has been a point of confusion within and outside of OBM. People often talk about BSA as if it were an intervention when it is actually a performance analysis framework. Yes, the results of the analysis should lead you to specific intervention choices – choices that are likely to be different from and/or more expansive than intervention choices indicated through PM analysis only – but BSA is, first and foremost, an approach to *analysis*. Part of the confusion likely stems from descriptions of BSA research, as described in the previous section. In empirical studies, the emphasis is on the effectiveness of a particular intervention on some measure of performance. In the BSA literature, those interventions choices were presumably based on the BSA work conducted, but this is often not the central theme of the publication (though it does tend to be the central theme in conceptual/theoretical papers and BSA books).

Given that analysis is central to BSA, all analysis and improvement efforts should follow a clear process that promotes analysis before change and evaluation throughout (Malott, 1974; Rummler, 2007). This analysis process generally comprises the following steps: (1) identify the system components relevant to the current level of analysis (see Levels of Analysis below), (2) identify issues or performance gaps within and across those components, and (3) create a prioritized list of recommended actions to close the identified gaps. Processes that are more specific exist within both BSA as well as other fields of performance improvement. For example, Malott (1974) recommended the ASDIER (Analyze, Specify, Design, Implement, Evaluate, and Recycle) process as a behavioral systems approach to organizational systems design. Rummler (2007) proposed the four-phase Results Improvement Process (RIP; desired results determined and project defined; barriers determined and changes specified; changes designed, developed, and implemented; and results evaluated and maintained or improved) for performance analysis and improvement projects.

Outside of BSA, the ADDIE (Analyze, Design, Develop, Implement, Evaluate) process, which is the gold standard for instructional systems design and training, is very similar to Malott's ASDIER process and Rummler's RIP (Molenda et al., 1996). This should not be too surprising given BSAs historical roots in programmed instruction. The Six Sigma DMAIC (Define, Measure, Analyze, Improve, Control) process is also similar to Malott's ASDIER process and Rummler's RIP. Again, this should not be too surprising, given that Six Sigma and the DMAIC process came out of Motorola in the 1980s, and that Six Sigma is based, in part, on Rummler's methodology, which was combined with Motorola's existing TQM methodology (Rummler et al., 2009).

LEVELS OF ANALYSIS

One of the primary differences between BSA and PM is BSA's emphasis on multi-level analysis and selection. The oldest and most widely accepted multi-level analysis is Rummler's three-level approach (Rummler, 2004, 2007; Rummler & Brache, 2013). Some BSA experts have proposed four (Addison et al., 2009), five (Malott, 2003), or even six levels of analysis (Gilbert, 2007). Advocates of more levels typically add a broader view above the organization level (macrosystem or world view) and/or a more micro view at the behavioral contingency level

TABLE 5.1
The Three Level Approach

Analyze this level...	*To understand and improve...*
ORGANIZATION LEVEL	• Environment in which the organization operates • How the organization is structured to support achievement of organization-level strategic and tactical goals
PROCESS LEVEL	• Workflow through which inputs are converted into outputs
JOB/PERFORMER LEVEL	• Job characteristics • Task/job responsibility performance • Antecedents, behaviors, and consequences of the individuals who work within the system

(Addison et al., 2009; Malott, 2003). Gilbert's six-level view is unique in that he recommended analyzing performance from different vantage points, starting at the philosophical level and moving down to the logistics level (Gilbert, 2007).

The three levels approach to BSA comprises the organization, process, and job/performer levels. Table 5.1 shows the purpose of analyzing each of the three levels. Analysis at each level typically involves gathering information in order to build one or more system maps. These maps represent current state performance at that level and are used to identify issues and opportunities for improvement or change.

Organization Level

The purpose of analyzing the organization level is to (a) understand the environment in which the organization operates, (b) assess whether the organizational structure supports the achievement of organization-level strategic and tactical goals.

Organization-Environment Analysis

Brethower's (1982) TPS (see Figure 5.2) is a useful system mapping tool for understanding the environment in which the organization operates. The TPS can actually be used at any level of performance, but we will restrict our discussion of it to the organization level. Readers interested in an expanded description of the TPS across levels are encouraged to read Brethower (1982). The TPS is a seven-component system diagram that, once created, provides a standard, shared language and tool for identifying business problems, designing performance improvement interventions, and delivering results. For optimal organizational health, each TPS component must be in place, without deficiencies, and without negatively impacting any of the other system components (Brethower, 2000). Table 5.2 provides descriptions of each of the seven system components of the TPS: (1) mission/goal, (2) products/services, (3) customers/stakeholders, (4) external feedback (customer measures), (5) processing system, (6) inputs, and (7) internal feedback (processing system measures).

Rummler (Rummler & Brache, 2013) added two important components (see Table 5.2) to the organization/environment analysis: external environmental variables and competition. Rummler's expanded version of the TPS is referred to as the Super-System (see Figure 5.2). These components are important because organizations operate within the context of larger community and industry systems and, as such, are subject to demands placed on them by those larger systems. For example, organizations are often subject to economic fluctuations, government or industry regulations, cultural demands and shifts, and nature-based variables

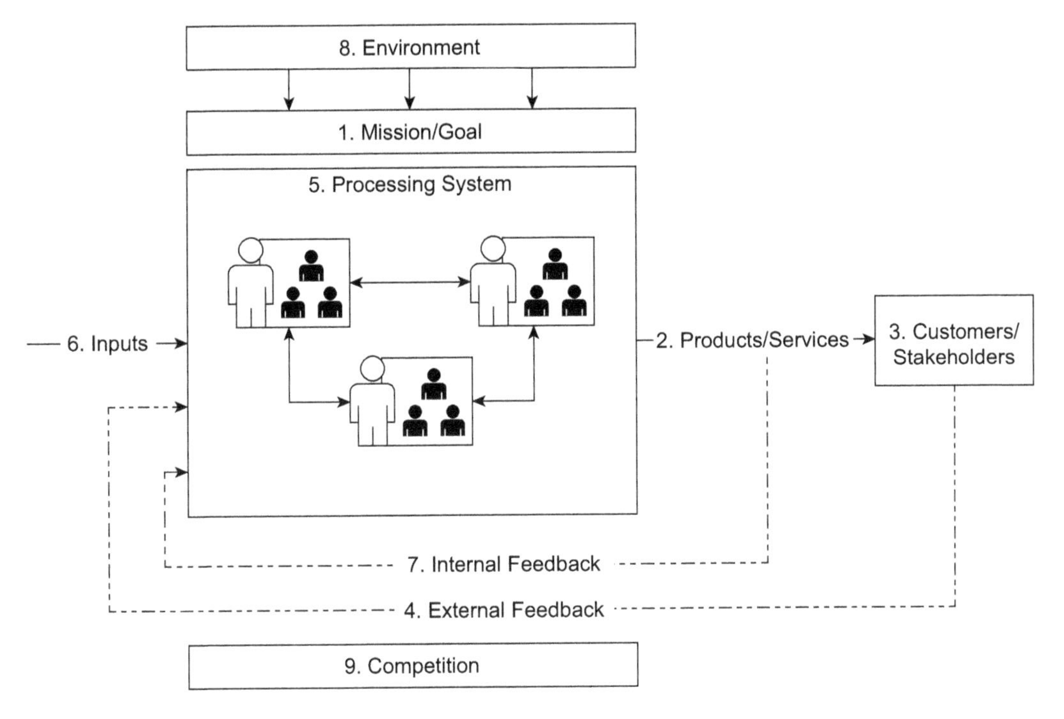

FIGURE 5.2 Total performance system/super-system.

TABLE 5.2
The TPS/Super System Components

COMPONENT	*QUESTIONS*	*DESCRIPTION*
1. MISSION/ GOAL	What is the overarching goal of the organization? What does it exist to accomplish/provide/do, for whom, and to what end?	All other system components exist to support the achievement of the mission and, therefore, any changes to the system should be functionally consistent (or "aligned") with the mission/goal.
2. PRODUCTS/ SERVICES	What are the products and/ or services produced by the organization?	Focusing on these organizational outputs helps you to see how the organization carries out its mission. Additionally, it is the sale of products/services to customers that creates the revenue required for organizational success.
3. CUSTOMERS/ STAKEHOLDERS	Who does the organization serve? Who are its customers? Who are the financial stakeholders of the organization?	Customers are those individuals who receive the product or service. Stakeholders are those who receive the financial outputs of the organization (e.g., parent company, stockholder, lending institution, employees). Without customers and stakeholders, the organization ceases to exist. Therefore, it is critical to assess this component early in your analysis.

(*Continued*)

TABLE 5.2
(Continued)

COMPONENT	*QUESTIONS*	*DESCRIPTION*
4. EXTERNAL FEEDBACK	How does the organization know if it is achieving its mission?	External feedback tells the organization the impact/value the product or service has on the customers and stakeholders. If customers are not satisfied, they might stop purchasing products or seeking the organization's services and the system will not thrive. If stakeholders are unhappy, they might begin to question their support of the organization.
5. PROCESSING SYSTEM	How does the organization convert inputs into outputs, in order to produce products/services that the customers value, in a way that satisfies the financial stakeholders?	Processing system effectiveness and efficiency is of critical concern, because organizational inputs and processing system activities are costs to the organization. The organization recoups its costs and makes at least a minimal profit (if it is a non-profit, more if it is a for-profit) by selling the outputs produced (products/services) to its customers.
6. INPUTS	What resources does the organization need in order to operate and produce the products/services?	The resources often include raw materials, capital, people, information, equipment & technology. According to Brethower (2000), inputs are a costly, but necessary, component of the organizational system.
7. INTERNAL FEEDBACK	How does the organization know if the processing system is performing effectively and efficiently?	Internal feedback provides information about processing system performance, and is a form of quality control. This feedback allows the organization to identify and correct system disconnects before the final products/services reach the customers, thus increasing the probability that system's products/services will be valued.
8. ENVIRONMENT	What external factors impact the organizational system (e.g., economy, government, culture, natural environment, marketplace)?	These variables tend to be outside the control of the organization, but can have a major effect on organizational performance. Organizational leaders should use environmental variables information to guide strategic & tactical decision-making.
9. COMPETITION	Who are the system's competitors? What other organizations are competing for customers and/or inputs/resources? What are the organization's current competitive advantages and disadvantages?	Organizational leaders should also use competitor analysis information to guide strategic & tactical decision-making.

such as climate, weather, and physical landscape. Additionally, organizations are subject to competition. Whether the organization is competing with another organization for customers, resources, or both, it is important to understand who those competitors are and in what areas the organization is outperforming or underperforming them.

Organizational Structure Analysis

Relationship mapping is a helpful tool for assessing whether the organization structure supports the achievement of organization-level strategic and tactical goals. Relationship

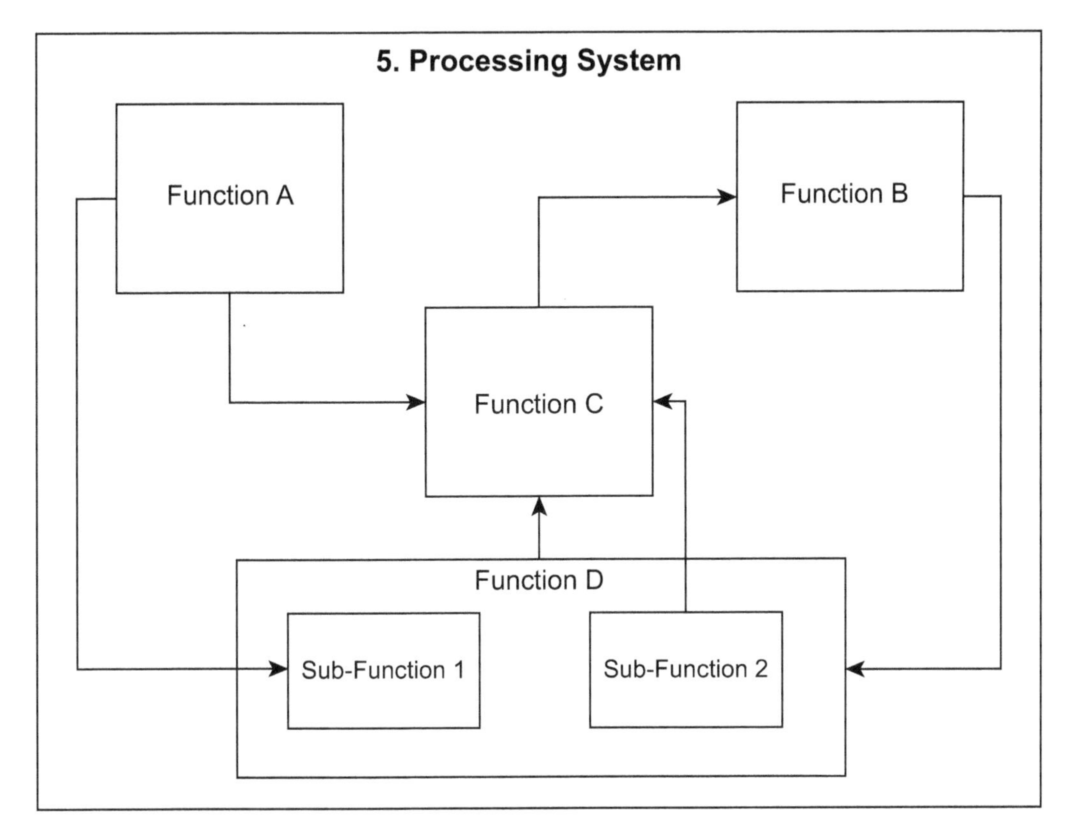

FIGURE 5.3 Relationship map.

mapping involves identifying (a) the various departments/functions of the organization, (b) the outputs of each of the functions and the receiving system/customers for each output, and (c) the inputs of each function and the suppliers of each input (see Figure 5.3). In this way, relationship mapping involves recognizing internal functions as suppliers and customers to one another and subsequently analyzing the relationships between and among those suppliers and customers. Doing this requires first defining the necessary input(s) for the customer function (what is needed from the supplier and what the customer's criteria for acceptable versus unacceptable are, typically in terms of quality, quantity, timeliness and/or cost). Next, define what is currently produced by the supplier function as an output and what the supplier's criteria for acceptable versus unacceptable are, again typically in terms of quality, quantity, timeliness, and/or cost). Goals and measures are created or adjusted to ensure that the needs of both the supplier function and the customer function are met and that the outputs are contributing to overall organizational goals. Of course, changes to functions require changes to behaviors. Therefore, organizational structure analysis will often lead to process analysis, where the individual steps and interlocking behavioral contingencies can be analyzed and improved.

Organization-Level Research

While BSA research at the organization level of performance is limited, there have been some studies that have demonstrated the effectiveness of intervention at this level (Brethower &

Wittkopp, 1988; Frederisken et al., 1985; Hyten, 2009; Strouse et al., 2004). One particularly interesting example of an organization-level study is Robertson and Pelaez (2016). They conducted an organization-level analysis and used the results to design and implement several solutions in a university setting. The Graduation Success Initiative (GSI) was created by Florida International University to address the student retention and delayed graduation of undergraduates, and other related issues that affected how much financial aid was provided to the university from the state. The authors used a systems approach to understand environmental variables that were critical to student success and align the organization both vertically and horizontally to solve the problems. From a vertical perspective, the GSI identified desired behaviors of students that were linked to graduation and retention and then aligned the behaviors of direct service providers to students all the way up the organization to administrators and trustees. This vertical systemic approach ensured that all behaviors of each level of the organization contributed to undergraduate success. From a horizontal perspective, the GSI analyzed different systems that influenced students across their educational lifecycle (e.g., admissions, advising, instruction) and determined changes that needed to be made to those systems to support the desired behavior of students. Through these behavioral systemic analyses and changes to critical functions, the GSI was able to substantially increase the on-time graduation rate for undergraduates.

Process Level

The purpose of analyzing the process level is to understand and improve workflow – how work gets done – within the processing system of the organization. In other words, process analysis involves analyzing how the organization converts inputs into outputs. This is typically accomplished by creating a cross-functional process map (Figure 5.4). A cross-functional process map shows the various functions involved in the process as individual rows, often called "swimlanes" (Rummler & Brache, 2013) within the map. Phases are typically listed across the top of the map, and steps are shown through a horizontal flowchart, with each step placed within the swimlane of the function responsible for completing that step. The overall map is read from left to right.

When analyzing processes, it is important to map them out exactly as they occur. This is referred to as "IS" or "Current State" process mapping (Rummler & Brache, 2013). Once mapped, the BSA practitioner analyzes the process to identify disconnects such as bottlenecks, redundant activities, rework loops, excessive reviews or approvals, or multiple variations on the process (Ramias, 2013). Once disconnects have been identified, a "SHOULD" or "Future State" process can be designed and implemented to address the issues.

Process vs. Function Analysis

Given that BSA practitioners typically start at the organization level and move down through the process and then performer levels from there, it might seem logical to move from analysis of the input-output relationships *between* departments/functions (organizational structure analysis, or relationship mapping) into an analysis of input-output relationships *within a specific department or function* (functional analysis). However, this is not the case. It is better to move directly from relationship mapping into an analysis of cross-functional processes. This is because attempting to improve single-function performance will likely lead to performance improvement within that function, but also to an overall sub-optimization of organizational performance as a whole – one part of the organization is improved at the expense of another part of the organization, which negatively impacts the organization as a whole (Rummler & Brache, 2013). It can also increase the likelihood that the organization is managed, analyzed,

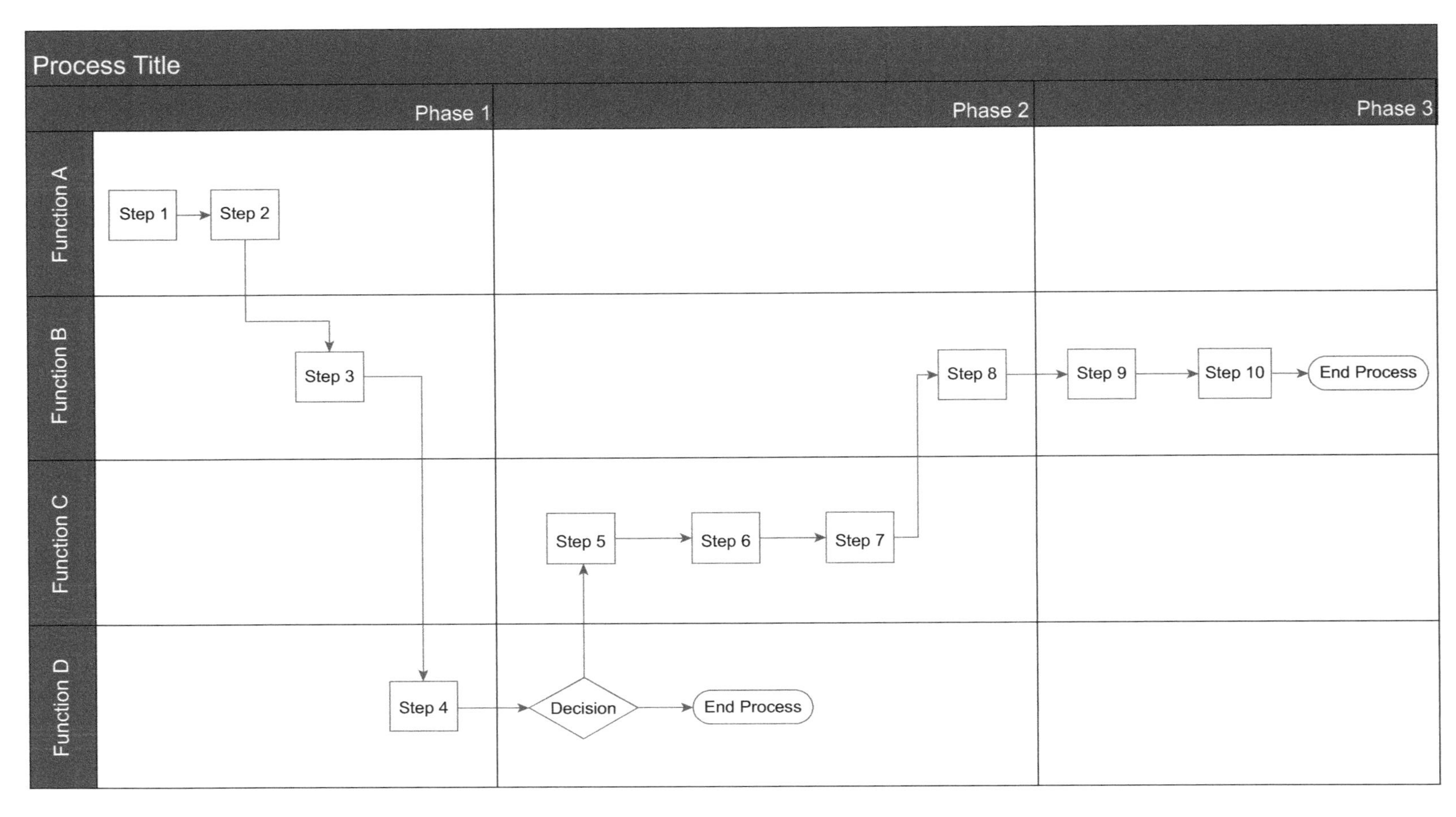

FIGURE 5.4 Process map.

and improved vertically, but not horizontally (see Vertical and Horizontal Alignment below). This leads to functional silos that operate independently of each other, as if they exist within a vacuum (which, of course, they do not). Even worse, it can lead to functions operating in direct competition with each other. This means that resources and rewards are allocated to functions, not processes, which can pit departments/functions against one another. Therefore, it is best to move from the organization level directly into the process level, and to analyze processes across functions.

Process-Level Research

Several studies have used process approaches to analyze and design interventions (Berglund & Ludwig, 2009; Clayton et al., 1997; Goomas, 2010, 2012a, 2012b; Hybza et al., 2013; Mihalic & Ludwig, 2009). A simple example of process analysis and optimization can be found in Kelley and Gravina (2018). The authors used process analyses and improvement to decrease the time that patients spent waiting for care in an emergency department (ED). The authors argued that longer wait times in EDs are associated with a number of adverse outcomes, including increased cost and reduced patient satisfaction scores. Because of these factors, hospital management was interested in decreasing the time it took for patients' entire visit (door-to-discharge) and the time it took for initial medical diagnostic tests to be completed (door-to-order), which were the two dependent variables of this study. During the assessment phase the authors reviewed the procedures through which patients were admitted and processed through the ED and mapped the process using an "IS" (current state) map. They found that a major bottleneck was the approval process for tests needed to diagnose patients. The nurses, who could see patients sooner than physicians, had to wait for the physicians to approve the order of diagnostic tests. By identifying the most common symptoms and the tests required for those symptoms, and arranging for pre-approval of those tests, they could lessen the bottleneck. After implementing the change, the ED saw a decrease in both door-to-order and door-to-discharge times. Providing performance feedback to nurses on adherence to the process change enhanced the intervention further. As a result of improved timeliness, the authors estimated a savings of $137,511.41 and an increase and stabilization of patient satisfaction scores.

Job/Performer Level

The purpose of analyzing the job/performer level (where the PM work occurs) is to understand and improve the (a) job characteristics; (b) task or job responsibility performance; and (c) antecedents, behaviors, and consequences of the individuals who work within the system. Because the scope of analysis at the job/performer level can vary so much, the BSA practitioner has many different choices when it comes to performance analysis tools.

Job Analysis

In traditional industrial/organizational psychology, job analysis (sometimes referred to as task analysis) refers to determining the activities that comprise a given job, the outputs/valued accomplishments produced by those activities, and the knowledge, skills, and abilities (KSAs) required to perform the activities successfully (Aamodt, 2016; Gatewood et al., 2016). In BSA, job analysis (sometimes referred to as the building a job model) also includes determining how those outputs/valued accomplishments are measured and the standards against which performance will be assessed, and may even include how the various accomplishments are weighted in terms of importance to overall job success (McGee & Diener, 2010; McGee & Diener-Ludwig, 2012; Rummler & Brache, 2013). Within BSA, job analysis is used to ensure that jobs are designed to support process and organization-level performance requirements (see Vertical and Horizontal Alignment).

Performance Analysis

A well-designed job is necessary but not sufficient for successful job performance. When the job model or task analysis shows that performance is occurring at below acceptable or desired levels, job-level performance analysis is required. The bulk of PM is dedicated to performance analysis and contingency analysis (see Behavior/Contingency Analysis); as such, several tools are available for each. At the level of job performance analysis, BSA (and PM) practitioners can choose from Abernathy's (2009, 2010) Performance Analysis/Performance Constraint Analysis, Austin's (2000) Performance Diagnostic Checklist (PDC), Binder's (1998) Six Boxes™, Gilbert's (1978, 2007) Behavior Engineering Model (BEM), Mager and Pipe's (1970) Performance Analysis Flow Diagram, and Rummler and Brache's (1996, 2013) Human Performance System (HPS), among others. While each tool differs slightly from the others in terms of organization (e.g., Austin's (2000) PDC is a checklist, while Mager and Pipe's (1970) Performance Analysis Flow Diagram is a flowchart), as well as the number of categories of sources of behavioral or system variation identified and the specific information or questions included under each category (e.g., Abernathy's (2009, 2010) Performance Constraint Analysis is broken into three general categories with three subcategories under each category, and two to three sources of variation under each subcategory, while Rummler and Brache's (1996) HPS is broken into six categories with one to four questions under each category), the general factors analyzed within each are: (a) job outputs/accomplishments, measures, and standards; (b) inputs, task support, and required resources; (c) consequences; (d) feedback; (e) KSAs, and selection and training systems; and (f) the performer's physical, mental, and emotional capacity (see Figure 5.5). Regardless of which one is chosen, these tools are best suited to investigating causes of performance gaps within a specific job responsibility (tasks and output/valued accomplishment) rather than overall job performance, though a tool can be used repeatedly if multiple gaps/deficiencies are found.

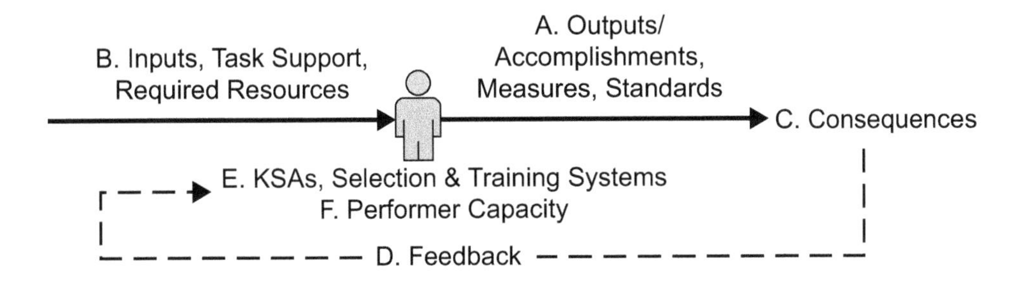

FIGURE 5.5 Job-level performance analysis diagram.

Behavior/Contingency Analysis

The final, and most molecular, analysis within BSA is the behavior or contingency analysis. As with job performance analysis, multiple tools are available, the most basic being a simple antecedent-behavior-consequence (ABC) analysis (Braksick, 2007; Daniels & Bailey, 2014). In an ABC analysis, the antecedents and consequences operating on a specific desired behavior and, when relevant, the competing, undesired behavior, are analyzed to determine the variables maintaining or suppressing behavior. Based on the results of the analysis, antecedents and consequences are added, altered, or removed as needed.

More sophisticated versions of the ABC analysis include Daniels and Bailey's (2014) PIC/NIC® (Positive/Negative, Immediate/Future, Certain/Uncertain) Analysis and Braksick's (2007) E-TIP™ (Effect, Timing, Importance, Probability) Analysis. In a PIC/NIC® Analysis, consequences are analyzed in terms of whether they are positive or negative, immediate or future, and certain or uncertain. Consequences that are immediate and certain are more powerful than those that are future and/or uncertain, so the goal is to design positive, immediate, and certain (PIC) consequences for desired behavior. The E-TIP™ Analysis is similar but also includes an analysis of the importance of the consequence from the performer's perspective.

Performer Level Research

Research on performer level analysis and interventions are numerous in the *Journal of Organizational Behavior Management* (Amigo et al., 2008; Doll et al., 2007; Eikenhout & Austin, 2005; Miller et al., 2014; Pampino et al., 2003; Rohn et al., 2002). LaFleur and Hyten (1995) used Gilbert's BEM as an assessment tool to determine performer level issues as they pertained to hotel banquet set up. The analysis uncovered several issues, including lack of formal training on procedures, no performance goals or performance feedback, lack of antecedents to prompt correct performance, suboptimal equipment location, and no consequences were in place to reinforce desired performance. The authors introduced a treatment package that consisted of optimal equipment set up, formal training, performance checklist development, job aids, goal setting, daily performance feedback and monetary bonuses for achieving quality performance. The treatment package resulted in near-perfect quality performance from staff.

VERTICAL AND HORIZONTAL ALIGNMENT

In addition to analyzing and improving performance at each of the three levels, it is critical to align performance across the levels to ensure everyone is working together to create organizational success. This requires both vertical and horizontal alignment. *Vertical alignment* refers to alignment of the goals, design, and management at the organization, process, and performer level (Rummler & Brache, 2013). This means that goals at the job-level support the achievement of goals at the process level, and the goals at the process-level support the achievement of organization-level goals and strategies. In order to achieve those goals, jobs must be designed to contribute to relevant processes effectively and efficiently, and processes must be designed to effectively and efficiently contribute to the production of the products and services that are sold to customers. Finally, Performance Management systems must be in place to ensure that supervisors are held accountable for supporting front-line worker performance, managers are held accountable for supporting supervisor performance, and leaders are held accountable for supporting manager performance.

Horizontal alignment refers to the alignment of goals, design, and management across jobs, processes, and functions. For example, if Job A produces outputs that are received by individuals within Job B, Job A is a supplier to Job B and Job B is a customer of Job A. Therefore, any job goals set for Job A must be based, in part, on the needs of its customer, Job B. The same is true of processes and functions throughout the organization. Viewing jobs, processes, and functions as internal supplier and customer relationships creates the necessary environment for building and maintaining horizontal alignment throughout the organization.

FUTURE TRENDS IN BSA

The world of work is always changing. A recent publication by Deloitte (2019) argued that workplace transformation occurs across three interrelated areas: work, workforce, and workplace. To achieve transformation across these three areas, organizations must consider the external factors driving change, the strategy or strategies they will employ to achieve the change (particularly digital strategy), and the work outputs required to achieve the strategy or strategies. Additionally, they must consider what work can be done by "smart machines, robots, and human-machine teams" (Deloitte, 2019, p. 5). For the work to be done by humans and human–machine teams, organizations must determine who can do the work and from where. They must also consider how the future of work and the workforce will affect and be affected by organizational design and leader and employee behavior, including relevant KSAs required for successful performance. Finally, Deloitte (2019) suggested that organizations must begin thinking about how their (a) work is delivered, (b) business is organized, (c) people experience work, and (d) work is enabled. Each of these strategies for addressing the future of work and the workplace can be approached from a BSA perspective. In this section, we will describe two specific future trends identified in Deloitte (2019) – digital transformation and strategic planning – that could be approached from a BSA perspective. We will additionally describe possible research in each of these areas.

BSA and Digital Transformation

The business and organizational landscape has changed significantly since the inception of behavioral systems analysis. Throughout the 2000s we have seen efforts to digitize, in other words, to convert analog information to digital (emails instead of memos, intranets instead of file cabinets). More recently, the exponential advancement of technology and the internet has created what is being called "digital transformation." According to the World Economic Forum (WEF), the combined value – to society and industry – of digital transformation until 2025 is estimated at $100 Trillion (World Economic Forum, 2016). An agreed-upon definition of digital transformation is elusive (Bloomberg, 2018), but generally it describes a change in the business structure to include digital technologies to enhance all aspects of the business (e.g., automation/robotics, machine learning, 3D printing, sensors, virtual and augmented reality, AI, blockchain, drones). What is uniform in all definitions of digital transformation is business strategy centered on customer engagement and feedback. In other words, addressing how customers have used, use, and will use products and services and incorporating user feedback into designing and delivering superior products or services.

In the modern business climate there are digitally native companies (Uber, Airbnb, Tesla) that have embraced digital transformation strategies – using technology to enhance the way they do business, and interact with their customers. In contrast to digital native organizations, there are legacy companies or analog companies that are established large

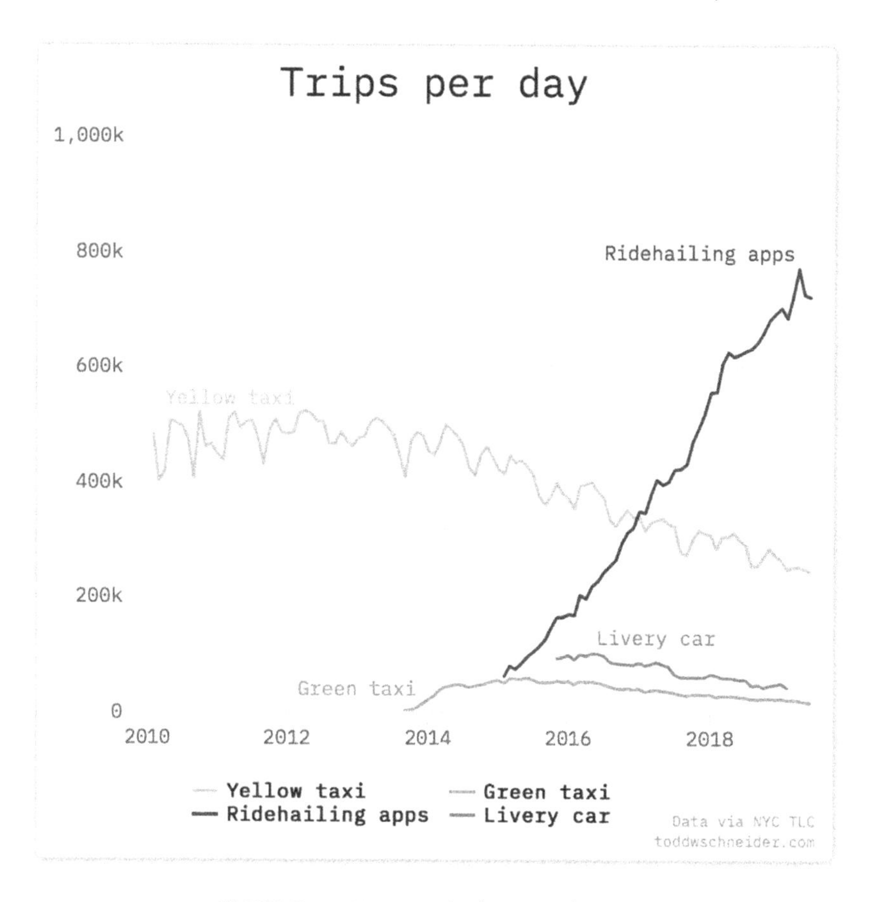

FIGURE 5.6 Trips per day by type of service.

organizations whose products and services can be disrupted by smaller, nimbler companies. Popular examples are ride-hailing companies and their disruption of taxicab services (e.g., Uber created a mobile phone application as an alternative to hailing a cab). Users can request a ride using their smartphones, enter the desired destination before the car arrives, and take care of payment all inside an application on their phone. The results of this application are less response effort and lower cost compared to hailing a taxi in the street, among other benefits. The result of this digital service has been a steady decrease in trips per day for established taxicab companies (see Figure 5.6). In an effort to remain relevant in the market, taxi companies have started to invest in applications to enhance their services (Wolford, 2019).

Large legacy companies can use BSA to understand how to adapt their businesses to be more flexible during the digital transformation era. By analyzing each level or their organization they can determine a digital strategy to transform the relevant parts, or the entire organization.

Organization Level

An organization-environment analysis can be useful in understanding how analog organizations can change to adapt to threats from smaller, digitally native organizations. Starting at a Super-System view, an organization can take into consideration where their competitors are excelling and develop a strategy to compete directly or decide on untapped markets or products that would differentiate themselves from competitors. Additionally, external environmental variables such as laws and policies surrounding data privacy could impact on how data is collected and used to create products and services. An assessment of emerging technologies and how they can fold into current or upcoming strategies would also inform at the organizational level. Another major environmental factor is the available workforce and whether or not they have the digital skills that are needed to deliver the strategy.

Given the size of many analog organizations an organization-level analysis could help determine the best method for pilot testing digital business models and ensuring the digital transformations are structured for success. The WEF (2016) suggests for analog organizations to develop digital innovation and experimentation at the edges of organizations as to not drastically change the core business. This strategy allows larger organizations to learn from digital transformation pilots to understand how the approach can be implemented at a larger scale.

Process Level

From a systems perspective, digital operating models need to be agile, flexible, and need to make decisions fast using reliable data sets. The existing processes and systems that are the core of the business need to reconcile cross-functionally with newer, leaner processes aimed at digital innovation (WEF, 2016). Christensen (1997) stated that a large barrier that existing firms struggle with is that their established business and process models that make them effective and efficient at their core business do not work for competing in the digital transformation space. Creating relationship maps between functions can help analog industries understand how innovative and agile processes work and how they are different from legacy practices. This information can inform changes within the organization to help shift from slow and effective processes to fast and efficient processes that deliver prototypes sooner. Internal processes in digital native organizations are also enhanced by analytics that prompt faster decision-making. Process analyses can help determine how analytics are currently used for decision-making, where those data come from, and the effects of certain decision-making processes.

Additionally, the organization must address how internal systems of the organization reconcile with digital initiatives such as automation. Automation, the use of robotic or automatic equipment in a production process, can be traced back to such early examples as the loom replacing textile workers in the 19th century and farming equipment taking the place of horses around the turn of the 20th century. Automation is excellent at performing "routine" tasks, that is, tasks that can be explicitly codified. Examples of "routine tasks" are bookkeeping, clerical tasks (sorting and computing data), and repetitive operations tasks (moving heavy car parts from one line to another). Automation is beneficial in these scenarios because it can outperform human counterparts in efficiency and accuracy, and does not succumb to repetitive stress injuries. Automation is, however, not well-suite to "non-routine" tasks such as flexibility, judgment and common sense (Autor, 2015). While it is easy to bemoan automation as a "job killer," it is more accurate to think of it as a "job transformer." Some jobs will, inevitably, be replaced. But as Bowen (1966) asserted, "the basic fact is that technology eliminates jobs, not work" (p. 9). This means that the type of jobs will be different, but there will be jobs. With these new jobs will come new KSA requirements, which means that new behaviors will have to be trained and maintained. Of course, this is an area that behavior analysts excel at. However, understanding which functions, processes, jobs, and KSAs will be affected, and how requires taking a broader view of performance than basic Performance Management of individual behavioral contingencies. In other words, this challenge will likely need to be met with a BSA approach.

Job/Performer Level

An analysis at the job/performer level could indicate changes in job description or role, and the environmental variables (antecedents, behaviors, and consequences) that must be in place to ensure individuals succeed in digital business models. For instance, an analysis of behavioral contingencies could help to illustrate how behavioral requirements, and therefore contingency requirements, will need to change to support switching from an analog work task to an agile, digital model. The analysis may uncover changes that need to be made in antecedents (training to increase digital skillset), behavior (what are the pinpointed behaviors that are aligned to the goal of the process and organization), and consequences (natural or designed) of working in a different system.

Digital Transformation Research Questions and Summary

The area of digital transformation not only provides opportunities for the practice of BSA, but also for additional BSA research. For example:

- Does the use of a particular pre-intervention assessment tool result in more effective and/or efficient behavioral interventions than either a different tool or no tool?
- Do process analysis and IBC interventions produce better performance outcomes (likely assessed through measures of aggregate products in addition to individual behavioral products) than individual performer analysis and change efforts? Do these two approaches produce greater effects when combined?
- Does an organization-environment analysis identify change opportunities or requirements that, if implemented, allow an organization to adapt more effectively and efficiently (likely assessed through profit and loss, products/services sold, or other business-level measures) than an organization that does not base changes on the results of such an analysis?

Given the economic impact of digital transformation, a systemic approach can provide opportunities for thoughtful analysis of all levels of an organization. A systems approach can help organizations assess digital competition and interpret laws and policies, which can affect how work is completed and goals are met. BSA can also help analog organizations adopt digital business models or processes, or to help digitally native organizations assess their current processes for enhancements.

BSA and Strategic Planning

According to the Balanced Scorecard Institute, strategic planning is a process undertaken at the leadership level to:

> [a] set priorities, [b] focus energy and resources, [c] strengthen operations, [d] ensure that employees and other stakeholders are working toward common goals, [e] establish agreement around intended outcomes/results, and [f] assess and adjust the organization's direction in response to a changing environment. ("Strategic Planning Basics," n.d.).

In their book *The Balanced Scorecard*, Kaplan and Norton (1996) asserted that 90% of organizations fail to implement their strategies successfully. Rummler and Brache (2013) argued that the reason for this failure is a lack of pre-planning around how the strategies should be implemented. Building BSA into the strategic planning process has the potential to produce a set of strategic goals that can be cascaded all the way down to the performer level. Additionally, it allows for identification of (a) the systems factors that will affect and be affected by those strategic goals, (b) how they will affect or be affected by the goals, and (c) the goals, design, and management changes that will need to occur at each level of performance to achieve the goals. An excellent means of managing performance related to cascaded goals is through the use of performance scorecards and organization-wide incentive systems (Abernathy, 2010, 2014; Daniels & Bailey, 2014). Figure 5.7 shows how one BSA tool, the Super-System diagram can encapsulate the six aims of the strategic planning process.

In typical strategic planning, the organization conducts a SWOT (Strengths, Weaknesses, Opportunities, and Threats) analysis to achieve these aims (Chermack & Kasshanna, 2007). Unfortunately, the structure of the SWOT analysis is typically left up to the organization (or consultant, if the organization has paid to bring one in for strategic planning purposes) and often results in a subjective, vague list with little regard to *how* to address the identified strengths, weaknesses, opportunities, and threats. One way to improve the SWOT analysis is to determine, in advance, how the SWOT components will be identified. We have found the organization-level tools (Super-System and Relationship Mapping) to be excellent sources of this information.

In the SWOT analysis, strengths and weaknesses are assessed by considering the organization's current competitive advantages and disadvantages, while opportunities and threats are assessed by looking at the organization's future "by accounting for the factors that exist in the external environment" (Chermack & Kasshanna, 2007, p. 384). In BSA, information regarding external environment factors is gathered while building the Super-System Map (see Figure 5.7), so the opportunities and threats should be easy to identify if this hasn't already been done as part of that analysis. We can identify the organization's current competitive advantages and disadvantages (strengths and weaknesses) by examining: (a) the products/services the organization sells to its customers; (b) the departments or functions involved in the design, development, and delivery of each product or service; (c) how the product or service is better or worse than that of the competitors; (d) what the organization does differently (either for the better or worse) from its competitors in the design, development, and delivery of the product/service; (e) and in what ways the organization excels or fails internally at supporting the product/service and its customers. This can be accomplished through reviewing the current Super-System and Relationship Maps and comparing those findings to what is known about the organization's top three competitors. Organizations could also consider conducting a formal competitor analysis to gather competitor information, but that is beyond the scope of this paper and is not always necessary – a surprising amount of information is available on the internet and through word-of-mouth.

Once we have a SWOT list based on an actual analysis of the organization rather than an unstructured brainstorming session, we still need to determine how to address the identified strengths, weaknesses, opportunities, and threats. Another popular tool from strategic planning, the TOWS (threats, opportunities, weaknesses, and strengths) analysis is useful for this step (Weihrich, 1982). In a TOWS analysis, we use the information gathered in the SWOT analysis to identify specific strategies for improvement or growth. While it does not require the use of a BSA tool, TOWS analysis can be made more effective by using BSA to first complete the SWOT analysis. Armed with the results of the SWOT, determine specific strategies by identifying how the organization can use its strengths to minimize threats and take advantage of opportunities and how it can improve weaknesses by taking advantage of opportunities and eliminate weaknesses to avoid threats. The more specific the results of the SWOT analysis, the easier it will be to identify these strategies.

The next step in the strategic planning process is the creation of strategic goals. We convert the TOWS strategies into specific goals. These goals must be actionable for implementation

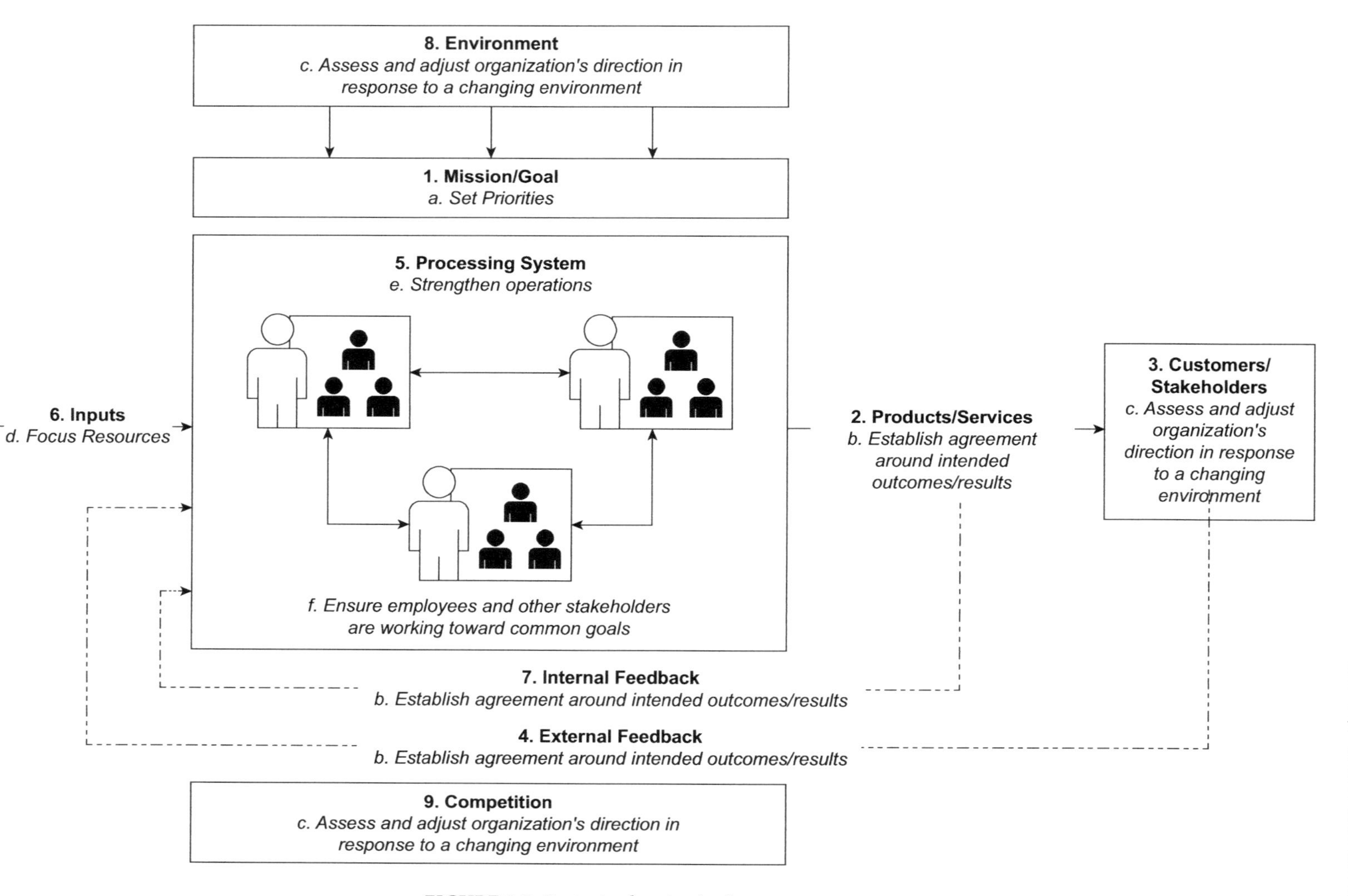

FIGURE 5.7 Strategic planning in the super-system.

to be successful, or even possible. Therefore, it is important to write SMART strategic goals: Specific, Measurable, Accountable, Realistic, and Time-bound (Doran, 1981). To write a SMART strategic goal, start by stating the direction of change (e.g., increase or decrease), then write out the accomplishment, followed by the desired amount of change and the deadline by when the change will have occurred (in strategic planning, this is typically three to five years out). Finally, to ensure accountability, assign an owner (only one owner – once two people are responsible for something, nobody is responsible for it) for that goal. This person is not expected to take all of the necessary actions to achieve the goal; rather, this is the person who will champion that goal and ensure that the actions are taken, when they need to be taken, by whoever needs to take them.

This is the point at which most strategic planning stops (though many organizations will have included a financial analysis of the goals as well). But, as stated previously, Rummler and Brache (2013) argued that this is the reason for strategic plan failure. We still have to determine how to achieve those goals. This is a critical, and typically missing, phase in the strategic planning process.

As previously stated, strategic goals are typically written three to five years out. Implementation planning requires (a) setting closer-in goals (organizational and cross-functional short-term and mid-term goals aligned with the long-term strategic goals), (b) establishing ongoing measures, and (c) determining specific actions to be taken. We start by breaking down the timeline for goal achievement. For any five-year strategic goals, determine where the organization will need to be at Years 4, 3, and 2 in order to hit the Year 5 goal. For any three-year strategic goals, determine where the organization will need to be at 30 months (Year 2.5), 24 months (Year 2), and 18 months (Year 1.5). These goals will likely be the same as the original strategic goal, except with smaller amounts and closer-in deadlines. Next, determine quarterly goals for Year 1 (now through one year from now). At this stage, the goals should comprise planning and implementation accomplishments rather than simply smaller amounts of the main accomplishment.

At this point, we have more actionable goals, but still no implementation plan (tactics) for reaching those goals. To determine tactics, we need to understand how the strategic goals impact various organizational system components and what changes, if any, will need to be made to those components and the system as a whole to support goal achievement. We cannot hope to achieve a newly set goal without making changes to what we are doing and, likewise, we cannot hope to achieve a strategic goal without making changes to our organizational system. What we have always done in our current organizational system will only produce more of what we are already getting; it will not produce something new. Once again, we will need to review the organization's Super-System and Relationship Maps.

We start this final phase of the analysis by asking how the strategic goal will impact, and be impacted, by new and existing customers and what system changes will be required to address or support that impact. We repeat this line of questioning for the organization's products/services, departments/functions, and inputs/resources. Once we understand the impact and required changes within these system components, we can determine specific actions to take to get started. We already have an end-of-year-one goal, so at this stage we are simply breaking down the first quarter goals into monthly (could even do weekly or daily) goals. Additionally, the level of specificity attained will allow the strategic goal owner and the rest of the leadership team to begin determining specific strategic goal team members. These are the individuals who will take on much of the action items related to researching and implementing the system changes.

We recommend that the leadership team meet monthly to discuss progress on the strategic goals and brainstorm solutions to any issues that arise. Additionally, either this team or the individual strategic goal teams should build a new quarterly plan in the third month of the current quarter throughout the course of the strategic plan implementation. This will ensure the level of plan specificity required for a successful implementation.

Strategic Planning Research Questions and Summary

As with digital transformation, the area of strategic planning not only provides opportunities for the practice of BSA, but also for needed BSA research. For example:

- Does having a strategic *implementation* plan increase the likelihood of goal achievement over simply having strategic goals?
- Does a BSA approach to strategic planning increase the likelihood of goal achievement over a non-BSA approach to strategic planning?

It should be noted that while we have presented digital transformation and strategic planning separately, digital transformation should actually be *part of* strategic planning. Because digital transformation is just that – an organization-wide transformation – it requires significant planning, resource allocation, behavior change, and Performance Management. Of course, there are other work trends that could be analyzed using BSA. We encourage the readers to identify trends in their own organizations and how a BSA approach might allow them to better understand and manage the performances affected by those trends.

CONCLUSION

While much work has been done in the area of BSA, we hope that this chapter makes clear that much more can and should be done to grow this OBM approach to performance analysis and improvement in complex behavioral systems. The extension of BSA applications to cover such trends as digital transformation and strategic planning is one opportunity for growth. Additionally, while some research exists to support the use of BSA in organizations, this research is limited in comparison to the PM research base (Johnson et al., 2014). We have provided several potential questions that BSA researchers could investigate. Further analysis of BSA concepts, such as metacontingencies and IBCs, coupled with research applying these concepts could help to demonstrate a better relationship between BSA, general systems theory, and behavior analysis. Finally, our examples have primarily focused on the application of BSA by consultants, primarily through the lens of the external consultant. Many organizations rely on internal experts for performance analysis and improvement. Rummler (2004) described the unique difficulties and opportunities present for the internal "consultant" and growth of BSA will require further investigation of these difficulties and opportunities, along with suggestions for reducing the difficulties and increasing the likelihood of capitalizing on the opportunities.

STUDY QUESTIONS

1. In what ways are both OBM and HPT rooted in Behavior Analysis?
2. Explain why it isn't accurate to describe BSA as though it were an intervention.
3. What are three of the levels of the multi-level BSA approach (in your own words)? How is this multi-level approach distinct from PM?
4. Distinguish between vertical and horizontal alignment.
5. What is the point where most strategic planning stops? (Hint: it is also argued that this is the reason why strategic planning may fail.)

REFERENCES

Aamodt, M.G. (2016). *Industrial/organizational psychology: An applied approach* (8th ed.). Cengage Learning.

Abernathy, W.B. (2009). Walden Two revisited: Optimizing behavioral systems. *Journal of Organizational Behavior Management, 29*, 175–192.

Abernathy, W.B. (2010, May/June). A comprehensive performance analysis and improvement method. *Performance Improvement, 49*(5), 5–17.

Abernathy, W.B. (2014). Beyond the Skinner box: The design and management of organization-wide performance systems. *Journal of Organizational Behavior Management, 34*(4), 235–254.

Addison, R., Haig, C., & Kearny, L. (2009). *Performance architecture*. Pfeiffer.

Amigo, S., Smith, A., & Ludwig, T. (2008). Using task clarification, goal setting, and feedback to decrease table busing times in a franchise pizza restaurant. *Journal of Organizational Behavior Management, 28*, 176–187. doi:10.1080/01608060802251106

Austin, J. (2000). Performance analysis and performance diagnostics. In J. Austin &
J.E. Carr (Eds.), *Handbook of applied behavior analysis* (pp. 321–349). Context Press.

Autor, D.H. (2015). Why are there still so many jobs? The history and future of workplace automation. *Journal of Economic Perspectives, 29*(3), 3–30.

Baer, D.M., Wolf, M.M., & Risley, T.R. (1968). Some current dimensions of applied behavior analysis. *Journal of Applied Behavior Analysis, 1*, 91–97.

Bailey, J. & Burch, M. (2002). *Ethics for behavior analysts: 2nd expanded edition*. Routledge.

Balanced Scorecard Institute (n.d.). Strategic planning basics. https://strategymanage.com/resources/strategic-planning-basics/

Berglund, K.M. & Ludwig, T.D. (2009). Approaching error-free customer satisfaction through process change and feedback systems. *Journal of Organizational Behavior Management, 29*(1), 19–46.

Binder, C. (1998, July/August). The Six Boxes™: A descendent of Gilbert's Behavior Engineering Model. *Performance Improvement, 37*(6), 48–52.

Bloomberg, J. (2018, April 29). Digitization, digitalization, and digital transformation: Confuse them at your peril. https://www.forbes.com/sites/jasonbloomberg/2018/04/29/digitization-digitalization-and-digital-transformation-confuse-them-at-your-peril/#1ef63c82f2c7

Bowen, H.R. (Chairman) (1966). Technological change and unemployment. *Report of the National Commission on Technology, Automation, and Economic Progress: Volume I*, (pp. 9–31). US Government Printing Office.

Braksick, L.W. (2007). *Unlock behavior, unleash profits* (2nd ed.). McGraw-Hill, Inc.

Brethower, D. (1972). *Behavior analysis in business and industry: A Total Performance System*. Behaviordelia.

Brethower, D.M. (1982). The total performance system. In R.M. O'Brien, A.M. Dickinson, & M.P. Rosow (Eds.), *Industrial behavior modification: A management handbook* (pp. 350–369). Pergamon.

Brethower, D.M. (2000). A systematic view of enterprise: Adding value to performance. *Journal of Organizational Behavior Management, 20*, 165–190.

Brethower, D.M. (2002). Behavioral systems analysis: Fundamental concepts and cutting edge applications. https://behavior.org/wp-content/uploads/2018/05/BSA-Brethower-PartV.pdf (Accessed: July 31, 2019)

Brethower, D.M. & Wittkopp, C.J. (1988). Performance engineering. *Journal of Organizational Behavior Management, 9*(1), 83–104. doi:10.1300/ J075v09n01_07

Chermack, T.J. & Kasshanna, B.K. (2007) The use and misuse of SWOT analysis and implications for HRD professionals. *Human Resource Development International, 10*(4), 383–399.

Christensen, C. (1997). *The Innovator's dilemma: When new technologies cause great firms to fail*. Harvard Business Review Press

Clayton, M.C., Mawhinney, T.C., Luke, D.E., & Cook, H.G. (1997). Improving the management of overtime costs through decentralized controls: Managing an organizational metacontingency. *Journal of Organizational Behavior Management, 17*(2), 77–98.

Corrigan, R.E. (1964). Programmed instruction as a systems approach to education. In G.D. Ofiesh, & W.C. Meierhenry (Eds.), *Trends in Programmed Instruction*. National Education Association and National Society for Programmed Instruction.

Daniels, A.C. & Bailey, J.S. (2014). *Performance management: Changing behavior that drives organizational effectiveness* (5th ed.). Performance Management Publications.

Deloitte (January, 2019). *Future of work: An introduction*. https://www2.deloitte.com/global/en/pages/human-capital/topics/future-of-work.html

Dickinson, A.M. (2000). The historical roots of organizational behavior management in the private sector: The 1950s–1980s. *Journal of Organizational Behavior Management, 20*(3–4), 9–58.

Doll, J., Livesey, J., McHaffie, E., & Ludwig, T.D. (2007). Keeping an uphill edge: Managing cleaning behaviors at a ski shop. *Journal of Organizational Behavior Management, 27*(3), 41–60. doi:10.1300/J075v27n03_04

Doran, G.T. (1981). There's a S.M.A.R.T. way to write management's goals and objectives. *Management Review, 70*(11), 35–36.

Eikenhout, N. & Austin, J. (2005). Using goals, feedback, reinforcement, and a performance matrix to improve customer service in a large department store. *Journal of Organizational Behavior Management, 24*(3), 27–62. doi:10.1300/J075v24n03_02

Frederisken, L.W., Riley, A.W., & Myers, J.B. (1985). Matching technology and organizational structure: A case study in white collar productivity improvement. *Journal of Organizational Behavior Management, 6*(3), 59–80.

Gatewood, R.D., Field, H.S., & Barrick, M. (2016). *Human resource selection* (8th ed.). Cengage Learning.

Gilbert, T.F. (1978). *Human competence: Engineering worthy performance.* McGraw-Hill.

Gilbert, T.F. (2007). *Human competence: Engineering worthy performance* (Tribute ed.). San Pfeiffer.

Glenn, S.S. & Malott, M.E. (2004). Complexity and selection: Implications for organizational change. *Behavior and Social Issues, 13*(2), 89–106.

Goomas, D.T. (2010). Replacing voice input with technology that provided immediate visual and audio feedback to reduce employee errors. *Journal of Organizational Behavior Management, 30*(1), 26–37.

Goomas, D.T. (2012a). The impact of wireless technology on loading trucks at an auto parts distribution center. *Journal of Organizational Behavior Management, 32*(3), 242–252.

Goomas, D.T. (2012b). Immediate feedback on accuracy and performance: The effects of wireless technology on food safety tracking at a distribution center. *Journal of Organizational Behavior Management, 32*(4), 320–328.

Hall, B.L. (1980). Editorial. *Journal of Organizational Behavior Management, 2*(3), 145–150.

Hawkins, R.P., Chase, P.N., & Scotti, J.R. (1993). Applied behavior analysis at West Virginia University: A brief history. *Journal of Applied Behavior Analysis, 26*(4), 573–582.

Hybza, M.M., Stokes, T.F., Hayman, M., & Schatzberg, T. (2013). Increasing medicaid revenue generation for services by school psychologists. *Journal of Organizational Behavior Management, 33*(1), 55–67.

Hyten, C. (2009). Strengthening the focus on business results: The need for systems approaches in organizational behavior management. *Journal of Organizational Behavior Management, 29*, 87–107. doi:10.1080/01608060902874526

Johnson, D.A., Casella, S.E., McGee, H., & Lee, S.C. (2014). The use and validation of preintervention diagnostic tools in organizational behavior management. *Journal of Organizational Behavior Management, 34*(2), 104–121.

Kaplan, R. & Norton, D. (1996). *The balanced scorecard.* Harvard Business Review Press.

Kaufman, R.A. (1964). The systems approach to programming. In G.D. Ofiesh, & W.C. Meierhenry (Eds.), Trends *in Programmed Instruction.* National Education Association and National Society for Programmed Instruction.

Kelley, D.P. & Gravina, N. (2018). Every second counts: Using process improvement and performance feedback to improve patient flow in an emergency department. *Journal of Organizational Behavior Management, 38*(2–3), 234–243.

Krapfl, J. (1982). Behavior management in state mental health systems. *Journal of Organizational Behavior Management, 3*(3), 91–105.

LaFleur, T. & Hyten, C. (1995). Improving the quality of hotel banquet staff performance. *Journal of Organizational Behavior Management, 15*(1–2), 69–93.

Mager, R.F. & Pipe, P. (1970). *Analyzing performance problems or "you really oughta wanna."* Fearon Publishers.

Maley, R.F. & Harshbarger, D. (1974). *Behavior analysis and systems analysis: An integrated approach to mental health.* Behaviordelia.

Malott, M.E. (2003). *Paradox of organizational change.* Context Press.

Malott, M.E. (2016). Selection of business practices in the midst of evolving complexity. *Journal of Organizational Behavior Management, 36*(2–3), 103–122.

Malott, R.W. (1974). A Behavioral systems approach to the design of human services. In R.F. Maley & D. Harshbarger (Eds.), *Behavior analysis and systems analysis: An integrated approach to mental health* (pp. 318–343). Behaviordelia.

Malott, R.W. (2016). Why is Dick so weird? In R.D. Holdsambeck & H.S. Pennypacker (Eds.) *Behavioral science: Tales of inspiration, discovery and service* (pp. 289–318). Cambridge Center for Behavioral Studies

Malott, M.E. & Glenn, S.S. (2006). Targets of intervention in cultural and behavioral change. *Behavior and Social Issues, 15*(1), 31–56.

McGee, H.M. & Diener, L.H. (2010). Behavioral systems analysis in health and human services. *Behavior Modification, 34*(5), 415–442.

McGee, H.M. & Diener-Ludwig, L.H. (2012). An introduction to behavioral systems analysis for rehabilitation agencies. *Journal of Rehabilitation Administration, 36*(2), 59–71.

Mihalic, M.T. & Ludwig, T.D. (2009). Behavioral system feedback measurement failure: Sweeping quality under the rug. *Journal of Organizational Behavior Management, 29*(2), 155–174.

Miller, M.V., Carlson, J., & Sigurdsson, S.O. (2014). Improving treatment integrity in a human service setting using lottery-based incentives. *Journal of Organizational Behavior Management, 34*, 29–38.

Molenda, M., Pershing, J.R., & Reigeluth, C.M. (1996). Designing instructional systems. In R. L. Craig (Ed.), *The ASTD training and development handbook: a guide to human resource development* (pp. 266–293). McGraw-Hill.

Ofiesh, G.D. & Meierhenry, W.C. (1964). *Trends in Programmed Instruction.* National Education Association and National Society for Programmed Instruction.

Pampino, R.N., Heering, P.W., Wilder, D.A., Barton, C.G., & Burson, L.M. (2003). The use of the performance diagnostic checklist to guide intervention selection in an independently owned coffee shop. *Journal of Organizational Behavior Management, 23*(2/3), 5–20.

Pershing, J.A. (2006). *Handbook of human performance technology: Principles, practices, and potential.* Pfeiffer.

Poling, A., Dickinson, A.M., Austin, J., & Normand, M.P. (2000). Basic behavioral research and organizational behavior management. In J. Austin & J.E. Carr (Eds.), *Handbook of applied behavior analysis* (pp. 295–320). Context Press.

Ramias, C. (2013, March). Seeing a process: The power of visual analysis. *BPTrends.* http://www.bptrends.com/bpt/wp-content/publicationfiles/03-05-2013-COL-Perf%20Improvement-Seeing%20the%20Process-Ramias-Wilkins-v1.pdf

Robertson, D.L. & Pelaez, M. (2016). Behavior analytic concepts and change in a large metropolitan research university: The Graduation Success Initiative. *Journal of Organizational Behavior Management, 36*(2–3), 123–153.

Rohn, D., Austin, J., & Lutrey, S. M. (2002). Using feedback and performance accountability to decrease cash register shortages. *Journal of Organizational Behavior Management, 22*(1), 33–46.

Rummler, G.A. (2004). *Serious performance consulting: According to Rummler.* International Society for Performance Improvement.

Rummler, G.A. (2007). The past is prologue: An eyewitness account of HPT. *Performance Improvement, 46*(10), 5–9. doi:10.1002/pfi.166

Rummler, G.A. & Brache, A.P. (1996). *Improving performance: How to manage the white space on the organization chart* (1st ed.). Jossey-Bass.

Rummler, G.A. & Brache, A.P. (2013). *Improving performance: How to manage the white space on the organization chart* (3rd ed.). Jossey-Bass.

Rummler, G.A., Ramias, A., & Rummler, R.A. (2009). *White space revisited: creating value through process.* John Wiley & Sons.

Skinner, B. F. (1953). *Science and human behavior.* Simon and Schuster.

Skinner, B. F. (1954). The science of learning and the art of teaching. *Harvard Educational Review, 24,* 86–97.

Skinner, B.F. (1958). Teaching machines. *Science, 128*(3330), 969–977.

Sigurdsson, S.O. & McGee, H.M. (2015). Organizational behavior management: systems analysis. In H. Roane, J.E. Ringdahl, & T. Falcomata (Eds.), *Clinical and organizational applications of applied behavior analysis* (pp. 627–647). Academic Press.

Smith, R.G. (1964). Programmed instruction and the technology of training. In G.D. Ofiesh & W.C. Meierhenry (Eds.), *Trends in Programmed Instruction.* National Education Association and National Society for Programmed Instruction.

Strouse, M.C., Carroll-Hernandez, T.A., Sherman, J.A., & Sheldon, J.B. (2004). Turning over turnover: The evaluation of a staff scheduling system in a community-based program for adults with developmental disabilities. *Journal of Organizational Behavior Management, 23*(2–3), 45–63.

Tosti, D.T. & Kaufman, R. (2007). Who is the "real" father of HPT?. *Performance Improvement, 46*(7), 5–8.

Von Bertalanffy, L. (December, 1972). The history and status of general systems theory. *The Academy of Management Journal, 15*(4), 407–426.

Weihrich, H. (1982), The TOWS matrix: a tool for situational analysis. *Long Range Planning, 15*(2), 54–66.

Wine, B. & Pritchard, J.K. (2018). Behavior analysis and organizations. In B. Wine & J.K. Pritchard (Eds.) *Organizational Behavior Management: The essentials.* Hedgehog Publishers.

Wolford, S. (2019, April 2). *Local cab companies look for ways to compete with rideshare.* https://news3lv.com/news/local/local-cab-companies-look-for-ways-to-compete-with-rideshare

World Economic Forum. (2016). *Digital transformation of Industries: Digital enterprise* [White paper]. http://reports.weforum.org/digital-transformation/wp-content/blogs.dir/94/mp/files/pages/files/dti-digital-enterprise-white-paper (Accessed August 5, 2019)

6

Paradox of Organizational Change

A Selectionist Approach to Improving Complex Systems[1]

Maria E. Malott

For many years, I have seen the frustration generated by the failure to succeed at organizational change. Initiatives are launched, people mobilized, resources allocated, and energy invested. With time, many of these initiatives are ignored. In the end, real change has not taken place. At best, what remains are partial records and distorted memories of the initiatives, unused technology, process documentation, or back-and-forth accusations of unmet promises. The underlying problems continue. Like a vicious cycle, similar initiatives are launched later to tackle the same underlying problems, just with different names and different players. Once again, commitments and resources are invested, and the cycle continues. Those who witness this repeated pattern over time grow tired, skeptical, and cynical of new change initiatives. Although they feel pressed to go along with the changes, they continue performing their jobs as they have all along.

In part the vicious cycle of organizational change is due to a lack of understanding of how systems evolve. Systems have paradoxical properties. They are complex and simple; dynamic and constant; chaotic and orderly. Let me explain these inherent contradictions.

Complex and Simple

Organizations have many parts. They are complex. Glenn and Malott (2004) described three types of complexity. One type consists of whole-part relations. Divisions contain departments, which contain processes, which contain sub-processes, and so on. Another type is component complexity. It refers to the number of units a process has. For instance, obtaining a mortgage requires relatively more steps than making a bank deposit. The third type is environmental complexity. Many factors from outside the boundaries of the organization affect its evolution. Other types of complexity can be identified. However, at the core of all organizations' complexities there are relatively simpler elements, the behavior of each individual.

Dynamic and Constant

Organizations and their parts are usually open systems with permeable borders. Their components are continuously interacting in nonlinear fashion with elements from their internal and external environments. But there is a constant source of their dynamic interactions: "contingencies of selection" (Glenn, 2004; Glenn et al., 2016). The behavior of

DOI: 10.4324/9781003198949-6

individuals is "occasioned and modified by the behavior of other individuals" (Glenn, 2004, p. 134). Glenn and Malott (2004) put it this way: "Relations between characteristics of organisms or behavior and their environments determine future frequencies of those characteristics" (p. 99).

Chaotic and Orderly

Organizations might seem in disarray because many unexpected events and relations develop unpredictably. "It is simply a miracle that the newspaper is out every day," a friend working for a news outlet once told me. He meant the process seemed out of control: unexpected events, last-minute changes, and general confusion were taking place continually. The daily edition might have included unplanned stories, might have been delayed, might have had errors. Yet, it was released every day. In the middle of the chaos, there is order. Processes more or less recur.

This chapter offers a method of organizational change that can end the vicious cycle of ineffective interventions. The method is based on the culturo-behavioral systems model presented in *Paradox of Organizational Change* (Malott, 2001, 2003). The model assumes that organizations are complex, dynamic, and chaotic, and it offers a systematic approach to change based on principles of environmental selection. The chapter is divided into two sections: first, it describes the model and illustrates it with an example; second, it offers guidelines for its application.

CULTURO-BEHAVIORAL SYSTEMS MODEL

The culturo-behavioral systems model (C-B Systems Model) centers on the metacontingency as a basic unit to analyze and improve organizations. A metacontingency consists of "a contingent relation between 1) recurring interlocking behavioral contingencies having an aggregate product and 2) selecting environmental events or conditions" (Glenn et al., 2016, p. 13). (For analyses of metacontingencies, also see Glenn, 1988, 1991, 2004; Glenn & Malott, 2004; Houmanfar & Rodrigues, 2006; Houmanfar et al., 2010; Malott, 2003, 2016a, 2016b; Malott & Glenn, 2006; Sandaker, 2009; Smith et al., 2011; Todorov, 2006.) Figure 6.1 illustrates the concept of metacontingency and its components.

Interlocking behavioral contingencies (IBCs) "involve the behavior of at least two participants, where any components of the behavioral contingency or the behavioral product of one participant interacts with elements of the behavioral contingency or product of other participants" (Glenn, 1988, p. 167). For instance, the actions of one player in a basketball game occasion or affect the behavior of another player.

An "aggregate product" (AP) consists of the compounded result of the actions and products of multiple individuals. In contrast, a "behavioral product" results from the actions of one individual. For instance, a transaction report is the AP of the interactions between several individuals working in a bank's branch, whereas a deposit slip is the behavioral product of a financial clerk's deposit transaction.

A "culturant" consists of IBCs and their AP (Hunter, 2012). The concept is helpful to narrow down the interactions that generate a specific product. Culturants have various levels of complexity. For instance, a culturant that produces a bank's transaction report embeds smaller culturants, each generating the transaction report of each branch. The larger the culturant, the farther removed from the behavior of an individual.

A "selector" refers to an external entity that affects the future occurrences of IBCs and their APs. Lineages of IBCs, that is their iterations, typically present some variation as some participants might be replaced and some might perform differently. As a result, the AP might

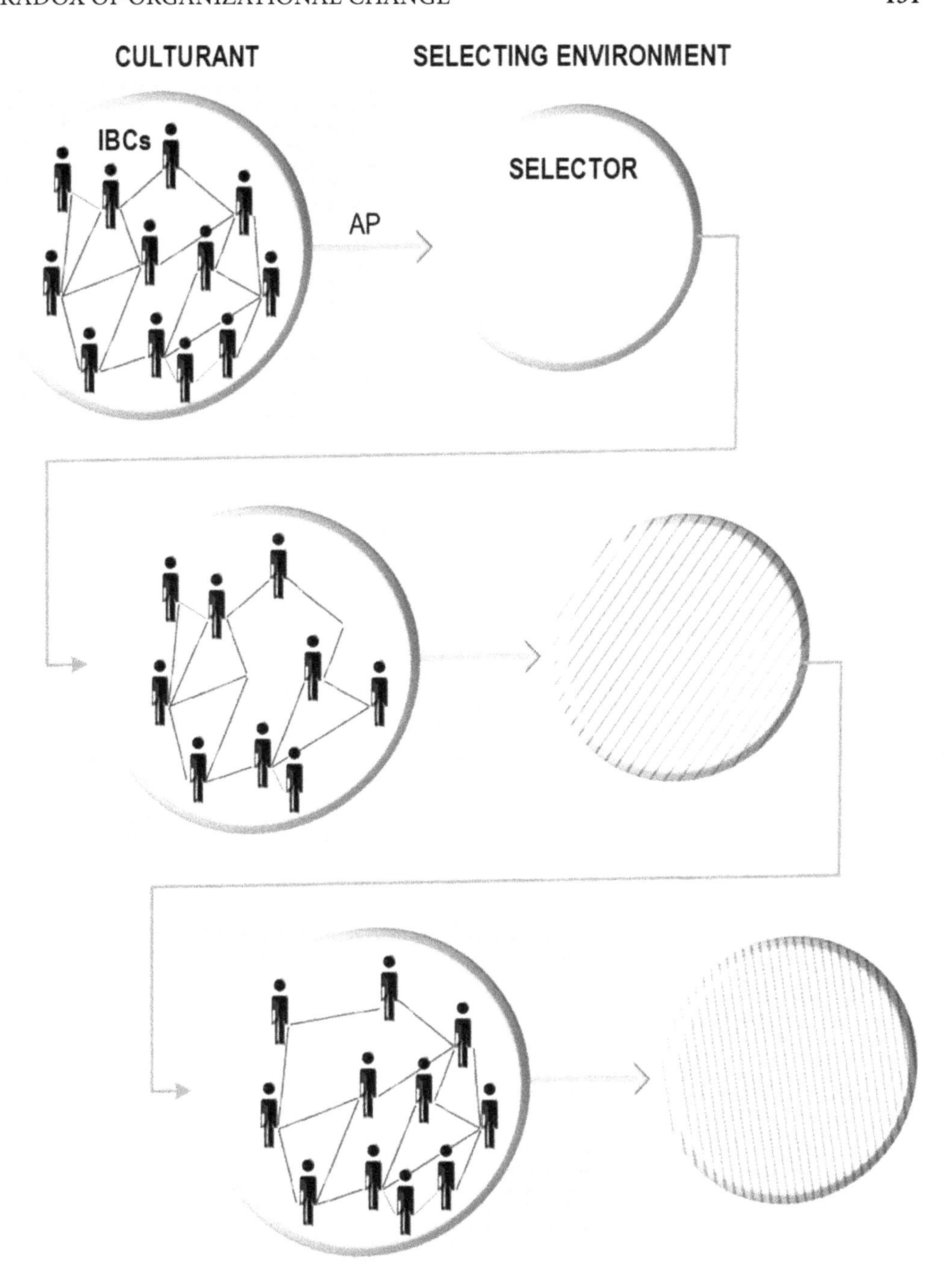

FIGURE 6.1 Metacontingency.

also vary. Figure 6.1 illustrates variation of each iteration by different configurations of the IBCs and variations of the selector by different patterns. The "selecting environment" consists of the circumstances that affect selection contingencies.

The culturo-behavioral systems model helps organizations to analyze their processes and implement change. "Culturo" refers to the selection of interactions of groups of individuals and their APs. "Behavioral" refers to the selection of individual behavior; that is, behavioral contingencies that form IBCs. "Systems" refers to a set of elements working together surrounding the actions of individuals. There is more to a behavioral system than individuals' actions, such as resources, technology, and regulations. These other elements need to be considered when attempting to improve organizations.

The C-B Systems Model has two parts: analysis and engineering. Analysis includes several levels: (1) macrosystem, (2) organization, (3) existing processes, and (4) existing IBCs. Engineering includes the next two levels: (5) new processes and (6) management. New processes involve mechanisms for continuous improvement and adjustment between metacontingencies. Figure 6.2 consists of a graphic representation of the C-B Systems Model.

I will present a complex example, based on a real case, to describe the C-B Systems Model; however, some of the details have been simplified or altered for better illustration. I will provide particulars of the case to clarify important points, hoping that they do not distract the reader from appreciating how the model could be used in different types of organizations.

Next time you buy cereal at a store, observe the display. You can choose from hundreds of cereals with different properties: grains (wheat, rice, oat, corn, barley); preparation (warm or ready-to-eat cold); health emphasis (e.g., high-fiber, sugar-free, gluten-free, fortified with vitamins); manufacturer (e.g., General Mills, Kellogg's, Post, Quaker); and other elements (e.g., shapes, colors, textures).

You can be sure that nothing in that display has been taken for granted: fixtures, store location, product assortment, adjacencies, number of facings (i.e., the number of units of each product type located in the front of the shelf, facing the customers), shelf heights, and shelf tags. The schematic of the display is called a "planogram" in the retail industry. Planograms are designed to attract shoppers and maximize sales and profits. After the planogram is implemented in the first set (i.e., the initial display), the shelf tags serve as physical prompts for stockers to identify the exact location of each product. As products are sold and empty spaces are evident, order writers scan the shelf tags each day to reorder the product sold.

Planogram compliance means that the actual displays precisely match the planogram's specifications (Harry, 2001; Lane, 2017; Wiles et al., n.d.). Planogram compliance is at the core of the retail business because if products are located in the wrong part of the display, the information feeding the replenishment, the sales, and the merchandising systems is inaccurate. Figure 6.3 illustrates the concept of planogram compliance. We shall see how an organization chose planogram compliance as a target area of improvement and how it developed an effective system that improved it.

Analysis

Analysis calls for navigating through the most to the least complex metacontingencies in the following levels: (1) macrosystem, (2) organization, (3) existing processes, and (4) existing IBCs. It is like peeling an onion. The larger metacontingencies include smaller ones, which in turn include even smaller ones. Ultimately the analysis leads to the IBCs and embedded behavioral contingencies that, if improved, could impact the organization's overall performance. Measures of APs at each level of analysis are the basis for identifying processes worth improving.

Macrosystem

An organization's competitiveness and survival depend in great part on what happens outside of it. That is why it is important to understand the macrosystem – the system that contains the organization of interest. Figure 6.4 illustrates Company Z's macrosystem as a metacontingency.

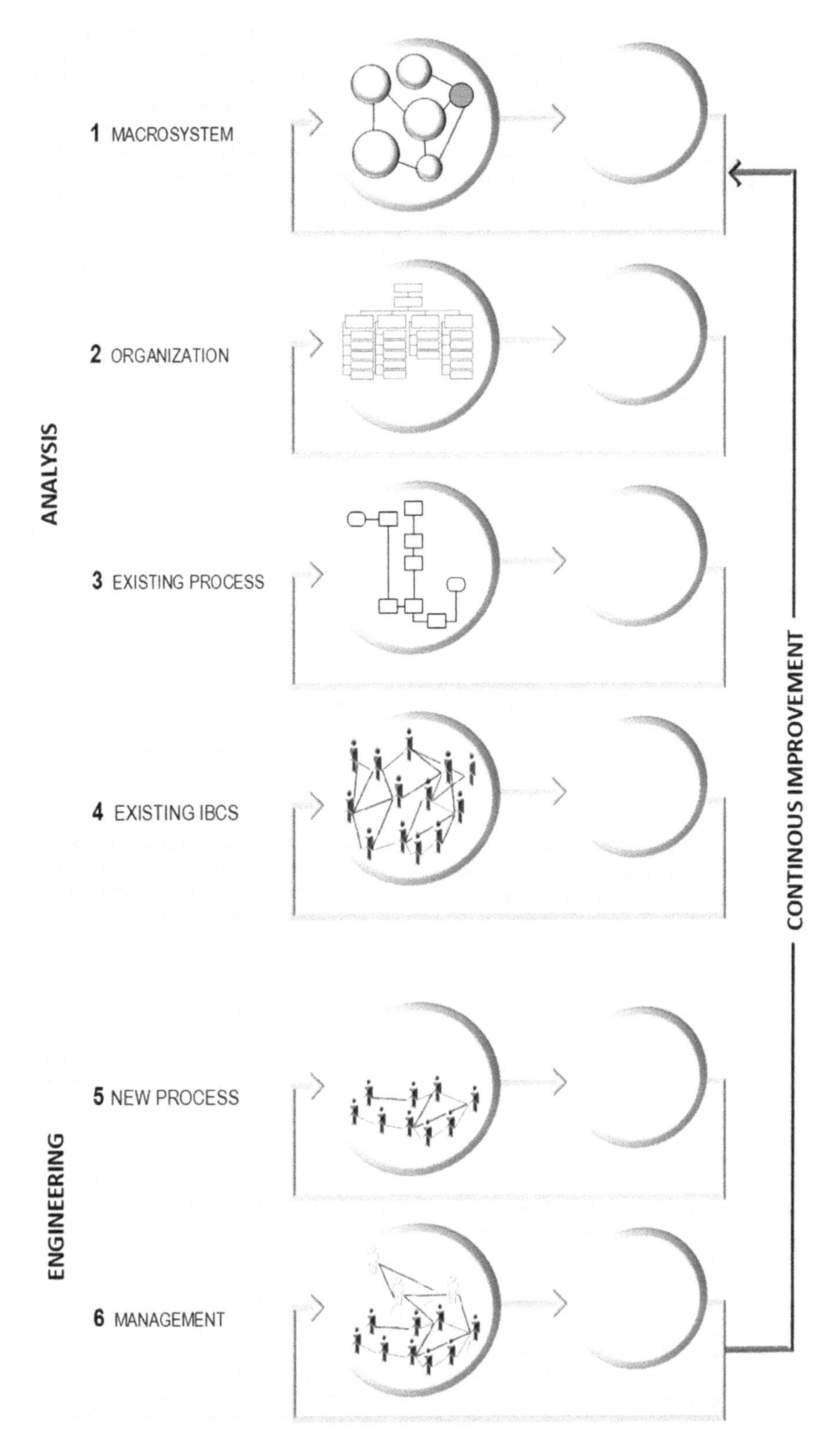

FIGURE 6.2 Culturo-behavioral systems model.

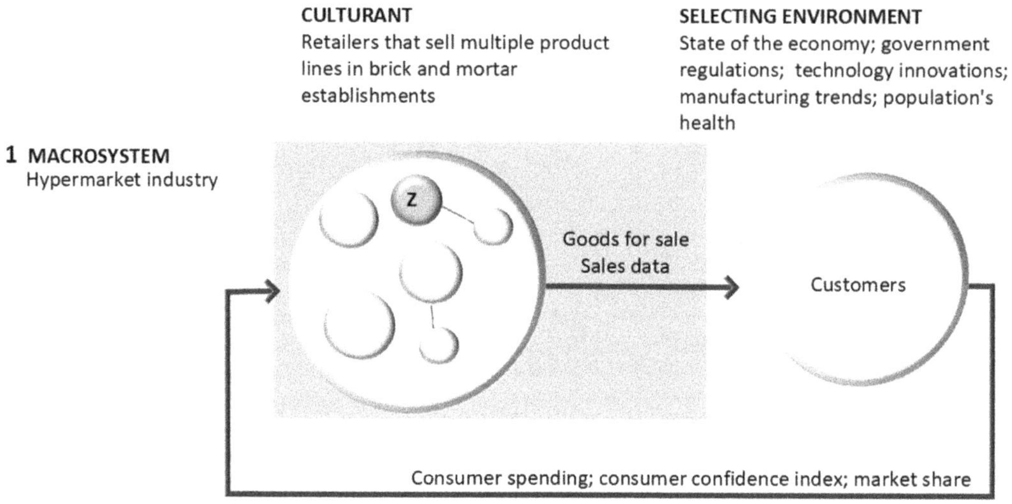

CULTURANT
Retailers that sell multiple product lines in brick and mortar establishments

SELECTING ENVIRONMENT
State of the economy; government regulations; technology innovations; manufacturing trends; population's health

1 MACROSYSTEM
Hypermarket industry

Z

Goods for sale
Sales data

Customers

Consumer spending; consumer confidence index; market share

FIGURE 6.3 Planogram compliance.

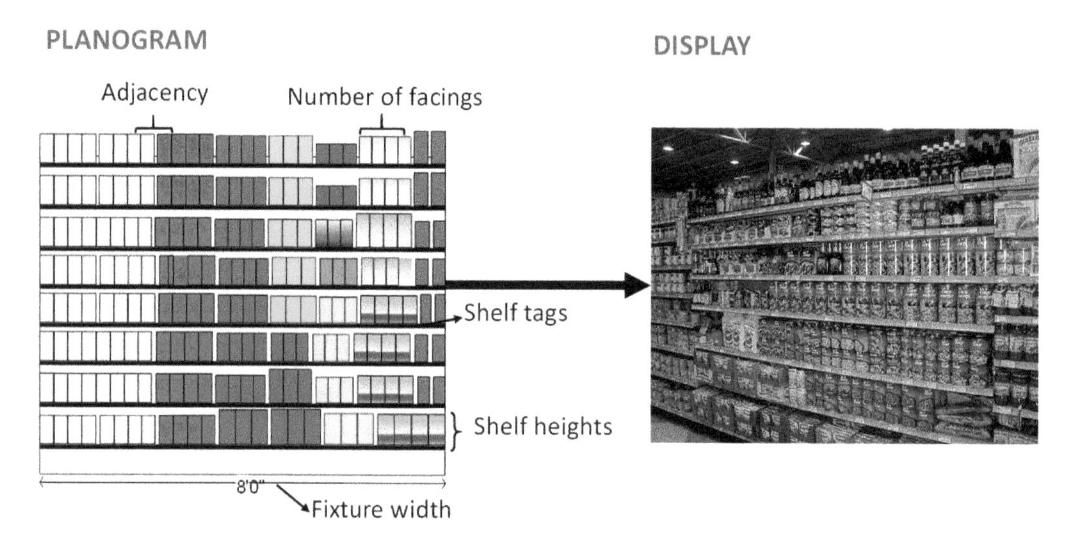

FIGURE 6.4 Macrosystem as a metacontingency.

Company Z's macrosystem is the hypermarket industry. Its culturant is formed by retailers that carry multiple product lines, combining supermarkets and department stores, such as Walmart, Target, and Kroger (*units*). They sell goods in brick and mortar establishments, offering a "one-stop shopping experience" under a single roof.

The *APs* consist of goods sold and sales data by the hypermarket industry. There are several sources of industry sales trends. For instance, the US Census Bureau lists 13 categories of retail sales (Amadeo, 2019) and collects data from 4,900 retailers (Amadeo, 2020). Hypermarket sales are compared to those of other retail segments, such as auto dealers, online merchants, hospitality, and leisure. Sales data are also aggregated by product lines across retail establishments. For instance, food sales trends are contrasted to those of clothing. As well, data are aggregated by product type, such as cereal, which, incidentally, has about 90% market penetration and generates a 40–45% profit margin. Supermarkets dominate the breakfast cereal market (Mayyasi, 2016).

Customers are *selectors*. They purchase goods sold in the hypermarket industry. There are several indicators of customers' preferences (i.e., feedback), such as consumer spending, consumer confidence index, and market share. Products that do not sell are permanently discontinued. Other factors from the *selecting environment* can cause product discontinuation and change in sales and profit trends, such as the state of the economy, government regulations, technology innovations, manufacturing trends, and the population's health (Treadwell, 2019).

Sales accuracy in the hypermarket industry relies on planogram compliance. Unfortunately, failure to meet compliance is a well-known industry problem. Gates (n.d.) reported that the total cost of noncompliance amounts to about 1% of gross product sales in food, drugs, and mass merchandising, which translates into lost opportunities of $10 to $15 billion in sales. He also referred to a study from the National Association of Retail Marketing Services (NARMS), which indicate that retailers' planogram compliance could increase 7.8% in annual sales and 8.1% in profit.

In summary, the analysis of the macrosystem provides a selectionist perspective of the system that contains the organization. It shows that planogram compliance is a challenge in the hypermarket industry and that, if improved, it could make Company Z more successful and competitive.

Organization

The complexities involved in a cereal display alone are enormous. Several departments and processes interrelate to produce the display, such as those that impact decisions surrounding product mix, orders, shipping and transportation, replenishment, and so on. The complexities grow exponentially when the organization has about 100 hypermarkets, each carrying about 200,000 products in four product lines: food (fresh produce and groceries), hard lines (e.g., toys), soft lines (e.g., clothing), and pharmacy. Such is the case of Company Z, which has about 90,000 employees. It operates about 100 hypermarkets located in several states. Figure 6.5 shows the organization as a metacontingency.

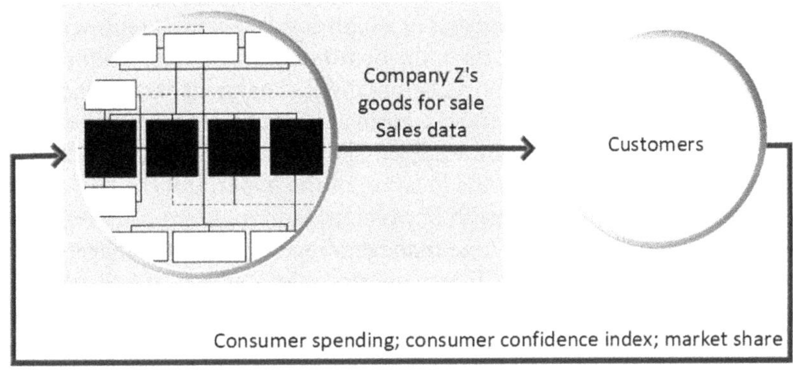

FIGURE 6.5 Organization as a metacontingency.

Company Z's *culturant* consists of a web of interrelated metacontingencies (*units*) that result in products sold and sales data (*APs*). Just as in the hypermarket industry, Company Z's *selectors* are its customers. Their preferences (feedback) determine Company Z's product mix, which vary by location. For instance, Wooddell (2020) reports cereal preferences by state, based on Google's search data. Warm cereal, like grits, might have a higher demand in some locations than others. Customer selection of Company Z's APs is affected by the same type of factors of the *selecting environment* that affect the hypermarket retailers: state of the economy, government regulations, technology innovations, manufacturing trends, and the population's health. As an example, health concerns (Peltz, 2016) are reflected in increasing trends of healthy choices in cereal, such as those with low sugar and high protein content. Millennials (individuals ages 18 to 34), on the other hand, consider expedience in their cereal choice. They prefer to carry their cereal as they go out the door and avoid cleaning dishes.

Objective measures at the organization's level guide areas of exploration and goal setting. Measures can be classified by type, such as volume, quality, cost, and timeliness. For instance, volume could be the number of items sold and number of data records; quality measures could be the accuracy of data (number of errors) and feedback from customers (number of complaints); cost-related measures could be the cost of goods sold and profit margins; timeliness measures could be on-time product deliveries and duration of order processing. Based on historical data and on benchmarks in the industry, performance standards are established for each measure.

A glance at Z's phone directory with pages and pages of names and departments provides a perspective of the company's complexity. Many employees do not know how the business is organized nor how it functions. They understand their jobs and those of individuals they work with. But they do not realize how their work affects other areas of the organization. Due to the unfamiliarity of jobs and political divisions with concentration of power, organizations develop walls between their components, ending in redundancies, dysfunctionality, and conflicting directions. These dynamics were well described by Rummler and Brache (1995) when they referred to the "white space in the organization chart."

Like other organizations in the hypermarket industry, Company Z shares the problem of the inaccuracy of planogram implementation. To improve Company Z's planogram compliance, it is necessary to understand how it is organized both structurally and functionally. The structural analysis is based on the traditional organizational charts, and the functional analysis is based on the interrelated dynamics between internal metacontingencies.

STRUCTURAL ANALYSIS

Organizational charts display hierarchical reporting units, such as regions, divisions, departments, and so on. Figure 6.6 consists of a high-level structural representation of Company Z.

Company Z's president reports to the board of directors, and senior vice presidents report to the president. Figure 6.6 shows Company Z's major departments, highlighted in black: Finance and Administrative Services, Human Resources, Merchandising, and so forth. Each major department is broken down into smaller divisions. For example, Operations is divided into regions corresponding to the location of the hypermarkets. A vice president of Region 1 oversees all the hypermarkets in her region. Store managers are responsible for the functioning of each hypermarket. Line managers report to store managers of a particular store; department managers report to line managers; sales staff report to department managers, and so on. Likewise, Merchandising is divided into smaller components; each one focused on the management of specific product lines, such as foods, fashion, and hard lines. Position titles include vice presidents, merchandise managers, buyers, and many others, all with specific reporting layers. In fact, Company Z has countless levels of reporting, not included because

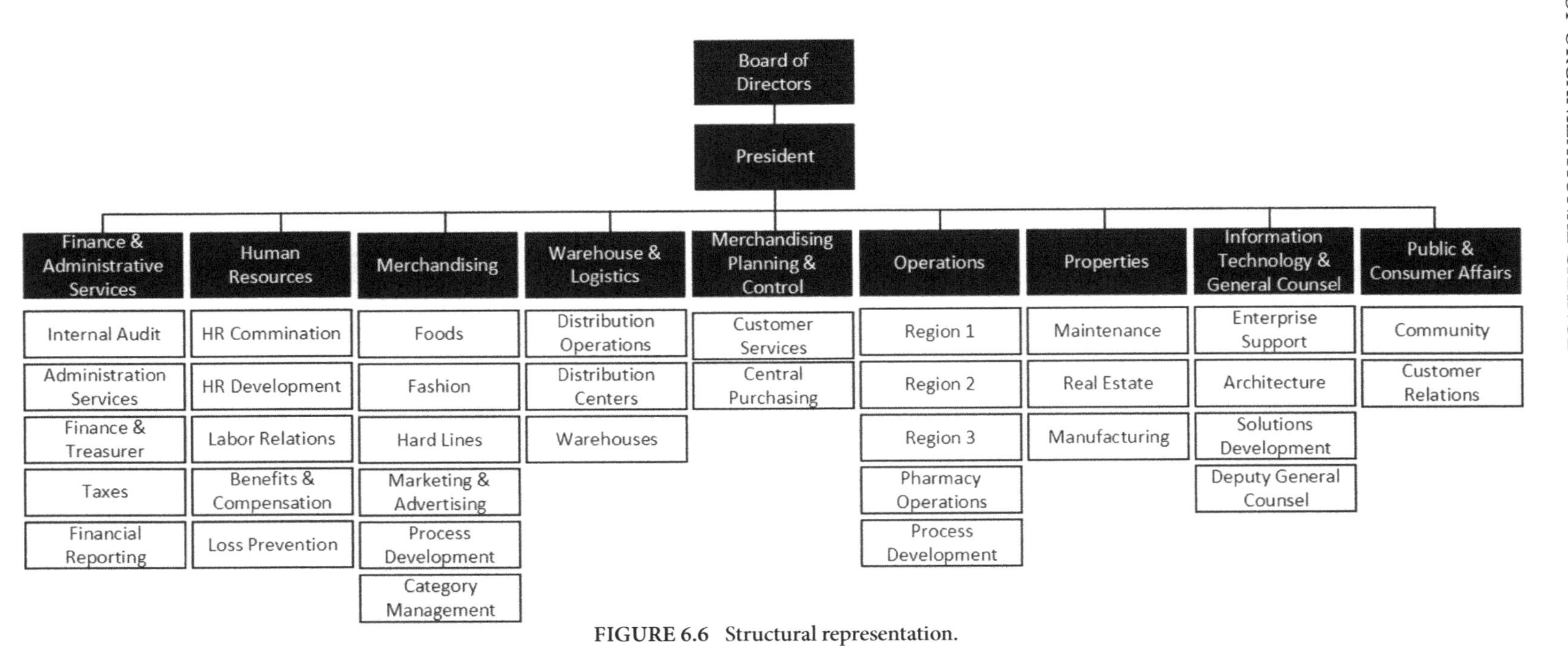

FIGURE 6.6 Structural representation.

of lack of space. The structural analysis shows the reporting lines and centers of decision making. It is also a foundation to investigate the concentration of power and understand the organization's political landscape.

FUNCTIONAL ANALYSIS

Internal units' relations are best captured in a functional format showing a web of interlocking metacontingencies. Some departments serve as a selector to other departments; others serve as input. Their culturants involves yet multiple smaller metacontingencies, which in turn involve others even smaller. Culturants, no matter their size, are selected by other functional units. Figure 6.7 consists of a higher-level functional representation of Company Z. The solid lines between the units identify relations between them – some serve as input providers, antecedents, or selectors. The dotted lines represent relations to external entities – vendors and customers.

Figure 6.7 shows that retail is in essence a throughput business: on one side there are vendors that produce the merchandise, and on the other side there are customers. The task of the business is to bring products from vendors to customers. Based on their functions, departments can be categorized as core, integrating, or support.

Core departments are essential for the business to succeed. In Company Z, Merchandising determines the customer product needs while meeting planned sales and profit margins. Its AP is the merchandising orders of products to be sold at the stores. Warehouse and Logistics receives the orders and arranges for transporting the products from the vendors to the stores,

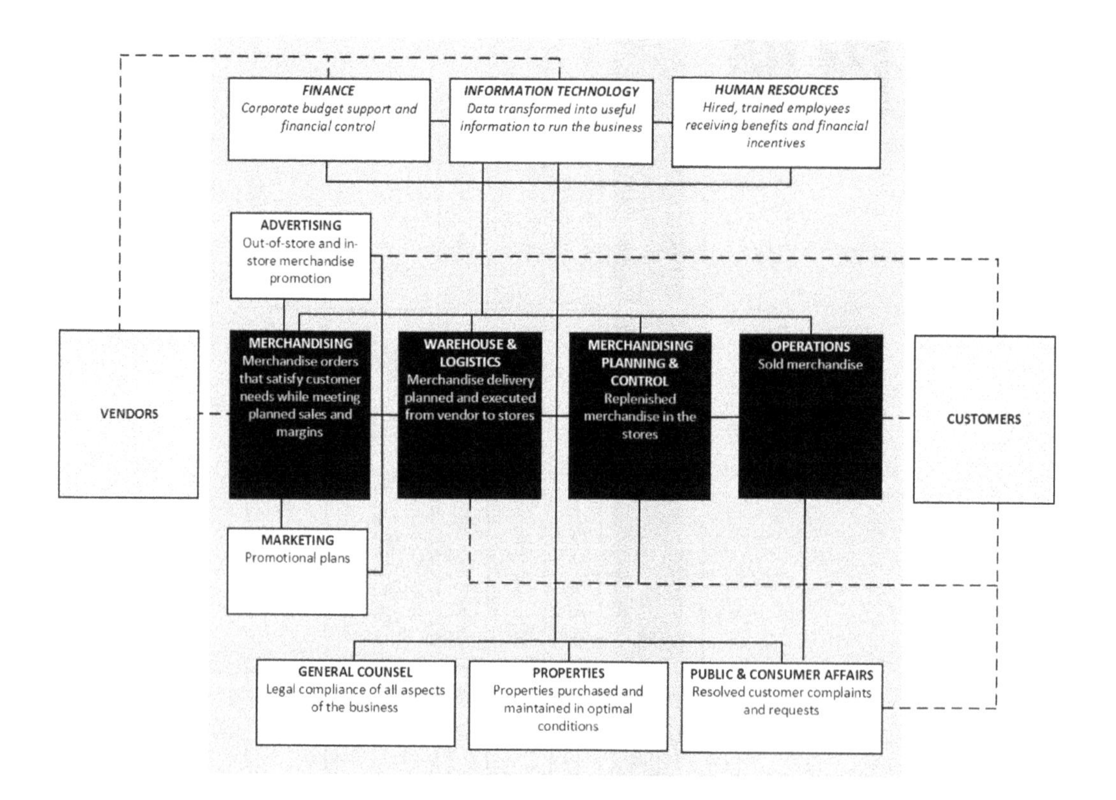

FIGURE 6.7 Functional representation.

warehouses, and distribution centers. The transportation schedule is received by Merchandising Planning and Control. This department keeps track of the inventory of the stores and plans the replenishing of products sold. Finally, the products are received in Operations (hypermarkets), where they are sold.

Integrating departments interact with all departments in the organization. For instance, Information Technology transforms data into information needed to run the business, and Finance coordinates all monetary transactions. Most activities in the business have financial implications. Human Resources recruits, hires, and manages benefits for all employees.

Support departments help some departments, but not all, with a specific function. For instance, Marketing generates in-store merchandise promotions, while Advertising focuses on out-of-store merchandise promotion. Both units are part of Merchandising.

The core of the organization should drive organizational change needs – those related to the processes that generate the product ultimately responsible for revenue. Unfortunately, most organizations – manufacturing, service, communications, and retail – have similar functional problems. The work is driven by the administrative structure rather than by integrated processes. Many departments act as if they were the core. Furthermore, departments at the core do not work cooperatively: support departments do not assist core departments, and integrating departments work independently. Personnel lose sight of their department's purpose. They do not understand the impact of their function on critical issues of the business. As a result, core departments have no support and must do much of the work that other departments should do for them. They acquire too many responsibilities to do a good job. Employees end up overwhelmed and ineffective.

The functional analysis shows the interactions between the metacontingencies involved in the organization – products of each department serve as resources for other departments. The analysis identifies the main functions or summaries of interlocking sets of behavioral contingencies, the aggregate products, and selector demands that take place inside of the organization. It also serves as a reference for process improvement initiatives.

In order to obtain planogram compliance, each department should work in concert and in support of the functions of other departments. To figure out the specific needs and products of each department in Company Z, it is necessary to dig deeper and examine the existing merchandise display process within this framework of the organization as a whole. And that is exactly what we do in the next level of analysis.

Existing Processes

The *process* of merchandise display involves several sub-processes (*units*) formed by smaller and interacting metacontingencies. The AP of one serves as antecedent, input, or selector of another. The *APs* are displays of merchandise and planogram implementation data in all product lines and hypermarkets. Figure 6.8 depicts the existing process as a metacontingency.

The existing process has several *selectors*: customers buy goods from displays; Merchandising obtains sales, profit, and planogram implementation data that influence future displays; Operations receives all components of the displays; Merchandise Planning & Control receives quantities by UPC codes to replenish; and vendors receive more orders. The *selecting environment* consists of factors that affect the merchandise display process. Examples are management priorities, turnover, product availability, and transportation conditions.

A cross-functional summary map, like the one in Figure 6.9, provides an overview of the process. The *name* of the process is Display of Merchandise. Its *scope* extends from the specification of product mix to obtaining feedback about display implementation.

CULTURANT
Subprocesses: **A.** Product selection; **B.** Display schematic; **C.** First set execution; **D.** Store rollout preparation; and **E.** Feedback

SELECTING ENVIRONMENT
Management priorities, turnover, product availability, transportation conditions

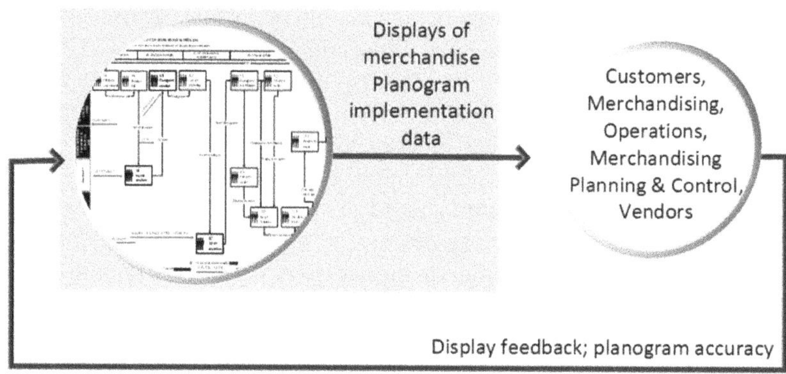

FIGURE 6.8 Merchandise display as a metacontingency

Departments involved in the process are identified on the left side of Figure 6.9. Not all individuals in each department participate in the Display of Merchandise process. The numbers are identified in parentheses: 71 from Merchandising (15 designers, 34 buyers, and 22 category analysts); 700 from Warehouse and Logistics; 23 from Merchandising Planning & Control (in Central Purchasing); 6,289 in Operations (5,800 stockers; 145 order writers, and 52 in-service group; 292 grocery team leaders); and 1,946 from vendors. In total the process of planogram implementation in the food lines involves 9,029 individuals.

Sub-processes are identified with a letter. "A" consists of product selection, which is based on data of category (e.g., cereal) sales, profit margins and market share, new products in the market, and customer preferences. "B" consists of display schematics, which involve the creation of the layout (the schematic of the shelf) and the planogram. "C" consists of the first set execution of the planogram in all stores. Buyers choose a vendor to implement the first set. Typically, this is done in a store assigned to this function – the model store. Present for the set are also a buyer, a category analyst, and operations staff. If needed, they adjust the physical display and finalize the planogram accordingly. "D" consists of the display rollout in all stores. This subprocess requires setting up reset stations in the back rooms of the stores before the scheduled day for the first set. Therefore, planograms are distributed, and fixtures, shelf tags, and products are ordered and delivered before the first set. And "E" consists of feedback on the display. Data on sales are collected each day by the order writer, who scans the shelf tags where a product is missing. These data feed all core departments.

Each subprocess includes culturants, which are identified with a number. For instance, A (product selection) includes 1.A, category assessment, and 2.A, product mix. Culturant 3.B, layout creation, is part of subprocess B (display schematic). Its APs are layouts, which are received by another culturant.

Duration is displayed at the bottom of Figure 6.9. Merchandise display takes an average of 28 weeks from beginning to end. The cross-functional summary map is an overview of the process. This is helpful in narrowing down the organization's complexity so that relevant IBCs can be identified and considered in the new process design, as we shall see at the next level.

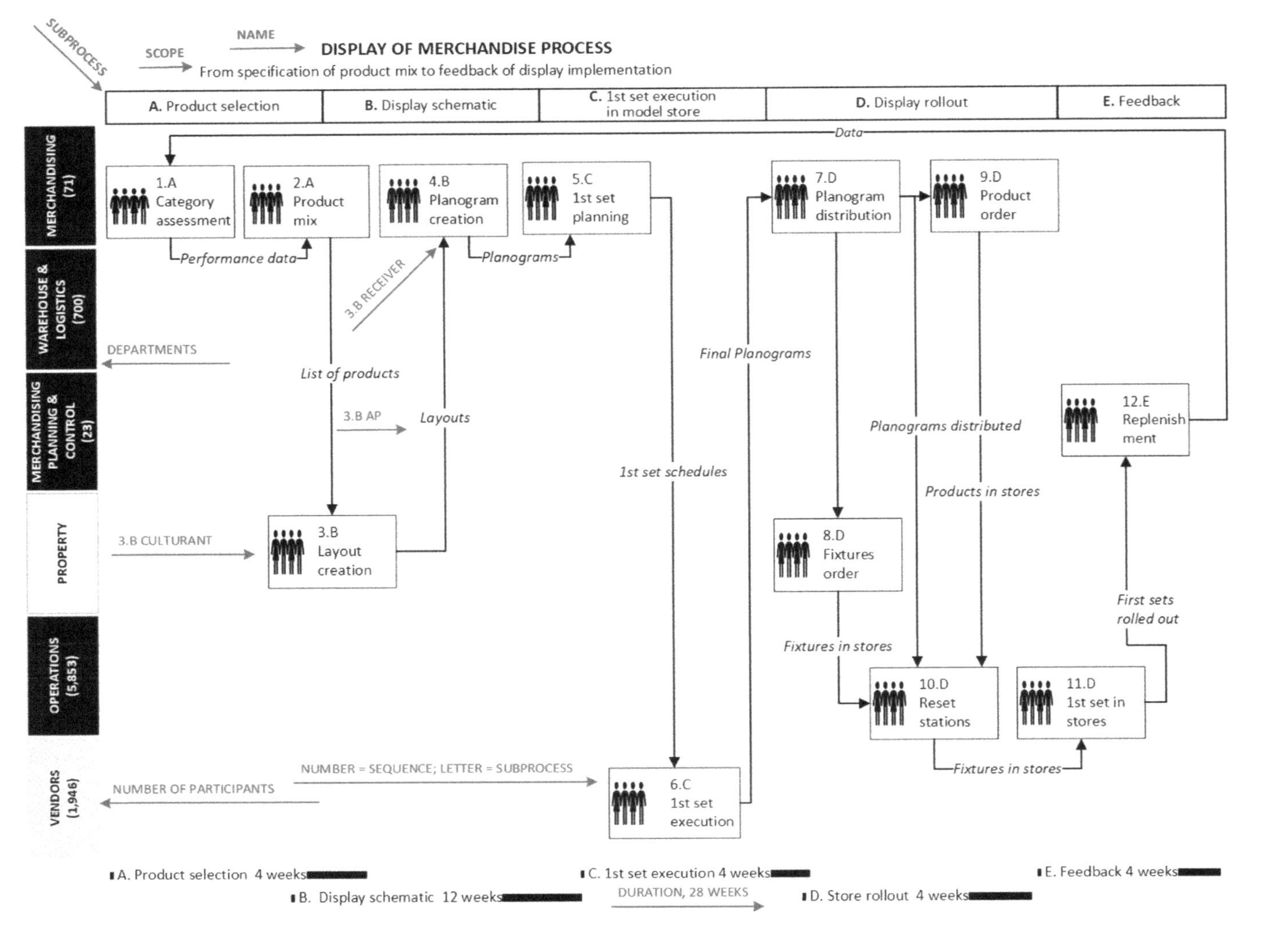

FIGURE 6.9 Cross-functional summary map.

Existing IBCs

Now it is time to gather data on the IBCs as they occur. The task might seem overwhelming, as Company Z sets 65,000 new displays a year. To narrow the scope, display processes can be studied for a sample of product categories, such as cereal. Figure 6.10 illustrates the analysis of existing IBCs as a metacontingency.

The existing *IBCs* in this analysis are formed by individuals interacting to produce the merchandise displays of representative categories (*culturant*). Their collaboration should produce planogram implementation data, but in the existing process such critical data are not collected. As in the existing process (Level 3 of the model), selectors are customers, vendors, and various departments of the organization. The selecting environment also involves factors similar to those in the existing process.

The process should be studied in its scope, from the selection of product mix through planogram implementation in all the stores for the sample product categories. Understanding what actually occurs in the process involves collecting IBC information, creating detailed cross-functional maps, and measuring the process and its AP.

COLLECT IBC INFORMATION

The objective is to follow the process as it typically occurs without judgment. Information is collected by interviewing participants, reviewing behavioral products, and engaging in direct observations. Participants are referred to as "performers" as they execute parts of the process. The smallest unit of analysis consists of the action of a performer that ends in an observable product. It is not necessary to capture steps taken without evident results. For instance, to print a planogram, a performer might open the computer, search a database, call someone, and so on. In this case, it is sufficient to document that she searches for a planogram (behavior) and prints it (product). In most cases, more details are distracting and unnecessary.

Within the IBCs, the actions of an individual's behavior or its product serve as antecedents or consequences to the behavior of others. Therefore, some performers function as selectors

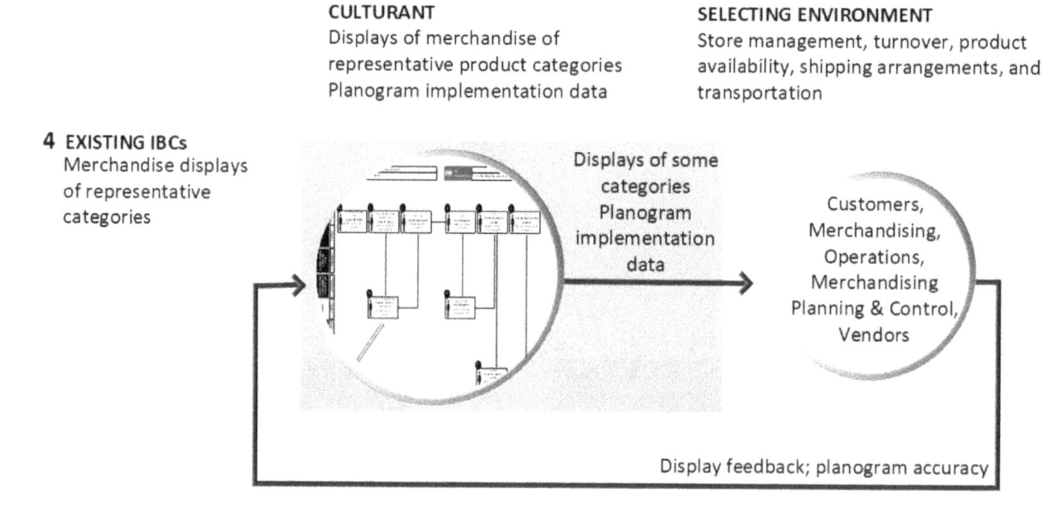

FIGURE 6.10 Merchandise display in sample product categories metacontingency.

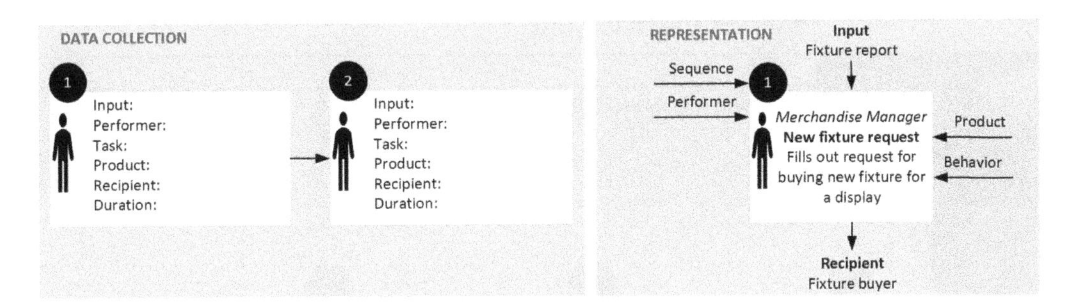

FIGURE 6.11 IBCs' data collection tool.

within the process. Figure 6.11 shows a tool for collecting components of IBCs and displaying them in detailed cross-functional maps.

The data collection tool provides a framework to answer basic questions for each action in the process: Who is the performer? What does the behavior consist of? What does it produce? Who is the recipient of the product? What input is needed to generate the product? Keep in mind that the recipient of a behavioral product is another performer in the process, that the product should be observable and quantifiable, that the input should be indispensable to generating the product, and that the behavior should be relevant to the process. Those using this tool should avoid getting sidetracked with details of related processes.

CREATE DETAILED CROSS-FUNCTIONAL MAPS

Relations between the actions of individuals and their products are illustrated in detailed cross-functional maps. Figure 6.12 details a sequence of 18 behaviors, their products, and the job titles of the performers involved in each part of the layout creation (step 3.B of Figure 6.9, Cross-Functional Summary Map). The display layout is the diagram of the store's floor space and the placement of the display fixtures. A new display might require moving other categories to a different store location or altering the space allocation.

The creation of the display schematic can be further divided into smaller sub-processes, such as 3.B.1, determine the accuracy of blueprints, and 3.B.2, order fixtures for a single display in the model store. The blueprint is a technical drawing of the aisle where the display is located, which matches that of the rest of the stores. New fixtures might need to be ordered or customized for the display.

The existing IBCs reveal that blueprints are inaccurate, requiring several steps to correct them. In addition, performers have to verify availability of fixtures in the model store. If a fixture needs to be manufactured for the first time, other steps are needed. These activities and many more take place before a first draft of a planogram is produced. A detailed cross-functional map should also capture variations between processes. For instance, a number of steps might not be needed for displays of fresh produce.

Creating the detailed cross-functional maps constitutes an intervention in itself. Performers can see how what they do impacts the work of others in other areas of the organization, and they can appreciate areas needing improvement.

MEASURE PROCESS AND APS

Measures of existing IBCs and the APs are the bases for assessing the effectiveness of a new or enhanced process. The existing IBCs might be assessed by duration and number of behaviors,

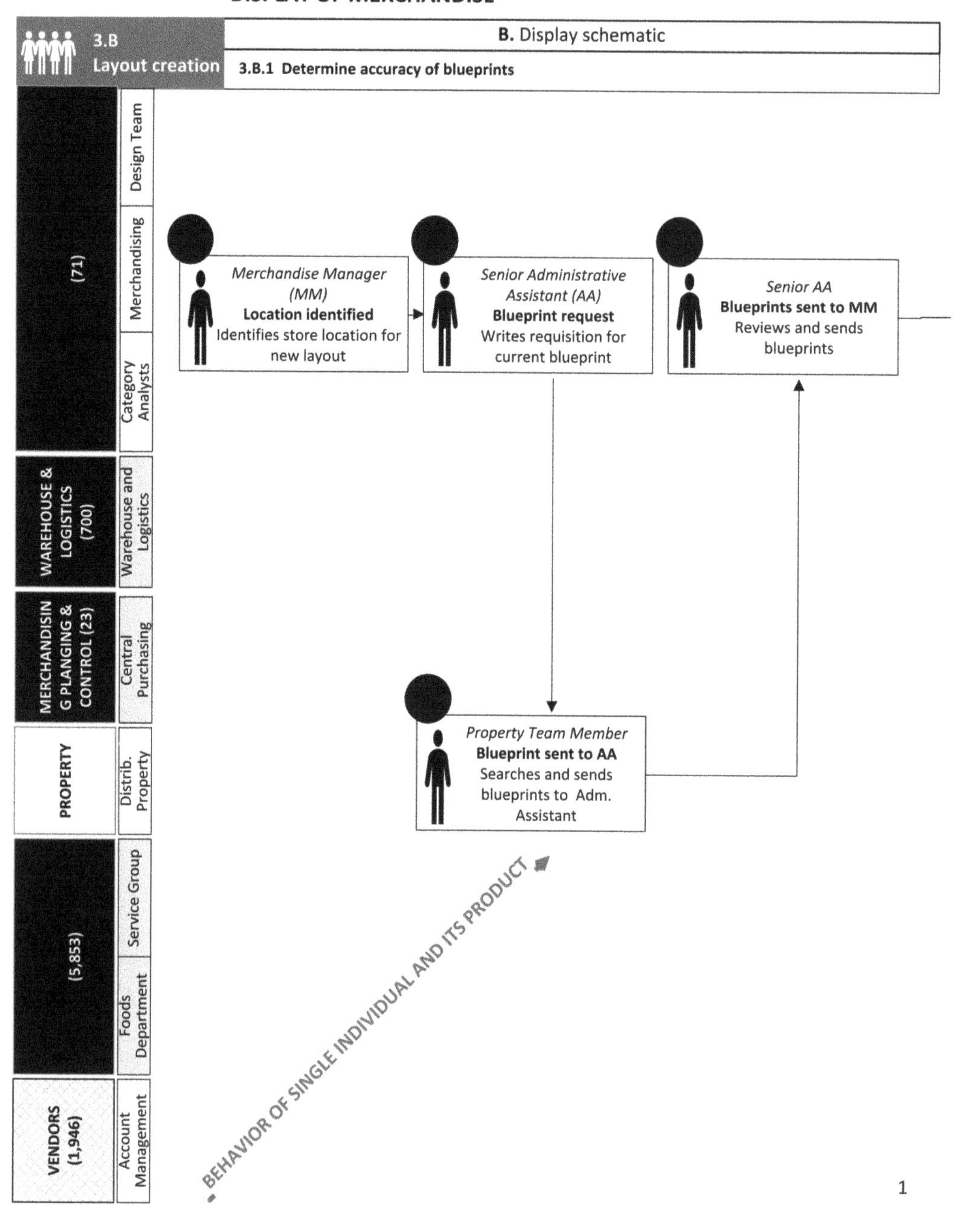

FIGURE 6.12 Detailed cross-functional process map.

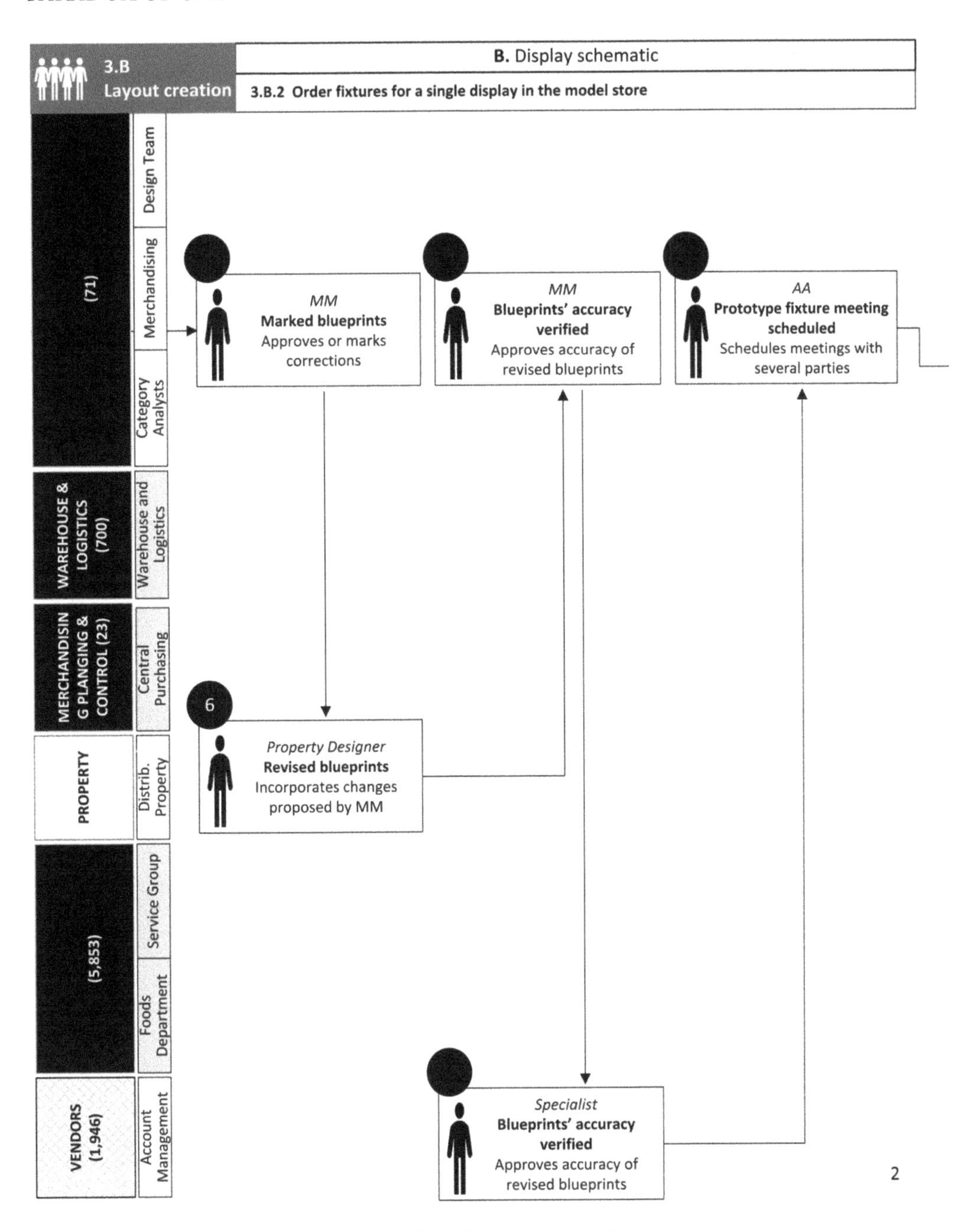

FIGURE 6.12 (Continued)

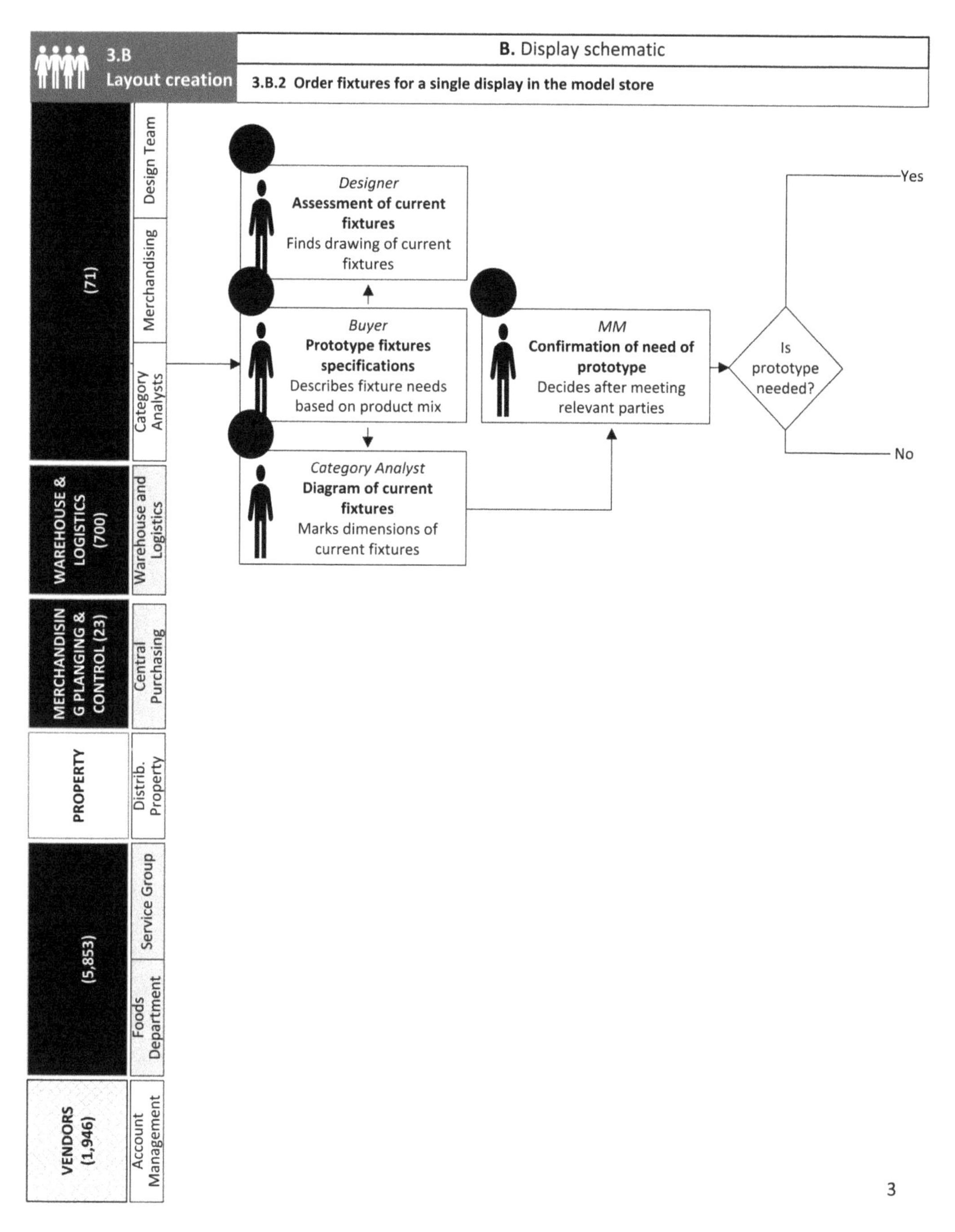

FIGURE 6.12 (Continued)

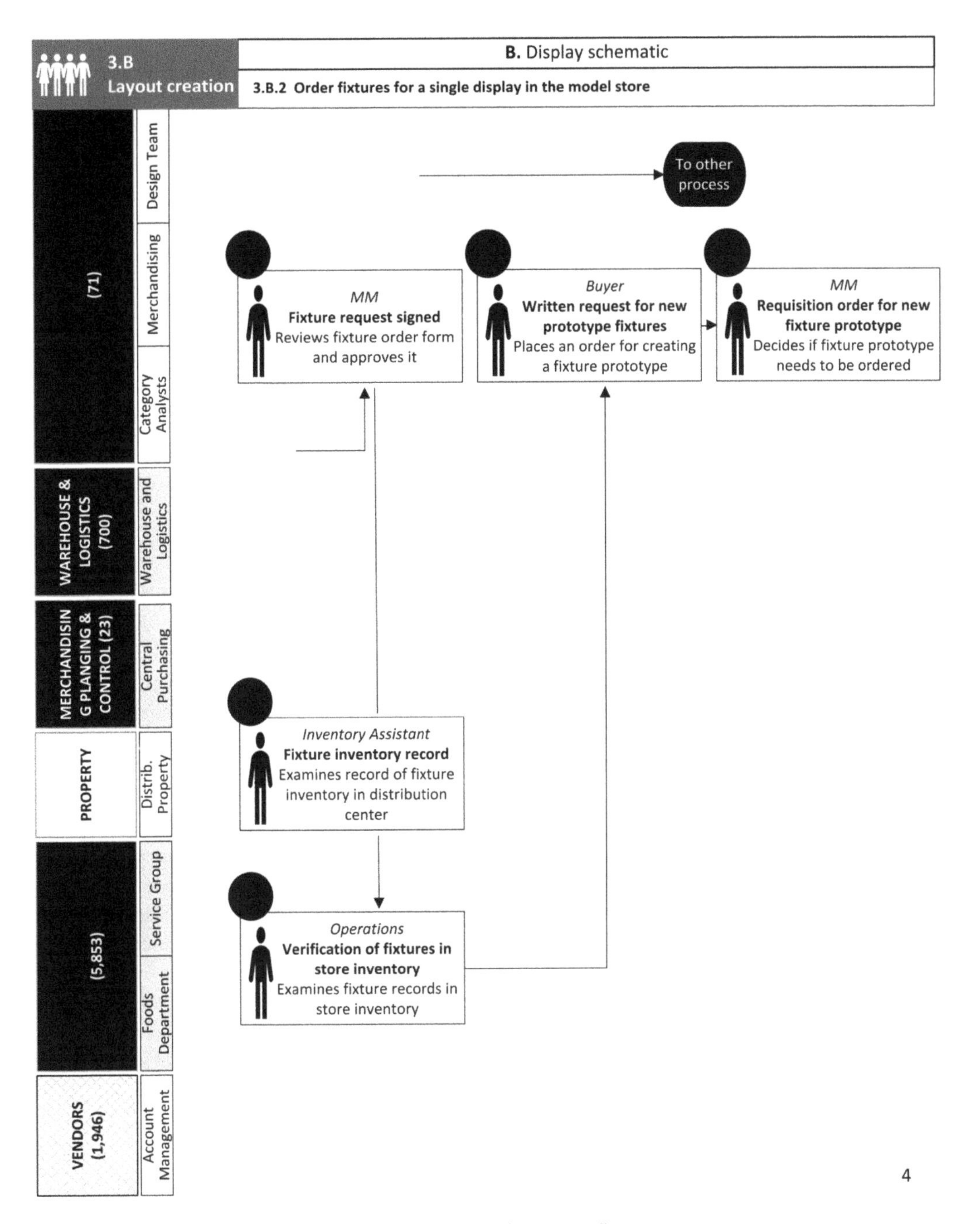

FIGURE 6.12 (Continued)

participants, and job classes involved. For instance, the process from beginning to end takes 28 weeks. Complete rollouts in food lines alone involve nearly 9,000 participants and about 30 job classes, as shown in Figure 6.13.

The AP of the existing IBCs is planogram compliance, which consists of the matching of planogram specifications to actual displays in terms of product location, number of facings, shelf tag locations, and shelf heights. Data can be summarized as the percentage of displays that meet planogram specifications and the frequency of the type of display error by product category or aggregated by all displays. In conclusion, the analysis of the existing IBCs reveals opportunities for improvement, benchmarks, potential savings, or gains of new processes. All of these conclusions are taken into consideration when engineering new processes.

Engineering

Engineering consists of designing and implementing new processes that would help the organization to compete effectively and adapt to ongoing internal and external changes. Engineering includes the generation of a new process (step 5) and its management system (step 6).

New Process

The new process should address areas of improvement and ensure planogram compliance. It should establish accountabilities for the behavior of critical performers and provide a supporting infrastructure. Its APs are merchandise displays and planogram implementation. The selector is the leadership who provide feedback and support. The selecting environment consists of organizational priorities that might favor or distract from the implementation of the new process. Figure 6.14 shows the new process as a metacontingency.

ACCOUNTABILITIES

In comparison to the existing process, in the new process some activities are kept, some are added, and some are altered or eliminated. The new process shall address a number of subcomponents that are related, for instance, to accessibility and accuracy of layouts and fixtures, properties of shelf tags, and many other factors. To illustrate how to approach designing a new process, this section focuses on the part of the process that pertains directly to planogram implementations. The existing process does not include specific accountabilities. Therefore, the new process includes accountabilities from Merchandising, Operations, and vendors. It specifies the actions of six job classes and two sub-processes: implementation of an accurate first set and maintenance of planogram compliance.

IMPLEMENTATION OF AN ACCURATE FIRST SET

A prerequisite for planogram compliance is accuracy in the implementation of the first set in the model store. This requires specific actions and accountabilities of performers from Merchandising, vendors, and Operations. *Merchandising* obligations rely on the buyers and the category analysts. *Buyers* are responsible for determining the product mix included in the display based on their analyses of sales, margins, and market share trends, as well as the introduction of new products in the marketplace. *Category analysts* are responsible for providing accurate planograms that fit properly in the store layout. The new process includes data collection on whether they have produced the accurate plan and planogram at the time of the first set. Participants in the display implementation collect data on the fulfillment of their

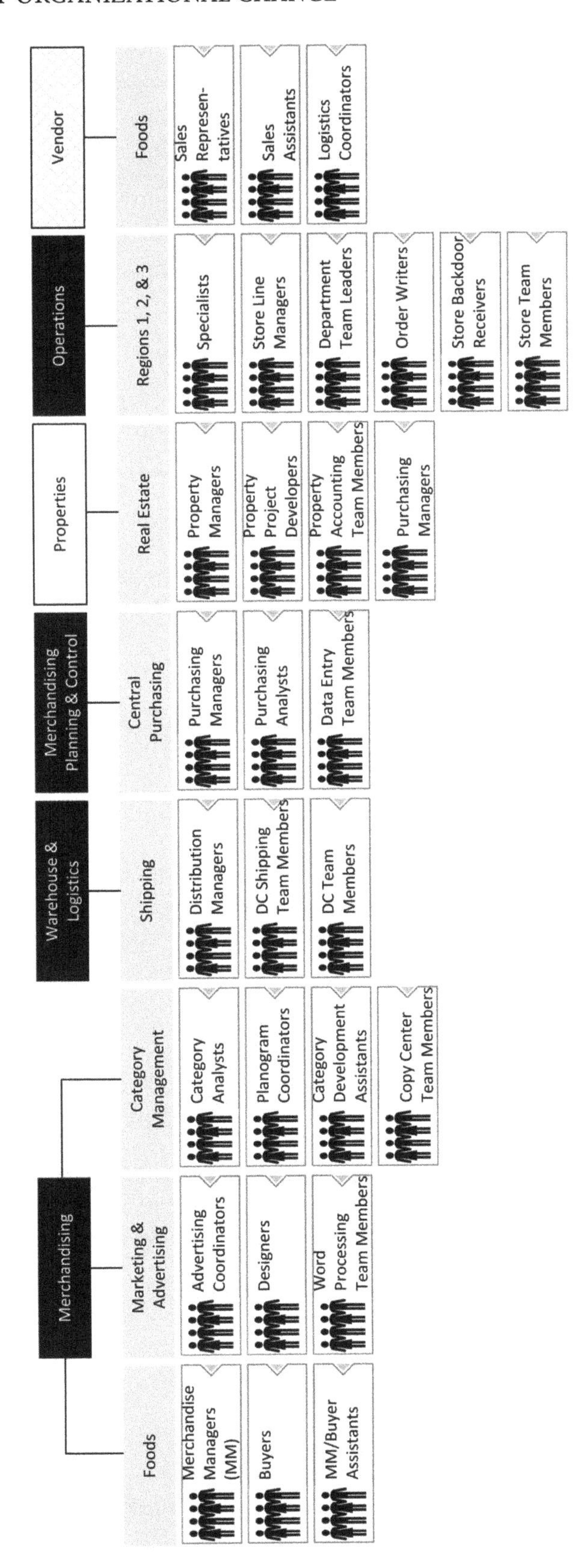

FIGURE 6.13 Job classes participating in merchandise display process.

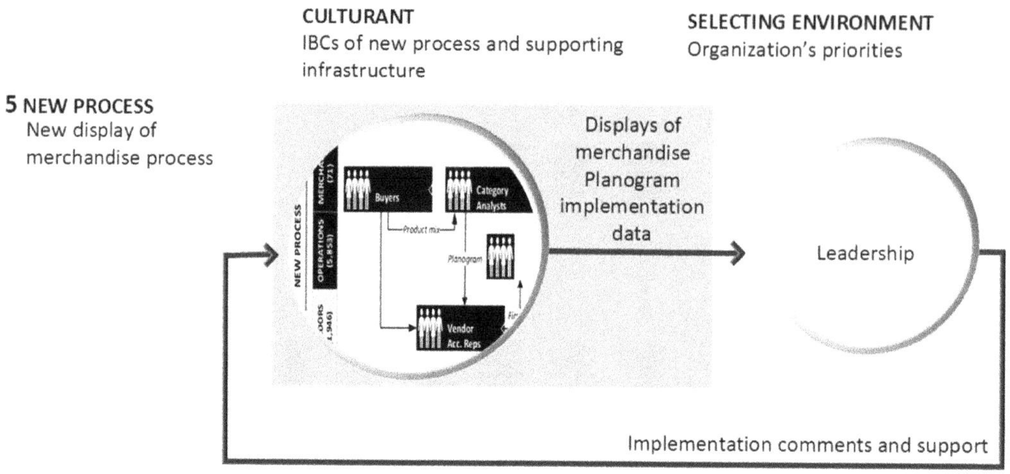
CULTURANT
IBCs of new process and supporting infrastructure
SELECTING ENVIRONMENT
Organization's priorities
5 NEW PROCESS
New display of merchandise process
NEW PROCESS
Buyers
Category Analysts
Vendor Acc. Reps
Displays of merchandise
Planogram implementation data
Leadership
Implementation comments and support

FIGURE 6.14 New process as a metacontingency.

respective accountabilities. A designated team member at the store verifies the data for each display. This evaluation includes the following questions:

☐ Yes ☐ No. Are there gaps in the planogram?
☐ Yes ☐ No. Does the planogram fit in the layout?
☐ Yes ☐ No. Is the footage listed correctly?
☐ Yes ☐ No. Are new items available?
☐ Yes ☐ No. Are shelf heights correct?

Vendor account representatives are responsible for creating the first set, matching the planogram precisely. They must use the correct version of the planogram and must ensure correct pricing and placement of items not included in the display in an assigned area. Their accountabilities are evaluated as follows:

☐ Yes ☐ No. Did the vendor use the planogram of the store?
☐ Yes ☐ No. Are new items priced?
☐ Yes ☐ No. Are non-eligible items placed in the assigned area?
☐ Yes ☐ No. Are back stock items placed in the assigned area?

In Operations, *team leaders* are responsible for independently verifying that the first set meets planogram specifications. They also must ensure that all items needed for the first set are available for the scheduled day. Team leaders' performance can be evaluated in terms of the following:

☐ Yes ☐ No. Is the planogram available?
☐ Yes ☐ No. Are shelf tags ready?
☐ Yes ☐ No. Are new items in the reset station?
☐ Yes ☐ No. Are fixtures available?

Answers to these process measures can be collected for the first set of each display. The data can be aggregated as the percentage of displays for which responsibilities were met.

PLANOGRAM MAINTENANCE

Maintenance pertains to the responsibilities of the stockers and the order writers. *Stockers* ensure that the right product is placed on the shelf according to the planogram and that empty shelf spaces are not filled with products not specified in the shelf tags. *Order writers* scan shelf tags to place orders of product sold on a daily basis and verify planogram compliance. If the wrong products were placed on the shelves, the data reported would be inaccurate and wrong information would feed the replenishment, finance, and merchandising systems. In addition, proof is needed regarding whether the order writer reported data on a daily basis or not and whether the data were accurate. That is why both the process team leader and the vendor sign off on the implementation of the first set.

PROCESS INFRASTRUCTURE

Leadership identifies new processes, gives direction and instructions, and assumes they will be implemented. When there is no compliance, performers are blamed. But it is often the case that failure of compliance is not due to lack of motivation, but to lack of adequate infrastructure. It is not reasonable to expect performers to implement a new process without providing them with what they need to do so (Gilbert, 1996). Brethower (2000) called the "processing system" the environment where the culturant exists (Brethower, 2000). Therefore, essential resources, technology, and jobs must support the new process.

Resources As an illustration, to implement the new process, performers need resources not readily available in the existing process: accurate blueprints, proper shelf tags, and items for the first set. As illustrated in the detailed cross-functional process map (Figure 6.12), Merchandising does not have accurate blueprints to prepare new layouts. Performers engage in a heavily administrative procedure to correct inaccurate blueprints. The new process requires a new electronic database system under Properties that provides easy access to accurate blueprints for all parties involved.

Shelf tags are another example. They are easily moved, so anyone could change their location, altering the physical prompts of the planogram. To solve this problem, a new type of shelf tag was identified that would not be glued to the shelf but could not be moved easily, making it challenging to remove during the first sets. It would take another process to get new shelf tags in all of Company Z's stores.

A final example: in the existing process, vendors could not find items needed to execute the first set. Therefore, the new process involves a system that allows store team members to place products, shelf tags, fixtures, and planograms in a designated space in the back room of the stores before the day of the first set.

Technology Company Z handles millions of data records daily. Information technology needs to enable the collection, distribution, and reporting of planogram process implementation and compliance. Technology packages are often acquired, but rather than facilitating the process; they often complicate it. That is why technologies need to be adapted or developed to meet new process needs.

Jobs As tasks are added, changed, or eliminated in the new process, the job functions and structures have to be adjusted accordingly. Sometimes process improvement results in certain positions no longer being needed, in which case participants are relocated elsewhere in the organization, where their skills match jobs needed. In some cases, additional staff need to be hired or current staff need to be trained. In addition to identification of the new process and infrastructure, a supporting management system needs to be part of the new process, as presented in the next section.

Management

Too often the responsibility of managing the job is given to performers with direct involvement in the core processes. The supervisors expect the performers to self-manage while they, themselves, are exempted from process implementation responsibilities. This is exactly the issue addressed in this component of the C-B Systems Model (see Figure 6.15).

Within the management support system, the *culturant* includes units of IBCs between process performers and a supporting management structure. The AP consists of accountability and feedback. *Selectors* are the top leadership who support and provide feedback on whether middle management supports the new process implementation. The *selecting environment* consists of factors that might affect the management structure implementation, such as strategic direction and leadership priorities.

MANAGEMENT INFRASTRUCTURE

Figure 6.16 illustrates the new process and the management infrastructure that supports it. The process and major outputs are at the bottom of the diagram in dark boxes. Major components are process performers, middle management, top leadership, and process management.

In the *new process*, performers are involved in interlocking behavioral contingencies. For instance, buyers set the occasion for category analysts to produce accurate planograms and for vendor account representatives to set the first set properly. Grocery team leaders serve as selectors for vendor account representatives to set up the first set and for order writers to comply with the planogram. Order writers, in turn, serve as selectors for stockers, who store products on the displays. *Middle managers* set the occasion and provide feedback based on

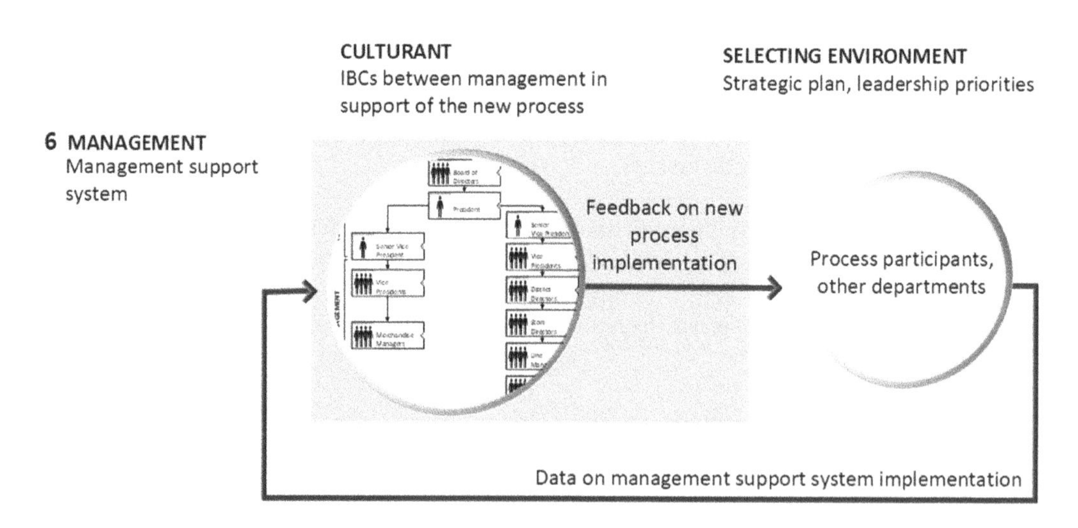

FIGURE 6.15 Management support system as a metacontingency.

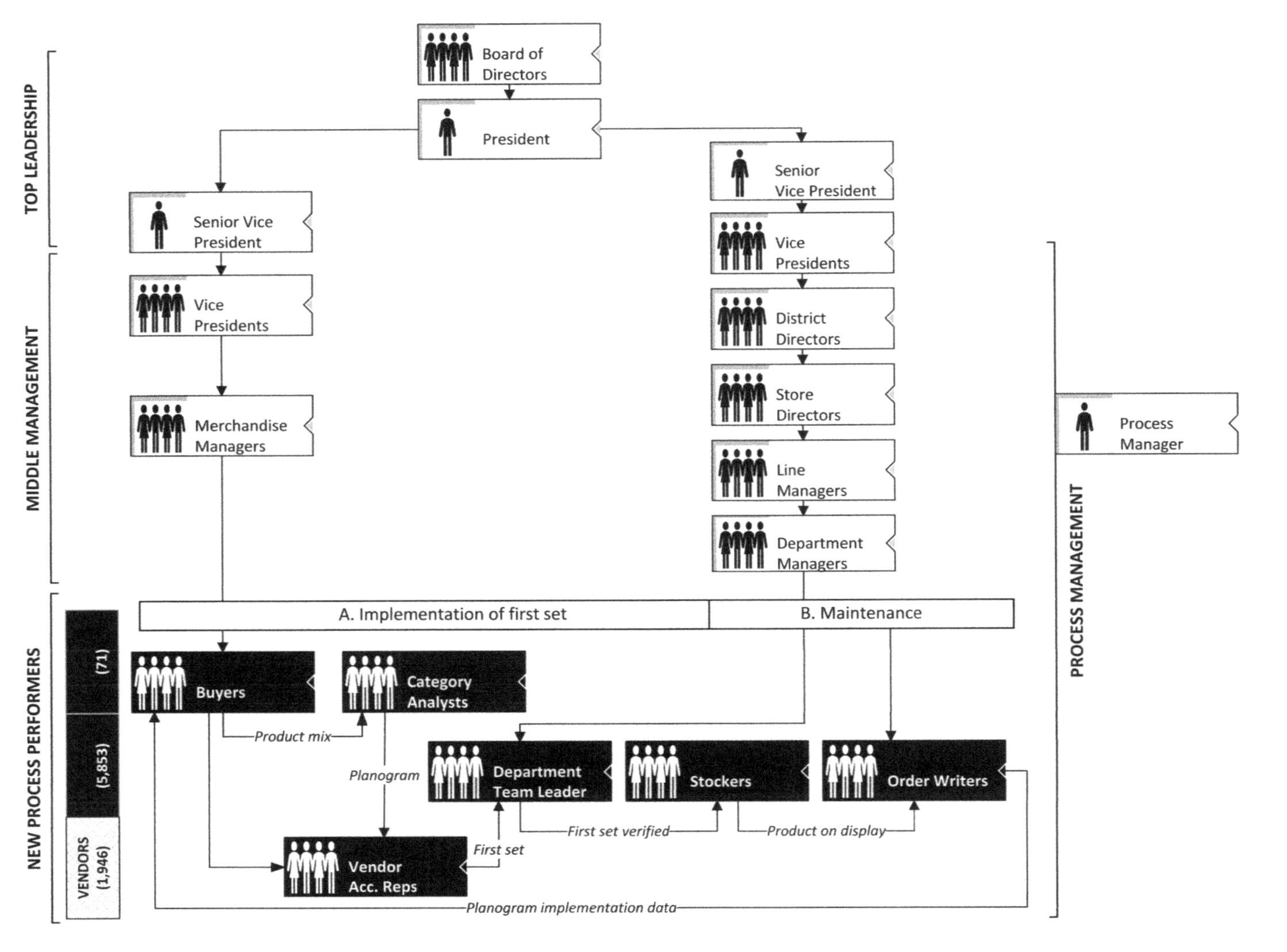

FIGURE 6.16 New process and management support system.

planogram compliance data. Merchandise managers provide feedback to buyers, vice presidents, and so on. *Top leaders* set the occasion and provide feedback to their direct reports on planogram implementation and measure of displays. In turn, they are accountable to the board of directors.

Depending on the complexity of the process, a *process manager* or team might also be needed to ensure implementation, feedback, and process improvement. This function coordinates the process across departments, ensuring that all interlocking contingencies function as a well-oiled machine. The function can be performed by someone within an existing job. However, some organizations have process improvement departments that ensure process compliance across departments.

PROCESS OF CONTINUOUS IMPROVEMENT

Change solutions are not permanent; they evolve with the vicissitudes of the organization and its environment. Therefore, new processes need to include ongoing assessment and continuous improvement so they can adapt and evolve. Navigating through the various systems of complexity, as shown with an example of the C-B Systems Model, would help with continuous improvement.

The new process, with its characteristics described here, was implemented in a hypermarket business. From conception to implementation across all of the hypermarket centers took approximately five years. In the analysis phase (prior to implementation of the new process), planogram compliance was measured in nine sampled categories. The data showed an average of 62% compliance. The error in these displays amounted to about $3 million. It took approximately four months to collect data from over 90% of all displays. Nearly 100% of the responsibilities identified were fulfilled by Merchandising, Operations, and vendors. With the new process in place, planogram compliance in the corporation increased to an average of 87%. Accuracy of aspects of the displays varied across features: displaying product on the correct shelf showed 92% accuracy; product locations, 90%; display footage, 95%; and number of facings, 92%. Improved but still with opportunities for improvement were shelf heights, with 72% accuracy, and shelf tag locations, with 81% accuracy. In addition, several systems were improved considerably. New changes would require this process to be adapted, such as the development of digital technologies to monitor the display of merchandising. Change is an ongoing process, not an end in itself. A number of other change initiatives were implemented during, before, and after this intervention addressing other critical processes, such as those involved in category analysis, pricing, promotion, and customer service, just to mention a few.

APPLICATION OF THE CULTURO-BEHAVIORAL SYSTEMS MODEL

Who would take on the task of doing the due diligence needed to lead change initiatives? That person could be you: someone working in the organization or a consultant who has the skill, knowledge, and commitment to do so. The facilitator needs to be able to navigate the organization's complexity from different perspectives. To reduce the perception of bias, there might be a preference for an outside facilitator or a member of an internal unit dedicated to facilitating change, such as a process improvement department.

Regardless of whether the facilitator is an outsider or an insider, two ingredients are essential to succeed in process change: leadership support and participant support. Improving an organization takes time and commitment; it often requires resources, technology, and job restructuring – all hard to obtain without leadership support.

But even with leadership backing, performers should be willing to participate. How do we gain leadership and participant support? And how do we face resistance to change? This section offers suggestions for a C-B Systems Model implementation gained from experience. The procedure offers guidelines and questions to be answered in (a) identifying targets of change that gain leadership support, (b) studying the existing process with an improvement team, (c) designing a new process that participants will embrace, and (d) implementing and continuously adjusting the new process.

Identifying Targets of Change That Gain Leadership Support

Countless opinions about what is wrong and what needs to change come from all sides of organizations: leadership, managers, and performers. They are based on their own experiences. Some recommendations are like those placed in "suggestions boxes," such as those that would improve the employees' environment, like increasing schedule flexibility or diversifying food offerings in the cafeteria. Others are more involved and point to what the organization, departments, or other individuals should do. Rarely do recommendations involve a change in the behavior of those making them. Many of these suggestions are perceived as unfounded and superficial, and they end up falling on deaf ears.

The C-B Systems Model offers steps of analysis that should be considered when attempting to identify targets worth pursuing: the macrosystem, the organization, and the existing process. An in-depth analysis involving these three levels is done before approaching the top organizational leadership for support. However, it helps to have a sponsor within the leadership team who appreciates the complexities of real change.

I have been surprised by how many senior leaders are unaware of factors outside their organization that impact its survival. Therefore, beginning with the study of the macrosystem (Level 1 of the C-B Systems Model) provides a perspective of the selecting environment and of the potential for the organization's differentiation from its competition. Key questions are: What variables affect the success of the industry? And what are the standards, measures, and benchmarks?

Many employees do not understand how the organization is constituted or where they stand in relation to the rest of the business. Understanding the organization (Level 2 of the model) provides the big picture of the organization. How is the organization structured (organizational chart), and how does it function? What are the core departments? What is the political structure of the organization, and does it get in the way of the function? If it does, how? What are the support departments, and are they really supporting the core? What are the integrating departments, and do they exert integrating functions or work in silos?

Process change needs to be identified in the context of the organization and its macrosystem (Level 3 of the model). Whether the target is to improve an existing process or to create a new one, this step should provide data-based answers to these questions: How does the target process affect the organization's performance overall and its competitiveness in the macrosystem that contains it? What departments or organizational units are directly involved in the target process, and how? What are some objective measures of the process and how do they compare to benchmarks? With the help of a sponsor, the remaining leaders of departments relevant to the target process can be convened to seek their endorsement and support for time and resources to study the existing process in detail and for assembling an improvement team.

If this step is done well, the answers to these questions would result in a convincing process improvement initiative that could gain support from the top leadership. The leadership would be more inclined to support process change if the anticipated results would help the organization to compete effectively.

Studying the Existing Process with an Improvement Team

Individuals working in one part of the organization do not realize how their actions and products affect others. That is why it is essential to understand the process as it occurs, along with the infrastructure that maintains it, without judgment (Level 4 of the model).

With the support of the leadership of the various units involved in the process, an improvement team, comprising performers, is assembled. The improvement team must be chosen carefully, as one of its critical tasks is facilitating buy-in of the change initiatives across the organization. The team members should be participants in the target process, be outstanding performers in their current jobs, and be respected by peers and management. In addition, they should be willing to be team members and commit to participating in all the steps of the process without exception. Sending substitutes to a team meeting is not acceptable. The team needs to move forward together in its understanding and troubleshooting; absences from the team activities slow the team's progress.

It is advisable to release a call for volunteers and request peer and management recommendations when recruiting members for the improvement team. A word of caution is that as soon as an initiative is announced, it is possible that too many people will want to participate, and large teams might be unmanageable. A team of about eight to ten people is ideal. Other willing members could participate in smaller components later on as part of the testing of implementation.

The facilitator identifies the frequency and duration of group meetings and activities beforehand, so expectations are clear. The facilitator is responsible for chairing meetings, gathering relevant information ahead of time, planning agendas, and serving as a liaison to the top leadership.

Once assembled, the improvement team studies the process from beginning to end and identifies areas of improvement. If the process is too complex, the team studies some components in detail, such as, in Company Z's case, the processes of displaying merchandise in some product lines.

Team members are expected to continue doing their regular jobs but are allowed flexibility and support to enable their participation; otherwise, working on the team becomes burdensome. These concessions necessitate management support. It should be clear that the objective is to improve processes, not to eliminate jobs, which would create resistance and fear.

At the conclusion of this phase, the improvement team presents a succinct summary of the analysis to the top leadership by answering the following questions: What are the major areas of opportunity for improvement within the process? What would be the gains and benchmarks of a new process? What elements of the infrastructure should be reviewed? This phase should conclude with leadership support and encouragement to design a new process and to form ad hoc solution teams, if needed.

Designing a New Process That Participants Will Embrace

The improvement team determines a new process and infrastructure (cross-functional summary map of Level 5 of the model) and the management system that will support it (Level 6 of the model). However, the team might not have the expertise needed to solve infrastructure challenges. In this case, short-term ad hoc solution teams are assembled. Their objective is to recommend solutions for specific components of the process infrastructure, including costs, benefits, and other implications. The improvement team evaluates the recommendations of the ad hoc solution teams and determines if adjustments to the new process need to be made.

The improvement team answers these questions: How does the new process benefit the organization in comparison to the existing one? What are the major steps, jobs involved, actions, and their interrelations? What additional systems or processes need to change, and what issues will these changes solve? What is the management structure that would support the new process, including performers, middle and top managers, and process manager, if needed?

This step ends with a brief presentation to the top leadership, showing a clear vision of the new process, costs, and benchmarks. At this time, the implementation team requests further support, resources, testing, and approval for implementation.

Implementing and Continuously Adjusting the New Process

Implementation involves testing the new process first and rolling it out across the organization second. If the organization is small, testing might not be needed; in which case, implementation begins with the rollout. In larger organizations, the new process is tested first to determine if it produces the expected results and to identify elements that would make the rollout effective, such as coordination and training. Members of the improvement team participate in these steps. They model for new participants engagement in processes that they would also adopt.

All elements of testing are planned ahead, including specification of areas, departments, and types of jobs. Proper tools, technologies, and training are also deployed. The improvement team monitors the testing closely to verify that all process components are implemented. As well, the team collects data on the implementation and impact of the process. If needed, elements of the new process are adjusted based on the test results. Additionally, the improvement team evaluates the process of implementation itself before rollout. Other tests might be needed until results are favorable.

In the corporate rollout, adjustments might be needed to adapt the new process to particular aspects of specific segments of the organization. For instance, process rollouts in international organizations might require adjustment to different countries' realities.

By the end of the implementation, the new process has been institutionalized. That means it has been incorporated into existing jobs, regulations, technologies, and so on. Then, the cycle continues. The new process eventually becomes the existing process, as new areas and components continue to change to adapt to new complexities and developments. This procedure of change takes time, commitment, and resources from conception to full execution. It might take years. Therefore, it is critical to choose the right process; otherwise, organizations might end up doing a lot of work with no impact, making people discouraged and continuing the vicious cycle of ineffective process change.

CONCLUSIONS

Organizational change efforts often result in vicious cycles. Initiatives are launched, resources are used, but in the end, substantial changes do not take place. Other change initiatives are launched afterward, with different names, in attempts to address the same unresolved issues. To avoid such an ineffective cycle, I presented an approach that leads to systemic change and meaningful results.

Organizational change is paradoxical because it involves properties with inherent contradictions: dynamic versus constant, complex versus simple, and chaotic versus orderly. The paradox comes from the fact that, in essence, organizations are complex dynamic systems; their components are constantly interacting and evolving. But change can be accounted for with elegant principles of environmental selection, which are the basis for the culturo-behavioral systems model.

Interactions between the behavior of several individuals and their APs are selected by their environment. For instance, an organization's products are selected by its customers; processes are selected by other departments; and interactions of individuals are selected by others. Such is also the case of the behavior and product of each individual in the group. Selection dynamics are influenced by environmental factors. These dynamic interactions and the factors that affect them can be analyzed at various levels of complexity with metacontingencies.

Metacontingencies are the fundamental unit of analysis of the C-B Systems Model. Although they are composed of behavioral contingencies, the focus on their IBCs facilitates navigating through complex systems, as opposed to starting with the behavior of single individuals. Of course, there are problems in organizations that can be addressed by manipulating behavioral contingencies without navigating complexity. For instance, the likelihood of late arrivals to work could be reduced with contingent reduction in compensation; smoking in a particular location could be affected by sanctions; recycling could increase with reinforcement from a supportive community. However, the types of issues addressed in this chapter are more complex and involve ongoing changing interactions among individuals and organizational units. The interactions between individuals and their APs are occasioned and altered by the actions and products of other groups.

The C-B Systems Model has two components: analysis and engineering. The analysis goes from general to specific metacontingencies – from macrosystems, to organization, to existing processes, and finally to existing IBCs. It concludes with identifying targets of intervention worth changing for the survival and competitiveness of the organization. Engineering consists of identifying key interrelations between participants, the supportive structures of those interrelations, and a management system that facilitates ongoing assessment and change. Organizational change necessitates support from the organization's leadership and performers involved in the process. I included some guidelines that can increase the likelihood of both when applying the C-B Systems Model.

Although I illustrated the application of the C-B Systems Model to a retail company, non-profit organizations are also complex systems, and the model applies to them as well. It also applies to any type of organization, regardless of its size and complexity, for instance, governmental and nongovernmental, public and private, and others. It is my hope that the C-B Systems Model and guidelines for its application presented in this chapter aid those interested in helping organizations to improve.

STUDY QUESTIONS

1. Explain the "vicious cycle of organizational change."
2. Define the following concepts with an example:
   a. Metacontingency
   b. Interlocking behavioral contingency
   c. Aggregate product
   d. Culturant
   e. Selector
3. Explain the two parts of the culturo-behavioral systems model described in this chapter.

4. Describe the difference between core, integrating, and support functions of departments?
5. Often times, when there is no compliance over time the performers are blamed. What's wrong with this/what is the more likely problem?

NOTE

1. The author thanks Dr. Ramona Houmanfar and her students at the Behavior Analysis Program of the University of Nevada, Reno, for the revisions of early drafts of this publication and their continued use and feedback of the Model here presented. The author also thanks Dr. Agustín Daniel Gómez Fuentes and his students at the Institute of Psychology and Education of the Universidad Veracruzana, Xalapa, Mexico, for their revisions and applications of the first publication of the text in Spanish (Malott, 2001).

REFERENCES

Amadeo, K. (2019, May 20). Retail sales and its components. *The Balance.* https://www.thebalance.com/what-is-retail-sales-3305722

Amadeo, K. (2020, July 17). US retail sales report, current statistics, and recent trends. *The Balance.* https://www.thebalance.com/u-s-retail-sales-statistics-and-trends-3305717

Brethower, D.M. (2000). A systemic view of enterprise: Adding value to performance. *Journal of Organizational Behavior Management, 20*(3/4), 165–190. doi:10.1300/J075v20n03_06

Gates, G. (n.d.). Best ways to fix poor planogram compliance. *Shopper Technology Institute.* Retrieved August 24, 2020, from https://www.shoppertech.org/ap091211.html

Gilbert, T.F. (1996). *Human competence: Engineering worthy performance.* HRD Press. (Original work published 1978)

Glenn, S.S. (1988). Contingencies and metacontingencies: Toward a synthesis of behavior analysis and cultural materialism. *The Behavior Analyst, 11*(2), 161–179.

Glenn, S.S. (1991). Contingencies and metacontingencies: Relations among behavioral, cultural, and biological evolution. In P.A. Lamal (Ed.), *Behavioral Analysis of Societies and Cultural Practices* (pp. 39–73). Praeger.

Glenn, S.S. (2004). Individual behavior, culture, and social change. *The Behavior Analyst, 27*(2), 133–151.

Glenn, S.S. & Malott, M.E. (2004). Complexity and selection: Implications for organizational change. *Behavior & Social Issues, 13,* 89–106. https://doi.org/10.5210/bsi.v13i2.378

Glenn, S.S., Malott, M.E., Andery Benvenuti, M., Houmanfar R., Sandaker, I., Todorov, J. C., ... Vasconcelos, L. (2016). Toward consistent terminology in a behaviorist approach to cultural analysis. *Behavior and Social Issues, 25,* 11–17. https://doi.org/10.5210/bsi.v25i0.6634

Harry, E. (2001). Change to merchandise, display to sell. *Dealerscope, 44*(1), 44.

Houmanfar, R. & Rodrigues, N. J. (2006). The metacontingency and the behavioral contingency: Points of contact and departure. *Behavior and Social Issues, 15,* 13–30.

Houmanfar, R.A., Rodrigues, N.J., & Ward, T.A. (2010). Emergence and metacontingency: Points of contact and departure. *Behavior and Social Issues, 19,* 78–103. doi:10.5210/bsi.v19i0.3065

Hunter, C.S. (2012). Analyzing behavioral and cultural selection contingencies. *Revista Lationomericana De Psicología, 44,* 43–54.

Lane, C. (2017, August 28). Planogram compliance. *Natural Insight.* https://www.naturalinsight.com/retail-dictionary/planogram-compliance.

Malott, M.E. (2001). *Paradoja de cambio organizacional: Estrategias efectivas con procesos estables.* Editorial Trillas.

Malott, M.E. (2003). *Paradox of organizational change: Engineering organizations with behavioral systems analysis.* Context Press.

Malott, M.E. (2016a). What studying leadership can teach us about the science of behavior. *The Behavior Analyst, 39*(1), 47–74. https://doi.org/10.1007/s40614-015-0049-y

Malott, M.E. (2016b). Selection of business practices in the midst of evolving complexity. *Journal of Organizational Behavior Management, 36*(23), 103–122. https://doi.org/10.1080/01608061.2016.1200511

Malott, M.E., & Glenn, S.S. (2006). Targets of intervention in cultural and behavioral change. *Behavior and Social Issues, 15*(1), 31–56. https://doi.org/10.5210/bsi.v15i1.344

Mayyasi, A, (2016, June 16). Why cereal has such aggressive marketing. *The Atlantic.* https://www.theatlantic.com/business/archive/2016/06/how-marketers-invented-the-modern-version-of-breakfast/487130/

Peltz, J.F. (2016, October 10). Why Americans are eating less cold cereal for breakfast. Los Angeles Times. https://www.latimes.com/business/la-fi-agenda-breakfast-cereals-20161010-snap-story.html

Rummler, G.A. & Brache, A.P. (1995). *Improving performance: How to manage the white space on the organizational chart.* Jossey-Bass.

Sandaker, I. (2009). A selectionist perspective on systemic and behavioral change in organizations. *Journal of Organizational Behavior Management, 29*(3), 276–293. https://doi.org/10.1080/01608060903092128
Smith, G.S., Houmanfar, R.A., & Louis, S.J. (2011). The participatory role of verbal behavior in an elaborated account of metacontingency: From conceptualization to investigation. *Behavior and Social Issues, 20*, 122–146.
Todorov, J.C. (2006). The metacontingency as a conceptual tool. *Behavior and Social Issues, 15*, 92–94.
Treadwell, L. (2019, January 31). The role of macro environment in the retail industry. *Chron*. https://smallbusiness.chron.com/role-macro-environment-retail-industry-33419.html
Wiles, S., Kumar, N., Roy, B., & Rathore, U. (n.d.). Planogram compliance: Making it work. Cognizant 20-20 Insights. https://www.cognizant.com/InsightsWhitepapers/Planogram-Compliance-Making-It-Work.pdf
Wooddell, B. (2020, March 6). In honor of National Cereal Day, these are the top cereals in all 50 states. WQA8, ABC. https://www.wqad.com/article/entertainment/in-honor-of-national-cereal-day-these-are-the-top-cereals-in-all-50-states/526-ab25a624-ad92-4c6b-8afc-116d8543725a

7

Consumer Behavior Analysis Meets the Marketing Firm[1]

Gordon R. Foxall

Ludwig von Mises has commented, speaking of production, that it

> is not something physical, material, and external; it is a spiritual and intellectual phenomenon. Its essential requisites are not human labor and external natural forces and things, but the decision of the mind to use these factors as means for the attainment of ends. What produces the product are not toil and trouble themselves, but the fact that the toiling is guided by reason. (von Mises, 1949, pp. 141–142)

If this is true of production, how much more so of marketing![2]

WHY?

Consumer behavior analysis brings together behavior analysis, microeconomics, and marketing science in a quest to better understand economic and social behavior (Foxall, 2016). It has been applied to such aspects of consumer choice as product and brand selection, store preference, the sensitivity of the quantity consumers purchase of a product to its price and the pattern of reinforcement it presents, and the determination of what it is that consumers actually purchase. The field is now attracting considerable research attention in fields such as food purchasing, healthy consumption, online consumer behavior, and travel (Foxall, 2017; see also, e.g., Fagerstrøm et al., 2017; Menon et al., 2019; Oliveira-Castro & Foxall, 2017). But the analysis of consumer behavior gives only one half of the picture. The firms and other marketing providers who supply consumers with products and services, retail outlets, and online shopping opportunities are also responsible for a large proportion of human economic and social behavior in affluent economies. A great deal of work has been done on this aspect of economic choice and has resulted in an account of *the marketing firm*, which complements the research on consumer choice. It is with this complementary component of the operant investigation of economic behavior in natural settings that this chapter is concerned.

There are several reasons why we, *as behavior analysts*, should be interested in the firm as a response to consumer choice. First, out of sheer intellectual concern with a fascinating component of society and the economy. Firms provide us with a number of conceptual opportunities to refine our tools of analysis. Given, for instance, that firms have a behavioral output of their own, which is sensitive to the consequences it produces, especially in terms of consumer response, can we treat the firm, or any other organization for that matter, as an operant system in its own right that can be understood in terms of the three-term contingency? Second, for

DOI: 10.4324/9781003198949-7

practical reasons, we may work in them, for them, and sometimes against them. Firms are ubiquitous. There is every reason therefore to understand why firms exist, what they do, how they do it, and the effects their operations have on those who work within them and those they claim to serve. Third, especially given that many of us are already interested in organizational behavior analysis, it is clear that in order to understand other organizations – non-firms – we have to understand how they resemble and differ from firms. Fourth, because we have concepts and techniques to offer students of the firm – and we have much to learn in return.

Above all, and uniting these reasons, it is important that behavior analysts make contact with other disciplines, not to the extent that we lose our distinctive mode of explanation but so that we expand the range of activities to which our experimental analyses and interpretations can be applied. The theme of this chapter is the nature of the organizations that meet consumer demand, the susceptibility of their behavior to operant explanation, and the consequences of treating them as operant systems. It draws on ideas from microeconomics and marketing science, as well as behavior analysis, in a nontechnical exploration of the sensitivity of corporate activity to contingencies of reinforcement. I argue that the concept of metacontingency is central to understanding the behavior of organizations such as marketing firms and that the idea of bilateral contingency is central to understanding why they exist and what their function is.

WHAT IS MARKETING?

At its simplest marketing is anything that comes between production and consumption, all the human activity involved in transportation and physical distribution, informing potential customers, and finding a mutually beneficial price for products and services. But I want to look at marketing from a broader perspective, that of the necessity of firms' responding to the "imperatives of customer-orientation," the social and economic forces that impose on firms the necessity of gearing production, marketing, and all the other functions of the firm toward the profitable satisfaction of customer requirements. Adam Smith wrote in *The Wealth of Nations* that "Consumption is the sole end and purpose of all production; and the interest of the producer ought to be attended to only so far as it may be necessary for promoting that of the consumer" (Smith, 1776, Book IV, Chapter 8, p. 49.) This provision, so often forgotten in the meantime, assumed renewed urgency with the overcoming of the problem of production that industrial nations experienced in the late 19th and early 20th centuries.

Whereas, prior to that, the problem had been to produce sufficient products and services to satisfy basic consumer wants, the possibility arose at that time of firms' being able to overproduce, to generate products in excess of the immediate requirements of the customers they served. Firms had the capacity to produce at such levels that the supply of commodities outstripped or potentially outstripped the demand for them. Especially since the end of the second world war, consumers' discretionary income, again in those industrial nations, has increased many times. Competition was refocused away from the traditional pattern in which firms manufacturing similar products engaged in rivalry within a given industry, toward *inter-industrial* competition in which, say, the producer of automobiles was competing not just with other auto manufacturers but with providers of luxury vacations, modern well-equipped homes, and international air travel. These elements of the modern economy add up to *consumer choice*, the first of the imperatives of customer-oriented management.

Consumer choice is reflected in the vast increase in commodities, products, and brands available in the marketplace coupled with an unprecedented capacity to purchase them. Most consumers have available to them extremely high levels of discretionary income compared with any previous age; most marketers face an industrial situation in which supply or the capacity to supply exceeds demand with the effect that competitors actively pursue branding strategies intended to enhance their offerings by increasing consumer involvement in purchasing a given firm's output. Most consumer innovations, albeit the majority are line extensions and continuous new products, are rejected at the stage of consumer purchasing despite vastly improved techniques of market research, market-based product testing, and test marketing; estimates agree on a proportion of 80–90%. For industrial products, estimations agree on a failure rate of approximately 40%. This picture is the result of high levels of competition not only within traditional industries but across industry boundaries. Consumer tastes are dynamic, not only as a result of cultural change and advertising practice, but because consumers themselves are inventive and innovative. The result is that it is the customer who is the final arbiter of what business the firm is in or should be in and, ultimately, of corporate success.

The other imperative is *consumer sophistication*, the phenomenon of the increasingly informed and erudite customer. It has always been said that buyers within firms were more sophisticated than final consumers: industrial buyers have expertise, are experienced and discerning procurers of goods and services, and have strict cost limits that govern what they can purchase. But final consumers have expertise too: they are aware of differences between brands, prices, and performances, and they actively discriminate in favor of those items that they judge to best suit their purposes. This is true of everyday products such as breakfast cereals and razor blades, but it also extends to consumer durables and along to the most sophisticated digital equipment and software. Consumers increasingly have state-of-the-art knowledge about the most complex products and services, sometimes to the point where they are ahead of the manufacturers. Consumers are the people who become entrepreneurs and give existing marketers a run for their money. These imperatives of customer-oriented management, consumer choice and consumer sophistication, have brought about the situation in which, in order to survive let alone meet their financial obligations, firms have to cater deliberately to the wishes of consumers.

Marketing-oriented management is an organization-wide philosophy that enjoins upon the entire firm the responsibility of profitably pursuing the fulfillment of customers' requirements. It is not an ideology for the aggrandizement of the marketing department or function but a unifying corporate perspective that leads to a distinctive strategy. The many definitions of strategy emphasize both the seeking of an optimal harmonization of intra-firm capabilities and external opportunities and threats, and the need to employ strategy in such a way as to achieve long-term prosperity. Andrews (1971, p. 48), for instance, portrays economic strategy in terms of "the best match between qualification and opportunity that positions a firm in its product/market environment," while the necessary link to profitability and survival is brought out by Simon and Fassnacht (2019, p. 42): "Strategy is the art and science of developing and deploying all of a company's resources so as to achieve the most profitable long-term survival of the company." Two extra-corporate influences make this marketing-oriented management imperative within this strategic context and within that of a modern affluent economy: the existence of massive consumer choice and the advent of a sophisticated consumerate (Foxall, 2015a).

The theory of the marketing firm is therefore the theory of a commercial organization obliged by competitive conditions to adopt the strategic philosophy of marketing- or customer-oriented management. It means that the firm is oriented toward satisfying customer needs profitably rather than trying to sell whatever it happens to produce. It means that every part of the organization is directed toward customer satisfaction rather than the fulfillment of internal requirements. In the past it was sufficient to assume customers would beat a path to one's door for a superior product or that customers could have any color they wanted as long as it was black. Given the imperatives I have described this is no longer the case.

I do not write, however, as an apologist of the marketing profession. I am not claiming that all firms actually behave in this way – only that there are strong pressures on those that value survival and profitability to do so. The theory of the marketing firm is what Chomsky calls a *competence* theory. Chomsky (1957, 1965) distinguishes competence theories of language from performance theories. The first refers to knowledge of the rules of language; the second, to the manifest use of language in actual situations. In this context, a competence theory is concerned with the structure of rules of grammar a person would ideally need to know in order to speak a language, while a performance theory involves itself with the ways in which everyday speech occurs in the process of interpersonal communication. I employ the idea of a competence theory in this chapter to refer to an idealized view of how a firm would need to behave in order to respond successfully to the social and economic factors that suggest that corporate performance is dependent on the pursuit of a strategy of customer-orientation. The theory seeks to identify the information needs and consequent decisions of a firm pursuing marketing-oriented management.

WHAT FIRMS DO

What the Firm is

The goal of the firm is profit maximization. We might debate whether this is profit maximization in the short- or the long-term and the precise nature of what is involved, but the principle is of maximizing the returns to entrepreneurship that the firm embodies. What is sure is that this goal of the firm is different from that of any of its stakeholders – its customers but also its owners, managers, or other employees. *Their* goal is consumption rather than profit maximization (Spulber, 2009). They may *prefer* to own or work for a firm that maximizes profit, but *their* goal is consumption. This factor makes the firm different from other organizations. Other organizations have goals that are not distinguishable from those of their stakeholders or members – consumer organizations, many cooperatives, many partnerships, and social marketing campaigns. In all these cases, the organization's goal is that of its members. Even organizations that aim to make a surplus or a profit are not profit-maximizers and their primary goal is consumption or the facilitation of consumption. Over and above this, they are not *marketing firms* since they *do not respond to the imperatives of customer-oriented management* – rather they are responses to social concerns, or the consumption interests of their members.[3]

Functions of the Firm

We have said that the marketing firm responds to the behavior of its customers. The central model of consumer behavior based on behavior analysis, behavioral economics, and marketing science is the Behavioral Perspective Model (CIRCS), which elaborates the three-term contingency by bringing it into the context of contemporary economies (Foxall, 2017). We can understand the role of the marketing firm more clearly by specifying the factors of which consumer behavior is a function. The stimulus field which influences consumer behavior comprises the discriminative stimuli and motivating operations that constitute the consumer behavior setting. The interaction of the consumer behavior setting with the consumer's learning history, particularly their consumption history, determine the consumer situation, which is the immediate precursor of consumer behavior. Consumer behavior eventuates in two kinds of reinforcement and punishment: utilitarian and informational. Utilitarian reinforcement consists of the functional benefits the consumer derives from owning and using products and services, the capacity of getting from A to B in the case of an automobile. Informational reinforcement refers to the social and symbolic benefits thereof – the status gained from owning and driving a prestigious marque of car, for instance. Some goods deliver just one of

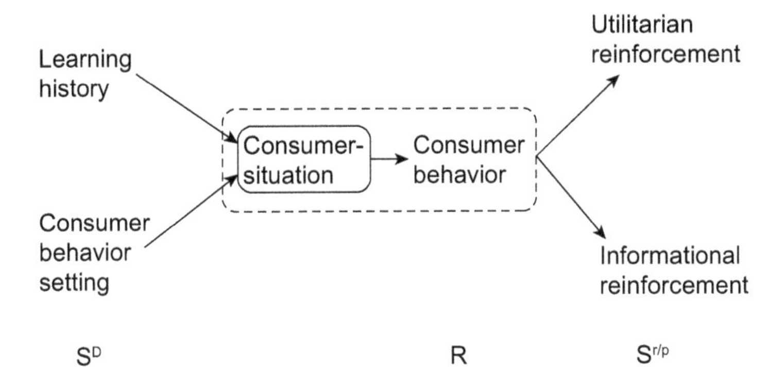

FIGURE 7.1 Summative Behavioral Perspective Model. The model is an elaboration of the three-term contingency – $S^D \rightarrow R \rightarrow S^{r/p}$ – in which the rate of responding CIRCS is a function of the discriminative stimuli (S^D) that prefigure the rewards (S^r) and punishers (S^p) that have previously accompanied the performance of similar behavior in similar circs.

these sources of reinforcement. A wedding ring and many ornamental products are primarily conveyors of informational reinforcement, for instance, while a drink of water offered to a thirst-wracked individual in the Sahara is entirely utilitarian (no one has asked "Is it *Perrier*?" before accepting such an item). The vast majority of goods contain elements of both utilitarian and informational reinforcement and our research indicates that what consumers maximize is a bundle of both kinds of reinforcer in optimal combination (Oliveira-Castro & Foxall, 2017). This finding contributes to our understanding of the nature of inter-industrial competition by suggesting that what consumers actually purchase and consume is not automobiles, exotic vacations, digital cameras, or space travel but particular bundles of utilitarian and informational reinforcement which are provided equally by firms that have not traditionally been seen as competitors.

We can now clarify what we mean by profit maximization. When we say that firms maximize profits, we mean that they seek to maximize the utilitarian and informational reinforcement that *they* receive as a result of trading in the marketplace. Corporate utilitarian reinforcement consists of sales, revenue, and profit, while corporate informational reinforcement inheres in reputation, trustworthiness and reliability.

Management Tasks of the Marketing Firm

Marketing firms uniquely attempt to manage the scope of the consumerate's behavior setting, manage patterns of reinforcement in order to influence consumer demand, and participate in marketing transactions through the marketing mix. The marketing mix comprises the instruments at the firm's disposal to attempt to modify consumer behavior. Broadly speaking these instruments are the famous "4Ps" of product, price, promotion, and place. The art of marketing mix management, however, is to present the consumer not with four separate elements but with a unified whole, for it is the marketing mix that creates sales rather than any particular component of it.

Marketing transactions have four characteristics. They are literal or objective exchanges in which legal titles are transferred between sellers and buyers. They entail prices that are set by competitive market forces. They embrace the entire marketing mix, all four of the 4P's, managed as a whole marketing offering. And, as follows from several of these, they take place in pecuniary markets. The marketing firm seeks to effect marketing transactions based on *exchange* and thereby creating customers. Marketing transactions entail literal exchange or transfer of legal title. A marketing transaction comprises mutual reinforcement based on literal exchange. In a marketing relationship based on economic exchange, the mutual reinforcement is typically accomplished by an item-for-item switch of valued items. The requirement that marketing transactions be understood as literal transfers entails that marketing firms operate in pecuniary markets. Each party to a marketing relationship provides the other with utilitarian and informational reinforcement: typically, goods that supply functional and social utilities are traded for money and marketing intelligence. The marketing intelligence provided by customers, information about what they have bought and their experience of it and their plans for the future provides informational reinforcement which guides the marketer's strategic planning and marketing management activities. The literalness of exchange in typical pecuniary trading is easily discerned, but the question arises what is actually exchanged in the case of intangibles such as services: the essence of a marketing transaction is mutual transfers of legal title to a product or the outcome of a service. Such exchange is a transfer of property rights (see, *inter alia*, Commons, 1924; Demsetz, 2014; Posner, 1995). Legal entitlement and contractual obligations are elements of the contingencies of reinforcement and punishment which influence behavior, just as the market itself is ultimately a source of mutually accepted and reciprocally binding contingencies (Foxall, 1999).

THE MARKETING FIRM AND METACONTINGENCY

Biglan (1995, p. 122) defines a metacontingency as "a contingent relation between a cultural practice and an outcome of that practice that affects the practice's subsequent probability." Metacontingency refers to the behavior of the firm as a whole which is over and above the aggregated behavior of its members. The firm's behavior has its own emergent consequences – such behavior evolves, i.e., there is feedback from the outcome of corporate practices that attracts consequences (consumer behaviors) that encourage the continuance or amendment or abandonment of those practices. By contrast, the combined behavior of a large collective is macrobehavior: it does not produce an additional/emergent output that has a consequential effect on the practices that make up the collective's behavioral repertoire.

Whereas an individual's behavior is typically predicted within an experimental paradigm according to the three-term contingency, an organization's behavior reflects its structure as a system of *interlocking behavioral contingencies* (IBCs). The operant nature of the supra-individual behavior of the organization is inferred from the consequences or outputs *it* generates *over and above the aggregate behaviors of its members* and the effects of the organization's behavior, *which is greater than the sum of its parts*, on *its* subsequent conduct. Biglan and Glenn (2013) speak of the relationships between IBCs, their products (or outputs), and the rewarding or punishing consequences enjoined by their external environments on these products, such as *metacontingencies*. The supra-personal behavior of the marketing firm consists of the marketing mixes that it generates, launches into the marketplace, and subsequently manages through their life cycles. The accent which the theory of the marketing firm places on exchange relationships as central to marketing transactions suggests the mechanism by which the marketing firm and its customer base are bound together, namely the concept of bilateral contingency, to which we shall return (Foxall, 1999, 2014a, 2014b, 2015b).

The metacontingency concept is a means of describing the interactions of individual consumers with firms, and of firms with other firms, as based on interwoven contingencies. Each entity is a contextual system in its own right, its behavior predictable from its learning history and behavior setting (Foxall, 2018). The idea of the marketing firm rests, moreover, on a distinction between the behavioral outputs of organizations that are metacontingencies and those of collectivities of persons who may form the firm's customer base (Foxall, 2015b;

see also Biglan & Glenn, 2013; Houmanfar et al., 2009). Hence, the import of a firm as a metacontingency derives from its behavioral output having emerged from, but nevertheless over and above, the combined actions of its members. This renders the output of the metacontingency qualitatively different from the aggregated behaviors of its members. Such metacontingent corporate behavior evolves in its own right as its consequences are selected or deselected by the environment, in this case by the firm's customers, and potential customers, who respond to the marketing mixes it presents. The behavioral output of the firm's consumers is, in contrast, the aggregated consequences of their several actions. While it is possible to perform statistical operations on measures of this behavior, as though it were an entity in its own right, it remains no more than a combination of individual operant responses (Biglan & Glenn, 2013). Crucially, this combined behavioral entity does not evolve: its future prevalence is not sensitive to any environmental consequences that it generates in toto since it produces no behavioral outputs in addition to those of consumers *en masse* that can be differentially acted on by a selective environment. Such behavior, the actions of a large collectivity, is termed macrobehavior (Glenn, 1991, 2004).

The marketing firm's output is the marketing mix – not a product alone but a fusion of the product and non-product instruments available to the firm to attempt to influence demand and which acts as a single entity to create a customer. For what produces sales is not the product alone or advertising alone but the mix of elements that the firm has at its disposal to convert consumer wants into consumer demand: product, price, promotion (including advertising), and place (representing distribution utilities). Therefore, comprehensive marketing mix management is a mandatory component of the output of the marketing firm in a competence theory for it is the marketing mix as a unified entity that creates customers. The kind of firm we are considering is only competent to market successfully if it employs all four elements of the marketing mix in optimal fashion. Social marketing campaigns by contrast rely heavily on persuasive communication – in fact, for many this is the sole element of the marketing mix employed. The deployment of a communications strategy is not marketing, and clearly it does not entail marketing mix management.

An organization other than a firm could evince metacontingency: many practices of non-firm organizations have outputs that are acted on by the wider community in ways that determine the probability of those practices. This might be true of public corporations, partnerships, marketing cooperatives, social marketing campaigns, but not of consumer cooperatives. But the marketing firm is a unique kind of metacontingency in that its goal of π-maximization, which it does not share with its stakeholder sets it apart from other organizations. It alone operates in a competitive marketplace with market-determined prices, it alone responds to the imperatives of customer-oriented management, it alone has a marketing mix as its emergent output, and manages the entrepreneurial process which it exists to encapsulate.

BILATERAL CONTINGENCY

A Nexus of Bilateral Contingencies

Bilateral contingency analysis concerns the overt relationships between the marketing firm and a customer, either a final consumer or a corporate purchaser (Figure 7.4). (Note that the bilateral contingencies that link the firm, its stakeholders, and consumerates include contractual relationships, e.g., between the firm and its customers, or the firm and its employees, and noncontractual relationships among all these parties that are both commercial and social in nature. The latter are termed "mutuality" relationships (see Foxall, 1999). The task of marketing management is to plan, devise, and implement marketing mixes that deliver satisfactions for the firm's customer base that are profitable for the firm. The components of the marketing

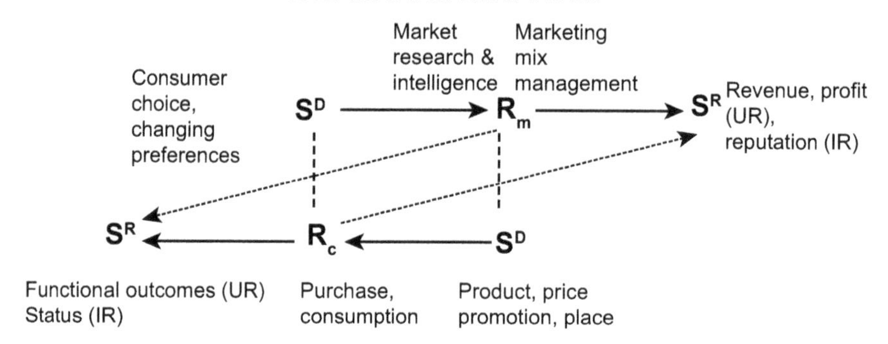

FIGURE 7.2 Bilateral contingency.

Source: Foxall, G. R. (2015b). Consumer behavior analysis and the marketing firm: Bilateral contingency in the context of environmental concern, *Journal of Organizational Behavior Management, 35*, 44–69. Reproduced by permission.

mix (product, price, promotion, and place utilities) appear in the marketplace initially as discriminative stimuli for the consumer behaviors of browsing, purchasing, and consuming. Purchasing includes the exchange of money for the ownership of the legal right to a product or service, and this pecuniary exchange acts as a source of both utilitarian reinforcement (in the form of resources that can be paid out or reinvested) and informational reinforcement (in the form of feedback on corporate performance) for the marketing firm. The efficacy of R_m (managerial behavior) in fulfilling the professional requirements of marketing management, namely the creation of a customer who purchases the product at a price level sufficient to meet the goals of the firm, is determined by the generation of profit and reputation for the firm (depicted by the dotted diagonal line in Figure 7.2.) This consumer behavior (R_c) also provides discriminative stimuli for further marketing intelligence activities, marketing planning and the devising and implementation of marketing mixes that respond to the stabilities and/or dynamic nature of the behavior of the customer base (Foxall, 1999, 2014a, 2014b; Vella & Foxall, 2011). At this level of market interaction between the enterprise and its customer base, managerial behavior can be viewed as maximizing a utility function, comprising a combination of utilitarian reinforcement and informational reinforcement. The firm is embedded in a nexus of bilateral contingencies, and the management of multilateral contingencies lies at the heart of its administrative task. This is not to say that the firm is *coterminous* with such a nexus but that it provides the nucleus of a network of interrelationships among its stakeholders.

THE MANAGEMENT OF THE STRATEGIC PROCESS

The central aspect of the management of strategic scope that defines the marketing firm's character is its responsibility for the management of the firm's strategic scope, which is the range of marketing mixes the firm can support and the consumerates it can serve with them. There are three elements to the management of this strategic process: the creation of marketing intelligence, the design of marketing strategy, and marketing mix management. In the first, the firm initially acquires data on existing and potential markets and then plans its marketing response. In this procedure, the firm establishes its feasible marketing scope. In the second element, which entails the formulation of marketing strategy, the firm assesses its strategic

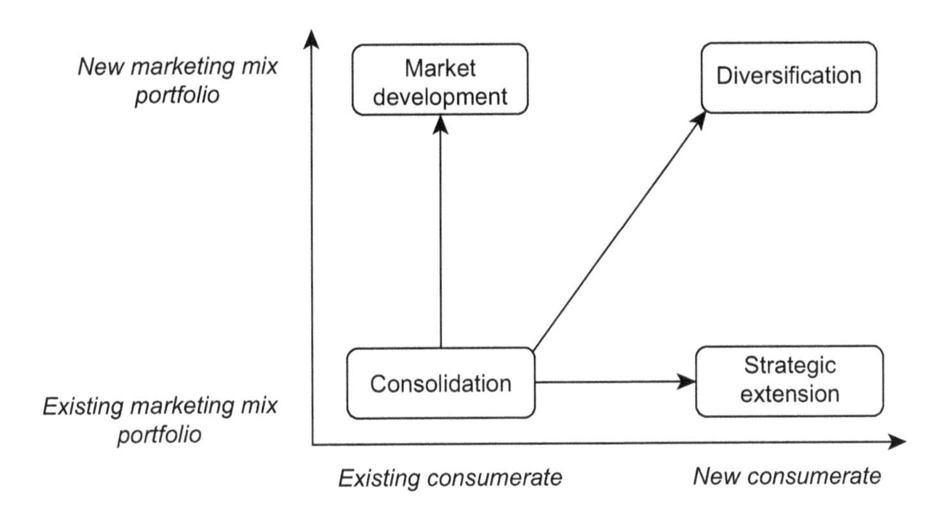

FIGURE 7.3 Strategic scope. Strategic scope defines the marketing mixes the firm can support and the consumerates it can serve with them.

environment and then finalizes its strategic scope aspirations. This procedure establishes the firm's planned marketing scope. In the third element, which comprises the management of the firm's portfolio of marketing mixes, there are also two stages: the design of the marketing mixes, which are intended to effect the firm's planned strategic scope and the administration of the marketing mix portfolio within the competitive marketplace. The endpoint of this element is the achievement of the firm's realized marketing scope.

The management of the strategic process is that of the firm's strategic scope, defined by the range of marketing mixes a firm can support and the spectrum of consumerates through whose service with them it can achieve its objectives of survival and profit maximization (Figure 7.3). Achieving a strategic scope that attains these objectives imposes three obligations on firms, each of which demands specific informational inputs and decision outputs. The resulting spheres of operation are the *creation of marketing intelligence* which typically involves market search and managerial response, reveals the potential (*feasible*) strategic scope of the firm given its capabilities and resources; the *formulation of marketing strategy*, concerned to determine the planned strategic scope of the firm, namely the markets it will serve, the marketing mixes with which it will seek to accomplish this, and expectations of further diversification and innovation. Another way of saying this is that it is activity that determines the *potential* strategic scope of the firm which the organization plans to achieve and it involves the detailed planning of the selection of product-market scope of the firm and how it will be resourced; and *marketing mix management*, the planning and implementation of the portfolio of marketing mixes through which the firm will seek to achieve its objectives developed in the course of the first two stages. This determines the *revealed* or *effective* strategic scope of the firm.

Creation of Marketing Intelligence

Possible incompleteness in the market is revealed by a market search (confined necessarily within the strategic scope of the firm, though one would hope with an eye to extraneous opportunities too). By revealing the feasible strategic scope of the firm, this should engender planning based on the fact that market incompleteness is the identification of a gap in the market which can be filled by product development, market development, or diversification (the last of which is diversification in Penrose's terms). There may be no response necessary to the intelligence so gathered and evaluated.

Formulation of Marketing Strategy

The firm assesses its strategic environment by considering the marketing opportunities available to it and the behaviors of consumers and competitors. This could be done with the aid of external consultants and agents. However, planned movement in any one of these directions reflects a change in the strategic scope of the firm (following on from decision-making on the basis of marketing intelligence and planning). This decision-making must recognize that, although the market search was undertaken within the strategic scope of the firm its results and revealed potentials have now got to be rigorously reexamined within the capabilities framework of the organization (Day, 2011). But the planning of future marketing scope must not be confined within the preexisting corporate policy and strategy: it ought also to impinge on and challenge that strategic position so that it is not a static straitjacket; if necessary, the firm's strategic scope must be modified and decisions made with respect to the resources the firm will employ and how it will utilize them.

Marketing Mix Management

The firm must design each of its marketing mixes as a unity of product, place, promotion, and price. It is the marketing mix that produces sales, not just any one part of it. It is feasible that external consultants or agents could assist in this stage. The firm must also manage its portfolio of marketing mixes as a single entity (Figure 7.4). This determines the actual strategic scope of the firm. Marketing mix management presents a more complex task than the product portfolio management that concentrates only on a single element of the marketing mix (Foxall, 2015c).

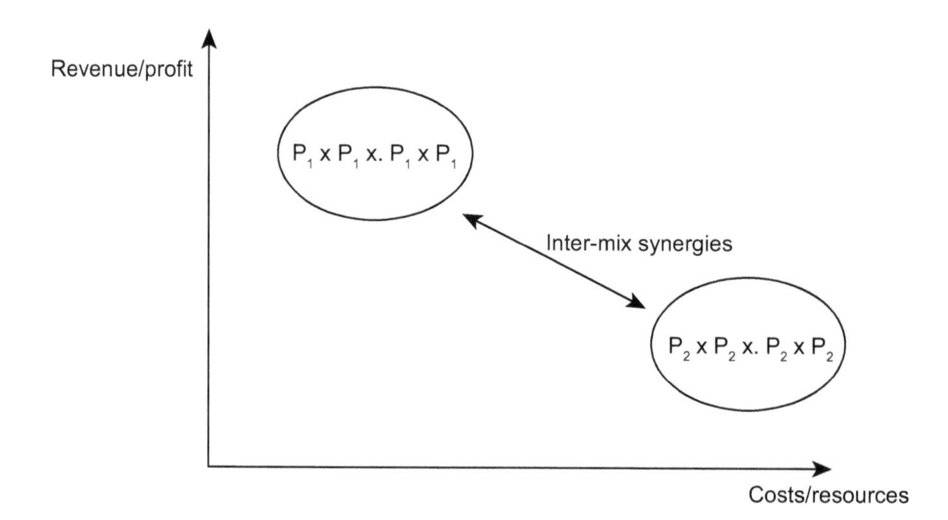

FIGURE 7.4 Portfolio of marketing mixes. The strategic scope represented by the portfolio of marketing mixes that the firm manages determines the extent to which the firm consolidates its market positions or diversifies into novel areas. The portfolio must be managed as a single entity. For simplicity, only two marketing mixes are shown.

The marketing firm is a means of identifying and responding to market incompleteness by altering its strategic scope (product/market development, diversification). The point about the firm's undertaking this is (i) to economize on transaction costs but also, and at least as important, (ii) to enhance sales (physical) and revenues (cash). Entrepreneurship is involved in all three of these marketing resources and the tasks that they entail. Entrepreneurship is the identification of market incompleteness, the response to it in light of the firm's current strategic scope, and the development and deployment of appropriate marketing mixes, which ensure that the firm's overall mix portfolio achieves its profit objectives. This does not necessarily mean it maximizes profit, only that it achieves sufficient profit to enable it to invest, satisfy shareholders, and survive and prosper. Entrepreneurship is the successful planning of profitable (in the above sense) feasible strategic scope and the implementation of the decisions that ensue with respect to the management of strategic scope. This can be undertaken only within the organization.

Some general comments are necessary. First, the management of strategic scope views the strategic process as a single entity, rather than three disjointed spheres of operation, which as a whole is concerned with the creation and implementation of the strategic scope of the firm. Its goal and content is the portfolio of marketing mixes that constitute the emergent output of the business organization, which influences, first, consumer behavior and, second, the fortunes of the firm itself and hence its subsequent behavior. Indeed, the management of a whole portfolio of marketing mixes in a unified and harmonious manner is the very embodiment of the firm as a metacontingency, and it rests on the concept of the bilateral contingencies that define marketing and mutuality relationships within and beyond the firm.

ENTREPRENEURIAL ENCAPSULATION

The entrepreneur in neoclassical microeconomics is both the owner and manager of the firm. However, given the concentration on states of equilibrium in the neoclassical model of the firm, the absence of change, there is little for the occupant of these roles to do. The firm is a price taker that generates a single product for which there is an assured market; consumers' tastes are invariable, perfect knowledge obtains, and the firm, like every other firm, inescapably earns a "normal" profit. The entrepreneur is thus spared the necessity of having to make decisions by the theoretically-prescribed contingencies of reinforcement that define the market in equilibrium. This state of affairs, which obviates the need for decision-making, innovation, or marketing, is firmly rejected by economists of the Austrian school (the initiators of which were indeed Austrian economists) for whom the presumption of omniscience, the unnecessity of innovation, and the static conditions of production are entirely at odds with the realities of the economic system as it exists. (The Austrian School is described very briefly in the box below.) Far from equilibrium being the norm, markets are constantly in flux and entrepreneurs discover opportunities for novelty in order to profit. The essence of entrepreneurship in this account lies in surprise and discovery, the alertness to the possibility of profiting through arbitrage, and thus achieving the returns due to the first-mover (Kirzner, 1980). Both calculation and management are, on this view, absent from entrepreneurship.

The Austrian Perspective in a Nutshell

The prevalent approach to economics, found in most basic and advanced texts, emphasizes economic behavior at equilibrium, and is concerned principally with economies that are in a state of static optimization. The focus is therefore on the end states that economic systems reach, rather than with how they reach them and what disturbs them.

Austrian economics, originated by a group of nineteenth-century economists (including Menger, 1976; von Mises, 2016; Hayek, 1949), adopts a realistic perspective, focusing on the marketplace as a process that is ever-changing rather than one that has reached an endpoint that reflects equilibrium. In terms of the behavior of economic actors, the Austrian approach does not make the simplifying assumption that these individuals are omniscient, having the perfect knowledge of prices and the behavior of other actors, with which neoclassical economists simplify their analyses. On the contrary, Austrian economics stresses the uncertainty which surrounds all attempts to base decisions on knowledge, and the consequent fallibility of economic actors like consumers and managers. They know some things but not everything and, in particular, they cannot be aware of what other economic actors know. Markets are not static but highly dynamic, preferences and behaviors change frequently, and the task of the economic actor is to discover, from her subjective viewpoint, what is happening and how to profit from it. Whereas the entrepreneur in neoclassical economics knows the structure of the market in which she operates, notably, how many buyers and sellers there are, and her options on how much to produce and at what price to offer it are prescribed by that structure, the entrepreneur in Austrian perspective must ascertain opportunities to profit through observation of what can be efficiently bought and sold (Kirzner, 1973; Sautet, 2000).

For useful and up-to-date introductions, see Holcombe, R. G. (2014). *Advanced introduction to Austrian economics*. Edward Elgar; Foss, N. J., Klein, P. G., & McCaffrey, M. (2019). *Austrian perspectives on entrepreneurship, strategy, and organization*. Cambridge University Press.

The Austrian perspective is much closer to the idea of business development and creative enterprise inherent in modern strategic management and marketing, as well as recent contributions to the theory of the firm. Drucker (1977, 2007), for instance, argues that marketing and innovation are the sole functions of the business organization, the objective of which is to create a customer. Entrepreneurship remains, however, a "special" function. For Penrose (2009, p. 31), "Entrepreneurial services are those contributions to the operations of a firm which relate to the introduction and acceptance on behalf of the firm of new ideas, particularly with respect to products ..." She contrasts entrepreneurship on this definition with managerial services, consisting as they do in "the execution of entrepreneurial ideas and proposals and the supervision of existing operations." Crucially, however, she notes that the same individuals may be involved in the provision of both kinds of service, a point to which I shall return.[4]

Entrepreneurship, seen as so decisive a mainspring of economic activity, requires protection from competitors. Also writing in the Austrian tradition, Holcombe (2007, 2013, 2014) stresses that entrepreneurial action requires internalization as it is a matter of securing personal or corporate advantage, and that firms therefore exist as "repositories of knowledge," knowledge which is necessarily tacit and decentralized. By preventing its availability to competitors, but also retaining a tacit understanding of production and marketing among those who can make effective use of it, the firm serves to encapsulate *innovative* knowledge and, indeed, entrepreneurship itself. Holcombe is making more than an abstract point here. There are tangible benefits to the firm that can safely make decisions to acquire productive inputs rather than generate them in-house because it has trust in the ability of a supplier to secure and safeguard vital tacit knowledge. The frequently febrile relationships between firms can, therefore, be an important determinant of the success or failure of an inter-organizational affiliation. An additional rationale of the firm inheres, then, in entrepreneurs' ability to operate within these business organizations by virtue of their being knowledge repositories. Firms are differentiated by the specialization of their tacit knowledge and according to Holcombe this helps maintain tacit knowledge within their boundaries. This is realized in the ability of entrepreneurial innovation to increase profits and this is why entrepreneurs benefit from organizing their activities within firms. The organization of production within firms enables the entrepreneur to benefit maximally from innovations due to tacit knowledge.

BILATERAL CONTINGENCY REVISITED

We have seen that bilateral contingency is a reciprocal interaction of the three-term contingencies that govern the behavior of two parties to a transaction or relationship (Foxall, 1999). It may also be seen as the dynamic interaction of two behavior settings. The behavior of one party supplies the reinforcing and punishing consequences of the other's behavior; in addition, the behavior of one party provides discriminative stimuli and motivating operations for the behavior of the other. The meshing of these reciprocal contingencies determines whether the relationship between the parties is of short- or long-term duration; it therefore determines whether one or the other party will engage in a search for alternative arrangements.

Extra-Firm Bilateral Contingency: Marketing Firm/Consumerate

The behavior of the marketing firm acts as reinforcing and aversive stimuli for the consumerate and vice versa – and these behaviors also provide discriminative stimuli and motivating operations for the other party to the transaction. In other words, each of the two parties impinges on the behavior setting of the other, attempting to alter its scope – usually by closing it (i.e., making a particular behavioral response more probable). Consumers' preferences, as identified in the marketing intelligence phase of marketing operations, provide the spur to the design and management of marketing mixes, leading to profit and reputation for the firm. The marketing mix provides discriminative stimuli and motivating operations for consumer behavior which results in utilitarian and informational reinforcement.

Intra-Firm Bilateral Contingency: Manager-to-Manager

We can use the same framework to analyze behavior within the firm, manager-to-manager, for instance. Manager-to-manager behaviors do not entail marketing transactions but constitute nevertheless a bilateral contingency: there is no literal exchange, no pecuniary markets and no marketing mix. This is not a commercial relationship but a professional one. It is what we might call a "mutual relationship."

Intra-Firm Bilateral Contingency: Principal–Agent

Next, we analyze the interactions of the owners of the firm who employ others to ensure the smooth and efficient running of operations – the well-known principal–agent relationship. Output can be increased if it is undertaken jointly – by people cooperating. The problem is that left to ourselves in small groups where everyone benefits from everyone else's output, there is a tendency sometimes to shirk, to free-ride on the efforts of others. If the joint working takes place within the confines of the firm, it becomes possible to monitor each person's effort and reduce the problem of free-riding. In other words, the firm makes principal–agent relationships manageable. The election of one manager to oversee the working arrangements of all laborers reduces free-riding and ensures that each employee's wages are closely related to the extra/marginal productivity of their output. Relationships within the firm between principal and agent are contractual, just like those of a consumer to a tradesperson. In the consumption case there is no question of authority, only the capacity of either party to the contract to refuse to trade further with the other.

Intra-Firm Bilateral Contingency: Function–Function

Also within the firm the relationships between functions can be analyzed in this way. How is marketing related to production, for example? Or the marketing intelligence operation to marketing mix management? Bilateral contingency provides a means of analyzing the behaviors of each in terms of the effects this has on the scope of the behavior setting of the other.

TOWARD PERFORMANCE THEORIES

Symmetrical and Asymmetrical Bilateral Contingencies

Competence theories such as the one I have outlined should generate performance theories that can be tested in natural settings. I would like to reach toward a conclusion by suggesting one sphere in which this might be possible.

Symmetrical Bilateral Contingency

Symmetrical bilateral contingency occurs when the parties to transactions both participate in metacontingencies, for instance, the marketing firm and a customer. Marketer behavior is met by that of the corporate customer – the marketing firm might have a whole gamut of strategic exploration and planning at its beck and call to tailor its offering to the specific needs of the customer. But in response the corporate customer has a purchasing strategy, formulated and refined within its own capabilities analysis and its knowledge of where the purchased item fits into its corporate strategy. And it can always choose to obtain the item from another supplier or even make it internally for itself. The organizations seem well-matched, and we can predict that such interactions will be stable, close, easily read by the parties involved and reliable.

Asymmetrical Bilateral Contingency

Less of a hypothesis for testing because it is too obvious is the relationship between an organization that participates in a metacontingency and the disparate individuals whose actions amount to macrobehavior (e.g., the marketing firm and its final consumerate). But it is also that situation where marketers become complacent, neglect innovation and entrepreneurship, and expect customers to remain loyal come what may, then the relationships with their consumers will become increasingly remote, difficult to read (or no one will be trying to read the contingencies) and fragile. The consumer will, if opportunities are available, seek alternative sources of supply.

Balanced Bilateral Contingency

A testable hypothesis for testing: that marketer– final-consumerate bilateral contingencies can be balanced rather than asymmetrical. Superficially, the final consumer seems to be in a poor place vis-à-vis the corporate organization but, if I am right, the imperatives of customer-oriented management ensure that the consumerate as a whole enjoys countervailing power through its ability to turn to competing suppliers, go off the whole idea, switch preferences, and so on. Given that 80 to 90% of new products in these markets fail, even after the most rigorous market testing, test marketing, and marketing mix strategizing, it would seem that consumers have some leverage here that makes the relationship balanced if not entirely symmetrical. (Principal reasons appear to be the sheer inability of businesses to anticipate the wants, preferences, and behaviors of their customers, who should according to the theory of the marketing firm be as close to the modern entrepreneurial firm as breathing, nearer indeed than hands and feet;[5] see, for further discussion, Foxall, 2015a). We can predict that such relationships would be stable (though changing in consumerate composition), easily read by the parties, distal, and reliable.

CONCLUSIONS

In conclusion, I have argued that the marketing firm differs from other organizations by virtue of goal separation, its responsiveness to the imperatives of customer-oriented management, its initiation of and participation in marketing transactions, its practice and encapsulation of entrepreneurship, and its being a metacontingency. The marketing firm is not unique in being based on metacontingencies, but it is a unique organization that differs from other organizations even though they evince metacontingency. The marketing firm is a multilateral contingency, a nexus of bilateral contingencies. The nature of these contingencies and the opportunities they present for the management of the marketing firm are fascinating, and go well beyond the present chapter. These topics, and their implications, are considered at length in a forthcoming text (Foxall, in preparation).

STUDY QUESTIONS

1. How has the role of marketing evolved in the era of consumer choice?
2. How does the firm goal of profit maximization differ from the goals of stakeholders, employees, etc.?
3. Distinguish between utilitarian and informational reinforcement with examples.
4. In your own words – describe a bilateral contingency. How does it differ from the traditional concept of the contingency?
5. Explain the three elements of the management of the strategic process.

NOTES

1. Based on an Invited Presentation at the 2019 Annual Conference of the Association for Behavior Analysis International, Chicago, IL, entitled "The Behavioral Economics of the Marketing Firm: Metacontingency, Bilateral contingency, and Agency." It draws also in part on Foxall, G. R. (2020). "The theory of the marketing firm," *Managerial and Decision Economics*, 41, 164–184.
2. At least as far as the designation "intellectual" is concerned: "spiritual" might be a value-judgment too far in both cases!
3. For critical views of Spulber's thesis, see Hart (2011), Walker (2017).
4. The full definitions are as follows: "Entrepreneurial services are those contributions to the operations of a firm which relate to the introduction and acceptance on behalf of the firm of new ideas, particularly with respect to products, location, and significant changes in technology, to the acquisition of new managerial personnel, to fundamental changes in the administrative organization of the firm, to the raising of capital, and to the making of plans for expansion, including the choice of method of expansion. Entrepreneurial services are contrasted with managerial services, which relate to the execution of entrepreneurial ideas and proposals and the supervision of existing operations. The same individuals may, and more often than not probably do, provide both types of service to the firm" (Penrose, 2009, Fn1, 31–32).
5. Apologies to Alfred Lord Tennyson, *The higher pantheism*.

REFERENCES

Andrews, K.R. (1971). *The concept of corporate strategy*. Irwin.

Biglan, A. (1995). *Changing cultural practices: A contextualist framework for intervention research*. Context Press.

Biglan, A. & Glenn, S.S. (2013). Toward prosocial behavior and environments: Behavioral and cultural contingencies in a public health framework. In G.J. Madden, W.V. Dube, T.D. Hackenberg, G.P. Hanley & K.A. Lattal (Eds.), *APA Handbook of behavior analysis* (Vol. 2, pp. 255–275). American Psychological Association.

Chomsky, N. (1957). *Syntactic structures*. Mouton.

Chomsky, N. (1965). *Aspects of the theory of syntax*. MIT Press.

Commons, J.R. (1924). *The legal foundations of capitalism.* Augustus M. Kelley.
Day, G.S. (2011). Closing the marketing capabilities gap. *Journal of Marketing, 75*, 183–195.
Demsetz, H. (2014). *The economics of the business firm: Seven critical commentaries.* Revised edition. Cambridge University Press.
Drucker, P.F. (1977). *Management.* Harper.
Drucker, P.F. (2007). *The practice of management.* Routledge.
Fagerstrøm, A., Pawar, S., Sigurdsson, V., Foxall, G.R., & Yani-de-Soriano, M. (2017). That personal profile image might jeopardize your rental opportunity! On the relative impact of the seller's facial expressions upon buying behavior on Airbnb. *Computers in Human Behavior*, 72, 123–131.
Foss, N.J., Klein, P.G. & McCaffrey, M. (2019). *Austrian perspectives on entrepreneurship, strategy, and organization.* Cambridge University Press.
Foxall, G.R. (1999). The marketing firm, *Journal of Economic Psychology, 20*, 207–234.
Foxall, G.R. (2014a). The marketing firm and consumer choice: Implications of bilateral contingency for levels of analysis in organizational neuroscience. *Frontiers in Human Neuroscience, 8*, 472. doi:10.3389/ fnhum.2014.00472
Foxall, G.R. (2014b). Cognitive requirements of competing neuro-behavioral decision systems: some implications of temporal horizon for managerial behavior in organizations. *Frontiers in Human Neuroscience*, 8 (184), 1–17. doi: 10.3389/ fnhum.2014.00184.
Foxall, G.R. (2015a). *Strategic marketing management.* Routledge. Routledge Library Edition.
Foxall, G.R. (2015b). Consumer behavior analysis and the marketing firm: Bilateral contingency in the context of environmental concern. *Journal of Organizational Behavior Management, 35*, 44–69.
Foxall, G.R (2015c). *Corporate innovation: Marketing and strategy.* Routledge. Routledge Library Edition.
Foxall, G.R. (2016). Operant behavioral economics. *Managerial and Decision Economics, 37*, 215–223.
Foxall, G.R. (2017). *Advanced introduction to consumer behavior analysis.* Edward Elgar.
Foxall, G.R. (2018). An economic psychology of the marketing firm. In: Lewis, A. (Ed.), *The Cambridge handbook of psychology and economic behaviour* (pp. 365–402). Cambridge University Press.
Foxall, G.R. (in preparation). *The theory of the marketing firm: Responding to the imperatives of customer-oriented management.* Palgrave Macmillan.
Glenn, S.S. (1991). Contingencies and metacontingencies: Relations among behavioral, cultural, and biological evolution. In P.A. Lamal (Ed.), *Behavioral analysis of societies and cultural practices* (pp. 39–73). Hemisphere.
Glenn, S.S. (2004). Individual behavior, culture, and social change. *The Behavior Analyst, 27*, 133–151.
Hart, O.D, (2011). Thinking about therefore firm: A review of Daniel Spulber's *The Theory of the Firm. Journal of Economic Literature*, 49, 101–113.
Hayek, F.A. (1949). *Individualism and economic order.* Routledge and Kegan Paul.
Holcombe, R.G. (2007). *Entrepreneurship and economic progress.* Routledge.
Holcombe, R.G. (2013). *Producing prosperity: An inquiry into the operation of the market process.* Routledge.
Holcombe, R.G. (2014). *Advanced introduction to the Austrian School of Economics.* Edward Elgar.
Houmanfar, R., Rodrigues, N.J., & Smith, G.S. (2009). Role of communication networks in behavioral systems analysis. *Journal of Organizational Behavior Management, 29*, 257–275.
Kirzner, I.M. (1973). *Competition and entrepreneurship.* Chicago University Press.
Kirzner, I.M. (1980). *The prime mover of progress.* London: Institute of Economic Affairs.
Menger, C. (1976). *Principles of economics.* New York: New York University Press.
Menon, R.G.V., Sigurdsson, V., Larsen, N.M., Fagerstrøm, A., Sørensen, H., Marteinsdottir, H. G., Foxall, G. R. (2019). How to grow brand post engagement on Facebook and Twitter for airlines? An empirical investigation of design and content factors *Journal of Air Transport Management*, 79, 1–10.
Mises. L. von (2016). *Human action.* Ludwig von Mises Institute.
Oliveira-Castro, J.M. & Foxall, G.R. (2017). Consumer maximization of utilitarian and informational reinforcement: Comparing two utility measures with reference to social class. *The Behavior Analyst, 42*, 457–476.
Penrose, E. (2009). *The theory of the growth of the firm* (4th ed.). Oxford University Press.
Posner, R.A. (1995). *Overcoming law.* Harvard University Press.
Sautet, F.E. (2000). *An entrepreneurial theory of the firm.* Routledge.
Simon, H. & Fassnacht, M. (2019). *Price management.* Springer.
Smith, A. (1776). *An inquiry into the nature and causes of the wealth of nations.* Methuen.
Spulber, D.F. (2009). *The theory of the firm: Microeconomics with endogenous entrepreneurs, firms, markets, and organizations.* Cambridge University Press.
Vella, K.J. & Foxall, G.R. (2011). *The marketing firm: Economic psychology of corporate behaviour.* Edward Elgar.
von Mises, L. (1949). *Human action.* Yale University Press.
Walker, P. (2017). *The theory of the firm: An overview of the economic mainstream.* Routledge.

8

Acceptance and Commitment Training

Improving Performance in Organizations with Applied Contextual Behavioral Science

Daniel J. Moran, Sonja Batten, Madison A. Gamble, and Paul Atkins

Laboring within organizations and industries is a major human endeavor. For many people, working comprises a significant portion of adult life. Working is behavior, and takes on many forms and functions differing between business sectors. There are differences between blue-collar and white-collar jobs, entrepreneurship and corporate employment, leadership positions or front-line worker positions, and a great deal of diversity between industries. This human endeavor is quite varied, and contextual behavioral science blended with Organizational Behavior Management can make a positive impact on workers' experiences and active engagement in the workplace.

When a Gallup poll (Gallup, 2019) investigated *active engagement* at the workplace – defined as people being "involved in, enthusiastic about, and committed to their work" (p. 1) – results showed that 34% of US workers met such dedicated criteria. The same report suggests "workers who have miserable work experiences," or *active disengagement*, is demonstrated by 13% of US workers. The rest of the study's cohort – 53% of the workers in the US – were "not engaged," yet could be construed as having reasonable work satisfaction, but not emotionally or cognitively connected to their work or workplace. This implies that the behavior of more than half of the US workforce could be accelerated to achieve the vision, mission, and goals for each organization. Modern applied behavioral science can assist with this endeavor while also aim to develop psychologically healthy workplaces that support optimal health for the worker.

The data from this most recent Gallup poll suggests engagement has increased over the last few years. Looking at previous Gallup polls, the percentage of actively disengaged employees was at an all-time high during the 2007–2008 US recession, and measured at 20% of those workers. On average, since Gallup started measuring workplace engagement in 2000, 17% of US employees were actively disengaged during the workday. These data are not likely to be shocking for most readers who observe performance in the workplace. If anything, they might appear to be underestimations. If you watch the behavior of people working in public, you can sometimes hear small talk among employees instead of focusing on their tasks. With the ubiquity of smartphones, you can see cashiers, crossing guards, and even ride-share drivers texting while they should be attending to their job. With the advent of social media, one can observe people's Facebook, Instagram, and Snapchat posts seem to continue during their workday. One can also surmise that workplace tasks do not impede an individual's high rate of this socially reinforced behavior, and infer that social media participation is emblematic of active disengagement at work.

DOI: 10.4324/9781003198949-8

Worldwide, the data are more concerning. According to an international poll sample "across 155 countries indicates that just 15% of employees worldwide are engaged in their job. Two-thirds are not engaged, and 18% are actively disengaged" (Gallup, 2019, p. 22). This calculates to approximately 340 million actively disengaged workers around the Gallup who were likely to be unproductive, unhappy, and disruptive. This study implies that humans spend so much time at work, but some of them spend very little of that time working. Since Gallup's definition of engagement included being "committed to their work," then an applied contextual behavioral science application focusing on *commitment* might help to influence this measure.

This widespread disillusionment with employment is not limited to commercial enterprises. Nurses, police, teachers and government staff (to name a few) also complain about excessive top-down attempts to control behaviors through administrative processes and coercion, and such workers are leaving in droves (Laloux, 2014). For the vast majority of people worldwide, the work dominating the majority of their waking hours does not enliven them.

ACTRAINING: A PRIMER

Acceptance and Commitment Training (ACTraining; Moran, 2011), which is the integration of Acceptance and Commitment Therapy (ACT; S.C. Hayes et al., 1999) applications in the workplace, can assist companies and employees to improve engagement, increase performance, and accelerate leadership skills while reducing burnout, stress, and injuries (Moran, 2015a). ACTraining can be integrated with applications of Industrial-Organizational (I/O) psychology and Organizational Behavior Management (OBM; e.g., the first section of this text), and other organizational psychology approaches, to change workplace processes and outcomes.

In both public and private sectors of government, industry, and business, I/O psychology and OBM create positive changes in business process improvement, leadership development, and workplace stress reduction through strategic consulting, corporate trainings, and executive coaching. OBM has the potential to improve the well-being of employees on an individual level as well as on a group level where success depends on sharing resources (see Hayes et al., Chapter 9 in this text). Utilizing the ideas of performance management (Daniels, 2000; Wilder et al., Chapter 1 in this text), along with classic applied behavioral science's focus on goal setting (Fellner & Sulzer-Azaroff, 1984) and feedback (Johnson et al., 2015), OBM initiatives can significantly influence key performance indicators (KPIs) in the business world. I/O psychology and OBM has also informed robust initiatives in behavior-based safety (Sulzer-Azaroff & Austin, 2000), Severe Incident Prevention (McSween & Moran, 2017), Behavioral Systems Analysis (Brethower, 2000), and leadership development (Daniels & Daniels, 2007). In the same manner in which ACT is a platform for integrating empirically supported treatments to address clinically-relevant concerns (Moran et al., 2018), ACTraining can be used as a platform for integrating proven organizational psychology applications. ACTraining has been successfully implemented in several organizational sectors (Moran, 2015a), and application manuals have been developed for worksite initiatives (Flaxman et al., 2013) and for industrial safety (Moran, 2013). Similar to ACT, ACTraining aims to increase psychological flexibility, and accelerating psychological flexibility has a significant impact on job-related measures. The following section focuses on psychological flexibility specifically, with particular attention to the implications of psychological flexibility for organizational behavior.

Defining and Assessing Psychological Flexibility at Work

Psychological flexibility may be defined as the skill to:

> Contact the present moment while also being aware of thoughts and emotions – without trying to change those private experiences or be adversely controlled by them – and depending upon

> the situation, persisting in or changing behavior in the pursuit of values and goals. (Moran, 2015a, p. 26)

To summarize the practical application of this construct, people who are rated with higher psychological flexibility are more focused on the here-and-now, dexterous when dealing with their feelings, and motivated to achieve personally significant objectives. Moreover, higher psychologically flexibility suggests that workers are keen to *change* their action plan when it stops leading to valued reinforcers, or *persist* in significant work tasks while on a lean schedule of reinforcement for such behavior.

Kashdan et al. (in press) define psychological flexibility as "the ability to pursue valued life aims despite the presence of pain" (p. 2), and developed the Personalized Psychological Flexibility Index (PPFI). This instrument assesses the individual's proclivities for either avoiding or accepting discomfort while engaging in measurable behaviors toward valued goals. The PPFI positively correlates with healthy personality traits, such as conscientiousness, open-mindedness, and self-control, while having a negative association with measures of problematic emotionality. Importantly for applied behavior analysis, the PPFI relates to overt responses, and alludes to "strivings" to add a more objective, behavioral perspective to the process and outcome of psychological flexibility. Kashdan et al. (in press) note:

> Specifically, the PPFI was associated with a greater tendency to select personal strivings that are central to a person's identity, provide a systematic framework for selecting goals and deal with competing options for allocating finite resources such as time and energy, and are part of a continual future-oriented plan. (p. 32)

ACTraining aims to increase psychological flexibility, which can be measured by the PPFI, and OBM professionals can look to measurable behavior change as a result.

In the ACTraining literature, the conventional assessment tool for psychological flexibility is the Acceptance and Action Questionnaire – Second Edition (AAQ-II; Bond et al., 2011). This tool is reported to measure "psychological inflexibility," and demonstrates large positive correlations with other measures of psychological distress. Bond et al. suggest:

> Psychological inflexibility, or experiential avoidance, is purported to be an important determinant of psychological distress and behavioral ineffectiveness (S. Hayes et al., 1996, 2006); thus, greater levels of inflexibility, indicated by higher AAQ-II scores, should be related to greater emotional distress (e.g., worse general mental health, as well as higher levels of depression, anxiety, and stress), and poorer life functioning (e.g., *show more absences from work*). (p. 683; italics added)

To encapsulate what the test developers are saying: the more psychologically inflexible one reports to be on the questionnaire, the more problematic their behavioral functioning will be, and this could be evidenced in the workplace.

The robust psychometric properties and utility of the AAQ-II, plus the understanding that psychological flexibility influences workplace performance, led to the development of the Work-Related Acceptance and Action Questionnaire (WAAQ; Bond et al., 2012). The test developers report the instrument "correlates significantly more strongly with work-specific variables" (p. 2), and provides "promising evidence that the WAAQ is a valid and reliable measure of psychological flexibility in relation to the workplace" (p. 15). The WAAQ was significantly associated with: "general mental health, neuroticism, conscientiousness, openness to experience, job satisfaction, the number of occasions people are absent from work, the work engagement factors of vigor, dedication, and absorption, as well as task performance" (p. 15). Explicating all of these workplace research constructs is beyond the scope of this chapter, but despite the fact that many of these data come from self-report paper-and-pencil tests, the variables are well-respected and practical in I/O psychology. The WAAQ is practical for OBM professionals because it was shown to be significantly correlated with *task performance* (i.e., overt behavior). Bond et al. (2012) suggest task performance is synonymous with work-related functioning, and measured this variable by asking three independent observers, each with experience in the work task, to rate the quality of performance. This suggests that the more psychologically flexible a person reports to be, the more likely they are performing well on the job task.

In addition, Holmberg et al. (2019) evaluated the psychometric characteristics of the WAAQ, and their "correlations illustrated a significant negative relationship between WAAQ and perceived stress, and a significant positive correlation with work engagement" (p. 103) for nursing staff. The WAAQ has been translated to Swedish, (Holmberg et al., 2019), Spanish (Ruiz & Odriozola-González, 2014), and Chinese (Xu et al., 2017), and shown that despite being administered in diverse areas, such as country, language, and work setting, the WAAQ continues to show negative correlations with psychiatric conditions, neuroticism, and burn-out, and positive correlations with task performance and work engagement. In summary, organizations and workers both benefit from employee psychological flexibility. The following section of the chapter focuses on the effects of ACTraining to increase this robust construct.

Investigating Psychological Flexibility's Influence in the Workplace

Bond and Bunce (2003) demonstrated that higher levels of psychological flexibility forecasted enhanced work performance and mental health, and Bond et al. (2011) showed that computer workers with higher scores on the AAQ-II were less likely to make input errors. This study also demonstrated a significant and positive correlation between acceptance and job satisfaction. When Bond and Flaxman (2006) applied their similar research protocol with a bank, higher levels of psychological flexibility continued to predict better mental health and job performance on new task demands. In addition, they showed that workers with higher psychological flexibility have a greater ability to react more productively to goal-related opportunities. When workers learn to perform a new skill, those who are not distracted by frustrations or stress will likely have better training outcomes, which suggested the utility for ACTraining in the workplace.

According to Bond et al. (2008) workers with higher levels of psychological flexibility professed that they had greater job control, defined as the perceived capability to influence one's work environment to make it more rewarding and less threatening. In addition to improving performance and job control, ACTraining, which aims to increase psychological flexibility, helps mitigate workplace stressors. In a randomized controlled trial (Bond & Bunce, 2000) workers were randomly assigned to either ACTraining or a control group aimed to help workers identify and change stressful events at work, or a waitlist group. ACTraining showed significantly greater improvements than both comparison groups on measures of stress and psychological health. Biron and van Veldhoven (2012) found that workers with higher psychological flexibility measures not only reported to have a greater ability to reduce exhaustion during stressful workdays, but also reported lower levels of emotional exhaustion at the end of their shift, as measured by the Utrecht Burnout Scale-General Version (Schaufeli & van Dierendonck, 2000). Lower measures of psychological flexibility have also been found to be a significant predictor of burnout (Vilardaga et al., 2011), and higher psychological flexibility helps the worker redirect their attention away from stressful feelings and more toward professionally relevant responsibilities. When Lloyd et al. (2013) implemented three half-day ACTrainings to workers, they demonstrated a significant increase in psychological flexibility, and a decrease in exhaustion when compared to a control group. ACTraining for stress management showed a significant effect for improving mental health for employees, and was specifically helpful for stressed workers (Flaxman & Bond, 2010).

Workers receiving ACTraining are more likely to adopt new initiatives in performing work tasks than workers not receiving ACTraining (Luoma et al., 2007; Varra et al., 2008). Additional research supports the use of ACTraining to mitigate stress levels for healthcare workers (Bethay et al., 2013; McConachie et al., 2014), university personnel (Hosseinaei et al., 2013), and early childhood special education teachers (Biglan et al., 2013). ACTraining delivered over the telephone showed workers more skillfully dealing with burnout and improving in performance on personal accomplishments (Luoma & Vilardaga, 2013), and an ACTraining smartphone app helped middle managers successfully deal with stress in the workplace (Ly et al., 2014). ACTraining can be delivered efficiently in the worksite using modern technology.

Overall, ACTraining is effectively designed to improve performance for workers and reduce job stress by increasing psychological flexibility. When employees are psychologically flexible, they can respond in the present moment, while mindful of their thoughts and emotions, and engage in committed actions that are linked to their values. This approach can lead to a more effective worker and greater workplace engagement. Up to this point we have focused on the relationship between psychological flexibility and meaningful behavior, and have provided a brief overview of studies that have demonstrated the effects of ACTraining on improving psychological flexibility. The following section provides an overview of ACTraining itself.

ACTRAINING: THE APPLICATION COMPONENTS

Acceptance and Commitment Therapy and ACTraining are both functionally based, applied science platforms for assessing and adaptably intervening in contexts where behavior change is a goal. ACT and ACTraining are not specific, formal, step-by-step, codified treatment packages, but rather, these platforms establish a context for other specific treatment packages to be functionally applied. Because applied behavioral science goals vary, there are several different ways the ACT model has been refashioned to more suitably fit these different challenges: The DNA-v Model (children and teens; L.L. Hayes & Ciarrochi, 2015), PEAK (people diagnosed with autism; Dixon, 2014), the Matrix (general use; Polk & Schoendorff, 2014), and Choice Point (weight loss; Ciarrochi et al., 2014) are a handful of derivations of the ACT model. This chapter will introduce ACT with the traditional ACT Hexagon Model (S.C. Hayes et al., 2016), and then discuss how to simplify the intervention for the workplace using The Mindful Action Plan (Moran, 2014), and the Safety Commitment Plan Worksheet (Moran, 2013).

The traditional ACT Hexagon Model (see Figure 8.1) promotes psychological flexibility by teaching a variety of skills across six interrelated areas: contacting the present moment, acceptance, defusion, perspective taking, values clarification, and committed action. Once learned, these skills can work together synergistically, promote workplace functioning, and create an effective context for both the employee and employer. While moving forward with reading each of these six components, please understand that the whole is greater than the sum of its parts. An applied behavior analyst using ACTraining at the workplace does not just select one out of these six components to influence a worker's behavior, but rather blends them all together for greater influence on the individual's repertoire. Let's turn to discussing each of these components.

Contact with the Present Moment

Behavior happens "now." All responses are emitted in the current moment. Verbal behavior often influences people to engage in language about the past or the future. In fact, Killingsworth and Gilbert (2010) show that people report that they are thinking about something

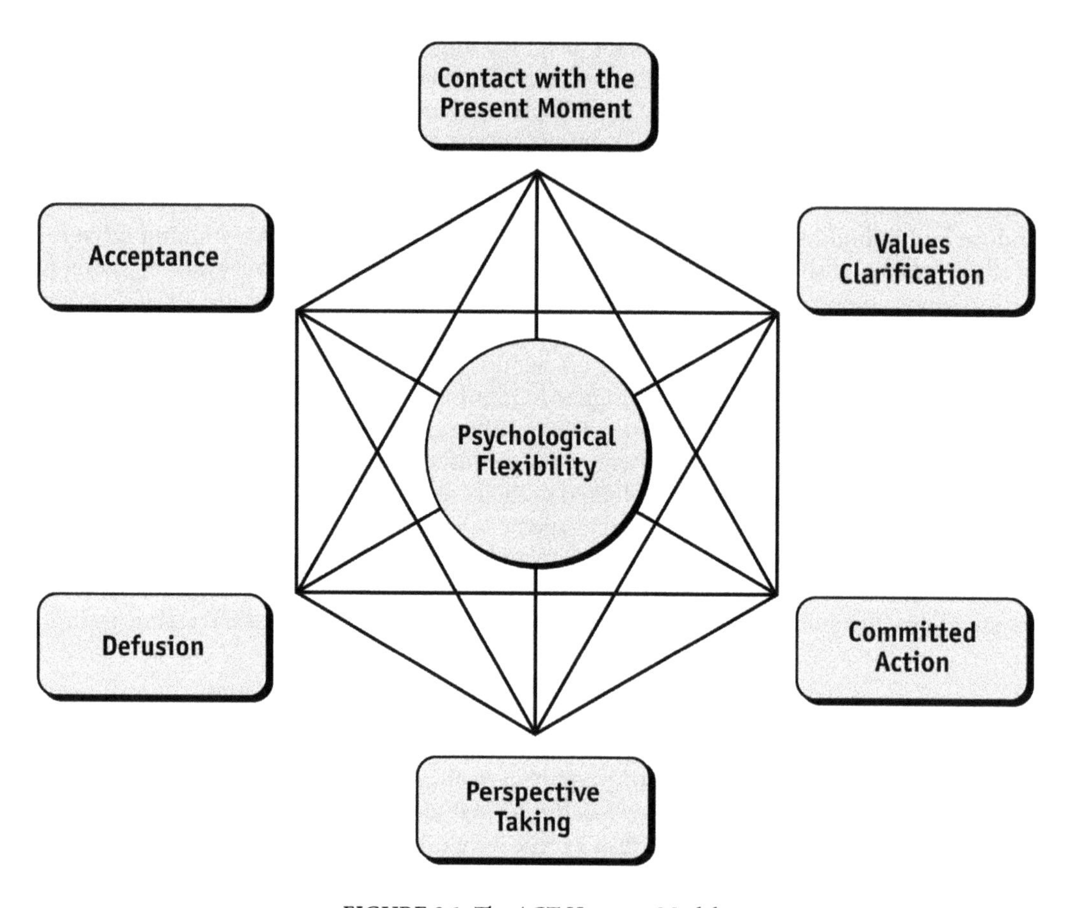

FIGURE 8.1 The ACT Hexagon Model.

other than what they are currently doing 46.9% of the time. This level of distraction takes a worker's engagement away from their job tasks, and may increase the likelihood of making mistakes or engaging in unsafe actions, and contributes to a lack of job satisfaction and diminishes performance. This is not to say that ACT practitioners believe people can constantly pay attention to the present moment 100% of the time. Most of the time, the meandering of private verbal behavior (thoughts) does not have a deleterious impact on a person's actions. However, if an OBM professional wanted to optimize behavior, they could utilize ACTraining to help the worker contact the present moment more regularly, which could increase their situational awareness and overall job performance.

According to Anbro et al. (2020), "Situational awareness is a critical skill within high-reliability organizations (HROs): organizations whose employees conduct highly technical operations in working conditions with varying levels of risk" (p. 2). When defining situational awareness, Endsley (1995a, 1995b) suggests there are three awareness levels that grow upon one another: Level 1 is the perception of elements in the current situation, Level 2 is the comprehension of the current situation, and Level 3 is the projection of the future status. Killingsworth et al. (2016) put behavioral terminology on this model, proposing that Level 1 is a combination of stimulus control, conditional discriminations, and observing responses, Level 2 occurs when the individual is tacting stimulus functions/features and the behavioral chains that follow, and Level 3 is verbally predicting responses and response generalization in different contexts.

Moran and Ming (2020, p. 5) suggest that "[c]ontact with the present moment relates to the core concepts of mindfulness and meditation training." The mindfulness movement in the West during the last decade has influenced how people behave in the workplace. Many organizations and industries have embraced meditation practices to help leaders and front-line workers focus on their actions in the current moment. Many of these mindfulness trainings and implementations are based on Eastern philosophical approaches, and include the ornamentation of these spiritual traditions. While this kind of approach to mindfulness might be helpful for some objectives, applied behavioral science can look for a core aspect of what is acquired during such exercises: the ability to continue engaging in the present-moment target behavior even in the presence of distracting public and private events.

Mindfulness exercises invite the individual to select some stimulus event, such as the behavior of breathing, and attend to that stimulus event exclusively. When other stimuli become present, such as thoughts about the future (e.g., where the person is going on vacation in three months) or the past (e.g., ruminating about a fight they had with their ex-boss from their old job), then the instructions from the mindfulness exercise encourage the person to bring their attending back to the target behavior of breathing. Mindfulness proponents may look at this way of explaining mindfulness as overly stripped-down because the practice has many other facets and processes to it. For the sake of introducing the application to the workplace for ACTraining, we will continue with the simplification of the process and outcome: people learn to attend to target behaviors (which only happen in the present moment), and when distracting private events arise (such as thoughts, emotions, and sensations), and external public events occur (such as noises or sights that have little to do with the target behavior), the person follows the instructions to notice those distracting events occurred, and begins attending to the chosen stimulus event again. This exercise can build a skill of contacting the present moment, and such a skill can be generalized. When a worker regularly practices focusing on breathing while letting go of distractors, this generalized operant of attending has a greater likelihood to be selected when working in a dynamic environment. A worker in a stressful situation could simply notice their private events related to stress, and simply notice external distractors of the noisy workplace and irritating coworkers' irrelevant complaining, and then bring their attending back to the target behavior of working successfully with the relevant stimulus events for the job.

Values Clarification

Values clarification encourages verbal behavior for establishing "verbally constructed consequences of ongoing, dynamic, evolving patterns of activity which establish predominant reinforcers for that activity that are intrinsic in engagement in the valued behavioral pattern itself" (Wilson & Dufrene, 2009, p. 64). Simply put, workers are invited to verbalize the qualities of their actions that are reinforcing just by engaging in such behavior. Oversimplified, but more practically said in an ACTraining intervention, values statements are developed with questions such as, "What do you want your life to be about? What is meaningful, vital, and purposeful to you? How do you want to be as a person while at the workplace?"

Since psychological flexibility was defined as "the ability to pursue valued life aims despite the presence of pain" (Kashdan et al., in press, p. 2), elucidating such valued aims is an important endeavor in ACTraining. In addition, values dignify accepting (see next section) the presence of the pain inherent in engaging in valued actions. Stress, interpersonal difficulties, and disappointment are just a few painful experiences that can occur in the workplace, and people engage in avoidance responses in the presence of such aversive experiences. Put colloquially, when stress arises at work, sometimes people deal with it by drinking alcohol, fighting with their coworkers, or other unproductive means of disengagement. However, values verbally construct and establish reinforcing consequences that increase the likelihood of engaging in chosen work behaviors, even if the behavior is related to the presence of such aversive events.

For example, Julie is a lighting designer for a university theater department. She has clarified for herself through years of personal exploration, and interacting with people in her artistic, verbal community that "illuminating the world to be a more interesting, beautiful, aesthetically pleasing place" is an occupation value for her. This verbal behavior influences even the mundane tasks related to her job to be a bit more reinforcing. Certainly, the behavior of being in the theater lighting booth on opening night for a play would be an appetitive stimulus event, and such an experience might be reinforcing for many people. However, because Julie has clarified her values, tasks such as choosing light bulbs, learning about electrical currents, and staying late after work while all her friends are at happy hour, are actually appetitive stimuli as well. Julie is demonstrating engagement. Verbal behavior can alter the reinforcing qualities of stimulus events, and ACTraining uses values clarification processes and capitalizes on such outcomes to lead to psychological flexibility and behavior change.

Acceptance

Because of the many different meanings of the term, ACT's perspective on acceptance is often misunderstood or misapplied. Acceptance does not mean liking or wanting one's experience and current conditions. When an ACTraining consultant teaches workers about dealing with stressful events, they do not suggest the workers simply enjoy their heart palpitations and muscle tension. In addition, ACTrainings do not focus on accepting "external" environmental events that can and should be changed. For example, when an ACTraining consultant is working with workplace safety, they would never tell the workers to simply accept dangerous conditions that could be engineered to be safer.

Instead, acceptance is "actively contacting psychological experiences, directly, fully, without needless defense, while behaving effectively" (S.C. Hayes et al., 1996, p. 1157). Workers are encouraged to demonstrate willingness to experience their urges, emotions, sensations, and other private events without engaging in avoidance responses to diminish or eliminate them. ACTraining highlights that private events naturally arise throughout the day, and engaging in actions to get rid of them actually exacerbate the problems (Boeschen et al., 2001; Roemer et al., 2001).

For example, Kim is a board-certified behavior analyst (BCBA®) and private practitioner who goes to children's homes to help them acquire language skills and behave more functionally with activities of daily living. As she is driving to see her next child, the parent cancels the appointment by text. Kim pulls over in a strip mall parking lot to read the text, but then checks her emails to find that someone else cancelled another appointment later that day. This means the billing is down for the day, and the progress of her clients will also be slowed down even though they were making solid progress. These events lead to her feeling dejected and sad.

She holds in her hand a source of a lot of immediately gratifying reinforcement: her cell phone. She starts to scroll through social media as she sits in the front seat of her vehicle, and looks at her friends' posts for the next 30 minutes. She is engaged in experiential avoidance, which is on the other end of the spectrum from acceptance, and is doing non-productive behavior with her free time in an attempt to not be in contact with the aversive emotions. Instead of writing up case notes, calling a new referral, or updating her website, she is engaged in an action that actually makes her situation worse: she sees other people posting their positive events while she is in the middle of that aversive event, which exacerbates her emotional struggle. She is "wasting" time with this distraction when she could be improving her entrepreneurial endeavor by doing other business-building actions. The ACTraining coach would teach her to allow herself to experience the dejection and sadness directly without defending against them while behaving effectively. The coach would also help her clarify her values to motivate her to move forward with such behaviors, even when faced with a lean reinforcement schedule, and to realize that "now" is the only time one can do valued actions. It would also be helpful if the coach used the other three components to ACTraining to which we now turn.

Defusion

Verbal behavior influences behavior change, and people can be their own listener. Language has an impact on overt responses, and sometimes people will say things to themselves that alter the reinforcing qualities of environmental events. Fusion occurs when people are significantly and rigidly influenced by their own rule-governed behavior. ACTraining uses defusion exercises to help the person mitigate just how influential such verbal behavior is on their repertoire.

Defusion skills help people notice their thoughts as stimulus events that they are not able to control from happening, and also as stimulus events that do not have to control their own behavior. For instance, a Registered Behavior Technician (RBT®) becomes angry because she was not given a certain amount of work hours at the clinic. Her private verbal behavior is, "I'm going to tell my BCBA® supervisor what I really think of her, and then I'm going to quit!" Under certain circumstances, people can be fused to their thoughts, and they actually overtly follow through on their verbal private events. Defusing from these verbalizations (as well as acceptance of her emotional state) can help the RBT® notice her thoughts as a language process that does not actually have to govern her measurable (and likely, intractable) responses.

In the aforementioned topic of contacting the present moment, mindfulness practices were mentioned as skill-building exercises to help people be more in the "here-and-now." Mindfulness can also assist with defusion. Many mindfulness scripts encourage the meditator to view their thoughts as distant from them, and when a thought arises, to see that thought as if it were a leaf on a stream floating on by. Practically speaking, these instructions in a mindfulness script are altering the influence of verbal behavior. Just because someone has a particular thought does not mean that they have to follow through on what they were thinking, and ACTraining uses defusion to help build psychological flexibility.

Perspective Taking

Steve Hayes, a co-developer of ACT, stated that basic ideas about perspective taking in his article on *Making Sense of Spirituality* (S.C. Hayes, 1984) are "historical seed corn" for ACT (S.C. Hayes, personal communication, October 6, 2017). Perspective taking is a skill for diminishing the impact of verbal behavior about the self. ACTraining practitioners will teach clients that people sometimes engage in language in such a way that limits responses and leads to inflexibility, especially when talking about one's self.

For example, a woodworker may tact, "I am not a good carpenter and I keep failing at my jobs," when their efforts to build a table do not meet the standards of the customer. This verbal behavior might limit their rate at attempts to build other projects, reduce the duration of working on tables, and increase the latency between a request to work on a new project and actually holding a saw and hammer in their hands. In other words, such language can lead to psychological inflexibility and work disengagement. However, the ACTraining coach will influence the language skill of perspective taking by teaching the woodworker that it is not necessary to be influenced by their own self-talk and unhelpful judgments about the self.

ACTraining suggests that there are three senses of the self in perspective taking: self-as-content, self-as-process, and the self-as-context. The self-as-content, also known as the conceptualized self, includes judgments and verbal descriptions of the person, such as, "I am not a good carpenter …" The self-as-process includes evaluations of what the person is doing in the present moment, such as, "I keep failing at my jobs." The self-as-context offers an experience that one's self is not something to be evaluated with language, but simply experienced as whole. The ACTrainer might point out to this woodworker that "not a good carpenter" and "failing at my jobs" are verbal behavior processes that do not actually have to have an impact on moving forward with valued actions. ACTraining encourages experiential exercises for people to learn that they are not their roles or their judgments, but that they simply *are*, and from that context they can begin to engage in values clarification and committed action.

Committed Action

Committed action is engaging in measurable responses in service of values, and is the focus of much of applied behavior analysis, especially in the workplace. "Committing means acting in the direction of what is important to you even in the presence of obstacles" (Moran, 2013, p. 27). This part of the hexagon model is "where the rubber hits the road" in ACT. In other words, committed action is when a worker demonstrates a connection with all the other parts of the model, getting traction from those components, and making forward movement toward valued goals. The "forward movement" is metaphorically speaking to what applied behavior analysts work for: behavior change.

The committed action component of the ACT Hexagon is firmly in the wheelhouse of behavior analysts. An effective ACTrainer will operationally define, or pinpoint, a target response, and then choose an effective measurement for such behavior. They will look at how to accelerate or decelerate the pinpointed behavior, or KPIs, according to the values of the client and the context surrounding the person, and begin measuring the rate, duration, latency, intensity, and/ or perseverance of this target response. Evidence-based interventions will be selected from the scientific literature, and individually applied with the behavioral principles and functional analysis guiding the implementation. ACTraining can supplement all of the applied behavioral science approaches mentioned earlier in the chapter (e.g., behavior-based safety, performance management, leadership practices) by assisting each working participant to build psychological flexibility.

Bringing it all together for committed action, ACTraining invites workers to be willing to experience uncomfortable emotions instead of avoiding them (acceptance), focus on the current opportunity to engage in a valued target behavior instead of being verbally caught up in the past and future (contact the present moment), notice private verbal behavior while not letting these stimulus events impede action (defusion), be similarly unimpeded by self-judgment (perspective taking), and then with clear, verbally constructed consequences for actions influencing the worker to have meaningful, reinforcing experiences (values clarification), the worker engages in measurable action toward their vital goals (committed action). In the work context, psychological flexibility involves all six of the core processes from the ACT Hexagon. By practicing this array of skills in a coherent way, the employee can begin to respond more flexibly to what is required in that moment in the work context, rather than becoming hooked on unhelpful thoughts that pull their focus away from the "here-and-now" or stymied by difficult feelings, memories, or physical sensations. ACTraining provides a new context for these uncomfortable feelings or thoughts, so that they are experienced as less powerful or toxic, and do not have to be avoided in order to engage in appropriate work actions.

Mindfulness-based skills building helps employees notice when they are pulled away from the present moment so they can bring themselves back to the present. When these skills are combined with a clear delineation of a worker's occupational and vocational values, the employee can be increasingly willing to experience whatever private events arise and mindfully engage in whatever actions are needed in the workplace at that moment. This interwoven approach is what is considered to be the application of psychological flexibility in the workplace. There are over 300 randomized controlled trials (RCTs) showing that ACT influences important clinically-relevant concerns, and ACTraining comes from that case conceptualization, and has been shown to be effective in dozens of RCTs at the workplace. The following section provides an overview of a model derived from ACTraining, The Mindful Action Plan.

MAKING ACTRAINING MORE USER-FRIENDLY WITH THE MINDFUL ACTION PLAN

The ACT Hexagon Model can be viewed as esoteric and strange. Encouraging people to embrace their difficult emotions, engage in mindfulness for practical reasons, and come in contact with the self-as-context can be peculiar for some people, especially at work. The implementation of ACTraining in the workplace is often a significant shift for the workers, and the applied behavior analyst using this approach would do well to make it user-friendly for the audience of workers. The method for executing an ACTraining must be done flexibly for two reasons: 1) teaching psychological flexibility in a rigid manner is poor modeling, and 2) effective applied behavioral science applications must be built from a functional analysis in order to fit the current challenging concerns. ACTraining can be done one-on-one in executive coaching, and also has been rolled out in corporate wide events, as well. As far as methods for corporate implementations, Flaxman et al. (2013) call their traditional manner for implementing ACTraining the "2 + 1" method of delivery, where they invite participants to attend two workshop-based trainings which occur in consecutive weeks, and then have a follow-up booster session within three months. This is the method that most of their research was based on, and it is also called the "333" method because there are three-hour trainings three times within three months.

One tool for introducing the ACTraining model in the workplace is *The Mindful Action Plan* (The MAP; Moran, 2015b). The MAP can be used to "guide" people on their journey to improving performance. This training tool summarizes ACT and the ACTraining approach with the following, easy to digest affirmation: "I am here now, accepting the way I feel and noticing my thoughts, while doing what I care about." Each of the six ACT components is covered in this one basic sentence that provides an employee with a simple reminder to operate in the present moment, letting go of restrictive self-concepts, without getting sidetracked by difficult thoughts or feelings, so that the worker can focus on doing what is important in order to be effective at work. The 333 training can focus on the 6 ACTraining processes, and the MAP can be the "take-home" tool so the participant can retain what has been learned, and continue to apply the skills in their environment. The MAP is a coherent approach allowing the worker to build a capacity for psychological flexibility and effective action in the workplace.[1]

The MAP is a checklist (see Figure 8.2) that is already partially completed with reminders of the main points of ACTraining. The "I am" portion of the MAP represents the *self-as-context*, while "here now" represents *contacting the present moment* from the traditional ACT Hexagon. The "accepting" obviously relates to *acceptance*, and instead of training the term *defusion* to workers, the MAP simply calls that skill "noticing." The blank parts of the MAP include "doing," and that is where the worker will write down pinpointed, measurable *committed actions* to take in order to complete a valued job task. This portion of the document can be viewed as a "To-Do" List For the worker. Another blank area of the MAP is the "what I care about" section, which represents the *values* domain in the traditional ACT Hexagon. Leaders and front-line workers alike are encouraged to clarify their values during ACTraining, and learn the skills of coming into contact with what is vital and meaningful in their life. While creating their To-Do List for the "doing" section of the MAP, workers also remind themselves

The Mindful Action Plan

I am here now,
accepting the way I feel and noticing my thoughts,
while doing what I care about.

	Addressing Internal-World Issues	✔
I Am	Notice if you are being influenced by any unhelpful self-descriptions. Let go of any problematic thoughts that you are believing about yourself.	
Here Now	Center your situational awareness on what you are doing. Notice what is happening here and now, and rather than getting wrapped up in events not in your present control, let go of these distracting events. Focus on what is relevant to your actions.	
Accepting	Allow yourself to acknowledge any emotions you are having without trying to control the emotions. Be willing to simply have those feelings while moving forward with valuable actions.	
Noticing	Prepare to simply notice thoughts that arise while moving forward with your valued actions. Let those thoughts go if they are not helpful. Treat distracting thoughts as disconnected from action while choosing to act in a meaningful manner.	
Doing	**To-Do List**	
What I Care About	**Values-Based Motivation**	
	– Personal Values: Describe your motivation for engaging in your chosen actions and why you aim for optimal performance.	

Designing Success with Performance Management

Make sure all required resources for successful actions have been acquired.	
Publicly announce your commitment to meet performance goals.	
Alert your accountability partner about your commitment and goals.	

Describe incentives, performance criteria, and deadlines:

FIGURE 8.2 The mindful action plan.

why they are doing those pinpointed actions, and writing those verbalizations on the MAP is a foundation for their motivation to work on their To-Do List. At the bottom of the MAP, the employee and an accountability partner incorporate the applications of performance management (Daniels, 2000) to undergird the entire process with the OBM applications related to performance criteria, incentives, and deadlines.

Not only has the MAP been discussed as contributing to executive coaching (Moran, 2015b), but it has also contributed to healthcare initiatives (Moran, 2015c), optimizing leadership (Moran, 2016a), group psychotherapy (Westrup & Wright, 2017), and sports teams (Moran, 2016b). The MAP demonstrates how malleable the ACTraining model can be to improve psychological flexibility, and creates a colloquial context for discussing the ACT principles and applications for individual workers.

An Example of The MAP at Work for the ABA Professional[2]

Patricia is a solopreneur who established her own ABA clinic working with children diagnosed with autism. She has been actively engaged in leading the organization's growth for over a decade, and the clinic has an excellent reputation among local health practitioners and educators. The employees and contractors are top-notch BCBA®s and RBT®s, and the data clearly show that their methods, even with more challenging clinical concerns, are effective. The company's mission statement – "To prepare children diagnosed with developmental delays for success in life" – is also related to Patricia's core values of being helpful, forthright, and scientifically based in her actions.

As with all business endeavors, there were challenges over her first ten years as a leader, and recently she has been struggling with giving feedback to people with whom she has grown fairly close. She believes that her relationships with some employees has led to her inability to delegate work to them, and impedes her from giving them feedback when they are not meeting the standards of KPIs. As a behavior analyst, she thought she would turn to another behavior analyst for help with her professional problem. She reached out to Scott, a licensed clinical psychologist and BCBA® with a background in ACTraining and Organizational Behavior Management. Scott agreed to perform executive coaching for Patricia, and corporate consulting for her company.

Patricia already had a solid understanding of how to run her business with a high-quality systems management approach utilizing performance management (Daniels, 2000). Her clinicians knew what behaviors were expected from them, and they were positively reinforced when completed in a timely manner. She incorporated behavioral objectives for basic management behavior (i.e., delegation, instruction, and feedback). The staff were well-trained, well-remunerated, and participated in an effective, healthy work culture. Patricia certainly benefited from Scott's outside review of her systems management approach, embraced some of Scott's minor tweaks to her methods, and felt validated that her approach fit the criteria of a well-run company from another OBM'er.

Her challenge centered on Astrid, a BCBA® whom she hired when the company was in the start-up phase. She had been a highly effective educator in the clinic for many years, and also quite productive when it was time to grow and expand the business. As the clinic became more successful, Astrid moved into supervisory roles, but was still required to carry a caseload of clients in order to justify her higher salary. Unfortunately, Astrid was not maintaining her standard number of billable hours in the last few months, and was asking for leeway from Patricia because of her outside commitments. Astrid was getting married soon, and was more focused on planning the wedding than generating billable hours. Patricia said that she understood that people have interests other than work, and even chatted with Astrid about dresses during the workday. Astrid seemed to be counting on Patricia's goodwill and their long interpersonal relationship so that Patricia would let her lower monthly numbers of billable hours slide. Patricia knew that the company would continue to survive, and maybe even thrive, without an optimal performance from Astrid, but she was concerned that she was taking advantage of her, and that other managers and therapists might follow suit. Patricia was becoming more disengaged from this part of leadership in the company. Scott pointed out that something needed to change, and that it would require altering how she interacted with Astrid around these issues.

Experienced applied behavior analysts know what to do as far as contingency management to address these concerns. Interventions discussed in other chapters in this book could be effective for Patricia's problems. Perhaps she could redefine pinpoints for Astrid, discuss expectations for such KPIs, develop creative and individually specific reinforcers for her (perhaps even something related to the wedding), and do so in a context of a high rate of non-contingent social reinforcers to maintain the healthy relationship. Patricia's problem is not an absence of knowing what to do from an OBM perspective, *but rather a lack of comfort with doing such actions* (i.e., Patricia was avoiding doing what she needed to do because of the uncomfortable feelings associated with it). What made Patricia successful (ABA skills and business acumen) was not what was going to get her through this next challenge: being psychologically flexible enough to manage the awkward interpersonal confrontation. Patricia and Scott agreed on what OBM processes to use to meet the practical goals she had set, but Patricia was still psychologically unprepared for enacting such work. Remember, ACTraining does not aim to replace evidence-based applications of applied behavioral science, but rather it aims to *enhance* them. Scott was using OBM to help Patricia's company, and ACTraining to help Patricia help herself.

Before their executive coaching started, Patricia gave informed consent to go through the experiential exercises related to ACTraining, and was educated about the coaching process. Scott started out the coaching with a brief discussion that their work together would be about specific behavior change, and Patricia was already on board with that approach given her background. They made a To-Do List together, with the ultimate target behavior being having a conversation with Astrid about increasing her productivity, and maintaining the behavior-based performance improvement process after the initial conversation. Scott and Patricia broke down the long-term goal into smaller defined pinpoints for the first week of the coaching: 1) Write down exactly what you want to say to Astrid, 2) Become fluent in vocally expressing what you want to say out loud by practicing five times per day, 3) Imagine how she might respond, and write these replies down, and 4) Become fluent in vocally responding to her reactions by spending five minutes a day rehearsing these replies out loud. These are steps that she can take to be more engaged in this workplace task, and ready for the conversation with Astrid. These also can be broken down into other smaller skills and objectives for Patricia to build her skills, but because she was familiar with fluency training, she already knew what these pinpoints required. Ultimately, her coach presented a hard copy of the MAP to Patricia, and they filled in the To-Do List portion next to the "Doing" component for the checklist with four pinpointed behaviors (see Figure 8.3).

> During their interactive coaching session, Scott asked Patricia,
>
> If the Association for Behavior Analysis International was going to give you a Lifetime Achievement Award, what would you like to be said during the award speech? What qualities of your behavior would you like to be highlighted when someone looks back at your career?

This is a tailor-made version of an oft-used values clarification exercise. This exercise is an invitation to look back on one's life and articulate what values you would like to have most emblematically represent your behavioral choices. This helps create an ability to articulate values for choices in the present moment, and can contribute to accelerating psychological flexibility.

Patricia and Scott had a thoughtful discussion about the "what I care about" portion of the MAP. She bandied about several values, and continued to return to talking about being helpful, forthright, and science-based as qualities for her actions. Ultimately, Scott summarized

Doing	To-Do List	
	Write down exactly what you want to say to Astrid	
	Become fluent in vocally expressing what you want to say out loud 5 times per day	
	Imagine how she might respond, write these replies down	
	Become fluent in vocally responding by spending 5 minutes a day rehearsing replies out loud	
What I Care About	Values-Based Motivation	
	-- Personal Values: Describe your motivation for engaging in your chosen actions and why you aim for optimal performance.	
	I choose to be a helpful person to other people in this world	
	I strive to be forthright with other people	
	I aim to make my vocational choices to be science-based.	

FIGURE 8.3 Completing the to-do list for "doing" component in the MAP, and the values-based motivation list for the "What I care about" component in the MAP.

what Patricia said and wrote it in the Values-Based Motivation section in the MAP to remind her of these motivational qualities when she looked at her To-Do List (see Figure 8.3). The "What I care about" section asks the worker to explore personal values, and "Describe your motivation for engaging in your chosen actions and why you aim for optimal performance." It is positioned in the checklist in a place that shows that "What I care about" provides a foundation and support for "Doing" one's target behaviors. When the session ended, the duo parted ways and planned to meet a week later, with Patricia committing to be more engaged as a leader, and do her To-Do List as homework for the week.

When Patricia returned the following week for the coaching session, she looked embarrassed and immediately blurted out, "I didn't do any of the homework!" The coach remained smiling and welcoming, and engaged in unconditional positive regard for Patricia, and asked what the obstacles were for her performance. He had indicated in the first session that they would be working on building up personal skills for keeping commitments, and reminded her, "Keeping a commitment means acting in the direction of what is important to you even in the presence of obstacles. What were some of the obstacles?"

Patricia went on to explain that as she *does not feel like* she is prepared for such a task, doesn't believe she has the mastery to be assertive with her friend, and said to the coach, "I am just not the kind of person who can confront people." With that statement, her coach began discussing perspective taking, the self-as-context, and engaged her in a mindfulness exercise called the *Observer Exercise* (cf., S.C. Hayes et al., 1999, p. 193). He encouraged her to examine her self-talk, and pointed out the "I am" portion of the MAP. They discussed the instructions to address her private verbal events that were impeding her psychological flexibility, and they read: "Notice if you are being influenced by any unhelpful self-descriptions. Let go of any problematic thoughts that you are believing about yourself." Scott and Patricia are both BCBA®s, and could have looked at this instruction as if it were not "behavioral enough" because it lacked the jargon and precision they were used to, but at the same time, embraced the colloquial nature of this checklist item. When Patricia can engage in the verbalization, "I am just not the kind of person who can confront people," *and* notice that it can have a diminished impact on her actions, she will become more psychologically flexible and increase her likelihood for giving feedback to Astrid.

The coach then asked, "What else are you perceiving as an obstacle to following through on the pinpoints we wrote last week in the 'Doing' portion of the MAP?" She immediately said,

"I just want to put it off. Maybe I can just wait until the wedding is over. Astrid will probably be more productive in the future! Besides, I have plenty of other things I have to worry about because school is going on summer break next month." Scott reminded her that behavior only happens in the present moment, and while planfulness can be helpful for entrepreneurs, their focus on what is actionable in the present moment is a workable way to successfully follow through on one's values. He assigned mindfulness exercises to her, and asked her to embrace doing them on a regular basis to help her to be more present focused. Then they reviewed the instructions for "here-and-now" in the MAP:

> Center your situational awareness on what you are doing. Notice what is happening here-and-now, and rather than getting wrapped up in events not in your present control, let go of these distracting events. Focus on what is relevant to your actions.

Scott reminded her that the MAP is a checklist, and can guide her to develop a more psychologically flexible repertoire, especially surrounding her assertiveness with employees.

Scott asked if she had other concerns that were impeding her from being more psychologically flexible, and Patricia replied, "I'm too nervous. Just thinking about having a crucial conversation with my long-time colleague makes me anxious." Her coach initiated a conversation about two approaches for dealing with anxiety, and both of them are consistent with ACTraining: 1) behavior therapy exposure exercises, and 2) acceptance skills. He got her permission to engage in imaginal exposure (Vrielynck & Philippot, 2009) in order to utilize evidence-based behavior therapy to address the anxiety responses. She complied and continued to do the exposure exercises outside of the session to help her with expanding her psychological flexibility around this anxiety response. Scott also educated Patricia about how the subculture in the West sets a context for following verbal rules to attempt to avoid emotional private events, and that such a repertoire can exacerbate behavioral problems. He suggested that the more she was unwilling to face the anxiety responses, and allow these feelings to influence her avoidance of the difficult interpersonal issue, the more likely they would have an impact on her. He used a traditional intervention from the ACT literature called *the Quicksand metaphor* (S.C. Hayes et al., 1999, p. 191) to teach her about the helpfulness, yet counterintuitive nature of acceptance. He explained that trying to avoid feeling anxious is like trying to get out of quicksand once you have stepped into it: the more you struggle, the faster you sink into it and eventually meet your demise. He explained that actually coming into contact with it, fully and without defense, actually would help in the long run. The more you are willing to be with this natural event, the more likely you will float on top of it rather than sink into it. They investigated the MAP instructions in the "Accepting" part of the checklist: "Allow yourself to acknowledge any emotions you are having without trying to control the emotions. Be willing to simply have those feelings while moving forward with valuable actions." Patricia's background in behavior analysis helped her understand how this could be applied to her situation.

Finally, Patricia opened up about her doubts and concerns related to the interpersonal issue with Astrid, "Being assertive won't work. It's too arduous of a task. Let sleeping dogs lie, right?" Patricia was being forthcoming with her fused content (i.e., the rule-governed behavior that was leading to psychological inflexibility), and said that she frequently had these judgments when she was about to engage in one of the pinpoints on the To-Do List. Scott pointed out, "Notice what your mind just did right there!" (Yes, he used the "mind", an explanatory fiction, to get his point across, but it was behavior analyst to behavior analyst, so the colloquialism was fully understood to mean "fluent private verbal behaving"). Scott continued,

> We all have thinking that we learn through our lifetime, and they get reinforced over the years, and then these thoughts, which might not be all that helpful, end up dominating our overt

> behavior. What if you can just notice that you had that thought, as if that thought 'Let sleeping dogs lie,' were painted on a poster board being carried by toy soldiers in a parade. And watch that thought drift away. Thoughts do not cause behavior!

Scott knew that Patricia's behavioral training would come to bear on this concept. He then turned to the section in the MAP for "Noticing" and read: "Prepare to simply notice thoughts that arise while moving forward with your valued actions. Let those thoughts go if they are not helpful. Treat distracting thoughts as disconnected from action while choosing to act in a meaningful manner."

After all of this, Scott once again pointed out the checklist function of the MAP, and also pointed out the sentence at the top of the document with is a summarization of all the skills combined. Each person using this ACTraining tool is encouraged to engage in the verbal behavior: "I am here now, accepting the way I feel and noticing my thoughts, while doing what I care about." This statement blends all six ACT domains and puts them in a personalized and practical format to be utilized as a tool for increasing psychological flexibility, while also acting as a task list, and reminder of long-term reinforcers for engaging in the pinpointed responses on the task list. Patricia dutifully did the experiential exercises, engaged in mindfulness practices, and followed the MAP to guide her through the difficult action of taking to Astrid. She accepted her emotions, defused from her thoughts, diminished the impact of negative evaluations she had of her self, and focused on the present moment opportunities to practice and also engage in the committed action of following through on her values to be forthright, helpful, and science-based. So, she spoke to Astrid in a professional manner and ultimately strengthened her relationship with her vulnerable action, and also established a clear set of Organizational Behavior Management guidelines with her colleague. Her OBM implementations were data-based, utilizing the ideas of performance management (Daniels, 2000), goal setting (Fellner & Sulzer-Azaroff, 1984), and feedback (Johnson et al., 2015), and ACTraining provided the platform for maintaining psychological flexibility while committing to this OBM approach. Patricia utilized contextual behavioral science to increase her psychological flexibility, follow through on a committed action, and was actively engaged at the workplace.

SUMMARY

ACTraining has been applied in the workplace in order to reduce stress, increase cooperation, improve productivity, reduce incidents and injuries, and accelerate leadership and innovation. The traditional ACT Hexagon Model has served as the foundation for dozens of empirical studies showing the efficacy of ACTraining in the workplace. The Mindful Action Plan is a nascent ACT intervention, and the ACTraining model has a great deal of room to grow in order to help people and organizations by improving psychological flexibility.

STUDY QUESTIONS

1. Distinguish between active engagement and active disengagement in your own words.
2. Explain the concept of psychological flexibility.
3. Describe some of the relationships between psychological flexibility and workplace behavior.
4. Describe two of the ACT processes reviewed in the chapter in your own words.
5. Describe a problematic issue you experienced at the workplace, and explain how the MAP may have been useful.

NOTES

1. Please visit D.J. Moran's website (www.drdjmoran.com) to obtain the free Mindful Action Plan in PDF form.
2. The following case study using the MAP was developed with authentic uses of the application, and also has been fictionalized to maintain the privacy of the professionals who utilized the tool.

REFERENCES

Anbro, S.J., Szarko, A.J., Houmanfar, R.A., Maraccini, A.M., Crosswell, L.H., Crosswell, F.C., Rebaleati, M., & Starmer, L. (2020). Using virtual simulations to assess situational awareness and communication in medical and nursing education: A technical feasibility study, *Journal of Organizational Behavior Management, 40*(1–2), 129–139. doi: 10.1080/01608061.2020.1746474

Bethay, J.S., Wilson, K.G., Schnetzer, L.W., Nassar, S.L., & Bordieri, M.J. (2013). A controlled pilot evaluation of acceptance and commitment training for intellectual disability staff. *Mindfulness, 4*(2), 113–121. doi: 10.1007/s12671-012-0103-8

Biglan, A., Layton, G.L., Jones, L.B., Hankins, M., & Rusby, J.C. (2013). The value of workshops on psychological flexibility for early childhood special education staff. *Topics in Early Childhood Special Education, 32*(4), 196–210. https://doi.org/10.1177/0271121411425191

Biron, M., & van Veldhoven, M. (2012). Emotional labour in service work: Psychological flexibility and emotion regulation. *Human Relations, 65*(10), 1259–1282. https://doi.org/10.1177/0018726712447832

Boeschen, L.E., Koss, M.P., Figuerdo, A.J., & Coan, J.A. (2001). Experiential avoidance and post-traumatic stress disorder: A cognitive mediational model of rape recovery. *Journal of Aggression, Maltreatment, & Trauma, 4*(2), 211–245. https://doi.org/10.1300/J146v04n02_10

Bond, F.W. & Bunce, D. (2000). Mediators of change in emotion-focused and problem-focused worksite stress management interventions. *Journal of Occupational Health Psychology, 5*(1), 156–163. doi: 10.1037/1076-8998.5.1.156

Bond, F.W., & Bunce, D. (2003). The role of acceptance and job control in mental health, job satisfaction, and work performance. *Journal of Applied Psychology, 88*(6), 1057–1067. doi:10.1037/0021-9010.88.6.1057

Bond, F.W. & Flaxman, P.E. (2006). The ability of psychological flexibility and job control to predict learning, job performance, and mental health. *Journal of Organizational Behavior Management, 26*(1–2), 113–130. doi: 10.1300/J075v26n01_05

Bond, F.W., Flaxman, P.E., & Bunce, D. (2008). The influence of psychological flexibility on work redesign: mediated moderation of a work reorganization intervention. *Journal of Applied Psychology, 93*(3), 645–654. doi: 10.1037/0021-9010.93.3.645

Bond, F.W., Hayes, S.C., Baer, R.A., Carpenter, K.M., Guenole, N., Orcutt, H.K., & Zettle, R. D. (2011). Preliminary psychometric properties of the Acceptance and Action Questionnaire–II: A revised measure of psychological inflexibility and experiential avoidance. *Behavior Therapy, 42*(4), 676–688. doi: 10.1016/j.beth.2011.03.007

Bond, F.W., Lloyd, J., & Guenole, N. (2012). The work-related acceptance and action questionnaire (WAAQ): Initial psychometric findings and their implications for measuring psychological flexibility in specific contexts. *Journal of Occupational and Organizational Psychology*, 1–25. doi: 10.1111/joop.12001

Brethower, D.M. (2000). A systematic view of enterprise: Adding value to performance. *Journal of Organizational Behavior Management, 20*(3/4), 165–190. doi: 10.1300/J075v20n03_06

Ciarrochi, J., Bailey, A, & Harris, R. (2014). *The weight escape: How to stop dieting and start living.* Shambala Publications.

Daniels, A.C. (2000). *Bringing out the best in people: How to apply the astonishing power of positive reinforcement.* McGraw-Hill.

Daniels, A.C. & Daniels, J.E. (2007). *Measure of a leader: The legendary leadership formula for producing exceptional performers and outstanding results.* McGraw-Hill.

Dixon, M.R. (2014). *PEAK relational training system: Direct training module.* Shawnee Scientific Press.

Endsley, M.R. (1995a). Toward a theory of situation awareness in dynamic systems. *Human Factors, 37*, 32–64. doi: 10.1518/001872095779049543

Endsley, M.R. (1995b). Measurement of situation awareness in dynamic systems. *Human Factors, 37*, 65–84. doi: 10.1518/001872095779049499

Flaxman, P.E. & Bond, F.W. (2010). Worksite stress management training: Moderated effects and clinical significance. *Journal of Occupational Health Psychology, 15*(4), 347. doi: 10.1037/a0020522

Flaxman, P.E., Bond, F.W., & Livheim, F. (2013). *The mindful and effective employee: An acceptance and commitment therapy training manual for improving well-being and performance.* New Harbinger Publications.

Fellner, D.J. & Sulzer-Azaroff, B. (1984). A behavioral analysis of goal setting. *Journal of Organizational Behavior Management, 6*(1), 83–90. https://doi.org/10.1300/J075v06n01_03

Gallup Press. (2019). *State of the global workplace.* Gallup.com.

Hayes, L.L. & Ciarrochi, J. (2015). *The thriving adolescent: Using acceptance and commitment therapy and positive psychology to help teens manage emotions, achieve goals, and build connection.* Context Press.

Hayes, S.C. (1984). Making sense of spirituality. *Behaviorism, 12*, 99–110

Hayes, S.C., Strosahl, K.D., & Wilson, K.G. (1999). *Acceptance and Commitment Therapy: The Process and Practice of Mindful Change.* Guilford Press.

Hayes, S.C., Strosahl, K.D., & Wilson, K.G. (2016). *Acceptance and Commitment Therapy: The Process and Practice of Mindful Change.* (2nd ed). Guilford Press.

Hayes, S. C., Wilson K. G., Gifford E. V., Follette V. M., Strosahl K. (1996). Experiential avoidance and behavioral disorders: a functional dimensional approach to diagnosis and treatment. *Journal of Consulting and Clinical Psychology, 64*(6), 1152–1168. https://doi.org/10.1037//0022-006x.64.6.1152

Holmberg, J., Kemani, M.K., Holmström, L., Öst, L.-G., & Wicksell, R.K. (2019). Evaluating the psychometric characteristics of the Work-related Acceptance and Action Questionnaire (WAAQ) in a sample of healthcare professionals. *Journal of Contextual Behavioral Science, 14*, 103–107.

Hosseinaei, A., Ahadi, H., Fata, L., Heidarei, A., & Mazaheri, M.M. (2013). Effects of group acceptance and commitment therapy (ACT)-based training on job stress and burnout. *Iranian Journal of Psychiatry and Clinical Psychology, 19*(2), 109–120.

Johnson, D.A., Rocheleau, J.M., & Tilka, R.E. (2015). Considerations in feedback delivery: the role of accuracy and type of evaluation. *Journal of Organizational Behavior Management, 35* (3–4), 240–258. doi: 108/01608061.2015.1093055

Kashdan, T.B., Disabato, D.J., Goodman, F.R., Doorley, J.D., & McKnight, P.E. (in press). Understanding psychological flexibility: A multimethod exploration of pursuing valued goals despite the presence of distress. *Psychological Assessment.*

Killingsworth, M.A. & Gilbert, D.T. (2010). A wandering mind is an unhappy mind. *Science, 330*, 932. doi: 10.1126/science.1192439

Killingsworth, K., Miller, S.A., & Alavosius, M.P. (2016). A behavioral interpretation of situation awareness: Prospects for organizational behavior management. *Journal of Organizational Behavior Management, 36*(4), 301–321. doi: 10.1080/01608061.2016.1236056

Laloux, F. (2014). *Reinventing organizations: A guide to creating organizations inspired by the next stage in human consciousness.* Nelson Parker.

Lloyd, J., Bond, F.W., & Flaxman, P.E. (2013). The value of psychological flexibility: Examining psychological mechanisms underpinning a cognitive behavioural therapy intervention for burnout. *Work & Stress, 27*(2), 181–199. doi: 10.1080/02678373.2013.782157

Luoma, J.B., Hayes, S.C., & Walser, R.D. (2007). *Learning ACT: An acceptance & commitment therapy skills-training manual for therapists.* New Harbinger Publications.

Luoma, J.B. & Vilardaga, J.P. (2013). Improving therapist psychological flexibility while training acceptance and commitment therapy: A pilot study. *Cognitive Behaviour Therapy, 42*(1), 1–8. doi: 1080/16506073.2012.701662

Ly, K.H., Asplund, K., & Andersson, G. (2014). Stress management for middle managers via an acceptance and commitment-based smartphone application: A randomized controlled trial. *Internet Interventions, 1* (3), 95–101. doi: 10.1016/j.invent.2014.06.003

McConachie, D.A.J., McKenzie, K., Morris, P.G., & Walley, R.M. (2014). Acceptance and mindfulness-based stress management for support staff caring for individuals with intellectual disabilities. *Research in Developmental Disabilities, 35*(6), 1216–1227. doi: 10.1016/j.ridd.2014.03.005

McSween, T. & Moran, D.J. (2017). Assessing and preventing serious incidents with behavioral science: Enhancing Heinrich's triangle for the 21st century. *Journal of Organizational Behavior Management, 37* (3–4), 283–300. doi: 10.1080/01608061

Moran, D.J. (2011). ACT for leadership: Using acceptance and commitment training to develop crisis-resilient change managers. *International Journal of Behavioral Consultation and Therapy, 7*(1), 66–75. doi: 10.1037/h0100915

Moran, D.J. (2013). *Building safety commitment.* Valued Living Books.

Moran, D.J. (2014). *The Mindful Action Plan.* https://www.pickslyde.com/wp-content/uploads/2017/05/TheMindfulActionPlan_2017.pdf

Moran, D.J. (2015a). Acceptance and Commitment Training in the workplace. *Current Opinion in Psychology, 2*, 26–31. doi: 10.1016/j.copsyc.2014.12.031

Moran, D.J. (2015b). Using the Mindful Action Plan to accelerate performance in the workplace. Invited address at the Association for Contextual Behavioral Science Southeast conference in Lafayette, LA

Moran, D.J. (2015c). Optimizing performance and reducing stress for healthcare professionals. http://www.pickslyde.com/wp-content/uploads/2016/03/Moran_WhitePaper_2016_03_cover_v6.pdf (Accessed November 2, 2017)

Moran, D.J. (2016a). Optimizing leadership commitment: Using the MAP for accelerating personal performance. Breakout session at the Behavior Safety Now conference, Jacksonville, FL

Moran, D.J. (2016b). Blending ACT and the Mindful Action Plan. Conference presentation sponsored by the Ascco Accademia di Scienze Comportamentali e Cognitive, Bressanone, Italy.

Moran, D.J., Bach, P., & Batten, S. (2018). *Committed action in psychotherapy practice: A guide to assessing, planning, and supporting change in your clients.* New Harbinger Press.

Moran, D.J. & Ming, S. (2020). The mindful action plan: Using the MAP to apply acceptance and commitment therapy to productivity and self-compassion for behavior analysts. *Behavior Analysis in Practice*, July 2020. https://doi.org/10.1007/s40617-020-00441-y

Polk, K.L. & Schoendorff, B. (2014). *The ACT matrix: A new approach to building psychological flexibility across settings and populations.* Context Press.

Roemer, L., Litz, B.T., Orsillo, S.M., & Wagner, A.W. (2001). A preliminary investigation of the role of strategic withholding of emotions in PTSD. *Journal of Traumatic Stress, 14*(1), 149–156. https://doi.org/10.1023/A:1007895817502

Ruiz, F.J. & Odriozola-González, P. (2014). The Spanish version of the Work-related Acceptance and Action Questionnaire (WAAQ). *Psicothema*, *26*, 63–68.

Schaufeli, W.B. & van Dierendonck, D. (2000). *UBOS: Utrechtse Burnout Schaal – Handleiding* [UBOS: Utrecht Burnout Scale – Manual]. Swets & Zeitlinger.

Sulzer-Azaroff, B. & Austin, J. (2000). Does BBS work? *Professional Safety*, *45*(7), 19–24.

Varra, A.A., Hayes, S.C., Roget, N., & Fisher, G. (2008). A randomized control trial examining the effect of acceptance and commitment training on clinician willingness to use evidence-based pharmacotherapy. *Journal of Consulting and Clinical Psychology*, *76*(3), 449–458. doi: 10.1037/0022-006X.76.3.449

Vilardaga, R., Luoma, J.B., Hayes, S.C., Pistorello, J., Levin, M.E., Hildebrandt, M.J., Kohlenberg, B., Roget, N.A., & Bond, F. (2011). Burnout among the addiction counseling workforce: The differential roles of mindfulness and values-based processes and work-site factors. *Journal of Substance Abuse Treatment*, *40*(4), 323–335. doi: 10.1016/j.sat.2010.11.015

Vrielynck, N., & Philippot, P. (2009) Regulating emotion during imaginal exposure to social anxiety: Impact of the specificity of information processing. *Journal of Behavior Therapy and Experimental Psychology*, *40*(2), 274–282. https://doi.org/10.1016/j.jbtep.2008.12.006

Westrup, D. & Wright, M.J. (2017). *Learning ACT for group treatment: An acceptance and commitment therapy skills training manual for therapists*. New Harbinger Publications.

Wilson K.G, Dufrene T. (2009) *Mindfulness for two: An acceptance and commitment therapy approach to mindfulness in psychotherapy*. New Harbinger.

Xu, X. & Liu, X. (2017). Psychological flexibility of nurses in a cancer hospital: Preliminary validation of a Chinese version of the Work-related Acceptance and Action Questionnaire. *Asia-Pacific Journal of Oncology Nursing*, *5*(1), 83–90.

9

Prosocial

Using an Evolutionary Approach to Modify Cooperation in Small Groups

Steven C. Hayes, Paul Atkins, and David Sloan Wilson

Suppose you are a subsistence farmer who owns a milk cow. You are one of a dozen families in the village, all of them also doing subsistence farming and owning a single cow, and together you all control the only good place locally to graze cattle: a very large grassy field. Everyone uses it to feed their cow. Everyone uses it in common and that's OK because the grass replenishes itself – there is enough for all.

One day a particular farmer decides to buy a second cow. Not to be outdone, within months you and all of the other village families follow suit, rationally concluding that the additional cow will bring more milk and meat to your family. There is no reason not to do it.

An observer sitting atop Mount Olympus might know that the field can only sustain 30 cows and after that it will be overgrazed and the grass will die out. On the ground, what the villagers know is that the field still grows enough grass to feed the now two-dozen cows. As a result, all is well and the village is more prosperous than ever.

The problem comes when you and your neighbors, each seeing your two cows fattening up nicely, make the rational decision to add just one more cow. Now the trap is sprung. Three dozen cows is too much. The field is overgrazed and before the grass can grow back, yet another cow is nibbling it down to nothing. The grass cannot sustain itself that way, and it all dies. Soon, so do all the cattle.

This famous parable of "The tragedy of the commons" was published by Garrett Hardin in *Science* magazine in 1968. The author concluded that common-pool resources such a forests, fields, fisheries, or water systems need to be protected, either by government regulation or private ownership, since "Freedom in a commons brings ruin to all" (Hardin, 1968, p. 1244). It is a very appealing metaphor for how individual contingencies and selfishness can lead to disaster at the level of collectives and group contingencies. Some of its incredible popularity and sticking power over more than 60 years might have come because it is a metaphor that appeals to the biases of both the left ("see, we need more top-down regulation!") and the right ("see, only private owners can protect the long term good!"). Both "command and control" and "invisible hand" economists can readily use "the tragedy of commons" story. In either case, however, it offers up a rather skeptical view of human cooperation: we cannot be trusted to work together to protect our common interests.

There is only one problem with this parable: it is not generally how people behave. Real people are well aware of the fragility of common-pool resources. Hardly a farmer exists who would know nothing of overgrazing, and it does not take a rocket scientist to predict the

DOI: 10.4324/9781003198949-9

increased risk of it, at least in broad terms. And real people know a lot about how to work together to achieve common ends.

We should. After all, we are neither the fastest nor the strongest; we have neither sharp claws nor strong bites; many non-human animals can defeat us easily one-on-one. But put people in groups and give them the tools needed to cooperate, and no other life form can compete with human beings. We are the super cooperators. Yes, not always. Yes, not everywhere. But often, and under specifiable conditions.

The late Elinor Ostrom (we will call her Lin, her preferred name of use) won the Nobel Prize for Economics in 2009 for her work in describing those conditions. Working with a variety of common-pool resource systems around the world, such as water systems among farmers in Nepal, Lin Ostrom found that people soon bend or break the rules of top-down regulation. Often this only makes good sense. After all, the "controller" is not local and may not have the best ideas. In a different way, private property rights sometimes lead owners to exploit the resource as rapidly as possible before moving on. Instead, what Lin Ostrom found was that in case after case, people can do very well, thank you, in controlling their common-pool resources for hundreds or even thousands of years without depletion or tragedy, but only if they arranged their interactions in a particular way. She distilled that wisdom into what has become known as the Core Design Principles or "CDPs."

Here are the core design principles that Ostrom derived for common-pool resource groups that enabled them to avoid the tragedy of the commons:

1. Groups that functioned well had *clearly defined boundaries*, that made it clear they were a group, what the group was about, and who was a member;
2. They had group practices that ensured that members experienced *proportional equivalence between benefits and costs*;
3. There were *collective choice arrangements* in place so that everybody affected by a decision had an opportunity to contribute to making that decision;
4. There was *monitoring*, preferably by members themselves, so that lapses in agreed-upon behaviors could be detected;
5. There were *graduated consequences* applied within the group so that lapses in agreed-upon behaviors were corrected, gently at first but with a capacity to escalate if necessary;
6. There were fast and fair *conflict resolution mechanisms* in place to resolve differences;
7. There was some *minimal recognition of rights to organize*, so that group members had the authority to manage their own affairs without external interference;
8. Finally, when systems became larger there was *polycentric governance*, with groups in multiple layers of nested enterprises, with each subgroup relating to other subgroups using principles 1 through 7.

There is nothing abstract or esoteric about this list – most people might see them as being common sense. Nevertheless, this does not mean that all groups implement the CDPs. Even common-pool resource groups vary in this regard, which is how Lin was able to derive the CDPs in the first place (Ostrom, 1990).

We can understand some of the reasons for groups failing to implement the CDPs as we appreciate the very reasons for their usefulness: CDPs specify the evolutionary conditions in which cooperative behaviors can be selected and strengthened. As with all adaptations that occur at higher levels of organization, the CDPs tend to be undermined by selfish processes at lower levels of organization – in this case at the level of individual group members. This is the insight that has led us to combine the CDPs with a psychological method drawn from contextual behavioral science (Acceptance and Commitment Training or "ACT"; Hayes et al.,

2012) in order to create a practical program for fostering prosociality in groups that we call "prosocial" (www.prosocial.world).

In this chapter, we will briefly describe that program, its intellectual basis, and why it might be of use to organization work in applied behavior analysis. A full book-length description is available (Atkins et al., 2019), so we will underemphasize practical matters and theoretical details in favor of a broad understanding. In this chapter, we will begin by describing the key features of multi-dimensional, multi-level evolutionary science. We will then use that framework to consider the elements of prosocial, revisiting and refining the CDPs and showing how ACT fits into that perspective. We argue that prosocial can be used now inside organizational behavior management.

AN EXTENDED EVOLUTIONARY SYNTHESIS

The core of evolutionary science is thinking broadly in terms of what Donald T.

Campbell called "variation and selective retention" (1960). Most behavior analysts will recognize that these terms do not apply to genes only. Evolutionary processes apply to all life dimensions at various time scales: cultures evolve; behavior evolves; symbolic learning evolves; epigenes evolve. Selection and retention operates across variations in all of these dimensions and more, and does so simultaneously. Importantly, selection also operates at multiple levels of organization simultaneously, and it is that fact that allows the CDPs to be understood and put to use in guiding the actions of small groups. Finally, if evolutionary principles are to be applied intentionally, there needs to be an understanding of the contextual features that determine whether or not given variations are successful.

We will begin with the most important feature of applied evolutionary science focused on small group behavior: selection can operate at different levels simultaneously.

Multi-Level Selection Theory

Multi-level selection is a kind of prodigal son of evolutionary science. Originally invoked by Darwin at the height of the gene-centric era, it was virtually cast into an ash heap of disproven ideas, along with Lamarkian evolution and other supposed falsehoods. Even today, it is hard to find textbooks that treat it fairly and accurately.

The core idea of multi-level selection (MLS) can be expressed very easily: "Selfishness beats altruism within groups. Altruistic groups beat selfish groups. Everything else is commentary" (Wilson & Wilson, 2007, p. 345). When competition is within groups, selection focuses on how individuals beat out individuals. But when competition is *between* groups, selection pressure can give an advantage to groups that work together effectively. The balance between these two levels of selection can be tipped toward cooperation and between-group selection if the individual can do relatively well as part of a larger organizational unit, but self-serving actions are restrained.

Consider your own body as an organized group of cells to see how these principles operate. While estimates vary, you have about 37 trillion native cells in your body. If even one begins to reproduce itself without restraint, you have cancer.

Your body continuously protects you against that possibility and must do so, or you would soon die. Mutations can occur with every cell division; your body is constantly correcting these errors to avoid pre-cancerous cells from forming. If that is not enough, when mutant cells first begin to reproduce faster than neighboring cells, your body attempts to detect this fact and to restrain or kill the mutants. Scientists are only beginning to understand the arsenal of cancer-preventing mechanisms that operate, but the bottom line is this: you get to succeed as an organism only if your cells do reasonably well overall as part of the collective called "you," but their self-interest is restrained.

These same facts apply to behavior. Behaviors that are for the good of the group often have costs for the individual and thus may not improve the relative fitness of the individual within the group. Even the smallest acts of kindness, such as opening a door for someone, typically require at least a small amount of time, energy, and risk on the part of the prosocial individual. For that reason, natural selection at the smallest scale – among individuals within a single group – can be *disruptive* as far as prosociality is concerned.

Multi-level selection is like a tug-of-war, with within-group selection pulling toward self-serving traits and between-group selection pulling toward group-serving traits. For cooperation to be selected, between-group selection needs to be strong enough to overcome the disruptive effects of within-group selection. This same tension applies to all levels of selection. Eukaryotic cells, for example, are themselves cooperative groups – the mitochondria in nucleated cells are literally a different life form. Even after most of a billion years to get it right, mitochondria still occasionally trick plants into producing only females since mitochondria are replicated only within the maternal line (Chase, 2007). The multi-level selection balancing act going on between cells and multicellular organisms is repeated within nucleated cells.

Prosociality and cooperation become central as we scale up into human behavior. Humans are faced with the same choice that we observe in the natural world, between individual self-interest and the interests of the collective. Individual human behavior can foster success at one level at the cost of success at another. What's good for you can be bad for your family.

What's good for your family can be bad for your clan. What's good for your clan can be bad for your nation. What's good for your nation can be bad for the world.

The general rule is this: adaptation at any level of a multi-tier hierarchy requires a process of selection at that level – and it tends to be undermined by selection at lower levels. When selection at lower levels is restrained, selection at higher levels can come to dominate.

Evolution in Multiple Streams

The discovery of genes as a mechanism of heredity was a major breakthrough in evolution science, but genes are hardly the *only* mechanism of inheritance (Jablonka & Lamb, 2006; Wilson et al., 2014). Parents and offspring typically share the same language, for example, which is not genetically inherited. Another inheritance mechanism involves changes in gene *expression* rather than gene *frequency*. Genes are up and down regulated, in part by epigenetic factors such as methylation of cytosine, making DNA transcription more difficult. Some of these epigenetic patterns can be passed across generations. Learning selects behavior within the lifetime of the individual, but it passes to other generations through social learning, symbolic learning, and cultural practices, and it alters the functioning of genes through epigenetic processes and through niche construction and selection. Ultimately every facet of human experience – the environments in which we live, our behavior, our cultural understandings and norms, our languages – are all continuously evolving using the same basic processes of variation, selection and retention.

PROSOCIAL AND APPLIED EVOLUTIONARY SCIENCE

Humans evolved in small bands and groups. That altered the evolutionary context to favor cooperation by shifting selection more toward between-group competition and less toward within-group competition. The other characteristic features of human functioning, cognition (Hayes & Sanford, 2014) and culture (Turchin, 2016), arguably followed as direct and indirect extensions of cooperation. If that is true, in some sense the small group is the primary unit of selection in human behavior, but it can be undermined by selection processes at lower levels of organization, namely the individual.

The deep lesson of multi-level selection is that evolution occurs at multiple levels at the same time, and thus behavior change needs to be thought of at multiple levels simultaneously. It is both/and not either/or. That might sound complicated, but we all manage it, all the time.

Balancing our needs with others is the warp and weft of daily life. Will I volunteer to help on someone else's project? Should I pick up my dog's poop? What should we do about refugees wanting to enter our country?

That is the reason we turned to contextual behavioral science and ACT in constructing prosocial as an intervention. Lin Ostrom was awarded the Nobel for showing that the CDPs accounted for group success, not for work showing how to get people to adopt these principles, nor to apply them in a flexible way. We needed principles of behavior change to accomplish that task, and it seemed to us that we should start with the processes that help explain and address the behavior of individuals since these would be key in preparing the way for the successful adoption of CDPs within groups.

It takes group actions to create the context in which cooperative behavior can be fostered, but it takes individual actions to create and to support such groups. Only individuals can ultimately decide to stay or leave; to participate or withdraw; to communicate or to remain silent, although they always do so in response to the context of the group. For that reason we will first describe the nature of ACT and psychological flexibility processes in the context of individuals before turning to how we use these processes in prosocial to foster the CDPs.

Managing Learning Processes

Operant learning principles provide the beginning of a useful theory of behavior that we can use to promote intentional change within and between groups. By operant, we simply mean that in a given *antecedent* context, particular variations in *behavior* produce particular *consequences* that select for that behavior in a particular *motivational* context. Shared understanding of this simple four-part process can be transformative for groups because it can make sense of previously incomprehensible or indefensible behavior.

Operant behavior is inherently purposeful, but in a limited sense of the term. As B.F. Skinner noted in *About Behaviorism*, the organism acts "in order to" produce consequences that have been secured in the past by various forms of action and thus "operant behavior is the very field of purpose and intention" (1974, p. 61). It is not the actual future that controls this kind of learning – it is the "futures" that have been experienced previously. We hardly need to extend the analysis of traditional behavioral principles in the present text, however, given the other chapters and the expected readership.

With the rise of relational learning (Hayes et al., 2001) a more generative learning process is established. Even human babies show a two-way street between names and objects by about age 12 months of age (Luciano et al., 2007). As the relational operants need to demonstrate stimulus equivalence forms, the number of learned relations quickly expands from sameness, to relations of difference, opposition, comparison, time, contingency, self, and so on. Relational framing of that kind can be applied to anything: in principle it is arbitrarily applicable.

Consider any verbal relation and you will note that they have a two-way quality that can then enter into networks. If Sally "is bigger than" Sam, you can derive that it is equally true that Sam "is smaller than" Sally. If you later learned that George was bigger than Sally, you could derive the relative size of all three.

This combinatorial property of relational networks is not only massively generative, it changes how we solve problems, such as how to get along in groups. Verbal problem-solving requires a symbolic description of events and their attributes entering into an if/

then relationship with imagined outcomes that can be compared: "Given this situation and its properties, if I do this I will get better outcomes than if I do that." In normal operant learning, the future purpose of action has actually been experienced in the past – in symbolic learning the past controls the relational framing of a purpose that may or may not have been experienced.

This new form of purpose (one based on relational framing instead of direct experience for the individual) creates a new contingency stream for evolution – not just contingencies of reinforcement, but also contingencies of meaning. Instead of just relying upon automatic reactions, thanks to the combinatorial property of relational networks people with a proper history can now plan ahead and create purpose symbolically.

Symbolic language is also a double-edged sword – a source of enormous variation but also enormous rigidity. The same symbolic relations that allow us to *solve* problems also allow us to *create* problems. For example, all animals will avoid not just direct sources of pain but also sources of pain based on classical conditioning. That makes perfect sense, and half a billion years is plenty of time to get good at it. But relational learning allows new forms – for example, a person might withdraw from a group to avoid thinking about a painful social rejection. A self-amplifying loop can easily be created in which avoiding possible pain of rejection and loneliness produces self-rules and encourages social behaviors leading to further withdrawal and loneliness. Relational learning processes can quickly become self-contradictory and self-amplifying. A problem-solving rule like "I have to fix my car or tomorrow will be terrible" is useful. "I have to get rid of my anxiety or tomorrow will be terrible" seems to be the same but is likely to cause harm because imminent terrible events *generate* anxiety, and in effect this rule means that anxiety is now something to be anxious about. Thus it both elicits anxiety and evokes avoidance of anxiety: a toxic combination.

This same double-edged quality applies to cognition in groups. Symbolic rules can be applied in ways that are coercive or that pull for excessive social compliance. Agreements that "this is how we do it here" or narratives about the supposed skill of the group ("We always win") can blind the entire group to healthy alternatives or to changing contexts that require new group practices. Members of a group can hold tightly to symbolic labels about who they are or what their role is in the group, which can induce behavioral rigidity that affects social relations (for example, "My boss did me wrong and I am going to find a way to get back at her"; "Joe is evil"; "I am just an introvert – I'm not good at being a leader").

Multi-level selection helps us think about the double-edged sword of human symbolic behavior and how it might be addressed. You can think of the "individual" as composed of a vast number of entities, including a variety of specific behavioral patterns, and so on. We all face selfishness from "groups within" when emotions or cognitions claim an unfair share of time and attention from us.

What psychological flexibility does is provide the skills and perspective needed to rein in internal selfishness that develops from the various thoughts, feelings, sensations, or memories that each of us contains. In effect, we shift from what's in the interests of parts of ourselves, such as our anxiety or suspicion, to what's in the interests of our whole person (Hayes, 2019).

Psychological flexibility consists of six processes:

1. Self: enhancement of the "deictic I" or perspective taking sense of self over the storied or conceptualized self;
2. Cognition: enhancement of cognitive defusion skills that allow the reduction of the automatic domination of verbal rules as opposed to the fused domination of verbal events over action;
3. Emotion: acceptance skills that allow emotion and sensation to be felt openly and without needless defense as distinct from experiential avoidance – attempting to change

the form, frequency, or situational sensitivity of private events even when that creates behavioral harm;
4. Presence: flexible, fluent, and voluntary attention to internal and external events in the now as opposed to domination by the conceptualized past or future as in rumination and worry;
5. Values: the establishment of chosen qualities of being and doing as reinforcers intrinsic to ongoing action; as opposed to fused, avoidant, or compliant verbal motivation;
6. Committed action: commitment to the creation of larger and larger patterns of values-based action as opposed to impulsivity, procrastination, and avoidant persistence.

Processes 1 and 4 are awareness processes that are designed to increase contextual sensitivity, thereby ensuring a more healthy selection of behaviors; Processes 2 and 3 are openness processes that are designed to increase healthy variability; Processes 5 and 6 are active engagement processes designed to foster healthy selection and retention processes.

Much as epigenetic processes alter how genotypes are expressed in the production of phenotypes, openness and awareness function are episymbolic processes that alter how our cognitive networks – our symbotypes, if you will – are expressed in our actions, and how we approach the challenges we face. We can have the thought that we *must* do something (for example, tell off a coworker) and respectfully decline to follow that self-rule; we can have the thought that we cannot do something (for example, give an important talk) and do it anyway.

Let's suppose we have a group member who has thoughts like "Oh, I can't do that because I'm not good at it, or It makes me too anxious to call volunteers. Find somebody else." That person could go to her grave declining to participate. But thoughts don't always have to have an automatic behavioral impact. For example, noticing thoughts with dispassionate curiosity dramatically reduces their automatic behavioral impact, such that a person might have the thought "It makes me too anxious to call volunteers" and still agree to do so.

Values-based actions in groups add positive moments to our lives, especially as group development is guided by the core design principles. The flexibility principles help you set up a social context for trust, and if these actions are supported by movement in a values-based direction, a self-amplifying process of effective group participation can ensue.

Although values are a symbolic event, values-based overt action is where the rubber meets the road. The benefit of dealing differently with internal barriers is that values can be put into practice through committed action.

Behavioral retention is fostered by two primary features of action: repetition leading to successful outcomes, and the integration of action into larger and more elaborate patterns that pay off in expressing values. As a shorthand, the prime tool for behavioral retention is practice and the creation of more integrated patterns of values-based action.

Using the Matrix to Foster Psychological Flexibility

The six flexibility processes comprise an integrated skill set. Both individuals and groups can be psychologically flexible. It is a skill set that supports prosocial behavior change and the deployment of the core design principles in part because these skills build key elements that undergird prosocial behavior: trust, a focus on longer term rather than immediate outcomes, and social value orientation.

In prosocial the prime method for working on psychological flexibility is called the *Matrix* (Polk et al., 2016). The Matrix is a process for thinking about two key dimensions of experience: moving *toward* consequences you want more versus the tendency to move *away* from consequences you want less, and "outside/inside," which represents the public physical world – what people can see, hear, taste, touch, and smell – versus private events, including thoughts, emotions, imagery, memories, and the like.

In this chapter we will present the Matrix in an upside-down version that allows these discriminations to be made very quickly using the metaphor of a person walking. Private events are analogous to what is in our hearts and heads: we have to tell others about these events for them to be known; public events are analogous to our hands and feet – anyone can see these because they are public.

We generally loop through the Matrix at least twice in the prosocial process. First, we look at clarifying individual goals, values, and concerns using the Matrix, and then we look at integrating those interests to craft a stronger sense of shared identity and purpose at the group level. Individuals or groups can complete the Matrix, and the process can be focused on one's own interests or the collective interests of the whole group.

The boxes in the figure are numbered. It is common to walk through them in this sequence, although it is by no means necessary and adapting to the context is encouraged. An individual might put words in these four sections such as 1. Authenticity; creativity; effectiveness 2. Fear of being ridiculed; fear of failure 3. Gossip; make jokes; avoid meetings 4. Coming to a meeting prepared, speaking up and sharing ideas.

Often in a group context there are privacy issues about the personal Matrix, so it is common to use online tools that present individual responses to the Matrix in anonymous form. If that approach is not used, the prosocial facilitator can ask if anybody would like to volunteer

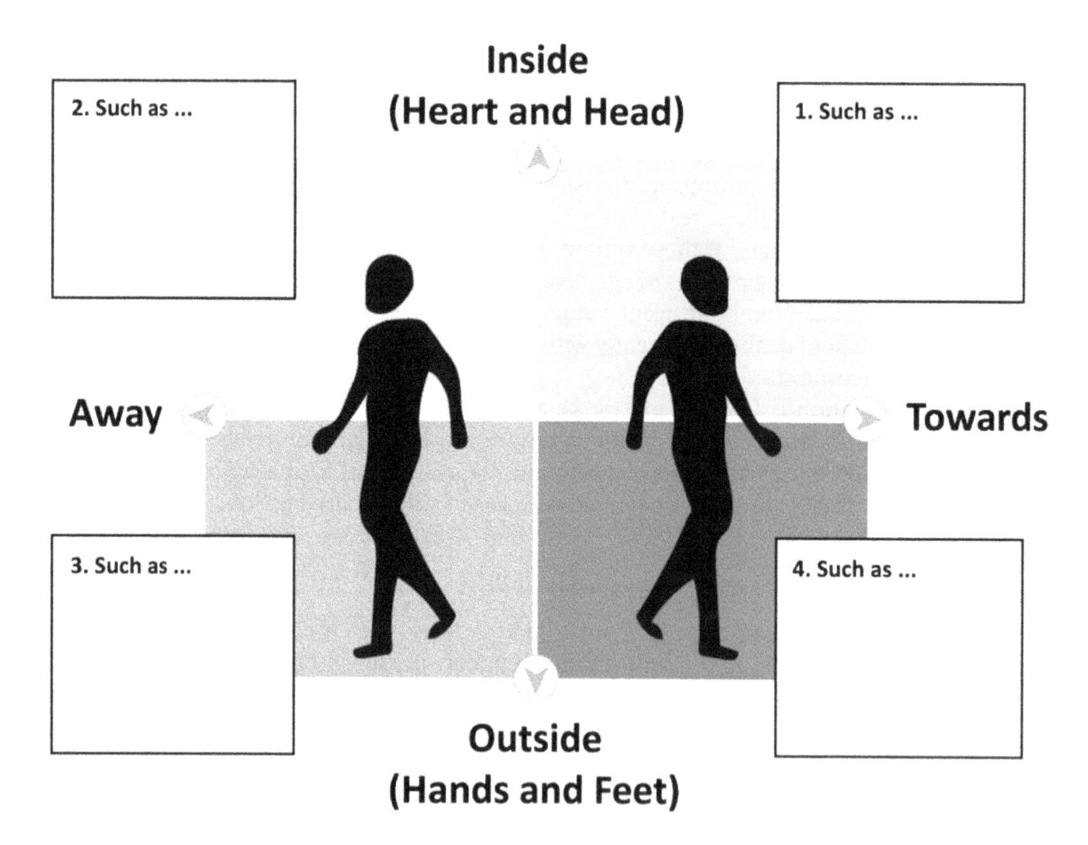

FIGURE 9.1 The steps of use of the Matrix, individually and in groups.

what they wrote down on their private map. In this way, group members choose what is most important, and safe, for them to share with the larger group, and a collective map of individual interests can be created.

Once the personal Matrix is done, a group Matrix is created. In this case we are looking at what we as a group want to move toward; what we as a group experience that draws us away; how that moving away looks publicly; and what we would see if we were all moving toward what we wanted this group to be about.

The cross in the middle of the Matrix represents conscious contact with the content of the Matrix itself. Thus, there is a rough correspondence between the Matrix and the six flexibility/inflexibility processes. The right side of the Matrix representing values and committed action; the left side representing the experiential avoidance and fusion; the cross in the middle representing awareness and the now.

What the Matrix process does that is useful for fostering group change will be explored in specific ways in the context of the CDPs to follow, but in general it fosters a personal consideration of values and vulnerabilities that are then shared in a safe context with others, fostering social connection and a feeling of belonging. It is very common for people to be surprised by the overlap of values and vulnerabilities within the group: people who may have felt that they are alone and disconnected frequently realize that others feel much the same way.

The collective Matrix fosters a sense of shared identity and group cohesion, and indicates places of disagreement that need to be worked on. In addition, it reveals concrete behavioral indicators of group functioning, both in a positive and negative direction.

THE CORE DESIGN PRINCIPLES

What follows is a discussion of the CDPs and how the group might be able to foster them. You will note that we have tweaked the definitions and labels for the CDPs in some areas in order for them to fit the full range of groups.

CDP 1: Shared Identity and Purpose

A group functions best when its purpose is clearly understood and perceived as worthwhile by its members. There should be a strong shared identity that helps group members to understand who is in or out of the group, and that coordinates behavior through shared norms and values.

In Ostrom's original study groups, the shared purpose was always sustainable management of a common-pool resource, which is why her original CDP1 focused on the issue of membership. Most other groups are defined more by their purpose and mere membership is not the issue. The key to this CDP is that members understand and care about the purpose of the group. That choice gives the group a shared sense of identity – creating a sense of belonging and caring for others in the group.

The Matrix is very helpful for CDP1 because it makes clear what group members most care about, both in terms of their stated values or goals, and also their concerns. It is a natural step for the group itself to then consider how they can create a sense of caring, belonging, and safety in the group.

When people share a purpose, they are more likely to care for the group and feel a sense of belonging. This makes them more likely to engage in prosocial behaviors, such as sharing information and helping others. You can see this happen automatically when a community experiences a natural disaster. As shared purpose becomes clear, people are more likely to exert effort to support collective action. Working to create a shared purpose *is* the very essence of clarifying and prioritizing the collective interests of the group over individual interests.

When the purposes of individuals within the group do not align with those of the group as a whole, a lot of time and energy is spent attempting to control individualistic behaviors. If a group can bring individual and collective purposes into alignment, a lot of this time and energy can be devoted to finding ways to better cooperate rather than to control individualism. An example of how this might be emphasized naturally using the Matrix is to begin the group process with questions like "What is *our* shared purpose? Who or what matters to *us*?" instead of the more individualistic question of "What matters most to *me* about the group?"

If your group seems to struggle with the question, you can deliberately shift a group's perspective to a future time frame. For example, we might ask this: "Imagine it's five years in the future, the group has been extraordinarily effective. What are we doing? Who are we serving?" and so on. From there it is but a short step to "What would we be most focused on as our common purpose?" It can also be helpful to ask questions that move people backward in time: What has enlivened and excited us in the past? When are we at our best?

It is important not to dive directly into the "how" questions of group functioning until the purpose is clear. CDP1 is first and foremost about why we are doing what we are doing. Once the "why" is evident, however, it is helpful to give purpose to life by embedding it in the concrete plans for the group. "What matters most in this situation?" or "What are we trying to achieve here?" are questions that put purpose inside group actions and plans.

Evidence for CDP1

There is abundant evidence from a variety of fields of study in support of core design principle 1. In terms of the positive benefits of a strong sense of shared identity and group cohesion (the degree to which the group sticks together and is unified in the pursuit of its goals), Chang and Bordia (2001) showed that group cohesion predicts group performance, while Mathieu et al. (2015) demonstrated that more cohesive groups perform better over time and better performance also enhances cohesiveness. Cohesion also enhances prosociality. De Cremer and Stouten (2003) demonstrated that contributions to a public good are higher when a person experiences the group as part of the self. Cohesive groups are more stable and members are more loyal (Van Vugt & Hart, 2004), while members of more cohesive groups are more likely to trust one another, share important information, and coordinate their actions more effectively (Ashforth & Mael, 1989). There are also impacts at the personal level. Group members feel more personal meaning in life when there is a strong sense of belonging in a group, because it expands their awareness to include a cause larger than themselves (Lambert et al., 2013).

Shared purpose also has a range of positive effects upon group members and groups. Workers whose purpose matches that of their organization produce 72% more output than unmatched workers (Carpenter & Gong, 2016) and workers are willing to be paid 44% less for the same job once they learned that their prospective employers had a social responsibility mission statement (Burbano, 2016). At least a part of what is going on here is a focus on approach rather than avoidance. When people are primed to focus on approach rather than avoidance, they are more proactive in contributing effort and ideas to a group, as well as managing their own needs (Kilduff & Galinsky, 2013).

CDP 2: Equitable Distribution of Contributions and Benefits

For groups to function well, the effort and other forms of contribution required of its members, and the benefits of that effort, need to be distributed fairly. Most people have a strong sense of equity that is violated when someone receives benefits disproportionate to their contributions. So perceived fairness – a fair balance between effort or workload and reward – is essential for good group performance. Sometimes, in groups that fall short of implementing this principle, perceived unfairness is "undiscussable"; sometimes, it is discussed endlessly but in ways that do not lead to positive change.

In general, a good way to implement this design principle is to have a discussion with each member of the group and each subgroup of members as to what they most want to get from the group and what they have most to give. If the arrangement seems fair to everyone at the end of the discussion, then both aspects of this design principles will be satisfied. Such an approach can often be more helpful than evoking unhelpful and biased frames of comparison by asking "Are you treated fairly" from the outset? The key outcome is that group members feel valued and rewarded for contributions.

There are two important aspects to fairness: are resources distributed among people fairly (e.g., who gets how much money; who gets promotional opportunities) and are there fair and transparent processes in which people are involved appropriately in decisions that affect them. CDP 2 is focused mainly on the first variety, sometimes referred to as distributive justice (Schäfer et al., 2015); CDP 3 (fair and inclusive decision-making) and 6 (fast and fair conflict resolution) are more focused on the second type, often called procedural justice (Bobocel & Gosse, 2015).

The most effective groups usually begin with a recognition that everybody deserves the opportunity to contribute to the fullest extent possible, if they so desire, and that benefits are fairly linked to contributions. By "contribution" we mean any form of adding to the good of the group through effort, hours, or resources. By "benefits" we mean anything that benefits the individual, such as salary, public recognition, learning opportunities, or social engagement.

Fairness can involve a sense of equality (e.g., benefits and workload are assigned equally), equity (benefits are linked to performance), or need (benefits are linked to need) or all three in combination. Once the ideas of distributive and procedural fairness, and the differences between equity, equality, and need-based norms of fairness, are introduced to groups, they are usually in a much better position to enrich their discussions of what really matters in relation to CPD 2, and to link issues of fairness to their shared purpose.

If fairness is a problem for a group, opening a conversation focused on fairness can often backfire because it primes self-interest and encourages biased and inaccurate estimates of contributions and benefits. Fairness grows from a group culture that's focused on "us" and how we all benefit, rather than one focused on me comparing my outcomes to your outcomes.

The individual and collective matrices are enormously helpful with this because they help build shared purpose and trust. When people are focused on their bigger and shared "toward" moves, there's less emphasis on the more self-protective "away" moves that are involved in social comparison. A conversation focused on "Are *we* working together effectively to achieve our shared purpose" is more likely to produce fairness as a by-product than a conversation focused directly on "Am *I* getting what I deserve?" This is particularly true when the dominant norm for fairness is equity – that is, benefits relative to contributions.

After reminding the group about their shared purpose, the focus of a fairness discussion might be on such issues as "What matters most to us about this situation?" When that is clear it can be helpful to move to "toward actions" if you think the group would benefit from getting more concrete about what fairness actually would look like in the group. It can also be helpful to move to the difficult thoughts and emotions that arise in the context of unfairness are more pressing and how they get expressed in action or inaction. Moving to perspective taking, practicing clear communication and focusing more on roles and tasks more than on personalities and individuals can all be helpful in breaking "fairness" log jams.

Evidence for CDP2

Colquitt and Rodell (2015) conducted a meta-analysis of 493 studies in the area. All forms of fairness significantly predicted social exchange quality (trust, perceived organizational support, leader-member exchange, and organizational commitment) which in turn significantly predicted task performance, organizational citizenship (prosociality), and negatively predicted counterproductive work behaviors (antisociality). They further showed that distributive, procedural and interactional justice predicted positive and negative affect in expected directions. In other words, not only does justice affect performance and prosociality, but it also significantly influences wellbeing.

In a meta-analysis of 190 studies with 65,000 participants, all forms of justice predicted organizational commitment, trust, and various measures of job and organizational satisfaction. Distributive and procedural justice strongly predicted organizational citizenship (i.e., prosocial) behaviors. Procedural justice was the strongest predictor of trust, job performance, and the extent of counterproductive work behaviors (Cohen-Charash & Spector, 2001). A meta-analysis of 166 studies of leadership and justice with 46,034 participants revealed that followers of leaders who were more fair (distributive justice) had significantly higher levels of job satisfaction (Karam et al., 2019).

In general, the vast literature on organizational justice seems to show that procedural justice (see CDP3 below) is more important than equity of outcomes (CDP2), but the issues are complex and both are clearly important. Viswesvaran and Ones (2002) conducted a meta-analysis of 16 studies (N = 4,696) that showed high correlations between distributive and procedural justice (r = .66). While both forms of justice were predictive of organizational commitment, organizational citizenship, productivity, and job satisfaction, and procedural justice was more predictive of all but the last of these constructs. One recent study (Cloutier et al., 2018) showed that violations of procedural justice had more effect upon distress than did violations of distributive justice. They concluded "The results highlight the greater need for workers to be valued and appreciated for who they are (consideration and esteem), rather than for what they do for their organization (distributive justice of rewards)" (Cloutier et al., 2018, p. 283). This may suggest that the key ingredient of fairness is that it serves as an indicator of respect for the members of the group, rather than as a kind of calculation as to whether benefits match contributions as suggested by earlier equity theory.

CDP 3: Fair and Inclusive Decision-Making

In well-functioning groups, members need to be involved in making decisions about the issues that affect them, particularly in their agreements about how the group itself runs. Giving people control over their own actions fosters wellbeing and effective action. Members need to know that their interests and perspectives have been considered fairly and efficiently. CDP 3 can take many different forms provided that individuals who are affected by the decisions have some influence over those decisions.

There are other benefits. Inclusive decision-making helps group members to develop crucial skills – not just the technical skills of learning about the issues and approaches to solving them, but the psychological skills of listening, perspective taking, self-regulating, making room for other points of view, and committing to action even when it's frightening.

Despite all the benefits of empowering group members, strong hierarchies of authority still persist in many groups, with decisions being made at the top and "pushed down" to those who are supposed to execute those decisions. Coercive behavior only gets worse when those in charge are threatened. Under time or resource pressures, the degree to which they rely upon their authority and power to enforce decisions only gets more intense.

Why is it like this? Surely if more devolved, inclusive decision-making is such an obviously good idea, then it ought to be selected for in the competitive world of organizational life, in community groups, even in day-to-day contexts such as parents engaging with the children that they love.

Hierarchies persist due to promises of more direction, protection, speed, and social order and, in nested groups, the ability of authorities to change leadership easily if that does not occur. The self-interest of leaders also sustains hierarchies. Authority figures are often afraid that they'll lose power if they try more inclusive decision-making. Leaders may believe their value lies in providing solutions, and engaging others in problem-solving and decision-making may reduce their self-perceived sense of value. The same is true in situations where knowledge is perceived to be power – "If I share my understanding then I lose my power and others gain it."

Hierarchies are well evolved for stable and relatively simple contexts that a single leader can understand, but they do not work well with the complex relationships, distributed information, and rapid change that are the hallmarks of the societies we now live in. Decisions propagated up through hierarchies take time and become increasingly disconnected from the information needed to make good decisions. If we want to create groups that balance individual and collective interests in the long term, we need to do the hard work of empowering people to make decisions and learning new ways of making decisions together.

The Matrix can prove useful when there is resistance to creating more inclusive forms of decision-making. If a group is to make progress with change, its members must not only talk about what they want to move toward, they must also have a way to talk about the positive and negative reinforcers that are keeping the system stuck. Using the Matrix groups can explore what is important to the group about fair and inclusive decision-making and a variety of alternatives can be considered. Examples include leadership not only seeking out multiple perspectives but encouraging group members to take real responsibility for finding workable solutions to group challenges, shifting the power to frame a decision to members of the group, or adopting a consent-based voting process (e.g., *Agree*: "I agree with this and approve of it moving forward"; *Abstain*: "I am happy for the group to decide without me"; *Disagree*: "I think we can probably do better"; and *Block*: "I have strong objections to this proposal and do not approve of it moving forward") among other options.

The Matrix can also be used to discuss the *content* of particular decisions. Simply start with this question: What is important to us about [decision]? Process issues can be examined by asking about such issues as "How can we make it more rewarding and less challenging for everybody to speak up?" A similar tactic can bring in the views of stakeholders. Sometimes groups have found it useful to use "circle talk," perhaps at the beginning of a meeting, allowing everyone the opportunity to reflect on how they are and what is important to them about the meeting, or at the end, so everybody gets a chance to comment on what has happened. Circles, even physical circles of seating, can do a lot to level the playing field in a meeting and encourage everyone's voice.

Evidence for CDP3

In the section on CDP2, we also reviewed the evidence for the benefits of CDP3 interpreted broadly as procedural justice. However, there is specific evidence that inclusion in decision-making is also beneficial in groups. In a meta-analytic review of 72 studies (N = 32,870), Slemp et al. (2018) showed that when leaders give followers choices and support them in executing those choices, they are happier, have less distress, are more productive at work, and are more intrinsically motivated to exert discretionary effort. In support of these findings, Chamberlin et al. (2018) conducted a meta-analysis of 151 samples (N = 53,200) and found that empowering people and giving them a voice improves job performance.

In a beautiful experimental study highlighting the specific effects of unilateral power upon cooperation (prosociality), Cronin et al. (2015) placed participants in hierarchical or non-hierarchical conditions, with or without power. Over nine sequential rounds, participants who had decisions made for them acted less and less cooperatively over time. Low power participants saw that there was little chance of them receiving a fair share of the proceeds, and so they withdrew their effort. Higher-ranked participants then had to work harder and harder to try to reach an agreement by making larger and larger contributions, but to no avail. Cooperation simply didn't happen as often in the groups with asymmetrical power as it did in the groups where power was balanced. This study replicates what is found in animal species. The strength of dominance hierarchies in animals varies. Species with strong hierarchies, such as chimpanzees, cooperate less than species with more relaxed, weaker hierarchies, such as cottontop tamarins.

Using a sample of 22,547 participants in the European Social Survey, participatory decision-making was shown to be associated with greater job satisfaction (Pacheco & Webber, 2016). Critically, lower than average participation had a larger marginal effect upon job satisfaction than a range of other variables, demonstrating the importance of participation in decision-making.

In a multi-level review Bashshur and Oc (2015) argued that having process and decision control is generally associated with improved performance, higher perceptions of justice, better job attitudes, improved relational outcomes (trust, liking, leader support, loyalty, etc.), and increased intention to stay in the group at the level of the individual. Most of the work at the level of the group appears to have been focused on voice as dissent. Having more minority dissent is associated with greater innovation (as long as people are involved in decision-making about implementation). However, it may also be disruptive for groups. At the level of the organization, voice tends to improve turnover, organizational learning and organizational performance while reducing wrongdoing.

CDP 4: Monitoring Behavior

For groups to function well, it's essential to have some way to monitor agreed-upon behaviors. In hierarchical organizations, monitoring agreed behaviors tends to be seen as the job of a manager or other authority. But such top-down monitoring is often coercive and serves the interests of the manager not of the person being monitored. It's also not very transparent, and self-serving behaviors increase when there is a lack of transparency. Ostrom's work suggested that monitoring is often better performed by peers as part of the normal interaction of group members. The point is to enhance the visibility of behaviors of group members to other members.

If a group is to cooperate effectively, members must know what others are doing. If group members don't notice and care about others' behavior, the group cannot appropriately coordinate its actions, discourage disruptive self-interested behavior, or encourage helpful, cooperative behavior. We use the term "monitoring" to describe observing with the intent to coordinate behavior. For some people, that word sounds a bit sinister because it's sometimes associated with powerful people attempting to control the behavior of others. But when we use "monitoring," we really just mean transparency of behavior – all members being able to see or notice what others are doing in the group. In this chapter, we'll explore what monitoring is and how you can build it into your group in a way that supports individual self-determination while also taking care of the needs of the collective.

The aim of monitoring is to capitalize on the positive reinforcement arising from cooperation rather than the negative processes of coercion and control. This CDP is about *transparency*, and caring about and noticing the work of others, not introducing a dead hand of control. This is why we emphasize that monitoring ideally include peers knowing what others are doing in the group. In some contexts, this might be as simple as regular meetings to discuss what members of the group are working on. In others, it might involve more formal systems of review, such as after-action reviews of team performance, performance appraisal discussions with a manager, or obtaining feedback from a survey of peers and subordinates in something like a 360-degree feedback process.

As with the other principles, this principle works at any scale. A virtual team must be able to see what everyone is doing in order to coordinate and perform, just as global arms control relies upon each nation being able to monitor nuclear testing and distinguish it from earthquakes.

Despite its obvious utility, as with all the principles, monitoring is not necessarily something that all groups do well. In our experience, groups do monitoring badly in three main ways:

- To the wrong extent: too much or too little relative to the purposes of the group
- Ineffectively: when either not enough information or the wrong information is gathered about behavior
- Coercively: when monitoring is used not to enhance mutual learning but instead to force behavior

There are two key practices to making behavior visible to others in the group. First, groups should share information about what members of the group are doing, either through meetings; online, asynchronous tools, such as project-management software; or other channels. Second, groups need to have processes for managing the performance of all employees that preserve the group's internal cooperation and prosociality.

An obvious way to make behavior more transparent in a group is to share information about progress made toward objectives using collaborative project-management tools, such as Trello or Asana. Many similar tools are available. Putting information online in a readily accessible format can be particularly important when members of the group work remotely, and the online shared space is sometimes the main means for getting information abou what others in the group are doing. This strategy primarily works to enhance coordination, but it can also tap into the other benefits of monitoring, such as by increasing prosociality, decreasing free-riding, and improving motivation.

To be useful, monitoring needs to be timely; focused on support and not coercive control; and mutual. Systems such as 360-degree feedback, with which staff can notice and comment upon manager behavior in the same way that managers notice and comment upon staff behavior, help to create norms of mutual accountability and shared continuous improvement.

The collective Matrix can be used to generate information about what needs to be monitored because it specifies valued individual and group behaviors as well as defensive individual and group behaviors that are likely to interfere with effective cooperation. For example, a group member might flag in the personal Matrix that they tend to go quiet and not volunteer their opinion when they feel unsure about something. This might work against effective cooperation if important dissenting voices are ignored. Given this information, other members of the group are in a better position to notice when the person might be avoiding speaking up and respond helpfully to include that person in the group discussion.

Evidence for CDP4

Bernstein (2017) conducted a review of the evidence for the benefits of monitoring and argued that being more able to see the work of others (transparency as monitoring) resulted in improved performance, communication/sharing of knowledge, learning, and more prosocial behavior through peer effects. He also noted, however, that when monitoring begins to feel like surveillance, it can easily be experienced as an invasion of privacy. Clearly monitoring must be done in a way that supports group members in achieving their purposes without excessive intrusion into their privacy. Negative evidence for this principle also comes from a study showing that when high trust leads to less monitoring, team performance tends to decline (Langfred, 2004).

There is also fascinating evidence that we have evolved to act more prosocially when monitoring is present. In a series of controlled studies, researchers showed that people are more likely to make voluntary donations when there is a picture of a pair of eyes on the wall than when there is not (Bateson et al., 2013; Bateson et al., 2006; Nettle et al., 2013). This basic finding in the lab has been replicated in a variety of contexts: the presence of watching eyes also increases charitable giving, decreases littering, increases the picking up of litter, and increases contributions to an "honesty box" in which people pay for coffee and other supplies in a shared kitchen.

CDP 5: Graduated Responding to Helpful and Unhelpful Behavior

No one is perfect when it comes to fulfilling the obligations of a group. Even the most capable and well-meaning members can fail, especially given competing demands upon their time and attention. While Ostrom was focused on graduated sanctions for misbehaviors the reinforcers were built-in: access to common-pool resources. In addition, Ostrom's groups tended to be stable and leaving was not a ready option. In order to generalize this principle, it needs to extend beyond just group responding meant to discourage unhelpful behavior and include responding meant to encourage helpful behavior. Without such positive reinforcement, there is little incentive to stay with the group and people either disengage or leave. The key issue is responding at an appropriate level of intensity to either encourage or discourage behaviors contributing or detracting from cooperation within the group.

Responding effectively to increase prosocial behaviors and decrease antisocial behaviors is not always easy, as seen in how often we get it wrong. The formal and informal processes put in place to respond to behavior should be focused on creating cooperation to move a group toward its shared purpose. As much as possible, such processes need to honor and preserve the degree to which people feel in control of their choices, their capacity to effect change, and their relationships.

Ostrom emphasized graded sanctions for negative behavior and sanctions that start small are far less likely to elicit strong emotional responses, counterattacks, or withdrawal from the group. By giving violators an easy way out, the sanctions also are likely to seem fairer and less indiscriminate.

In the successful groups that Ostrom studied, if violations persisted, the sanctions escalated; for example, if gossip might be followed by a visit from village elders. Often increased sanctions include guidance about what to do to avoid future sanctions.

If strong sanctions are applied immediately, instead of after a more mild sanction, it can undermine trust and provoke retaliation. Nobody wants to be in a group in which, literally or figuratively, the smallest violation could result in your head being cut off. Graduated sanctions can have the opposite effect, because others see that abusive and costly forms of selfishness will not be tolerated and thus their own cooperative steps are likely to be reciprocated.

The ultimate sanction of being cast out of the group gives gentle warnings part of their punch. We've probably all been in workgroups in which we felt a sense of relief or gratitude when a chronically toxic staff member was finally let go.

At the same time, a greater emphasis on positive reinforcement for helpful behavior avoids many of the negative risks of sanctions. It is important to encourage collective "toward" behaviors wherever possible rather than just focusing on individuals and behaviors that are not wanted. Rewards that are integral to the task itself are less likely to land poorly than crude use of external rewards. Within-group competition can be destructive if the gains that result from increased winner motivation are canceled out by losses in motivation on the part of losers. Focusing responding on behaviors and achievements that support shared purpose and identity, equity, and inclusiveness bolster the group against these dangers.

One of the many benefits of the Matrix is that it reveals what members of the group will consider reinforcing. Everybody is different, and we can never assume that a particular behavior will be reinforcing. The Matrix can also be used to explore what is important to us about this CDP; how we might implement it; what hooks might show up and get in the way of implementing the principle; or what the group might do in light of these hooks and defensive behaviors.

It is usually best to explore responding to helpful and unhelpful behavior separately, because the values and concerns are often quite different. Often groups know what works for responding to unhelpful behavior in a graduated way, such as by first asking the person why they did what they did, followed by things like skills training in responding constructively. Eventually, however, the group hits a sense that they don't know what to do, that the response might escalate conflict, or fear of confrontation and social disapproval. Walking inside these barriers in a values-based way is necessary to see full progress. This might include reorienting to the purpose of consequences, taking the perspective of the other person, defusing from judgments about what happened, and creating openness to gathering new data. It is also important to separate out evaluations that are subjective from actual observations.

Evidence for CDP5

There are large bodies of evidence both for graduated sanctions and, obviously in this context, appropriate reinforcement in enhancing prosocial behavior in groups. In terms of graded sanctions, people are more cooperative when opportunities to altruistically punish uncooperative behavior are present than when they're absent (Fehr & Gächter, 2002). Just the threat of sanctions via exclusion for "bad apples" decreases antisocial behaviors (Kerr et al., 2009). Sanctions are not just beneficial at the individual level, at the organizational level Gürerk et al. (2006) showed that institutions that had sanctions outcompeted institutions without sanctions by attracting members and cooperating more effectively.

That begin said, it has long been known that sudden reductions of positive reinforcement or sudden presentation of aversive consequences will produce increases in aggression in humans and non-human animals alike (e.g., Frederiksen, & Peterson, 1977). Meta-analyses show, for example, that social use of intense negative consequences (e.g., parental corporal punishment) increases compliance short term – but it also increases aggression longer term (Gershoff, 2002).

Interactions between sanctions and trust are complicated. On the one hand, sanctions appear to be particularly important in environments where there is lower generalized trust (Yamagishi, 1988). On the other hand, in a meta-analysis of 83 studies involving 7,361 participants across 18 societies (Balliet & Van Lange, 2013), levels of trust and the enforcement of social norms were reciprocally related such that each increased the other. Sanctions work more effectively when there's trust. For example, in high-trust societies such as Denmark and China, the prospect of punishment for failing to contribute to shared public goods promotes cooperation more effectively than in low-trust societies.

CDP 6: Fast and Fair Conflict Resolution

Any group that involves committed individuals acting authentically will inevitably encounter conflict as people have different interests and information. It is best to plan for conflicts and their resolution from the beginning. Successful groups have ways of reaching timely resolution or accommodation of differences in ways that honor individual differences in values and perspectives.

Conflict is normal and inevitable in any high-performing group. Group members perceive situations differently – noticing different "facts" and putting them together in different, sometimes self-serving, ways. This network of beliefs and evaluations is simply our symbolic relational repertoire in action. We create and derive networks of meaning to understand and predict the behaviors of others. But our networks of meaning can easily become rigid when we see them as the only possible truth rather than a perspective. The sense we make of situations tend to be self-serving – we seek out and process information in ways that will confirm our existing views.

If a group is to find a way through conflicts, it needs to ensure it has an effective capability at three levels:

1. Interpersonal skills such as listening well and speaking assertively not aggressively
2. Personal skills such as emotion regulation and perspective taking
3. Group-level agreements and processes for managing conflict efficiently and effectively.

Healthy conflict tends to be focused on tasks and includes legitimate differences of opinion, values, perspectives, or expectations. Unhealthy conflict tends to be more focused on labeling or judging individuals. It often involves people competing for scarce resources or power, conflicts between individual and collective goals, and poor communication patterns.

Healthy task conflict can be seen as a sign of a thriving, autonomy-supportive environment where people are encouraged to think for themselves and voice their opinions. Task conflict might arise because members perceive value issues differently, or because they bring different types of expertise to a task, leading them to see different solutions. Healthy disagreement can contribute to creativity, learning, and better solutions overall. Groups that experience no conflict, not even task conflict, are usually composed of highly avoidant members who are deferential to the leader.

Relationship conflict tends to be much more emotional, and it involves tension, annoyance, and animosity between people. Negative and rigid evaluations and judgments of others fuel relationship conflict. Whereas task conflict tends to produce more effective group decisions, relationship conflict is usually associated with poorer group decisions. Furthermore, relationship conflict usually creates disconnections between people as they avoid one another, leading to failures to transmit information and coordinate activity. The second author of this chapter once worked with a surgical team, the members of which were locked in relational conflict to the extent that they weren't passing on information about the treatment and current condition of patients at the handover between shifts, creating extreme risk for patients. Relational conflict also consumes a huge amount of emotional energy, distracting people from the task and causing them to waste time gossiping and disagreeing.

To the extent that a safe and trusting environment exists within a group, there is a lower likelihood of people hearing disagreement as criticism, as well as an increased willingness to speak up, knowing that disagreement will be less likely to blow up into emotionally charged relational conflict.

The overwhelming strategy most people use to manage the difficult feelings and thoughts associated with conflict is to simply avoid having it. Work teams learn what is "undiscussable," whether it be the manager's behavior, a team member's free-riding on the efforts of the rest of the team, or the lack of feasibility of a poorly thought through strategic plan.

If conflict is not dealt with effectively, it can undermine all the other principles. Conflict resolution includes (Fisher et al., 2011):

1. Separating the people from the problem.
2. Focusing on the shared interests of both parties.
3. Developing many options that can be used to solve the problem.
4. Evaluating the options using objective criteria.

The Matrix provides an effective tool for implementing these four recommendations and creating more integrative solutions. Mapping out the values and overarching goals espoused by each participant, and having recognized that they had much in common, sets an effective stage for exploring the fears and concerns. When making specific recommendations for action conflict, it's possible to think more abstractly about shared values to see if there's a way to come up with a specific action that will meet the needs of both sides.

When your group members seem to be stuck in conflicting positions, the Matrix can help identify the underlying interests through questions such as these:

- What is most important to you about getting X?
- What matters most to you here?
- What would you like to accomplish by getting X?
- What is it about this that really matters to you in the longer term?
- If you got what you are asking for, what interests and needs would that satisfy?

Focusing on interests tends to shift the focus from the unchangeable past or present to what we want for the future, which is the only place where changes can be made. Flexibility skills such as learning to take the perspective of others, empathize with them, and tolerate the pain of conflict helps transform the meaning of conflict from something to be avoided into something to be used for learning and growth.

A more helpful stance is to objectify the problem rather than the person, and to assume that everyone in the relationship has understandable intentions, at least from their own point of view. From this perspective, we can stand side by side instead of being squared off against one another, and thus work on solving the problem together.

Aside from developing personal and interpersonal skills to manage conflict effectively, having agreed-upon principles and processes that everyone can trust can greatly help the process of conflict resolution.

It is important that conflict management occurs in a timely manner. Typically, effective conflict resolution begins as an informal conversation between the parties involved. If participants have learned some of the skills of emotional self-regulation, perspective taking, listening effectively, speaking assertively not aggressively, and holding a conversation to a clear purpose, it's often possible for them to simply work through differences in open conversation. Beyond that initial conversation, it's quite common to encounter conflict-escalation processes that move through stages as required, from one-on-one conversation to a mediated conversation to some kind of informal arbitration process to an external arbitration process, for example. If groups successfully manage task conflict so that it doesn't become relational, they can improve not only the level of cooperation within the group, but also the levels of creativity and performance.

Evidence for CDP6

Relational and process-related conflict is generally unproductive while task-related conflict is productive as long as group members feel psychological safe (Bradley et al., 2012). A meta-analysis of 116 studies examining 8,800 teams showed relationship- and process-related conflict was associated with poor group outcomes. Unlike earlier studies, this analysis did not show a negative relationship between task conflict and group outcomes (de Wit et al., 2012). Teams with high task conflict and low relationship and process conflict are more effective at resolving conflict and perform more effectively (O'Neill et al., 2018).

One example of the ways that poorly managed conflict can undermine all the other principles is the effects of conflict upon teams that are structured for equitable (CDP2) and inclusive decision-making (CDP3). Self-managed teams restructure themselves in response to unmanaged conflict. Over time, people share less information with one another, were less trusting of giving others autonomy to make decisions, and avoided others with whom they were supposed to be cooperating, all of which eventually undermined many of the benefits of giving a group authority to manage itself (Langfred, 2007). But the effects can run the other way as well. More group cohesion (CDP1) moderates the effects of conflict upon team performance (Nesterkin, 2016) and having more voice in organizational dispute resolution (CDP3) results in more effective conflict resolution, which in turn results in lower turnover intentions (Van Gramberg et al., 2017).

CDP 7: Authority to Self-Govern

The seventh design principle shifts the focus away from the internal social organization of the group and toward external relations. Every group is embedded in a larger society that can limit its ability to govern its own affairs. These constraints can interfere with the objectives of the group and the implementation of CDPs 1–6. For example, state educational policy might impose limitations on how classes can be taught or a military group might be forced to get permission from a chain of command before they can act in an emergency situation. To create really high-performing groups, it is essential to provide an environment that does not excessively interfere with their capacity to implement principles 1 through 6.

In a sense, this principle is the same as CDP 3 (fair and inclusive decision-making), but at the group rather than individual level. Both CDP 3 and CDP 7 involve rights and responsibilities associated with autonomy – the right to have a voice and the responsibility to put forward one's perspective and expertise.

Energy and creativity can be unleashed when larger-scale entities, such as governments, corporations, and even the military, make it easier rather than harder for groups to form and manage their own affairs, and in a way that also contributes to the welfare of the larger-scale entity. The collective Matrix can work with a group to explore options for increasing authority to self-govern.

However hard it might be for a group to become more autonomous, the results are likely to speak for themselves. If you're fighting for autonomy, try to get your "superiors" to let you try self-governance on a pilot basis.

Evidence for CDP7

As currently framed, it is somewhat complex to assemble evidence specifically for this principle. As we use prosocial, we are increasingly conceiving this principle as an absence of interference from outside the group in CDP's 1–6. Put simply, if a team is unable to implement principles 1–6 effectively because of a hostile or even benevolently controlling environment, they will be unlikely to succeed for all the reasons given in the previous sections.

But there is more specific evidence for this principle from studies that compare teams that are relatively autonomous (self-managing) with those that exist within more traditional hierarchies. As just one example, Kirkman and Rosen (1999) showed that "empowered" teams were "more productive and proactive than less empowered teams and had higher levels of customer service, job satisfaction, and organizational and team commitment." Another empirical study of government departments showed that self-management contributed to job satisfaction and resource attainment, but it was less important than just having effective teamwork (i.e., principles 1–6) (Yang & Guy, 2011).

CDP 8: Collaborative Relations with Other Groups

This principle can be seen as a kind of meta-principle that allows all the other principles to be scaled to groups of groups. It concerns the way a group relates to the others with which it is in contact. If we are to build systems of cooperation, a group needs not only to practice principles 1–7 itself but also relate to other groups using principles 1–7. This can go wrong in two ways: a) other groups may not cooperate with you (e.g., they don't include your group in important decisions, behave in ways that can't be monitored, and so on), or b) your group may not cooperate well with other groups. In this fashion, the same design principles are relevant at all levels of a multi-tier hierarchy of social units. What is key is that group relations throughout systems of interest embody principles 1–7. In that context it is important to determine whether groups have purposeful, equitable, inclusive, transparent, responsive, harmonious and autonomy-supportive relations with other groups.

Multi-level selection theory casts the necessity of managing between-group interactions in particularly sharp relief. The general rule of multi-level selection is that adaptation at any given level requires a process of selection *at that level* and tends to be *undermined* by selection at lower levels. Many social pathologies are examples of lower-scale cooperation that's disruptive for higher-scale social units. For example, cooperation among relatives can become nepotism.

Cooperation among friends can become cronyism. Policies based on "my nation first" can be toxic for the planet. CDP 8 leads us to a necessary conclusion: a full-scale evolutionary approach inevitably leads to global concerns and considerations.

Selection at the upper levels of a multi-tier hierarchy of groups might seem inherently more difficult than that at lower levels. Perhaps, but consider that each of us, as multicellular organisms, are already groups of groups of groups – in fact, we are multispecies ecosystems when you take our microbiomes into account!

The concept of polycentric governance has the same quality of common sense as do the CDPs 1–7 for single groups. Yet, polycentric governance does not spontaneously evolve – it must be mindfully constructed, similar to relations among individuals within single groups.

A central insight for polycentric governance done right is that the core design principles are *scale independent*. Polycentric governance offers a fractal view of groups as organisms in their own right, allowing conversations to shift to how those entities might implement principles 1 through 7 in their relationships with one another. Groups of groups also need their own shared sense of identity and purpose (CDP 1); they must distribute contributions and benefits fairly among their member groups (CDP 2); all groups should take part in decision-making (CDP 3); agreed-upon behaviors should be monitored (CDP 4); there should be praised for good behavior and graduated sanctions for deviant behavior (CDP 5); there should be ways to resolve conflicts among groups that are fast and fair (CDP 6); and the group of groups should have the authority to manage its own affairs (CDP 7). The same can be said of groups of groups of groups – created appropriate relations at still larger scales, potentially to the scale of the entire earth. In this sense, CDP 8 is less a separate principle and more about the applicability of principles 1 through 7 at any level of organization.

There are several practical implications of CDP 8. First, when a single group grows in size, it must differentiate its members as groups of groups in order to function well. Think about how many groups compose a school system, a corporation, a hospital, or a government agency. In these cases, there's a lot of scope for implementing polycentric governance for the whole organization.

Second, if your group or multigroup organization has become prosocial enough to function as a corporate unit, then you can work with like-minded groups to form prosocial consortia that thrive in competition with less-organized groups. A number of enlightened business corporations are taking impressive steps in this direction, as we will describe.

Third, the more this false and destructive narrative can be replaced by a more scientifically validated narrative based on multi-level selection theory, then the more the CDPs will "make sense" at all scales.

Evidence for CDP8

Once again, it is not a trivial matter to assemble evidence for this principle. A central tenant of multi-level selection theory is that between-group competition can enhance within-group cooperation (see, e.g., Majolo & Maréchal, 2017 for an example in children) over time. But this does not mean that we must always be condemned to living within constantly warring small groups. The genius of Ostrom's principles lies in their capacity to be enacted at any scale. The Prosocial Model framing of CDP8 is that principles 1–7 will also work at group, and systemic levels. That is, to work effectively, groups of groups must also have shared purpose, equity, inclusive decision-making, transparency, effective feedback, effective conflict management and appropriate autonomy from broader systemic forces in order to cooperate effectively. One could argue that science as a whole is a prime example of a polycentric system. It is highly value-centric, driven by ideals such as objectivity and replicability. There is no centralized governing body, no global leader of science. But there are massive and highly effective global networks of cooperation (Aligica & Tarko, 2011).

What is really needed is solid evidence that each of the principles 1–7 apply equally to between-group relations as they do to within-group relations. Such evidence is available for some of the principles. For example, superordinate goals (CDP1) reduce intergroup conflict (Sherif, 1958), although superordinate identities may not be optimally effective.

There is value in retaining and celebrating subgroup autonomy and distinctiveness (CDP7) (Hogg, 2015). Similarly, studies have shown that between-group equity (Vincente & Carolina, 2017) and between-group monitoring (i.e., transparency, CDP4) (Bernstein, 2017) are key to system health. But this is an area that needs more research.

GOAL SETTING FOR ACTION

It is essential that setting concrete goals for action follow the discussions of the CDPs. It is here that prosocial begins to flow seamlessly into organizational behavior management. If you've used the collective Matrix to explore the different CDPs, then you will have derived concrete goals from the various matrices you've conducted. If you have simply discussed how to enhance the implementation of each of the CDPs, that process will have also given you a raw set of concrete goals. Either way, you'll need a process for compiling and prioritizing the goals of the group over the short and medium term. You will need an action plan.

Goals are important for groups because they help them to coordinate action in a shared direction, and because they motivate people to initiate and sustain effort, even when the going gets tough. But, done well, goals can also serve another critical purpose: they can help people to learn and adapt over time.

Goals that are difficult and challenging on the one hand but attainable with effort on the other are more likely to lead to improved performance than goals that are either too easy or impossibly hard. By definition, improved performance requires group members to change behavior. If they can accomplish the goal too easily with minimal or even no change in behavior, then goal setting is beside the point. Conversely, members will think it unlikely that they can reach goals that are too difficult. If even major changes in behavior would leave them far from a goal, then it's unlikely that the motivational impact of possible goal achievement would take hold.

Goals needs to be relevant to individual and group learning and performance: people need to see that the goal fits within their domain of responsibility, and that it matters. For goals to work they need to be meaningful to group members and, ideally, inspiring. If goals are not consistent with collective and personal values, then groups are less likely to achieve them. When setting goals, members need to take into account the individual strengths of members rather than implement the goal in a "one size fits all" fashion. Relevant goals are worthwhile, and timely; they fit with the other efforts of the group and with the current environment, and the right people and resources are present to accomplish the goal with effort.

The well-known acronym SMART (Locke & Latham, 1990, 2002, 2006) summarizes goals that take into consideration the important issues. A SMART goal is:

- *S*pecific
- *M*easurable
- *A*ttainable with effort
- *R*elevant
- *T*ime-bound

SMART goals emerge naturally from prosocial. We've had good results with the following approach, sometimes called "brain writing": After the facilitator shares the topic and ideas from the Matrix with the team, each member writes down ideas individually and then shares them with the facilitator and the group. This reduces the bias toward early ideas and gives everyone a voice, essentially allowing ideas to be generated in a broad way across the whole group before discussion.

Once a set of ideas has been generated, the group can discuss each and begin to refine and prioritize them, fitting them into SMART form wherever possible and examining their costs and benefits, and whether the group has the necessary capability and resources. To act as guides for immediate action, goals should be consistent with the group's longer-term vision but be something that can be attained in the next quarter to year.

Once goals are prioritized they should be allocated to people, with parameters for accountability. While it is certainly possible for a small group to have accountability for completing a goal, it's often useful to hold just one person accountable for ensuring that the goal moves forward. Shared accountability can sometimes lead to nobody feeling any particular pressure to complete the goal. For that reason, it's usually best to assign the responsibility for making sure goals are completed to people or small groups before ending the prosocial session.

Groups that have created SMART goals using the prosocial process usually find value in continuing to use the Matrix, and in reviewing the steps to implement the CDPs as members pursue the tasks required to meet their goals.

EVIDENCE FOR PROSOCIAL

Throughout this article we have provided extensive evidence for each of the individual principles. But it is of course important to consider the evidence for the ACT relevant components of prosocial, as well as prosocial as a whole. Focusing on evidence for the ACT relevant aspects, we can easily find studies demonstrating, for example, the positive effects of psychological flexibility upon emotional exhaustion (Biron & van Veldhoven, 2012) and the seminal work of Bond and his colleagues demonstrating positive effects of ACT interventions upon workplace health and effectiveness (Bond & Bunce, 2003; Bond et al., 2008; Bond et al., 2010; Donaldson-Feilder & Bond, 2004; Flaxman & Bond, 2010).

But while this work is excellent, the effects of ACT training that is solely focused upon psychological flexibility may not be optimized for the contexts and purposes of group cooperation. Just as applying ACT to depression involves behavioral activation and ACT for anxiety involves exposure, ACT interventions may need to be explicitly tailored toward consideration of the components of cooperation in order to maximally influence behavior change. We believe that the core design principles are just these components of cooperation. In small groups you need to also focus upon training specific skills related to functions such as resolving conflict, giving feedback and making decisions in order to foster trust and cooperation.

To date there have not been any randomized controlled trials on the effects of prosocial upon groups and this is certainly a situation we are working to rectify. However, we do have emerging evidence for the effectiveness of prosocial. In a naturalistic setting, (Styles, 2016) was able to compare a government department that received a combination of prosocial and strategic visioning training with the rest of the entire Australian public service between 2014 and 2015 on a series of measures of morale, job satisfaction and leadership. He found that, while the Australian public service trended downwards across the year on all these measures, the department with which he worked generally improved. In another study (Wilson et al., in preparation) showed that workgroups on average scored lower on implementation of the CDPs than non-work groups, and that the CDP's were highly correlated with group outcomes such as group satisfaction, commitment and trust. While this evidence is consistent with the extensive evidence reviewed earlier for all the elements of prosocial, further research is obviously required to test the efficacy of prosocial in a variety of contexts.

CONCLUSION

The integration of psychological flexibility principles and the core design principles allows a new approach to enhancing human cooperation. prosocial is a coherent set of methods that can be used to improve the cooperation of small groups.

STUDY QUESTIONS

1. Describe the tragedy of the commons in your own words.
2. Describe two of the core design principles listed in the chapter.
3. What are some of the benefits of creating a shared purpose and inclusive decision-making?
4. How do the authors use the word *monitoring* and why is this important?
5. Distinguish between healthy and unhealthy conflict.

REFERENCES

Aligica, P.D. & Tarko, V. (2011). Polycentricity: From Polanyi to Ostrom, and Beyond. *Governance, 25*(2), 237–262. doi: 10.1111/j.1468-0491.2011.01550.x

Ashforth, B.E. & Mael, F. (1989). Social Identity Theory And The Organization. *Academy of Management Review, 14*(Jan), 20–39.

Atkins, P., Wilson, D.S., & Hayes, S.C. (2019). *Prosocial: Using evolutionary science to build productive, equitable, and collaborative groups*. Context Press / New Harbinger Publications.

Balliet, D. & Van Lange, P.A.M. (2013). Trust, Punishment, and Cooperation Across 18 Societies: A Meta-Analysis. *Perspectives on Psychological Science, 8*(4), 363–379. doi:10.1177/1745691613488533

Bashshur, M.R. & Oc, B. (2015). When Voice Matters. *Journal of Management, 41*(5), 1530–1554. doi: 10.1177/0149206314558302

Bateson, M., Callow, L., Holmes, J.R., Redmond Roche, M.L., & Nettle, D. (2013). Do images of "watching eyes" induce behaviour that is more pro-social or more normative? A field experiment on littering. *PLOS ONE, 8*(12), e82055. doi: 10.1371/journal.pone.0082055

Bateson, M., Nettle, D., & Roberts, G. (2006). Cues of being watched enhance cooperation in a real-world setting. *Biology Letters, 2*(3), 412–414. doi: 10.1098/rsbl.2006.0509

Bernstein, E.S. (2017). Making Transparency Transparent: The Evolution of Observation in Management Theory. *Academy of Management Annals, 11*(1), 217. http://annals.aom.org/content/11/1/217.abstract

Biron, M. & van Veldhoven, M. (2012). Emotional labour in service work: Psychological flexibility and emotion regulation. *Human Relations, 65*(10), 1259–1282. doi:10.1177/0018726712447832

Bobocel, D.R. & Gosse, L. (2015). Procedural justice: A historical review and critical analysis. In R.S. Cropanzano & M.L. Ambrose (Eds.), *The Oxford handbook of justice in the workplace* (Vol. 1, pp. 51–87). Oxford University Press.

Bond, F.W. & Bunce, D. (2003). The Role of acceptance and job control in mental health, job satisfaction, and work performance. *Journal of Applied Psychology, 88*(6), 1057–1067.

Bond, F.W., Flaxman, P.E., & Bunce, D. (2008). The influence of psychological flexibility on work redesign: Mediated moderation of a work reorganization intervention. *Journal of Applied Psychology, 93*(3), 645–654. doi: 10.1037/0021-9010.93.3.645

Bond, F.W., Flaxman, P.E., Van Veldhoven, M.J.P.M., & Biron, M. (2010). The impact of psychological flexibility and Acceptance and Commitment Therapy (ACT) on health and productivity at work. In J. Houdmont & S. Leka (Eds.), *Contemporary occupational health psychology: Global perspectives on research and practice* (Vol. 1). Wiley-Blackwell.

Bradley, B.H., Postlethwaite, B.E., Klotz, A.C., Hamdani, M.R., & Brown, K.G. (2012). Reaping the benefits of task conflict in teams: The critical role of team psychological safety climate. *Journal Applied Psychology, 97*(1), 151–158. doi: 10.1037/a0024200

Burbano, V.C. (2016). Social responsibility messages and worker wage requirements: Field experimental evidence from online labor marketplaces. *Organization Science, 27*(4), 1010–1028. doi: 10.1287/orsc.2016.1066

Campbell, T.D. (1960). Blind variation and selective retention in creative thought and other knowledge processes. *Psychological Review, 67*, 380–400.

Carpenter, J. & Gong, E. (2016). Motivating agents: How much does the mission matter? *Journal of Labor Economics, 34*(1), 211–236. doi:10.1086/682345

Chamberlin, M., Newton, D.W., & LePine, J.A. (2018). A meta-analysis of empowerment and voice as transmitters of high-performance managerial practices to job performance. *Journal of Organizational Behavior, 39*(10), 1296–1313. doi: 10.1002/job.2295

Chang, A. & Bordia, P. (2001). A multidimensional approach to the group cohesion-group performance relationship. *Small Group Research, 32*(4), 379–405. doi:10.1177/104649640103200401

Chase, C.D. (2007). Cytoplasmic male sterility: a window to the world of plant mitochondrial- nuclear interactions. *Trends in Genetics, 23*(2), 81–90. doi: 10.1016/j.tig.2006.12.004

Cloutier, J., Vilhuber, L., Harrisson, D., & Béland-Ouellette, V. (2018). Understanding the effect of procedural justice on psychological distress. *International Journal of Stress Management, 25*(3), 283–300. doi: 10.1037/str0000065

Cohen-Charash, Y. & Spector, P.E. (2001). The role of justice in organizations: A meta analysis. *Organizational Behavior and Human Decision Processes, 86*(2), 278–321. doi: 10.1006/obhd.2001.2958

Colquitt, J.A. & Rodell, J.B. (2015). Measuring justice and fairness. In R. Cropanzano & M.L. Ambrose (Eds.), *The Oxford handbook of justice in the workplace* (Vol. 1, pp. 187). Oxford University Press.

Cronin, K.A., Acheson, D.J., Hernández, P., & Sánchez, A. (2015). Hierarchy is detrimental for human cooperation. *Scientific Reports, 5*, 18634. doi: 10.1038/srep18634

De Cremer, D. & Stouten, J. (2003). When do people find cooperation most justified? The effect of trust and self–other merging in social dilemmas. *Social Justice Research, 16*(1), 41–52. doi: 10.1023/A:1022974027023

de Wit, F. R., Greer, L. L., & Jehn, K. A. (2012). The paradox of intragroup conflict: A metaanalysis. *Journal of Applied Psychology, 97*(2), 360–390. doi: 10.1037/a0024844

Donaldson-Feilder, E. J. & Bond, F. W. (2004). The relative importance of psychological acceptance and emotional intelligence to workplace well-being. *British Journal of Guidance & Counselling, 32*(2), 187–203.

Fehr, E. & Gächter, S. (2002). Altruistic punishment in humans. *Nature, 415*, 137. doi: 10.1038/415137a

Fisher, R., Ury, W., & Patton, B. (2011). *Getting to yes: Negotiating agreement without giving in* (Rev. ed.). Penguin Books.

Flaxman, P.E. & Bond, F.W. (2010). Acceptance and commitment training: Promoting psychological flexibility in the workplace. In R.A. Baer (Ed.), *Assessing mindfulness and acceptance processes in clients: Illuminating the theory and practice of change* (pp. 282–306). Context Press/New Harbinger Publications.

Frederiksen, L.W. & Peterson, G.L. (1977). Schedule-induced aggression in humans and animals: Comparative parametric review. *Aggressive Behavior, 3*(1), 57–75. doi: 10.1002/1098-2337

Gershoff, E.T. (2002). Corporal punishment by parents and associated child behaviors and experiences: A meta-analytic and theoretical review. *Psychological Bulletin, 128*(4), 539–579. doi: 10.1037//0033-2909.128.4.539

Gürerk, Ö., Irlenbusch, B., & Rockenbach, B. (2006). The competitive advantage of sanctioning institutions. *Science, 312*(5770), 108. doi:10.1126/science.1123633

Hardin, G. (1968). The tragedy of the commons. *Science, 162*(3859), 1243–1248. doi: 10.1126/science.162.3859.1243

Hayes, S.C. (2019). *A liberated mind: How to pivot toward what matters.* Avery.

Hayes, S.C., Barnes-Holmes, D., & Roche, B. (2001). *Relational frame theory: A post-Skinnerian account of human language and cognition.* Plenum Press.

Hayes, S.C. & Sanford, B. (2014). Cooperation came first: Evolution and human cognition. *Journal of the Experimental Analysis of Behavior, 101*, 112–129. doi: 10.1002/jeab.64

Hayes, S.C., Strosahl, K., & Wilson, K.G. (2012). *Acceptance and commitment therapy: The process and practice of mindful change* (2nd ed.). Guilford Press.

Hogg, M.A. (2015). Constructive leadership across groups: How leaders can combat prejudice and conflict between subgroups. In *Advances in Group Processes* (Vol. 32, pp. 177–207). Emerald Group Publishing Limited.

Jablonka, E. & Lamb, M.J. (2006). *Evolution in four dimensions: genetic, epigenetic, behavioral, and symbolic variation in the history of life.* MIT Press.

Karam, E.P., Hu, J., Davison, R.B., Juravich, M., Nahrgang, J.D., Humphrey, S.E., & Scott DeRue, D. (2019). Illuminating the "face" of justice: A meta-analytic examination of leadership and organizational justice. *Journal of Management Studies, 56*(1), 134–171. doi: 10.1111/joms.12402

Kerr, N.L., Rumble, A.C., Park, E.S., Ouwerkerk, J.W., Parks, C.D., Gallucci, M., & van Lange, P.A.M. (2009). "How many bad apples does it take to spoil the whole barrel?": Social exclusion and toleration for bad apples. *Journal of Experimental Social Psychology, 45*(4), 603–613. doi: 10.1016/j.jesp.2009.02.017

Kilduff, G.J. & Galinsky, A.D. (2013). From the ephemeral to the enduring: How to approach oriented mindsets lead to greater status. *Journal of Personality and Social Psychology, 105*(5), 816–831. doi:10.1037/a0033667

Kirkman, B.L. & Rosen, B. (1999). Beyond self-management: Antecedents and consequences of team empowerment. *The Academy of Management Journal, 42*(1), 58–74. http://www.jstor.org/stable/256874

Lambert, N.M., Stillman, T.F., Hicks, J.A., Kamble, S., Baumeister, R.F., & Fincham, F.D. (2013). To belong is to matter: Sense of belonging enhances meaning in life. *Personality and Social Psychology Bulletin, 39*(11), 1418–1427. doi: 10.1177/0146167213499186

Langfred, C.W. (2004). Too much of a good thing? Negative effects of high trust and individual autonomy in self-managing teams. *Academy of Management Journal, 47*(3), 385–399. doi:10.2307/20159588

Langfred, C.W. (2007). The downside of self-management: A longitudinal study of the effects of conflict on trust, autonomy, and task interdependence in self-managing teams. *Academy of Management Journal, 50*(4), 885–900. doi: 10.5465/amj.2007.26279196

Locke, E.A. & Latham, G.P. (1990). *A theory of goal setting and task performance.* Prentice-Hall.

Locke, E.A. & Latham, G.P. (2002). Building a practical useful theory of goal setting and task motivation. *American Psychologist, 57*, 705–717.

Locke, E.A. & Latham, G.P. (2006). New Directions in Goal-Setting Theory. *Current Directions in Psychological Science, 15*(5), 265–268.

Luciano, C., Gómez-Becerra, I. & Rodríguez-Valverde, M. (2007). The role of multiple exemplar training and naming in establishing derived equivalence in an infant. *Journal of Experimental Analysis of Behavior, 87*, 349–365.

Majolo, B. & Maréchal, L. (2017). Between-group competition elicits within-group cooperation in children. *Scientific Reports, 7*(1), 43277. doi:10.1038/srep43277

Mathieu, J.E., Kukenberger, M.R., D'Innocenzo, L., & Reilly, G. (2015). Modeling reciprocal team cohesion-performance relationships, as impacted by shared leadership and members' competence. *Journal of Applied Psychology, 100*(3), 713–734. doi: 10.1037/a0038898

Nesterkin, D. (2016). Conflict management and performance of information technology development teams. *Team Performance Management, 22*(5/6), 242–256. doi: 10.1108/TPM-05-2016-0018

Nettle, D., Harper, Z., Kidson, A., Stone, R., Penton-Voak, I. S., & Bateson, M. (2013). The watching eyes effect in the Dictator Game: it's not how much you give, it's being seen to give something. *Evolution and Human Behavior, 34*(1), 35–40. doi: 10.1016/j.evolhumbehav.2012.08.004

Ostrom, E. (1990). *Governing the commons: The evolution of institutions for collective action.* Cambridge University Press.

O'Neill, T.A., McLarnon, M.J.W., Hoffart, G.C., Woodley, H.J.R., & Allen, N.J. (2018). The structure and function of team conflict state profiles. *Journal of Management, 44*(2), 811–836. doi: 10.1177/0149206315581662

Pacheco, G. & Webber, D. (2016). Job satisfaction: how crucial is participative decision making? *Personnel Review, 45*(1), 183–200. doi: 10.1108/pr-04-2014-0088

Polk, K.L., Schoendorff, B., Webster, M., & Olaz, F.O. (2016). *The essential guide to the ACT Matrix: A step-by-step approach to using the ACT matrix model in clinical practice.* New Harbinger Publications/Context Press.

Schäfer, M., Haun, D.B., & Tomasello, M. (2015). Fair is not fair everywhere. *Psychological Science, 26*, 1252–1260. doi: 10.1177/0956797615586188

Sherif, M. (1958). Superordinate goals in the reduction of intergroup conflict. *American Journal of Sociology, 63*(4), 349–356. Retrieved from http://www.jstor.org/stable/2774135

Slemp, G.R., Kern, M.L., Patrick, K.J., & Ryan, R.M. (2018). Leader autonomy support in the workplace: A meta-analytic review. *Motivation and Emotion*, *42*(5), 706–724. doi:10.1007/s11031-018-9698-y

Styles, R. (2016). Outstanding evidence for PROSOCIAL in a government agency setting. http://magazine.prosocial-groups.org/outstanding-evidence-for-prosocialin-a-government-agency-setting/

Turchin, P. (2016). *Ultrasociety: How 10,000 years of war made humans the greatest cooperators on earth.* Beresta Books.

Van Gramberg, B., Teicher, J., Bamber, G.J., & Cooper, B. (2017). A changing world of workplace conflict resolution and employee voice: An Australian perspective. Paper presented at the Conflict and its Resolution in the Changing World of Work: A Conference and Special Issue Honoring David B. Lipsky, Ithaca, NY.

Van Vugt, M. & Hart, C. M. (2004). Social identity as social glue: The origins of group loyalty. *Journal of Personality and Social Psychology*, *86*(4), 585–598. doi: 10.1037/0022-3514.86.4.585

Vincente, M.-T. & Carolina, M. (2017). *Justice in teams.* Oxford University Press.

Viswesvaran, C. & Ones, D.S. (2002). Examining the construct of organizational justice: A meta-analytic evaluation of relations with work attitudes and behaviors. *Journal of Business Ethics*, *38*(3), 193–203. http://www.jstor.org/stable/25074792

Wilson, D.S., Hayes, S.C., Biglan, T., & Embry, D. (2014). Evolving the future: Toward a science of intentional change. *Behavioural and Brain Sciences*, *34*, 395–416. doi: 10.1017/S0140525X13001593

Wilson, D.S. & Wilson, E.O. (2007). Rethinking the theoretical foundation of sociobiology. *Quarterly Review of Biology*, *82*, 327–348.

Wilson, D.S., Philip, M., & Atkins, P.W.B. (in preparation). What all business groups need.

Yamagishi, T. (1988). The provision of a sanctioning system in the United States and Japan. *Social Psychology Quarterly*, *51*(3), 265. doi: 10.2307/2786924

Yang, S.-B. & Guy, M.E. (2011). The Effectiveness of self-managed work teams in government organizations. *Journal of Business and Psychology*, *26*(4), 531–541. doi: 10.1007/s10869-010-9205-2

10

The Nurture Consilience

A Framework for Intentional Cultural Evolution[1]

Anthony Biglan and Magnus Johansson

Despite considerable increases in the economic wellbeing of people in many countries, it would be hard to argue that human evolution is on a wholly beneficial pathway. First among the challenges to our future wellbeing is climate change. Many of the predictions regarding climate change that were made 15 or 20 years ago underestimated the extent, rapidity, and severity of the changes that are occurring (Cheng et al., 2019; Oppenheimer et al., 2019; Scherer, 2012). Only in recent years have we seen a more concerted effort starting to reflect the urgency of the issue at hand. It is conceivable that this will be an irreversible process even if all human-caused emissions of greenhouse gases are eliminated (Solomon et al., 2013). We face the very real prospect that warming will accelerate to an extent that significant portions of the earth will no longer be habitable.

Even in the absence of climate change, societies around the world have problems that are diminishing the wellbeing of millions of people. Following a several-decades-long trend of improvement, life expectancy has fallen in many countries, most significantly in the UK and USA (Smith, 2018). The number of children living in poverty in the USA has increased in the last decade (Child Trends Databank, 2019). Obesity has almost tripled in the USA during the last 40 years (Hales et al., 2020). Faced with such threats to human wellbeing, one would hope that democratic countries would cooperate to address these problems. But in recent years the opposite seems to be happening. Political polarization has increased in many countries (Boxell et al., 2020), perhaps most significantly in the USA (Jurkowitz et al., 2020; Pew Research Center, 2016). Democracy and the rule of law are being undermined in many countries – including the United States, Hungary, India, Poland, Russia, and Brazil (Abramowitz, 2018). A major reason for this trend is the rise of social media, which was initially expected to promote democracy and public support for science-based solutions to our problems, but has instead contributed to the proliferation of antisocial and anti-science beliefs, values, and acts (Haidt & Rose-Stockwell, 2019; Marantz, 2019).

Over the past 50 years the behavioral sciences have accumulated an enormous body of knowledge that has the potential to vastly improve human wellbeing (Biglan, 2015). Unfortunately, these developments are still not widely recognized outside the behavioral science community. It would seem that behavioral scientists and practitioners need to play a more assertive role in influencing the further evolution of societies. The present chapter is written in the hopes that it can contribute to the advancement of a pragmatic science of human behavior that will enable world societies to do a better job not only of enhancing the wellbeing of their members, but in ensuring the sustainability of life on the planet.

DOI: 10.4324/9781003198949-10

THE NURTURE CONSILIENCE

The evolutionary biologist David Sloan Wilson has characterized the human sciences as a vast archipelago, each island of which is isolated from the other islands of knowledge (Wilson, 2007). He has been a leader in integrating knowledge from these different disciplines within an evolutionary framework (Wilson, 2005, 2012, 2019) and showing how this framework could guide the intentional evolution of cultural practices (Wilson et al., 2014). We find it useful to refer to this integration as the nurture consilience (Biglan et al., in press).

The basic principles of evolutionary theory are applicable to every living process. Variation and selection, and in some manner reproducing the selected variants, explains not only the selection of genes (Jablonka & Lamb, 2014), but also the selection of behavior (Skinner, 1981), the evolution of human language abilities (Hayes et al., 2017), and the practices of groups and organizations (Atkins et al., 2019; Wilson et al., 2013).

Extensive evidence from clinical psychology, developmental psychology, social psychology, prevention science, and evolution shows that humans are most likely to thrive in nurturing environments that minimize toxic biological and social conditions, limit influences and opportunities for the development of antisocial behavior, richly reinforce diverse forms of prosocial behavior, and promote psychological flexibility, which involves a pragmatic approach to living one's values even in the context of troubling psychological and environmental obstacles (Biglan, 2015; Biglan et al., 2012).

Wilson's analysis of multi-level selection (Wilson et al., 2013, 2014) is particularly important. According to multi-level selection theory, all life consists of units within units. For example, multicellular organisms evolved out of single-celled organisms as a result of the single-celled organisms cooperating to the point where a single more complex organism evolved. The analysis is relevant to understanding how humans developed the cooperative capacities that have enabled us to dominate most of the world (for better or for worse). The challenge for evolving societies involves aligning the consequences of the actions of individuals, groups, organizations, and governments to select mutually beneficial outcomes.

Much of behavioral science research focuses on the behavior of individuals. However, Wilson shows that the behavior of the individual is heavily influenced by the social groups they are in and that the development of prosocial behavior needs to be understood in terms of its role in facilitating the survival and success of the group (Wilson, 2019).

The definition of prosocial behavior is partially dependent on context, but some characteristics may be universal. Prosociality can be seen as individuals' behavior that contributes to their group's survival and thriving. When Wilson et al. (2009) investigated adolescents' prosociality from an evolutionary perspective, they used a rating scale from the Developmental Assets Profile to measure prosociality. This scale includes items such as "I am helping to make my community a better place," "I am sensitive to the needs and feelings of others," and "I am serving others in my community." They also measured perceived social support, divided into several contexts such as family, school and neighborhood. They found that support from each of these contexts contributed to the level of prosociality among adolescents. In a contextual, multi-level analysis, we cannot separate the individual from the group, nor isolate the group from other groups.

Behavior that benefits one's own group, thus being labeled "prosocial," could in fact be antisocial when seen in a larger context where there could be detrimental effects to another group or a higher-level group. For instance, backing up a member of your political in-group by acting aggressively toward your political opponents would be seen as positive by the in-group, but contributes to polarization in the larger context, undermining the functioning of the larger group, such as the community. When assessing the benefit of a particular constellation of behaviors, we need to be concerned about its impact not only on the group engaged in the behavior, but also its impact on the rest of society.

Humans have also evolved the ability to survive in harsh and threatening environments by adopting more antisocial patterns of behavior (Dishion & Snyder, 2016). This suite of antisocial behaviors includes the development of impulsive, aggressive and uncooperative behavior, substance use, academic failure, and early childbearing (Ellis et al., 2012; Ellis & Bjorklund, 2012). These behavioral tendencies appear to make it more likely that a person will survive and procreate in the harsh environment. However, their long-term benefit to the individual and those around them is generally lacking (Biglan et al., 2019).

Public Health

Another facet of the nurture consilience is public health. Public health focuses on the incidence and prevalence of problematic (or positive) events in a defined population. Most aspects of human wellbeing can be measured. This includes physical disease, mental health, and life satisfaction (Diener, 2013). It also includes the measurement of the incidence and/or prevalence of risk factors for targeted problems, such as poverty, economic inequality, discrimination, and the marketing of harmful products (Biglan & Embry, 2013). Finally, it can include the measurement of positive events, such as acts of kindness, graduation rates, and longevity. In short, we can track the wellbeing of the people in a given community, state, or nation with some precision. Such tracking is foundational for any effort to improve wellbeing. We can assess the impact of policies, programs, or trends in behaviors or organizational practices in terms of their impact on measures of population wellbeing.

This same perspective is relevant to the measurement of cultural evolution. Virtually any aspect of culture can be assessed in terms of its incidence and prevalence. This includes not only the incidence or prevalence of the behavior of individuals, but the actions and products of groups and organizations. Here are some examples:

- The incidence of companies adopting the standards of B Corporations (Loewenstein, 2016). These standards require companies to systematically assess the impact of their practices on employees, customers, suppliers, and society as a whole – in addition to their impact on investors.
- The prevalence of B corporations in a region, nation or across the world.
- The prevalence of corporations that systematically assess their impact on the wellbeing of customers, employees, and communities in which they operate.
- The incidence of externalities caused by business practices (Biglan, 2009).

By measuring the incidence and prevalence of corporate practices and their impact over time we can gauge how well we are doing in evolving a system of capitalism that works for everyone.

A Choice of Values

The social psychologist Tim Kasser has summarized a wealth of evidence indicating that people tend to endorse one of two contrasting value systems (Kasser, 2016). One involves materialistic values that are characterized by a desire to accumulate wealth and prestige – "I want to be rich; I want to be famous." The other involves prosocial or communitarian values – caring for others and one's community and growing as a person. The research he reviews suggests that people are unlikely to embrace both sets of values.

Kasser's analysis is consistent with the nurture consilience. Prosocial values are promoted by nurturing environments, whereas materialistic values are made more likely by threatening conditions as well as by the promotion of materialism due to marketing.

Each of these value sets are verbally and socially constructed; they are cultivated by contrasting social environments. Groups instill prosocial values through a combination of modeling and reinforcement of prosocial behavior and the suppression of antisocial behavior through criticism, gossip, ostracism, and gradually more severe punishment. On the other hand, environments that have high levels of coercion have been shown to promote antisocial behavior.

There is, at the same time, evidence accumulating from research in clinical psychology that shows that people are able to choose and articulate values that become the criteria for the selection of their behavior (Hayes, 2019). Numerous studies have shown that people who are trying to cope with psychological and behavioral problems such as depression or overeating benefit from becoming clear about what they most value, making goals that are in the service of those values, and evaluating what they do in terms of its contribution to or interference with their living consistent with their values (Barrett et al., 2019; Reilly et al., 2019). Obviously, success in living consistent with one's values is affected by the person's social milieu.

Functional Contextualism

The approach we take to behavioral science is guided by the philosophy of science called Functional Contextualism (Hayes et al., 2012). In this approach, the goal of research is the prediction-and-influence of the act-in-context. This means that our intention is not only to predict behavioral phenomena but to identify malleable variables that influence behavior. And by "behavior" we mean anything that a person, group, or organization does.

THE EVOLUTION OF MORE NURTURING SOCIETIES

At the present moment in our cultural evolution we seem to be in a worldwide struggle between prosocial and antisocial values and actions. Examples of antisocial values and actions that threaten wellbeing include:

- The actions of corporations that are profitable to the corporation but harmful to significant segments of the population (Biglan, 2020f). Well documented examples include:
  - the tobacco industry (Biglan, 2020d)
  - the arms industry (Biglan, 2020e)
  - the food industry (Biglan, 2020b)
  - the pharmaceutical industry (Biglan, 2020a)
  - the fossil fuel industry (Biglan, 2020c)
  - the technology industry (McNamee, 2019)
- The ascendancy of free-market ideology that has encouraged the belief that wellbeing will best be served by limiting the government's size and ability to regulate and encouraging individuals to pursue their own economic gain. The result has been a sharp increase in poverty and economic inequality, particularly in the United States (Biglan, 2020f).
- Networks of racist hate groups that have greatly accelerated the number of people who are willing to engage in racist rhetoric, public policies, and violence thanks to the ability of the internet to amplify what were once much more isolated small groups of antisocial individuals (Marantz, 2019).
- Political parties within nations that promote the wellbeing of some segments of the population at the cost to other segments (Biglan, 2020f).
- Political actors who promote the perception of outside threats, increasing xenophobia and protectionism (Mutz, 2018; Setzler & Yanus, 2018).

- Well-intended but counterproductive efforts such as "safe spaces" that seem to increase polarization and threaten free speech (Lukianoff & Haidt, 2019; Rose, 2017; Swan, 2017).
- Nations that are using technology to undermine democracy and wellbeing in other countries (Cadwalladr, 2020; Wylie, 2019).

All of these examples have in common the fact that actions are selected by the short-term benefits that accrue to these actors despite the fact that they do harm to others. The generic problem therefore is how we can change the consequences of harmful and beneficial actions so that the incidence and prevalence of harmful actions decline and beneficial actions increase. The analysis applies to the behavior of individuals, the behavior of groups, the actions of organizations, and the actions of nations. In what follows we give examples of strategies for changing these contingencies. We start at the level of individuals since there has been a lot more research on selecting the behavior of individuals than on selecting the actions of groups and organizations.

Increasing the Incidence of Prosocial Behavior in the Population

In this section we briefly describe four types of interventions that have the potential to increase the incidence and prevalence of prosocial behavior in populations.

Family and School Interventions

There is a huge body of evidence showing that we can promote prosocial behavior and prevent antisocial behavior through family and school-based programs and practices (Biglan, 2015). Numerous family interventions have been shown to promote effective parenting practices and to prevent the development of most of the psychological and behavioral problems children and adolescents can develop, including aggressive and uncooperative behavior, academic failure, substance use, risky sexual behavior and early childbearing (Leslie et al., 2016; Van Ryzin et al., 2015). The common features of these family interventions include reducing the use of harsh and inconsistent discipline, richly reinforcing all types of prosocial behavior, monitoring and setting effective limits on children's behavior, communicating in warm and patient ways, and problem-solving. There is also some evidence that family interventions that encourage young people to think about the future provide additional benefits (Van Ryzin et al., 2016).

There is an equally rich and extensive body of evidence showing how schools can nurture successful prosocial development and prevent the psychological and behavioral problems that undermine child and adolescent wellbeing (Biglan, 2015; Biglan & Embry, 2013). The critical ingredients in these interventions include the replacement of punitive practices with programs and practices that promote emotional regulation, cooperation, and empathy. Long-term benefits of programs that promote emotional regulation and cooperation have been shown. For example, the Good Behavior Game, which rewards small groups of elementary school children for working together cooperatively, has been shown to increase the likelihood that children will graduate from high school and attend college at the same time that it prevents aggressive behavior and substance use (Bradshaw et al., 2009; Kellam et al., 2011, 2012).

Although further research would be useful in determining the degree to which these interventions promote a lifelong orientation toward prosociality, the documented benefits of these interventions are sufficient to justify their widespread implementation; they promote prosocial behavior and prevent antisocial behavior. We believe that the spread of these interventions will prove to be one important step in evolving societies with more people who have prosocial orientations. There are already numerous examples of the successful dissemination of these programs (National Academies of Sciences, Engineering, and Medicine, 2019). However, we have reached only a tiny sliver of the population in any country, let alone worldwide.

Increasing the Prevalence of Psychological Flexibility

Research in clinical psychology has shown the importance of psychological flexibility for people's wellbeing. Psychological flexibility consists of an orientation toward living that is guided by conscious and intentional efforts to live according to a chosen set of values. It involves a set of skills that include the ability to be in the present moment as opposed to thinking about the past or future. It includes the skill of observing and accepting thoughts and feelings as thoughts and feelings, rather than seeing the world through the lens of those thoughts and feelings. Finally, it involves changing or persisting in one's course of action depending on its contribution to valued ends. Psychological flexibility is a skill set that can be improved with practice (Hayes, 2019).

The evidence that psychological flexibility (PF) is important for human wellbeing comes largely from treatment research that has shown that the remediation of diverse psychological and behavioral problems is mediated by increases in PF (Hann & McCracken, 2014; Hayes et al., 2012; Krafft et al., 2017). There is also evidence from etiological studies showing that psychological inflexibility is a risk factor for psychological and behavioral problems (Kashdan & Rottenberg, 2010; Levin et al., 2014). In Switzerland, Andrew Gloster and colleagues (2017) surveyed a representative sample of the adult Swiss population and found that PF moderated the influence of stress on health and wellbeing, with higher levels of flexibility providing more protection. Similarly, a recent study in Portugal found that PF moderated the effects of major life events on depression (Fonseca et al., 2019). Studies on self-help interventions have shown promising results for improving PF (French et al., 2017; Hofer et al., 2018; Wersebe et al., 2018), which could prove to be a cost-effective way to scale up availability to larger populations.

We are unaware of any research evaluating community-wide efforts to increase psychological flexibility. However, Levin et al. (2016) suggested testing whether the approach that Sanders and colleagues have taken (Sanders et al., 2017) in promoting effective parenting in entire populations could be useful in promoting psychological flexibility. Sanders and colleagues have evolved a comprehensive system for reaching parents in communities with help on common problems of child behavior. It is called Triple P or the Positive Parenting Program. The approach consists of a set of levels of intervention that start with the minimal interventions such as publicity in the media and single brief group sessions for parents. The next level consists of a set of tip sheets for common behavior problems (e.g., tantrums in supermarkets). Parents with multiple behavior problems can get more intensive support. In a randomized trial across 18 counties in South Carolina, the implementation of Triple P in nine of those counties resulted in significantly lower levels of child abuse (Prinz et al., 2009).

Levin et al. (2016) suggest that one could identify the most common problems that adults (or teens) experience and create tip sheets that help people cope with their problems through psychological flexibility techniques. The self-help interventions mentioned earlier (Hofer et al., 2018) could be used as a source for developing content for tip sheets to be studied experimentally.

Promoting Prosocial Behavior Within Organizations

Workplaces have a large influence on the wellbeing of employees and thus public health. As an example, during the last decade mental health-related sick leave has been steadily rising to the point of being the number one reason for long-term sick leave in Sweden (Hagström, 2019).

The reasons for such a development can be manifold, but are likely to be found in contextual factors. While interventions that target an individual's capacity to handle stress generally show positive results (Frögéli et al., 2016; Khoury et al., 2015; Ly et al., 2014; Richardson & Rothstein, 2008), and psychological flexibility helps protect against negative effects of work stress (Bond et al., 2008; Bond & Bunce, 2000), work environment factors also need to be improved. It is unlikely that higher rates of stress-related sick leave are caused by a sudden lack of stress tolerance or psychological flexibility. The domains of nurturing environments are likely to be as relevant for adults at work as for children and youth in their formative years (Johansson et al., in press). These include increasing prosocial interactions, minimizing toxic social and physical/safety events, and improving strategies for limiting the risk of developing problems.

Although psychological flexibility has almost exclusively been targeted at the individual level, there are recent efforts to transfer the concept to whole organizations (Gascoyne, 2019) and groups (Johansson & Biglan, 2019). Tip sheets could be useful in the work context as well. The Triple P tip sheets include topics such as "coping with stress" and "balancing work and family," and of course other tip sheets relevant to organizational settings could be constructed. Many managers struggle with how to deal with conflicts and manage difficult conversations with employees. While the effects of a tip sheet might be modest in terms of effect size as measured by Cohen's *d*, it could still produce low cost and significant benefit on a larger scale, compared to no support at all.

Affecting Individual Wellbeing Through Public Policy

Public policies that reduce family poverty, economic inequality, and discrimination may also increase the proportion of people who value prosociality. The evidence is less clear on this point. Family poverty is a risk factor for the development of antisocial behavior (Van Ryzin et al., 2018). So is economic inequality (Wilkinson & Pickett, 2017). And there is some evidence that when a family's economic wellbeing is suddenly and substantially increased, children in that family are less likely to have diagnosable psychological disorders (Costello et al., 2003). Research is needed on whether the implementation of policies that affect family poverty or economic inequality reduce the proportion of young people who develop antisocial behavior and values.

Affecting the Practices of Corporations

Over the past two centuries, corporations have evolved because they enabled profitable business activities that would have been difficult or impossible for individuals or small firms to achieve. For example, railroads that have to work across great distances benefited from the size, organization, and ability to raise capital that corporations could achieve. Although corporations have brought many benefits, they can also cause the kinds of harm that were enumerated above.

The practices of corporations as well as those of other organization evolve as a function of their consequences. The primary selecting consequence for corporations has traditionally been profit. Indeed, Milton Friedman, a Nobel Laureate in economics, argued that the only goal of a corporation should be to achieve profits (M. Friedman, 1970). However, as the examples cited above show, corporations may design and market products that are profitable to the corporation but harmful to customers. They may engage in practices that are harmful to their employees and to the communities in which they operate. They may engage in public relations, lobbying, and political activity that are designed to prevent regulation of their practices, reduce their taxes, and enhance their political influence (Biglan, 2020f). So long as the only goal of a corporation is to maximize its profits, any legal practice that enhances or protects profits – including lobbying, tax evasion and political influence – will be selected. And, at least in the United States, as corporations have succeeded in amassing considerable political power through practices that are legal, yet harmful to many, public policy has increasingly favored the interests of large corporations (Biglan, 2020f).

The problem is not insurmountable. At least in the US, business has gained so much control over policymaking that the enactment of laws that would restrain harmful corporate practices are difficult to achieve. This is because, over the past 50 years, advocacy for free-market economics has convinced policymakers and a large proportion of the population that government regulation of business is counterproductive. Recent books have documented just how thoroughly business interests have dominated public beliefs about government and government regulation (Biglan, 2020f; Mayer, 2016; Pierson & Hacker, 2016).

Efforts have arisen to get corporations to not only benefit their investors, but to select practices also on the basis of their impact on employees, customers, suppliers, and the communities in which they operate (Mackey & Sisodia, 2013). Public policies could be enacted that required all corporations to measure their impact on each of these constituencies and take steps to minimize the harm that they do. Given the current political power of corporations, it will be necessary to develop a large and effective reform movement that works to make the wellbeing of every member of society the fundamental value that guides public policy.

One of the critical contingencies that needs to be established might be called a "no profit principle." Often, when a corporation engages in harmful practices it is fined. However, in most cases the fines are simply the cost of doing business; the practice remains profitable even after the fines are paid. What is needed is a law that requires that all of the profits from a demonstrably harmful practice must be forfeited by the company. In this way, there would be no incentive to engage in a harmful practice.

The current situation is an example of multi-level selection and of an evolutionary mismatch. In an evolutionary mismatch, a species, industry, group, or culture has evolved in a way that may have been beneficial during that evolution, but is now harmful. For example, the human capacity to be reinforced by sugar evolved under circumstances when sugar was hard to come by in large amounts. But now sugar is so readily available that we have an epidemic of obesity.

The mismatch we have in mind regarding corporations involves the expansion of the number, size, power, and political influence of corporations. The practices of the network of conservative business interests that have successfully advocated for free-market principles over the past 50 years were selected by their contribution to the economic success of the owners of these corporations. Figure 10.1 documents the economic success of this advocacy in the United States. What has been selected is an increasingly large and sophisticated network of people and organizations. This has created an evolutionary mismatch; no similarly large and sophisticated entity has been selected that could counter the harms this network of corporations is doing.

Groups and organizations opposing various harmful corporate practices have tended to work on the individual industries doing harm. There is one movement to reduce tobacco use, while other groups and organizations are working to reduce gun violence. Still others are working to reduce the use of fossil fuels, unhealthful food, the marketing of alcohol to young people, and the incarceration of nonviolent offenders.

In every case, the practices that are harmful have been selected by the profits to those who engage in those practices. What is needed is a coalition of all of the advocacy organizations to work for a set of policies that would prevent any corporate practice that can be shown to be harmful to a significant proportion of the population. This coalition would advocate for a public health approach to the impact of corporate practices. It would measure the impact on the population of practices such as the marketing of tobacco, alcohol, unhealthful food,

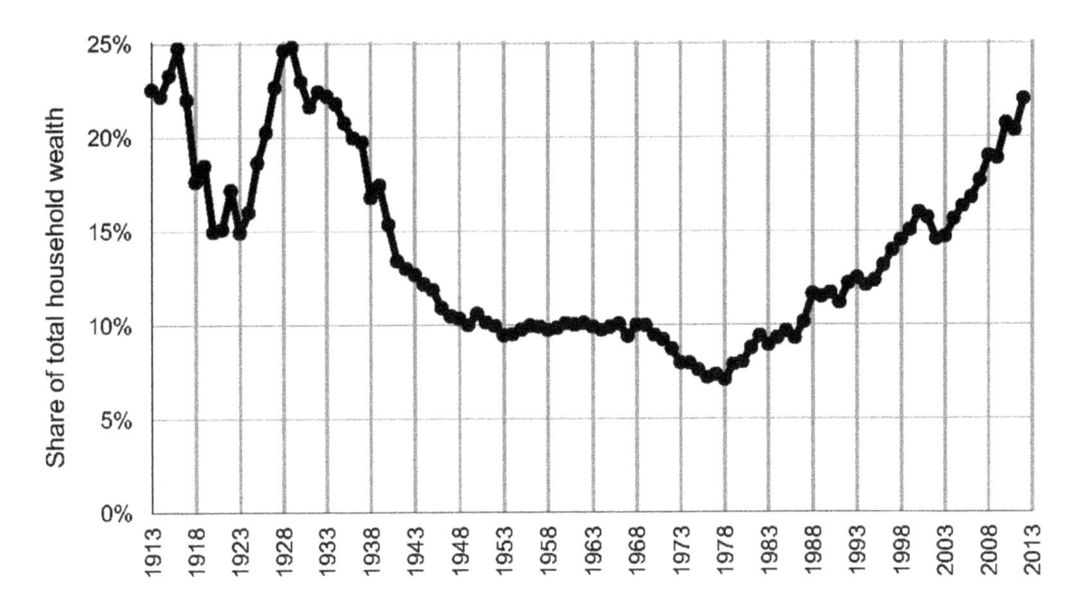

FIGURE 10.1 Top 0.1% Wealth share in the United States, 1913–2012.

Note: Figure from Saez & Zucman (2016), used with permission.

or guns. It would advocate for policies that ensure that no profits accrue to companies that engage in harmful practices.

An interesting example is described in a forthcoming publication that investigated the effects of public posting of fines dealt out by the Occupational Safety and Health Administration (OSHA) in the USA (Johnson, in press). When OSHA issued a press release about fining a company a substantial amount of money for substandard safety practices, local press would often pick that up and spread the information along. The study found that press releases on average reduced safety violations by 73%, compared to when no press release was issued. One caveat was that the effect was only found in areas with above-median labor unionization.

EVOLVING THE MOVEMENT THAT IS NEEDED TO REFORM SOCIETIES

Social reform movements have been a critical feature of cultural evolution for centuries. Their achievements have included the abolition of slavery, universal suffrage, the advancement of civil rights, and liberation from colonial rule (*World Protest and Reform Movements*, 2018). Given the challenge of combating climate change and the divisiveness of the current era, we need a worldwide movement bigger than any that has ever been mounted. There is ample reason to doubt that we can create such a movement. However, it may not be necessary to convince millions of people that we can definitely achieve change. Research on psychological flexibility has shown that our lives become more meaningful when we commit to trying to achieve big and bold goals (Hayes, 2019).

One reason for thinking that such a movement is possible consists of all of the evidence presented above. We know what human beings need to thrive and we have learned a lot about how to create the conditions that foster thriving. The spreading of this knowledge and implementing implicated practices is itself a movement that is already underway. Around the world, thousands, perhaps millions of people, have become committed to a simple basic value: evolving environments that ensure the wellbeing of every person.

There is a spiritual dimension to this value. It transcends us as individuals. Research on human perspective taking shows that people are able to transcend their own sense of self by becoming in touch with our common humanity (Hayes, 2019). The transcendence can go beyond our connection with other humans to our connection with all living things – a transcendence that is vital to our saving the planet from ourselves.

The nurture consilience includes the evidence that people who embrace prosocial values are not only kinder and more compassionate to others, they are more compassionate to themselves. This is another reason for optimism that we can motivate people to join a movement.

The Reform of Every Sector of Society

If human evolution is going to move in a direction that steadily increases the wellbeing of the population, it will require a reform of every sector of society. In our view, change will require both top-down and bottom-up strategies. We need to increase the proportion of people who are living in environments that nurture prosociality and prevent antisocial behavior. Presumably, the more people who embrace prosocial values and goals, the more support there will be for the institutions of society to adopt policies that minimize harmful practices and promote beneficial ones. At the same time, any policy that advantages general wellbeing will create fertile ground for the promotion of individual prosociality.

What follows is a brief summary of the reforms needed. In every sector, our *modus operandi* should be to examine how well that sector is contributing to the general wellbeing as opposed to acting in the interests of subsets of the population at the expense of other sectors. An effective reform movement would clearly document specific harmful practices and propose changes in policy or practice to replace harmful practices with beneficial ones. One way to combine top-down and bottom-up approaches is to involve stakeholders at multiple levels in developing, testing and implementing changes in their communities.

Business

Thanks in large measure to advocacy for free-market ideology, capitalism has evolved into a system that limits government and restricts regulation of business so that it serves special interests rather than the public (Aligica & Tarko, 2014; Khatri et al., 2006). The trend is especially true in the United States, but the belief that unfettered markets will necessarily benefit society has been spreading throughout the world.

Perhaps the core belief that has underpinned the recent evolution of capitalism is the principle that a corporation's only duty is to maximize its profits. The Business Roundtable, an organization of major American corporations, adopted this principle in the 1990s (The Business Roundtable, 1997). Since then, the Roundtable have, at least on paper, embraced the prosocial principles that corporations' practices should be evaluated in terms of their impact, not only on investors, but on employees, customers, suppliers, and the society as a whole (Gelles & Yaffe-Bellany, 2019). It would be very useful to develop reliable measures of these impacts, so that quarterly profits would no longer be the only numbers published openly and discussed in relation to how a corporation is doing and what its value is. Such measures would likely affect stock valuation in the long run.

One of us has enumerated corporate practice in six industries that are doing substantial harm, which should be targeted for reform (Biglan, 2020a, 2020b, 2020c, 2020d, 2020e; Marantz, 2019). Rather than addressing each harmful industry by itself, a reform movement would push against the dominant view the corporate regulation is always harmful. It would counter with the more empirically accurate public health and evolutionary principle that practices should be selected that benefit or harm and that we need to have a regulatory system that measures harm, implements consequences that minimize harm, and supports beneficial practices.

As we suggested above, the business community is likely to become more supportive of this principle to the extent that we are able to increase psychological flexibility, empathy, and compassion in the business community.

Higher Education

Universities can be an engine of cultural change. But for them to influence evolution in a direction that nurtures prosociality, we will need to ask probing questions at every university to understand how well higher education is contributing to the evolution of greater nurturance. Is it doing research that contributes to solving the world's most pressing problems? Or research on how to increase the prevalence of compassion, caring, and psychological flexibility in the population? Research on reducing greenhouse gas emissions? Research on reducing poverty, economic inequality, and discrimination? Research on how to disseminate and implement evidence-based practices? Conversely, is it doing research that contributes to climate change, economic inequality, or the reduction in individual liberties?

In the United States, higher education is not doing nearly what it needs to. If leaders in higher education adopted the principle that higher education should measure its worth in terms of its benefit to the society as whole, it would have to ask how well its teaching and research are contributing to this outcome. In the US, tuition fees have increased dramatically in recent years and many students are saddled with huge debts (Z. Friedman, 2017). In addition, universities are not doing as much as they could to train people to work in their communities to provide effective behavioral health and preventive interventions that can prevent the most common and costly problems of children and adolescents.

Jane Mayer (2016) has documented how successful free-market advocates were in funding programs and universities that contributed to the conservative ascendancy that has advantaged corporations and wealthy individuals, while diminishing the wellbeing of millions of others. The free-market advocates did this by funding programs in the social sciences, law, and economics that promoted free-market ideas and principles.

The reforms needed in higher education will be advantaged to the extent that the values and principles for ensuring everyone's wellbeing are promoted. One way of doing this will be to have strong programs of applied behavioral science research that are consistent with the nurture consilience described above. Those programs need to train a generation of young people who are skilled in implementing the practices that can increase the prevalence of prosocial values and behaviors in the population.

Health Care

Here too, the principle that the healthcare system should minimize harm and maximize benefit would select practices that steadily improve wellbeing. Particularly in the United States, the healthcare system most often simply waits until people are ill and seek help, and then treats them. The impact of stressful environments, poverty, economic inequality, discrimination, and the marketing of harmful food, tobacco, and alcohol are largely ignored. Yet it is these social determinants of health that account for a huge proportion of the illnesses that the system simply waits to treat (Adler et al., 2016; Allen et al., 2014; Bambra et al., 2010).

The evolution of a more effective healthcare system would become more likely if the leaders in this sector embraced prosocial values that make the contribution of these actors to the wellbeing of the population more important than the accumulation of wealth.

Media

A recent analysis of social media (Biglan, 2020f) led us to conclude that the advent of social media is one of the most profound developments in cultural evolution since the invention of the printing press. It is as though social media has given every person on the planet a radio station. This has enabled far right-oriented individuals and state actors to use social media to promote outrage and antipathy toward outgroups (Coppins, 2020; Haidt & Rose-Stockwell, 2019). Many people who are appalled by these developments have unwittingly contributed to the problem. Commenting or sharing inflammatory posts increases their spread thanks to the algorithms that many social media platforms use.

There are several things that can be done to counter these developments. First, we need to strengthen the network of prosocial actors and organizations such that they are liking sharing and otherwise promoting posts and social media that recognize and approve of prosocial behavior and organizational actions to promote prosocial reality. Second, we need to become more sophisticated about the most effective ways to promote prosociality in the context of the profusion of racist, anti-Semitic, and hateful social media. One way to do this is helping those in your in-group to do better at vetting information, ideally before spreading it, but also after the fact to improve future interactions.

Third, we need to communicate in a way that appeals to a broad audience where political or ideological views can be overcome. The work of Jonathan Haidt (2012) describes six "moral foundations" and shows that liberals/progressives most often ignore three of them, namely group loyalty, respect for authority, and sense of sanctity, while conservatives are often better at utilizing all six of the moral foundations. The three underused foundations could be leveraged by liberals to communicate better with a wider audience and increase the likelihood of establishing collaborative efforts on improving nurturance in society. A recent report by the Century Foundation (Greer & Kahlenberg, 2020) draws similar conclusions, arguing that progressives have more or less abandoned what once was mainstream values. Experimental research has shown how this can be turned around. One experiment tested ways to frame progressive economic policy and it was found most effective to have a political candidate emphasize conservative values such as family, patriotism and respecting tradition (Voelkel & Willer, 2019). This framing increased support significantly with both conservatives and moderates with no significant changes in support from progressives, compared to a framing that emphasized liberal values such as social justice and equality.

Recently, Thomas Edsall (2020) summarized research on the most effective ways to appeal to voters described as "persuadable" (*The Race-Class Narrative Project*, 2018) who feel threatened by demographic changes, such as immigration. These voters can respond quite readily to divisive messaging, but by appealing to a broader set of shared values they can also be convinced by a more prosocial message.

Creating a Grand Coalition Around the Nurture Consilience

The principle that unites reform efforts in each sector of society is the valuing of the wellbeing of every person. As we have described, the world is faced with an evolutionary mismatch. International corporations have amassed power and influence that is beyond the ability of individual states to effectively regulate. As long as the dominant view is that regulation is necessarily harmful, it will be difficult to achieve the regulation that is needed.

The antidote to this problem is to create a coalition among the organizations working to reform individual sectors of society. The movement that we envision is one in which people concerned about the practices in any given sector or any given country unite with people working in other sectors and countries around the basic principle that we want a society that is working for the wellbeing of everyone. Greater detail about how such a coalition can be created is provided in the book *Rebooting Capitalism: How We Can Forge a Society That Works for Everyone* (Biglan, 2020f).

Action Implications for Behavioral Practitioners and Scientists

If you want to contribute to the nurture consilience, here are some things you can consider doing:

- Look at the B corp practices (https://bcorporation.net) and see how they might be relevant, particularly if you run a business yourself.
- Consider ethical issues in your work and collaborations. Talk to clients and collaborators about values and long-term goals from a multi-level perspective.
- Identify stakeholders within and outside the organization you work with, and discuss relationships with other groups and possible externalities. This can be used to make change processes work better, or just improving participatory practices in general.
- Refrain from working with those that disregard the damaging consequences of their business practices.
- Visit the Open Mind platform (https://openmindplatform.org), an online tool to bridge differences and communicate better across differentiated opinions, based on Jonathan Haidt's research. Perhaps you can use it with your students?
- Assess the degree to which your university is doing research and training relevant to the most pressing problems of human behavior. Analyze the budgets of each department and document the degree to which research in the university was contributing to the reduction of significant problems and the degree to which students are being trained to work in settings such as schools, communities, and human services using evidence-based practices.
- Create interdisciplinary research addressing important social problems, such as climate change, racism, and discrimination that have as their goal changes in the incidence and prevalence of behavior in entire populations. In addition, in keeping with the need to influence policymakers and citizens to make use of behavioral science, these programs should do research and teach methods for advocating for the use of behavioral science and methods.

CONCLUSION

If you are reading this chapter, it is likely that you are a student or faculty member in a behavior analytic or contextual behavioral science program. Over the past ten years, there has been considerable expansion of interest in addressing problems that go beyond those that behavior analysis has devoted the majority of its attention to (developmental disorders and organizational behavior). Interest in clinical interventions (Hayes et al., 2012) and cultural evolution (Mattaini, 2019) are prominent examples. At the same time, conceptual and empirical developments in the contextual behavioral science community have enriched behavior analysis.

As noted above, we subscribe to a particularly expansive view of behavioral science (Wilson et al., 2014). In line with Skinner's vision of a science of human behavior that could effectively address every problem that involves human behavior (Skinner, 1953), we believe that it is useful to analyze any aspect of behavior in terms of the principles of variation and selection. In keeping with a multi-level analysis of selection, we include the behavior of dyads, groups, organizations, and even nations.

The first author recently participated in a panel discussion at an ABAI conference on the relationship between behavior analysis and the rest of behavioral science. As with many other discussion and publications, the emphasis was on how we can get other areas of behavioral science to recognize the achievements of behavior analysis and make use of our knowledge. In our view, this question should be heavily modified. While behavior analysis certainly can contribute to other sciences, it also needs to learn from other fields how to address a broader set of societal issues in a fashion that attracts long-term funding and widespread dissemination. Many behavior analysts wish that the field was doing more about pressing social problems such as racism and poverty. But for a behavior analyst to contribute to the solution of these problems, they would first have to master the existing empirical evidence on these problems, much of which is not taught in BA programs.

The USA and the world have entered a period of unprecedented upheaval. Over the past 50 years the United States has been on a downward trajectory in which the wellbeing of a large proportion of Americans has steadily declined and political power has stopped being responsive to their needs (Biglan, 2020f). Our failures to address climate change, racism, and the economic wellbeing of half of Americans call for a great awakening, in which millions of Americans take action to create a democracy that works to advance everyone's wellbeing.

We need to build interdisciplinary programs in our universities that are organized around the goal of ameliorating one or more of our most pressing problems. Such programs need to be explicitly focused on developing and disseminating knowledge about the contextual conditions that influence these problems. They need to experimentally evaluate the impact of comprehensive interventions on problems such as climate change, discrimination, and poverty. They should be evaluated in terms of how well they are contributing to improving population wellbeing. An example of this direction is the effort of the Coalition of Behavioral Science Organizations to organize a nationwide effort to reduce concentrated disadvantage in American neighborhoods (Biglan et al., 2020).

For behavior analysts, a modest step in the direction we advocate would be to ensure that BA students are trained to use and integrate empirical evidence that is not labeled as behavior analytic. BA programs could have a course at the beginning of graduate school on how *any* empirical fact about human behavior is valuable for building societies that nurture wellbeing. The goal of such a course would be to (a) increase students' facility in understanding facts from non-behavior analytic studies in terms of contextual principles and (b) prepare students to study research on human behavior that was not done by behavior analysts so that they can incorporate useful knowledge into their repertoire without feeling that they are abandoning the pragmatic focus of contextual behavioral science on prediction *and influence*.

Consider the evidence from Kasser's work on materialistic values that was cited above (Kasser, 2016). Superficially, it might seem that this work is inconsistent with a functional contextualist approach to behavior. However, his work on materialism vs. prosocial behavior gets at the prevalence and importance of these two constellations of behavior in the population. Kasser's analysis describes the relationship between these two constellations and numerous psychological and behavioral problems, and the contextual conditions that make materialistic values and behaviors more likely. All of this points to the conditions, such as threat and coercion, whose prevalence we must reduce if we are going to reduce the prevalence of materialistic values.

Behavioral science has the potential to help solve the many intertwined problems that we face. Yet, it will not happen unless we abandon traditional divisions within the field and boldly create a science that is pragmatically focused on where we need to go rather than where we have been.

STUDY QUESTIONS

1. Describe two trends that seem to be signs of diminished wellbeing around the world.
2. Explain how both prosocial and antisocial values develop?
3. Describe the concept of an "evolutionary mismatch" and provide an example of a current mismatch with problematic consequences.
4. Explain how social media has contributed to societal problems. What can be done about it?
5. Describe three steps practitioners and researchers alike could take to contribute to the nurture consilience.

NOTE

1. No funding was used to write this book chapter.

REFERENCES

Abramowitz, M.J. (2018). *Democracy in Crisis*. Freedom House. https://freedomhouse.org/report/freedom-world/2018/democracy-crisis

Adler, N.E., Cutler, D.M., Fielding, J.E., Galea, S., Glymour, M.M., Koh, H.K., & Satcher, D. (2016). Addressing Social determinants of health and health disparities: A vital direction for health and health care. *NAM Perspectives*, *6*(9). https://doi.org/10.31478/201609t

Aligica, P.D. & Tarko, V. (2014). Crony capitalism: Rent Seeking, institutions and ideology. *Kyklos*, *67*(2), 156–176. https://doi.org/10.1111/kykl.12048

Allen, J., Balfour, R., Bell, R., & Marmot, M. (2014). Social determinants of mental health. *International Review of Psychiatry*, *26*(4), 392–407. https://doi.org/10.3109/09540261.2014.928270

Atkins, P.W.B., Wilson, D.S., & Hayes, S.C. (2019). *Prosocial: Using Evolutionary science to build productive, equitable, and collaborative groups*. Context Press.

Bambra, C., Gibson, M., Sowden, A., Wright, K., Whitehead, M., & Petticrew, M. (2010). Tackling the wider social determinants of health and health inequalities: Evidence from systematic reviews. *Journal of Epidemiology & Community Health*, *64*(4), 284–291. https://doi.org/10.1136/jech.2008.082743

Barrett, K., O'Connor, M., & McHugh, L. (2019). A Systematic review of values-based psychometric tools within acceptance and commitment therapy (ACT). *The Psychological Record*, *69*(4), 457–485. https://doi.org/10.1007/s40732-019-00352-7

Biglan, A. (2009). The Role of advocacy organizations in reducing negative externalities. *Journal of Organizational Behavior Management*, *29*(3–4), 215–230. https://doi.org/10.1080/01608060903092086

Biglan, A. (2015). *The nurture effect: How the Science of human behavior can improve our lives and our world*. New Harbinger Publications.

Biglan, A. (2020a). Big Pharma and the death of americans. *The Evolution Institute*. https://evolution-institute.org/big-pharma-and-the-death-of-americans

Biglan, A. (2020b). How and why the food industry makes Americans sick. *The Evolution Institute*. https://evolution-institute.org/how-and-why-the-food-industry-makes-americans-sick

Biglan, A. (2020c). The fossil fuel industry: The greatest threat to human well-being. *The Evolution Institute*. https://evolution-institute.org/the-fossil-fuel-industry-the-greatest-threat-to-human-well-being

Biglan, A. (2020d, March 5). How Cigarette marketing killed 20 million people. *The Evolution Institute*. https://evolution-institute.org/how-cigarette-marketing-killed-20-million-people/

Biglan, A. (2020e, March 12). The right to sell arms. *The Evolution Institute*. https://evolution-institute.org/the-right-to-sell-arms/

Biglan, A. (2020f). *Rebooting capitalism: How We can forge a society that works for everyone*. Values to Action.

Biglan, A., Elfner, K., Garbacz, S.A., Komro, K., Prinz, R.J., Weist, M.D., Wilson, D.K., & Zarling, A. (2020). A Strategic plan for strengthening America's families: A Brief from the coalition of behavioral science organizations. *Clinical Child and Family Psychology Review*, *23*(2), 153–175. https://doi.org/10.1007/s10567-020-00318-0

Biglan, A. & Embry, D.D. (2013). A framework for intentional cultural change. *Journal of Contextual Behavioral Science*, *2*(3–4), 95–104. https://doi.org/10.1016/j.jcbs.2013.06.001

Biglan, A., Flay, B.R., Embry, D.D., & Sandler, I.N. (2012). The critical role of nurturing environments for promoting human wellbeing. *American Psychologist*, *67*(4), 257–271. https://doi.org/10.1037/a0026796

Biglan, A., Johansson, M., Van Ryzin, M.J., Embry, D.D. (in press). Scaling up and scaling out: consilience and the evolution of more nurturing societies. *Clinical Psychology Review*.

Biglan, A., Van Ryzin, M.J., Moore, K.J., Mauricci, M., & Mannan, I. (2019). The socialization of boys and men in the modern era: An evolutionary mismatch. *Development and Psychopathology*, *31*(5), 1789–1799. https://doi.org/10.1017/S0954579419001366

Bond, F.W. & Bunce, D. (2000). Mediators of change in emotion-focused and problem-focused worksite stress management interventions. *Journal of Occupational Health Psychology*, *5*(1), 156–163. https://doi.org/10.1037/1076-8998.5.1.156

Bond, F.W., Flaxman, P.E., & Bunce, D. (2008). The influence of psychological flexibility on work redesign: Mediated moderation of a work reorganization intervention. *Journal of Applied Psychology*, *93*(3), 645–654. https://doi.org/10.1037/0021-9010.93.3.645

Boxell, L., Gentzkow, M., & Shapiro, J.M. (2020). *Cross-Country trends in affective polarization* (Working Paper No. 26669). National Bureau of Economic Research. https://doi.org/10.3386/w26669

Bradshaw, C.P., Zmuda, J.H., Kellam, S.G., & Ialongo, N.S. (2009). Longitudinal impact of two universal preventive interventions in first grade on educational outcomes in high school. *Journal of Educational Psychology*, *101*(4), 926–937. https://doi.org/10.1037/a0016586

Cadwalladr, C. (2020, January 4). Fresh Cambridge Analytica leak "shows global manipulation is out of control." *The Observer*. https://www.theguardian.com/uk-news/2020/jan/04/cambridge-analytica-data-leak-global-election-manipulation

Cheng, L., Abraham, J., Hausfather, Z., & Trenberth, K.E. (2019). How fast are the oceans warming? *Science*, *363*(6423), 128–129. https://doi.org/10.1126/science.aav7619

Child Trends Databank. (2019). Children in poverty. *Child Trends*. https://www.childtrends.org/indicators/children-in-poverty

Coppins, M. (2020, March). The Billion-dollar disinformation campaign to reelect the president. *The Atlantic*. https://www.theatlantic.com/magazine/archive/2020/03/the-2020-disinformation-war/605530/

Costello, E.J., Compton, S.N., Keeler, G., & Angold, A. (2003). Relationships Between poverty and psychopathology: A natural experiment. *JAMA*, *290*(15), 2023–2029. https://doi.org/10.1001/jama.290.15.2023

Diener, E. (2013). The remarkable changes in the science of subjective well-being. *Perspectives on Psychological Science*, *8*(6), 663–666. https://doi.org/10.1177/1745691613507583

Dishion, T.J. & Snyder, J.J. (2016). *The Oxford Handbook of coercive relationship dynamics*. Oxford University Press.

Edsall, T.B. (2020, February 26). Opinion | Does Anyone have a clue about how to fight back against Trump's racism? *The New York Times*. https://www.nytimes.com/2020/02/26/opinion/trump-racism-democrats.html

Ellis, B.J. & Bjorklund, D.F. (2012). Beyond mental health: An evolutionary analysis of development under risky and supportive environmental conditions: An introduction to the special section. *Developmental Psychology*, *48*(3), 591–597. https://doi.org/10.1037/a0027651

Ellis, B.J., Del Giudice, M., Dishion, T.J., Figueredo, A.J., Gray, P., Griskevicius, V., Hawley, P.H., Jacobs, W.J., James, J., Volk, A.A., & Wilson, D.S. (2012). The evolutionary basis of risky adolescent behavior: Implications for science, policy, and practice. *Developmental Psychology*, *48*(3), 598–623. https://doi.org/10.1037/a0026220

Fonseca, S., Trindade, I.A., Mendes, A.L., & Ferreira, C. (2019). The buffer role of psychological flexibility against the impact of major life events on depression symptoms. *Clinical Psychologist*, *n/a*(n/a), 1–9. https://doi.org/10.1111/cp.12194

French, K., Golijani-Moghaddam, N., & Schröder, T. (2017). What is the evidence for the efficacy of self-help acceptance and commitment therapy? A systematic review and meta-analysis. *Journal of Contextual Behavioral Science*, *6*(4), 360–374. https://doi.org/10.1016/j.jcbs.2017.08.002

Friedman, M. (1970). The social responsibility of business is to increase its profits. *New York Times*. https://graphics8.nytimes.com/packages/pdf/business/miltonfriedman1970.pdf

Friedman, Z. (2017, February 21). Student loan debt In 2017: A $1.3 trillion crisis. *Forbes*. https://www.forbes.com/sites/zackfriedman/2017/02/21/student-loan-debt-statistics-2017/

Frögéli, E., Djordjevic, A., Rudman, A., Livheim, F., & Gustavsson, P. (2016). A randomized controlled pilot trial of acceptance and commitment training (ACT) for preventing stress-related ill health among future nurses. *Anxiety, Stress, & Coping*, *29*(2), 202–218. https://doi.org/10.1080/10615806.2015.1025765

Gascoyne, A.C. (2019). *The development and validation of a measure of organisational flexibility*. ACBS Conference, Dublin, June 2019.

Gelles, D. & Yaffe-Bellany, D. (2019). Shareholder value is no longer everything, top C.E.O.s say. *The New York Times*. https://www.nytimes.com/2019/08/19/business/business-roundtable-ceos-corporations.html

Gloster, A. T., Meyer, A. H., & Lieb, R. (2017). Psychological flexibility as a malleable public health target: Evidence from a representative sample. *Journal of Contextual Behavioral Science*, *6*(2), 166–171. https://doi.org/10.1016/j.jcbs.2017.02.003

Greer, S. & Kahlenberg, R.D. (2020, February 26). *How Progressives can recapture seven deeply held American values*. The Century Foundation. https://tcf.org/content/report/progressives-can-recapture-seven-deeply-held-american-values/

Hagström, K. (2019). *Samhällsförlusten av sjukskrivningar: 64 miljarder kronor*. https://www.skandia.se/om-oss/nyheter/nyhetsarkiv/2019/sverige-forlorar-64-miljarder-pa-sjukskrivningar---psykisk-ohalsa-star-for-varannan-diagnos/

Haidt, J. (2012). *The righteous mind: Why good people are divided by politics and religion*. Knopf Doubleday Publishing Group.

Haidt, J. & Rose-Stockwell, T. (2019, December). The dark psychology of social networks. *The Atlantic*. https://www.theatlantic.com/magazine/archive/2019/12/social-media-democracy/600763/

Hales, C.M., Carroll, M.D., Fryar, C.D., & Ogden, C.L. (2020). *Prevalence of Obesity and severe obesity among adults: United States, 2017–2018* (No. 360; NCHS Data Brief). https://www.cdc.gov/nchs/products/databriefs/db360.htm

Hann, K.E.J. & McCracken, L.M. (2014). A systematic review of randomized controlled trials of acceptance and commitment therapy for adults with chronic pain: Outcome domains, design quality, and efficacy. *Journal of Contextual Behavioral Science*, *3*(4), 217–227. https://doi.org/10.1016/j.jcbs.2014.10.001

Hayes, S.C. (2019). *A liberated mind: How to pivot toward what matters*. Avery.

Hayes, S.C., Barnes-Holmes, D., & Wilson, K.G. (2012). Contextual behavioral science: Creating a science more adequate to the challenge of the human condition. *Journal of Contextual Behavioral Science*, *1*(1–2), 1–16. https://doi.org/10.1016/j.jcbs.2012.09.004

Hayes, S.C., Strosahl, K., & Wilson, K.G. (2012). *Acceptance and commitment therapy: The process and practice of mindful change*. Guilford Press.

Hayes, S.C., Sanford, B.T., & Chin, F.T. (2017). Carrying the baton: Evolution science and a contextual behavioral analysis of language and cognition. *Journal of Contextual Behavioral Science*, *6*(3), 314–328. https://doi.org/10.1016/j.jcbs.2017.01.002

Hayes, S.C., Strosahl, K., & Wilson, K.G. (2012). *Acceptance and commitment therapy: The process and practice of mindful change*. Guilford Press.

Hofer, P.D., Waadt, M., Aschwanden, R., Milidou, M., Acker, J., Meyer, A.H., Lieb, R., & Gloster, A.T. (2018). Self-help for stress and burnout without therapist contact: An online randomised controlled trial. *Work & Stress*, *32*(2), 189–208. https://doi.org/10.1080/02678373.2017.1402389

Jablonka, E. & Lamb, M.J. (2014). *Evolution in four dimensions: Genetic, Epigenetic, behavioral, and symbolic variation in the history of life* (Revised ed.). The MIT Press.

Johansson, M. & Biglan, A. (2019, June 29). *Measuring nurturance in work environments – an instructive assessment for improving social work environments*. ACBS World Conference 17, Dublin. https://contextualscience.org/wc17_symposium_detail

Johansson, M., Biglan, A., & Embry, D.D. (in press). The PAX good behavior game: One Model for evolving a more nurturing society. *Clinical Child and Family Psychology Review*.

Johnson, M.S. (in press). Regulation by shaming: Deterrence effects of publicizing violations of workplace safety and health laws. *American Economic Review*, 80.

Jurkowitz, M., Mitchell, A., Shearer, E., & Walker, M. (2020, January 24). U.S. Media polarization and the 2020 election: A nation divided. *Pew Research Center's Journalism Project*. https://www.journalism.org/2020/01/24/u-s-media-polarization-and-the-2020-election-a-nation-divided/

Kashdan, T.B. & Rottenberg, J. (2010). Psychological flexibility as a fundamental aspect of health. *Clinical Psychology Review*, *30*(7), 865–878. https://doi.org/10.1016/j.cpr.2010.03.001

Kasser, T. (2016). Materialistic values and goals. *Annual Review of Psychology*, *67*(1), 489–514. https://doi.org/10.1146/annurev-psych-122414-033344

Kellam, S.G., Mackenzie, A.C.L., Brown, C.H., Poduska, J.M., Wang, W., Petras, H., & Wilcox, H.C. (2011). The good behavior game and the future of prevention and treatment. *Addiction Science & Clinical Practice*, *6*(1), 73–84. http://www.ncbi.nlm.nih.gov/pmc/articles/PMC3188824/

Kellam, S.G., Wang, W., Mackenzie, A.C.L., Brown, C.H., Ompad, D.C., Or, F., Ialongo, N.S., Poduska, J.M., & Windham, A. (2012). The impact of the good behavior game, a universal classroom-based preventive intervention in first and second grades, on high-risk sexual behaviors and drug abuse and dependence disorders into young adulthood. *Prevention Science*, *15*(1), 6–18. https://doi.org/10.1007/s11121-012-0296-z

Khatri, N., Tsang, E.W.K., & Begley, T.M. (2006). Cronyism: A cross-cultural analysis. *Journal of International Business Studies*, *37*(1), 61–75. https://doi.org/10.1057/palgrave.jibs.8400171

Khoury, B., Sharma, M., Rush, S.E., & Fournier, C. (2015). Mindfulness-based stress reduction for healthy individuals: A meta-analysis. *Journal of Psychosomatic Research*, *78*(6), 519–528. https://doi.org/10.1016/j.jpsychores.2015.03.009

Krafft, J., Ferrell, J., Levin, M.E., & Twohig, M.P. (2017). Psychological inflexibility and stigma: A meta-analytic review. *Journal of Contextual Behavioral Science*. https://doi.org/10.1016/j.jcbs.2017.11.002

Leslie, L.K., Mehus, C.J., Hawkins, J.D., Boat, T., McCabe, M.A., Barkin, S., Perrin, E.C., Metzler, C.W., Prado, G., Tait, V.F., Brown, R., & Beardslee, W. (2016). Primary Health care: Potential home for family-focused preventive interventions. *American Journal of Preventive Medicine*, *51*(4, Supplement 2), S106–S118. https://doi.org/10.1016/j.amepre.2016.05.014

Levin, M.E., Lillis, J., & Biglan, A. (2016). The Potential of community-wide strategies for promoting psychological flexibility. In R.D. Zettle, S.C. Hayes, D. Barnes-Holmes, & A. Biglan (Eds.), *The Wiley handbook of contextual behavioral science*. Wiley. https://doi.org/10.1002/9781118489857

Levin, M., MacLane, C., Daflos, S., Seeley, J.R., Hayes, S.C., Biglan, A., & Pistorello, J. (2014). Examining psychological inflexibility as a transdiagnostic process across psychological disorders. *Journal of Contextual Behavioral Science*, *3*(3), 155–163. https://doi.org/10.1016/j.jcbs.2014.06.003

Loewenstein, M. (2016). *Benefit corporations: A challenge in corporate governance* (SSRN Scholarly Paper ID 2746203). Social Science Research Network. https://papers.ssrn.com/abstract=2746203

Lukianoff, G. & Haidt, J. (2019). *The coddling of the American mind: How good intentions and bad ideas are setting up a generation for failure* (Reprint ed.). Penguin Books.

Ly, K.H., Asplund, K., & Andersson, G. (2014). Stress management for middle managers via an acceptance and commitment-based smartphone application: A randomized controlled trial. *Internet Interventions, 1*(3), 95–101. https://doi.org/10.1016/j.invent.2014.06.003

Mackey, J. & Sisodia, R. (2013). *Conscious capitalism: Liberating the Heroic spirit of business.* Harvard Business Review Press.

Marantz, A. (2019). *Antisocial: Online extremists, techno-utopians, and the hijacking of the American conversation.* Viking.

Mattaini, M.A. (2019). Out of the lab: Shaping an ecological and constructional cultural systems science. *Perspectives on Behavior Science, 42*(4), 713–731. https://doi.org/10.1007/s40614-019-00208-z

Mayer, J. (2016). *Dark money: The hidden history of the billionaires behind the rise of the radical right.* Doubleday.

McNamee, R. (2019). *Zucked: Waking up to the Facebook catastrophe.* Penguin Press.

Mutz, D.C. (2018). Status threat, not economic hardship, explains the 2016 presidential vote. *Proceedings of the National Academy of Sciences, 115*(19), E4330–E4339. https://doi.org/10.1073/pnas.1718155115

National Academies of Sciences, Engineering, and Medicine. (2019). *Fostering Healthy mental, emotional, and behavioral development in children and youth: A national agenda.* National Academies Press.

Oppenheimer, M., Oreskes, N., Jamieson, D., Brysse, K., O'Reilly, J., Shindell, M., & Wazeck, M. (2019). *Discerning experts: The Practices of scientific assessment for environmental policy.* University of Chicago Press.

Pew Research Center. (2016). *Partisanship and political animosity in 2016* (p. 105). https://www.people-press.org/wp-content/uploads/sites/4/2016/06/06-22-16-Partisanship-and-animosity-release.pdf

Pierson, P. & Hacker, J.S. (2016). *American amnesia: How the war on government led us to forget what made America prosper [Elektronisk resurs].* Simon & Schuster.

Prinz, R.J., Sanders, M.R., Shapiro, C.J., Whitaker, D.J., & Lutzker, J.R. (2009). Population-based prevention of child maltreatment: The U.S. Triple p system population trial. *Prevention Science, 10*(1), 1–12. https://doi.org/10.1007/s11121-009-0123-3

Reilly, E.D., Ritzert, T.R., Scoglio, A.A.J., Mote, J., Fukuda, S.D., Ahern, M.E., & Kelly, M.M. (2019). A systematic review of values measures in acceptance and commitment therapy research. *Journal of Contextual Behavioral Science, 12*, 290–304. https://doi.org/10.1016/j.jcbs.2018.10.004

Richardson, K.M. & Rothstein, H.R. (2008). Effects of occupational stress management intervention programs: A meta-analysis. *Journal of Occupational Health Psychology, 13*(1), 69–93. https://doi.org/10.1037/1076-8998.13.1.69

Rose, F. (2017, March 30). *Safe Spaces on college campuses are creating intolerant students.* HuffPost. https://www.huffpost.com/entry/safe-spaces-college-intolerant_b_58d957a6e4b02a2eaab66ccf

Saez, E. & Zucman, G. (2016). Wealth inequality in the United States since 1913: Evidence from Capitalized income tax data. *The Quarterly Journal of Economics, 131*(2), 519–578. https://doi.org/10.1093/qje/qjw004

Sanders, M. R., Burke, K., Prinz, R.J., & Morawska, A. (2017). Achieving Population-level change through a system-contextual approach to supporting competent parenting. *Clinical Child and Family Psychology Review, 20*(1), 36–44. https://doi.org/10.1007/s10567-017-0227-4

Scherer, G. (2012, December 6). Climate science predictions prove too conservative. *Scientific American.* https://www.scientificamerican.com/article/climate-science-predictions-prove-too-conservative/

Setzler, M. & Yanus, A.B. (2018). Why did women vote for Donald Trump? *PS: Political Science & Politics, 51*(3), 523–527. https://doi.org/10.1017/S1049096518000355

Skinner, B.F. (1953). *Science and human behavior.* Macmillan.

Skinner, B.F. (1981). Selection by consequences. *Science, 213*(4507), 501–504. https://doi.org/10.1126/science.7244649

Smith, R. (2018, August 17). *Life expectancy dropped in multiple countries, new study finds.* CNN. https://www.cnn.com/2018/08/16/health/life-expectancy-uk-us-drop-study-intl/index.html

Solomon, S., Pierrehumbert, R.T., Matthews, D., Daniel, J.S., & Friedlingstein, P. (2013). Atmospheric Composition, irreversible climate change, and mitigation policy. In G.R. Asrar & J.W. Hurrell (Eds.), *Climate science for serving society: Research, Modeling and prediction priorities* (pp. 415–436). Springer Netherlands. https://doi.org/10.1007/978-94-007-6692-1_15

Swan, L. (2017, March 20). *Safe spaces can be dangerous.* Psychology Today. https://www.psychologytoday.com/blog/college-confidential/201703/safe-spaces-can-be-dangerous

The Business Roundtable. (1997). Statement on corporate governance. http://www.ralphgomory.com/wp-content/uploads/2018/05/Business-Roundtable-1997.pdf

The Race-Class Narrative Project. (2018, May 21). Demos. https://www.demos.org/campaign/race-class-narrative-project

Van Ryzin, M.J., Fishbein, D., & Biglan, A. (2018). The promise of prevention science for addressing intergenerational poverty. *Psychology, Public Policy, and Law, 24*(1), 128–143. https://doi.org/10.1037/law0000138

Van Ryzin, M.J., Kumpfer, K.L., Fosco, G.M., & Greenberg, M.T. (2015). *Family-based prevention programs for children and adolescents: Theory, Research, and large-scale dissemination.* Psychology Press.

Van Ryzin, M.J., Roseth, C.J., Fosco, G.M., Lee, Y., & Chen, I.-C. (2016). A component-centered meta-analysis of family-based prevention programs for adolescent substance use. *Clinical Psychology Review, 45*, 72–80. https://doi.org/10.1016/j.cpr.2016.03.007

Voelkel, J.G. & Willer, R. (2019). *Resolving the progressive paradox: Conservative value framing of progressive economic policies increases candidate support* (SSRN Scholarly Paper ID 3385818). Social Science Research Network. https://papers.ssrn.com/abstract=3385818

Wersebe, H., Lieb, R., Meyer, A.H., Hofer, P., & Gloster, A. T. (2018). The link between stress, wellbeing, and psychological flexibility during an Acceptance and Commitment Therapy self-help intervention. *International Journal of Clinical and Health Psychology, 18*(1), 60–68. https://doi.org/10.1016/j.ijchp.2017.09.002

Wilkinson, R.G. & Pickett, K.E. (2017). The enemy between us: The psychological and social costs of inequality. *European Journal of Social Psychology, 47*(1), 11–24. https://doi.org/10.1002/ejsp.2275

Wilson, D.S. (2005). Evolution for everyone: How to increase acceptance of, interest in, and knowledge about evolution. *PLoS Biology, 3*(12). https://doi.org/10.1371/journal.pbio.0030364

Wilson, D.S. (2007). *Evolution for everyone: How Darwin's theory can change the way we think about our lives*. Delacorte Press.

Wilson, D.S. (2012). Consilience: Making contextual behavioral science part of the United Ivory Archipelago. *Journal of Contextual Behavioral Science, 1*(1–2), 39–42. https://doi.org/10.1016/j.jcbs.2012.09.005

Wilson, D.S. (2019). *This View of life: Completing the Darwinian Revolution*. Pantheon.

Wilson, D.S., Hayes, S. C., Biglan, A., & Embry, D. D. (2014). Evolving the future: Toward a science of intentional change. *Behavioral and Brain Sciences, 37*(04), 395–416. https://doi.org/10.1017/S0140525X13001593

Wilson, D.S., O'Brien, D.T., & Sesma, A. (2009). Human prosociality from an evolutionary perspective: Variation and correlations at a city-wide scale. *Evolution and Human Behavior, 30*(3), 190–200. https://doi.org/10.1016/j.evolhumbehav.2008.12.002

Wilson, D.S., Ostrom, E., & Cox, M.E. (2013). Generalizing the core design principles for the efficacy of groups. *Journal of Economic Behavior & Organization, 90*, S21–S32. https://doi.org/10.1016/j.jebo.2012.12.010

World Protest and Reform Movements. (2018, March 7). Readex. https://www.readex.com/content/world-protest-and-reform-movements

Wylie, C. (2019). *Mindf*ck: Cambridge Analytica and the Plot to Break America*. Random House.

11

Organization and Leadership in Resistance Movements

Constructing Justice[1]

Mark A. Mattaini and Kathryn M. Roose

The sub-discipline of organizational behavior management (OBM) has increasingly been intertwined with social issues in recent years. Interspersed between important research on improving employee productivity, safety, and efficiency have been articles addressing organizational responsibility toward the environment, employee wellbeing, and broader social issues. Conceptual and experimental work in OBM has laid a foundation that can be leveraged to address large-scale societal issues of social significance; the same scientific principles that describe effective business practices can be applied to social issues and resistance movements. A special section on Leadership and Cultural Change in the *Journal of Organizational Behavior Management* poses the call to action, "[t]he challenge ahead for the behavior science community is to do the extensive and difficult behavioral systems research needed to pinpoint the variables that will bring about massive, yet crucial, changes in individual behavior and organizational action" (Houmanfar, 2017, p. 121). More is possible by extending our attention to "post-Skinnerian theoretical advances and laboratory discoveries that emphasize derived stimulus relations to scaled-up, impactful, and evidence-based technologies for use by members of the society" (Dixon et al., 2018, p. 242), and providing initial guidance for harnessing those technologies.

The challenges are enormous. Modern societies often fail to respond adequately to structural injustice, human rights violations, or environmental degradation, resulting in tremendous human and global costs, while supporting ecologies of disengagement and violence (Roose & Mattaini, in press). Global populations experience worldwide unrest as citizens demand equity, freedom, and remedies for injustice in economic conditions and civil rights for historically marginalized groups. Challenging such deeply entrenched and complex conditions demands responses that go beyond or challenge established community and political norms. At such times, the committed – those who refuse to ignore or participate in injustice – have the collective potential, and often the moral obligation, to refuse cooperation, most powerfully as members of resistance movements. A common refrain from this group is "silence is violence," making clear the view that ignoring injustice or staying silent is essentially complicity with injustice.

Recent examples of resistance movements include Women's Marches, Occupy Wall Street, Arab Spring, Me Too, Yellow Vests, and Black Lives Matter, all of which have mobilized large and often committed numbers of citizens. Creative tactics often need to be developed "on the spot" (though actually with careful if rapid planning). A notable example is the Black Lives

DOI: 10.4324/9781003198949-11

Matter (BLM) movement, originally emerging in 2013, but experiencing an unprecedented resurgence in 2020 with almost nonstop protests, sit-ins, marches, and other events across the country and the world. Peaceful protests and nonviolent resistance were joined by violence, riots, and looting in some areas as clashes between police and protesters occurred, and as non-supporters took advantage of the unrest to engage in destructive behaviors, ostensibly for personal gain (e.g., looting), or in some cases, to bring negative attention toward the movement.

In a stunning example of the evolution of a resistance movement, several new movements emerged in support of BLM. The Wall of Moms appeared in Portland, Oregon, in response to disturbing examples of law enforcement and federal agent retaliation against protesters, stating "we moms would take some physical hits in hopes our Black and Brown kids, friends, neighbors, and loved ones will be spared some pain" (Wamsley, 2020, n.p.). Notably, representatives from the Wall of Moms report that they take direction from the leaders of the BLM movement, as they recognize the importance of coordination and organization (Wamsley, 2020). The Wall of Moms was followed by the "PDX Dad Pod" (PDX = Portland) who organized to lend additional support to BLM and the Wall of Moms, bringing leaf blowers to protests to blow away tear gas (Impelli, 2020). The next group to join the movement was the Wall of Vets, indicating that their role is to "ensure our citizens did not have their right to free speech and their right to protest and right to assemble taken away from them" (Moreno, 2020). Such protective movements have predecessors over many centuries (McCarthy & Sharp, 1997). Nonviolent resistance has proven powerful in thousands of cases globally (McCarthy & Sharp, 1997; Sharp, 2005) – consistently more powerful than violent alternatives for achieving social change, and usually with fewer casualties, especially to noncombatants. In fact, the inclusion of any level of violent responses in resistance campaigns greatly reduces the chances for success (Chenoweth & Stephan, 2011).

Unfortunately, however, a great deal of resistance effort is and has been wasted due to the lack of knowledge of the extensive history of effective strategic nonviolent struggle (McCarthy & Sharp, 1997; Sharp, 2005), or of the principles underlying that history. The intent of resistance movements is nearly always to have a meaningful impact on governmental or cultural practices, typically by advocating for policy or structural changes, thereby "turning protest into policy." Such change requires a firm grounding in values and ethics consistent with nonviolent action, a culturo-behavioral understanding of the dynamics of the policy process, and behavioral repertoires that offer analytic and strategic options for framing and sustaining change (Mattaini et al., in press). Values and ethical commitments necessary to such advocacy are extremely demanding, beginning with textured understandings of social and environmental justice, structural violence, and contextual variables. While integrity is required in all forms of behavior analytic work, temptations to manipulate messaging in less than fully honest ways depending on the audience, or to omit or exaggerate research findings, are common risks for those contributing to social movements (Fawcett et al., 1988). If serious injustice or oppression is identified and the advocate has the knowledge and capacity to intervene, such intervention becomes a serious ethical obligation. Other value dilemmas and ethical challenges may emerge within movements due to the intense human interactions involved.

RESISTANCE ORGANIZATIONS AS CULTURAL SYSTEMS EMBEDDED IN COMPLEX CONTEXTS

Behavioral systems analysis (Mattaini, 2013) and cultural systems analysis (Mattaini, in press) are discussed in several chapters of this volume, so our discussion here will emphasize only a few points that are particularly relevant for resistance movements as organizations. First, the networks of environments within which such organizations operate are in nearly all cases highly complex, with many systems, actors, cultural and geographic factors, value systems, organizational tensions, and resource pools involved. The ecology that produces and supports a resistance movement is much like biological ecologies in which the single organism is embedded in systems embedded in systems embedded in systems. Such complexity tends to be progressive as movements and contexts evolve over time (see Mobus & Kalton, 2015 for an extensive discussion of progressive complexity). Given these realities, social movements in context are best viewed as organic rather than mechanical. Resistance movements typically operate within constantly shifting contexts where new supporters and opponents may emerge unexpectedly, political or health events may demand immediate responses, and levels of commitment within the movement may intensify or attenuate in response to internal or external variables.

Opponents to justice movements cannot operate without the support of multiple other networks. Helvey (2007), for example, provided an extensive analysis of "pillars of support" without which governments cannot sustain their power, indicating that "in a strategic nonviolent conflict, the operational focus for planners is primarily about the alignment and capabilities of pillars of support" (p. 9). Included on Helvey's pillars are the police, the military, civil servants, media, the business community, youth, "workers," religious organizations, non-governmental organizations (NGOs), and many other organizations and less formal community groups. Somewhat similar pillars support commercial, religious, or educational systems (cf. Skinner, 1987), and in fact a similar list can be developed for supports needed, or that can be valuable, for resistance movements. Identification of such pillars supporting movements, and those needed to do so, is an important leadership exercise.

Actors (persons or systems) in each pillar are in most cases not entirely in agreement, and each pillar is embedded in its own networks of supporting or opposing systems which may affect their involvement in the movement. In addition, groups within networks may form their own cultures (self-organization). Adequate analysis therefore often requires the ability to form an integrated, active image of current situations and possible shifts in forces that may assist or impede the movement, and creatively take steps to imagine and construct possible alternatives. As Willems (1974) noted, unexpected or unnoticed "other variables" may be key to understanding behavior or events. In cases where many relevant variables operate and interact simultaneously, approaches based on Goldiamond's nonlinear behavior analysis (1984; Layng, 2009) and cultural systems analysis (Mattaini, 2013, in press, Chapter 4) may be required to construct adequate strategic plans.

MOBILIZATION AND ORGANIZATION IN RESISTANCE MOVEMENTS

Strategic theorists of nonviolent power generally argue that most successful nonviolent campaigns require carefully coordinated action among many individuals, often over a considerable period of time, to build and sustain organizational strength. Long-time activist Saul Alinsky, who led the Industrial Areas Foundation, asserted that "power and organization are one and the same" (1971, p. 113). Similarly, Peter Ackerman and Christopher Kruegler argue that "a key task for nonviolent strategists is to create new groups, or turn preexisting groups and institutions into efficient fighting organizations" (1994, p. 26). Frances Fox Piven and Richard Cloward, often viewed as politically radical, "argue that channeling disruptive protest into organizational development weakens poor people's movements and impedes social progress" (Cortright, 2010, p. 194, commenting on comments by Piven & Cloward, 1979). Later, however, Piven (2006) maintained that contributions of many individuals "must be coordinated for the effective mobilization of disruptive power," and that achieving that coordination is the "classic problem of solidarity, or organizing for joint action" (p. 29).

Mobilization is important, but often insufficient to conquer the injustices resistance movements wish to challenge. For example, "[y]outh movements fizzle when they fail to forge broad-based alliances, sustain pressure on power holders or organize around a compelling alternative vision. Organization is the pathway to power" (Stephan & Thompson, 2018). Mobilization alone can increase public awareness and may lead to minor accommodations by oppressive opponents intended to deflect attention, but movements advocating for major structural change typically require sustained, coordinated strategic efforts. For example, the resistance movement that led to the resignation of Hosni Mubarak has been criticized for lacking planning for an alternative to Mubarak, resulting in similarly repressive leadership. Similarly, the Occupy Wall Street movement has been criticized for being heavy on mobilization, but light on organization, including a lack of proposals for concrete legislative action (Stephan & Thompson, 2018). The course of Black Lives Matter in the United States has offered multiple examples of how mobilization and organization can support each other. For example, less than two months into the 2020 resurgence of the Black Lives Matter movement, 368 bills regulating police practices had been introduced in 29 states, with more expected when state legislatures resume their regular sessions (CSG Justice Center Staff, 2020). Without continued advocacy, however, history teaches that many will not be passed.

Before moving on to explore effective organizational models grounded in, or consistent with, behavior science, the use of electronic and social media tools for mobilization and organizing requires attention. The potential for coordinating and organizing through social media, the internet, and other electronic means has received considerable attention for over a decade (Lee, 2020; Young et al., 2019). Certainly, the use of cellular phones to document repressive acts has been a powerful tool supporting social justice. There are several important limitations and cautions related to electronic options, however. Repressive governments (local or national) have often either interrupted or intercepted messaging, or tracked positional locations using cell technology (Mattaini, 2013); no form of electronic communication should be regarded as entirely secure for participants in and supporters of resistance movements, and alternatives often need to be established as backups. Further, opponents of justice movements regularly provide false information through social media, which can interfere with planning.

A valuable discussion of the limits of electronic tools, and an important call for direct action, was Malcolm Gladwell's (2010) historical review. He notes that while social media (as long as not hijacked) has often been valuable for coordination, every successful resistance movement facing serious oppression has required participants to commit to serious physical and legal risks, to in some way take to the streets together. Strong personal ties have consistently been needed to marshal and sustain genuine participation; as lifelong activist Barbara Deming noted, "one fire kindles another" (1971, p. 254). ("Virtual" contact, as became widespread during the COVID-19 pandemic, can assist in building such ties, particularly if both the audio and video channels are engaged. The power of literally standing together, however, should not be dismissed, particularly for the most challenging issues.)

Not surprisingly, there is great interest in the potential for social media to bring worldwide attention to social causes. Recruitment, fund-raising, communication, and dissemination of information can all be facilitated by social media, offering the potential to enhance the strength and spread of social movements, as was the case during Arab Spring. Despite such examples (sometimes labeled Twitter or Facebook revolutions), as Gladwell (2010), Young et al. (2019), and others convincingly establish, social media was not a substantial factor in the final success in any of those cases. Despite the enormous contemporary expansion of social media, tweeting or messaging alone have only minimal power for overcoming committed, well-resourced, and often armed opponents.

EFFECTIVE ORGANIZATIONAL MODELS

Ackerman (founding chair of the International Center on Nonviolent Conflict) and Kruegler's (1994) research into nonviolent struggles around the world identified three functional strata required to support organizational strength in resistance organizations. The three strata are (a) the leadership, (b) the operational corps, and (c) the wider civilian population. The role of leadership is described as twofold: "to make the primary decisions that will shape the conflict, and to service as a rallying point for inspiration, courage and clarity of purpose" (p. 27). The history of resistance movements provides many examples of strong, singular leadership. For example, Gandhi and Martin Luther King, Jr.'s leadership styles "were founded on their ability to inspire large groups of people by communicating a vision of change" (Krapfl & Kruja, 2015, p. 30). Although it is commonly believed that such charismatic leadership is essential for success, Ackerman and Kruegler (1994) found that a committee or a similar group was the most common structure in resistance groups.

Network or even cellular leadership groups can be highly resilient and difficult to infiltrate and destroy. At the same time, however, without intensive contact structures, focusing power and maintaining common goals and discipline become more challenging. Charismatic leaders like Martin Luther King, Jr. or Nelson Mandela carry undeniable advantages in providing inspiration, rallying courage, and accessing resources, including third-party supporters. There is, however, too much to be done in any resistance struggle to rely on a single leader, and movements with a single inspirational leader can be vulnerable to decapitation. With singular leadership, personal weaknesses (or false charges of alleged weaknesses) can damage movements. Years of efforts to discredit US civil rights leaders, including Dr. King, Malcolm X, and Bayard Rustin continue into the present. Some once-inspiring leaders at later times in life may act in ways that damage their own reputations, and sometimes their movements. For example, Aung San Suu Kyi's lifelong efforts to overcome authoritarian government in Burma were genuinely inspiring; her minimal response to the later persecution of the Muslim Rohingya population, however, has been deeply disturbing to many. Leadership networks, discussed later, appear in most cases to be optimal.

The second level of organization in the Ackerman and Kruegler (1994) model, the operational core, carries a challenging range of responsibilities. They are responsible for disseminating leadership decisions and information to the broader population, instructing and nurturing support among that population, serving in intelligence roles, and performing "highly specialized and sometimes particularly dangerous operations" that cannot be expected of the general population (Ackerman & Kruegler, 1994, p. 28). The instructional role is central to the development and sustainment of shared stimulus relations within the broader population. Solidarity, discipline, and courage among the broader population emerging from shared forms of relational responding are nearly always required for movement success. (Discipline is often based on enforcing a common code of conduct; an example is the "CORE Rules for Action," available in Mattaini, 2013, p. 106.) Each of those roles is complex and challenging. The operational corps therefore requires extensive support from leadership.

Nonviolence theory and extensive research (see, for example, Chenoweth & Stephan, 2011; Schell, 2003) confirm that power ultimately lies in the hands of the general population – "the functions of the leadership and operational corps are designed to engage, focus, and leverage that power" (Mattaini, 2013, p. 119). In nonviolent struggle, ultimately, "the collective choices of masses of citizens become decisive" (Ackerman & Kruegler, 1994, p. 29). The task in building a movement therefore is to gain the support, recruit the participation, and maintain the solidarity of the population. Resistance movements may extend over lengthy periods of time, another reason that while nonviolent struggle can be powerful, it is often very challenging.

Sources of Strategic Capacity

Sharp and Raqib (2010), experts in strategic resistance who collectively spent decades studying and consulting with movements around the world, determined that three types of knowledge are generally necessary to craft an adequate grand strategy for a resistance struggle facing dedicated, well-resourced opponents (clarifications in brackets are from the current authors):

1. Knowledge of the conflict situation, the opponents, and the society and its needs. [deep personal grounding in local conditions]
2. In-depth knowledge of the nature and operation of the technique of nonviolent action. [technical understanding of the dynamics of and available options for conditions like those in the current situation]
3. The knowledge and ability required to analyze, think, and plan strategically. [core problem analysis and strategic development repertoires] (p. 16)

Sharp and Raqib clarify that simply bringing together several persons, each of whom has some of that knowledge is not adequate; those in strategic leadership need substantial mastery of all three, particularly in the most challenging struggles. For this reason, a major effort of organizations like the Industrial Areas Foundation or the American Friends Service Committee often place a heavy emphasis on providing opportunities for members of local communities to learn core skills for organizing and strategic analysis. Behavior science and cultural systems preparations could be of particular value in enhancing those skills within interdisciplinary resistance efforts. This work need not be viewed as distinct from other actors in the movement; Sharp (a political scientist and lifelong activist) included a brief and convincing analysis of the similarities of approaches for defeating violence identified by B.F. Skinner and Gandhi in his book *Social power and political freedom* (1980, Appendix C).

In the 2009 book *Why David sometimes wins: Leadership, organization and strategy in the California Farm Worker Movement*, Marshall Ganz of Harvard focused on "strategic capacity" within the movement, extracting principles inductively from comparative analyses of competing campaigns of the United Farm Workers, the AFL-CIO, and the Teamsters, all of whom wanted to represent the farmworkers. Ganz's work, which has much in common with cultural systems analysis, provides a strong example of movement complexity – it was not just a case of workers vs. growers. His research suggested that strategic capacity emerges from two sets of factors, what he called "biographical" and "organizational" sources. In the first group, strength emerged from the distinctive *combined identities* of individual members of the leadership team, the outside *social networks* of which individuals were members, and the *diversity of tactical repertoires* that emerged from their individual movement (and life) histories. Diversity across these three dimensions offered a variety of perspectives and life experiences, connections (for example, with other progressive groups), and potential options for developing and implementing tactical and strategic planning, all of which could enrich strategic planning exercises. In order to keep these sources of strategic capacity active, a number of desirable practices that should be shaped and reinforced emerge, including ongoing recruitment and welcoming of new members to the leadership group, establishing the equivalence {new members ≈ increased power} rather than {new members ≈ threats to personal influence}, in part through open discussion of the inescapable challenges of accepting changes in leadership dynamics.

The three organizational sources of strategic capacity, *processes of deliberation and decision-making*, *resources*, and *accountability structures* complement the biographical. Ganz found that effective resistance movements rely to a great extent on *processes of shared power* in which all voices are respected in deliberations, and established procedures to make decisions after all are heard, and to maintain discipline around those decisions once made. According to Ganz' data, diversity of thinking tends to be lost over time as minorities tend to take on majority perspectives unless continuous respectful challenging is reinforced. Circle processes (described in the following section) provide one option for encouraging such thoughtful deliberation. Further, when members of leadership bring personal and outside *resources* (e.g., willingness to pay dues, contacts with potential allied groups, access to funding sources, or those in influential political positions) additional options are made available. And finally, structures and processes supporting *accountability*, both for the extent to which decisions and commitments are honored, and for the effectiveness of resistance actions taken, are an essential source of strategic capacity, and are areas in which culturo-behavior analysis and associated research methods are potentially particularly strong.

Leadership Networks and Circle Processes

In OBM the focus has typically been on the ability of leaders to analyze and guide interlocking behavioral contingencies that together produce the desired aggregate product of the organization. Goltz and Hietapelto (2003) suggest that leadership is a function of two factors:

> (1) the power holder's skill in determining, in a complex environment, what workgroup, departmental, or organizational responses will be reinforced, and (2) his or her skill in using antecedents and reinforcement dimensions he or she controls to direct members of a workgroup toward making those responses. (p. 8)

This has proven to be an effective model in traditional business settings. Due to the complex nature of the environments within which social movements operate, and the just-discussed need for distributed and shared leadership, a broader scope is commonly required (Mattaini & Holtschneider, 2017). Large-scale social movements are not in most cases effectively managed by centralized leadership in the ways that corporations are managed by an executive team. Resistance movements often rely on networks of largely autonomous units, including for decision-making. Helvey (2007) noted that

> in a crisis situation [common in resistance movements] decision-making often needs to be pushed to the lowest level so that action can proceed in a timely way; this requires that such skills are in people's repertoires and have been encouraged in advance. (p. 114)

Military counter-insurgency forces recommend a similar process, to the extent possible pushing down responsibility for decision-making to those closest to the action (The United States Army and Marine Corps, 2007).

Because of these unique characteristics, collective leadership is often the better choice (Ganz, 2009; Mattaini & Holtschneider, 2017; Sharp, 2005). Such collective leadership notably appears in Skinner's (1948) utopian novel *Walden two* in which decisions are made by a Board of Planners. Such a structure is supported by research that indicates that collective problem-solving is more effective at addressing complex issues (Lee et al., 2010; Nemeth & Ormiston, 2007; Wuchty et al., 2007). One such method of collective problem-solving is the circle process. Found in aboriginal and First Nations cultures around the world, circle processes are becoming increasingly familiar in a variety of contemporary contexts, including classrooms, correctional systems, and organizational settings. Restorative circle methods are often used as alternatives to punishment, instead giving the perpetrator the opportunity to make amends with their victim(s) and repair harm. The research on the effectiveness of restorative justice practices is encouraging, although still emerging. The model is well established in schools, where the evidence is clear that alternatives such as suspension and expulsion are linked to higher rates of involvement with the criminal justice system – but also increasingly within a wide range of organizations and communities (Mattaini & Holtschneider, 2017). Circle specialists (e.g., Ball et al., 2010; Riestenberg, 2012) offer guidelines for basic circle planning processes at community levels, including planning for community building, decision-making, conflict resolution, and accountability, all of which can be and have been useful in multiple ways for movement building. Mattaini and Holtschneider offer a behavioral perspective on these processes:

> Circles are a method of dialogue rooted in the values of interconnectedness, equality, and respect – principles that are often absent in contemporary decision-making among persons of different cultures and power differentials. Circles bring together affected stakeholders through an organized behavioral process that can dramatically increase the probability that divergent perspectives can be understood, evaluated, and collectively incorporated into planning and problem-solving. (p. 130)

As an example, Figure 11.1 highlights key practices structured into a problem-solving circle as might be used in meetings of members of all three of Ackerman and Kruegler's (1994) strata, especially at the most stressful times. Mattaini and Holtschneider (2017) note that well-implemented circle processes are highly consistent with behavioral systems principles, constructing a network of collective practices within circle cultures, including:

- Practices encouraging empathy
- Practices encouraging acceptance and commitment to action, grounded in common values (standard emphases in Acceptance and Commitment training in OBM, Moran, 2011)

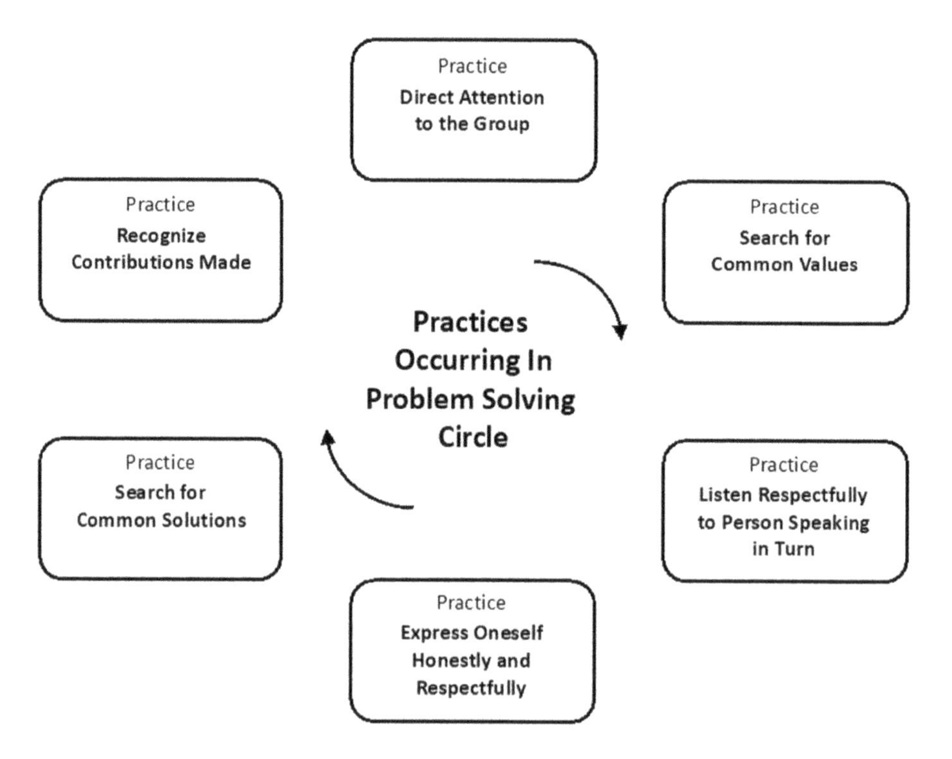

FIGURE 11.1 Practices shaped in a successfully organized problem-solving circle. Adapted with permission from Mattaini and Holtschneider (2017).

- Practices maximizing opportunities for reinforcing cooperation and innovation
- Practices minimizing aversives while encouraging expressions of differences in perspectives

Organizations characterized by Ganz's (2009) principles supporting strategic capacity and building a culture of practices like those incorporated in circles offer promising support for strategic advance.

ESSENTIAL LEADERSHIP PRACTICES

Much has been written about effective leadership in OBM. For example, Krapfl and Kruja (2015) provide two key features of leadership which should not be a surprise to behavior scientists: the behaviors of the leaders, and the context in which they take place. Additionally, Krapfl and Kruja describe common characteristics of leaders, including setting the mission and/or vision, ethical values, execution skills, innovation/creativity, communication skills, enabling skills, team-building skills, confronting adversity, tenacity, and culture-building skills. Conceptual work has placed emphasis on setting the mission and/or vision: "leaders create new verbal relations between the current and future states of the organization" (Houmanfar et al., 2015, p. 15) and creating an environment to support and motivate employees to execute the mission and vision set by leadership (Daniels & Daniels, 2004).

While there is substantial organizational literature discussing "key traits" or "characteristics" of effective leaders, behavior scientists think instead in terms of key practices and repertoires. This shift implies potential for learning, and is supported in much of the resistance movement literature. For example, Robert Helvey in particular, drawing on his own strategic military experience and the nonviolent resistance literature, focuses on repertoires like "set the example," "know the people you expect to lead," and "give others credit for success" (2007, pp. 107–115). There is considerable technical literature and research on leadership, particularly in OBM, that can provide general guidance that may be adapted for local situations. Just a note, however: the language of "behavior management" may be problematic in many resistance settings due to relational framing {behavior management ≈ oppression} to the many who have often experienced those in control as disempowering and oppressive. References framed as effective leadership practices and repertoires are more likely to evoke positive responses.

Clarity and Communication

Effective communication is essential to effective leadership. There is a robust research base on the importance of leadership in OBM, much of it including a focus on verbal behavior (e.g., Houmanfar et al., 2009). Effective communication is clearly necessary for leaders of social change. Most importantly, leaders are responsible for communicating the vision and mission, specifying the behaviors necessary to achieve them, and providing feedback to reinforce goal-directed behavior (targeted communication). Studies find that in the face of ambiguity, individuals will self-generate their own rules based on their observations, which may in some cases prove counterproductive (Houmanfar et al., 2009). Within such organizational networks, ambiguity can also lead to the emergence of independent self-organizing units with their own networks of relational processes that may change the very structure of the organization.

Effective leadership communication involves the specification of rules in the technical sense – description of the consequences of behavior. The environments of resistance movements are, by their nature, ambiguous, and explicit rules reduce environmental ambiguity. A key leadership function under such conditions is to elaborate rules that are sufficient, only as explicit and complex as necessary, and accurate. Movement networks often require tight discipline, which requires communication and monitoring, especially in cases where the danger of injury or death is high (Mattaini, 2013; Sharp, 2005). In cases where networks are widely dispersed, communication between cells can be challenging, and considerable local creativity may be required to remain in contact – one reason knowledge of local conditions is so critical.

Structuring Recognition and Reinforcement

A constructive (or "constructional" to use Goldiamond's (2002) term) approach, as proposed by Goldiamond, emphasizes constructing and reinforcing new patterns of behavior to replace undesired or problematic behavior, as opposed to simply trying to suppress undesired or problematic behavior. According to Mattaini (2013):

> On the practical side, he [Goldiamond] concluded, as had B.F. Skinner before him, that the data demonstrated that constructing new patterns supported by arranged or preferably natural reinforcement was (a) more acceptable to people and (b) more likely to result in lasting change, whereas suppressive strategies did not take away the inclination to act and therefore were ever fragile. (p. 61)

Effective leaders provide high levels of monitoring in the beginning, fading over time, and relatively immediate consequences that emphasize recognition of positive contributions, encouragement, and – very valuable for resistance communities – opportunities to describe how one or one's group achieved positive outcomes (Komaki & Apter-Desselles, 1998). Many leaders believe they provide much more recognition than their followers report they are receiving (Daniels & Daniels, 2004). Some minimize the importance of recognition because they believe followers should participate out of commitment, without requiring thanks or praise, but in fact in situations where "success" may be far distant, effective reinforcement is what maintains and deepens involvement.

Research on schedules of reinforcement in laboratory and applied settings provides guidance for social and environmental movements as well; for example, intermittent schedules assist in maintaining commitment and momentum. The reinforcers involved are often different than in other settings, however; in resistance movements, social reinforcers are primary – and essential. Merely indicating generically that everyone is doing great is seldom effective, and may well be read as insincere or even manipulative. Instead, reinforcement should be detailed, genuine, and tailored to the individual. Mattaini (2013) indicates:

> The best course is to develop a culture in which participants regularly encourage each other, but leaders need to pay attention to make sure this encouragement does not fade too drastically, since there is a natural tendency among humans to reduce effort over time. (p. 126)

Attention to discretionary action that goes beyond the norm is particularly important as such action can often advance progress in the campaign, and serve as a motivating antecedent (establishing operation), for both the individual and peers. Komaki and Apter-Desselles (1998) and Daniels and Daniels (2004) provide additional useful guidance for managing recognition.

Aversive Practices and Strategic Components

Given the high level of stress that is common for movement leadership, and the high levels of aversive and coercive control in many contemporary societies, it is understandable that threats or scolding may slip into leaders' repertoires, often responding with threats or scolding. Subjecting members of the movement to aversive tactics would likely have a devastating impact on morale and commitment to the group. Aversive control over time inevitably evokes a continuum of behavior ranging from withdrawal or emotional behavior to acts of counter control by the followers (Mattaini, 2013). Thus, leaders of resistance movements should be cautioned, and should caution themselves, to refrain from frequent aversive interactions. There are serious conditions in which honestly delivered correction or retraining may be required, and even in which participants must be dropped from the movement organization. Collective procedures like circle processes and mentoring can often help in resolving issues within the group in less aversive ways. Remembering that the goal is to construct a culture of encouragement and recognition within the movement, and to have an impact on the issue for which the group was formed, aversive interactions should be defused whenever possible.

Most Western people and communities rely on aversives to exercise coercive control; rates of aversives within families, schools, governments, criminal justice, and many other institutions are extremely high (Sidman, 2001). It is therefore not surprising that resistance movements often consider using aversive methods to coerce compliance from opponents. This is a complex issue. Nonviolent aversive action is involved in cases where, for example, protest is a strategically chosen option, even if usually in combination with persuasion (Mattaini, 2013, Chapter 8). The extent of aversive action to engage in is a key decision in many protest movements; protest alone can often produce a change in the actions of opponents, but those changes are often very fragile, especially if other powerful forces oppose them. Counter-controlling aversive responses rather than compliance are common in such cases. Often additional strategic choices therefore need to be considered, including, for example, alternative persuasive tactics, constructive noncooperation, disruptive noncooperation, or resource disruption (Mattaini, 2013).

This leaves us with one critical question related to coercion which we can only cover briefly here: questions of violent action or property damage as resistance tactics. In many resistance efforts in which threats of or actual violence are used by opponents, it may seem only natural to strike back, riot, or loot. The data on responding to violence with violence are very clear, however; in most cases it will fail, typically both immediately and over the long term. The opponent typically has many more resources for such situations, legitimacy of the movement among the larger population is weakened or lost, discipline within the resistance group is likely to break down entirely, and noncombatants are more likely to be injured (Chenoweth & Stephan, 2011; Mattaini, 2013). Maintaining discipline and avoiding any violence is sometimes very challenging, but essential. Strategic nonviolence is more effective in the long run; the most successful are the toughest, those willing to "stand in the fire."

The question of property damage in resistance efforts has been ethically challenging over at least the past six decades. The best analyses suggest that, for example, disabling a military-style attack vehicle that is about to be used against nonviolent protesters may be justifiable or even necessary (Deming, 1971). Most other property damage, including the kind of damage that occurs in looting is not surprising as a response from oppressed people, but has two risks: the loss of legitimacy among the broader population whose support is often essential, and distraction within the resistance group from their justice-focused goals. Relying primarily on aversives by resistance movements is therefore as complex and often problematic as in clinical or regular organizational settings.

Directing Attention to Social and Environmental Justice

Actions directing attention to injustice and the structures contributing to it are themselves important leadership practices, both within the organization and to the larger public. This is a shared responsibility of both resistance leaders (often in the media), and behavior scientists in their research, publications, and also in the media. For example, publications in the *Journal of Organizational Behavior Management* have tackled issues relating to the role and responsibility of business and industry relating to "negative externalities" such as environmental pollution, the impact of corporate practices on employee health, and poverty as a result of corporate lobbying (Biglan, 2009, 2020); consumer practices that may influence organizational values (Houmanfar et al., 2015; Foxall, 2015); and wellbeing (Geller, 2015). According to Biglan (2009), "externalities continue precisely because there is no cost to the organizations for practices that impose these costs on third parties" (p. 215). He recommends that societies evolve cultural practices to address the real problems of negative externalities. Under some circumstances, consumers have power to direct organizational attention toward sustainability, and social and environmental justice. "Customers are *selectors*, and, along with the income they generate, they constitute the *selecting environment*" (Malott, 2016, p. 106). Where this dynamic is present, industries are more likely to be responsive to consumer demand, whether the demand is for a higher quality of products, lower prices, or for organizations to engage in practices in line with social movements. Consumers are increasingly paying attention to the social practices of the brands they buy and the services they use.

Resistance movements have harnessed this power, made stronger with their numbers, in their attempts to garner public support. In recent examples, companies have faced both backlash and surges of support for making statements in relation to Black Lives Matter. This has been called brand activism, and a recent survey found that 64% of consumers would reward companies (with their dollars) for engaging in socially significant behavior (Duarte, 2020). Resistance movements can in some cases harness the pressure of capitalism to garner support for their movements and to push their agendas. This includes support in the form of funding (e.g., Livingston, 2020), or in the form of social pressure, as in a recent example of Nike pulling all merchandise for the Washington Redskins football team due to movements demanding the end of cultural appropriation in sports (Grimes, 2020).

The challenges that remain are substantial. Marginalized and oppressed populations often have fewer resources than those with strong political connections, and therefore typically experience limited commercial or media power. Consumers, often including those experiencing injustice, generally carry relational frames directly or indirectly encouraging purchases and options that are often inconsistent with social and environmental justice. Such actions are encouraged by corporate narratives of the value of consumerism – narratives that result in increased poverty and injustice, devastate the environment, and inflame political divisions (Biglan, 2020). The political system and political actors also often support the cause of corporate capitalism to their own benefit, even when that damage is clear. Alternative narratives (for example, Grant, 2011) supporting resistance through alternative lifestyles are possible, and can be encouraged through resistance movements and resistance communities leveraging action for justice, and among coalitions of such movements working to convincingly offer such alternatives to the general public.

EXPERIMENTATION

Culturo-behavior science can offer valuable resources for resistance movements and other forms of action supporting social and environmental justice, as reflected in this chapter and other work the authors have done. Still, this is very early science, and there is much more to learn. Gandhi (1970) described himself as a scientist, and explicitly thought of and described his work as an intentional series of moral experiments. He stated,

> I claim for them nothing more than does a scientist who, though he conducts his experiments with the utmost accuracy, forethought, and minuteness, never claims any finality about his conclusions, but keeps an open mind regarding them. I have gone through deep self-introspection, searched myself through and through, and examined and analyzed every psychological situation. Yet I am far from claiming any finality or infallibility about my conclusions. (p. 51)

This remains the best stance for the present: all personal and collective action should be viewed as experimental in nature. As we attempt to contribute to resistance movements, it is useful to think of our goals as recursively examining a broad range of existing data, exploring observationally, developing conceptual models from those observations, and – with movement participants – developing experiments where possible to test those models (Bates, 1950, Chapter 18). As we learn more about both practices in movement cultures and practices within oppressive opponents, it should become increasingly possible to refine our methods. One advantage for behavior science is that our research methods, especially but not limited to small-N studies and community-level time-series designs, have the potential to offer real contributions to resistance movements as we advance together toward justice, equity, and increments in global wellbeing.

STUDY QUESTIONS

1. Describe the relationship between resistance movements and organizational behavior management.
2. Explain two of the authors' points regarding the conceptualization of resistance movements as organizations.
3. The authors state that "Mobilization is important, but often insufficient ..." Explain this in your own words.
4. Describe some of the authors' main points regarding the use of social media in resistance movements (at least two).
5. What are "circle practices" and why might they be helpful in organizing resistance movements?

NOTE

1. Some of the content in this chapter has been adapted with permission from Mattaini, 2013, © Mark A. Mattaini.

REFERENCES

Ackerman, P. & Kruegler, C. (1994). *Strategic nonviolent conflict: The dynamics of people power in the twentieth century.* Praeger.
Alinsky, S.D. (1971). *Rules for radicals: A pragmatic primer for realistic radicals.* Vintage.
Ball, J., Caldwell, W., & Pranis, K. (2010). *Doing democracy with circles: Engaging communities in public planning.* Living Justice Press.
Bates, M. (1950). *The nature of natural history.* Princeton University Press.
Biglan, A. (2009). The role of advocacy organizations in reducing negative externalities. *Journal of Organizational Behavior Management, 29*(3–4), 215–230. doi: 10.1080/01608060903092086
Biglan, A. (2020). *Rebooting capitalism: How we can forge a society that works for everyone.* Values to Action.
Chenoweth, E. & Stephan, M.J. (2011). *Why civil resistance works: The strategic logic of nonviolent conflict.* Columbia.
Cortright, D. (2010). *Gandhi and beyond: Nonviolence for a new political age.* Paradigm.
CSG Justice Center Staff (2020, July 17). States taking action: Law enforcement. *The Council of State Governments: Justice Center.* https://csgjusticecenter.org/states-taking-action-law-enforcement/?mc_cid=eeb849f869&mc_eid=%5bUNIQID%5d&mc_cid=eeb849f869&mc_eid=91e5c1a01c
Daniels, A.C. & Daniels, J.E. (2004). *Performance management: Changing behavior that drives organizational effectiveness.* Performance Management Publications.
Deming, B. (1971). *Revolution and equilibrium.* Grossman.
Dixon, M.R., Belisle, J., Rehfeldt, R.A., & Root, W.B. (2018). Why we are still not acting to save the world: The upward challenge of a post-Skinnerian behavior science. *Perspectives on Behavior Science, 41*(1), 241–267. doi: 10.1007/s40614-018-0162-9
Duarte, F. (2020, June 12). Black Lives Matter: Do companies really support the cause? *BBC.* https://www.bbc.com/worklife/article/20200612-black-lives-matter-do-companies-really-support-the-cause
Fawcett, S.B., Bernstein, G.S., Czyzewski, M.J., Greene, B.F., Hannah, G.T., Iwata, B.A., Jason, L.A., Mathews, R.M., Morris, E.K., Otis-Wilborn, A., Seekins, T., ... Winett, R.A. (1988). Behavior analysis and public policy. *The Behavior Analyst, 11*(1), 11–25. doi: 10.1007/BF03392450

Foxall, G.R. (2015). Consumer behavior analysis and the marketing firm: Bilateral contingency in the context of environmental concern. *Journal of Organizational Behavior Management, 35*(1–2), 44–69. doi: 10.1080/01608061.2015.1031426

Gandhi, M.K. (1970). *Gandhi: Essential writings*. Edited by V. V. Ramana Murti. Gandhi Peace Foundation.

Ganz, M. (2009). *Why David sometimes wins: Leadership, organization, and strategy in the California Farm Worker Movement*. Oxford University Press. doi: 10.1093/acprof:oso/9780195162011.001.0001

Geller, E.S. (2015). Seven life lessons from humanistic behaviorism: How to bring the best out of yourself and others. *Journal of Organizational Behavior Management, 35*(1–2), 151–170. doi: 10.1080/01608061.2015.1031427

Gladwell, M. (2010, October 4). Small change: Why the revolution will not be tweeted. *The New Yorker*. https://www.newyorker.com/magazine/2010/10/04/small-change-malcolm-gladwell

Goldiamond, I. (2002). Toward a constructional approach to social problems: Ethical and constitutional issues raised by applied behavior analysis. *Behavior and Social Issues, 11*, 108–197. Originally published in *Behaviorism, 2*, 1–84. doi: 10.5210/bsi.v11i2.92

Goldiamond, I. (1984). Training parents and ethicists in nonlinear behavior analysis. In R.F. Dangel & R.A. Polster (Eds.), *Parent training: Foundations of research and practice* (pp. 504–546). Guilford.

Goltz, S.M. & Hietapelto, A. (2003). Using the operant and strategic contingencies models of power to understand resistance to change. *Journal of Organizational Behavior Management, 22*(3), 3–22. doi: 10.1300/J075v22n03_02

Grant, L.K. (2011). In response: Can we consume our way out of climate change? A call for analysis. *The Behavior Analyst, 34*(2), 245–266. doi: 10.1007/BF03392256

Grimes, P.J. (2020, July 2). Nike removes Redskins name, apparel from its website. *NBC Sports*. https://www.nbcsports.com/washington/redskins/nike-removes-redskins-name-apparel-its-website

Helvey, R.L. (2007). *On strategic nonviolent conflict: Thinking about the fundamentals*. Albert Einstein Institution.

Houmanfar, R.A., Alavosius, M.P., Morford, Z.H., Herbst, S.A., & Reimer, D. (2015). Functions of organizational leaders in cultural change: Financial and social well-being. *Journal of Organizational Behavior Management, 35*(1–2), 4–27. doi: 10.1080/01608061.2015.1035827

Houmanfar, R.A. (2017). Organizational behavior management & socio-cultural issues: Do we have a role to play? *Journal of Organizational Behavior Management, 37*(2), 121–125. doi: 10.1080/01608061.2017.1331103

Houmanfar, R., Rodrigues, N.J., & Smith, G.S. (2009). Role of communication networks in behavioral systems analysis. *Journal of Organizational Behavior Management, 29*(3–4), 257–275. doi: 10.1080/01608060903092102

Impelli, M. (2020, July 22). Portland dads with leaf blowers join Wall of Moms to blow back tear gas from police. *Newsweek.*: https://www.newsweek.com/portland-dads-leaf-blowers-join-wall-moms-blow-back-tear-gas-police-1519673

Komaki, J.L. & Apter-Desselles, M. (1998). *Leadership from an operant perspective*. Routledge.

Krapfl, J.E. & Kruja, B. (2015). Leadership and culture. *Journal of Organizational Behavior Management, 35*(1–2), 28–43. doi: 10.1080/01608061.2015.1031431

Layng, T.J. (2009). The search for an effective clinical behavior analysis: The nonlinear thinking of Israel Goldiamond. *The Behavior Analyst, 32*(1), 163–184. doi: 10.1007/BF03392181

Lee, K., Brownstein, J.S., Mills, R.G., & Kohane, I. S. (2010). Does collocation inform the impact of collaboration? *PLOS One, 5*(12), e14279, 1–6. doi: 10.1371/journal.pone.0014279

Lee, S.C. (2020). Social work and social media: Organizing in the digital age. *Journal of Public Health Issues and Practices, 4*(1), 1–6. doi: 10.33790/jphip1100158

Livingston, M. (2020, June 16). These are the major brands donating to the Black Lives Matter movement. *cnet*. https://www.cnet.com/how-to/companies-donating-black-lives-matter/

Malott, M.E. (2016). Selection of business practices in the midst of evolving complexity. *Journal of Organizational Behavior Management, 36*(2–3), 103–122. doi: 10.1080/01608061.2016.1200511

Mattaini, M.A. (2013). *Strategic nonviolent power: The science of satyagraha*. Athabasca University Press.

Mattaini, M.A. (in press). Cultural systems analysis. In T.M. Cihon & M.A. Mattaini (Eds.), *Behavior science perspectives on culture and community*. Springer.

Mattaini, M.A., Esquiredo-Leal, J.L., Ardila Sánchez, J.G., Richling, S.M., & Ethridge, A.N. (in press). Public policy advocacy in culturo-behavior science. In T.M. Cihon & M.A. Mattaini, (Eds.), *Behavior science perspectives on culture and community*. Springer.

Mattaini, M.A. & Holtschneider C. (2017). Collective leadership and circles: Not invented here. *Journal of Organizational Behavior Management, 37*(2), 126–141. doi: 10.1080/01608061.2017.1309334

McCarthy, R.M. & Sharp, G. (1997). *Nonviolent action: A research guide*. Garland.

Mobus, G.E. & Kalton, M.C. (2015). *Principles of systems science: Understanding complex systems*. Springer. doi: 10.1007/978-1-4939-1920-8

Moran, D.J. (2011). ACT for leadership: Using acceptance and commitment training to develop crisis-resilient change managers. *International Journal of Behavioral Consultation and Therapy, 7*(1), 66–75. doi: 10.1037/h0100928

Moreno, J.E. (2020, July 25). "Wall of Vets" joins protests in Portland. *The Hill*. https://thehill.com/homenews/state-watch/509047-wall-of-vets-grandparents-join-protests-in-portland

Nemeth, C.J. & Ormiston, M. (2007). Creative idea generation: Harmony versus stimulation. *European Journal of Social Psychology*, *37*(3), 524–535. doi: 10.1002/ejsp.373
Piven, F.F. (2006). *Challenging authority: How ordinary people change America*. Rowman & Littlefield.
Piven, F.F. & Cloward, R.A. (1979). *Poor people's movements: Why they succeed, how they fail*. Vintage.
Riestenberg, N. (2012). *Circle in the square: Building community and repairing harm*. Living Justice Press.
Roose, K.M. & Mattaini, M.A. (in press). Challenging violence: Toward a 21st century, science-based "Constructive Programme." In T.M. Cihon & M.A. Mattaini, (Eds.), *Behavior science perspectives on culture and community*. Springer.
Schell, J. (2003). *The unconquerable world: Power, nonviolence, and the will of the people*. Metropolitan Books.
Sharp, G. (1980). Skinner and Gandhi on defeating violence (Appendix C). In G. Sharp, *Social power and political freedom*. Extending Horizons Books.
Sharp, G. (with contributors) (2005). *Waging nonviolent struggle: Twentieth-century practice and twenty-first-century potential*. Extending Horizons Books.
Sharp, G. & Raqib, J. (2010). *Self-liberation: A guide to strategic planning for action to end a dictatorship or other oppression*. Albert Einstein Institution.
Sidman, M. (2001). *Coercion and its fallout*. Authors Cooperative.
Skinner, B.F. (1948). *Walden two*. Macmillan.
Skinner, B.F. (1987). Why we are not acting to save the world. In B. F. Skinner, *Upon further reflection* (pp. 1–14). Prentice-Hall.
Stephan, M.J. & Thompson, T.P. (2018, April 4). Why you should never underestimate a bunch of well-organized teenage protesters. *The Washington Post*. https://www.washingtonpost.com/news/democracy-post/wp/2018/04/04/why-you-should-never-underestimate-a-bunch-of-well-organized-teenage-protesters/?noredirect=on&utm_term=.597f132f1587
The United States Army and Marine Corps. (2007). *Counter-insurgency field manual*. University of Chicago Press.
Wamsley, L. (2020, July 22), In Portland, a "Wall of Moms" and leaf blowers against tear gas. *NPR*. https://www.npr.org/sections/live-updates-protests-for-racial-justice/2020/07/22/894197681/in-portland-a-wall-of-moms-and-leaf-blowers-against-tear-gas
Willems, E.P. (1974). Behavioral technology and behavioral ecology. *Journal of Applied Behavior Analysis*, *7*(1), 151–165. doi: 10.1901/jaba.1974.7-151
Wuchty, S., Jones, B.F., & Uzzi, B. (2007). The increasing dominance of teams in production of knowledge. *Science*, *316*(5827), 1036–1039. doi: 10.1126/science.1136099
Young, A., Selander, L., & Vaast, E. (2019). Digital organizing for social impact: Current insights and future research avenues on collective action, social movements, and digital technologies. *Information and Organization*, *29*(3), 1–6. doi: 10.1016/j.infoandorg.2019.100257

12

Interbehavioral Psychology and Organizational Behavior Management

Mitch Fryling, Linda J. Hayes, and Will Fleming

Organizational behavior management (OBM) is a subfield of Applied Behavior Analysis (ABA) that focuses on the study of behavior within organizational settings (Wilder et al. in this text). As a distinct area of application within ABA, OBM has many unique features. For instance, while it may be argued that all settings are complex in the sense that they are multi-factored, behavior occurring in organizational settings may be especially prone to influence from contextual factors. Though the field of behavior analysis may be increasingly interested in studying contextual variables, the study of behavior in organizations *requires* us to think more contextually than many in behavior analysis are accustomed to doing. Moreover, this complexity is related to how we think about behavior more generally, including *what* we are studying and how we go about studying it. We draw attention to these conceptual hurdles not only because they are relevant to the development and refinement of the philosophical foundation of ABA and OBM specifically, but also because humans spend much of their lives behaving in organizational settings and organizations are involved in many of the most important issues in society today. As such, getting a better grasp on what we are studying in OBM has social implications, influencing the focus of research and the development of applied technology.

The aim of the present chapter is to highlight some themes in the OBM literature, emphasizing the conceptual problems they raise, and to propose potential solutions and future directions. Our chapter is conceptual in nature, and is informed by interbehaviorism (Kantor, 1953) and Interbehavioral Psychology (Kantor, 1958). In particular, we address matters related to the complexity of the subject matter in OBM, the relationship of OBM to basic behavioral principles, and interdisciplinary science.

ORGANIZATIONS AS COMPLEX SETTINGS

Behavior analysts working in the area of OBM have made a great deal of progress over the years (e.g., Dickinson, 2001; VanStelle et al., 2012). For example, interventions focused on providing feedback (e.g., Alvero et al., 2001), clarifying tasks (e.g., Tittelbach et al., 2007), providing behavior-based training (e.g., Gravina et al., 2013), and more, have all been addressed in the OBM literature (Wilder et al. Chapter 1 of this text). While these lines of research have proven useful and have provided the field with many tools to assess and improve employee performance, it is also the case that much of this work does not focus on the aforementioned complexity entailed in organizational settings. Indeed, a recent review of the literature on OBM research in human service settings found that the majority

DOI: 10.4324/9781003198949-12

of the research in this area has focused on front line staff engaging in relatively repetitive tasks (Gravina et al., 2018). In short, although organizational behavior is likely to occur in complex contexts, the research in OBM hasn't always focused on and/or captured this context specifically. At the same time, several lines of work in the field suggest that OBM is moving toward an increased focus on this complexity. In the following section we provide a brief overview of these lines of work.

Research Focusing on Organizational Complexity in OBM

Behavioral Systems Analysis

One longstanding area of scholarship and application in OBM that seems to be focused on organizational complexity is behavioral systems analysis (BSA; e.g., Malott, 2003; McGee & Cowley-Koch, Chapter 5 in this text). While providing a thorough overview of BSA is far beyond the scope of the present chapter, we note that all BSA models place emphasis on a much larger context than is typically done in behavior analytic work. Generally speaking, the BSA approach involves considering various *levels of analysis*, with the exact number of levels depending on the particular model. For example, BSA often involves consideration of the organizational level, the process level, and finally, the job-performer level. Interestingly, the majority of research and application in OBM focuses on the job-performer level and, as such, falls within the purview of what is considered Performance Management. Although BSA is considered to be behavior analytic in nature, there is little focus on traditional contingency constructs (e.g., discriminative stimuli, reinforcers, extinction, etc.) in these models. This is not surprising as there is no reason to assume that principles derived from the study of individual behavior would operate similarly at a systems level. Still, it is noteworthy that much of the terminology used within BSA is unique to BSA and is not used in other divisions of the discipline of behavior analysis.

Metacontingencies

The topic of metacontingencies also seems to be focused on the sort of complexity present in organizational settings, and there has been much interest in this area within behavior analysis over the years (Zilio, 2019). While different models emphasize various factors that contribute to cultural and organizational circumstances (Glenn, 2004; Glenn et al., 2016; Houmanfar et al., 2010; Malott, Chapter 6 of this text), all metacontingency models describe how occurrences of culturants are controlled by selecting events or receiving systems. Unlike operants, *culturants* refer to classes of interlocking behavioral contingencies (i.e., functionally related behavior of multiple individuals) that result in *aggregate products* (i.e., outcomes of interlocking behavioral contingencies; Hunter, 2012) that can be selected by external environments. By identifying the culturant as the unit of selection (see L.J. Hayes & Houmanfar, 2004), metacontingencies offer a versatile and scalable approach for understanding how group interactions and their products are controlled by cultural consequences (i.e., events contingent on the production of aggregate products that select culturants; Tadaiesky & Tourinho, 2012; Vichi et al., 2009) without having to perform more molecular analyses regarding how group members interact with one another. Although earlier conceptualizations of metacontingencies reflect two- and three-term contingency constructs (Glenn, 1988; Glenn, 2004; Houmanfar & Rodrigues, 2006) and experimental preparations were similarly aligned in this way (e.g., Hunter, 2012), the metacontingency enterprise has since developed constructs (Glenn et al., 2016), analytical logic (Baia & Sampaio, 2019), and experimental procedures (e.g., Soares et al., 2019) that are not shared with behavior analysis at large.

Derived Stimulus Relations/Acceptance and Commitment Training

An additional line of research aimed at expanding the scope of research and practice in OBM pertains to derived stimulus relations and Acceptance and Commitment Training (e.g., Bond & Flaxman, 2006; S.C. Hayes et al., 2006; Moran, 2015; Moran et al., Chapter 8 of this text). Included in this category is work on values in OBM (e.g., Herbst & Houmanfar, 2009). While it is beyond the scope of the present chapter to describe this area of work in detail, there is an emphasis on understanding the extent to which derived stimulus relations are involved in organizational behavior, and on interventions targeting these derived relations to improve cooperation, establish relations between work behavior and values, and more. This work stands out because it represents a focus on aspects of behavior that are not commonly addressed in the OBM literature. In addition, this literature also involves a great deal of terminology that is not typically involved in traditional behavior analytic work.

Cultural Science

Similar to the other lines of work we have described thus far, research and scholarship in the area of cultural science also represents a move to understand the complexities of group and organizational settings (e.g., Cihon & Mattaini, 2019; Mattaini, 2019). This work is unique in that it specifically suggests a more interdisciplinary or transdisciplinary path to behavior analytic work on organizational complexity. Like the aforementioned areas, this work also attempts to expand upon traditional contingency analyses, incorporates new terms, and more (e.g., even new disciplines). This line of work seems to be somewhat distinct from the others in that there is an explicit call for interdisciplinary and/or transdisciplinary work to address complexity in groups and organizations.

While there are other lines of work within OBM that are focused on improving the understanding of organizational and group complexity (e.g., Foxall, Chapter 7 of this text), these examples highlight the extent to which work in this area requires behavior analysts to think differently about their subject matter than they may be accustomed to. We will elaborate on this theme more later in the chapter. In the following section we review an additional area of work within OBM, which also raises the question of *what* is being studied in OBM.

BASIC BEHAVIORAL PRINCIPLES IN ORGANIZATIONAL SETTINGS

Behavior analysis has long aspired to be a single integrated science comprised of various sub-domains. While some may debate the boundaries among these domains, it is generally agreed that behavior analysis involves theory and philosophy, basic research in the experimental analysis of behavior (EAB), Applied Behavior Analysis, with practice sometimes being considered an additional area and/or extension of the applied domain (Moore & Cooper, 2003). These domains are thought to interact and influence one another in various ways. For example, the experimental analysis of behavior aims to understand basic behavioral processes and how they operate in various circumstances, with the assumption that those processes will have implications for theory development and application in socially important circumstances. Applied Behavior Analysis involves studying those basic processes in socially important contexts, and practice involves using the resulting technology in service delivery (e.g., in clinical work in the field). Theory and philosophy are typically held as being the foundation of all of these areas of work. Assuming that this is the case, that each of these areas work together in some sort of organized harmony, one might assume that there is be some sort of relationship between these various areas of work. For example, one might assume that work in the experimental analysis of behavior would be cited by workers in Applied Behavior Analysis, and vice versa, and that both would abide by established behavioral theory and philosophy.

While aspirations to achieve and sustain relations among the various sub-divisions of the behavior analytic enterprise seems to be common among the workers in these sub-domains, there has long been concern that the field is not as integrated as one might hope. In 1981 Poling et al. (1994) assessed the extent to which research published in applied journals cited literature from the experimental analysis of behavior and found that there were few citations from the experimental analysis of behavior in the applied literature. In fact, the authors found that the applied and experimental analysis of behavior seemed to be becoming increasingly separate areas. This circumstance hasn't seemed to change over time, as similar findings have been discovered over many years (e.g., Elliott et al., 2005; Poling et al., 1994). While the relationship between EAB and ABA has been of particular interest, the relationship between other areas of behavior analysis has also been considered (e.g., theory/philosophy and application; Fryling, 2013; Pierce & Epling, 1980). Thus, while it might be assumed that the different sub-domains of behavior analysis would interact and participate in the larger science of behavior, this is not how things have unfolded thus far. The separation among the various domains may be owing to many factors. For example, we have argued that part of the reason for this may pertain to how behavior analysis is conceptualized as a discipline (L.J. Hayes et al., 2009). This topic continues to be of considerable interest to behavior analysts. For example, Kyonka and Subramaniam (2018) recently described a model of research across the basic-applied spectrum.

Similar themes have also been explored in the OBM literature. For example, Normand et al. (1999) explored the extent to which research published in the *Journal of Organizational Behavior Management* (*JOBM*) was described in terms of behavioral principles. Specifically, Normand and colleagues reviewed research articles and case study reports published in *JOBM* between 1992 and 1997. Articles were examined to see whether behavioral principles were mentioned in the introduction or discussion. The authors found that 35% of the studies reviewed discussed behavioral principles. It is noteworthy that while basic experimental studies were fewer in number, they were more likely to discuss behavioral principles relative to applied studies (55% of basic studies, 32% of applied studies). In discussing the results of their analysis in the context of Pierce and Epling's (1980) critique of the *Journal of Applied Behavior Analysis*, as well as recent trends in the OBM literature at the time (e.g., Balcazar et al., 1989), Normand and colleagues wondered whether *JOBM* should be called the *Journal of Applied Feedback* (p. 54). The authors concluded their analysis by providing possible recommendations, including the creation of different categories of articles that focus more or less on behavioral principles.

More recently, DiGennaro Reed et al. (2016) examined the role of behavioral principles in the OBM literature in more detail. The authors first identified articles published in *JOBM* between the years of 2006–2015, and then included articles that a) involved a research or case study, b) mentioned a behavioral principle in the introduction or discussion, and c) included a description of functional relations among those principles and the effects of an intervention (simply mentioning a principle in the introduction or discussion was not enough to be included) in their analysis. Once these articles were identified, the authors then coded whether or not the study was conducted in a laboratory or field setting, and which behavioral principles were referenced.

DiGennaro Reed et al. (2016) noted an overall increase in the number of articles that mentioned behavioral principles in the introduction or discussion, with 52.8% of the articles doing so, compared to 35% in the Normand et al. (1999) analysis. When looking at *which* behavioral principles were mentioned most often, reinforcement was included in 71.6% of the articles, followed by discriminative stimulus (34.3%), and motivating operations (31.3%). Similar to the analysis by Normand and colleagues (1999), articles conducted in laboratory settings, while fewer in number when compared to field studies, were more likely to involve behavioral principles. DiGennaro Reed et al. (2016) noted that the increased interest in translational research in the field more generally may partly account for the increase found in *JOBM*. Still, the authors noted that the percentage could be higher, and that *JOBM* could address this by requiring a consideration of behavioral principles as a condition of publication. The authors also commented that it was interesting that reinforcement was the most frequently mentioned principle, and that rule-governed behavior was not examined more often (only 19% of the articles). This stands out because reinforcement most likely participates in the generation of rules, pertains to rule-following, and more within organizational settings.

The analyses of both Normand et al. (1999) and DiGennaro Reed et al. (2016) highlight some general themes within the OBM literature. Interestingly, while strategies to improve the percentage of studies articulating the work in behavioral terminology were proposed in both articles, the possibility that the principles themselves were not aligned with the dynamics of organizational settings was not considered. In other words, it's possible that the principles of behavior derived from observations of individuals, often in less than fully naturalistic settings, may not lend themselves to the analysis of behavior in organizational settings. That is, the results of these analyses may also point to something more fundamental about *what* is being studied in OBM. Taken together with the converging movements we described in the previous section, it seems like an alternative means of conceptualizing the subject matter of behavior analysis and its implications for OBM, is worth considering.

Summary

In our perspective, each of these areas of research and scholarship point to potential deficiencies with traditional conceptualizations of behavior. Indeed, each of these areas of work highlight the extent to which contingency constructs may fail to capture the complexities of behavior in organizational settings. From our perspective traditional continency constructs fail us in the area of complex behavior more generally (also see Kantor, 1970), and some of the areas of research and scholarship we described earlier in the chapter may represent a sidestepping of important issues related to the subject matter of the field itself. To us, an alternative to this sidestepping is to reconsider what we are studying in behavior analysis more fundamentally. Fortunately, an alternative conceptualization is already available – it is the field construct described by J.R. Kantor (Kantor, 1958). The following section describes the interbehavioral field, and especially draws attention to setting conditions, which are critical to understanding behavior in organizational settings.

THE INTERBEHAVIORAL FIELD

Interbehavioral psychology is a relatively little known approach to the science of behavior. While there are many features of both interbehaviorism (a philosophy of science; Kantor, 1953) and interbehavioral psychology (a specific approach to the science of psychology; Kantor, 1958) that are relevant to behavior analysis (e.g., Fryling & L.J. Hayes, 2018), interbehavioral psychology is especially known for the field construction. The interbehavioral field or psychological event (these terms are used synonymously) is Kantor's way of conceptualizing the subject matter of behavior science. There are many unique features of the field construct, and it is an especially distinct alternative to more common ways of conceptualizing the subject matter in behavior analysis. For example, the term *inter*behavior itself, as opposed to behavior, represents a shift in emphasis away from behavior and toward a more specific focus on *relations* among stimulation and responding. It is for this reason that interbehaviorists prefer the

Sf←→Rf double-headed arrow as opposed to the S→R or S→R→Sr linear type models which are common in behavior analysis. The Sf←→Rf interaction is only part of the subject matter in the interbehavioral perspective, however. The psychological event construct is represented by the following formula – PE = C (k, sf, rf, st, hi, md). Here PE stands for the psychological event, C for the integrated nature of all of the factors comprising the event (i.e., that the psychological event is *one* integrated whole), k for the unique configuration of factors in each and every event, sf for stimulus function, rf for response function, st for setting conditions, hi for interbehavioral history, and md for medium of contact (Kantor, 1958, p. 14).

Implications for Behavior Analysis and OBM

One of the most distinguishing features of the psychological event (PE) pertains to its being one integrated happening; it is one event. This feature of the PE is represented by the C in the aforementioned formula. Psychological stimulation (sf), responding (rf), interbehavioral history (hi), setting conditions (st), the medium of contact (md), and the unique configuration of all of these factors (k) occur in one moment, as one, unitary happening. Indeed, the various factors involved in the PE are distinguished only for analytical purposes. In other words, there is no stimulation without responding, no stimulation absent setting conditions, no setting conditions absent an interbehavioral history, and so on.

For example, an employee working in an organization may be considered from the perspective of the PE. First, the individual's behavior is occurring in a setting – there are many setting conditions present. These likely involve the method by which the employee is paid, the role the individual has, the relation of this role to other roles in the organization, the work hours and how they are distributed throughout the week, variability in tasks, benefits associated with the job, and so on. Moreover, the employee may have had a recent evaluation that was only moderately positive, and a recent argument with a peer. The employee may be working on a task (e.g., analyzing data) which has been associated with a great deal of aversive stimulation in the past (e.g., comments from a supervisor), such that the stimulus functions of the task are more than they might seem to an observer. This is to say that the task has acquired the substitute stimulus functions of the aversive experiences associated with it. These experiences may be complex, and the employee's interbehavioral history is always present in the situation. There may also be a deadline associated with completing the task (an additional setting factor), adding to the complexity of the PE. These are only some of the factors that might be considered from the perspective of the PE. As this brief description highlights, there are many factors that may be taken into account when employee behavior is conceptualized from the perspective of the PE.

This analysis stands in contrast to other ways of thinking about behavior in behavior analysis. For example, in respondent conditioning, stimuli are conceptualized as preceding responding, and moreover to *elicit* or otherwise "cause" responding to occur (S→R). Constructs involved in operant conditioning follow a similar linear sequence, where behavior occurs and is followed by a consequence (e.g., a reinforcer or a punisher), which impacts the evocative functioning of antecedent stimuli (e.g., discriminative or s-delta) in the future (S→R→Sr). Even the motivating operation construct depends upon this linear way of thinking (see L.J. Hayes & Fryling, 2014). By contrast, the PE construct does not follow this sort of linear sequence. Importantly, this does not mean that the PE is ahistorical. Quite the contrary, interbehavioral history is a participating factor. It is just that this history is participating in the *present* psychological event, and as this event evolves, so does the history. From the perspective of the PE, all psychological happenings are happening here in the present, including references to the past and future (i.e., the implication being that there is no past or future distinct from the present; see Fryling & L.J. Hayes, 2010; L.J. Hayes, 1992).

Moreover, given that each factor outlined in the PE is a participant in a unitary happening, none of its "parts" are held to be causing others of its "parts" (Fryling & L.J. Hayes, 2011; L.J. Hayes et al., 1997). One implication of this is that a more detailed consideration of the factors participating in the current event is encouraged. By contrast, operating in terms of traditional operant constructs leads to a more or less exclusive emphasis on understanding the consequences of behavior. Given the emphasis on the consequences of behavior in behavior analysis, including OBM, it should come as no surprise that a significant amount of research has explored the use of feedback contingent on employee behavior (e.g., Alvero et al., 2001). However, to reiterate, from the perspective of the PE, behavior is not conceptualized as distinct from stimulation, history or the setting, the implication being that all such factors are worthy of the same consideration as is given to consequences in behavior analysis.[1]

Another feature of the PE warrants further consideration. Kantor's PE construct involves stimulus and response *functions* (Kantor, 1958). The inclusion of the word *function* is critical: interbehavioral psychology makes a distinction between stimulus objects and stimulus functions, and similarly, between the movements of an organism and response functions, whereby attention is drawn to the psychological aspects of both stimulating and responding. These distinctions permit an analysis of responding with respect to stimuli that are psychologically but not physically present or, in Kantor's terms, responding with respect to substitute stimulation. These constructions facilitate the analysis of a wide range of behavior that is often assumed to be private or otherwise unavailable for study in mainstream behavior analysis. While this is not the specific focus of the present chapter, it does have implications for research in OBM that focuses on studying derived stimulus relations, values, and related topics.

As we have described thus far the PE construct places emphasis on all of the factors participating in psychological happenings. We have long been interested in this construct because of the many implications it has for improving the study of complex behavior in natural science perspective, and for developing a more coherent philosophical foundation for work in behavior analysis (e.g., L.J. Hayes & Fryling, 2018; Fryling & L.J. Hayes, 2018). Given the interest in addressing more of the complex circumstances in organizational settings, we believe the PE construct also has implications for expanding the scope of work in OBM, and to provide a foundation for researchers involved in these various areas of scholarship to converge upon.

To some extent, the PE construct may have already influenced both theory and research within OBM. Houmanfar and colleagues' (2010) elaborated five-term contingency was constructed on the basis that, like PEs, sociological events or SEs (i.e., interlocking behavior between group members that produces aggregate products) are composed of interrelated factors that should not be considered independent of one another and cannot be reduced to events below the sociological level of analysis (or cultural level, see Glenn, 2010). Although this approach – based on differentiating SEs from PEs – has been shown to be useful for understanding organizational complexity in important areas such as leadership (Houmanfar et al., 2015), the participation of rules and policies (Houmanfar et al., 2009; Smith et al., 2011), and cultural resiliency (Ardila Sánchez et al., 2019; Houmanfar et al., in press), the PE construct has more to offer than a useful template of characteristics for other event constructs. Organizations can be considered to be irreducible units that operate on the sociological level, but they necessarily involve PEs in which individuals behave on the psychological level (Houmanfar et al., 2010). While this work is influenced by interbehavioral thinking in some ways, it is noteworthy that the premise for all of this work is the contingency construct, albeit an elaborated version of that contingency. Contingency constructs, regardless of how they are elaborated upon, maintain the traditional linear thinking associated with those constructs and cannot be confused with the field perspective of interbehavioral psychology. While we could emphasize various aspects of the PE and consider their impact on organizational behavior, the following section considers the topic of setting conditions specifically.

SETTING CONDITIONS IN ORGANIZATIONAL SETTINGS

Setting conditions (Kantor, 1924; Kantor & Smith, 1975) may consist of various contextual factors, such as an individual being very tired or sick, the weather, being inside a busy restaurant or café, or more specific to the present chapter, aspects of an organizational context (including factors both internal and external to the organization). Like all factors in the PE, the participation of setting conditions is important to consider as the presence or absence of particular setting conditions amounts to an entirely different event. That is, the addition or removal of a particular setting factor changes the organization of the other factors comprising the PE. In the context of understanding organizational behavior, setting conditions may consist of rules, regulations, and laws pertaining to the organization. For example, a particular leader within an organization may make a decision to allocate more or less of the annual budget to a particular department within an organization (e.g., marketing), having implications for the budgets of other departments (e.g., training). Many of these changes may be external to the organization. For example, an institution receiving government funding of some sort may be greatly impacted by political efforts and regulations of various sorts (e.g., funding or defunding particular organizations, or placing restrictions on what sort of work receives funding and what doesn't). We consider some examples of setting conditions within the context of higher education below, a setting with which the authors are particularly familiar.

Higher Education

Institutions that provide post-secondary instruction are complex entities with a multitude of setting conditions participating in the behavior life of all of those involved in the organization. While many individuals behave within higher education organizations, for present purposes we generally refer to staff, faculty, administrators, and students in our examples.

Funding

Exactly how higher education is paid for varies from country to country, state to state, institution to institution, and even across programs within particular institutions. For example, some higher education institutions rely almost exclusively on money generated from student tuition, and the behavior of many individuals involved in the institution are impacted by this setting condition. Administrators are immediately tasked with how much they should charge for tuition, as all other aspects of the institution depend on this number. This includes the sorts of buildings they might need for classes, how many support staff and faculty are hired, how much those individuals should be paid, how much the school is able to spend on marketing, and other operations. Further, this sort of setting condition puts undue emphasis on increasing enrollment. In other words, additional enrollment is likely to be encouraged. This example stands in contrast to organizations that rely on government funding or state tuition dollars, which have their own host of setting conditions that may impact the behavior of all involved.

Accreditation and Certification/Licensure Standards

Many programs, especially those where professional training is provided, have to contend with degree standards and requirements from the university/college as well as from accreditation and certification/licensure boards. For example, some accreditation bodies have requirements specifying the number of full-time faculty that must be employed in support of a particular program. This sort of requirement has implications for administrators who must weigh the pros and cons of accreditation and commit to having the appropriate number of faculty to maintain accreditation. Other accreditation standards may pertain to the student to faculty ratio in a given program at a given time, with implications for the number of students that may be enrolled. The presence or absence of these setting conditions impact the behavior of many involved in the educational enterprise. For example, faculty and students may be less likely to conduct quality work in circumstances where the ratio of students to faculty is too high. Alternatively, a standard requiring a lower student to faculty ratio may serve to prevent faculty from being overly burdened with instructional demands and permit more opportunities to focus on research and scholarship. This, in turn, will have implications for the experiences of students, faculty, staff, the reputation of the program, and so on.

Accreditation and Licensure/Certification standards can also impact *what* is taught within a particular degree program. This can range from how many courses are required for a given program to the specific content of those courses. For example, behavior analytic training programs have had numerous changes in standards from certification boards over the years, with a resulting impact on the behavior of many within the program (e.g., administrators involved in curriculum design, faculty teaching courses, students pursuing certification, etc.). The more extensive and detailed these conditions are, the less room for decision-making by individuals within the institution. Extensive requirements of these sorts may function as a setting condition preventing the differentiation of programs in the field. Rules and regulations pertaining to clinical supervision can also impact those involved in training programs. For example, placing a cap on the number of individuals who may be involved in a group supervision meeting has implications for the cost of providing that training, for the work of the supervisor, the experience of the students, and so on. We provide only some examples here; clearly, accreditation and licensure/certification standards impact the behavior of many involved in organizations that offer professional training programs.

Rules and Regulations Within Institutions

There are many ways in which rules, regulations, and practices within organizations can function as setting conditions for behavior in the workplace. For example, decisions about how resources are allocated, or how an organization responds to an issue from the outside, may have implications for employee behavior. Importantly, these setting conditions may operate at several levels. For example, a department may have a spending budget for the year, and how the department goes about deciding how to spend money allocated to it may impact employee behavior. Sometimes leaders make resource allocation decisions on their own, eliminating input from those involved in the group. At the other extreme are circumstances where decisions are made entirely by the group, perhaps voted upon, etc. The implications of these setting conditions may be far-reaching. For example, individuals may be more or less interested in efforts to cut costs within the organization if they have no say in how that money is used when it is saved. At the same time, depending on one's role within an organization, they may have varying perspectives as to how particular decisions may impact the group over time, including neighboring groups, and so on.

As these brief examples highlight, setting factors are an important area for further research and practice in OBM. We have only touched upon select issues pertinent to higher education. There are many additional setting factors present and relevant to behavior analytic training programs, including the job market for students in particular areas. The fast-paced, ever-changing world that most organizations operate in requires OBM to consider setting conditions more carefully. Looking at organizational behavior from the perspective of the PE may facilitate this work.

It should also be noted that organizational practices may be considered to be cultural in nature from an interbehavioral perspective, emphasizing the participation of setting factors in the evolution of cultures. According to Kantor (1982), cultural behavior refers to institutional stimulus-response functions in which responses with respect to the same stimulus objects are shared across individuals and acquired under group auspices (i.e., the group participates in the development of these shared stimulus functions). As such, interactions among individuals not only participate in the performances of cultural behavior but also in its development; group auspices are important for understanding the processes by which cultural behavior evolves. However, as Kantor (1982) points out, group auspices are not limited to those operating from a psychological perspective, but from others as well, including sociological and anthropological perspectives.

This suggests that constructing an interdisciplinary account of organizational and cultural behavior may be warranted, echoing similar advocations from within behavior analysis (Glenn, 1988; Mattaini, 2019). To this end, we offer a word of caution to behavior analysts considering interdisciplinary endeavors.

INTERDISCIPLINARY SCIENCE

While the majority of this chapter has focused on reconceptualizing the subject matter of behavior analysis in an effort to improve our understanding of behavior in organizational settings, an additional means of improving our understanding of this complexity pertains to interdisciplinary sciences. Indeed, there is no question that the disciplines of sociology and economics, among others, have something to teach us about behavior in groups. Our perspective on interdisciplinary sciences is informed by a few key assumptions derived from Kantor's philosophy of science, interbehaviorism (Kantor, 1953). First, disciplinary sciences distinguish themselves from other sciences by identifying a unique feature of the natural world to study, a unique relation to focus upon. This is not to suggest that disciplinary subject matters are distinct from one another *in principle*. Identifying a unique subject matter is indeed an arbitrary procedure. Still, it is an important step as it pertains to the extent to which a disciplinary science provides an orientation to something *new* about the constellation of factors comprising the world of natural happenings. It also involves identifying subject matter boundary conditions, particularly with respect to neighboring sciences, so as to avoid the collapsing of all of the sciences, especially neighboring sciences, together into one. Important to remember here is that something new may emerge from the disciplinary science, which may be lost when subject matter boundaries are not respected. The focus on something new has implications for how interdisciplinary sciences may be conceptualized, too. In short, genuine interdisciplinary relationships involve studying the *relationship between two or more disciplinary subject matters*. This relationship is a *new relationship*, and because of this, interdisciplinary enterprises focused upon such a relationship may result in the discovery of something unique, something new.

Still, interdisciplinary sciences are not often conceptualized this way, and there are a number of problematic conceptualizations of interdisciplinary science that may limit the extent to which these efforts result in the understanding of something new. For instance, collaborative efforts, wherein two disciplines are working in a parallel manner, can sometimes be misconstrued as being interdisciplinary in nature. From our perspective, while additional disciplinary progress may occur under these arrangements, nothing *new* emerges, nothing which may be considered interdisciplinary in nature. In other cases, interdisciplinary efforts involve compromising one of the participating science's boundary conditions, as when a behavior scientist and biologist work together on what amounts to a study on something biological in nature. Here, something is learned about the subject matter of the science of biology, but nothing is gained about the subject matter of behavior science. The outcome of this is that the value of one of the disciplines (in this case behavior science) is diminished; the relationship is one of helping the other discipline make progress.

These sorts of interdisciplinary arrangements occur for several reasons. For example, it may be that one of the participating disciplines has a lack of clarity as to its specific subject matter and how it relates to the subject matter of neighboring sciences. It might also be a matter of failing to appreciate the cumulative nature of disciplinary sciences, and/or a misunderstanding of disciplinary sciences more generally. Importantly, none of this is to suggest that interdisciplinary sciences are problematic in principle; rather that they may be pursued in ways that prevent the discovery of something new, something unique and distinct from that discovered in participating disciplinary sciences themselves. The interbehavioral approach to both disciplinary and interdisciplinary sciences highlights important issues to consider as we pursue interdisciplinary research and practice (see L.J. Hayes & Fryling, 2009 for a more elaborate discussion of these issues).

CONCLUSION

The aim of the present chapter was to consider the implications of J.R. Kantor's interbehavioral psychology, and especially the psychological event construct, for the field of organizational behavior management. We first reviewed several areas of research and scholarship in OBM, including the ongoing assessment of the extent to which behavioral principles are considered in OBM research. We then reviewed the psychological event construct in detail, highlighting its unique features and distinguishing it from more traditional ways of conceptualizing and studying behavior within behavior analysis and OBM. We placed special emphasis on setting conditions, and described examples of various setting conditions in organizational contexts (specifically higher education). We concluded the chapter with brief comments on valid interdisciplinary relationships from an interbehavioral perspective.

STUDY QUESTIONS

1. In your own words, what are some of the main points the authors are making in the section that reviews different areas of research focusing on organizational complexity?
2. Describe two of the themes identified by the authors in the section on basic behavioral principles in OBM.
3. Compare and contrast the interbehavioral field construct and more traditional operant-contingency constructs in behavior analysis.
4. Provide an original example of a setting condition that is relevant to understanding organizations.
5. How do the authors conceptualize interdisciplinary sciences? What are two problematic conceptualizations of interdisciplinary sciences from the authors perspective?

NOTE

1. This is not to suggest that feedback and training are not important and useful areas of research and application, just that they are not the *only* important issues. Conceptualizing behavior as a PE draws attention to additional factors to consider, with implications for both research and practice.

REFERENCES

Ardila Sánchez, J.G., Houmanfar, R.A., & Alavosius, M.P. (2019). A descriptive analysis of the effects of weather disasters on community resilience. *Behavior and Social Issues*, *28*(1), 298–315. doi: 10.1007/s42822-019-00015-w

Alvero, A.M., Bucklin, B.R., & Austin, J. (2001). An objective review of the effectiveness and essential characteristics of performance feedback in organizational settings. *Journal of Organizational Behavior Management*, *21*, 3–29. doi: 10.1300/J075v21n01_02

Baia, F.H. & Sampaio, A.A.S. (2019). Distinguishing units of analysis, procedures, and processes in cultural selection: Notes on metacontingency terminology. *Behavior and Social Issues, 28*(1), 204–220. doi: 10.1007/s42822-019-00017-8

Balcazar, F.E., Shupert, M.K., Daniels, A.C., Mawhinney, T.C., & Hopkins, B.L. (1989). An objective review and analysis of ten years of publication in the *Journal of Organizational Behavior Management. Journal of Organizational Management, 10*, 7– 37. doi: 10.1300/J075v10n01_02

Bond, F.W. & Flaxman, P.E. (2006). The ability of psychological flexibility and job control to predict learning, job performance, and mental health. *Journal of Organizational Behavior Management, 26*, 113–130. https://doi.org/10.1300/J075v26n01_05

Cihon, T.M. & Mattaini M.A. (2019). Editorial: Emerging cultural and behavioral systems science. *Perspectives on Behavior Science, 42*, 699–711. doi: 10.1007/s40614-019-00237-8

Dickinson, A.M. (2001). The historical roots of organizational behavior management in the private sector: The 1950s–1980s. *Journal of Organizational Behavior Management, 3-4*, 9–58. doi: 10.1300/J075v20n03_02

DiGennaro Reed, F.D., Henley, A.J., Rueb, S., Crabbs, B., & Giacalone, L. (2016). Discussion of behavioral principles in *Journal of Organizational Behavior Management*: An update. *Journal of Organizational Behavior Management, 36*(2–3), 202–209. doi: 10.1080/01608061.2016.1200938

Elliott, A.J., Morgan, K., Fuqua, R.W., Ehrhardt, K., & Poling, A. (2005). Self- and cross-citations in the Journal of Applied Behavior Analysis and the Journal of the Experimental Analysis of Behavior: 1993–2003. *Journal of Applied Behavior Analysis, 38*, 559–563. doi: 10.1901/jaba.2005.133-04

Fryling, M.J. (2013). Philosophy, theory, and the practice of applied behavior analysis. *European Journal of Behavior Analysis, 14*, 45–54. doi: 10.1080/15021149.2013.11434444

Fryling, M. J. & Hayes, L. J. (2010). An interbehavioral analysis of memory. *European Journal of Behavior Analysis, 11*, 53-68. https://doi.org/10.1080/15021149.2010.11434334

Fryling, M.J. & Hayes, L.J. (2011). The concept of function in the analysis of behavior. *Mexican Journal of Behavior Analysis, 37*, 11–20. doi: 10.5514/rmac.v37.i1.24686

Fryling, M.J. & Hayes, L.J. (2018). J.R. Kantor and behavior analysis. *Conductual, 6*, 86–94. http://conductual.com/articulos/J.%20R.%20Kantor%20and%20Behavior%20Analysis.pdf

Glenn, S.S. (1988). Contingencies and metacontingencies: Toward a synthesis of behavior analysis and cultural materialism. *The Behavior Analyst, 11*(2), 161–179. doi: 10.1007/BF03392470

Glenn, S.S. (2004). Individual behavior, culture, and social change. *The Behavior Analyst, 27*, 133–151. doi: 10.1007/BF03393175

Glenn, S.S. (2010). Metacontingencies, selection, and OBM: Comments on "Emergence and metacontingency." *Behavior and Social Issues, 19*(1), 104–110. doi: 10.5210/bsi.v19i0.3220

Glenn, S.S., Malott, M.E., Andery, M.A.P.A., Benvenuti, M., Houmanfar, R.A., Sandaker, I., Todorov, J.C., Tourinho, E.Z., & Vasconcelos, L.A. (2016). Toward consistent terminology in a behaviorist approach to cultural analysis. *Behavior and Social Issues, 25*(1), 11–27. doi: 10.5210/bsi.v25i0.6634

Gravina, N.E., Loewy, S., Rice, A., & Austin, J. (2013). Evaluating behavioral self-monitoring with accuracy training for changing computer work postures. *Journal of Organizational Behavior Management, 33*(1), 68–76. doi: 10.1080/01608061.2012.729397

Gravina, N., Villacorta, J., Albert, K., Clark, R., Curry, S., & Wilder, D. (2018). A literature Review of organizational behavior management interventions in human service settings From 1990–2016. *Journal of Organizational Behavior Management, 2–3*, 194–224. doi: 10.1080/01608061.2018.1454872

Hayes, L.J. (1992). The psychological present. *The Behavior Analyst, 15*, 139–144. https://doi.org/10.1007/BF03392596

Hayes, L.J., Adams, M.A., & Dixon, M.R. (1997). Causal constructs and conceptual confusions. *The Psychological Record, 47*, 97-112. https://doi.org/10.1007/BF03395214

Hayes, L.J., Dubuque, E.M., Fryling, M.J., & Pritchard, J.K. (2009). A behavioral systems analysis of behavior analysis as a scientific system. *Journal of Organizational Behavior Management, 29*(3/4), 315–332. doi: 10.1080/01608060903092169

Hayes, L.J. & Fryling, M.J. (2009). Toward an interdisciplinary science of culture. *The Psychological Record, 59*, 679–700. doi: 10.1007/BF03395687

Hayes, L. J., & Fryling, M. J. (2014) Motivation in behavior analysis: A critique. *The Psychological Record, 64*, 339-347. https://doi.org/10.1007/s40732-014-0025-z

Hayes, L.J. & Fryling, M.J. (2018). Psychological events as integrated fields. *The Psychological Record, 68*, 273–277. doi: https://doi.org/10.1007/s40732-018-0274-3

Hayes, L.J. & Houmanfar, R. (2004). Units and measures: A response to Glenn and Malott. *Behavior and Social Issues, 13*(2), 107–111. doi: 10.5210/bsi.v13i2.379

Hayes, S.C., Bond, F.W., Barnes-Holmes, D., & Austin, J. (2006). *Acceptance and mindfulness at work: Applying Acceptance and Commitment Therapy and Relational Frame Theory to Organizational Behavior Management.* Taylor & Frances.

Herbst, S.A. & Houmanfar, R. (2009). Psychological approaches to values in organizations and organizational behavior management. *Journal of Organizational Behavior Management, 29*, 47–68. doi: 10.1080/01608060802714210

Houmanfar, R.A., Ardila Sánchez, J.G., & Alavosius, M.P. (in press). Role of cultural milieu in cultural change: Mediating factor in points of contact. In T.M. Cihon and M. Mattaini (Eds.), *Behavior science perspectives on culture and community*. Springer.
Houmanfar, R., A., Alavosius, M.P., Morford, Z.H., Herbst, S.A., & Reimer, D. (2015).
Functions of organizational leaders in cultural change: Financial and social well-being. *Journal of Organizational Behavior Management, 35*(1–2), 4–27. doi: 10.1080/01608061.2015.1035827
Houmanfar, R. & Rodrigues, N.J. (2006). The metacontingency and the behavioral contingency: Points of contact and departure. *Behavior and Social Issues, 15*, 13–30. doi: 10.5210/bsi.v15i1.342
Houmanfar, R., Rodrigues, N.J., & Smith, G.S. (2009). Role of communication networks in behavioral systems analysis. *Journal of Organizational Behavior Management, 29*(3), 257–275. doi: 10.1080/01608060903092102
Houmanfar, R., Rodrigues, N.J., & Ward, T.A. (2010). Emergence and metacontingency: Points of contact and departure. *Behavior and Social Issues, 19*(1), 78–103.
Hunter, C.S. (2012). Analyzing behavioral and cultural selection contingencies. *Revista Latinoamericana de Psicología, 44*(1), 43–54.
Kantor, J.R. (1924). *Principles of psychology (Vol. 1)*. Principia Press.
Kantor, J.R. (1953). *The logic of modern science*. Principia Press.
Kantor, J.R. (1958). *Interbehavioral psychology*. Principia Press.
Kantor, J.R. (1970). An analysis of the experimental analysis of behavior (TEAB). *Journal of the Experimental Analysis of Behavior, 13*, 101–108. doi: 10.1901/jeab.1970.13-101
Kantor, J.R. (1982). *Cultural psychology*. Principia Press.
Kantor, J.R. & Smith, N.W. (1975). *The science of psychology: An interbehavioral survey*. Principia Press.
Kyonka, E.G.E. & Subramaniam, S. (2018). Translating behavior analysis: A spectrum rather than a road map. *Perspectives on Behavior Science, 41*, 591–613. doi: 10.1007/s40614-018-0145-x
Malott, M.E. (2003). *Paradox of organizational change: Engineering organizations with behavioral systems analysis*. Context Press.
Malott, M.E. & Glenn, S.S. (2006). Targets of intervention in cultural and behavioral change. *Behavior and Social Issues, 15*, 31–57. doi: 10.5210/bsi.v15i1.344
Mattaini, M.A. (2019). Out of the lab: Shaping an ecological and constructional cultural systems science. *Perspectives on Behavior Science, 42*, 713–731. doi: 10.1007/s40614-019-00208-z
Moore, J. & Cooper, J.O. (2003). Some proposed relations among the domains of behavior analysis. *The Behavior Analyst, 26*, 69–84. doi: 10.1007/BF03392068
Moran, D.J. (2015). Acceptance and Commitment Training in the workplace. *Current Opinion In Psychology, 2*, 26–31. doi: 10.1016/j.copsyc.2014.12.031
Normand, M., Bucklin, B., & Austin, J. (1999). The discussion of behavioral principles in *JOBM*. *Journal of Organizational Behavior Management, 19*(3), 45–56. doi: 10.1300/J075v19n03_04
Pierce, W.D. & Epling, W.F. (1980). What happened to analysis in applied behavior analysis? *The Behavior Analyst, 3*, 1–9. doi: 10.1007/BF03392287
Poling, A., Alling, K., & Fuqua, R.W. (1994). Self-and cross-citations in the *Journal of Applied Behavior Analysis* and the *Journal of the Experimental Analysis of Behavior*: 1983–1992. *Journal of Applied Behavior Analysis, 27*, 729–731. doi: 10.1901/jaba.1994.27-729
Soares, P.F.R., Martins, J.C.T., Guimarães, T.M.M., Leite, F.L., & Tourinho, E.Z. (2019). Effects of continuous and intermittent cultural consequences on culturants in metacontingency concurrent with operant contingency. *Behavior and Social Issues, 28*(1), 189–202. doi: 10.1007/s42822-019-00009-8
Smith, G.S., Houmanfar, R., & Louis, S. (2011). The participatory role of verbal behavior in an elaborated account of metacontingency: From conceptualization to investigation. *Behavior and Social Issues, 20*, 122–146. doi: 10.5210/bsi.v20i0.3662
Tadaiesky, L. T. & Tourinho, E. Z. (2012). Effects of support consequences and cultural consequences on the selection of interlocking behavioral contingencies. *Revista Latinoamericana de Psicología, 44*(1), 133– 147.
Tittelbach, D., Deangelis, M., Sturmey, P., & Alvero, A. M. (2007). The effects of task clarification, feedback, and goal setting on student advisors' office behaviors and customer service. *Journal of Organizational Behavior Management, 27*(3), 27–40. doi: 10.1300/J075v27n03_03
VanStelle, S.E., Vicars, S.M., Harr, V., Miguel, C.F., Koerber, J.L., Kazbour, R., & Austin, J. (2012). Publication history of the *Journal of Organizational Behavior Management*: An objective review and analysis: 1998–2009. *Journal of Organizational Behavior Management, 32*, 93–123. doi: 10.1080/01608061.2012.675864
Vichi, C., Andery, M.A.P.A., & Glenn, S.S. (2009). A metacontingency experiment: The effects of contingent consequences on patterns of interlocking contingencies of reinforcement. *Behavior and Social Issues, 18*, 41–57. doi: 10.5210/bsi.v18i1.2292
Zilio, D. (2019). On the function of science: An overview of 30 years of publications on metacontingency. *Behavior and Social Issues, 28*, 46–76. doi: 10.1007/s42822-019-00006-x

13

High-Reliability Organizations

A Technical Context to Coordinate Behaviors

Mark P. Alavosius and Ramona A. Houmanfar

ORGANIZATIONAL CONTEXT

Throughout the chapters of this text there is much discussion of behavior (B) and how expansive understanding of principles of behavior enable the design of interventions to improve organizational performance. Principles of behavior inform discussion of how this scientific foundation of selection processes contributes to behavior assessment and management practices. Relatively less discussion in OBM, over the decades of its development as a discipline, has addressed the nuances of design of organizational settings (O) and the cultural context in which behavior is managed (M), although that is advancing with consideration of interlocking behavioral contingencies, macro- and metacontingencies and systemic selection processes at multiple levels such as individual, group, and culture (Glenn, 1988; Glenn, 2004; Malott & Glenn, 2006; Houmanfar et al., 2010). An assumption seems implicit in much OBM theorizing that contingencies that manage individual behavior are easily transported across organizational models employed in various industries and sectors of the economy. There appears to be less analysis toward assessing the target organization's structure and level of maturity within an industry. Cursory descriptions of industry and setting are seen as sufficient to foster generalization of OBM interventions as those manipulations coordinate processes fundamental to human behavior.

The chapters of this book reveal the status of the OBM discipline in 2020. The extent to which this tendency to not explicate organizational structures, levels of coordination, their maturity path and control systems is enabling or disabling advances in organized behavior change is a provocative area to explore. We posit that deeper exploration of organizational models, their developmental history and their control systems within the context of broad social factors are areas for more work to enrich OBM.

Trends in Work Environment

Several trends are evident that are shaping future directions in reaserch on the work environment (see Chapter 2 in this text for a discussion in relation to health and safety). Automation is replacing human conduct in many workplaces and workers, like machine operators and food workers, are hard hit. COVID-19 is accelerating this transformation. Many occupations are vulnerable as automation affects vast numbers of workers who will need to transfer to new industries. The Mckinsey Global Institute (Manyika et al., 2017) projects that 400 to 800 million jobs will be replaced globally by robotic automation by 2030. Basic repetitive work

DOI: 10.4324/9781003198949-13

behaviors, like assembling parts during manufacturing, are completed by robots. Supervisory behaviors to evaluate variation in operations and direct solutions (e.g., schedule route changes in transportation/distribution networks) are increasingly completed by machines, some of which use AI to learn how to improve. The role of humans at work in automated processes is not entirely eliminated but is evolving in significant ways. Humans are called upon to monitor the processes, detect issues, and interact with other humans within such systems and become part of a complex, learning system that adapts, modifies itself and evolves toward more effective and efficient operations.

Globalization is another trend shaping organizations, their supply chains, and markets. Global employers need to operate with much diversity (e.g., regulatory environments, populations, etc.) to align operations across many countries and cultures. Following a globalized manufacturing process from raw materials to a product purchased by consumers (e.g., sports apparel) reveals a chain of coordinated steps conducted by an army of workers from cotton fields in Bangladesh that harvest raw materials to looms in Thailand that weave fabric to factories in China that sew garments that are then shipped to distribution centers across the globe to be sold by vendors everywhere. Purchasers in a trendy store may not be aware of the intricate coordination of labor across a far-flung enterprise needed to bring this year's fashion to their nearby stores. Organizational leaders are immersed in these challenges. The market selects the product produced by the most efficient and affordable production process and savvy leaders look to adjust their organization to maximize efficiency, profit, and perhaps meet other goals like environmental protection. The globalization process is orderly as it selects effective models. Organizational leaders' choices as to where to locate various elements are driven by value propositions. The consumer may not see much of this as the unsavory aspects are camoflaged, but it is foundational to the design of work organizations.

The birth and growth of worldwide organizations crucial to providing essential goods and services to vast populations reveal that organizational structures vary from command-control models with strong centralized leadership to distributed network models that involve teamwork with sub-elements having much autonomy. Organizational models evolve over time to adapt to contexts. Start-up companies may begin as small, centrally controlled organizations that innovate and gain footing to compete. Centralized control enables accountability and leaders' intimate contact with all facets of the operation. As small organizations develop, acquire wealth and market share, organizational design evolves to structures that standardize successful operations and maintain quality. Companies, perhaps under regulatory pressure, operate under established standards that dictate complexity. Supply chains providing raw materials, energy, logistical support and even human capital develop to sustain the industry. The innovating organization that captures market share from competitors transforms into the standard bearer. Tolerance for operational drift reduces. The location of a company in its developmental history is relevant to the goals of the organization, how it is designed, and how it is managed. Along its growth trajectory, which changes as a company progresses from birth to maturity to potential decline, are values that guide governance, investment, evaluation, and management.

Organizational variations at different waypoints distinguish leaders in an industry from the pack that follows. These organizational designs are essential platforms to support human (behavioral) factors that affect operational integrity, control drift, foster innovation, propel growth, or limit expansion (Houmanfar et al., 2015). The composition of the leadership team, their competencies and values, roles and responsibilities are influential as leaders guide development (Krapfl & Kruja, 2015). Start-up companies benefit from leaders who attract talent, seek investments, and propel innovation. Established organizations benefit from leaders who standardize effective operations, sustain quality, and minimize drift. Komisar (2001) describes a succession of leaders, with varying essential competencies, that are probable as a company develops from start-up to mature operation. The wellbeing of organizational members, those in the local community, and consumers are influenced by a multitude of factors that interlock organizational levels and entrench organizations within the supply chains and receiving system. Examination of OBM initiatives within this organizational context may expand OBM concepts and procedures as the discipline matures. The boundaries of the organizational unit being addressed in OBM set the parameters for assessment (e.g., by OBM practitioners). For example, consider the sports apparel company that outfits the affluent weekend adventurer. Does the OBM practitioner address issues in the storefronts only to examine how customers value the current offerings and adjust the behavior of salespeople to increase sales? If so, the analysis does not examine issues like child labor used in the plantations, overworked, underpaid laborers in sweatshops making the backpacks, and transit of product via environmentally hazardous trade routes. The boundaries of the analysis frame behavioral targets, OBM interventions, and expected results.

In some sectors of the economy, such as transportation, the energy sector, communications, and distribution systems, for example, we see mature, established organizations that are increasingly technical, with automated contexts where work behaviors are repetitive, high-rate, and standardized in complex processes to reduce variation from designed procedures. In these mature, leading organizations, failure can be catastrophic to workers, the community and environment. Consider disasters in transportation, refineries, pipelines, railroads, oil rigs, and nuclear power plants that are infrequent but devastating. High-risk industries such as these are increasingly automated, but the human elements which remain have the potential to either avert or assist the evolution of a disaster and sustain or collapse the enterprise. As engineering controls become increasingly effective, hyper-efficiency is achieved. Variations in human behavior emerge as the greatest threat to operational integrity. Analysis of this is a worthy target for OBM.

HIGH-RELIABILITY ORGANIZATIONS

High-reliability organizations (HROs) are interesting and unique settings in which managerial and operational behaviors are intricately interlocked across levels of the organization. A complex network of human and machine-controlled contingencies coordinate behavior. HROs are notable for formal, systematic efforts to measure operations with great precision, learn from incidents and accidents, and institutionalize corrections to improve health, safety, and quality performance (Dekker & Woods, 2009). The learning curve at this level of organizational maturity involves human learning and machine learning that propels progress toward measurable levels of excellence. The pace of learning is accelerated relative to less technically advanced organizations as massive data collection tracks changes and guides improvement. Artificial intelligence contributes to pattern detection and understanding sources of variability that contribute to unsatisfactory performance. The surveillance systems in HROs measure, often in real time, characteristics of behaviors (e.g., speed, accuracy, duration, latency of responding, etc.) of humans and machines as they conduct complex operations. For example, members of a flight crew flying from Los Angeles to London are tracked by a variety of sensors and their every action is measured with high fidelity. Data are monitored by flight controllers, and their behavior is similarly tracked. Vast data sets are stored in "black boxes" for later analysis. Commercial aviation maintains an extraordinary level of reliability and safety. Incidents are infrequent and those that do occur shock us as they are unexpected. Operators of nuclear power reactors similarly work in a highly surveilled system in which the organization is more than a passive venue for the behavior. The organization includes elements that track behaviors, alert operators to emerging issues, stream instructions to avert anomalies, and may take coordinated action (e.g., automated shutdown, de-energize, divert effort) to manage unplanned events (Carvalho et al., 2012; Hamilton et al., 2013; Kim & Byun, 2011; Preischl & Hellmich, 2016; Yang et al., 2012). Operators on drilling rigs bore wells that may be miles deep, then turn and run horizontally for miles and reliably hit a target (pocket of oil or gas in a formation) the size of a basketball while maintaining the integrity of the well. The behaviors of rig crews are coordinated by a drilling plan, standard instructions, and data from multiple sensors throughout the well being constructed. The BP Macondo disaster in the Gulf of Mexico and the Piper Alpha fire in the North Sea are rare examples of how this human–machine interaction can go wrong with devastating impact.

HROs institutionalize behavioral contingencies that precisely measure operations, select behaviors, and correct deviation. Highly engineered work controls monitor processes and include redundancies, fail-safes, and back-up systems so that deviation is detected early and nearly error-free technical operations can be sustained. In such environments, failures are more likely to result from a complex set of interwoven, organized factors, including human behavior, rather than some single component fault. HROs are uniquely challenging work environments as behavior management is accomplished by human action of supervisors and machines that work together to monitor and correct behavior, and this interaction is transforming rapidly. COVID-19 has accelerated automation to reduce human contacts at work and this is evident in HROs. In the latest design of oil rigs, crew members' behaviors on the rig interact with elaborate dashboards that enable their situational awareness of events happening miles below the surface of the earth. Off-site personnel and automated expert systems track progress in relation to a drilling plan and sustain the integrity of drilling processes. Perhaps ten people are needed on the newest off-shore rig where formerly hundreds were required. Digitalization is transforming the oil fields. HROs organize contexts that emphasize maintaining operational integrity in the face of challenges inherent in continuous, 24 hours/day operations (e.g., aviation, nuclear power plants, medical settings, and oilrigs run continuously). Human factor challenges addressed by OBM in these environments are perhaps uniquely complex as workers' repertoires need to adjust to the rapidly advancing technologies. Progress in OBM and behavior systems analysis research is enabled by the wealth of observational data generated by the surveillance systems that allow demonstration of lawful behavior within complex technical settings.

Big Data

The surveillance systems in HROs, to a greater or lesser extent, generate massive data sets that challenge human comprehension. "Big data" (Brynjolfsson & McAfee, 2014; Houmanfar et al., 2019) are characterized by a massive volume of data points, collected at high velocity, from multiple sources which may vary in veracity. The data may be collected in real time from many locations, often refreshed and streamed to relational databases. Variability is embedded in measures that might be analyzed in a multitude of relations so that sources of deviation can be detected with advanced statistics. These can be multi-variate, concurrent time series that "realize" the operational processes over their life cycle. Oil rigs drill continuously for months to create a well. From rigging up at the start to finishing with an operational wellhead, data streams in real time along a time/depth curve depicting every instant in the process. These data are examined in real time and used to make decisions throughout months of drilling (Capote et al., 2018). AI systems apply algorithms to assess the meaning of complex patterns. Human operators also monitor the data and are challenged to comprehend meaning and predict what may happen as anomalies are encountered (Endsley, 1995a, 1995b). In some cases, the data streamed to operators is feedback delivered akin to percentile schedules to guide responding. In rare cases, the anomaly exceeds the limits of the software and humans need to determine when and how to override automated systems. To avert disaster, solutions are applied, often in an iterative search for resolution. Data displays visualizing the patterns and trends are crucial to humans' effective management of such processes. As humans interact with big data and AI systems, it is convenient to categorize the challenges to analysis as five data Vs – volume, velocity, variability, veracity, and visualization. Examining human fluency within analysis and decision-making in such systems is an area rich in research opportunities. Simulations, gamification (Morford et al., 2014), and VR preparations permit controlled examination of the human experience in such organized settings.

HROs rely on competent humans to monitor data streams, comprehend patterns in complex data, respond to alarms and signals, and sometimes approve or override automated adjustments. This often occurs within time constraints, so fast, accurate, fluent responding (Binder, 1996) is crucial to maintain situational awareness (Killingsworth et al., 2016). Pilots of commercial aircraft monitor preset flight plans run by autopilot and relatively infrequently manually control flight maneuvers. A similar role is developing for surgeons, locomotive engineers, nuclear power plant operators, oil rig personnel and other managers of HROs where expert technologies increasingly conduct many operations. The behavioral challenges to workers in HROs are perhaps unique as the context for work is highly organized, increasingly automated and sources of behavioral variance are within the complexity of interlocked contingencies. The human working in an automated environment is often a passive observer of ongoing processes and unpredictably called to act. To put this change in perspective, the Mckinsey Global Institute (Manyika et al., 2017) projects in the US that 39 to 73 million jobs will be eliminated in the next ten years forcing workers to transfer to new jobs or other industries. Many of the new jobs will entail that human oversight function. The shift has advanced in HROs under COVID-19 impacts. It will happen in many industries and occupations. This trend entails massive re-imagining of how and where people work. OBM contributes to rethinking how to assess organizational environments, organize labor, develop talent and competencies, and transition the population to these workforce dynamics.

Goals of HROs

HROs aspire to be hyper-reliable and hyper-efficient. They benchmark themselves against the best run companies on earth to set measurable objectives. This is not an academic exercise. Metrics reveal rates of breakdowns, losses, costs per some unit of production such as miles driven, barrels produced, megawatts of power generated, and so on. For example, oil services are global companies that develop land-based and marine oil and gas fields. They aspire to performance levels achieved by the best HROs in terms of operational hours without incidents. Management systems are refined so that disasters such as the BP event in the Gulf of Mexico (Deepwater Horizon Study Group, 2011) are averted (Flin & O'Connor, 2001; IOGP, 2014a, 2014b). Other high tech industries are leading the way with the development of replicable methodologies to prevent human error and avoid system failure. Transfer of behavioral technologies across industries (Simon et al., 2000) offers opportunities to OBM researchers to study and understand work behaviors within the context of highly organized processes and further articulate multi-level selection processes to foster systematic replication. Commercial aviation is the exemplar HRO as they were at the forefront of important developments (Craig, 2012; Moriarity, 2015; Savage, 2013; Wagener & Ison, 2014). Airlines maintain excellent (in relation to other industries) safety records across millions of hours of operation. Much of this is the result of sophisticated automated flight controls; some is the highly developed competencies of flight crews trained in high-fidelity simulators who learn to step in when automation reaches the limit of its design in a particular situation. The extraordinary example of the pilot, who landed his disabled airliner in the Hudson River with no loss of life, illustrates how humans can fluently interact with technology to quickly solve seemingly insurmountable problems (Sullenberger & Zaslow, 2009).

Industries aspiring to be top tier HRO's adopt behavior scientific methodologies into their industry's technologies that resemble those developed in aviation, but systematically adapt them to the idiosyncrasies of their industry. Medicine, for example, is emulating aviation with the development of simulators of surgery and patient care (Zeltser & Nash, 2010; Simon et al., 2000). Behavior science provides a coherent framework for identifying sources of behavioral variation in these settings and helps to develop effective interventions that establish and sustain operational integrity by medical teams (Danielsson et al., 2014; Epps & Levin, 2015; Gaba et al., 2001; Gillepsie et al., 2013; Howard et al., 1992; Morey et al., 2002; Ward et al., 2015). Presently, 400,000 patients die prematurely in the US due to medical error. COVID-19 cases are overwhelming hospitals, placing enormous stress on healthcare workers, and likely increasing mortality rates due to human error. This fatality rate is unimaginable in the leading HROs. In a range of dynamic contexts such as transportation industries (e.g., commercial aviation, railways), medicine (e.g., anesthesia, surgical teams), and nuclear power (e.g., nuclear power plants) a challenge to managers is integrating highly trained personnel with advancing technologies. Events external to organizations may be unpredictable and highly influence organizational behavior. For example, since 1975, Baker Hughes Tool Company posts a monthly count of active drilling rigs worldwide (https://rigcount.bakerhughes.com/rig-count-overview). This is a metric of how the petroleum industry coordinates producers and its suppliers of oil and gas to meet consumer demand. In September 2020, they reported 702 active rigs. This is 429 fewer rigs than in September 2019 before the COVID-19 pandemic. Oilrigs are distributed across the planet both on land and at sea and their workforce is often multicultural. Crew members' behaviors required to operate these rigs must interlock at team-level efforts and also engage with off-site personnel (e.g., suppliers, engineers, etc.) who provide ancillary services. Imagine the challenges to the industry leaders to lower rig count by 40%, reduce the labor force, and maintain the integrity of remaining drilling operations during the pandemic. Senior personnel with much experience are being released and replaced by younger workers who lack the learning history required for expert performance. Note that similar challenges impact the airline industry. That no catastrophic loss has occurred as these industries suffer the worst downturn in their history is evidence that the organizational systems are resilient and behavior management within supports is able to weather enormous shocks to the industry.

Two Organizational Challenges

Leaders of HRO settings face two fundamental challenges to the behavior management of critical processes. First, leaders need to maintain procedural integrity and ensure that organizational members adhere to intricate and precise procedures to sustain their business. Control of deviations from desired practice is paramount as team members conduct prescribed duties within defined parameters. Work behaviors combine in tasks within workflows in processes. These may be organized in business units that interlock to yield a good or service. On oil rigs, for example, workers follow a prescribed drilling plan that is engineered to reach oil reserves that can be thousands of meters below the earth's surface. The drilling plan dictates parameters (e.g., depths, pressures) of operations conducted by shifts of workers who drill continuously for weeks or months until the reserve is tapped. Oil rig workers' behavior is channeled by rigid parameters that greatly constrain deviation. The behaviors on the rig are conducted as tasks within drilling processes to drill to depth while maintaining well control. The Ghawar oil field in Saudi Arabia is the world's largest oil field. There are thousands of active wells. Many rigs are drilling at any one time to explore the geologic formation and tap more reserves. Thus each rig can be seen within a fleet of rigs under the control of Saudi Aramco, the national oil company. Each rig is connected to some extent with the others, so they share knowledge of the formation and plan accordingly. Pipelines deliver the oil and gas to transit centers that then pass the oil to refineries that produce fuel and other products, which are used by consumers. The entire process from raw materials (e.g., crude oil) to consumable product (e.g., gasoline) is designed to reduce variability and prevent catastrophic loss. As you fill your tank at your local gas station, contemplate the intricate organization of oil and gas exploration, drilling, pipelines, refineries, and service stations, making this volatile product available round the clock to consumers across the globe.

The second challenge to workers in HROs is that, on occasion, leaders must manage unanticipated events (e.g., on oil rigs, excessive pressures threaten well control, pipelines rupture in the distribution chain, or downturn in the market necessitates shutdown of active wells and containment of the reserves) that disrupt well-laid plans. These deviations may escalate to crisis-level events that threaten not just the task at hand but the lives of the crew and the environment in which they operate. Such was the case on the Deepwater Horizon where the crew lost control of the well and a blowout occurred that could not be contained by engineered fail-safe systems. In these crisis situations, the leader and crew must detect and track the changing context and adapt their responses to address the emerging crisis. Failure to adjust in a timely way can be catastrophic. During crises, rules that formerly were effective may be incorrect for the emerging conditions. Flexible repertoires are needed to (1) stop current action, (2) assess the altered environment, (3) troubleshoot sources of variation, and (4) take corrective action. These four events happen at various vantage points in an organization such that effective action likely requires coordination of multiple actors and synthesis of information on many variables. The event could happen on one rig (e.g., loss of well control due to pressure) and involve the rig crew interacting with data analysts off rig. Other events (e.g., terrorist attack) may occur in a region and disrupt multiple rigs in an entire oil field. Leaders of these operations rely on the organization of roles and responsibilities that interlock crewmembers. These crewmembers follow standard work instructions for routine operations and then switch to emergency responses to handle the crisis. Thus the organization and human competencies are designed for rigid rule-following with the capacity for flexibility when circumstances require novel behavior.

Teamwork: Crew Resource Management

Crew Resource Management (CRM) was developed in aviation as a behavioral system to coordinate flight crews and controllers and meet both challenges. CRM entails two response classes: rigid adherence to standardized work and flexing to alternative responses when conditions change and standard work is no longer effective. CRM deployment in HROs was spurred by catastrophic losses in commercial aviation, nuclear power, oil exploration, and medicine where standard work generally achieves the desired result, but on occasion conditions emerge which require nonstandard responses to achieve the goals of safe operations. The behavioral challenges in sustaining routine operations, but also adapting to rapidly changing conditions are considerable (Alavosius et al., 2005; Alavosius et al., 2017) and call for a competency model in HROs that bridges these two fundamental features of CRM (rigid compliance with rules, and flexibility in tracking changing conditions and adapting to them (see Wulfert et al., 1994 for a discussion of rule-governed rigidity; see Alavosius et al., 2017 for a detailed description of CRM competencies). CRM is generally examined in the context of a relatively small team of people managing an operation within tight boundaries (e.g., surgical team in an operating room), but analyses suggest that the principles of behavioral coordination apply to larger ensembles within larger systems. The extent of generalization of these competencies within an operational system is an important area for OBM and behavior systems research.

CRM is a systemic model of training and behavior change that results in a reduction of human error by crewmembers working in a highly engineered environment (e.g., cockpit, surgical suite, nuclear power control room, oil rig, etc.) by arranging relevant and available resources to standardize behaviors (Kanki et al., 2010). From its origin in aviation, CRM targets several key processes or skills: situation awareness, communication skills, teamwork, task allocation, and decision-making. The list of key processes or skills differs in organizations somewhat, but all focus on defining optimal interpersonal interactions of crewmembers working cooperatively within a dynamic environment. To facilitate analysis of critical variations in CRM behavior, these skills can be grouped together into six core skill sets that can be measured as crews interact with their operational environments (Alavosius et al., 2017):

1. Communication,
2. Situational awareness,
3. Decision-making,
4. Teamwork,
5. Management of limits of crewmembers' capacities, and
6. Leadership.

Each of these six competency domains can be deconstructed into more molecular definitions of behavior within some defined context. Behavioral assessment can occur within the routine sequences by which a team completes a task. Alavosius et al. (2017) describe CRM as a cascading chain of behavioral events where the leader and crewmembers effectively utilize available resources to:

1. Plan a work process,
2. Brief everyone on roles/functions,
3. Monitor the process as it occurs,
4. Detect & report deviations from the plan,
5. Communicate corrections from the top-down,
6. Adjust actions as needed,
7. Debrief moments (at significant change or conclusion of work),
8. Learn to refine the human-machine interface.

Thus CRM orchestrates cooperation among crewmembers that have different vantage points on the dynamic process. Individuals' combined perspectives optimize adaptive behaviors by all members of the team and may include the input of remote personnel who monitor the process from afar (e.g., from mission control settings). The behaviors involved in CRM are continuous but can be observed in several key events involved in managing a complex and dynamic process. A chain of CRM behaviors often begins with a briefing meeting during which the team leader informs the crewmembers of the task ahead, reviews their individual and collective roles and responsibilities and provides objectives to gauge progress. Following the briefing, the crewmembers conduct the task and work together to assess progress and meet project objectives. In HROs, operations are guided by standard work instructions that describe optimal behavior. Unexpected events may thwart progress and crewmembers communicate their observations, perhaps in the format of a debriefing meeting, to decide on an adjusted course of action. Upon completion of the task or other significant event (e.g., handoff to another crew at shift change) a debriefing is held to share updates on progress, review actions taken and summarize lessons learned for future operations. These three events (briefing, operations, debriefing) provide useful vantage points for assessors to examine competency by leaders and crewmembers in context as they adhere to rules and track the effects of their actions. Some of this is evaluated in simulators; some is assessed in the field. Leadership serves an essential integrative function of all elements, without which CRM would not culminate in desirable outcomes in an organization.

Cooperative Fluency

Crew Resource Management is a systemic intervention that focuses on the reduction of human error through training, behavior change, and design of organizational contextual resources available to assist in these aims. Many different organizations across high-reliability industries have proposed their own account of what skills constitute effective CRM. We posit that these skills can be grouped together into six broad behavioral classes that combine in what might be termed "cooperative fluency": communication, situational awareness, decision-making, teamwork, managing human capacity, and leadership. Each of these behavioral events can be examined from a behavioral perspective and viewed as an ongoing interaction of crewmembers with each other in an organized context to complete a complex task. Automation and AI elevates mechanical control to the status of a crewmember when those machine controls learn from experience.

Aviation is the exemplar industry with the most mature CRM processes enabled by high-fidelity simulators and a well-established competency framework to assess crew capability. The nuclear power industry also has an impressive safety record with advanced training and simulators. Medicine is challenged by a culture of under-reporting, likely as a result of malpractice issues, with uncertain metrics on patient safety and medical error. Medicine is pursuing CRM and looks to aviation and military applications for inspiration. Medical simulators and VR technologies are used to train competencies and develop support systems (Anbro et al., 2020). Oil field services are initiating formal CRM training and developing a competency framework to gauge the ability of Well Site Leaders for CRM, although rig simulators are relatively low fidelity when compared to those used in aviation. Advances are rapid with VR technologies aiding simulations.

Effective training and maintenance of these CRM and leadership behavioral classes helps create and maintain an organizational culture with an emphasis on respect, communication, perspective taking, and safety. Effective implementation of CRM allows organizations to address pro-social behavior in regards to keeping their own employees safe to preventing major catastrophes with wide-scale environmental impact. The role of leadership in creating and fostering an organizational culture, which effectively utilizes CRM, is essential. From organizational leaders' power to implement change across an entire system down to instances of leadership from a member of a crew in promotion of CRM, the function of leadership is essential to sustaining the shift to (and continued use of) CRM in any given organization. Such a shift is especially critical in high-risk industries with the potential for catastrophic loss. Leading industries implementing CRM demonstrate impressive results: aviation, aerospace and nuclear power are exemplars. The oilfield services industry is following suit even as that industry is in decline and alternative energy sources are developed. Medicine seeks to create work environments that are safer for both their employees, patients and the communities in which they operate. High-risk industries span the globe, employ vast numbers of workers, serve countless consumers and therefore, the potential impact of improved behavior management is quite substantial.

Focus on crew behavior in the context of CRM is a useful approach for behavior analysis. By analyzing communication networks, instructions (e.g., SOPs) and other rules, verbal coordination of behaviors, accuracy and latency of responding, and the interlocked behaviors in context seen in team dynamics, we can objectively measure skills of CRM and test supports. By adding objective measurement elements to CRM skills, behavior analysis is extending the conceptual literature from cognitive psychology that explores human-machine interactions via cognitive models. Analyzing key behaviors in their context allows OBM to develop measures of competency that can be used to inform organizational leaders with respect to training, employee feedback, policy changes, and other pragmatic adjustments to the work environments in HROs. As the digitalization of work advances, humans inspect complex, dynamic data displays to detect variation in processes and comprehend what those deviations mean. Comprehension is often a shared activity in which crewmembers communicate their perspectives and arrive at a consensus understanding.

TEAM DYNAMICS

Recent research in the area of team dynamics has demonstrated that the communication within and among teams provides critical data associated with team members' understanding and engagement with the work situation (Houmanfar et al., 2009; Houmanfar et al., 2010; Maraccini et al., 2018; Smith et al., 2012). Moreover, research findings suggest that implicit attitudes and biases of team members occurring under time pressure and stress significantly influence cooperation (Ghezzi et al., 2020; Rafacz et al., 2018). These studies focused on objective measurement and analysis of implicit biases in relation to effective communications as related to clarity, accuracy, level of ambiguity, shared meanings, and value-based actions. The assessment approach utilized in these studies has informed the development of measurement tools to assess the values of team members, analyze audience segmentation, and craft rules of engagement aligned with their biases and values (see Chapter 14 in this text for a detailed discussion of biases and values in organizations).

The dynamic nature of HROs necessitates the coordinated behaviors of multiple individuals performing multiple job functions simultaneously to achieve safe and effective results. Observation systems track moment-to-moment variation. Desired results cannot be achieved consistently without effective planning and communication to interlock behaviors. It is important to note that in these dynamic environments, communication is not just top-down, but across levels of a networked workforce. The purpose of targeting communication processes among employees is to break through potential barriers that have been established through hierarchies. It is interesting to contemplate the biases inherent in human-machine interactions where AI algorithms are operating. Both the human and AI function as crewmembers and all may be biased as a function of their learning curves.

Skinner's analysis of verbal behavior (1957) can be used as a foundation for our understanding of communication. Skinner describes verbal behavior as the behavior of an individual (speaker), which results in the behavior of another individual (listener) interacting with the environment in a manner consistent with the behavior of the first individual (speaker). Reinforcement in such instances is indirect; rather than the direct manipulation of the environment producing reinforcement, the speaker's behavior is reinforced by the listener's direct manipulation of the environment. The speaker and listener roles can fluctuate quite rapidly in everyday life; this is also evident in dynamic, high-risk work environments. With regards to the analysis of communication, a majority of the literature focuses on the topographical characteristics that focus primarily on the verbal behavior of the speaker. In many organizational settings, the dynamic interaction of teams requires our focus on ways by which verbal behavior and its products may affect the listener's behavior. This approach to the analysis of language and communication is mostly captured by the functional account of verbal behavior. Relational Frame Theory (Hayes et al., 2001) provides an empirically supported functional approach to the analysis of language. RFT emphasizes that when we learn to relate events and objects in certain ways, such as comparing them, the function (or meaning/properties) of one event or object transfers to (rubs off on) the other. This transformation of stimulus functions helps explain why we can say we are emotional, for example, when we hold a pocket watch that we received as a gift during a fun winter holiday: the functions of holiday music, friends, laughter and food are not only related to the timepiece (that is, we think about the holiday when we hold the watch), but the watch has also acquired the sentimental stimulus function of the holiday (Flaxman et al., 2013).

Houmanfar et al. (2009) and Houmanfar and Rodrigues (2012) note that many communications serve to alter the function of stimuli in the workplace, which in turn impacts employee behavior. Rules or statements that change the reinforcing or punishing effectiveness of consequences (in much that same way the establishing operations nonverbally alter the effect of consequences) have been called augmentals (Houmanfar et al., 2009, Maraccini et al., 2016; Stewart et al., 2006). In high-risk industries, the moment by moment responding by team members may have a detrimental or positive impact on the outcome of team performance. Some potentially catastrophic change occurs in the environment, and it is up to the team in that environment to detect variation and alter their behavior in such a way as to avoid an escalating event. Adhering to instructions for "normal operations" is a common response. Team members follow rules and repeatedly try established behavior that is now ineffective (Alavosius et al., 2005). They find themselves in a hole, but the tendency is to keep digging. Communication between crewmembers in such a situation can allow for the generation of motivating operations (MOs; Michael, 1993, 2000) that may evoke novel responding and problem-solving behavior. MOs may be statements that alter the effectiveness of stimuli by altering a consequential function (Blakely & Schlinger, 1987) and can be used to increase the importance of team goals while communicating a clear connection between the team actions and goals (Houmanfar et al., 2009)

From a behavior analytic perspective (Houmanfar & Johnson, 2003), team communication can be defined as a psychological event in which team members engage in verbal interactions to adhere to the presented rule(s) of operations or problem solve under the antecedent and consequential control of an absence of effective rules or presence of heuristic rules. Based on conceptual discussions (Houmanfar & Johnson, 2003; Houmanfar et al., 2009) and experimental analyses pertaining to different configurations of rules such as no rule and/or implicit rather than explicit (Smith et al., 2012) and inaccurate rather than accurate (Smith et al., 2012), rules can generate environmental ambiguity. Experimental findings demonstrate that environmental ambiguity associated with no rule or ambiguous/inaccurate ones were found to occasion problem-solving behavior, which in turn led to reduced performance and self-generation of inaccurate organizational rules on the part of verbal participants. Conversely, explicit and accurate rules, which minimize environmental ambiguity, were found to produce greater and longer-lasting levels of performance.

With regard to HROs, effective communication involves verbal interactions between team members from different levels of a hierarchy. Potential systemic barriers to effective communication must be overcome in order to promote the safety of team members. Such barriers include environmental obstacles such as a loud work environment, or interpersonal obstacles, such as rigid adherence to hierarchical structures and perceived status granted by such structures for certain roles. In a medical emergency situation, if the nurses notice a potential problem, they need to communicate that to the doctor in charge, whose responsibility is to then attend to the communicated information and factor that into decision-making. The doctor has the authority to make the decision, with team members' input, and communicate an action plan to all. Note that leadership shifts, moment-to-moment, from the nurses detecting the problem to the doctor formulating an action plan and is shared by the team in what might be regarded as cooperative fluency. There are component interpersonal behaviors in this that might be brought to high, sustained rates and generalization to novel circumstances enabled by environmental supports like heuristic rules and real-time data displays.

The traditional approach to leadership consisting of the chain of command (top-down) approach has to be revisited in the context of team dynamics in HROs. Instead, leaders have to take into consideration the ever-evolving external environment and verbally evaluate the potential adaptations the organization can make to those possible futures. These relations are based on verbally constructed outcomes that, for the leader at least, bear some connection with the current situation. However, these relations must be communicated effectively to the rest of the people in the team if they are to behave in accordance with said relations (Houmanfar et al., 2009). Software that analyzes the current status of a dynamic process, compares it to previous similar situations, and forecasts likely trajectories enable effective action.

As discussed by Houmanfar and Szarko in Chapter 14 in this text, individuals' histories of relational networks significantly influence how a collectivity of individuals in given interlocked contingencies respond to organizational information generated by each other through communication networks. This interaction between relational networks and communication networks can be captured through the phenomenon of self-organization that is one characteristic of social systems. As discussed by Houmanfar et al. (2009), the verbal networks formulated by members of an organized team depend on their prior history of already established verbal relations. New relations are more easily formed if they are in accordance with existing relational networks. Due to the role of coherence (consistency of Derived Relational Responding in the absence of explicit reinforcement) as a reinforcer (Dean et al., 2006; Festinger, 1957; Hayes et al., 2001), relational networks are often generated without external input or interference. In other words, the dynamics of relational responding are such that an individual's relating tends to become more ordered over time, even in the absence of external consequences. This inherent dynamic is referred to as self-organization in other sciences and is one of the defining characteristics of a complex system (Bar-Yam, 1997; Kauffman, 1993). Relational networks, as well as the communication networks within an organization seem to display this feature of self-organization. Thus, communication networks may develop in organizations without being specifically put in place by leadership. People with access to more information, through social links or by virtue of their position within the organization, may function as hubs in these networks (Sandakar, 2009). Similarly, rumor and gossip may proliferate through many parts of the company in the absence of external feedback (Houmanfar & Johnson, 2003; Kauffman, 1993).

CONCLUSION

Many different organizations across high-reliability industries have proposed their own account of what skills constitute effective communication and team dynamics. As organizations develop and mature, goals are refined, sources of variation identified and controls are orchestrated and sometimes automated. Review of the literature indicates that many HRO's are developing expertise in behavior science applications to enhance team dynamics within increasingly technical contexts. The initiatives reveal common directions and areas for cross industry dissemination.

Effective training and maintenance of effective communication will help create and sustain an organizational culture with an emphasis on respect, safety, and wellbeing (Houmanfar et al., 2015). The role of leadership in creating and fostering an organizational culture, which effectively utilizes communication, is essential (Houmanfar et al., 2009). From organizational leaders' power to implement change across an entire system down to instances of leadership from a member of a team in promotion of effective team performance, the function of leadership is essential to sustaining the shift to (and continued use of) team coordination in any given organization. The focus on team performance in the context of CRM is a useful level for behavior analysis within complex, interlocking contingencies (Alavosius et al., 2017). By analyzing communication networks, instructions (e.g., SOPs) and other rules, verbal coordination of behaviors, accuracy and latency of responding, and the interlocked behaviors seen in team dynamics, we can objectively measure behaviors within teams and sources of variation. Analyzing key CRM behaviors in organized teams allows us to develop measures of competency that inform organizational leaders with respect to training, employee feedback, policy changes, and other pragmatic adjustments to the work environments in HROs. Behavior is lawful and a function of the environment (Gilbert, 1978, 2007). HROs offer uniquely engineered environments with exquisite data systems, mature management systems, high social utility and opportunities for OBM researchers to explore high-performance settings and examine multi-level selection processes.

STUDY QUESTIONS

1. Outline the main steps/locations used to produce a product (from raw materials to finished item) you favor (e.g., your phone, laptop, apparel). Speculate why organizational leaders might want consumers to be unable to describe the process required to provide this to you.
2. Define and give an example of human-machine learning in an HRO.
3. Define CRM as a cascading chain of interlocked behaviors.
4. Describe ways the interaction between relational networks and communication networks can be captured through the phenomenon of self-organization in organized teams.
5. Compare the role of leadership in the context of team dynamics and cooperative fluency in HROs in relation to the traditional approach to leadership consisting of a chain of command (top-down). Provide an example.

REFERENCES

Alavosius, M.P., Houmanfar, R., Anbro, S. Burleigh, K, & Hebein, C. (2017). Leadership and crew resource management in high reliability organizations: A competency framework for measuring behaviors. *Journal of Organizational Behavior Management*, *37* (2) 142–170.

Alavosius, M.P., Houmanfar, R., & Rodriquez, N.J., (2005). Unity of purpose/unity of effort: Private-sector preparedness in times of terror. *Disaster Prevention and Management*. November, *14/5*, 666–680.

Anbro, S.J., Szarko, A.S., Houmanfar, R.A., Maraccini, A.M., Crosswell, L.H., Harris, F.C., Rebaleati, M., & Starmer, L. (2020). Using virtual simulations to assess situational awareness and communication in medical and nursing education: A technical feasibility study. *Journal of Organizational Behavior Management*, *40*(1–2), 129–139. doi: 10.1080/01608061.2020.1746474

Bar-Yam, Y. (1997). 1997). *Dynamics of complex systems*. Addison-Wesley.

Binder, C. (1996). Behavioral fluency: Evolution of a new paradigm. *The Behavior Analyst*, *19*, 163–197.

Blakely, E. & Schlinger, H. (1987). Rules: Function-altering contingency-specifying stimuli. *The Behavior Analyst*, *10*(2), 183–187.

Brynjolfsson, E. & McAfee, A. (2014). *The second machine age*. W.W. Norton & Company.

Capote, W., Boz, A., Lopez, J.C., Noya, V., Bordage, P., Febles, N., Hebein, C., Houmanfar, & R., Alavosius, M. (2018). An applied behavior science project; Rig floor safety. In: *Proceedings of 2018 SPE Conference on Health, Safety, Security, Environment, and Social Responsibility*. Abu Dhabi, UAE. DOI: https://doi.org/10.2118/190610-MS

Carvalho, P.V.R. d., Benchekroun, T.H., & Gomes, J.O. (2012). Analysis of information exchange activities to actualize and validate situation awareness during shift changeovers in nuclear power plants. *Human Factors and Ergonomics in Manufacturing & Service Industries*, *22*(2), 130–144. doi:10.1002/hfm.20201

Craig, C. (2012). Improving flight condition situational awareness through human centered design. *Work*, *41*, 4523–4531. doi: 10.3233/WOR-2012-0031-4523

Danielsson, E., Alvinius, A., & Larsson, G. (2014). From common operating picture to situational awareness. *International Journal of Emergency Management*, *10*(1), 28–47.

Dean, W.C., Johnston, M.D., & Saunders, K.J. (2006). Intertrial sources of stimulus control and delayed matching-to-sample performance in humans. *Journal of the Experimental Analysis of Behavior*, *86*, 253–267

Dekker, S.W. & Woods, D.W. (2009). The high reliability organization perspective. In E. Salas & D. Maurino (Eds.), *Human Factors in Aviation* (2nd ed.) (pp. 123–146). Wiley.

Deepwater Horizon Study Group (2011). Investigation of the Macondo Well Blowout Disaster. http://ccrm.berkeley.edu/pdfs_papers/bea_pdfs/dhsgfinalreport-march2011-tag.pdf

Endsley, M.R. (1995a). Toward a theory of situation awareness in dynamic systems. *Human Factors, 37*, 32–64. doi: 10.1518/001872095779049543

Endsley, M. R. (1995b). Measurement of situation awareness in dynamic systems. *Human Factors, 37*, 65–84.

Festinger, L. (1957). *A theory of cognitive dissonance*. Stanford University Press.

Epps, H.R. & Levin, P.E. (2015). The TeamSTEPPS approach to safety and quality. *Journal of Pediatric Orthopedics, 35*(5), S30–S33. doi: 10.1097/BPO.0000000000000541

Flaxman, P.E., Bond, F.W., & Livheim, F. (2013). *The mindful and effective employee: An Acceptance & Commitment Therapy training manual for improving wellbeing and performance*. New Harbinger Publication, Inc.

Flin, R. & O'Connor, P. (2001). Applying crew resource management in off-shore oil platforms. In E. Salas, C.A. Bowers, & E. Edens (Eds.). *Improving teamwork in organizations: Applications of resource management training* (pp. 217–233). Erlbaum.

Gaba, D., Howard, S., Fish, K., Smith, B., & Yasser, S. (2001). Simulation-based training in anesthesia crisis resource management (ACRM): A decade of experience. *Simulation & Gaming, 32*(2), 175–193.

Ghezzi, E.L., Houmanfar, R.A., & Crosswell, L (2020). The motivative augmental effects of verbal stimuli on cooperative and conformity responding under a financially competing contingency in an analog work task. *The Psychological Record, 70*, 411–431. doi: 10.1007/s40732-020-00400-7

Gilbert, T.F. (1978, 2007). *Human Competence: Engineering Worthy Performance*. Publication of the International Society for Performance Improvement. Pfeiffer.

Gillespie, B.M., Gwinner, K., Fairweather, N., & Chaboyer, W. (2013). Building shared situational awareness in surgery through distributed dialog. *Journal of Multidisciplinary Healthcare, 6*, 109–118.

Glenn, S.S. (1988). Contingencies and metacontingencies: Toward a synthesis of behavior analysis and cultural materialism. *The Behavior Analyst, 11*, 161–179.

Glenn, S.S (2004). Individual behavior, culture, and social change. *The Behavior Analyst, 27*, 133–151.

Hamilton, W.I., Kazem, M.L.N., He, X., & Dumolo, D. (2013). Practical human factors integration in the nuclear industry. *Cognition, Technology & Work, 15*(1), 5–12. doi: 10.1007/s10111-012-0213-z

Hayes, S.C., Barnes-Holmes, D., & Roche, B. (2001). *Relational frame theory: A post-Skinnerian account of human language and cognition*. Guilford Press.

Houmanfar, R. A., Alavosius, M. P., Binder, C., Johnson, K. (2019). Human Competence Revisited: 40 Years of Impact. *Journal of Organizational Behavior Management, 39*, 1–16.

Houmanfar, R.A., Alavosius, M.P., Morford, Z.H., Herbst, S.A., & Reimer, D. (2015). Functions of organizational leaders in cultural change: Financial and social wellbeing. *Journal of Organizational Behavior Management, 35*, 4–27.

Houmanfar, R. & Johnson, R. (2003). Organizational implications of gossip and rumor. *Journal of Organizational Behavior Management, 23*, 117–138.

Houmanfar, R.A. & Rodrigues, N. J. (2012). The role of leadership and communication in organizational change. *Journal of Applied Radical Behavior Analysis. N1, 22–27.*

Houmanfar, R.A., Rodrigues, N. J., & Smith, G. S. (2009). Role of communication networks in behavioral systems analysis. *Journal of Organizational Behavior Management, 29*, 257–275.

Houmanfar, R.A., Rodrigues, N.J., & Ward, T.A. (2010). Emergence and metacontingency: Points of contact and departure. *Behavior and Social Issues, 19*, 78–103.

Howard, S., Gaba, D., & Fish, K. (1992). Anesthesia crisis resource management training: Teaching anesthesiologists to handle critical incidents. *Aviation, Space, and Environmental Medicine, 63*(9), 763–770.

IOGP. Report 501. (2014a). *Crew Resource Management for Well Operations Teams*. Project commissioned by OGP's Safety Committee and the Well Experts Committee to the University of Aberdeen.

IOGP. Report 502. (2014b). *Guidelines for Implementing Well Operations Crew Resource Management Training*. Well Experts Committee. Training, Competence & Human Factors Task Force.

Kanki, B., Helmreich, R., Anca, J., & ScienceDirect (Online service). (2010). *Crew resource management* (2nd ed.). Academic Press/Elsevier.

Kauffman, S. (1993), *Origins of order: Self-organization and selection in evolution*. Oxford University Press

Killingsworth, K., Miller, S.A., & Alavosius, M.P. (2016). A behavioral interpretation of situational awareness: Prospects for organizational behavior management. *Journal of Organizational Behavior Management, 36*(4), 301–321. doi: 10.1080/01608061.2016.1236056

Kim, S.K. & Byun, S.N. (2011). Effects of Crew Resource Management training on the team performance of operators in an advanced nuclear power plant. *Journal of Nuclear Science and Technology, 48*(9), 1256–1264. doi: 10.1080/18811248.2011.9711814

Komisar, R. (2000). *The monk and the riddle*. Harvard Business School Press.

Krapfl, J.E. & Kruja, B. (2015). Leadership and culture. *Journal of Organizational Behavior Management, 35*, 28–43.

Malott, M.M. & Glenn, S.S. (2006). Targets of intervention in cultural and behavioral change. *Behavior and Social Issues, 15*, 31–56.

Manyika, J., Lund, S., Chul, M., Bughin, J., Woetzel, J., Batra, P., Ko, R. & Sanghyi, S. (2017). Jobs lost, jobs gained: What the future will mean for jobs, skills and wages. Mckinsey Group. https://www.mckinsey.com/featured-insights/

future-of-work/jobs-lost-jobs-gained-what-the-future-of-work-will-mean-for-jobs-skills-and-wages (Accessed November 27, 2020)

Maraccini, A.M., Houmanfar, R.A., & Szarko, A. (2016). Motivation and complex verbal phenomena: Implications for organizational research and practice. *Journal of Organizational Behavior Management, 36*, 282–300.

Maraccini, A.M., Houmanfar, R.A., Kemmelmeier, M., Piasecki, M., & Slonim, A.D. (2018). An inter-professional approach to train and evaluate communication accuracy and completeness during the delivery of nurse-physician student handoffs. *Journal of Interprofessional Education & Practice, 12*, 65–72. doi: 10.1016/j.xjep.2018.06.003

Michael J. (1993). Establishing operations. *The Behavior Analyst, 16*, 191–206.

Michael J. (2000). Implications and refinements of the establishing operation concept. *Journal of Applied Behavior Analysis, 33*, 401–410.

Morey, J.C., Simon, R., Jay, G.D., Wears, R.L., Salisbury, M., Dukes, K.A., & Berns, S.D. (2002). Error reduction and performance improvement in the emergency department through formal teamwork training: Evaluation results of the MedTeams project. *Health Services Research, 37*(6), 1553–1581.

Morford, Z.H., Witts, B., Killingsworth, K., & Alavosius, M.P. (2014). Gamification: The intersection between behavior analysis and game design technologies. *The Behavior Analyst, 37*, 25–40.

Moriarity, D. (2015). *Practical human factors for pilots*. Elsevier.

Preischl, W. & Hellmich, M. (2016). Human error probabilities from operational experience of German nuclear power plants, Part II. *Reliability Engineering & System Safety, 148*, 44–56. doi: 10.1016/j.ress.2015.11.011

Rafacz, S., Houmanfar, R., Smith, G., & Levin, M. (2018). Assessing the effects of motivative augmentals, pay for-performance, and implicit verbal responding on cooperation. *The Psychological Record, 69*, 49–66. doi: 10.1007/s40732-018-0324-x

Sandaker, I. (2009). A selectionist perspective on systemic change in organizations. *Journal of Organizational Behavior Management, 29*, 276–293.

Savage, I. (2013). Comparing the fatality risks in United States transportation across modes and over time. *Research in Transportation Economics, 43*(1), 9–22. doi: 10.1016/j.retrec.2012.12.011

Simon, R., Langford, V., & Lock, A. (2000, October). A successful transfer of lessons learned in aviation psychology and flight safety to health care: The MedTeams system. In *Safety Initiative 2000: Spotlight strategies, sharing solutions*.

Skinner, B.F. (1957). *Verbal behavior*. Appleton-Century-Crofts.

Smith, G.S., Houmanfar, R., & Denny, M. (2012). Impact of rule accuracy on productivity and rumor in an organizational analog. *Journal of Organizational Behavior Management, 32*, 3–25.

Sullenberger, C. & Zaslow, J. (2009). *Highest duty: My search for what really matters*. William Morrow & Company.

Stewart, I., Barns-Holmes, D., Barnes-Holmes, Y., Bond, F.W., Hayes, S.C. (2006). Relational frame theory and industrial/organizational psychology. *Journal of Organizational Behavior Management, 26*, 55–90.

Wagener, F. & Ison, D. (2014). Crew resource management in commercial aviation. *Journal of Aviation Technology and Engineering, 3*(2), 2–13.

Ward, M., Zhu, X., Lampman, M., & Stewart, G. (2015). TeamSTEPPS implementation in community hospitals. *International Journal of Quality Assurance, 28*(3), 234–244.

Wulfert, E., Greenway, D.E., Farkas, P., Hayes, S.C., & Dougher, S.C. (1994). Correlation between self-reported rigidity and rule-governed insensitivity to operant contingencies. *Journal of Applied Behavior Analysis, 27*(4), 659–671.

Yang, C.W., Yang, L.C., Cheng, T.C., Jou, Y.T., & Chiou, S.-W. (2012). Assessing mental workload and situation awareness in the evaluation of computerized procedures in the main control room. *Nuclear Engineering and Design, 250*, 713–719. doi: 10.1016/j.nucengdes.2012.05.038

Zeltser, M.V. & Nash, D.B. (2010). Approaching the evidence basis for aviation-derived teamwork training in medicine. *American Journal of Medical Quality, 25*(1), 13–23. doi: 10.1177/1062860609345664

14

Value-Based Governance in Organizations and Beyond

Ramona A. Houmanfar and Alison J. Szarko

WELLBEING IN ORGANIZATIONS AND BEYOND: VALUE-BASED GOVERNANCE

As industries continue to adopt bureaucratic systems of labor in search of profit, it is important to consider the impact these systems have on the wellbeing of workers and the quality of services that arise under these systemic frameworks. A behavior scientific discussion of organizational conditions in the context of different management approaches is relevant not only in terms of organizational financial profits, but also for the continued maintenance and growth of societal and psychological wellbeing for workers and consumers.

Houmanfar et al. (2015) define boundaries that depict the level of human wellbeing in terms of the following:

1. One's verbal behavior with respect to one's other behavior and environment
2. The sets of direct-acting contingencies operating in one's environment
3. The level of coercive control in one's environment
4. The degree to which individuals have an optimal level of choice

Houmanfar et al.'s (2015) analysis of wellbeing promotes a prosocial approach to the design and implementation of governance within organizations. By drawing upon Biglan and Glenn's (2013) perspective, Houmanfar et al. (2015) define prosocial behavior as any behavior, verbal or non-verbal, that contributes to the wellbeing of others and/or to society as a whole. This category of practices includes any behavior that:

1. Operates in the context of positive reinforcement contingencies for others
2. Minimizes aversive or coercive conditions and contingencies of others
3. Aids others in identifying or achieving optimal levels or choice

Biglan and Glenn (2013) offer a number of utilitarian suggestions for improving human wellbeing, including reducing toxic and aversive conditions, reinforcing prosocial behavior, teaching and promoting prosocial norms and values, setting limits on opportunities for problem behavior, and promoting psychological flexibility. Each of these suggestions rests on changing the behavior of individuals such that change leads to measurable improvements for others. However, larger scale applications are needed if behavior analysts are to help achieve the larger outcomes required to address problems confronting humanity in today's world.

DOI: 10.4324/9781003198949-14

TABLE 14.1
Glossary of definitions

	Definition
Burnout	a syndrome resulting from chronic workplace stress that has not been successfully managed consisting of three psychological dimensions: 1) feelings of energy depletion or exhaustion; 2) having negative, callous, or excessively detached thoughts and feelings toward clients, customers, and/or colleagues; and 3) thoughts and feelings of incompetence and lack of achievement at work.
Derived Relational Responding	operant responding to the relations among properties of two or more stimuli that have not been directly trained.
Ply	a rule that specifies a consequence that will be delivered by another person or people.
Track	a rule that specifies a consequence that occurs naturally as part of the interaction with the environment.
Augmentals	rules that change the reinforcing or punishing effectiveness of consequences (in much that same way establishing operations nonverbally alter the effect of consequences).
Value-based governance	an organization is said to practice value-based governance when the workers are granted the opportunity to change the organizational environment in ways that improve it and are reinforced for doing so.
Cultural milieu	the collection of the distinctive stimulus functions influencing the acquisition and maintenance of IBCs and behaviors of individuals that interact with the associated aggregate products material.
Cultural-organizational milieu	comprised of the cultural milieu factors such as properties of materials, resources, policies, rules, values, traditions, institutions, technological progress, art, other organized groups, competition, and individuals (e.g., society leaders) that influence organizational policies, rules, IBCs, & aggregate products
Interlocking behavioral contingency	comprised of operant contingencies in which behavior of two or more people functions as environmental events for the behavior of the others.
Metacontingency	depicts the contingent relation between interlocking behavioral contingencies (IBCs), their aggregate product, and the environmental demand.

In this chapter we expand on Houmanfar et al.'s (2015) discussion of wellbeing as related to traditional approaches to organizational governance by first providing a summary of popular definitions of stress and burnout as psychological phenomena associated with wellbeing in organizations (see Table 14.1). We will then discuss ways a scientific behavior analysis of rule governance in the context of different management approaches may influence psychological, social, and financial wellbeing in organizations. We chose stress and burnout as the primary indicators of psychological and social wellbeing as the problems are global, involve workers' behaviors influenced by their team and leadership actions, and are illustrative of problems requiring systemic change. Lastly, we call for future work in behavior analysis, emphasizing the importance of organizational management practices that support value-based actions, and eliminates aversive conditions within behavioral systems (see Malott, 2003 for an overview of behavioral systems; also see Chapter 5 by McGee & Crowly-Koch and Chapter 2 by Alavosius & Burleigh in this text for behavioral safety).

Epidemiology of Burnout and Bureaucracy

The phenomenon of burnout seems to have emerged in response to the many customary organizational practices that took place during the Industrial Revolution (Schaufeli et al., 2009).

Specifically, burnout appears to be a cultural response to bureaucratically-rooted organizational systems (Schaufeli et al., 2009). As highlighted by Schaufeli et al. (2009), bureaucratic systems are maintained by a strict arrangement of hierarchical power dynamics within the organizational environment. This approach reduces individual autonomy and exerts limits on behavioral variation.

If left untreated, burnout can lead to worker health problems, depression, and a reduction in productivity, as well as an increase in organizational absenteeism and turnover (Lloyd et al., 2013). Within the field of applied behavior analysis (ABA), early-career BCBA's may be disproportionately at risk of developing burnout (Fiebig et al., 2020). Excessive work demands have also been positively correlated with high levels of ABA provider burnout and low levels of job satisfaction (Dounavi et al., 2019). Perceived supervisory and collegial support seems to decrease the likelihood of clinically significant levels of burnout and increase the degree of ABA provider job satisfaction (Dounavi et al., 2019). Perceived supervisor support may also play a central role in predicting low levels of ABA provider burnout and increasing levels of ABA provider self-efficacy (Gibson et al., 2009).

While the concept of burnout is beginning to gain traction within the field of ABA, it is a well-known phenomenon in the biomedical healthcare profession (Rotenstein et al., 2018; Shanafelt et al., 2017; Song & Waline, 2020). It is estimated that more than 50% of physicians experience clinically significant levels of burnout in the United States (Shanafelt et al., 2017). Clinically significant levels of healthcare professional burnout have also been reported in other countries, making burnout a global issue (Song & Waline, 2020). Burnout in the context of medicine has been linked to lower quality patient care, reduced professionalism, a higher rate of substance abuse for physicians compared to the general population, and a higher risk of medical errors (Golda, 2019; Shanafelt et al., 2017; Swensen et al., 2016). It is estimated that physician burnout costs the United States healthcare system $4.6 billion annually (Han et al., 2019). Therefore, the need for a coherent and comprehensive behavior analytic account of this complex phenomenon is critical, in order to improve the conditions under which healthcare workers provide patient care.

Defining Burnout

The World Health Organization (WHO) defines burnout as "a syndrome ... resulting from chronic workplace stress that has not been successfully managed" consisting of three psychological dimensions: "1) feelings of energy depletion or exhaustion; 2) increased mental distance from one's job, or feelings of negativism or cynicism related to one's job; and 3) reduced professional efficacy" (WHO, 2020). The WHO (2020) highlights that burnout is specific "to phenomena in the occupational context and should not be applied to describe experiences in other areas of life." Although an occupational context is typically a setting in which one acquires monetary capital in exchange for their labor, burnout can also occur when labor is voluntary and/or not monetarily compensated (e.g., community service, activism, emotional labor, domestic labor, etc.). Therefore, it is important to consider one's work, as not only the actions one takes solely in exchange for monetary capital, but rather as the conglomerate of actions that are taken *in service of* a verbally specified desired outcome (e.g., psychological capital, social capital, and/or monetary capital). In the current context of the COVID-19 pandemic, wherein many individuals are now working from home, occupational stress may be more likely to invade the home environment. Accordingly, family members and/or roommates of burned-out workers are also more likely to contact aversive contextual circumstances, which were formerly exclusively located at some other workplace location.

In 1976, Maslach was researching the coping strategies of human service workers (Schaufeli et al., 2009). She observed and described a pattern in her research on participant's responses to questions about their working behavior and clustered those responses into three main categories. Based on this work (see Figure 14.1), burnout can be defined as:

- Emotional exhaustion– the experience of being emotionally overextended and depleted of emotional resources (e.g., "It's the end of my shift and I have nothing left to give.")
- Depersonalization – having negative, callous, or excessively detached thoughts and feelings toward clients, customers, consumers, or colleagues (e.g., "I could care less about what the patient wants, I'm going to do what I know is best.")
- Reduced Personal Accomplishment–recurring thoughts and feelings of incompetence and lack of achievement at work (e.g., "I need to study more, I'm not as smart as everyone in class." or "No one appreciates how hard I work.")

Maslach and colleagues have also developed the most well-known measure of burnout, the Maslach Burnout Inventory (MBI). The MBI is a Likert-scale self-report measure (Maslach et al., 1996–2019). There are five versions of the MBI that focus on: human service workers, medical personnel, educators, students, and general workers (Maslach et al., 1996–2019). Other self-report measures for capturing this phenomenon have also emerged. For example, the Well-Being Index (WBI) is a nine-item, yes/no, self-report measure developed by the Mayo Clinic to capture burnout specifically in the context of the medical profession (Dyrbye et al., 2013). The emerging behavior scientific research related to wellbeing across different settings (e.g., clinical and organizational) has resulted in the development of tools that can guide the assessments and interventions associated with stress and burnout. The following section provides a brief overview of said behavioral assessment and training tools.

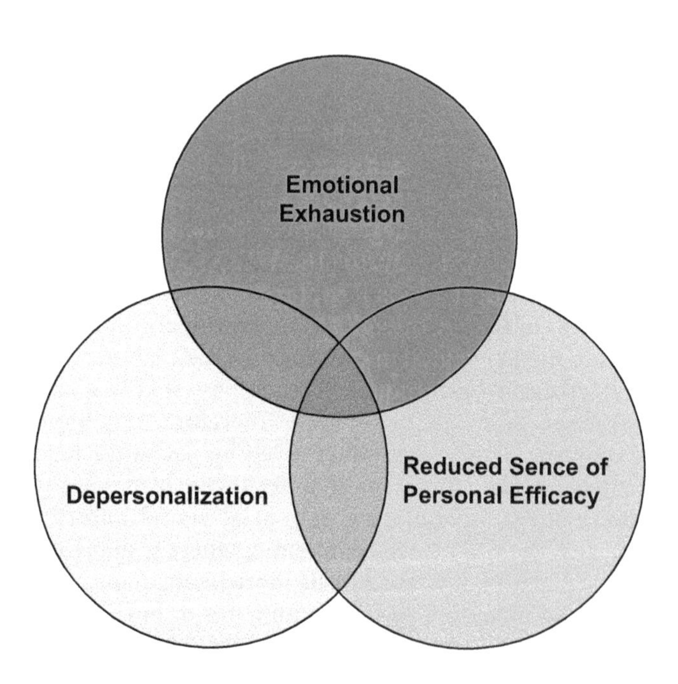

FIGURE 14.1 Three variables of burnout.

Behavioral Assessment of Burnout

When referring back to the original root metaphor of "burnout," the notion of "energy depletion" may be understood as a state of organismic deprivation. There is a large body of literature within the field of behavioral science dedicated to investigating the impact of motivational variables on responding and learning, which may aid in behavior analysts' abilities to understand the burnout construct in practice (Hayes & Fryling, 2014; Lewon et al., 2019; Michael, 1993). Within the area of behavioral economics, researchers demonstrate that individuals are more likely to predominantly respond in relation to implicit heuristics (i.e., relational frames with strong histories of reinforcement) when they are: fatigued, stressed, multitasking, and under time pressure (Kahneman, 2011).

Those within the medical field have suggested utilizing a modified systemic version of Abraham Maslow's Hierarchy of Needs Theory to inform healthcare network interventions for reducing burnout and improving provider wellbeing (Shapiro et al., 2018). The core assumption to the Hierarchy of Needs Theory – whether applied at the individual or group level – is the notion that individuals are more likely to engage in value-based action when their basic needs have been met (i.e., food, water, sleep, safety, etc.). It is easier to attend to the social contingencies of one's environment when one is well-rested, fed nutrient-rich food, given access to clean water, and provided healthy and safe living, as well as healthy and safe working conditions. On the other hand, it is difficult to attend to value-based, prosocial, cooperative action when one is deprived of basic resources for survival. Shapiro et al. (2018) recommend conducting basic needs assessments within clinical working environments to ensure healthcare workers continuously have the sufficient amount of sleep, food, water, safety, etc. that is required for them to work cooperatively and effectively with their healthcare teams and patients.

In their (2017) *Implicit bias review*, The Kirwan Institute for the Study of Race and Ethnicity define *implicit bias* as "the attitudes or stereotypes that affect our understanding, actions, and decisions in an unconscious manner; activated involuntarily, without awareness or intentional control; can be either positive or negative; everyone is susceptible" (p. 10). From a scientific behavior perspective, the term translates most synonymously with the definition of a *brief immediate relational response* (BIRR) within a Relational Frame Theory account, specifically, the Relational Elaboration and Coherence (REC) Model (Barnes-Holmes et al., 2010). The REC model views relational responses:

> like all behaviors, [they] unfold across time. Thus, when a stimulus is encountered, a relational response may occur relatively quickly and be followed by additional relational responses. These additional responses may occur toward the stimulus itself or toward the initial response to the stimulus. With sufficient time, these additional relational responses will likely form a coherent relational network. (Barnes-Holmes et al., 2010, p. 102)

The REC model classifies two categories of arbitrarily applicable relational responding. BIRRs are behaviors that occur consistently under time pressure and are often synonymous with features typically used to describe the cognitive construct "implicit bias." Extended elaborated relational responding (EERRs) are responses that occur in the absence of time pressure and are often synonymous with the features typically used to describe the cognitive construct "explicit bias." Hughes and Barnes-Holmes (2013) note: "It is important to appreciate that both are behavioral patterns, and thus they may interact in a dynamic manner" (p. 102).

Consistent with the above, implicit bias can be behaviorally interpreted as brief immediate relational responses that occur consistently and quickly under time pressure (Barnes-Holmes et al., 2010). These responses are verbal and occur under relative quick time pressure (e.g., ~3 seconds or less latency of responding toward the verbal referent of interest) (Baker et al., 2015). Theoretically, when one considers the precision teaching literature, a verbal repertoire may also meet some temporal criteria of "fluent," if fluency is also defined by the REAPS criteria of mastery (i.e., retention, endurance, application, and stability) (Binder, 1996). Implicit responses can be interpreted as occurring as a product of the individual's history of reinforcement for particular ways of relationally responding under specified social contexts. A quicker more consistent latency of responding may suggest a denser history of reinforcement with a particular stimulus class when the latency is measured using contextually relevant parameters (Smith, 2013). However, it is important to note that the empirical research on this topic is limited (Ghezzi et al., 2020). Further basic manipulations of this construct from a behavioral perspective are needed to verify the postulates of the REC model's theoretical assumptions as related to cooperation, situational awareness, and conflict management (Alavosius et al., 2017; Ghezzi et al., 2020; Rafacz et al., 2019).

It is also important to consider the relationship between burnout and implicit bias. When individuals are placed under conditions conducive to long-term states of stress and fatigue, the symptoms of burnout are likely to emerge – which, if detected and measured, can be used as a form of organizational feedback to those in charge of policy decision-making and organizational-level remediation. When individuals are experiencing symptoms of burnout (i.e., emotional exhaustion, depersonalization of others, and a lack of personal efficacy), they may become less sensitive to the direct-acting contingencies of their present moment experiences and may be more likely to act with respect to deeply conditioned social biases (i.e., BIRRs).

Said another way, individuals may behave on "autopilot" and/or become more psychologically rigid (Törneke et al., 2008). Depending on the individual's vocation, this type of rigidity could lead to an increase in errors in workplace settings (Maraccini et al., 2018). For example, excessively rigid rule-following due to worker burnout may lead to increases in healthcare disparities, plane crashes, treatment provider errors, and/or environmental disasters, such as the British Petroleum (BP) oil spill or an unintended forest fire. As mentioned earlier researchers demonstrate that individuals are more likely to respond in relation to implicit heuristics (i.e., relational frames with strong histories of reinforcement) when they are: fatigued, stressed, multitasking, and under time pressure (Kahneman, 2011). Behavioral technologies such as Acceptance and Commitment Training (ACT) have been suggested as a strategy to help individuals and organizations manage symptoms of burnout and implicit bias, in service of maintaining healthy, cooperative working environments (see Chapter 8 by Moran et al. and Chapter 9 by Hayes et al. in this text).

In a longitudinal study at the University of Nevada, Reno School of Medicine, Baker et al. (2015) utilized the Implicit Relational Assessment Procedure (IRAP) to collect data pertaining to a range of target concepts, which allowed for the design of specific curricular interventions to address specific areas of social bias. For example, trainings were developed to teach medical students how to manage and augment their implicit biases toward diverse members of medical teams as well as how to manage and augment their implicit biases toward specific patient populations (e.g., weight bias, biases toward English-as-a-Second Language patients, etc.). The group-level analyses of the two classes of medical students indicated that the Year 1 students generally did not exhibit implicit biases associated with being burned out. However, the Year 3 students exhibited implicit biases, which were associated with a greater degree of burnout relative to the Year 1 students for the majority of the burnout stimuli assessed.

In a recent follow-up study, Smith et al. (under review), further explored the relationship between the longitudinal student burnout measures using the IRAP and their explicit measure of burnout (using MBI) over the first two years of medical school. Three successive cohorts of medical students completed both implicit and explicit measures of burnout at several time points during their first two years of medical school at UNR School of Medicine. Both assessments were conducted via the internet during the first week of medical school, the end of the first year of medical school, and the end of the second year, though not all cohorts were able to complete the assessments at all time points. Mixed linear models were used to compare the two measures directly, as well as to evaluate changes over time in each measure separately. Minimal correspondence was observed between the implicit and explicit measures of burnout on a within-subject basis. However, when analyzed separately, all subscales of both measures detected significant change over time in the direction of greater levels of burnout, particularly during the first year of medical school. The IRAP also detected a consistent increase in positive implicit responding toward medical training during students' second year, which was not detected by the MBI. As part of the intervention efforts, the Performance System Technologies lab at UNR, in collaboration with UNR School of Medicine, have incorporated content on ACT (Hayes et al., 1999; see Chapters 8 and 9 in this text) within the medical school curriculum (e.g., race, gender, weight, cooperation, sexual orientation, socio-economic status, & lifestyle; see Baker et al., 2015). The leadership team members at UNR School of Medicine have utilized these data to inform their decision processes associated with their curricular programs.

Burnout and Bureaucracy

In a bureaucratic system, there is a large degree of administrative record-keeping and clerical work required for maintaining effective communication with all stakeholders (Schaufeli et al., 2009). Top-down hierarchical decision-making is also common within a bureaucratic system, which in turn, limits the degree of in-the-moment autonomy for the workers contributing labor to that organization (Abernathy, 1996, 2009). Generally, as the amount of bureaucracy increases within an organization, the higher the likelihood there is for a delay in communication between those responsible for the distribution of organizational resources and those providing services (Bar-Yam, 1997; Houmanfar et al., 2009). As discussed in behavior scientific literature on rule governance and communications in behavioral systems, the hierarchical structure facilitates the development of rigid communication and management by negative reinforcement (Bar-Yam, 1997; Houmanfar et al., 2009). Burnout is an unintended consequence of rigid communication and management by aversive control and can be viewed as an internality of the organization rather than an individual mental health syndrome for an individual worker. If one individual is experiencing symptoms of burnout within an organizational setting, it is very likely that many other individuals working under the same environmental conditions within that organization are concurrently experiencing a similar degree of stress and burnout. An internality is a long-term side-effect of an organization's systemic structure, which can have positive or negative impacts on worker wellbeing (Reimer & Houmanfar, 2017). Table 14.3 provides an overview of work-related conditions that may influence individual experience across the dimensions of burnout.

According to the behavior scientific literature, higher levels of job control predict greater learning, better job performance, and positive mental health outcomes (Bond & Flaxman, 2006; Bond et al., 2008; Terry & Jammieson, 1999). There is overwhelming evidence that higher ratings of stress and demand are correlated with a higher risk for illness and death (Labbe & Fobes, 2010; Taylor, 2008). The persistent imbalance of demands in relation to the resources available to adequately fulfill a service is a critical factor in the analysis of burnout within a bureaucratic system (Schaufeli et al., 2009). For example, within a clinical setting, there may be too many clients to serve and not enough clinicians available to adequately provide compassionate, person-centered care. Other examples of an insufficient amount of resources include a lack of functional personnel equipment, a lack of service-related supplies, and/or a lack of space to meet operational demands (Schaufeli et al., 2009; Shapiro et al., 2018). There may also be an insufficient amount of opportunities for workers to rest and regenerate their depleted energy between work shifts. For example, overscheduling workers, under-staffing, a limited amount of personal vacation days, and/or assigning too many recurring back-to-back deadlines (Shapiro et al., 2018). The direct experiences of healthcare workers around the globe to combat the COVID-19 pandemic provides a multitude of real-life scenarios that highlight how the arrangement of an organizational system can influence not only a consumer's wellbeing but also the wellbeing of those directly providing a service (Smith et al., 2020).

Monetary resources may even be allocated toward motivating organizational workers to engage in practices that are advantageous to the survival of the bureaucratic system, but detrimental to the employees working within those systems. An example of this involves providing overtime compensation as a means of maintaining a continuous flow of production or bonuses that are contingent upon individual worker output. In theory, this approach may lead to an initial increase in production output. However, over time workers may begin to become dependent on this pay-for-performance source of compensation to maintain their quality of life outside of work due to societally-determined factors that impact monetary inflation (e.g., corporate-level impacts on the national GDP) and the pressures of social capital (e.g., marketing, materialism). Accordingly, socio-cultural, intersectional factors are important for consideration when arranging organizational contingencies related to monetary distribution. In this context, intersectional factors constitute multiple social identities such as race, gender, sexual orientation, socio-economic status, and disability that intersect at the micro level of individual experience to reflect interlocking systems at the macro social-structural level (Crenshaw, 1989).

The additional hours consistently spent working overtime or competing against one's own performance for a higher compensation may contribute to a disproportionate distribution of worker fatigue if external societal conditions are not considered when arranging these incentive programs within organizational settings. One worker within this environment may be a middle-aged, single, Brown, English-as-a-Second Language, Latinx, cisgender mother providing for three children on her single-family income – where her *work* does not end the moment she arrives home. Rather, her "second shift" (i.e., paternal and domestic labor) is just beginning when she arrives home (Richter et al., 2014). In contrast, her colleague hired on in the same position may be a young, single, White, gay, childless, affluent, cisgender male with no dependents. The degree to which each of these individuals is likely to experience stress, fatigue, and burnout is multifactorial and intersectional. While the contingencies operating within the workplace are technically *equal*, the conditions under which these two individuals are operating under – in terms of what motivates them to obtain monetary capital – may be different. The conditions under which they are also likely to experience chronic exposures to stress within and outside of their workplace environments is also different. Monetary incentive programs, designed without these considerations in mind, may be perpetuating a culture of disproportionate wealth distribution if socio-cultural factors are not considered.

Additionally, the market pressure to produce a never-ending, large amount of services and products within a competitive, monetarily incentivized socio-cultural environment has detrimental effects on the quality of life for organizational workers and consumers when ethical parameters of capitalism are not considered (Biglan, 2011, 2020). The question then becomes: how critical is it for an organization to continuously produce a product or service, and at what point does this pressure to produce monetary capital lead to a detrimentally impact on workers and consumers quality of life?

Due to the nature of the hierarchical decision-making process inherent within a bureaucratic system – there is also a temporal delay in the communication between those in supervisory roles and those in supervisee roles (Houmanfar et al., 2019). Subordinates within these dichotomous relationships may engage in rigid, compliant, rule-governed behavior in relation to their supervisor, which in turn artificially restricts the worker's ability to adjust and adapt to their present moment environmental conditions (Törneke et al., 2008). For example, a Board-Certified Behavior Analyst (BCBA®) might be unable to make a pediatric clinical treatment decision until their BCBA-D Clinical Director can review and approve a written proposal on the rationale for the treatment change. At first glance, this may seem like a beneficial layer of accountability and quality control for services. However, if the Clinical Director falls behind on their proposal reviews, due to the continuous, capitalistically-driven demand for a large clientele, the child receiving services in this context is delayed critical time-sensitive treatment. If the Clinical Director works below a Regional Director, they may be under pressure as their supervisor's superordinate to increase the speed at which they review and approve treatment proposals so that the company can take on *even more* consumers for the sake of profit. This bureaucratically-rooted process may inadvertently result in a lower quality review of treatment proposals by the Clinical Director, making the very purpose of the quality control practice dysfunctional and in need of organizational process remediation.

With regards to our discussion of rule-governed behavior, styles of leadership and team management are believed to function as important factors in the design and implementation of effective organizational contingencies. For instance, leadership and team management practices may promote environmental ambiguity that is defined as incomplete or inaccurate information regarding the work-related matters that lack a clear or accurate description of contingencies and their context (Houmanfar & Johnson, 2003). The literature indicates that level of ambiguity influences the incidence and prevalence of problem-solving behaviors that may negatively affect interrelated or coordinated behaviors of individuals, stress management, resistance to change, individuals' performance outcomes, and eventually the efficiency by which organizational products are generated (Houmanfar & Johnson, 2003; Kolvitz, 1997). Therefore, in order to promote a healthy level of problem-solving practices, organizations should acquire and/or maintain a balance between high productivity, a commitment to organizational members, and practice open communication. In that regard, the remaining sections of this paper will include a discussion on how understanding the nature of verbal rules may contribute toward an understanding of the issues involved in re-engineering behavioral systems in the face of continued socio-economic and cultural demands. This discussion will include an analysis of organizational leadership and team management in developing a value-based governance approach to promote wellbeing as related to psychological health and team dynamics in organizations.

RULE GOVERNANCE IN ORGANIZATIONS

As discussed by Houmanfar et al. (2009), the purpose of management is to develop and implement rules and policies to guide behavior, both individually and collectively, to be more efficient and productive. Traditionally, behavior analysis has considered rules to be contingency specifying stimuli (Skinner, 1953, 1957). Rules are thought to affect behavior by their description of a contingent relationship between antecedents, responses, and consequences (Malott, 1992; Weatherly & Malott, 2008). This definition of rules, however, does not explain why some rules are effective and why some are not. In other words, it does not provide a technical account of rules and their effect on the behavior of the listener (Hayes et al., 1989).

The functional account of rule governance (Hayes et al., 1989) suggests that rules are understood by way of the frames they imply and their influence on derived relational responding (i.e., responding to a stimulus is based on its relation to other stimuli). For example, consider a rule that may be communicated at a hospital: "The nurse who receives the highest percentage of patients' positive comments related to the discharge process this month will be granted use of the convenient parking spot in front of the hospital." According to this perspective, the rule relies on frames of coordination (sameness) between the word "positive comments" and the behaviors associated with the discharging process. The rule also relies on an if-then frame of the relation between the process of "discharging a patient" and the potential outcome of a "convenient parking spot." The behaviors associated with the discharge process undergo a transformation of function due to the relation between "highest number of patients' positive comments" and "convenient parking spot." This relational response (i.e., frame of coordination that is established via the transformation of stimulus function) is likely to be reinforced by the social community, and thus the rule is likely to maintain its reinforcing effect. During the course of the month, a nurse might evaluate their behaviors throughout each patient's discharge process by placing verbal statements about them in frames of comparison with other nurses: "Taylor ended up with 25% more positive feedback than I did." Statements like these may lead to further relational responding that may result in other generated rules such as: "It is easier for me to connect with kids. So, I should work on being assigned to the pediatric unit moving forward to increase my overall rating."

We can also define a rule according to its influence on the listener or recipient (Hayes et al., 1989; Houmanfar et al., 2009). A ply is a rule that specifies a consequence that will be delivered by another person or people (i.e., the consequence is socially mediated). For example, a healthcare worker is told that the shift manager disapproves of the medical team's use of cell phones during hospital shifts. Alternatively, a track is a rule that specifies a consequence that occurs naturally as part of the interaction with the environment. For example, a healthcare worker is told that the use of cell phones can promote distraction and result in medical errors. Both kinds of rules can be effective; however, a ply is less likely to be effective when the social context is absent, suggesting a diminished likelihood of contacting the social consequence. A track, on the other hand, retains its effectiveness regardless of the presence or absence of a social context.

As discussed by Houmanfar et al. (2009), beyond rules, communication serves to alter the function of stimuli in organizational settings, which in turn impacts behavior. Statements that change the reinforcing or punishing effectiveness of consequences have been called augmentals. Formative augmentals establish a previously neutral stimulus as a reinforcer or punisher. For example, in a medical context, "If we keep patients' positive feedback over 80% for the month, everyone will receive a shared bonus." This statement will probably result in the medical team seeking records on patients' feedback, possibly a previously neutral stimulus, and attempting to achieve the stated goal. Motivative augmentals, on the other hand, influence the effectiveness of stimuli by altering a consequential function. For example, "Patient's satisfaction is the backbone of our hospital reputation. If we don't promote medical team-patient rapport, we will miss our accreditation." This statement may alter a verbal stimulus (patient's satisfaction) that already functioned as a reinforcer for medical teams by temporarily increasing its reinforcing effectiveness when this new rule is generated.

ENVIRONMENTAL AMBIGUITY

Utilizing effective rules in order to reduce environmental ambiguity can be a vital practice on the part of leadership and team management, but the design of rules is not a simple process of just describing contingencies. In many cases, the source of a rule may have quite a different history and perspective from those of the rule followers, and this discrepancy may explain the often-seen mismatch between the rule author's intended function and the rule followers' understanding of the verbal stimuli. Recent conceptual and experimental analyses of rule governance have discussed a variety of factors that may affect a listener's responding. For example, whether or not there is no rule, and/or an implicit rather than explicit rule, a simple or complex rule, and/or an inaccurate rather than an accurate rule (Houmanfar & Johnson, 2003; Johnson et al., 2010; Smith et al., 2012). The combination of these factors generates various levels of environmental ambiguity for a rule follower. As discussed by Houmanfar and Johnson (2003), environmental ambiguity can occasion problem-solving behavior, which in turn can lead to induced stress, conflict, reduced performance, and the listener generation of inaccurate organizational rules. Conversely, explicit and accurate rules minimize environmental ambiguity and can produce greater and longer lasting levels of worker performance.

A relational understanding of the verbal products that are communicated through organizational networks can enhance our ability to craft these verbal products so as to render them more suitable to the needs of specific organizations, departments, and teams. Providing individuals with simple, accurate rules that come from a reliable source can help to improve the effectiveness of organizational functioning while reducing the possibility of a mismatch in shared stimulus function occurring between those providing the rules within the organization and those that are operating in relation to the organization's rules.

Shared Stimulus Function

As noted by many in behavior science, verbal behavior does not emerge within a vacuum. We each engage in verbal behavior as a product of our unique socio-cultural histories and present moment circumstances. How we learn to follow rules depends upon our histories with rule-following and our present moment environmental circumstances (Houmanfar et al., 2009). The abovementioned account of rule governance highlights the importance of functional characteristics of rules in the team management of organized group practices. With regards to topography and function of rules, organizational rules are said to be institutional stimuli that correspond to a shared response from a group (Houmanfar et al., 2009; Kantor, 1967, 1982). Therefore, as highlighted by Houmanfar et al. (2009), the institutional nature of organizational rules requires our focus on not only the shared function they serve among workers but also the topographical characteristics that mediate stimulus control among the collective of individuals. A shared stimulus function is demonstrated when a given stimulus functions similarly for one individual as it does for another individual under similar contextual circumstances due to both individuals having a similar enough history of reinforcement with that stimulus object.

An example of a shared verbal stimulus function within an organizational setting may involve two workers that grew up in similar social communities and have experienced similar histories of reinforcement. Worker A and worker B have learned through their individual histories that rules provided by their supervisor are likely to match the contingencies of the workplace. Therefore, worker A's and worker B's behavior tend to quickly come under the stimulus control of the instructions provided by their supervisor. Given that both individuals respond similarly in the presence of their supervisors' instructions, the stimulus function between worker A and worker B is shared. In contrast, worker C may have a drastically different history where rules provided by their supervisors in the past have frequently been inaccurate with the contingencies of the workplace. Worker C's behavior may be less likely to come under the control of their supervisor's instructions. If worker C responds noticeably different than worker A and B to their supervisors' instructions, there is likely a lack of shared stimulus function between the workers with respect to their supervisors' instructions.

Shared verbal stimulus function likely evolved in human phylogeny out of a necessity for small groups to survive and adapt to their changing environmental conditions. Modern evolutionary scientists examine evolutionary processes from four dimensions of inheritance: genetic, epigenetic, behavioral, and cultural (i.e., symbolic) (Jablonka & Lamb, 2005). It is posited that cultural or symbolic communication repertoires among humans emerged due to survival advantages for a eusocial species (Hayes & Sanford, 2014). The ability to cooperate is a human adaptation that evolved within small groups prior to the development of language and cognition. Cooperation among small groups then set the conditions under which a shared symbolic communication repertoire (i.e., language and cognition) would be selected within human phylogeny.

Despite our endowments to engage in cooperative, prosocial behavior, cultural drift may occur: "when such original survival contingencies can no longer serve as standards against which to evaluate the adequacy of practices, practices become susceptible to other influences" (Houmanfar & Johnson, 2003, p. 125). In work environments, the influences that are most likely shaping an individuals' practices are the workplaces' "organizational stimuli" (Houmanfar et al., 2009, p. 259). These stimuli are the rules, policies, statements, and other members within the organization. When effective, "organizational rules are institutional stimuli that correspond to a shared response from a group" (Houmanfar et al., 2009, p. 267).

When a lack of shared stimulus function is present in the organizational communication processes, the likelihood for miscommunication to occur between individuals is increased. Research has shown that miscommunication or "inaccurate rules" in an analog work setting increases the frequency and duration of rumor behavior as well as decreases levels of productivity (Houmanfar & Johnson, 2003; Smith et al., 2012). There are also safety risks involved with a lack of shared stimulus function (see Chapter 2 by Alavosius & Burleigh in this text). For example, faulty group communication has been correlated with increases in the frequency of commercial airliner crashes, increases in the frequency of environmental disasters from energy providers, and increases in the frequency of medical errors within hospital settings (Alavosius et al., 2017; Maraccini et al., 2018). Many of these instances result in death or long-term injury for both the workers and for consumers of these organizations' aggregate products. A lack of shared stimulus function within a group becomes additionally problematic when common pooled resources (e.g., clean water, energy, food, etc.) are limited. In these circumstances, individuals may be more likely to act with respect to their own self-interests (e.g., selecting a smaller, sooner, individual reward) rather than conserving common pool resources (e.g., selecting a larger, later, group reward). This leads us into a discussion on self-interest as it relates to individual rule governance.

Self-Rules: Individual Rule Governance

As noted, the capability to engage in rule-governed behavior is a product of one's social conditioning. We posit that the capability to engage in rule-governed behavior with respect to one's own behavior is also a product of social conditioning. McHugh and Steward (2012) defines the "self" as comparable to the definition of deictic relational responding (i.e., I/YOU, HERE/THERE, and NOW/THEN relations). The goal of many language-based clinical services is to aid an individual's capability to transform maladaptive deictic relational framing into more contextually sensitive, flexible, adaptive frames, such that an individual is more capable in their abilities to achieve self-identified value-based action. In this context, values are defined as overarching life reinforcers (e.g., the type of person we want to be, what we stand for, what is important to us) that guide our actions (Hayes et al., 1999; Herbst & Houmanfar, 2009).

Törneke et al. (2008) highlights the ways in which rigid responding toward self-generated rules can lead to an increase in psychological problems for an individual, depending upon the circumstance. That is not to say all forms of rigid rule-following are unhealthy, just that it depends on the context. Given that the environment is *always* comprised of some level of variability, to suggest that someone should *always* follow a particular set of rules is in violation of natural human dynamics. We are part of nature. Like nature, we evolve and are inevitably going to be exposed to conditions of environmental ambiguity, wherein making a flexible, adaptive response that is in opposition to a rule may be the action that is most necessary and most aligned with an individual's and/or organization's values. Individuals with a history of rigid rule-following, whether the source of said rule is the self or another, are at an increased risk for exhibiting psychological problems (Törneke et al., 2008). Refer to Törneke et al. (2008) for a further elaboration on the ways in which rule-governed rigidity is related to psychological problems.

In contrast, Atkins and Styles (2016) explore the ways in which self-rules can predict psychological wellbeing. They define a self-rule as a rule used "to describe how a person should behave in particular circumstances to achieve particular outcomes" which is derived from the I/HERE/NOW-YOU/THERE/THEN deictic frame (Atkins & Styles, 2016, p. 73). It is "a description of an 'if-then' contingency specifying a person's response and/or desired outcome to a given experience or context, where the verbal stimulus allows a frame of coordination between the rule and actual behavior" (Atkins & Styles, 2016, p. 73). The authors note, "The person following a rule can detect the rule is being followed (or not) because what is being done corresponds (or not) with the rule" (Atkins & Styles, 2016, p. 73). Said another way, there is congruence between the action that is specified in the self-rule and the action that is actually taken by the person.

For example, Taylor may verbally state to herself, "I will spend more time in the pediatric unit to improve my patient satisfaction rating." If Taylor then spends more time in the pediatric unit and improves their patient satisfaction rating, there is congruence between Taylor's desired outcome (i.e., improved satisfaction rating) and their action (i.e., spending more time in pediatrics). Taylor may be more likely to follow rules that are derived in relation to the deictic relational repertoire frequently classified as the "self."

Self-Rules Promoting of Burnout or Wellbeing

Atkins and Styles (2016) categorize self-rules into two categories: control-oriented and values-oriented. *Control-oriented self-rules* are rules about "taking action in order to create an experience that is less aversive" (Atkins & Styles, 2016, p. 73). The inferred function of these rules is experiential avoidance, maintained by negative reinforcement. These types of self-rules are also rigid in nature. For example, Taylor may state, "I want a high patient satisfaction score to avoid getting in trouble with my supervisor" In this context, Taylor is spending more time in the pediatric unit to improve their patient satisfaction score, such that they can avoid being reprimanded and can avoid an aversive experience with their supervisor.

In contrast, *values-oriented self-rules* are rules about "taking action in order to create more experience of value" that occasion value-based action (Atkins & Styles, 2016, p. 73). The inferred function is access to positive reinforcement. These types of self-rules are more flexible in nature, likely due to their appetitive function. For example, Taylor may state, "I want a high patient satisfaction score because my patient's experiences are important to me and I can make a real difference in the pediatric unit with my understanding of pediatric healthcare." In this context, Taylor is spending more time in the pediatric unit not only to improve their patient satisfaction score but also to increase their access to the self-identified positive reinforcement contingencies associated with pediatric care.

VALUE-BASED GOVERNANCE

The main challenge for organizations in the 21st century is to interact with the increasing environmental demands that are not only financial but also social in nature. The current experiences of healthcare workers around the globe to combat the COVID-19 pandemic provides a multitude of real-life scenarios that highlight how the arrangement of an organizational system can influence not only a consumer's wellbeing but also the wellbeing of those directly providing a service. Similarly, there is evidence to suggest that post-COVID-19 changes such as the increased demand for telehealth services and the use of online platforms may positively affect millennial and generation X workers in avoiding aversive working conditions, while also presenting particular challenges for health care providers and those maintaining more traditional, in-person vocational positions (Agnew, 2013; Schawbel, 2013). With the expanding role of social networks in our global landscape (e.g., Facebook, Twitter, etc.), opportunities for intra- and inter-individual transmission of prosocial behavior inside and outside of organizations are limitless. We see examples of this across the globe as communication technologies orchestrate social action in response to governments' restrictions of freedoms and other affronts to social groups.

With regard to behavioral technology, evidence from Organizational Behavior Management demonstrates the utility of primarily using positive reinforcement in the workplace (Abernathy, 1996, 2000, 2009; Daniels & Daniels, 2005; see chapters by Moran et al. and Hayes et al. in this text). This brings us to the discussion of ways by which moving from a purely rule-governed approach – which is conducive to rigid responding and aversive control – toward a value-based governance approach – which allows for persons' increased access to positive reinforcement via promotion of opportunities for adaptive responding, can be critical to well-being in organizations. As discussed by Houmanfar et al. (2009), a relational understanding of the verbal products that are communicated through organizational networks can enhance our ability to craft rules to render them more suitable to the needs of specific organizations, departments, and teams. Providing workers with simple, accurate rules that come from a respected, trusted source can help to improve the effectiveness of their behavior while reducing the likelihood of workers deriving (and disseminating) self-rules that may turn out to be inaccurate (Alavosius et al., 2005; Houmanfar & Johnson, 2003; Smith et al., 2012). Recognizing the nature of different departments and teams and their relation to the organization can guide team management in presenting formative and motivative augmentals that produce shared goals and hence improved cooperation within the organization, and increased access to positive reinforcement.

According to Skinner (1990, p. 112), "values" is used when someone behaves with respect to contingencies arranged by others, so that an individual's behavior reinforces the behavior of the person or persons who manages those contingencies (Skinner, 1990, p. 112). For example, the leadership of a health and wellness center might arrange contingencies that reinforce attendance and healthy behaviors (e.g., exercise, mindfulness exercises, etc.), and may provide constructive support for reducing the behaviors of social avoidance, as well as unhealthy food and alcohol consumption. One is then said to have values when he or she attends the health and wellness center events, engages in physical and psychological flexibility exercises, and avoids situations in which over-consumption of food or drugs are likely. Applying this to organizational leadership, Houmanfar et al. (2015) and Herbst and Houmanfar (2009) argued that organizational leadership demonstrates values when it creates an environment in which workers are encouraged to manage their own environment in accordance with a set of organizational goals and are reinforced for doing so. In other words, an organization is said to practice value-based governance when the workers are granted the opportunity to change the organizational environment in ways that improve it and are reinforced for doing so. By adoption of this approach, members of the organized groups including leaders, managers, and members of their teams:

1. Operate in the context of positive reinforcement contingencies for others.
2. Minimize aversive or coercive conditions and contingencies of others. Leaders' actions and management practices in this context not only affect the wellbeing of organizational members (e.g., their safety, health, financial security, etc.) but also bear a positive or negative impact on consumer practices and community wellbeing (e.g., education, obesity, cancer, safe or green driving, energy conservation, diversity-based healthcare, etc.).
3. Aid others in identifying or achieving optimal levels of choice.

The abovementioned overview of value-based governance aligns with Abernathy's Positive Leadership Model (Abernathy, 1996, 2000, 2009). Abernathy (2000, 2009) describes four approaches to management: autocratic, absentee, paternalistic, and positive leadership (see Table 14.2). By describing different types of management approaches, Abernathy emphasizes how aversive control is inherent in the rule-governed style of supervision within bureaucratic organizations (hierarchical behavioral systems). He in turn introduces the alternative management approach called "positive leadership," which allows the manager to take on the role of a team leader (instead of a supervisor) who arranges their self-managing team's access to positive reinforcers in their environment and provides positive social and financial consequences.

Autocratic managers may provide effective antecedents, but they rely heavily on the use of aversive consequences. An individual working under the supervision of autocratic management may frequently engage in control-oriented self-rules to regulate their behavior, as a means of avoiding punishment and coercion from their supervisor. Results are obtained through intimidation, private and public criticism, ridicule, and other aversive techniques. Quality of life for individuals working under an autocratic management style is likely to be low due to the use of coercion.

TABLE 14.2
Management Approaches & Associated Actions

Types of Leadership	*Actions*
Autocratic	• Is result oriented and provides specific direction and feedback. • Results are obtained through intimidation, private and public criticism, ridicule and other aversive techniques. • May provide effective antecedents, but relies heavily on aversive consequences.
Absentee	• Little time spent "on the floor." • Fails to provide workers assistance and recognition to improve job satisfaction. • Does not provide clear direction, feedback or positive reinforcement for getting the job done. • The result is poor-performing areas with absenteeism.
Paternalistic	• The supervisor is a "people person" who is involved with workers and concerned about meeting their needs. • The emphasis is on worker satisfaction and retention rather than their performance. • Fails to provide worker direction and performance feedback. • Provides positive consequences without effective direction and feedback.
Positive Facilitative	• Provides clear and consistent direction. • Provides constructive and consistent feedback. • Provides positive social and financial consequences for success.

An absentee supervisor may spend very little time interacting directly with the individuals they oversee. They fail to provide workers with assistance and recognition for improved performance. They do not provide clear direction, feedback, or positive reinforcement for getting the job done. It is likely that the quality of performance is poor under absentee supervision. Individuals working in relation to this type of management style may follow either control-oriented self-rules or values-oriented self-rules, depending on the level of aversion the absentee leader creates when they are actually present. Alternative "leads" within a team may be socially selected among the group to provide more direct guidance and management. However, the individual(s) that gets assigned to be an unofficial "lead" of the group, under the supervision of an absentee supervisor, will likely have their labor exploited by the system they serve – doing the job of a leader while continuing to be compensated and labeled as a subordinate.

In contrast to the absentee management style, there is the paternalistic approach. A paternalistic manager is typically labeled as a "people person" who is involved with workers and concerned about meeting their needs. They place an emphasis on worker satisfaction and retention rather than worker performance. They fail to provide worker direction and performance feedback. The paternalistic manager provides positive consequences without effective direction and feedback. This type of manager may also be excessively involved in the personal lives of those they oversee, in an attempt to maintain rapport among themselves and the workers they oversee. While involved in the work process, the paternalistic leader may not be very effective in improving performance. Individuals may engage in control-oriented self-rules to avoid interactions with the paternalistic leader, if the interactions are too frequent to the point of creating an aversion for the worker. If the individual workers do have a personal rapport developed with this type of leader, they may engage in values-oriented self-rules to increase their contact with said leader, which may interfere with their ability to accomplish other aspects of their job.

Abernathy's positive leadership approach (1996, 2009, 2014) advocates for team managers to adopt a facilitative approach and to demonstrate value-based governance. As mentioned earlier, this approach calls for the manager to take on the role of a team leader (as opposed to a supervisor), arrange their self-managing team's access to positive reinforcers in their environment, and provide positive psychological, social, and financial consequences. This style of management is most synonymous with many of the teaching strategies taught to ABA behavioral technicians who work directly on the frontline with individuals receiving ABA services. Specifically, it is similar to Natural Environment Training (NET) used in clinical settings. Those that utilize a positive, facilitative leadership approach provide clear, accurate rules to workers. They provide consistent feedback to shape worker behavior by using positive reinforcement techniques. The positive, facilitative leader also ensures the working environment is arranged, such that workers have access to all the resources they need to accomplish the jobs they have been assigned. If workers do not have resources, the facilitative leader adjusts the environment accordingly.

Abernathy (2001) examined the effects of the positive leadership approach by providing monthly performance scorecards and incentive pay on workers performance in a variety of organizations. Twelve organizations were examined with a combined 4,289 workers and 2,195 objective performance measures. The most important implication of Abernathy's study was the effect of feedback and influence of the level of control workers had over their assigned performance measures. Individual and small team measures produced improvement, hourly workers improved more than salaried, more controllable measure types displayed more improvement, and a low number of changes in scorecard parameters increased improvement.

As behavioral scientists, we are not suggesting anyone is inherently an autocratic, absentee, paternalistic, or facilitative leader. Nor are we suggesting these leadership styles are

TABLE 14.3
Organizational Conditions & Burnout based on Schaufeli, W.B., Leiter, M.P., & Maslach, C. (2009)

Burnout Symptom	*Organizational Conditions*
Emotional exhaustion	Degree of Bureaucracy Ability to Self-Govern
Depersonalization/cynicism	Case Load Distribution of Resources
Lack of personal efficacy	Financial Contingencies tied to Performance Amount of Socially Mediated Positive Reinforcement

fixed, concrete, and to be found within someone's personality. The above descriptions are simply a framework for individuals interested in working in organizational settings to aid in identifying characteristic features of a behavioral repertoire. It is likely that many of us engage in all four of these leadership approaches, depending on the context and the individuals we are responding in relation to. However, we advise those interested in applied organizational work to consider a positive, facilitative leadership approach whenever possible, as it is most aligned with the values of applied behavioral analysis – use positive reinforcement and create the conditions under which those you work with are most likely to succeed.

It is important to note that as organizational leadership moves from primarily rule governance to value-based governance, self-organization may increase. It would therefore be more effective for management to attempt to provide a modicum of organization to the organization's communication networks while simultaneously recognizing and taking advantage of the communication dynamics that self-organize within the organization (Houmanfar et al., 2009). To this end, gaining constant feedback from the workers about the effectiveness of management efforts is necessary (see Table 14.3).

Impact of Value-Based Governance Beyond Organizational Boundaries

Beyond the benefits that may directly accrue to organizations that adopt a value-based governance approach, there should be benefits to the consumers' practices, which ultimately act as the selective mechanism for those entities (Houmanfar et al., 2010). In addition to previously cited literature on burnout, numerous studies have found a predictive relationship between experienced work stress and substance abuse (e.g., Chopko et al., 2013; Dawson et al., 2005; Grunberg et al., 1999), though it should be noted that direct relationships are not always found (e.g., Hodgins et al., 2009). Further, researchers have also pinpointed relationships between career work stress and domestic violence (e.g., Cano & Vivian, 2003; Stith et al., 2004). Though it is beyond the scope of this chapter to exhaustively review the literature pertaining to the relationship between workplace stress and societal problems, even a brief review points to the effects that creating an environment in which workers experience minimal stress would have significant effects on the wellbeing of overarching culture more generally.

When considering organizational values, however, one might look beyond how organizational leadership behaves toward the people managed within the organization and toward the implications their leadership and management practices have for the culture more generally. Therefore, one can argue that an organization demonstrates values not only through the practices it has toward its workers, but through the outcomes its practices have in relation to the culture more broadly. As such, we consider value not only in terms of the reinforcers inherent in the product or service delivered, but the delayed consequences that organizational practices may have for the health of its members, their families, their communities, and the broader environment in which the organization operates. This broader perspective on the boundaries of assessments in Organizational Behavior Management (OBM) calls for enhancements to measures such as Gilbert's (2007) potential for improving performance ("the PIP") to include functional assessment of the societal impact of leaders' actions (Houmanfar et al., 2019). Value-based governance, much like value-based action (see Chapter 8 by Moran et al. and Chapter 9 Hayes et al. in this text), is not something that can be captured in isolation. As behavioral scientists, we are interested in patterns of behavior over time (i.e., observable and verifiable organizational and individual characteristics).

In much the same way that rules can govern behavior as part of the associated behavioral contingencies, leadership values, societal values and beliefs about the future – be it the economy, a richer, more diverse middle-class, competition, advocacy organizations, or other factors – can also guide the design of organizational products or provision of human services, which consumers may or may not select or purchase. This relationship can be circular in that the consumers' interaction with products and services often alters the cultural environment resulting in a different set of strategies for organizational practices that are altered by their leaders.

As discussed by Houmanfar et al. (2009), organizational change is addressed theoretically through metacontingency analysis (Glenn, 1991, 2004; Houmanfar et al., 2010; Malott, 2003; Malott & Glenn, 2006; Mawhinney, 1992, 2001). Theories of selection and metacontingencies are also applied within the framework of behavioral systems analysis (Malott, 2003; see Malott's Chapter 6 in this text). In short, there is a contingent relation between a cultural practice (a set of similar interlocking behavioral contingencies across an industry) in an organization, the outcome of that practice (i.e., aggregate product) and the environmental demand (which maintains the future production of organizational product). According to this perspective, which is based on general system theory, organizations are behavioral systems that are formed by individuals' interaction (IBCs) toward a common objective (production of an aggregate product). This interaction toward a common objective occurs within the context of the organization's interaction with a broader cultural and economic environment (Brethower, 1982, 1999, 2000; Glenn & Malott, 2004; Malott, 2003; Malott & Glenn, 2006; Rummler, 2001; Rummler & Brache, 1995). According to Houmanfar et al.'s elaborated account of the metacontingency (2010, 2020) the selecting environment includes cultural milieu, which are the values; prevailing beliefs/opinions that persons acquire across the three environmental tiers (biological, anthropological, and psychological) are shared by members of communities (cultural groups), systems of IBCs, and associated community of consumers. And, they are comprised of the collection of functional properties inherent in objects, actions, events, and persons. These distinctive stimulus functions influence the development and maintenance of IBCs and behaviors of individuals (consumers) that interact with the associated aggregate products (e.g., ABA services, training technologies, etc.), in addition to institutions (political, religious, economic, etc.), policies, rules, technological progress, environmental competition, etc. (Ardila et al., 2019). Behaviors of consumers in this context can be discussed as macrobehavior (socially learned operant behavior observed in the repertoires of several members of a cultural system) and the associated cumulative effect on the environment (i.e., macrocontingency). Organizational milieus are influenced by cultural milieu, and they affect organizational policies, rules, IBCs, and aggregate products, and hence are referred to as the cultural-organizational milieu. Similar to the earlier discussion of organizational rules, the shared stimulus functional properties of cultural-organizational milieu are acquired through the interaction with individuals who have similar histories of reinforcement. In short, the design of a product and its generation rely not only on selection by consumers but also on the cultural milieu and the associated cultural-organizational milieu (see Figure 14.2).

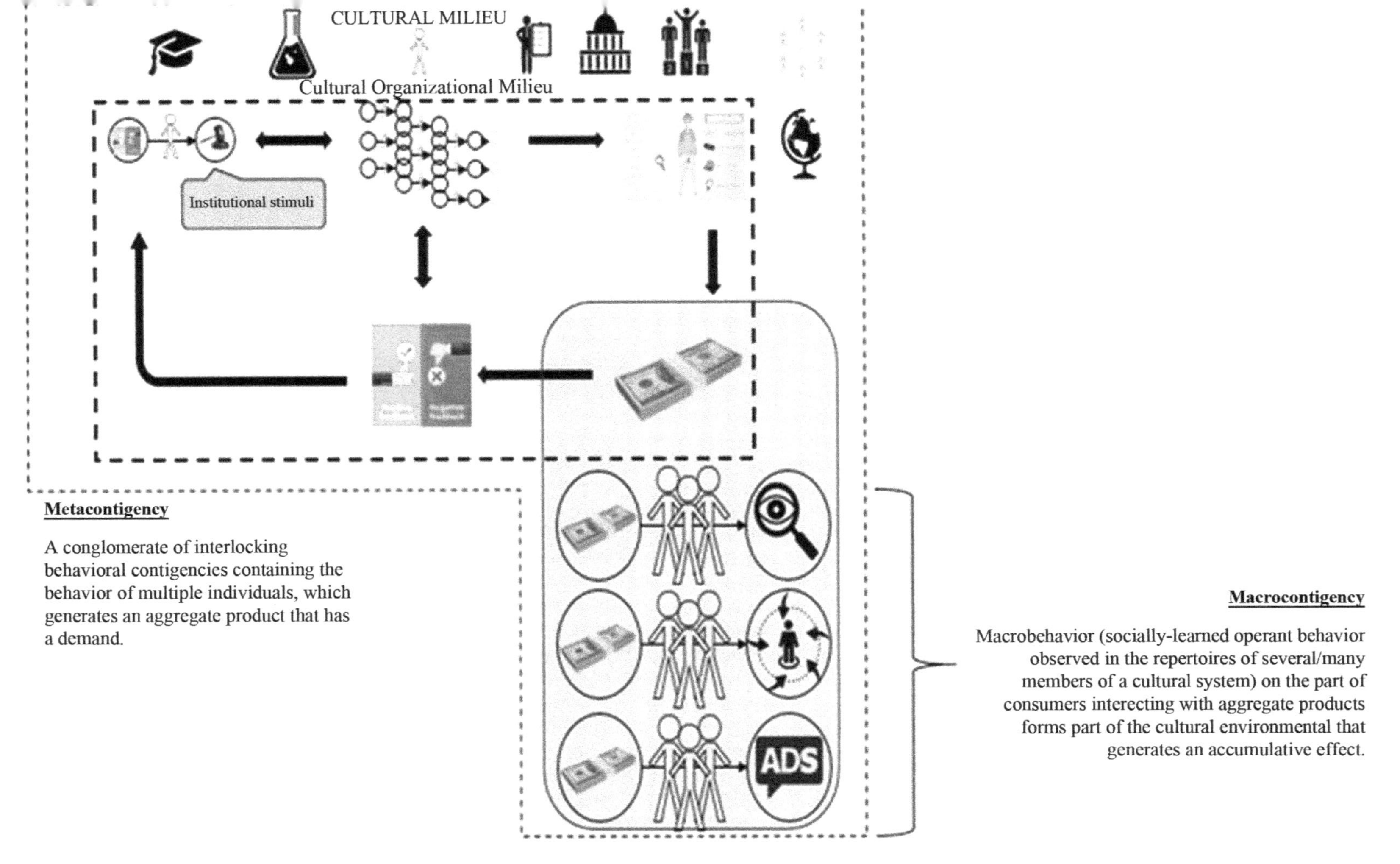

FIGURE 14.2 Naturalistic and selectionist account of socio-cultural phenomena begins with the identification of the circumstances under which metacontingencies and macrocontingencies occur. The cultural milieu constitutes the collection of the distinctive stimulus functions influencing the acquisition and maintenance of IBCs and behaviors of individuals that interact with the associated aggregate products.

As institutions move toward value-based governance, they must hold themselves accountable for developing organizational processes that serve their cultural environment (e.g., local, regional, national, or global communities). For example, Patagonia, Inc. is an outdoor gear and clothing company whose stated values (one of the cultural-organizational milieu factors) are: to build the best product, cause no unnecessary harm, use business to protect nature, and not be bound by convention (Patagonia, 2020b). In alignment with their value to "build the best product," the management team released a statement to their workers and consumers on April 27, 2020, explicitly stating they would be utilizing their core values to guide their actions as the COVID-19 pandemic unfolds and would be utilizing the Fair Labor Association's Guidance to inform their policies and procedures. The Fair Labor Association is "a collaborative effort of universities, civil society organizations and socially responsible companies dedicated to protecting workers' rights around the world" (Fair Labor Association, 2020). In alignment with the cultural milieu of "cause no unnecessary harm" – the philosophy to reduce any unnecessary harm to the environment as a result of operations – the company stated they were "working in partnership with our supplies with the aim of minimizing the impacts on suppliers and workers" (Patagonia, 2020a, 2020b). To align with the value of "using business to protect nature" (cultural milieu stimulus object), the organization has an entire department dedicated to climate-change-related activism, which has taken the form of suing the 45th U.S. president, soliciting signatures for petitions, disseminating climate-change education via community forums, and implementing their "self-imposed Earth tax" (cultural milieu factor) – by donating 1% of their annual profits to environmental nonprofits. Lastly, in alignment with Patagonia's core value of "not bound by convention" (cultural-organizational stimulus), the organization made the executive decision on March 13, 2020, to close their stores, while continuing to pay all workers until more information was known about the spread of the COVID-19 virus, being one of the first private sector organizations to implement this procedure (Yakowicz, 2020). While Patagonia is one of many leading groups for fair labor practices, the bulk of their supply chains and factories are located outside of the United States, and audits reveal human trafficking and exploitation, particularly within the suppliers of raw materials sent to factories. This reveals the complexities associated with managing the network of value-based governance in the context of far-flung global operations of the supply chain, factories and distributions (White, 2015).

Moreover, consumers' knowledge of misaligned practices in a network of organizational practices is also critical in our analysis of value-based governance. The consumer side of an organization has been largely ignored within behavior analysis. Fortunately, a few ideas about this area lay the substantial groundwork for an advanced analysis of consumer behavior (e.g., see the Chapter 7 by Foxall in this text; also Foxall, 2001, 2010, 2015; Hantula et al., 2008). Most consumer research disregards the effect of the consumer setting on behavior and is often not grounded in empirically demonstrated principles.

Behavior scientists working in economics would benefit from empirical explorations of consumer behavior, particularly in the areas of choice and alternative selections. The above example in addition to our discussion of value-based governance demonstrates the critical role of organizational leaders in the analysis of organizational practices as they serve as the primary source for decision-making in organizations. The analysis also draws upon the nature of rules and the way these verbal stimuli can influence the promotion of value-based governance in organizations. Implementation of value-based governance in alignment with stated objectives challenges leaders, especially within the global networks in which many companies operate, which is an area in need of more research. The extent to which standards, regulations, work instructions, and other bureaucratic variables are needed to support core prosocial values to ensure wellbeing is informed by behavioral systems analyses of the organizational and cultural milieu.

CONCLUSION

This chapter provided an overview of ways a behavior scientific discussion of rule governance as related to leadership and team management practices may influence psychological, social, and financial wellbeing in organizations. Job stress and burnout were discussed as indicators of psychological and social wellbeing as the problem is global, involves workers' behaviors influenced by leadership actions, and is illustrative of problems requiring systemic change.

The discussion of wellbeing in organizations calls for future work in behavior analysis, emphasizing the importance of organizational leaders' decision-making behaviors in establishing organizational practices that support value-based actions, and eliminate aversive conditions within behavioral systems. We believe that further focus on empirical analyses associated with specification and demonstration of rule governance and value-based governance as related to wellbeing in organizations (and beyond) is a challenge that is worth the direct attention of researchers and practitioners who are interested in the application of behavior science in organizations.

STUDY QUESTIONS

1. Describe burnout as a cultural response to bureaucratically-rooted organizational systems, and provide an overview of work-related conditions that may influence an individual's experience across the dimensions of burnout.
2. Provide an overview of ways shared stimulus function can be discussed in our analysis of rule governance and environmental ambiguity in organizations.
3. Discuss control-oriented self-rules in comparison to values-oriented self-rules in the analysis of wellbeing in the organization.
4. What are some of the critical components of value-based governance? How does this perspective interact with Abernathy's discussion of different types of management?
5. Describe the elaborated account of metacontingency and discuss its utility in the analysis of value-based governance in organizations and beyond.

REFERENCES

Abernathy, W.B. (1996). *Sin of wages.* PerfSys Press.

Abernathy, W.B. (2000). *Managing without supervising: Creating an organization-wide performance system.* PerfSys Press

Abernathy, W.B. (2001). An analysis of twelve organizations' total performance system. In L.J. Hayes, J. Austin, R. Houmanfar, & Clayton, M.C. (Eds.), *Organizational Change* (pp. 239–272). Context Press.

Abernathy, W.B. (2009). Walden two revisited: Optimizing behavioral systems. *Journal of Organizational Behavior Management, 29,* 175–192. doi: 10.1080/01608060902874567

Abernathy, W.B. (2014). *The liberated workplace: Transitioning to Walden three.* Performance Management Publications.

Agnew, J. (2013). *Managing millennials: Can science help?* Aubrey Daniels International. http://aubreydaniels.com/pmezine/managing-millennials-can-science-help

Alavosius, M.P., Houmanfar, R., & Rodriquez, N.J. (2005, November). Unity of purpose/unity of effort: Private-sector preparedness in times of terror. *Disaster Prevention and Management, 14*(5), 666–680. doi: 10.1108/09653560510634098

Alavosius, M.P., Houmanfar, R.A., Anbro, S., Burleigh, K., & Hebein, C. (2017). Leadership and crew resource management in high-reliability organizations: A competency framework for measuring behaviors. *Journal of Organizational Behavior Management, 37,* 142–170. doi: 10.1080/01608061.2017.1325825

Ardila Sánchez, J.G., Houmanfar, R.A., & Alavosius, M.P. (2019). A descriptive analysis of the effects of weather disasters on community resilience. *Behavior and Social Issues, 28,* 298–315. doi: 10.1007/s42822-019-00015-w

Atkins, P.W.B. & Styles, R.G. (2016). Measuring self and rules in what people say: Exploring whether self-discrimination predicts long-term wellbeing. *Journal of Contextual Behavioral Science, 5*(2), 71–79. doi: 10.1016/j.jcbs.2016.05.001

Baker, T., Schwenk, T., Piasecki, M., Smith, G.S., Reimer, D., Jacobs, N., Shonkwiler, G., Hagen, J., Houmanfar, R.A. (2015). Cultural change in a medical school: A data-driven management of entropy. *Journal of Organizational Behavior Management, 35,* 95–122. doi: 10.1080/01608061.2015.1035826

Barnes-Holmes, D., Barnes-Holmes, Y., Stewart, I., & Boles, S. (2010). A sketch of the implicit relational assessment procedure (IRAP) and the relational elaboration and coherence (REC) model. *The Psychological Record, 60,* 527–542. doi: 10.1007/BF03395726

Bar-Yam, Y. (1997). *Dynamics of complex systems.* Addison-Wesley.

Biglan, A. (2011). Corporate externalities: a challenge to the further success of prevention science. *Prevention science: the official journal of the Society for Prevention Research, 12*(1), 1–11. doi: 10.1007/s11121-010-0190-5

Biglan, A. (2020). *Rebooting Capitalism: How We Can Forge a Society That Works for Everyone.* Values to Action.

Biglan, A. & Glenn, S. S. (2013). Toward prosocial behavior and environments: Behavioral and cultural contingencies in a public health framework. In G.J. Madden (Ed), *APA handbook of behavior analysis* (pp. 255–275). American Psychological Association.

Binder, C. (1996). Behavioral fluency: Evolution of a new paradigm. *The Behavior Analyst, 19*(2), 163–197. doi: 10.1007/BF03393163

Bond, F.W. & Flaxman, P.E. (2006). The ability of psychological flexibility and job control to predict learning, job performance, and mental health. *Journal of Organizational Behavior Management, 26*(1–2), 113–130. doi: 10.1300/J075v26n01_05

Bond, F.W., Flaxman, P.E., & Bunce, D. (2008). The influence of psychological flexibility on work redesign: Mediated moderation of a work reorganization intervention. *Journal of Applied Psychology, 93*, 645–654. doi: 10.1037/0021-9010.93.3.645

Brethower, D.M. (1982). The total performance system. In R.M. O'Brien, A.M. Dickinson, & M.P. Rosow (Eds.), *Industrial behavior modification: A management handbook* (pp. 350–369). Pergamon Press.

Brethower, D.M. (1999). General systems theory and behavioral psychology. In H.D. Stolovitch & E.J. Keeps (Eds.), *Handbook of human performance technology*, (pp. 67–81). Jossey-Bass Pfeiffer.

Brethower, D.M. (2000). A systematic view of enterprise: Adding value to performance. *Journal of Organizational Behavior Management, 20*, 165–190. doi: 10.1300/J075v20n03_06

Cano, A. & Vivian, D. (2003). Are life stressors associated with marital violence? *Journal of Family Psychology, 17*, 302–314. doi: 10.1037/0893-3200.17.3.302

Chopko, B.A., Palmieri, P.A., & Adams, R.E. (2013). Associations between police stress and alcohol use: Implications for practice. *Journal of Loss and Trauma, 18*(5), 482–497. doi: 10.1080/15325024.2012.719340

Crenshaw, K. (1989). Demarginalizing the intersection of race and sex: A Black feminist critique of antidiscrimination doctrine, feminist theory and antiracist politics. *University of Chicago Legal Forum, 1989*(8). https://chicagounbound.uchicago.edu/uclf/vol1989/iss1/8

Daniels, A.C. & Daniels, J.E. (2005). *Measure of a leader.* Performance Management Publications.

Dawson, D.A., Grant, B.F., & Ruan, W. (2005). The association between stress and drinking: Modifying effects of gender and vulnerability. *Alcohol and Alcoholism, 40*, 453–460. doi: 10.1093/alcalc/agh176

Dounavi, K., Fennell, B, & Early, E. (2019). Supervision for certification in the field of applied behavior analysis: Characteristics and relationship with job satisfaction, burnout, work demands, and support. *International Journal of Environmental Research and Public Health, 16*, 2098. doi: 10.3390/ijerph16122098

Dyrbye, L.N., Satele, D., Sloan, J., & Shanafelt, T.D. (2013). Utility of a brief screening tool to identify physicians in distress. *Journal of General Internal Medicine, 28*(3), 421–427. doi: 10.1007/s11606-012-2252-9

Fair Labor Association. (2020). https://www.fairlabor.org/about-us

Fiebig, J.H., Gould, E.R., Ming, S., & Watson, R.A. (2020). An invitation to act on the value of self-care: Being a whole person in all that you do. *Behavior Analysis in Practice.* doi: 10.1007/s40617-020-00442-x

Foxall, G.R. (2001). Foundations of consumer behaviour analysis. *Marketing Theory, 1*, 165–199. doi: 10.1177/147059310100100202

Foxall, G.R. (2010). Invitation to consumer behavior analysis. *Journal of Organizational Behavior Management, 30*, 92–109. doi: 10.1080/01608061003756307

Foxall, G. (2015). Consumer behavior analysis and the marketing firm: Bilateral contingency in the context of environmental concern. *Journal of Organizational Behavior Management, 35*(1–2), 44–69. doi: 10.1080/01608061.2015.1031426

Ghezzi, E.L., Houmanfar, R.A., & Crosswell, L (2020). The motivative augmental effects of verbal stimuli on cooperative and conformity responding under a financially competing contingency in an analog work task. *The Psychological Record, 70*, 411–431. doi: 10.1007/s40732-020-00400-7

Gibson, J.A., Grey, I.M., & Hastings, R.P. (2009). Supervisor support as a predictor of burnout and therapeutic self-efficacy in therapists working in ABA schools. *Journal of Autism and Developmental Disorders, 39*, 1024–1030. doi: 10.1007/s10803-009-0709-4

Gilbert, T. (2007). *Human competence: Engineering worthy performance* (Tribute ed.). Pfeiffer.

Glenn, S.S. (1991). Contingencies and metacontingencies: Relations among behavioral, cultural, and biological evolution. In P.A. Lamal (Ed.), *Behavioral analysis of societies and cultural practices* (pp. 39–73). Hemisphere.

Glenn, S.S. (2004). Individual behavior, culture, and social change. *The Behavior Analyst, 27*, 133–151. doi: 10.1007/BF03393175

Glenn, S.S. & Malott, M.M. (2004). Complexity and selection: Implications for organizational change. *Behavior & Social Issues, 13*, 89–106. doi: 10.5210/bsi.v13i2.378

Golda, N. (2019). Setting our sights on the right target: how addressing physician burnout may be a solution for improved patient experience. *Clinics in Dermatology, 37*(6), 685–688. doi: 10.1016/j.clindermatol.2019.07.022

Grunberg, L., Moore, S., Anderson-Connoly, R. & Greenberg, E. (1999). Work stress and self-reported alcohol abuse: The moderating role of escapist reasons for drinking. *Journal of Occupational Health Psychology, 4*, 29–36. doi: 10.1037/1076-8998.4.1.29

Han, S., Shanafelt, T.D., Sinsky, C.A., Awad, K.M., Dyrbye, L.N., Fiscus, L.C., ... Goh, J. (2019). Estimating the attributable cost of physician burnout in the united states. *Annals of Internal Medicine, 170*(11), 784–790. doi: 10.7326/m18-1422

Hantula, D.A., DiClemente Brockman, D., & Smith, C.L. (2008). Online shopping as foraging. The effects of increasing delays on purchasing and patch residence. *IEEE Transactions on Professional Communication, 51*, 147–154. doi: 10.1109/TPC.2008.2000340

Hayes, L.J. & Fryling, M.J. (2014). Motivation in behavior analysis: A critique. *The Psychological Record, 64*, 339–347. doi: 10.1007/s40732-014-0025-z

Hayes, S.C. & Sanford, B.T. (2014). Cooperation came first: Evolution and human cognition: cooperation and cognition. *Journal of the Experimental Analysis of Behavior, 101*(1), 112–129. doi: 10.1002/jeab.64

Hayes, S.C., Strosahl, K.D., & Wilson, K. G. (1999). *Acceptance and Commitment Therapy: An experiential approach to behavior change.* Guilford Press.

Hayes, S.C., Zettle, R.D., & Rosenfarb, I. (1989). Rule-following. In S. C. Hayes (Ed.), *Rule- governed behavior: Cognition, contingencies, and instructional control* (pp. 191–218).Plenum Press.

Herbst, S.A. & Houmanfar, R. (2009). Psychological approaches to values in organizations and organizational behavior management. *Journal of Organizational Behavior, 29*, 47–68. doi: 10.1080/016080/01608060802714210

Hodgins, D.C., Williams, R., & Munro, G. (2009). Workplace responsibility, stress, alcohol availability and norms as predictors of alcohol consumption-related problems among employed workers. *Substance Use & Misuse, 44*, 2062–2079. doi: 10.3109/10826080902855173

Houmanfar, R. & Johnson, R. (2003). Organizational implications of gossip and rumor. *Journal of Organizational Behavior Management, 23*, 117–138. doi: 10.1300/J075v23n02_07

Houmanfar, R.A., Rodrigues, N.J., & Smith, G.S. (2009). Role of communication networks in behavioral systems analysis. *Journal of Organizational Behavior Management*, 29, 257–275. doi: 10.1080/01608060903092102

Houmanfar, R., Rodrigues, N.J., & Ward, T.A. (2010). Emergence and metacontingency: Points of contact and departure. *Behavior and Social Issues, 19*, 53–78. doi: 10.5210/bsi.v19i0.3065

Houmanfar, R.A., Alavosius, M.P., Morford, Z.H., Herbst, S.A., & Reimer, D. (2015). Functions of organizational leaders in cultural change: Financial and social wellbeing. *Journal of Organizational Behavior Management, 35*, 4–27. doi: 10.1080/01608061.2015.1035827

Houmanfar, R. A., Alavosius, M. P., Binder, C., Johnson, K. (2019). Human competence revisited: 40 years of impact. *Journal of Organizational Behavior Management, 39* (1–2). doi: 10.1080/01608061.2019.1599165

Houmanfar, R., A. Ardila Sánchez, J.G., & Alavosius, M.P. (2020). Role of cultural milieu in cultural change: mediating factor in points of contact. In T. Cihon, & M.A. Mattaini (Eds.). *Behavior Science Perspectives on Culture and Community.* Springer

Hughes, S. & Barnes-Holmes, D. (2013). A functional approach to the study of implicit cognition: the implicit relational assessment procedure (IRAP) and the relational elaboration coherence (REC) model. In S. Dymond & B. Roche, *Advanced in relational frame theory: research and application.* (pp. 95–125). New Harbinger Publications.

Jablonka, E. & Lamb, M.J. (2005). *Evolution in four dimensions: Genetic, epigenetic, behavioral, and symbolic variation in the history of life.* MIT Press.

Johnson, R.A., Houmanfar, R., & Smith, G.S. (2010). The effect of implicit and explicit rules on customer greeting and productivity in a retail organization. *Journal of Organizational Behavior Management, 30*, 38–48. doi: 10.1080/01608060903529731

Kahneman, D. (2011). *Thinking, fast and slow.* (First ed.). Farrar, Straus and Giroux.

Kantor, J.R. (1982). *Cultural psychology.* Principia Press, Inc.

Kantor. J.R. (1967). *Interbehavioral psychology.* Principia Press, Inc.

Kolvitz, M. (1997). Donald T. Tosti, Ph.D. and Stephanie F. Jackson, M.A.: The organizational scan, performance levers, and alignment. In P.J. Dean & D.E. Ripley, *Performance improvement pathfinders: Models for organizational learning systems* (pp. 124–141). The International Society for Performance Improvement.

Kirwan Institute for the Study of Race and Ethnicity (2017). *Implicit bias review.* The Ohio State University.

Labbe, E.E. & Fobes, A. (2010). Evaluating the interplay between spirituality, personality and stress. *Applied Psychophysical Biofeedback, 35*, 141–146. doi: 10.1007/s10484-009-9119-9

Lewon, M., Spurlock, E. D., Peters, C.M., & Hayes, L.J. (2019). Interactions between the effects of food and water motivating operations on food- and water-reinforced responding in mice. *Journal of the Experimental Analysis of Behavior, 111*(3), 493–507. doi: 10.1002/jeab.522

Lloyd, J., Bond, F.W., & Flaxman, P.E. (2013). The value of psychological flexibility: Examining psychological mechanisms underpinning a cognitive behavioural therapy intervention for burnout. *Work & Stress, 27*(2), 181–199. doi: 10.1080/02678373.2013.782157.

Malott, R. (1992). A theory of rule governed behavior and organizational management. *Journal of Organizational Behavior Management, 12*, 45–65. doi: 10.1300/J075v12n02_03

Malott, M.E. (2003). *Paradox of organizational change: Engineering organizations with behavioral systems analysis.* Context Press.

Malott, M.E. & Glenn, S.S. (2006). Targets of interventions in cultural and behavioral change. *Behavior and Social Issues, 15, 31–56.* doi: 10.5210/bsi.v15i1.344

Mawhinney, T.C. (1992). Evolution of organizational cultures as selection by consequences: The gaia hypothesis, metacontingencies, and organizational ecology. In T.C. Mawhinney (Ed.), *Organizational culture, rule-governed behavior and organizational behavior management* (pp. 1–26). The Haworth Press, Inc.

Mawhinney, T.C. (2001). Organization-environment systems as OBM intervention context: Minding your metacontingencies. In L.J. Hayes, J. Austin, R. Houmanfar, & M.C. Clayton (Eds.), *Organizational change* (pp. 137–166). Context Press.

Maraccini, A.M., Houmanfar, R.A., Kemmelmeier, M., Piasecki, M., & Slonim, A.D. (2018). An inter-professional approach to train and evaluate communication accuracy and completeness during the delivery of nurse-physician student handoffs. *Journal of Interprofessional Education & Practice, 12,* 65–72. doi: 10.1016/j.xjep.2018.06.003

Maslach, C., Jackson, S.E., & Leiter, M.P. (1996–2019). *Maslach Burnout Inventory Manual (Fourth Edition).* Mind Garden, Inc.

McHugh, L. & Stewart, I., 1971. (2012). *The self and perspective taking: Contributions and applications from modern behavioral science.* Context Press/New Harbinger Publications.

Michael, J.L. (1993). Establishing operations. *The Behavior Analyst, 16,* 191–206. doi: 10.1007/BF03392623

Merriam-Webster. (n.d.). Wellbeing. In *Merriam-Webster.com dictionary.* https://www.merriam-webster.com/dictionary/well-being (Accessed June 30, 2020)

Patagonia (2020a). http://www.patagoniaworks.com/press/2020/4/27/patagonia-statement-regarding-covid-19-and-our-supply-chain

Patagonia (2020b). https://www.patagonia.com/core-values/

Rafacz, S., Houmanfar, R., & Smith, G., Levin, M. (2019). Assessing the effects of motivative augmentals, pay for-performance, and implicit verbal responding on cooperation. *The Psychological Record*, 69, 49–66. doi: 10.1007/s40732-018-0324-x

Reimer, D. & Houmanfar, R.A. (2017). Internalities and their applicability for organizational practices, *Journal of Organizational Behavior Management, 37,* 5–31. doi: 10.1080/01608061.2016.1257969

Rotenstein, L.S., Torre, M., Ramos, M.A., Rosales, R.C., Guille, C., Sen, S., & Mata, D.A. (2018). Prevalence of burnout among physicians: A systematic review. *Journal of the American Medical Association*, 320(*11*), 1131–1150. doi: 10.1001/jama.2018.12777

Richter, A., Kostova, P., Harth, V., & Wegner, R. (2014). Children, care, career – a cross-sectional study on the risk of burnout among German hospital physicians at different career stages. *Journal of Occupational Medicine and Toxicology, 9,* 41–41. doi: 10.1186/s12995-014-0041-6

Rummler, G.A. & Brache, A.P. (1995). *Improving performance: How to manage the white space on the organizational chart* (2nd ed.). Jossey-Bass.

Rummler, G. A. (2001). Performance logic: The organization performance rosetta stone. In L. J. Hayes, J. Austin, R. Houmanfar, & M.C. Clayton (Eds.), *Organizational change* (pp. 111-132). Context Press.Schaufeli, W.B., Leiter, M.P., & Maslach, C. (2009). Burnout: 35 years of research and practice. *Career Development International, 14*(3), 204–220. doi: 10.1108/13620430910966406

Schawbel, D. (2013, 16 December). 10 ways millennials are creating the future of work. *Forbes.* http://www.forbes.com/sites/danschawbel/2013/12/16/10-ways-millennials-are-creating-the-future-of-work/

Shanafelt, T.D., Dyrbye, L.N., West, C.P. (2017). Addressing physician burnout: The way forward. *Journal of Academic Medicine, 317*(9), 901–092. doi: 10.1001/jama.2017.0076

Shapiro, D.E., Duquette, C., Abbott, L.M., Babineau, T., Pearl, A., & Haidet, P. (2018). Beyond burnout: A physician wellness hierarchy designed to prioritize interventions at the systems level. *The American Journal of Medicine, 132*(5). doi: 10.1016/j.amjmed.2018.11.028

Skinner, B.F. (1953). *Science and human behavior.* New York: Free Press.

Skinner, B.F. (1957). *Verbal behavior.* Copley Publishing Group.

Skinner, B.F. (1990). Beyond freedom and dignity. Bantam Books. (Original work published 1971).

Smith, B.M., Twohy, A.J., & Smith, G.S. (2020). Psychological inflexibility and intolerance of uncertainty moderate the relationship between social isolation and mental health outcomes during COVID-19. *Journal of Contextual Behavioral Science, 18,* 162–174. doi: 10.1016/j.jcbs.2020.09.005

Smith, G.S., Houmanfar, R., & Denny, M. (2012). Impact of rule accuracy on productivity and rumor in an organizational analog. *Journal of Organizational Behavior Management, 32,* 3–25. doi: 10.1080/01608061.2012.646839

Smith, G.S. (2013). Exploring the predictive utility of implicit relational assessment procedure (IRAP) with respect to performance in organizations. Unpublished doctoral dissertation. University of Nevada, Reno.

Smith, G.S., Houmanfar, R.A., Jacobs, N.N., Froehlich, M., Szarko, A.J., Smith, B.M., Kemmelmeier, M., Baker, T.K., Piasecki, M., & Schwenk, T.L. (under review). Assessment of medical student burnout: Toward an implicit measure to address current issues. *Advances in Health Sciences Education.*

Song, P.P. & Waline, J.H. (2020). Physician burnout: a global crisis. *The Lancet, 10221*, 333. doi: 10.1016/S0140-6736(19)32480-8

Stith, S.M., Smith, D.B., Penn, C.E., Ward, D.B., & Tritt, D. (2004). Intimate partner physical abuse perpetration and victimization risk factors: A meta-analytic review. *Aggression and Violent Behavior, 10*, 65–98. doi: 10.1016/j.avb.2003.09.001

Swensen, S., Kabcenell, A., & Shanafelt, T. (2016). Physician-organization collaboration reduces physician burnout and promotes engagement: The mayo clinic experience. *Journal of Healthcare Management, 61*(2), 105–127. doi: 10.1097/00115514-201603000-00008

Taylor, S.E. (2008). *Health Psychology* (7th ed.). New York, NY: McGraw-Hill.

Terry, D.J. & Jimmieson, N.L. (1999). Work control and employee wellbeing: A decade review. In C.L. Cooper & I.T. Robertson (Eds.), *International review of industrial and organizational psychology* (pp. 95–148). John Wiley & Sons.

Törneke, N., Luciano, C., & Salas, S.V. (2008). Rule-governed behavior and psychological problems. *International Journal of Psychology & Psychological Therapy, 8*(2), 141–156.

Weatherly, N.L. & Malott, R.W. (2008). An analysis of organizational behavior management research in terms of three-contingency model of performance management. *Journal of Organizational Behavior Management, 28*, 260–285. doi: 10.1080/01608060802454643

White, G. (2015, June). All your clothes are made with exploited labor. *The Atlantic*. https://www.theatlantic.com/business/archive/2015/06/patagonia-labor-clothing-factory-exploitation/394658/

World Health Organization. (2020). *ICD-11 – mortality and morbidity statistics*. World Health Organization (WHO). https://icd.who.int/browse11/l-m/en

Yakowicz, W. (2020). At billionaire-owned Patagonia outdoor clothing chain, employees to be paid despite store closures amid coronavirus. https://www.forbes.com/sites/willyakowicz/2020/03/16/at-billionaire-owned-patagonia-outdoor-clothing-chain-employees-to-be-paid-despite-store-closures-amid-coronavirus/

Index

Page numbers in *italics* reference figures and page numbers in **bold** reference tables.